American English Spelling

D. W. CUMMINGS

American
English
Spelling

An Informal Description

The Johns Hopkins University Press

Baltimore and London

This book has been brought to publication with the generous assistance of the Andrew W. Mellon Foundation.

The Johns Hopkins University Press
701 West 40th Street
Baltimore, Maryland 21211
The Johns Hopkins Press Ltd., London

The paper used in this publication meets
the minimum requirements of American
National Standard for Information Sciences—
Permanence of Paper for Printed Library
Materials, ANSI Z39.48-1984.

Library of Congress Cataloging-in-Publication Data

Cummings, D. W. (Donald Wayne), 1935–
  American English spelling.

  Bibliography: p.
  Includes indexes.
  1. English language—United States—Orthography and spelling. I. Title.
PE2817.C86 1988   421'.54   86-30537
ISBN 0-8018-3443-0 (alk. paper)

Contents

Detailed Table of Contents   vii
Preface   xxv
Notes on Usage   xxxi

Analysis   **1**
1. Spelling as System   3
2. The Explication of Written Words   32

Tactics   **67**
3. Sequences and Distributions   69
4. String Patterns and Rules   90
5. Suffix Rules   112
6. VCV in Disyllables   123
7. The Third Syllable Rule   131

Procedures   **143**
8. Silent Final *e* and Its Deletion Rule   145
9. The Twinning Rule   161
10. Assimilated Prefixes   177

Correspondences   **199**
11. The Sounds and Letters of English   201
12. Short *a*, /a/   213
13. Short *e*, /e/   217
14. Short *i*, /i/   222
15. The Short *o*'s, /ä/ and /ȯ/   231
16. High Short *u*, /u̇/   241
17. Low Short *u*, /u/   244

18. Long *a*, /ā/   249

19. Long *e*, /ē/   258

20. Long *i*, /ī/   271

21. Long *o*, /ō/   280

22. The Simple Long *u*, /ū/   288

23. The Complex Long *u*, /yū/   297

24. The Diphthongs, /ȯi/ and /aȯ/   301

25. Vowels before /r/   307

26. The Front Stops: /b/, /p/, /d/, and /t/   327

27. The Velar Stops, /g/ and /k/   350

28. The Simple Fricatives /v/, /f/, /th/, /<u>th</u>/, and /h/   373

29. The Simple Fricatives /z/ and /s/   391

30. The Palatal Sibilants: /sh/, /ch/, /j/, and /zh/   407

31. The Nasals: /m/, /n/, and /ŋ/   423

32. The Liquids, /l/ and /r/   439

33. The Semivowels, /w/ and /y/   456

34. Conclusion   461

Bibliography   465
Index of Words   475
General Index   539

Detailed Table of Contents

Preface   xxv

Notes on Usage   xxxi

ANALYSIS   1

Chapter 1. Spelling as System   3
    1.1 Introduction   3
    1.2 The Systematicity of American Spelling   4
    1.2.1 Performance and Code   4
    1.2.2 Self-regulation and Self-reorganization   5
    1.3 Spelling Rules   9
    1.4 Unity, Variety, and Analogy   10
    1.5 Demands and Contentions   12
    1.5.1 The Phonetic Demand   13
    1.5.2 The Semantic Demand   14
    1.5.3 The Etymological Demand   17
    1.5.4 Standardization and the Growing Visual Bias   21
    1.5.4.1 Spelling Pronunciations   22
    1.5.4.2 The Public Uses of Writing   24
    1.6 The Principle of Preferred Regularity   25
    1.7 Well-formed and Ill-formed Spellings   26
    1.8 Accepted, Unaccepted, and Unrecorded Spellings   27
    1.9 Goals of This Description   29
    1.9.1 Minimum and Maximum Simplicities   29
    1.9.2 System-centered versus Use-centered Descriptions   30

Chapter 2. The Explication of Written Words   32
    2.1 The Theory of Explication   32
    2.2 The Explication of Elements   33
    2.2.1 Elements and Morphemes   33
    2.2.2 Prefixes, Bases, and Suffixes   33
    2.2.3 Meaning and Content   35
    2.2.4 Stems   35
    2.2.5 Free and Bound Elements   36

2.2.6 Primes   36
2.2.7 Terminative and Nonterminative Elements   37
2.3 The Explication of Sets   39
2.3.1 The Set [+ *sume, sumpt* +]   39
2.3.2 The Set [*tend, tense, tent*]   41
2.3.3 The Set [*verse, vert*]   42
2.3.4 Immediate and Mediate Explicata   44
2.3.5 Sets and Connate Groups   45
2.3.6 Nonterminative Suffixes   46
2.4 The Explication of Particles   47
2.4.1 The Linking Particles   47
2.4.2 The Initial Particle   48
2.5 Explication versus Other Lexical Analyses   49
2.5.1 Explication versus Etymological Analysis   50
2.5.2 Explication versus Generative Analysis   51
2.6 On Orthographic Concepts   52
2.6.1 Silent Letters   54
2.7 Problems and Questions   55
2.7.1 The Explication of Form and Content   55
2.7.2 Element and Particle Boundaries   56
2.7.3 The Rule of Syllabicity   59
2.7.3.1 Lexical Simplification   61
2.7.4 Merging   61
2.7.4.1 Subelemental Patterning   62
2.7.5 Two Examples of Explication   63
2.7.5.1 The Set [*gym, gymn* + , *gymnasi* +]   63
2.7.5.2 The Set [*ly* + , *lyse*, + *lyte*]   64
2.8 Summary   66

TACTICS   **67**

Chapter 3. Sequences and Distributions   **69**
3.1 Tactics and Tactical Patterns   69
3.2 Consonant Sequence Rules   71
3.2.1 Digraphs, Clusters, and Concatenations   71
3.2.1.1 Digraphs   71
3.2.1.2 Clusters   72
3.2.1.3 Concatenations   73
3.2.2 The Mixed Voicing Rule   73
3.2.2.1 Voicing in Clusters   74
3.2.2.2 Voicing in Concatenations   75
3.2.3 The Initial Doublet Rule   76
3.2.4 Final Doublet Constraints   76
3.2.5 The Triplet Rule   77

3.2.6 Doublets within Larger Clusters and Concatenations 77
3.2.6.1 Holdouts 79
3.3 Vowel Sequence Rules 81
3.3.1 The Vowel Doublet Rule 81
3.4 Distribution Rules 82
3.4.1 The Final *s* Rule 82
3.4.1.1 Holdouts 82
3.4.2 The Final *z* Rule 83
3.4.3 The Tactics of *y* and *i* 84
3.4.3.1 The *y*-to-*i* Rule 86
3.4.3.2 Holdouts 86
3.5 The Short Word Rule 87
3.5.1 Holdouts 89
3.6 Summary 89

Chapter 4. String Patterns and Rules **90**
4.1 On the Term *String* 90
4.2 The Minor Strings 91
4.2.1 The V.V Rule 91
4.2.2 The VC# Rule 93
4.2.3 The V*e*# Rule 94
4.3 The Major Strings 96
4.3.1 The VCC/VCV Contrast 96
4.3.2 A Short History of the VCC/VCV Contrast 97
4.3.2.1 The Development of Silent Final *e* 99
4.3.2.2 Latin "Position" and VCV/VCC 99
4.3.3 The VCC Pattern 100
4.3.3.1 Holdouts 101
4.3.4 The VCV Pattern 107
4.3.4.1 The VCV Pattern in Monosyllables 107
4.3.4.2 Consonant Digraphs in VCV Strings 108

Chapter 5. Suffix Rules **112**
5.1 Introduction to the Shortening Rules 112
5.2 The Suffix -*ity* Rule 112
5.2.1 Introduction to the Rule 112
5.2.2 Holdouts 114
5.2.2.1 Long *u* 114
5.2.2.2 V.V 115
5.2.3 The Final Rule 115
5.3 The Suffix -*ic* Rule 115
5.3.1 Introduction to the Rule 115
5.3.2 Holdouts 116
5.3.3 The Final Rule 118
5.4 The Suffix -*ion* Rule 118

5.4.1 Introduction to the Rule   118
5.4.2 Holdouts   119
5.4.3 The Final Rule   119
5.5 The Suffix *-it* Rule   120
5.6 The Suffix *-id* Rule   120
5.6.1 Holdouts   120
5.6.2 A Second *-id*   121
5.6.3 The Final Rule   121
5.7 The Suffix *-ish²* Rule   121
5.7.1 Holdout   122
5.7.2 The Final Rule   122
5.8 The Suffix *-ule* Rule   122

Chapter 6. VCV in Disyllables   **123**
6.1 Introduction   123
6.2 Iambs and Trochees   123
6.3 Regular VCV Trochees   124
6.3.1 Summary   126
6.4 The Nonregular VCV Trochees   127
6.4.1 The Stress Frontshift Rule   127
6.4.2 The Consonant *v* in VCV Strings   128
6.4.3 Further VCV Holdouts   129
6.4.3.1 Holdouts to the Stress Frontshift Rule   129
6.5 Summary   130

Chapter 7. The Third Syllable Rule   **131**
7.1 Instances of the Rule   131
7.1.1 The Old English Third Syllable Rule   133
7.2 Preemptors of the Third Syllable Rule   134
7.2.1 Long *u*   134
7.2.2 V.V   135
7.2.3 The Strong VCVV String   135
7.3 A Special Instance of the Third Syllable Rule   138
7.4 The Third Syllable Rule and Conservative Analogy   139
7.5 Some Tentative Conclusions   141

PROCEDURES   **143**
Chapter 8. Silent Final *e* and Its Deletion Rule   **145**
8.1 The Functions of Silent Final *e*   145
8.1.1 Marking Long Vowels   145
8.1.2 Marking Soft *c* and Soft *g*   146
8.1.3 Marking Voiced *th*   147
8.1.4 Insulating Nonterminative Letters   147
8.1.5 Silent Final *e* and the Short Word Rule   148
8.1.6 Fossil *e*'s   148
8.1.6.1 French Fossil *e*'s   148

8.1.6.2 Native Fossil *e*'s 149

8.1.7 Some Special Cases 149

8.1.7.1 The Ending *le* 149

8.1.7.2 The Suffix *-ate* and De-stressing 151

8.1.7.3 The Suffix *-ile* 152

8.1.7.4 The Suffix *-ine* 152

8.1.7.5 The Suffix *-ure* 153

8.1.7.6 The Suffix *-ite* 154

8.2 Silent Final *e* Deletion 154

8.2.1 Holdouts 156

8.3 Silent Final *e* Deletion in V*e*# Strings 157

8.4 Suffixes Starting with Consonants 158

8.5 The Logic of Silent Final *e* Deletion 159

Chapter 9. The Twinning Rule   **161**

9.1 Introduction to Twinning 161

9.2 Instances of the Rule 162

9.3 An Extended Example: *+fer* Words 168

9.4 Apparent Nonregular Twinnings 170

9.4.1 Nonterminative Bound Bases 170

9.4.2 Suffix Rules 172

9.4.3 Stress-waver 173

9.5 Holdouts to the Twinning Rule 174

9.5.1 Nonregular Twinnings 174

9.5.2 Nonregular Nontwinnings 174

9.6 The Final Form of the Twinning Rule 175

Chapter 10. Assimilated Prefixes   **177**

10.1 Introduction to Assimilation 177

10.2 The Prefix *com-* 178

10.2.1 The Assimilations 178

10.2.2 The Productive Prefix *co-* 179

10.2.3 Holdouts 180

10.3 The Prefix *ex-* 181

10.3.1 The Assimilations 181

10.3.2 Holdouts 182

10.3.3 Some "Converted" *ex-*'s 182

10.4 The Prefix *sub-* 183

10.4.1 The Assimilations 183

10.4.2 Simple Addition in Recent *sub-* Words 185

10.4.3 Two Unusual *sub-*'s 186

10.5 The Prefixes *in-*[1] and *in-*[2] 186

10.5.1 The Coform *en* 187

10.6 The Prefix *ad-* 188

10.6.1 The Influence of the Full Assimilation of *ad-* 191

10.6.2 Some Only Apparent *ad-*'s 192

10.6.3 Lost *ad-*'s   193
10.6.4 Summary   193
10.7 The Prefix *dis-*   193
10.7.1 Lost and Apparent *dis-*'s   194
10.8 The Prefix *ob-*   195
10.9 The Prefix *ab-*   196
10.10 The Prefix *syn-*   197

CORRESPONDENCES   199

Chapter 11. The Sounds and Letters of English   201
11.1 The Sounds   201
11.1.1 Phones, Phonemes, Morphophones   201
11.1.2 English Morphophones   203
11.2 The Letters   207
11.2.1 The English Alphabet   207
11.2.1.1 The Roman Influence   207
11.2.1.2 The Runic Influence   209
11.2.2 Consonant Digraphs   209
11.3 Vowels and Consonants   210

Chapter 12. Short *a*, /a/   213
12.1 Historical Sources   213
12.2 The Major Spelling of /a/   214
12.2.1 /a/ = *a*   214
12.3 Holdouts to the /a/ = *a* Correspondence   215

Chapter 13. Short *e*, /e/   217
13.1 Introduction   217
13.2 Historical Sources   217
13.3 The Major Spellings of /e/   217
13.3.1 /e/ = *e*   217
13.3.2 /e/ = *ea*   219
13.4 The Minor Spellings of /e/   220
13.4.1 /e/ = *ai, ay*   220
13.4.2 /e/ = *ie, ei*   220
13.4.3 /e/ = *u*   221
13.4.4 /e/ = *eo*   221
13.4.5 /e/ = *ae*   221

Chapter 14. Short *i*, /i/   222
14.1 Historical Sources   222
14.2 Stressed and Unstressed /i/   222
14.3 The Major Spellings of /i/   223
14.3.1 /i/ = *i*   223
14.3.2 /i/ = *y*   226
14.4 The Minor Spellings of /i/   228

14.4.1 /i/ = *e*   228
14.4.2 /i/ = *o*   228
14.4.3 /i/ = *u*   228
14.4.4 /i/ = *ee, ea*   229
14.4.5 /i/ = *ei, ie*   229
14.4.6 /i/ = *ui*   229

Chapter 15. The Short *o*'s, /ä/ and /ȯ/   **231**
15.1 Introduction   231
15.2 The Spellings of /ä/   231
15.2.1 The Major Spellings of /ä/   232
15.2.1.1 /ä/ = *a*   232
15.2.1.2 /ä/ = *o*   233
15.2.2 The Minor Spellings of /ä/   235
15.2.2.1 /ä/ = *ow*   235
15.2.2.2 /ä/ = *ah*   235
15.2.2.3 /ä/ = *e*   235
15.3 The Spellings of /ȯ/   236
15.3.1 The Major Spellings of /ȯ/   236
15.3.1.1 /ȯ/ = *aw*   236
15.3.1.2 /ȯ/ = *au*   237
15.3.2 The Minor Spellings of /ȯ/   238
15.3.2.1 /ȯ/ = *o*   238
15.3.2.2 /ȯ/ = *a*   239
15.3.2.3 /ȯ/ = *ou*   239
15.3.2.4 /ȯ/ = *oa*   240

Chapter 16. High Short *u*, /u̇/   **241**
16.1 Introduction   241
16.2 Historical Sources   241
16.3 The Major Spellings of /u̇/   242
16.3.1 /u̇/ = *oo*   242
16.3.2 /u̇/ = *u*   242
16.4 The Minor Spellings of /u̇/   243
16.4.1 /u̇/ = *ou*   243
16.4.2 /u̇/ = *o*   243
16.5 The Spellings of /u̇/ Summarized   243

Chapter 17. Low Short *u*, /u/   **244**
17.1 The Major Spellings of /u/   244
17.1.1 /u/ = *u*   244
17.1.2 /u/ = *o*   245
17.2 The Minor Spellings of /u/   247
17.2.1 /u/ = *oo*   247
17.2.2 /u/ = *ou*   247

Chapter 18. Long *a*, /ā/   **249**

    18.1 Historical Sources 249
    18.1.1 Middle English Long *a* 249
    18.1.2 Two Middle English Diphthongs 250
    18.1.3 From Middle to American English 250
    18.2 The Major Spellings of /ā/ 251
    18.2.1 /ā/ = *a* 251
    18.2.2 /ā/ = *ai, ay* 252
    18.2.3 Summary 254
    18.3 The Minor Spellings of /ā/ 254
    18.3.1 /ā/ = *ei, ey* 254
    18.3.2 /ā/ = *eigh, aigh* 255
    18.3.3 /ā/ = *ea* 256
    18.3.4 /ā/ = *et* 256
    18.3.5 /ā/ = *e, ee* 256
    18.3.6 /ā/ = *ae, ao, au* 257

Chapter 19. Long *e*, /ē/   **258**

    19.1 Historical Sources 258
    19.2 The Major Spellings of /ē/ 260
    19.2.1 /ē/ = *e* 260
    19.2.2 /ē/ = *y* 262
    19.2.3 /ē/ = *i* 262
    19.2.4 /ē/ = *ea, ee* 264
    19.3 The Minor Spellings of /ē/ 267
    19.3.1 /ē/ = *ie, ei* 267
    19.3.2 /ē/ = *ey* 268
    19.3.3 /ē/ = *ae, oe* 268
    19.3.4 /ē/ = *eo* 270
    19.3.5 /ē/ = *agh, ah* 270
    19.3.6 /ē/ = *ay* 270

Chapter 20. Long *i*, /ī/   **271**

    20.1 Historical Sources 271
    20.2 The Major Spellings of /ī/ 272
    20.2.1 /ī/ = *i* 272
    20.2.2 /ī/ = *y* 276
    20.3 The Minor Spellings of /ī/ 278
    20.3.1 /ī/ = *ie* 278
    20.3.2 /ī/ = *ei* 278
    20.3.3 /ī/ = *eigh* 278
    20.3.4 /ī/ = *ai* 279
    20.3.5 /ī/ = *ay* 279
    20.3.6 /ī/ = *ey* 279
    20.3.7 /ī/ = *uy* 279
    20.3.8 /ī/ = *oy* 279

Chapter 21. Long *o*, /ō/   **280**

21.1 Historical Sources   280
21.2 The Major Spellings of /ō/   281
21.2.1 /ō/ = *o*   281
21.2.2 /ō/ = *oa*   284
21.2.3 /ō/ = *ow*   284
21.3 The Minor Spellings of /ō/   285
21.3.1 /ō/ = *ou, ough*   285
21.3.2 /ō/ = *eau, au*   286
21.3.3 /ō/ = *oo, oh, ew, eo*   286
21.4 The Spellings of /ō/ Summarized   287

Chapter 22. The Simple Long *u*, /ū/   **288**

22.1 Introduction   288
22.2 Historical Sources   288
22.3 The Major Spellings of /ū/   289
22.3.1 /ū/ = *oo*   289
22.3.2 /ū/ = *u*   290
22.3.2.1 The Correspondence /ū/ = *u* and the
             Third Syllable Rule   291
22.3.3 The Major Spellings of /ū/ Summarized   291
22.4 The Minor Spellings of /ū/   291
22.4.1 /ū/ = *o*   291
22.4.2 /ū/ = *oe*   293
22.4.3 /ū/ = *ou*   293
22.4.4 /ū/ = *ew*   295
22.4.5 /ū/ = *eu*   295
22.4.6 /ū/ = *ui*   296
22.4.7 /ū/ = *uo, uh, w*   296

Chapter 23. The Complex Long *u*, /yū/   **297**

23.1 The Distribution of /yū/ and /ū/   297
23.1.1 Initial /yū/   297
23.1.2 /yū/ after Labials and Velars   297
23.1.3 /ū/ after Liquids   298
23.1.4 /ū/ after Fricatives   298
23.1.5 /yū/ and /ū/ after Dentals   299
23.2 The Spellings of /yū/   299
23.2.1 /yū/ = *u*   299
23.2.2 /yū/ = *ew*   299
23.2.3 /yū/ = *eu*   300
23.2.4 Other Spellings of /yū/   300

Chapter 24. The Diphthongs, /ȯi/ and /aú/   **301**

24.1 On Diphthongs   301
24.2 The Spellings of /ȯi/   301

24.2.1 The Major Spellings of /òi/   302

24.2.1.1 /òi/ = *oy* in Final Position   302

24.2.1.2 Initial and Medial /òi/ = *oi*   302

24.2.1.3 Holdouts, Apparent and Real   302

24.2.2 The Minor Spellings of /òi/   303

24.3 The Spellings of /aù/   303

24.3.1 The Major Spellings of /aù/   303

24.3.1.1 /aù/ = *ow* in Final Position   304

24.3.1.2 /aù/ = *ow* before Vowels   304

24.3.1.3 /aù/ = *ow* before *l* and Final *n*   305

24.3.1.4 /aù/ before /d/ and /z/   305

24.3.1.5 /aù/ = *ou*   305

24.3.2 The Minor Spellings of /aù/   306

Chapter 25. Vowels before /r/   **307**

25.1 /r/ Coloring   307

25.2 The /âr/ Field   308

25.2.1 The Major Spellings of /âr/   308

25.2.1.1 /âr/ = *ar*V#, *ar*VV   308

25.2.1.2 /âr/ = *ar*VC, *arr*   309

25.2.1.3 /âr/ = *err, er*VC   310

25.2.1.4 The Major Spellings of /âr/ Summarized   310

25.2.2 The Minor Spellings of /âr/   310

25.3 The /ôr/ Field   311

25.3.1 The Major Spellings of /ôr/   311

25.3.1.1 /ôr/ = *orr, or*VC   311

25.3.1.2 /ôr/ = *or#, or*C   312

25.3.1.3 /ôr/ = *war*C, *war*#   313

25.3.1.4 /ôr/ = *or*VV, *or*V#   313

25.3.1.5 /ôr/ = *ar*C, *ar*#   314

25.3.1.6 The Major Spellings of /ôr/ Summarized   314

25.3.2 The Minor Spellings of /ôr/   314

25.4 The /êr/ Field   315

25.4.1 The Major Spellings of /êr/   316

25.4.1.1 /êr/ = *er*VV, *er*V#   316

25.4.1.2 /êr/ = *irr, ir*VC, *ir*VV   316

25.4.2 The Minor Spellings of /êr/   317

25.4.2.1 /êr/ = *eer*   317

25.4.2.2 /êr/ = *ear*   317

25.4.2.3 /êr/ = *ier*   318

25.4.2.4 Other Minor Spellings of /êr/   318

25.5 The Spellings of /īr/   318

25.5.1 The Major Spellings of /īr/   319

25.5.1.1 /īr/ = *ir*V#, *ir*V   319

25.5.2 The Minor Spellings of /īr/   319

25.6 The Spellings of /ùr/ and /yùr/   320
25.6.1 The Major Spellings of /ùr/ and /yùr/   320
25.6.1.1 /ùr/ = *ur*V   320
25.6.1.2 /yùr/ = *ur*V   320
25.6.2 The Minor Spellings of /ùr/ and /yùr/   321
25.7 The /ur/ Convergence   321
25.7.1 Historical Sources   321
25.7.2 The Major Spellings of /ur/   323
25.7.2.1 /wur/ = *wor*   323
25.7.2.2 /ur/ = *er*C, *er*#   323
25.7.2.3 /ur/ = *ir*C, *ir*#   324
25.7.2.4 /ur/ = *ur*C, *ur*#   324
25.7.2.5 The Major Spellings of /ur/ Summarized   325
25.7.3 The Minor Spellings of /ur/   325

Chapter 26. The Front Stops: /b/, /p/, /d/, and /t/   **327**
26.1 Introduction   327
26.2 The Spellings of /b/   328
26.2.1 Overview   328
26.2.2 The Minor Spelling of /b/   328
26.2.3 The Major Spellings of /b/   328
26.2.3.1 The Major Spellings of /b/ Summarized   328
26.2.3.2 /b/ = *b* at Simple Boundaries   330
26.2.3.3 /b/ = *b* in Shortened VCV Strings   330
26.2.3.4 /b/ = *b* in Consonant Clusters and Concatenations   331
26.2.3.5 /b/ = *b* after Vowel Digraphs   331
26.2.3.6 /b/ = *b* after Long Vowels   331
26.2.3.7 /b/ = *bb* at Complex Boundaries   332
26.2.3.8 /b/ = *bb* after Short Vowels   332
26.2.3.9 /b/ = *bb* between Short Vowels and *le*   333
26.2.3.10 /b/ = *b* after Reduced Vowels   333
26.3 The Spellings of /p/   333
26.3.1 Overview   333
26.3.2 The Minor Spellings of /p/   334
26.3.3 The Major Spellings of /p/   335
26.3.3.1 /p/ = *p* at Simple Boundaries   335
26.3.3.2 /p/ = *p* in Shortened VCV Strings   335
26.3.3.3 /p/ = *p* in Consonant Clusters and Concatenations   336
26.3.3.4 /p/ = *p* after Vowel Digraphs   336
26.3.3.5 /p/ = *p* after Long Vowels   336
26.3.3.6 /p/ = *pp* at Complex Boundaries   336
26.3.3.7 /p/ = *pp* after Short Vowels   337
26.3.3.8 /p/ = *pp* between Short Vowels and *le*   337
26.3.3.9 /p/ = *p* after Reduced Vowels   337
26.4 The Spellings of /d/   337

26.4.1 Overview   337

26.4.1.1 The Flapped *d*   338

26.4.2 The Minor Spellings of /d/   338

26.4.3 The Major Spellings of /d/   339

26.4.3.1 /d/ = *d* at Simple Boundaries   339

26.4.3.2 /d/ = *d* in Shortened VCV Strings   340

26.4.3.3 /d/ = *d* in Consonant Clusters and Concatenations   340

26.4.3.4 /d/ = *d* after Vowel Digraphs   340

26.4.3.5 /d/ = *d* after Long Vowels   341

26.4.3.6 /d/ = *dd* at Complex Boundaries   341

26.4.3.7 /d/ = *dd* after Short Vowels   341

26.4.3.8 /d/ = *dd* between Short Vowels and *le*   342

26.4.3.9 /d/ = *d* after Reduced Vowels   342

26.5 The Spellings of /t/   342

26.5.1 Overview   342

26.5.2 The Minor Spellings of /t/   343

26.5.3 The Major Spellings of /t/   346

26.5.3.1 /t/ = *t* at Simple Boundaries   346

26.5.3.2 /t/ = *t* in Shortened VCV Strings   347

26.5.3.3 /t/ = *t* in Consonant Clusters and Concatenations   348

26.5.3.4 /t/ = *t* after Vowel Digraphs   348

26.5.3.5 /t/ = *t* after Long Vowels   348

26.5.3.6 /t/ = *tt* at Complex Boundaries   349

26.5.3.7 /t/ = *tt* after Short Vowels   349

26.5.3.8 /t/ = *tt* between Short Vowels and *le*   349

26.5.3.9 /t/ = *t* after Reduced Vowels   349

Chapter 27. The Velar Stops, /g/ and /k/   **350**

27.1 Introduction   350

27.2 The Spellings of /g/   350

27.2.1 Overview   350

27.2.2 Hard and Soft *g, gu,* and *gg*   350

27.2.3 The Minor Spellings of /g/   351

27.2.4 The Major Spellings of /g/   352

27.2.4.1 /g/ = *g* at Simple Boundaries   352

27.2.4.2 /g/ = *g* in Shortened VCV Strings   353

27.2.4.3 /g/ = *g* in Consonant Clusters and Concatenations   353

27.2.4.4 /g/ = *g* after Vowel Digraphs   354

27.2.4.5 /g/ = *g* after Long Vowels   354

27.2.4.6 /g/ = *gg* at Complex Boundaries   354

27.2.4.7 /g/ = *gg* after Short Vowels   354

27.2.4.8 /g/ = *gg* between Short Vowels and *le*   355

27.2.4.9 /g/ = *g* after Reduced Vowels   355

27.3 The Spellings of /k/   355

27.3.1 Historical Sources   355

27.3.2 The Minor Spellings of /k/   356

27.3.2.1 /k/ = *cc*   356

27.3.2.2 /k/ = *kk*   356

27.3.2.3 /k/ = *ch, cch*   356

27.3.2.4 /k/ = *q, qu*   358

27.3.2.5 /k/ = *cq, cqu*   360

27.3.2.6 /k/ = *x*   360

27.3.2.7 /k/ = *lk*   360

27.3.2.8 /k/ = *kh*   361

27.3.2.9 /k/ = *sc*   361

27.3.2.10 /k/ = *gh, kg*   361

27.3.3 The Major Spellings of /k/   361

27.3.3.1 The Major Spellings of /k/ Summarized   361

27.3.3.2 /k/ = *k* before *e, i,* and *y,* but *c* before *a, o,* and *u*   362

27.3.3.3 The Regular Settings for /k/ = *k*   362

27.3.3.4 The Regular Settings for /k/ = *c*   364

27.3.3.5 /k/ = *c* in Shortened VCV Strings   365

27.3.3.6 /k/ = *c* after Reduced Vowels   366

27.3.3.7 /k/ = *c* in the Cluster /kt/   366

27.3.3.8 The Spellings *c* and *k* in Other Consonant Clusters and Concatenations   366

27.3.3.9 The Spelling *ck* Summarized   368

27.3.3.10 /k/ = *ck* after Short Vowels   368

27.3.3.11 Word-final /k/ = *ck* after a Stressed Short Vowel   369

27.3.3.12 Sometimes Word-final /k/ = *ck* after Reduced Vowels   369

27.3.3.13 /k/ = *ck* and the *k*-Insertion Rule   370

27.3.3.14 The Cluster /ks/   370

Chapter 28. The Simple Fricatives /v/, /f/, /th/, /<u>th</u>/, and /h/   **373**

28.1 The Spellings of /v/   373

28.1.1 Historical Sources   373

28.1.2 The Minor Spellings of /v/   375

28.1.2.1 /v/ = *vv*   375

28.1.2.2 /v/ = *lv*   376

28.1.2.3 /v/ = *f*   376

28.1.3 The Major Spelling of /v/   376

28.1.4 The Spellings of /v/ Summarized   377

28.2 The Spellings of /f/   377

28.2.1 Historical Sources   377

28.2.2 The Minor Spellings of /f/   378

28.2.2.1 /f/ = *ph*   378

28.2.2.2 /f/ = *pph*   379

28.2.2.3 /f/ = *gh*   379

28.2.2.4 /f/ = *lf*   380

28.2.2.5 /f/ = *ft*   380

28.2.3 The Major Spellings of /f/ 380

28.2.3.1 The Major Spellings of /f/ Summarized 380

28.2.3.2 /f/ = *ff* in Word-final Position 381

28.2.3.3 /f/ = *f* at Simple Boundaries 381

28.2.3.4 /f/ = *f* in Shortened VCV Strings 382

28.2.3.5 /f/ = *f* in Consonant Clusters and Concatenations 382

28.2.3.6 /f/ = *f* after Vowel Digraphs 382

28.2.3.7 /f/ = *f* after Long Vowels 382

28.2.3.8 /f/ = *ff* at Complex Boundaries 383

28.2.3.9 /f/ = *ff* after Short Vowels 383

28.2.3.10 /f/ = *ff* between Short Vowels and *le* 384

28.2.3.11 /f/ = *f* after Reduced Vowels 384

28.3 Spelling /th/ and /<u>th</u>/ 384

28.3.1 Historical Sources 384

28.3.2 The Minor Spellings 385

28.3.3 The Major Spelling 385

28.3.3.1 /th/ = *th* 385

28.3.3.2 /<u>th</u>/ = *th* 385

28.4 The Spellings of /h/ 386

28.4.1 /h/ = *h* 386

28.4.2 /h/ = *wh* 387

28.4.3 /hw/ = *wh* 388

28.4.4 The Spellings of /h/ Summarized 389

28.4.5 Silent *h* 389

Chapter 29. The Simple Fricatives /z/ and /s/ 391

29.1 The Spellings of /z/ 391

29.1.1 Historical Sources 391

29.1.2 The Minor Spellings of /z/ 391

29.1.3 The Major Spellings of /z/ 391

29.1.3.1 *z* versus *zz* 392

29.1.3.2 *s* versus *ss* 394

29.1.3.3 *zz* versus *ss* 396

29.1.3.4 *z* versus *s* 396

29.2 The Spellings of /s/ 397

29.2.1 Historical Sources 397

29.2.2 The Minor Spellings of /s/ 397

29.2.2.1 /s/ = *sc* 397

29.2.2.2 /s/ = *ps* 399

29.2.2.3 Other Minor Spellings of /s/ 399

29.2.3 The Major Spellings of /s/ 400

29.2.3.1 /s/ = *ss* in Word-final Position after Short Vowels 401

29.2.3.2 /s/ = *s* at Other Simple Boundaries 401

29.2.3.3 /s/ = *s* in Shortened VCV Strings 402

29.2.3.4 /s/ = *s* in Consonant Clusters and Concatenations 402

29.2.3.5 /s/ = *s* after Vowel Digraphs 402

29.2.3.6 /s/ = *s* after Long Vowels 403

29.2.3.7 /s/ = *ss* at Complex Boundaries 403

29.2.3.8 /s/ = *ss* in VCC Strings 404

29.2.3.9 /s/ = *ss* between Short Vowels and *le* 404

29.2.3.10 /s/ = *s* after Reduced Vowels 404

29.2.4 /s/ = *c* 405

29.2.4.1 /s/ = *c* in Element-initial Position 405

29.2.4.2 /s/ = *c* in Element-medial Position 405

29.2.4.3 /s/ = *c* in Element-final Position 406

29.2.4.4 /s/ = *c* in Consonant Clusters 406

Chapter 30. The Palatal Sibilants: /sh/, /ch/, /j/, and /zh/ **407**

30.1 Introduction 407

30.2 The Spellings of /sh/ 407

30.2.1 The Minor Simple Spellings of /sh/: *ch* and *sch* 407

30.2.2 The Major Simple Spelling of /sh/: *sh* 408

30.2.3 The Palatalized Spellings of /sh/ 409

30.2.3.1 /sh/ = *t* 410

30.2.3.2 /sh/ = *s* 410

30.2.3.3 /sh/ = *ss* 411

30.2.3.4 /sh/ = *sc* 411

30.2.3.5 /sh/ = *c* 412

30.3 The Spellings of /ch/ 412

30.3.1 The Minor Simple Spellings of /ch/ 412

30.3.2 The Major Simple Spellings of /ch/: *ch* and *tch* 412

30.3.2.1 /ch/ = *tch* Regularly in Word-final Position 413

30.3.2.2 /ch/ = *ch* at Other Simple Boundaries 414

30.3.2.3 /ch/ = *ch* in Shortened VCV Strings 414

30.3.2.4 /ch/ = *ch* in Consonant Clusters and Concatenations 414

30.3.2.5 /ch/ = *ch* after Vowel Digraphs 415

30.3.2.6 /ch/ = *tch* in VCC Strings 415

30.3.2.7 /ch/ = *ch* after Reduced Vowels 415

30.3.3 The Palatalized Spelling of /ch/: *t* 415

30.4 The Spellings of /j/ 417

30.4.1 Historical Sources 417

30.4.2 The Minor Simple Spellings of /j/: *dj* and *gg* 418

30.4.3 The Major Simple Spellings of /j/ 418

30.4.3.1 /j/ = *dg* in Word-final Position 418

30.4.3.2 /j/ = *g* at Other Simple Boundaries 419

30.4.3.3 /j/ = *g* in Shortened VCV Strings 419

30.4.3.4 /j/ = *g* in Consonant Clusters and Concatenations 419

30.4.3.5 /j/ = *g* after Vowel Digraphs 420

30.4.3.6 /j/ = *g* after Long Vowels   420
30.4.3.7 /j/ = *dg* in VCC Strings   420
30.4.3.8 /j/ = *g* after Reduced Vowels   420
30.4.3.9 The Correspondence /j/ = *j*   420
30.4.4 The Palatalized Correspondence /j/ = *d*   421
30.5 The Spellings of /zh/   421
30.5.1 Historical Sources   421
30.5.2 The Simple Spellings of /zh/   422
30.5.2.1 /zh/ = *g*   422
30.5.2.2 /zh/ = *j*   422
30.5.3 The Palatalized Spellings of /zh/: *s, z,* and *t*   422

Chapter 31. The Nasals: /m/, /n/, and /ŋ/   **423**

31.1 Introduction   423
31.2 The Spellings of /m/   423
31.2.1 The Minor Spellings of /m/   423
31.2.1.1 /m/ = *mb*   423
31.2.1.2 /m/ = *lm*   424
31.2.1.3 /m/ = *mn*   425
31.2.1.4 /m/ = *gm*   425
31.2.1.5 Other Minor Spellings of /m/   426
31.2.2 The Major Spellings of /m/   426
31.2.2.1 /m/ = *m* at Simple Boundaries   426
31.2.2.2 /m/ = *m* in Shortened VCV Strings   427
31.2.2.3 /m/ = *m* in Consonant Clusters and Concatenations   427
31.2.2.4 /m/ = *m* after Vowel Digraphs and Long Vowels   428
31.2.2.5 /m/ = *mm* at Complex Boundaries   428
31.2.2.6 /m/ = *mm* in VCC Strings   429
31.2.2.7 /m/ = *m* after Reduced Vowels   429
31.3 The Spellings of /n/   429
31.3.1 The Minor Spellings of /n/   430
31.3.1.1 /n/ = *kn*   430
31.3.1.2 /n/ = *gn*   430
31.3.1.3 /n/ = *pn*   431
31.3.1.4 Other Minor Spellings of /n/   431
31.3.2 The Major Spellings of /n/   432
31.3.2.1 /n/ = *n* at Simple Boundaries   432
31.3.2.2 /n/ = *n* in Shortened VCV Strings   432
31.3.2.3 /n/ = *n* in Consonant Clusters   433
31.3.2.4 /n/ = *n* after Long Vowels and Vowel Digraphs   433
31.3.2.5 /n/ = *nn* at Complex Boundaries   433
31.3.2.6 /n/ = *nn* in VCC Strings   434
31.3.2.7 /n/ = *n* after Reduced Vowels   434
31.4 The Spellings of /ŋ/, "eng"   435
31.4.1 Historical Sources   435

31.4.2 /ŋ/ = *n*   436
31.4.2.1 /ŋ/ = *n* before /k/ = *k*   436
31.4.2.2 /ŋ/ = *n* before /k/ = *c*   436
31.4.2.3 /ŋ/ = *n* before /g/ = *g*   436
31.4.2.4 /ŋ/ = *n* before /k/ = *ch*   436
31.4.2.5 /ŋ/ = *n* before *x*   436
31.4.2.6 /ŋ/ = *n* before *qu*   437
31.4.3 /ŋ/ = *ng*   437
31.4.4 Two Complications to the /ŋ/ Rule   438

Chapter 32. The Liquids, /l/ and /r/   **439**
32.1 Introduction   439
32.2 The Spellings of /l/   439
32.2.1 The Minor Spellings of /l/   439
32.2.1.1 /l/ = *sl*   439
32.2.1.2 /l/ = *ln*   440
32.2.2 The Major Spellings of /l/   440
32.2.2.1 American Variants and the Emerging Pattern   440
32.2.2.2 The Spellings *l* versus *ll* Summarized   441
32.2.2.3 /l/ = *l* in Initial Position   442
32.2.2.4 /l/ = *ll* in Word-final Position   442
32.2.2.5 /l/ = *l* in Word-final Position   444
32.2.2.6 /l/ = *l* in Shortened VCV Strings   444
32.2.2.7 /l/ = *l* in Consonant Clusters   445
32.2.2.8 /l/ = *l* after Long Vowels and Vowel Digraphs   445
32.2.2.9 /l/ = *ll* at Complex Boundaries   446
32.2.2.10 /l/ = *ll* in VCC Strings   447
32.2.2.11 /l/ = *l* after Reduced Vowels   447
32.3 The Spellings of /r/   447
32.3.1 The Minor Spellings of /r/   448
32.3.1.1 /r/ = *wr*   448
32.3.1.2 /r/ = *rh, rrh*   448
32.3.1.3 Other Minor Spellings of /r/   449
32.3.2 The Major Spellings of /r/   450
32.3.2.1 Variant Spellings with *r* and *rr*   450
32.3.2.2 The Spellings *r* versus *rr* Summarized   450
32.3.2.3 /r/ = *r* in Initial Position   451
32.3.2.4 /r/ = *r* in Word-final Position   451
32.3.2.5 /r/ = *r* in Shortened VCV Strings   451
32.3.2.6 /r/ = *r* in Consonant Clusters   452
32.3.2.7 /r/ = *r* after Long Vowels and Vowel Digraphs   453
32.3.2.8 /r/ = *rr* at Complex Boundaries   453
32.3.2.9 /r/ = *rr* in VCC Strings   454
32.3.2.10 /r/ = *r* after Reduced Vowels   454

Chapter 33. The Semivowels, /w/ and /y/   **456**

    33.1 Introduction   456
    33.2 The Spellings of /w/   456
    33.2.1 The Minor Spellings of /w/   456
    33.2.2 The Major Spellings of /w/   457
    33.2.2.1 /w/ = *u*   457
    33.2.2.2 /w/ = *w*   458
    33.3 The Spellings of /y/   459
    33.3.1 The Consonantal /y/   459
    33.3.2 The Glide /y/   459

Chapter 34. Conclusion   **461**

    Bibliography   **465**
    Index of Words   **475**
    General Index   **539**

Preface

During the last two decades much important work has been done on the study of English orthography, enough that Michael Stubbs can say in his *Language and Literacy* that we now understand the English spelling system and that it is morphophonemic—that is, it relates "orthographic units not only to phonemes, but also to morphemes, and therefore to grammatical and semantic units" (43). Stubbs alludes here to the morphophonemically based work of Richard Venezky, Noam Chomsky and Morris Halle, Carol Chomsky, and K. H. Albrow. These people, and others—such as Robert Oswalt in his short but insightful study—use different versions of morphophonemic theory to find order where for four hundred years critics could see only confusion and whimsy.

In this book I argue that orthography, like morphology or syntax or phonology, is an autonomous and self-governing system, both self-regulating and self-reorganizing. Orthography is not autonomous in the sense of being utterly independent, for it and the other systems interdepend in complex ways. Their interdependent autonomy can be suggested through a metaphor: Morphology, phonology, syntax, and orthography are like poles of force in a complex magnetic system. Their interdependence is like the designs etched into iron filings sprinkled on a sheet above them. The poles are autonomous centers, but their fields of effect so interdepend that at their peripheries it is impossible to tell when you have moved from the field of influence of one clearly into the field of influence of another. Orthography, then, my argument goes, is one autonomous but interdependent system within the larger system of systems that makes up American English. This book describes that autonomy and interdependence, though its major concern is with that systematicity.

Some opening disclaimers are in order. The title, *American English Spelling,* is meant to be taken literally. This is a study of English as it is spelled in America. There is no attempt to speak in an orderly way of spelling in any of the other English-speaking areas. The reasons have little to do with the way in which words are actually spelled, for the differences between American and, say, British English spelling are quite modest. Perhaps the largest among these differences has to do with the British tendency to twin final consonants in unstressed syllables while American English is more insistent that the syllable receive at least secondary stress (see 9.1)—as in *medallist,* usually qualified as "chiefly British," versus *medalist.* Beyond that, there are the old stand-bys: the British predilection for *-our* where American English more regularly has *-or* (see Aronoff 1978); the word-final *re* versus *er* difference. A short visit to New Zealand led to the following list of British spellings that seemed odd to American eyes: *tonnes, tyre, programme, cheque, honour, centre, jewellery, nett (weight), enquiries*—a modest list at worst. The major reason for restricting this study to American English is the marked difference in pronunciation that is found in the other varieties of English, especially in the pronunciation of the vowels. Trying to write sound-to-spelling correspondences for the range of American pronunciations is trying at times; to add, say, British to it would render the job much more difficult.

The subtitle, *An Informal Description,* is meant to suggest that this book is not the kind of modern linguistic science that speaks in algorithmic, formal terms. It is offered, rather, as humanistic scholarship. I take some solace in a work like *On Explaining Language Change,* in which Roger Lass argues convincingly for a view of language and language study based on complementarity. Lass warns us of the potential for delusion in a relentless insistence on deductive formalism. He has helped me feel somewhat less quaint and anachronistic in claiming to study language in the spirit of humanistic scholarship rather than scientific formalism.

I do not deal with proper names in any sustained or orderly way, owing to the fact that each proper name can be pretty much a rule unto itself. This is not to say that proper names are not orthographically interesting and important. Far from it. More than one good and useful book could be written using proper names to demonstrate, among other things, the way the orthographic system has changed across the centuries.

Nor do I attempt to analyze the spelling of schwa or any of the partially reduced vowels, such as unstressed short *i* or the barred *i* recognized in some linguistic analyses. Since any vowel letter and nearly any vowel digraph and trigraph can spell schwa, to try to do reduced vowels justice would have added too much to what is already a lengthy book. A description of the orthography of reduced vowels will have to wait. There is, however, one exception to the omission of unstressed vowel spellings in the following chapters: the first of a pair of vowels in hiatus—a pair that is discussed as the V.V pattern (see 4.2.1) and in which the first vowel is treated as long, even when unstressed, as in the case of the first *e* in *create* or the *i* in *hiatus*.

Unlike Richard Venezky's *Structure of English Orthography*, and, for that matter, nearly all work in orthography, this one does not deal with spelling-to-sound correspondences. It deals instead with sound-to-spelling correspondences. It examines the problem from the standpoint not of the reader but rather of the writer—or at least the speller. Readers start with letters for which they must find the sounds, while spellers start with sounds for which they must find the letters. This book is an example, I believe, of what Z. Šaljapina and V. Ševoroškin had in mind at the end of their review of Venezky's work when they commented on the potential usefulness of a study of English orthography that, unlike Venezky's analytic study, was synthetic.

And finally, this book does not say anything directly to the huge problems of teaching and learning English orthography, in either the reading or the spelling classroom. This silence is somewhat ironic in that my original interest in English spelling grew out of the problems of teaching remedial spelling to college-age students, a project in which I am still much involved. The one thing that I would say about the role of orthography in the classroom is that probably it is better for the teacher to know more rather than less. If we can begin to understand the English orthographic system better, then we should be better able to understand the relationship between that system and the manifold problems of teaching people to read and write our language. Then we should be able to do a better job in the classroom.

The book is divided into four sections. The first, consisting of chapters 1 and 2, presents the approach to orthographic analysis upon which the entire description is based. Chapter 1 sets out a theoretical basis for viewing American English spelling as systematic. Chapter 2 describes the analysis, or explication, of written words into their elements, particles, and processes.

The second section, consisting of chapters 3–7, describes orthographic tactics and tactical rules. Chapter 3 describes the constraints placed on the distribution and sequencing of English vowels and consonants in written words. Chapters 4–7 describe the important tactical strings of vowel and consonant letters. Chapter 4 sets out the major and some of the minor string patterns. Chapter 5 describes the shortening effects of certain suffixes on preceding strings that would normally be expected to contain long vowels. Chapter 6 describes the behavior of one of the two most important strings—VCV, or vowel-consonant-vowel—in disyllables, including the shortening produced by stress frontshifting in words adopted from French. And chapter 7 describes the shortening of VCV strings in the third or fourth syllable from the end of words, especially in Romance adoptions and adaptations.

The third section, consisting of chapters 8–10, describes three major procedural rules that affect the way elements combine: the final *e* deletion rule (chapter 8), the final consonant twinning rule (chapter 9), and the assimilation rules for the final consonant in certain prefixes (chapter 10).

The fourth section is the largest, consisting of chapters 11–33. It describes in some detail the major and minor correspondences between the sounds of American English and their spellings. Chapter 11 discusses the analysis of English sounds and the development of the English alphabet. Chapters 12–17 describe the short vowels; chapters 18–23, the long vowels. Chapters 24 and 25 describe the complex vowels—that is, the diphthongs and vowels colored by a following /r/ sound. Chapters 26–33 describe the eight groups of consonants recognized in this analysis: the front stops, the velar stops, the two groups of simple fricatives, the palatalized fricatives, the nasals, the liquids, and the semivowels.

Chapters 12–33 refer repeatedly to the frequency of occurrence of certain sound-to-spelling correspondences. The source for these figures is the computer study *Phoneme-Grapheme Correspondences as Cues to Spelling Improvement,* by Hanna et al. (1966). Their phonemic analysis has been criticized (by Ney 1974, for instance), and a number of changes have been made to bring it into line with the analysis of English sounds used in this study. But the work of Hanna et al. remains very useful if we remember that the percentages they offer represent an abstract scaling of the occurrence of the variant correspondences. Their figures say nothing about the frequencies the readers and writers of English actually encounter in the written language. Their figures are based on about 14,000 high-frequency word types. In actual written discourse, word types occur as tokens with widely differing frequencies. For instance, in the *American Heritage Word Frequency Book,* which speaks not only in terms of types but also in terms of tokens actually encountered in print, the 100 most common word types cited represent nearly 50 percent of the 5,088,721 word tokens in its tally. Hanna et al. do not describe written English as it is experienced. Still, their figures are useful for comparing and arbitrarily scaling the different correspondences. (Godfrey Dewey's *Relative Frequency of English Spellings* does contain a frequency count that is based on the occurrence of spellings in word tokens rather than word types [1970, 28–47].)

In any work of this kind the two great dictionaries, the *Oxford English Dictionary* (*OED*) and *Webster's Third New International* (*W3*), are the major sources. The debt owed them can never be adequately reflected in the documentation. The next most important source for this study, especially in its historical discussion, is the work of Otto Jespersen. *Sounds and Spellings,* the first part of his *Modern English Grammar,* remains after all these years a remarkable work. Much of importance has been done in the history of English speech sounds since Jespersen's day—for instance, by A. A. Prins (1972) and E. J. Dobson (1957). And yet Jespersen's description remains reliable in its outlines and in the great majority of its details. Further, the organization of Jespersen's *Sounds and Spellings* makes it particularly useful to orthographers. Jespersen's name occurs more often than any other in the documentation of this study, and yet it could well have occurred much more often than it does, so valuable has his work been.

The first sustained work on this book was made possible by a sabbatical year granted to me by Central Washington University. For that I thank Central, its Professional Leave Committee, and the taxpayers of the state of Washington.

I thank Eric Halpern, Humanities Editor at The Johns Hopkins University Press, for his support and advice. To Penny Moudrianakis, whose copyediting skill and good spirit made both this book and its writing much happier enterprises, Εὐχαριστῶ παρὰ πολύ.

And I thank my wife, Carol, who finally convinced me that a sabbatical leave was something to pursue, and once it was granted, that to do such work one should be well away from home and its interruptions and in a place lovely to the soul. Thus, much of the first draft of this book was written in Hawaii, Rarotonga, and Tahiti, and for the memories of those places one also must give thanks.

D. W. Cummings
Central Washington University

Notes on Usage

The Pronunciation Symbols

Most studies such as this one use versions of the International Phonetic Alphabet or of the system devised by George Trager and Henry Lee Smith. But since this study is intended to be useful to teachers and others who are deeply engaged with English spelling without necessarily being trained linguists, it seemed better to use a system of pronunciation symbols that was less technical and perhaps less intimidating. *Webster's Third New International Dictionary of the English Language Unabridged* is the standard for American dictionaries, and so I chose to use the Merriam-Webster system, with two exceptions. Unlike Merriam-Webster, I have not used schwa to represent the stressed vowel in words like *dug*. I have restricted schwa to vowels that are unstressed and reduced, and have represented the stressed full vowel of *dug* as /u/. Also unlike Merriam-Webster, I have not used the diaresis to mark long *u*, preferring instead the macron that is used with the other long vowels. Finally, the equivalences between the pronunciation symbols of the International Phonetic Alphabet and those I have used in this text are given in the table on page xxxii. For more details on the analysis of speech sounds used in this study and on the symbols used to represent those sounds, see section 11.1.2.

Other Symbols

In addition to those discussed above, the following symbols are used throughout the text:

In Pronunciations. A syllable with primary stress is shown with a preceding high-set mark: /ə'lōn/. A syllable with secondary stress is shown with a preceding low-set mark: /'daun̩bēt/. Unstressed syllables are not marked.

IPA	Symbol Used Here	Example	IPA	Symbol Used Here	Example
æ	a	bat	ŋ	ŋ	sing
e	ā	bait	o	ō	boat
ɑ:, ɑ	ä	bother	ɔ	ȯ	bought
aʊ	aù	bout	ɔɪ	ȯi	boy
b	b	bob	p	p	pop
tʃ	ch	church	r	r	roar
d	d	did	s	s	sass
ɛ	e	bet	ʃ	sh	shush
i	ē	beet	t	t	tot
f	f	fluff	θ	th	thin
g	g	gag	ð	t̲h̲	then
h	h	hat	ʌ	u	but
ɪ	i	bit	ʊ	u̇	book
aɪ	ī	bite	u	ū	boot
dʒ	j	judge	v	v	vat
k	k	kick	w	w	wit
l	l	lull	j	y	yet
l̩	ᵊl	little		yū	butte
m	m	mum	z	z	zap
n	n	nun	ʒ	zh	azure
n̩	ᵊn	lighten	ə	ə	alone

In Explications. In the analysis, or explication, of written words into their elements, parentheses indicate word boundaries, plus signs indicate element boundaries within words, and overstruck virgules indicate the deletion of letters. For instance, *explication* would be shown as (ex + plic + ate̸)ion), indicating that it consists of the prefix *ex-*, the bound base *plic +*, and the two suffixes *-ate* and *-ion*, with the *e* in *-ate* being deleted when the *-ion* is added. The close parenthesis after *ate̸* indicates that *explicate* is a word within the derived word *explication*. Because the open and close parentheses are not nested, explications do not show the order in which elements are thought to have been concatenated.

When representing bound bases, a preceding plus sign indicates a terminative base—that is, one that can come at the end of a word. A plus sign after the base represents a nonterminative base—that is, one that cannot come at the end of, or terminate, a word. Thus, *+pete* (as in *compete*) is terminative, *plic +* (as in *explicate*) is not.

In Sets.   Sets of coforms are italicized and enclosed in square brackets, as, for instance, [+ *mit,* + *miss*], the terminative bound bases in such related words as *remit* and *remission.*

In Spellings.   Accepted spellings are italicized. Incorrect, unrecorded, or unexpected spellings are marked with a preceding asterisk: *repare versus *repair.* A following asterisk—as in *sawyer*—indicates that the word has a variant spelling (or pronunciation, or both) relevant to the point at hand.

Usually, elements—that is, prefixes, bases, and suffixes—are italicized, as are individual letters, characters from the IPA, and runes. Elements given in explications are not italicized.

Optional letters in accepted variant spellings are enclosed in parentheses. Thus *gue(r)rilla* represents the two variants *guerilla* and *guerrilla.*

In Letter Sequences.   In representing canonical sequences of letters, V represents any vowel letter, C any consonant, and # represents the end of the word. Primes indicate identical letters. Specific letters are given in lowercase italics. For instance, VC'C'*le*# represents any vowel letter followed by any double consonant followed by word-final *le,* as in *addle.*

In Arrays.   For ease of reading, words and elements listed in the simple arrays are not italicized. Words cited as words in the discursive arrays are italicized, however.

ANALYSIS

1 Spelling as System

The right writing of our English . . . is a certain reasonable course to direct the pen by such rules as are most conformable to the propriety of sound, the consideration of reason, and the smoothing of custom jointly.
—Richard Mulcaster, *The Elementarie* (1582)

1.1 Introduction

More than four hundred years ago in Elizabethan London, Richard Mulcaster, headmaster of the Merchant-Taylors' School, published his spelling text, *The Elementarie*. The Elizabethans were an argumentative lot, and Mulcaster was disturbed by people who even then were claiming that the English spelling system was nonsensical and needed reform. He was particularly disturbed by people like Thomas Smith, John Hart, and William Bullokar, who argued that the English alphabet needed to be made more phonetic. For Mulcaster recognized that a mature spelling system has to do more than spell sounds. Sounds are too changeable and diverse, and to follow them alone can lead to great confusion.

More recently, linguists have pointed out much the same thing—rediscovering, as it were, Mulcaster's four-hundred-year-old insight. But Mulcaster, besides being the first to make the point, was also the one who made it most memorably. The Elizabethans, as we might expect of the subjects of the formidable Queen Elizabeth I, tended to see things in political terms. And Mulcaster, good Elizabethan that he was, presented his argument in the form of a political allegory:

In the beginning Sound was King, with complete dominion over spelling. But the sounds of speech vary a great deal from person to person, from place to place, from time to time. And eventually in the Kingdom of Sound, orthography—or, as Mulcaster called it, "right writing"—grew confused and confusing. The unhappy people petitioned their King for relief, though only with great fear and hesitation. King Sound was predic-

3

tably put off by their petition, but in time they convinced him to agree to have Custom and Reason join him in the rule of spelling. It was only with considerable reluctance that King Sound gave up his complete dominion, and the price for his agreement was his remaining the primary member of the triumvirate. Sound would have to remain the primary rule, but now English spelling would be controlled by "the propriety of Sound," "the smoothing of Custom," and "the consideration of Reason"—jointly. Sound remained primary, but his vagaries were made more sensitive to convention and word history because of the influence of informed Custom and more regular and ruly because of the influence of orderly Reason (Mulcaster [1582] 1970, 64–77).

1.2   The Systematicity of American English Spelling

American English spelling is part of the English language, which, like any language, cannot function unless it is systematic. Thus, the American English spelling system is just that—a system. Spelling is affected by the same systemic demands that are intrinsic to any complex system: the demand to be predictable, consistent, patterned and ruly, nonrandom, and economical; to integrate misfits and holdouts; to resist and yet accommodate change.

Like any other system, the English spelling system is a rule-ordered whole. Its ruliness has been pointed out a number of times recently by a number of different people. Noam Chomsky and Morris Halle in *The Sound Pattern of English* (1968) allude to it repeatedly (see, for example, 46, 48–49, 69, 80n, 131n, 148, 174n, 221). In 1971, in an article in the *Harvard Educational Review*, Carol Chomsky outlined it in clear and convincing terms. Insight into this ruliness informs the work of people like Richard Venezky and Ruth Weir, Fred Brengelman, Michael Stubbs, Robert Dixon and his colleagues, Paul and Jean Hanna and their colleagues, Richard Hodges, Robert Oswalt, and K. H. Albrow. The English spelling system is not an aggregate of different words and spellings; it is a whole that is different from the sum of its parts. And as a system it is affected by the demands necessarily made of any system: the demands for stability, regularity, and organization—in spite of the howls of its critics and would-be reformers.

1.2.1   Performance and Code

Like any linguistic system, the American English spelling system has two aspects. On one hand, there is the abstract **code,** general, conservative, and relatively constant, which all who use the system must learn and

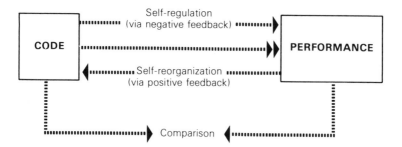

Figure 1-1. Feedback between Performance and Code

share. On the other hand, there is the concrete, particular **performance**, varied and innovative, that arises when someone actually puts the code to use. It was the diversity of this performance that led to the confusions in the Kingdom of Sound in Mulcaster's allegory.

The code is the conservative force in the system; the performance is the source of innovation and change. The history of the system is in large part the story of the interaction between the code and its tendency toward invariance with the performance and its tendency toward variation.

1.2.2 Self-regulation and Self-reorganization

The American English spelling system is both self-regulating and self-reorganizing. Four hundred years ago Mulcaster used a political allegory to make his point; today we are less inclined toward political allegory and more inclined toward such things as the language and imagery of cybernetics and systems theory. Today we are more inclined to say that our spelling system incorporates a feedback loop that monitors the output of the system and compares that sample of output with the expectations and norms of the code. This comparison determines the match between the features of the living performance and the expected norms within the code. It can be visualized as illustrated in figure 1-1.

There are three possible results of the monitoring and comparing via the feedback loop.

First, the performance may match the expected norms of the code, in which case the system remains essentially stable, with no changes in either code or performance.

Second, the performance may not match the expected norms of the code, and the invariant norms of the code may be mapped into the performance so that the change detected in the performance is "brought into line." This is an example of negative feedback. It is a complex, cultural version of the mechanical negative feedback that causes a thermostat to react to an environment cooler than the expected norms by turning on the heat, thereby raising the temperature in the environment to at least the minimum set down in the norms. The invariant norms of the "code"—by which the operation of the thermostat is defined—are mapped into the changing environment. Another way of saying this is that in the process of negative feedback a mismatch between code and performance leads to a change in performance. This process is called **self-regulation.** It is the usual process involved in language-learning: An individual's performance is found not to match the expectations of the code—for instance, he misspells a word on a spelling test—and various devices are used to bring his future performance into line with the expected norms of the code. His spelling is "corrected." In the process of self-regulation the changing performance gives way to the invariant demands of the code.

But in some instances the mismatch between performance and code has a third, quite different result: The variation found in the performance is mapped into the invariants of the code. The mismatch is resolved not by bringing the performance into line with the code as before, but rather by bringing the code into line with the performance. The code is changed. This is an instance of positive feedback, and its effects can be termed **self-reorganization.**

Self-reorganization occurs, usually, as older forms are replaced by newer but more ruly forms that enter the language as variants and then, invoking the power of the pattern they exemplify—invoking, that is, their own ruliness—replace the older, less ruly forms.

An example is the word *millionaire*. Originally the English spelled it as it is spelled in French: *millionnaire,* with two *n*'s. But in the English spelling system the second *n* is an anomaly: The stem is clearly *million,* with the suffix *-aire,* and there is no easy way to account for the second *n*. The second *n* was a fossil, a carry-over from French spelling. So in time it was dropped, making the word more regular and integrating it more into the English spelling system: *million + aire = millionaire.* With this modest orthographic change a form that had been only partially integrated into the English spelling system became more fully integrated. Josef Vachek speaks of linguistic features that are only partially integrated as being **peripheral** to the system of the language, while those that are more fully integrated are more **central,** more typical of the regularities of the system, more influenced by the stabilizing pressures of the linguistic system (1965, 1966a; see also Daneš 1966). In the modest evolution from *millionnaire to millionaire* a more ruly spelling displaced a less ruly one. Such evolutionary changes—sometimes modest as in *millionaire,* at other times considerably more ambitious—lead to greater integration and stronger patterns and processes within the spelling system. (We might hope that in time the same integration will occur with similar French fossil *n*'s, as in *questionnaire, legionnaire,* and, less obviously, *mayonnaise*.)

A somewhat more complex example of the way in which the American English spelling system reorganizes itself involves the two variant spellings of the past tense of the verb *leap—leapt* and *leaped. Leapt,* the less regular form, is also the older. The use of the final *t* in this word goes back to at least the thirteenth century; the use of the final *ed,* to only the sixteenth. The more regular *-ed* suffix is displacing an older suffix that shows up in only a few old past tense verbs, like *slept, crept,* and, more complexly, *left.* The displacement of *leapt* by *leaped* is particularly interesting because in this word the *-ed* suffix is, like *-t,* pronounced /t/. So pronunciation is not motivating the change in spelling. The change is a product of the system's attempt to reorganize itself by making a patterned element, the past tense suffix *-ed,* more stable in its function, more ruly.

Another example of self-reorganization involves the modal auxiliaries *could, would,* and *should,* a group of words whose spellings have become more similar over the centuries, thus foregrounding their functional parallelism:

(Array 1-1)

Old English	Middle English	American English
cūthe	couthe, coude	could
sceolde	scholde	should
wolde	wolde	would

These two processes—self-regulation and self-reorganization—are essential to the viability of the code within a changing environment. On one hand, the code—as a conservative locus of invariance and predictability—must maintain stability; it must slow down the rate of change. This it does via negative feedback and self-regulation. On the other hand, the code must also remain resilient enough to adapt to truly relentless pressures for change from the environment. If it did not, the code would simply become irrelevant to the reality of the living performance. The code avoids irrelevance via positive feedback and the process of self-reorganization.

In *The Flamingo's Smile* (1985) biologist Stephen Jay Gould suggests that a gradual but steady "reduction of variation—particularly the elimination of extremes" may be characteristic not only of all natural systems but also of "any system free to experiment but ultimately regulated by good and workable design" ("Riddles," 259, 258). He uses this notion of "early experimentation and later standardization" to explain the evolutionary shift from "few species in many groups to many species in few groups." (In another essay of that volume ["Losing the Edge"] he uses it to explain the mysterious extinction of the .400 hitter in professional baseball.) Moreover, he suggests that "this principle of diversity—early experimentation and later standardization—may be a true mark of history, producing trends towards decreased variation in basic designs of life" ("Riddles," 260). This principle is much like the statistician's notion of regression to the mean—the raw statistical fact that any event that diverges markedly from the mean is likely to be followed by another event that is closer to the mean.

The history of the English spelling system is marked by just such a reduction and regression. In Middle English there was great variation in spelling, and the variation flourished even after the rise of Written Standard English in the Early Modern period. Variation began to decline in the late sixteenth century and declined markedly in the seventeenth century, encouraged, according to Fred Brengelman (1980), by the efforts of early British orthoepists and orthographers like Mulcaster. This reduction in variation represented a steady process of self-reorganization, of code-changing, brought on by positive feedback that was provided at least in part by those orthoepists and orthographers as they described, taught, and encouraged the emerging patterns and ruliness of the English spelling system. They, figuratively speaking, were describing the mean toward which the orthographic system was regressing. They provided the centering that made that surge of positive feedback and self-reorganization possible, gradually eliminating extremes and reducing variation.

A spelling system evolves over the centuries, through a constant process of change that affects now the performance, now the code. Changes in performance are well illustrated in the process of the individual's language learning. Changes in the code are also constant, though less immediately apparent, involving such things as the respelling of *millionaire, leaped,* and *could, should,* and *would,* and the reduction of variation and extremes in general.

But the issue is really larger than the interaction between the performance and the code. It involves an interaction between the code and its total environment. This environment contains, as perhaps its single most important constituent, the performance. But it also contains other important constituents—specifically, various demands, including the systemic demands discussed earlier. Other demands—phonetic, semantic, and historical—will be discussed later. We can picture the code within its environment as shown in figure 1-2. The code's environment consists of the

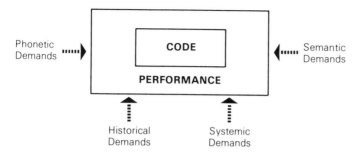

Figure 1-2. The Code in Its Environment

performance plus the various demands, which are mediated to the code via the performance. The performance is the opening in the system. The living performance is the energy source that makes the spelling system open rather than closed.

With this larger sense of environment as performance plus demands, we can describe the life of the spelling system as the ongoing interaction and interdependence between code and environment. As negative feedback arises in the matching of code and environment, self-regulation takes place—hence, language learning. As positive feedback arises in the matching of code and environment, self-reorganization takes place—thus, language change. (For discussion of systems approaches see Laszlo 1972, Ashby 1968, Parsons 1968, and Rapaport 1968.)

1.3 Spelling Rules

Part of the systematicity of American English spelling is the too-often-maligned spelling rule. Spelling rules come in at least two types: tactical and procedural. **Tactical rules** deal with strings of sounds and letters. They describe expected sequences and clusters; they describe patterned regularities in the system. Thus it is a tactical rule that states that the digraph *ck* occurs only after short vowel unigraphs. Contrast, for example, *rock* and *stick* with *broke, rook,* and *stink. Rule* here means simply "a careful description of a conventionalized set of expectations within the system."

Procedural rules govern the way elements—prefixes, bases, and suffixes—are combined to form written words. An example of such a process is the twinning of final consonants in certain stems when certain suffixes are added. Thus the Twinning Rule, a procedural rule, underlies such expected and conventionalized spellings as *running, run + n + ing,* rather than simply *runing, *run + ing. Procedural rules are more like rules in the ordinary sense of prescriptions for expected, or required, behavior, as in the rules of a game. Procedural rules, like Max Black's **instructions,** describe "how to do it," while tactical rules, like Black's **uniformities** (1962, 109–15; see also Gumb 1972, 21–24), describe regularities that result from "how it has been done."

Important products of these tactical and procedural rules are **correspondences,** the conventionalized relationships that exist between sounds and their spellings. It is a correspondence, for instance, that describes the complex sound /kw/ as regularly being spelled *qu* in English, the only known holdouts occurring in *choir, coif,* and *coiffure.* Another correspondence describes the sound /ŋ/ as being spelled *n* before the sounds /k/ or /g/, and *ng* everywhere else.

In the present study, tactical rules will be discussed in chapters 3–7, procedural rules will be discussed in chapters 8–10, and correspondences will be discussed in chapters 12–33.

1.4   Unity, Variety, and Analogy

In any language, as in any other system, there are certain forces that, if left unchecked, could reduce the system to chaos. One such force, the drive for unity and simplicity, arises from the human mind's natural inclination to unity. The mind searches relentlessly for links and unities amidst apparent confusion and diversity, striving to discern ways in which two things can be said to be the same, or can be treated so as to be more the same.

This drive for unity is in fact a drive for analogy, a drive to perceive similarity in the midst of difference. In his *Short History of English* ([1914] 1957), Henry Wyld states well the case for the importance of analogy:

> By the side of sound change the other great factor in the development of language is *Analogy.* This principle has long been recognized among students of language, but a distinction was formerly made by Grammarians between "true" and "false" Analogy. The former was supposed to be a legitimate and natural process, the latter a corrupt and erroneous one. This distinction can no longer be maintained, and whatever the results may be, whether conservative and in accordance with past habits in the language, or whether, on the other hand, they lead to new departures, and, historically speaking, "incorrect" forms, the process of Analogy is now recognized as being a perfectly natural one, of the same essential nature in all cases, and one which at every period of every language is necessarily in operation.
>
> Briefly, Analogy is the process whereby, in the first instance, words are associated in the mind in groups, whether it be according to *meaning, grammatical function, resemblance of sound* [or, we would add, *spelling*], to a

combination of two of these, or even of all three [or four]. When once words have become associated together in the mind there is a tendency to connect them still more intimately and treat them as far as possible in the same way. (49; see also Householder 1971, 61–80)

But this drive for analogy and unity, if carried to excess, could create radical linguistic problems. In time too many things would be the same as too many others; everything, in a sense, would be equal to everything else; distinctions would be impossible to maintain, and the language would not function. There is a contending force, a tendency toward variety or the multiplication of distinctions and different forms—written, spoken, semantic, syntactic. This drive for variety, carried to extremes, would create its own kind of linguistic problems. It would make the language so complex in time that learning it and using it would be extremely, perhaps even debilitatingly, difficult. The contention between the drive for unity and the drive for variety, which reduce down to the drives to declare things similar or different, is an important check and balance in the system of the English language.

Our major concern here is analogy and its role in the drive for unity. Analogy underlies the process of categorizing, without which there could be no language at all. For instance, from a strictly physical and existential point of view, no two spoken sounds can be exactly the same. People's voices differ; acoustical settings differ; even the voice of an individual differs from one moment to the next. But by categorizing we can declare that certain sounds belong to the same category and are, in spite of their differences, functionally "the same."

Thus we get the distinction between **phones** (actual physical spoken sounds, an infinite set in English) and **phonemes** (in English a set of about forty categories of sounds, the members of each of which are taken to be "the same sound" in spite of inevitable physical differences). Behind this categorizing of phones into phonemes lies the power of analogy. In general, analogy leads to simplification as it makes physically different sounds or referents functionally the same. It reduces distinctions. By increasing simplicity and decreasing distinctions, analogy is one of the major forces toward unity in the English language.

Analogy also motivates many of the patterns and processes in the English spelling system. One type of analogy—what we will call **conservative analogy**—is particularly important to English spelling. Conservative analogy differs from general analogy in that where general analogy simply treats certain things *as if* they were equivalent, conservative analogy works to *make* them so. Conservative analogy works to keep the spelling of functionally equivalent elements the same.

Thus, for instance, conservative analogy motivates the most important process involved in the combining of elements in English spelling—the process we call **simple addition,** by which two or more elements, when combined to form a stem or word, simply add together with no changes in spelling. Most combinations of elements are controlled by simple addition, and thus by conservative analogy. The most straightforward instance is the formation of compound words, where almost without holdout simple addition prevails: the constituent stems and elements add together with no change in their spelling, as in *firearm* (fire)(arm) and *redeye* (red)(eye). Simple addition, and thus conservative analogy, also hold in the formation of most complex words, as in *unblushingly* (un(blush)ing)ly) and *reseeded* (re(seed)ed).

The term *conservative analogy* makes use of the double sense of *conservative:* on the one hand, "preserving or saving"; on the other hand, "minimizing." Both senses are useful here, for the equivalent form of functionally equivalent things is preserved or saved, while the number of different but equivalent forms is kept to a minimum. (The term *conservative analogy* is from Otto Jespersen, though at times he called it *preservative analogy,* at other times *preventive analogy* [(1909) 1954, 1:18].) The role of conservative analogy is quite complicated. Sometimes it preempts other processes and patterns, and sometimes it itself is preempted. We will return to this topic later, in subsequent discussions of tactics and processes.

1.5   Demands and Contentions

American English spelling is a system that is flexible and responsive to contending forces and the demands they create. The interaction of these demands determines the system's shape and its complexity. Any adequate description of American English spelling must do justice to these contentions, must recognize them and show how they are resolved. In addition to the **systemic demands** for regularity and order, there are, at the core of the American spelling system, demands stemming from the old dichotomy of language—sound and sense, or expression and content. We call these the **phonetic** and **semantic demands.** Put rather simply, the phonetic demand urges that a given sound be spelled consistently from word to word. The semantic demand urges that a given unit of semantic content be spelled consistently from word to word. In addition to the phonetic and semantic demands, a third—the **etymological demand**—urges that a word be spelled so as to reflect its etymological source (or, more accurately, its user's notion of its etymological source). Brengelman (1980) sketches out the way sixteenth- and seventeenth-century orthographers described and heightened the four core demands. In addition, in the English language we find a growing visual bias and increased standardization, which lead to even more regularity and predictability in American English spelling.

1.5.1 The Phonetic Demand

In terms of Mulcaster's allegory the phonetic demand was the only one at work when Sound was in sole control of Right Writing. In historical terms the same is essentially true of Old English and early Middle English, both of which were considerably more phonetic in spelling than is American English. But in a spelling system in which the only demand is the phonetic one—that each sound be spelled consistently from word to word—you would have, not too surprisingly, a purely phonetic alphabet, such as the International Phonetic Alphabet used by linguists.

In a certain sense the phonetic demand is basic, or at least prior, to others. Back in the early Middle Ages, when the Christian monks first began to write down Old English in their modified Latin alphabet, their main appeal had to be to the ear. They had to find ways to relate the Latin letters they had brought to Britain with the Germanic sounds they heard there. Sound, as Mulcaster would say, was King.

All people who learn to read and write go through a similar phase in which the phonetic demand is dominant. They come to the job of learning to read and write already knowing how to speak the language. Their job during these early stages is primarily one of learning to associate sounds and spellings.

In a strongly phonetic system of spelling, what is written down is a dialect. And if there are sharp dialect differences within a language, the spelling of one dialect can be nearly incomprehensible to the speakers (and thus the readers) of another dialect. In Old English times there were marked dialect differences, but the apparent difficulties were held down somewhat by the fact that most of the important writing that has survived time and the Vikings was done in Wessex, in the West Saxon dialect. However, by Middle English times, though the dialect differences continued, literacy had spread, so the differences in dialect led to sharp differences in spelling. Today we think of Middle English primarily in terms of Chaucer and his *Canterbury Tales,* written in the dialect of late fourteenth-century London. However, many manuscripts have survived in other dialects, and the problems of comprehension that they pose, even to a reader skilled in Chaucer's dialect, attest to the fact that Middle English readers from one dialect area must have had considerable difficulty with the spelling from other areas. It was not uncommon for Middle

English scribes to report that they had "translated" the text from one dialect—say, the northern—to another, in order to make it more accessible to the new intended readership. This translation was in large part a matter of respelling (Craigie [1946] 1969, 116–17). In Mulcaster's terms, the sole dominion of Sound was breaking down, proving itself to be unworkable.

Adding to the breakdown of Sound's sole dominion was the fact that the scribes who were doing most of the spelling did tend to repeat old spellings—that is, to pay less attention to their ears and more to their eyes. Such is the natural, even inevitable, course of events. It is easier to use one's earlier spellings as a source of simplicity and unity, a source that cuts through, even ignores, the complexity and variety of different pronunciations. This tendency is part of the reason we find proofreading so difficult.

The historical referent of Mulcaster's allegorical merging of Sound, Custom, and Reason was the rise of Written Standard English. In fifteenth-century Westminster, in the offices of Chancery, Chancery English, the English of government officialdom, arose. It appears to have developed out of the merging of two earlier, more localized written standards—that from the Wycliffite centers in the central midlands, and that which had developed in fourteenth-century London with the help of writers like Chaucer (Fisher 1977, Samuels 1963). With the rise of this Written Standard, writing—and spelling—began to escape from the variation of dialect and the tyranny of Sound. At this point the phonetic demand began to contend in earnest with the semantic and etymological demands.

1.5.2 The Semantic Demand

The rise of the semantic demand with the rise of the Written Standard in fifteenth-century England is repeated in microcosm in the development of any individual's writing and reading skills. In time, demands other than the phonetic begin to assert themselves, and things get more complex than the simple injunction that a given sound be spelled consistently from word to word. There arises, for instance, the semantic demand that a given unit of semantic content be spelled consistently from word to word.

Usually there is no problem in the interaction of the two demands, phonetic and semantic. For usually semantic units tend to be pronounced the same from one word to another, and so long as sound and semantic content remain constant, the spelling system has no problems. For instance, the simple semantic unit *cat* sounds essentially the same in isolation as it does in the complex word *cats*, or in compounds like *catfish* and *wildcat.* In each instance it is /k/, /a/, /t/ spelled *c, a, t.* The same is true of the semantic unit *dog* in *dogs, dogfish, underdog.*

However, because of rules at work in English pronunciation, it is not unusual for a certain semantic unit to be pronounced differently from one setting to another. For instance, in the two complex words *dogs* and *cats* the second element in each is the plural suffix *-s,* which adds the semantic content "more than one" to the singular noun. But in *cats* the *-s* is pronounced /s/ and in *dogs* it is pronounced /z/. The reason for the difference is regular and systematic: the English language tends to avoid juxtaposing voiced consonants with voiceless ones. The /t/ at the end of *cat* is voiceless, so the *-s* takes on a voiceless pronunciation, /s/, to make the voiceless concatenation /ts/. But the /g/ at the end of *dog* is voiced, so the *-s* takes on a voiced pronunciation, /z/, making the voiced concatenation /gz/. (For more on the clustering and concatenating of voiced and voiceless consonant sounds, see 3.2.2.)

The sounds and spelling of the plural suffix in *dogs* and *cats* is an example of how the simple phonetic demand for a one-to-one relationship between sound and letter can be preempted by the demand for a consistent spelling of a semantic unit from word to word. The resolution of the phonetic demand can be complicated by the semantic demand. The twinning of *n* in *running* is an example of how, on the other hand, the semantic demand can in turn be preempted by the demand for a consistent spelling of a sound, namely, the short *u* in *run* and *running.* One result of that twinning is that the *u* retains the "look" of a short vowel. Another result is that the semantic demand is complicated: the semantic unit that is spelled *run* in the base form *run* appears to be spelled *runn* in the complex *running.* In this sense the semantic demand has been preempted by the phonetic. But a third result of that systematic twinning is that the phonetic demand itself is complicated: the sound /n/, normally spelled *n,* is thereby spelled *nn.*

Another example of the complication of the phonetic demand by the semantic involves the base element spelled *sign:* Used alone as a word, it is pronounced /sīn/ (rhyming with *dine*). With the addition of the suffix *-al* in the word *signal,* it is pronounced /sig/ + /n/ (more or less rhyming with *diggin'*). With the addition of the prefix *de-* in *design,* however, the base *sign* is pronounced /zīn/. And if to *design* we add the suffix *-ate* to form the verb *designate,* the base is now pronounced a fourth way, /zig/ + /n/. In four different settings the same semantic unit has four different pronunciations, which the phonetic demand, left to itself, would render in four different ways. There are reasons, rather complex ones, for the changing pronunciations, but the spelling system cuts through the complexity by spelling the same semantic unit the same way each time, regardless of the systematic changes in its pronunciation. It is always *s, i, g, n*—and again the semantic demand overrides the phonetic. As a result of this accommodation, the sound-to-spelling relationships at work in the phonetic realm are complicated: sometimes *s* spells the sound /s/, sometimes /z/; sometimes the *i* spells a long vowel sound, sometimes a short one; sometimes the *g* is pronounced, sometimes not.

Another result of the accommodation of phonetic demand to semantic is more subtle: the meaning unit spelled *sign* has been dissociated somewhat from the basic sound sequence /sīn/. It is no longer the case that the four letters are simply spelling sounds. They are now spelling a semantic unit that has various pronunciations that are interrelated in a systematic and patterned way. The written word has begun to move away from the spoken word.

At the beginning of his *On Interpretation* Aristotle states that "spoken words are the symbols of mental experience and written words are the symbols of spoken words" (16a). Since alphabetic literacy was relatively new in Aristotle's day, his statement could reflect as much a lingering discomfort with the new written word as a serious semantic analysis (Havelock 1963; Ong 1982, 23–24). But though modern linguists have tended to reject much of the linguistic work done by the Greeks, they have perpetuated this one assertion. Ferdinand de Saussure echoes it in his *Course in General Linguistics* ([1915] 1959), setting the tone for most modern linguists: "Language and writing are two distinct systems of signs; the second exists for the sole purpose of representing the first. The linguistic object is not both the written and the spoken forms of words; the spoken forms alone constitute the object" (23–24). Similarly reductive definitions of writing can be found in Edward Sapir (1949, 19–20) and Leonard Bloomfield (1933, 21, 282).

Yet this assertion that the written language is somehow secondary, merely a record of the primary spoken language, is clearly too easy. Such an easy explanation can work for the early stages of literacy, in both languages and individuals, but in time, after sustained literacy, the written language begins to take on a reality and primacy of its own. The protocol is no longer from writing to sound to meaning. In time it goes directly from writing to meaning, with the sound growing less and less important. Mature readers do not sound out each word, nor do mature spellers. Beginning readers and spellers do, as do mature readers and spellers confronted by some new or temporarily forgotten word that puzzles them. But in time the written language is dissociated from the spoken, and the interaction of the phonetic and semantic demands in cases such as the suffix -*s* and the base *sign* is part of the motivation for that dissociation (see Bissex 1980, 3–100). The ability to ignore sound is a sign of mastery of one's literacy.

Nearly a hundred years ago Henry Bradley argued for the parallel status of speech and writing. Forty years ago Dwight Bolinger (1946) challenged the by-then-common reductionist view. More recently Fred Householder (1971) also has challenged it. Today this rejection of the earlier reductionist view of writing informs the work of Josef Vachek, Eric Havelock, Jack Goody, Walter Ong, and Michael Stubbs. It is also important to the work of modern orthographers like Richard Venezky and K. H. Albrow, as it was much earlier to that of Richard Mulcaster.

The two core linguistic demands on the English spelling system—the phonetic and the semantic—usually pull together, but often they contend with each other. And surrounding this core are other forces, which make their own demands of the system. Most important in this surrounding group is the etymological demand.

1.5.3   The Etymological Demand

The etymological demand is that to the extent possible, a word's spelling reflect its sources. The etymological demand is clearly part of what Mulcaster meant by *Custom* in his allegory. This demand can get very complicated in a language such as English, which has adopted—and adapted—so many words from so many different languages. (In general, an **adoption** is a word brought into the language with no or very little orthographic change. An **adaption,** on the other hand, is a word brought into the language with enough orthographic change to produce at least some, and in many cases total, integration. Obviously, the distinction between adoption and adaptation must remain something of a subjective judgement call.)

By and large the etymological demand parallels the semantic, but it can do violence at times to the phonetic demand, considerably complicating English tactics and sound-to-spelling correspondences. A good case in point is the word *debt*. In Middle English this noun was spelled *dette* and was probably pronounced quite "phonetically": /'detə/, since in Middle English the final *e* was usually pronounced. The word was also spelled *dette* in Old French, from which it was adopted. Later, in sixteenth-century English, it began to be spelled *debte,* and by the eighteenth century it was *debt*. The *b* was introduced, apparently, as part of the Classical Revival of the sixteenth century, for the Latin source of the French word was *dēbitum*. The pronunciation remained what it had traditionally been, but the spelling was changed to reflect more directly the classical origin of the word. In his etymological dictionary Walter Skeat (1882) called *debt* "a bad spelling of *dett*, M.E. *dette*"—which is perhaps due not so much to a phonetic bias on his part as to his generalized impatience with what he saw as sometimes ignorant, sometimes pedantic (and sometimes both!) tinkering with his etymologist's vision of reality. In any case, the modern spelling of *debt* is an instance of the etymological demand contending with and to a certain extent dominating the phonetic. In a sense its sixteenth-century respelling from *dette* is an instance of disintegration or antiadaption.

There are many, many instances of such historical respellings, many of which do a kind of violence to the tactics and correspondences of English. Some examples:

(Array 1-2)

American English	Middle English	French	Latin
indict	enditen	enditer	indictare
chronicle	cronicle	cronique	chronica
fault	faute	faute	fallita
language	langage	langage	lingua
column	columpne	colompne	columna
solemn	solempne	solempne	solemnis

In cases such as these, the American English spelling is a reflection of the way things were in Latin and thus is historically quite accurate. Sometimes the historical reconstructions are less accurate and more imaginative. When done by individual classicists and scholars, this kind of change is called, by philologists such as Skeat, "pedantic interference," and when it is the product of the mind of the populace simply trying to get a semantic and historical handle on a puzzling form, it results in a special kind of adaptation called "folk etymology." But the results tend to be the same: the modern spelling attempts to reflect what are taken to be the etymological sources (and the semantic relationships) of the word. Examples of respelling based on etymological mistakes or folk etymology are *scissors, scythe, ptarmigan,* and *crayfish.*

Scissors in Middle English was *sisoures*, from Old French *cisoires*, from Latin *cīsoria*. In the sixteenth century the word was probably confused with the etymologically unrelated Latin *scindēre* 'to cut' and perhaps the Latin *scissor,* for that is when *sc* first appeared in English. *Scythe*—from Middle English *sithe, sythe*, from Old English *sīthe*—suffered a similar fate.

Ptarmigan was in earlier English spelled *termigant*, from Gaelic *tarmachan*. The *p* was added due to the mistaken notion that the first syllable must reflect a Greek element, *pter-* meaning "wing," as in *pterodactyl* and *helicopter.* This is one of the few mistaken respellings for which responsibility can be levied. In the *Oxford Dictionary of English Etymology* (1966) C. T. Onions identifies the culprit, or culprits, as Sibbald in his *Scotia Ilustrata* (1684) and consequently Pennant in his *Zoology* (1768).

Crayfish earlier was *crevis,* in Middle English *crevise,* adopted from Old French. It provides a standard example of folk etymology: The syllables of *crevise* do not hook up semantically or historically with any other elements in English, and the users of a language tend to reject singletons, misfits, to make them fit somehow; the second syllable of *crevis* is phonetically similar to *fish;* and the creature in question is somewhat like a fish; so *fish* it became. The *cray* can be seen as an adaptation of *cre,* though the variant *crawfish* has always seemed to me to be more appropriate (suggesting, as it does, crawling and claws).

The point here is that "pedantic interferences," be they correct or mistaken, as well as the steady anonymous adaptation by folk etymology, must be seen as important parts of the evolution of the spelling system. They reflect the human factor at work, and as such they remind us that language is a human creation, for use by and for humans. At the same time, they represent the relentless movement of the language toward more complex unities, tighter patterns, more regularity, less variation, and finally, in one sense, greater simplicity. These "pedantic" or "folk" historical respellings are clear instances of the etymological—or, more generally, the historical—demand at work on the spelling system, the demand that the spelling somehow reflect the historical sources and relationships of the word, or at least the user's notions of those sources and relationships.

As new words are brought into the language, through either simple adoption or more complex adaptation, they tend either to confirm the existing system, leading to greater pattern and predictability, or to challenge the system, introducing spellings that run counter to existing patterns and expectations. Some adaptations, with changes designed to make them look and sound more English, can and do confirm the system. Examples would be perfectly English-looking recent adaptations such as *moose* (from Natick *moos*), *soy* (from Japanese *shōyu*), *carboy* (from Persian *garāba*), *dervish* (from Turkish *dervis*), and *caddy* and *paddy* (from Malay *kati* and *padi*). The Malay word *kechup* has produced the following variant spellings, different attempts at adaptation and integration: *ketchup, catchup, catsup.*

But some adaptations, though they move closer to the established patterns of American English spelling, are still unusual enough to complicate those patterns and to challenge our expectations. An example is a word like *gnu*. It is adapted from the Kaffir word *qnu*, and is considerably more English-looking than its source. But the word-initial /n/ = *gn* correspondence and the word-final *u* are rare enough in English that *gnu* still challenges our expectations and complicates at least one tactical rule, which deals with avoiding word-final *u* (see 8.1.4).

Adoptions do not entail an attempt to adapt the word to the English spelling system at all. The word is simply brought into English and spelled as it was spelled in the original—sometimes doing violence to American English tactics, procedures, and correspondences. Fairly well known examples are *poi* (with the unusual word-final *oi*), *llama* (with the unusual word-initial *ll*), and *ski* (with the unusual final *i*). Less well known are words like the technical Greek adoptions *cnida* and *phthalein*, the Maltese *dghaisa*, and the Maori *ngaio*. Such unadapted, unintegrated adoptions pose genuine challenges and create genuine complications for English spelling. Most unintegrated, peripheral words are such adoptions. (Craigie discusses a number of such unadapted and exotic forms in his *English Spelling* [(1927) 1974, 74–91].)

Particularly complicating are those adoptions that might be called "cultural" or "status words." Brengelman (1971) has pointed out that one of the functions of the English spelling system is to mark various registers in the lexicon. Commonly cited instances of this include the Greek spellings that are retained in words from the technical register (for instance, *ph* for /f/, *rh* for /r/, *ch* for /k/, as in *physics, rheostat, chloride*); the foreign-looking Italian spellings that are retained in the musical register (*pianissimo, allegretto, concerti*); and the adoptions from French that deal with cooking or with the arts or high fashion (*flambé, vinaigrette, ballet, revers, bis*). All are adoptions that have resisted integration and have retained in large measure their original sounds and spellings. They all remain at the periphery of and complicate the English spelling system.

Dis-integration, or antiadaptation, as with the respelling of *dette* to *debt*, occurs when a once-integrated word is reintroduced into the language with its foreign spelling. The word *debonnaire* was brought into the language quite early, deriving from Old French *debonaire*. In Middle English it had some variant spellings, including the quite integrated *debonair*. However, in the seventeenth century the word became popular again, this time being influenced by the Modern French spelling, *debonnaire*, with its extraneous *n*. Thus today we have three variant spellings showing a scale from the most to the least integrated and adapted: *debonair, debonaire, debonnaire*.

1.5.4 Standardization and the Growing Visual Bias

In earlier centuries readers had a definite aural bias. Medieval readers read more in terms of the ear and the sounded word. Even readers who read to themselves read aloud, slowly and carefully (Chaytor 1950, 10–21; Clanchy 1979, 202–20; McLuhan 1960). Silent speed-reading is a quite recent development, a development that reflects the growing visual bias of readers. As has been said before, the protocol no longer need run from written word to sound to meaning (as it did in earlier centuries). It can now run the shorter route, directly from written word to meaning. As this happens, the written word grows more autonomous, and the user's bias shifts away from the aural and toward the visual.

A specific instance of this shifted bias has to do with the legal status of surnames. In the early seventeenth century Shakespeare signed his will with two different spellings. There was nothing unusual about this variation because in those days one's surname was taken to be a sound rather than a written form. It could be spelled any number of ways, just so long as the spelling could be interpreted as the spoken name. Today the situation is reversed. Today you can change the pronunciation of your name quite casually, but changing its spelling requires legal action. If, for instance, you had the somewhat unfortunate last name *Snortin,* you could declare that the *s* was silent and that your name should be pronounced as if it were spelled *Norton,* and assuming that you could convince enough people that that was how you wanted your name pronounced, that is how it would be pronounced. However, if you wanted to change the written form, the spelling, from *Snortin* to *Norton,* you would have to take legal action, for today a person's legal name is no longer a spoken form, or pronunciation; it is now a written form, a spelling. The bias has shifted, from aural to visual.

This shift, in turn, has led to more concern for a standardized, consistent spelling. Today people named *Shakespeare* must settle on one spelling and stick with it. And what is true of one surname is true of the lexicon in general. In Middle English there were variant spellings, sometimes many variant spellings, for nearly all words. A look at the lists of spelling forms at the head of entries in the *OED* quickly confirms that statement. For instance, the *OED* shows these variants, some of them occurring up into the seventeenth century, for the primer standby *cat: catt, catte, kat, katt, katte.* For *husband* it shows over thirty variants, including *husbonde, husebande, husebonde, hosebaunde, hosband, housbond, hosbon, huszbande, housebande, hisband,* and (!) *housebounde.* By Early Modern English times (the fifteenth and sixteenth centuries), the number of variants

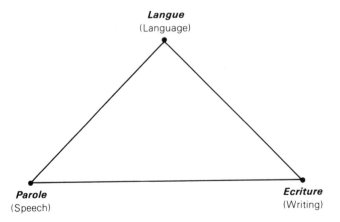

Figure 1-3. Goody's Trichotomy

had declined. In Modern English, including American English, it has declined even more. Though still far more than most teachers like to admit, the number of variant spellings is much smaller than it used to be, and smaller than many spellers would like to see. This increased predictability and invariance, though it makes things more difficult for the speller, is absolutely essential to today's silent speed-reader.

The rise of a standardized orthography and the growing visual bias suggest some limitations to Saussure's important dichotomy between *langue* 'language' and *parole* 'speech' (1959, 7–15). Jack Goody, who rejects the reductionist view of the written word, expands Saussure's dichotomy to a trichotomy (see figure 1-3) (1977, 77). Goody's trichotomy is a useful one, and even more useful if we think of the vertical sides of the triangle as representing the interaction and interdependence of the three components: speech and writing are the realms of linguistic performance, while language is the realm of linguistic code. Positive and negative feedback occur along the two vertical sides of the triangle. Thus speech, reflecting the phonetic demand and acting through positive feedback, affects the language code, which in turn, through negative feedback, affects the written performance. But the reverse is also true: writing, through positive feedback, affects the language code, which in turn affects speech, as, for instance, in spelling pronunciations.

1.5.4.1 Spelling Pronunciations

Spelling pronunciations are one symptom of the shift from the aural to the visual bias. In spelling pronunciations speakers change the sound of a word by bringing it more in line with its spelling. For instance, the older pronunciation of *forehead*, the only pronunciation given in the *OED*, is with no /h/ sound. *W3*, however, shows a newer pronunciation with the /h/ suggested by the spelling. A sampling of spelling pronunciations provided by Householder includes the following, all of which have modern pronunciations that are closer to their spelling than were their older, traditional pronunciations: *yesterday, Wednesday, diphtheria, diphthong, harass, kiln, victuals, conch, draught, certain, author, yes, housewife, gold, bomb, jaunt, laundry, sewer* (1971, 252–53).

Though underestimated, spelling pronunciation is an important and respectable factor in language change. Jespersen ([1909] 1954) says that spelling pronunciation has affected the pronunciation of all the following words: *second* (1:25); *nephew* (1:42); *theater, apothecary, catholic, throne* (1:45); *humble, host, inherit, heretic, heresy, homely, hypocrite, hypocrisy, hospital, heritage, heritor, humor, hermit, hotel* (1:61–62); *novel* (1:91); *periwig* (1:105); *registrar* (1:198); *assoil, precise* (1:204); *wassail* (1:268); *fault, vault, assault, Walter, altar, fealty, moult, cauldron, baldric, herald, ribald, emerald, soldier, falcon, realm* (1:295–97). In many cases he is, like Householder, offering examples from larger groups, and in more general terms he suggests that spelling pronunciation has restrained palatalization "in rare or literary words" (1:342) and has helped keep alive the insistence on the /hw/ pronunciation of *wh*-words, like *whale* and *which* (1:374–75). (For a discussion of the role of spelling pronunciation in the history of /h/ see Stubbs 1980, 36–40. See also Bolinger and Sears 1981, 95–97; Heller and Macris 1968; Kerek 1976; Levitt 1978; Skousen 1982; Smith and Baker 1976.) It seems likely that something like spelling pronunciation was part of the process that led to the leveling of dialect differences in late Middle and Early Modern English. Michael Samuels says that "the evolution and spread of standard English in the fifteenth and sixteenth centuries was primarily through the agency of writing, not speech" (1963, 87).

The most obvious effect of spelling pronunciations is to bring the sound of words into line with the predominant sound-to-spelling correspondences, thus simplifying and regularizing these correspondences even more. Spelling pronunciations are more typical of American English than British English, perhaps because of the national predisposition among Americans to follow the written word more than the spoken.

With the rise of the Written Standard in the fifteenth century, writing—and spelling—began to escape from the variation of dialect. This escape encouraged the shift to a visual bias, which in turn made spelling pronunciations possible. And spelling pronunciations represent the completion of an important reversal of energies: Whereas before the spoken dialect determined what was written, now what was written began to affect what was spoken. The rise of a written standard—working together, to be sure, with the mass media and other technological innovations—leads to the rise of a spoken standard, particularly in the United States.

One effect of this spoken standard has been to level pronunciation in the United States—and, to a certain extent, pronunciation in all English-speaking countries of the world. Dialect differences tend to disappear in what might be called the Midwesternizing of American speech. Even the weather ladies on Boston television sound as if they are speaking to and from Indianapolis. This leveling of dialect differences may have little direct effect on the spelling system, in the sense of changing the way words are spelled, but by leveling differences in pronunciation, it helps simplify and heighten sound-to-spelling correspondences.

1.5.4.2   The Public Uses of Writing

In one sense the demands arising from the public uses of writing are closely related to the changing bias discussed earlier. In general, as the written word is put to more and more public uses, the need for standardization and ruliness increases. This is true not only of the history of the written language itself but also of the history of individuals' uses of language. Children who "write" in private scripts decipherable only to themselves are not concerned with standardization. They are in a position much like that of Lewis Carroll's caterpillar: just as the caterpillar's words mean whatever he wants them to mean, infant spellers' scribbles spell whatever they want them to spell. As the individual moves from this purely private use of written language ("private" because the writer is also the sole reader) to more social uses of language, where there are other readers, but readers who are close to and share much with the writer, who can understand and even expect idiosyncrasy, the need for standardization increases but is still not fully developed. Only a churl corrects spelling errors in a love letter.

However, when the individual speller moves beyond the private and social uses of writing to the more public uses of school and job, the pressures of standardization become very strong, much stronger than logic would require if comprehension and legibility were the only criteria. In the public uses of writing, correctness becomes a mark of competence, of status, and, alas, even of something like moral rectitude. Standardization is immensely, even inordinately, important. And this puts extra pressure on the spelling system to be regular, patterned, and predictable.

1.6 The Principle of Preferred Regularity

A spelling is correct if it is recorded by reputable dictionaries as *the* spelling or as *one* of the variant spellings of a word. But the several fine and reputable dictionaries with which American English is blessed do not always agree on which spellings to list as accepted variants. It seems wise to take what might be called the "loose constructionist" view of correctness: a spelling is correct if it is recorded as an accepted variant by even only one current and reputable dictionary. (By "reputable dictionary" we mean *W3* or any of the standard college dictionaries used in Donald Emery's study of variant spellings [1973].)

Three points to remember about variants are: (1) all are equally correct, but (2) not all are equally common, and (3) not all are equally regular.

Orthographically, a variant's relative commonness is not so important as its relative regularity. Faced with variants, a speller's most sensible approach would seem to be to choose the most regular. This approach is known as the **Principle of Preferred Regularity.** If the dictionaries give us the variants *busing* and *bussing,* the Principle of Preferred Regularity leads us to prefer *bussing* because it is a regular instance of the Twinning Rule: (bus)s + ing). So, too, *bussed* and *busses.* Preferring the spellings with *ss* implies nothing about the relative frequency of the variants. In fact, the variants with *s* are probably more common than those with *ss*. This difference in frequency is suggested by the fact that the spellings with *s* occur as first entries in *W3* and in the *American Heritage, New Collegiate, New World,* and *Standard Collegiate* dictionaries. The *ss* spellings occur as first entries in only one dictionary, *Random House.*

Just as preferring *bussing* to *busing* implies nothing about the relative frequency of the two spellings, neither does it imply anything about their relative correctness. Both, since they are recognized and recorded variants, are equally correct. All that preferring *bussing* to *busing* implies is that the former is more regular in terms of the procedures and tactics of American English. By adhering to this principle, we assist the spelling system in its systemic evolution toward greater regularity and simplicity. (For more on *bussing* and *busing* see Bowman 1966.)

In the orthographic system, repeated specific events tend to lead to patterned general processes. As the patterned process grows stronger through the accumulation of specific events, it reaches out via the power of analogy to attract events that may not be related to it in any historical or rigorously logical sense. What is important is the emerging pattern. Recognition of the pattern leads to greater understanding of the events

involved, greater rationality. Also, by recognizing that emerging pattern
and staying out of its way by invoking the Principle of Preferred Regularity, we encourage (or at least allow) the orthographic system to evolve.
For instance, the word *mileage* was sometimes spelled *milage* in the
eighteenth century. (The *OED* shows a quotation from Benjamin Franklin
without the first *e*.) But the spelling *mileage* predominated in the nineteenth and twentieth centuries, so that *milage* is now a rather rare variant,
and is not even recorded in all American dictionaries. However, the
pattern that has been emerging in English spelling since the Middle Ages
would call for *milage* as the ruly spelling: *milage* = *milé* + *age*. A final *e*
whose only function is to mark a preceding vowel as long should be
deleted when a suffix is added that starts with a vowel. So *mileage* is a less
ruly spelling than *milage*, which the Principle of Preferred Regularity
would lead us to choose.

Admittedly, with some variants it is difficult to know which, if any, is
the most regular. For instance, *bogeyman, boogeyman, bogyman, boogieman*, and *boogyman* all are recorded as variants. To prefer one over the
other on the grounds of greater regularity seems risky at best. But, on the
other hand, since we are given a choice between, say, *cancellation* and
cancelation, the Principle of Preferred Regularity would lead us to choose
cancelation since it fits the Twinning Rule, while *cancellation* is excep-
tional, even though it is the first entry in *W3* and in all dictionaries in
Emery's compilation and even though the *Random House* and *Webster's
New World* do not even list *cancelation* as a variant (see chapter 9 for the
Twinning Rule).

1.7   Well-formed and Ill-formed Spellings

Closely related to this concern with relative regularity is the distinction
between well-formed and ill-formed spellings. A spelling is well formed to
the extent that it satisfies the following conditions: (1) it contains elements
appropriate to the intended meaning and use; (2) it spells the individual
elements consistently with the known sound-to-spelling correspondences;
(3) it spells the total word consistently with the known tactical and
procedural rules.

A word is ill formed if it fails on any one or a combination of these three
features. Thus, *repare, a common spelling up into the seventeenth century, though it would today be called "incorrect," is well formed because
it obviously consists of the proper selection of elements and is consistent
with the known principles of affixation that apply. It also spells the base
element *pare* in a way that is not only consistent with sound-to-spelling

correspondences but is even consistent with the other members of the *pare* group: *prepare, separate, apparatus, parade, apparel, disparate*. On the other hand, *repair,* though accepted as correct, is from our point of view ill formed to the extent that its spelling of *pare* is idiosyncratic and inconsistent with its spelling everywhere else in the *pare* group. *Repair* is well formed to the extent that it is consistent with the known and relevant principles of affixation, and its idiosyncratic spelling of *pare* is at least consistent with the sound-to-spelling patterns for /âr/, as in *stair, air, chair, lair.* Obviously, the distinction between well-formed and ill-formed words is a scaled polarity rather than a dichotomy like our notions of correctness in spelling. Unlike the typical notion of correctness, the distinction between well-formed and ill-formed words is not binary.

1.8   Accepted, Unaccepted, and Unrecorded Spellings

We can also distinguish between spellings that are accepted as correct and those that are unaccepted. Many, many words in American English have more than one accepted spelling (see Emery 1973). As noted earlier, our criterion for an accepted correct spelling will be that the spelling must occur as an accepted variant in at least one of the current reputable American dictionaries. The modifier *current* is important, for the notion of what are and are not accepted variants changes over time. A spelling is unaccepted if, logically enough, it is not listed as the spelling or as an accepted variant spelling in any current American dictionary.

That last statement is accurate enough if the spelling contrasts with some other spelling that *is* listed. For instance, we know that *repare is not an accepted spelling, not just because we do not find it listed in any dictionary, but also because we do find *repair.* But a spelling may not be listed in any dictionary, and thus may not be compared with some other spelling that is listed, simply because the word, though used and recorded in the past, is no longer in use. The *OED* and the *Dictionary of American English* contain hundreds and hundreds of words that were once used in English but that have disappeared from the everyday language and the current dictionaries. Or a spelling may not be listed owing to the fact that it has not been used as yet, or perhaps because it was used but was never caught by any of the dictionary compilers, or perhaps because it was used, was caught, but was not recorded, simply because the editor decided that it was too local or rare or otherwise too insignificant an item to consume important space in the dictionary. In short, we have a number of well-formed spellings that are neither accepted nor unaccepted; they are simply not currently recorded.

These well-formed but unrecorded spellings become quite important later in this study, in the explication of complicated words. This explication will try to unfold the elements that are contained within a longer, complicated word. (See chapter 2.) Without worrying too much for the time being about the technicalities involved, we would explicate the word *competition* as (com + pete̸) + ite̸ + ion), which means that the prime word in the noun *competition* is the verb *compete*, which itself consists of the prefix *com-* and the base *+pete*. At the next level we encounter the spelling *competite*, which consists of the verb *compete* plus the suffix *-ite*, with the final *e* in *compete* being deleted when the suffix is added. *Competite* is a spelling that is well formed but that has apparently never been recorded. It is a potential word, parallel with the adjective-noun *composite*, which would also explicate to a verb plus *-ite:* (com + pose̸) + ite), which could then take *-ion* to form *composition*, parallel with *competition*.

The English word-formation system is so rich that we cannot make use of all of the potential it offers. We already have the adjectives *competitive* and *competing;* we do not feel a need for *competite*—or at least so far we have not. It is quite possible that at some point a distinction will arise that will lead to the use of *competite*, probably via back-formation from *competition*, but for now it remains a potential accepted spelling, well formed but never recorded.

So we have two distinctions—the first a two-way distinction between well-formed and ill-formed spellings, the second a three-way distinction among accepted, unaccepted, and not currently recorded spellings.

As we think about the interaction of these distinctions, we must realize, first of all, that not all accepted spellings are well formed. As was pointed out earlier, *milage* is an instance of an ill-formed but accepted spelling. *Repair* is another example; another ill-formed but accepted spelling is *forty*, which in view of *four, fourteen*, and the parallel with *six, sixteen*, and *sixty*, and other sets, really ought to be spelled with an *ou*. The anomalous French double *n*'s in words like *questionnaire, legionnaire*, and *debonnaire* are also instances of accepted ill-formedness.

We can summarize the types of spellings, then, as follows:

Group 1. Accepted Spellings
    a. Spellings that are well formed and accepted
    b. Spellings that are ill formed but accepted
Group 2. Potentially Accepted Spellings
    c. Spellings that are well formed and were accepted and
       recorded in the past but are no longer recorded

      d. Spellings that are well formed but have never been
         recorded
Group 3. Unaccepted Spellings
      e. Spellings that are well formed, that may have been
         accepted and recorded in the past but are currently not
         accepted spellings of the intended words (example:
         *repare)
      f. Spellings that are ill formed and unaccepted

1.9   Goals of This Description

1.9.1   Minimum and Maximum Simplicities

American English orthography consists, then, of interacting and interdependent linguistic forces and their demands—systemic, phonetic, semantic, etymological. Sometimes these demands work together, but very
often they contend with one another. American English orthography is
marked by a growing visual bias, increasing standardization, and increasing regularity and pattern. It includes accepted spellings that are ill
formed and well formed, unaccepted spellings that are ill formed and well
formed, and unrecorded spellings, many of which are at least potentially
well formed within current orthographic rules and patterns. In order to
describe American English spelling adequately, we must organize all of
this so as to make these rules and patterns more understandable and all of
the information contained within American English orthography and its
words more accessible.

    The Gestalt psychologists spoke of certain principles of organization
that control the mind's quest for a good Gestalt—that is, a good form or
organization. Important principles in this good Gestalt are simplicity,
symmetry, regularity, and pattern, together with closure and the best and
tightest organization possible with the material given (see Katz 1950,
Kohler 1959, Koffka 1935, Wertheimer 1950). An analysis and description
of the American English spelling system should try to resolve the often
contending demands of the system into the simplest organization possible. But the Gestaltists spoke of two kinds of simplicity (Koffka 1935,
171–74). The first, called **minimum simplicity,** is the simplicity rendered by
applying a principle of homogeneity, so that one of the demands is allowed
to dominate all others. An example of a minimum simplicity would be that
purely phonetic spelling yearned for by so many spelling reformers over
the centuries. Such a reform would produce a minimum simplicity because it would take a complex and dynamic system and reduce it to one

single, arbitrary principle. Minimum simplicities lead to bad Gestalts, to unsatisfying and finally unstable organizations. In Mulcaster's allegory the realm of King Sound, with its minimum simplicity, proved to be unstable.

For a more satisfying and stable organization, we need turn to the second kind of simplicity, **maximum simplicity,** which Koffka describes as the simplicity of "perfect articulation," wherein all the contending demands are taken into account and allowed their full interaction, somewhat as in the conclusion of Mulcaster's allegory, with Sound, Custom, and Reason working together jointly.

Thus, a good description of American English spelling should strive for the stability and power of a maximum simplicity, for as thorough as possible an articulation of the demands and contentions in the system.

1.9.2 System-centered versus Use-centered Descriptions

If the output of the American English spelling system is represented by the six groups described in 1.8, the question then becomes, to which of the six should a description of the system be held to account? A description that accounted systematically for well-formed words only might be called a system-centered description, one that emphasized regularity and system at the expense of holdouts and misfits. A description that accounted for and described the individual accepted words within the lexicon, minimizing any regularity and systematicity at work, might be called a use-centered description. It is fair to say that scholarly technical treatments, such as Venezky's *Structure of English Orthography* (1970) and (less directly) Chomsky and Halle's *Sound Pattern of English* (1968) tend in the first direction, toward system-centeredness. But textbooks and similar, more popular treatments—especially proreform manifestos—tend to be use-centered, even to the extent of denying that any real system exists at all, at least insofar as they often deny the existence of any true and reliable spelling rules.

Descriptions and rules that are rigorously system-centered should lead only to well-formed spellings. Those that are rigorously use-centered should lead only to accepted spellings. The following description hovers somewhere between these two extremes. Its general end will be to rationalize spellings as much as possible, in the sense of making more rational, or giving the reasons for. It will do this on the assumption that what can be made more rational will become better understood and more accessible. To do this it will follow an ordered list of desiderata:

First, it will attempt to include a given spelling within a pattern or process that is universal within the system and as reliable as that high level of generality allows. Examples of universal patterns are the VCC Pattern, a tactical pattern defining stressed short vowels (see 4.3.3), and the Twinning Rule (see chapter 9).

Second, failing the first, it will attempt to include a given spelling within a subpattern or subprocess, which though perhaps quite local, can still be made rational. The *k* insertion in words like *picnicking* and *trafficker* is an instance of a very localized subpattern.

Third, failing the first and second, it will present the historical basis for the peculiarity represented by the given spelling—including a description of how, though accepted, it is ill formed or in some sense anomalous. Examples are words like *debt* and *indict*.

Fourth, failing the first, second, and third desiderata, it will simply list the spelling, again showing its ill-formedness or anomaly and relating this anomaly to the larger, more rational patterns and rules within the system—as, for instance, with the hard-core holdout *forty*.

In short, although this description will stress rational system, pattern, and regularity, it will also use that system to describe accepted but ill-formed spellings that represent holdouts to the patterns and regularities.

The following chapters—dealing with orthographic analysis, tactical rules, procedural rules, and sound-to-spelling correspondences—try to take into account the self-regulation and self-reorganization taking place in the system and to articulate into the Gestaltists' maximum simplicity the contentions among the phonetic, semantic, and etymological demands. They try to describe accurately, if tentatively, the interplay of tactical and procedural rules which informs the sound-to-spelling correspondences in American spelling. They attempt to treat the American English spelling system—or, as Mulcaster would have it, "the right writing of our English"—as "a certain reasonable course to direct the pen by such rules as are most conformable to the propriety of sound, the consideration of reason, and the smoothing of custom jointly."

2 The Explication of Written Words

2.1 The Theory of Explication

Explication is a specific strategy for analyzing written words. To explicate words is to analyze them into the smallest written parts that contribute semantic content. These smallest written parts are called elements. In addition to analyzing words into their elements, explication also reveals the relatively few particles and processes that are of orthographic importance. Explication is explanation in something like the etymological sense: "an unfolding, a folding out of the infolded parts." Explication tries to make explicit the information that lies implicit and folded within the written word so that it can become part of our lexical understanding. In their psychological study of English spelling patterns, Philip Smith and R. G. Baker comment that even "linguistically unsophisticated subjects can squeeze a large amount of information out of a word's spelling" (1976, 284–85). Explication is meant to build from and add to this ability.

The theory of explication is meant to support our efforts to teach and learn the written English language—how to spell it, how to read it, how to understand better the structure and function of its words. Since its motivation is finally, in the broadest sense, pedagogical, explication strives for concreteness and accessibility in its descriptions. *Accessibility* is being used here much as Charles Read recently used it to refer to "the relative ease with which a learner or a user can grasp and manipulate" the entities identified in an analysis (1983, 153).

This chapter discusses the two major classes of fundamental entities in the explication of written words: elements and particles. **Elements,** again, are the smallest parts of written words that contribute semantic or syntactic content. Elements are either **free** or **bound;** that is, they either can or cannot stand alone as separate words. They are also either **terminative** or **nonterminative;** that is, they either can or cannot stand at the end of words. There are three types of elements: **prefixes, bases,** and **suffixes.** All prefixes and suffixes are bound. Some bases are bound, some are free. Some bases are terminative, some are not.

Some elements—called **coelements**—come in **sets** of two or more and work together as orthographic teams. An example is the set containing the *-s* and *-es* forms of the plural suffix, as in *hugs* and *kisses*.

Particles are letters that are inserted between elements in a word. Particles contribute neither semantic nor syntactic content. Examples are the *o* in the compound *speedometer* and the second *t* inserted in *hitter.*

2.2 The Explication of Elements

2.2.1 Elements and Morphemes

Elements are the written language's parallel to the spoken language's morphemes. Their parallelism with morphemes is very close, but it is still better to distinguish the two with different names. For example, linguists recognize a plural morpheme that has three forms, or allomorphs: /s/, /z/, and /iz/—as in *cats* /kats/, *dogs* /dȯgz/, and *foxes* /'fäksiz/. This morphemic analysis is based on the way things sound. But explication into elements is based on how things look, and it treats the plural suffix as an element with two coforms, spelled *s* and *es*—as in *cats* and *foxes*. We can then go on to point out that these two different forms of the plural suffix have three different pronunciations, as in *cats, dogs,* and *foxes.*

Instead of a single morpheme with three allomorphic forms, explication describes a set of two coelements—with three pronunciations. This lack of correspondence with so simple an instance as the plural suffix is enough to impress on us that morphemes and elements are quite different things, parallel but different, and that we ought to keep them separate in our minds. Thus, we speak no more in terms of morphemes but rather in terms of elements, defined, again, as the smallest parts that contribute semantic content to the written word.

2.2.2 Prefixes, Bases, and Suffixes

In most situations the user of English has no problem at all recognizing prefixes, bases, and suffixes. For instance, in the sentence, "They re-painted the old car" the complex word *repainted* obviously contains three elements—a prefix, a base, and a suffix: *re* + *paint* + *ed.* The base *paint* is the word's semantic core, the starting place for describing what the word is being used to mean in a given utterance. The prefix and suffix add semantic content to that core, the prefix *re-* adding the content "again," and the suffix *-ed* adding "in the past."

Prefixes function in several different ways in words: Often they function like negative or reversive adverbs—the *in-* and *un-* in *insufferable* and *unlace*, for instance. Often they function rather like prepositions, adding content concerning direction or position: the *trans-*, *sub-*, and *com-*, for instance, in *transoceanic*, *subhuman*, and *composition*. Often they function like adjectives: the *super-* in *superman*, the *bi-* in *bisexual*, the *omni-* in *omnidirectional*. (For listings of prefixes see Quirk et al. 1985, 1540–46; Marchand 1969, 129–208; Partridge [1958] 1983, 821–33; Jespersen 1946, 6:464–533.)

It is traditional to distinguish between two kinds of suffixes: inflectional and derivational. In general, inflectional suffixes simply add bits of semantic content to their words, information that answers such questions as How many? When? How much? Although Old English was a heavily inflected language, by the time of the reemergence of English in the fourteenth century, most of the inflectional suffixes had been stripped away in the transition from Old to Middle English. The only inflectional suffixes left in American English are (1) the noun plural suffixes *-s* and *-es;* (2) the genitive suffix *-'s;* (3) the verb tense markers *-s, -es, -ed;* (4) the verb participle markers *-ed* and *-ing;* and, less convincingly, (5) the comparative and superlative suffixes *-er* and *-est*.

The list of derivational suffixes is considerably longer, running to more than eighty in even Marchand's rather conservative listing. Whereas inflectional suffixes simply add bits of content to their words, derivational suffixes characteristically shift the word's grammatical function. For instance, the derivational suffix *-ic*, added to the noun *class*, produces the adjective *classic*, which can then be converted to serve as a different kind of noun. This new noun can take another derivational suffix, *-al*, to form a new adjective, *classical*. The derivational suffix *-ly*, added to the adjective *classical*, produces the adverb *classically*. The adjective *classical* can also take the derivational suffixes *-ist, -ism,* and *-ity* to form different nouns, or even *-ize* to form the verb *classicalize*, which is then free to take on the compound derivational suffix *-ation* to form yet another noun, *classicalization*. (For lists of suffixes see Quirk et al. 1985, 1546–58; Marchand 1969, 209–358; Partridge [1958] 1983, 835–66; Jespersen 1946, 6:208–464.)

There are some problems with this distinction between inflectional and derivational suffixes. For instance, the genitive inflection *-'s* actually behaves much like a derivational suffix, causing a function shift: *dog* is a substantive, but *dog's*, as in "the dog's dish," is a modifier. Also, some so-called derivational suffixes do not seem to differ much from some so-called inflections. It is hard, for instance, to see any radical difference between a so-called inflection like *-est*, which adds the content "most" to words like *calmest*, and a so-called derivational suffix like *-let*, which adds the meaning "little" to words like *piglet*. But in spite of the blurring of the distinction between inflectional and derivational suffixes, it is still a useful distinction to maintain.

2.2.3 Meaning and Content

It is easy to speak of elements as contributing "meaning" to written words, but elements do not themselves have meaning to contribute. In fact, words (and thus elements) do not have meanings; people do. And people use words (and elements) to represent and attempt to communicate the meanings they themselves have in mind. Meanings are in the mind, not in the word. What words (and elements) do have, and what makes it possible for them to be used to express people's meanings, is **content.** The content of a word is what the dictionary tries to describe in its definitions of the word's various senses. It can be useful to distinguish between semantic and syntactical content, even though the distinction is finally difficult to maintain. Semantic content is what we have in mind when in everyday language we ask, "What does this word mean?" Semantic content is information that has to do, more or less directly, with our world as it is organized and represented in our language—its things, events, qualities, and relationships. Syntactical content, on the other hand, is information that has to do with the functioning of the word within the sentence in which it occurs. Although the distinction is not completely sharp, the major carriers of semantic content in words are the prefixes and bases. The major carriers of syntactical content are the suffixes, both derivational and inflectional. Most derivational suffixes contribute at least some semantic content to a word, but their major contribution is syntactic. Inflectional suffixes contribute semantic content to a word, too, but they also function as important syntactical markers.

Semantic content can be thought of as an element's semantic load, the source of the contribution it makes to its word. The content of a word is its shared and agreed upon potential for representing meaning. Whereas meaning is nearly always conjunctive—that is, A and B and C—content is disjunctive—A or B or C. This disjunctive content makes it possible for people to represent their conjunctive meanings through words when they speak or listen, read or write.

2.2.4 Stems

A **stem** is that element or string of elements to which a prefix or suffix is being added or from which a prefix or suffix is being subtracted. A stem always contains at least one base. Some stems contain one base and one base alone, but more often when we use *stem,* we will be referring to a base plus one or more prefixes or suffixes to which we are going to add, or from which we are going to subtract, a prefix or suffix. *Stem*, then, is a handy general term: it can refer to a lone base, or a base plus a suffix, or a prefix plus a base, or a prefix plus a base plus a suffix, or a base plus two suffixes, and so on. The two main points to remember are (1) that the stem always contains a base, and (2) that the stem is the string to which we are going to add, or from which we are going to subtract, prefixes or suffixes.

For example, in a word such as *unquestioningly,* if we subtract the prefix *un-,* the stem will be *questioningly.* But if, instead, we subtract from *unquestioningly* the suffix *-ly,* the stem will be *unquestioning.* Subtracting the prefix *un-* from *unquestioning* results in the stem *questioning.* If we then subtract the suffix *-ing,* the stem will be *question.* If we then subtract the suffix *-ion,* the stem will be *quest,* which is also the base.

2.2.5   Free and Bound Elements

An important distinction is made between bound elements and free elements. A **free element** can stand alone as a word—like *dog, zebra, word, free,* or like the base *paint* in *repainted.* A free element can have a word boundary immediately before *and* after it, simultaneously. A **bound element,** however, must have one or more elements added to it before it can stand free as a word. An example would be the bound base spelled *sumpt* in such words as *assumption, consumption, resumption, sumptuous.* There is no such word as *sumpt; there is only the bound base spelled *sumpt,* which, before it can function freely as a word, must have one or more other elements added to it. Another example of a bound element is the base spelled *sume* in *assume, consume, resume.* You can assume something, consume something, resume something, but you cannot simply *sume it. The base spelled *sume* cannot stand free as a word; it is bound.

Prefixes and suffixes are always bound. It is true that prefixes and suffixes can be made to stand free as words through a process of clipping. For instance, the word *pro* 'expert' was originally a prefix, clipped from the word *professional.* However, when a prefix is freed like this, it is better to think of it as no longer a prefix. The *pro* that is used to mean "expert" is a word and is now a free base. The prefix *pro-* still exists, but there is now also a free base *pro* as well.

2.2.6   Primes

Stems also are either free or bound. One type of free stem is of particular concern to the explication of written forms: the shortest free stem in a word, its **prime.**

Because accessibility is one of the key goals of explication and because free stems tend to be more concrete and accessible than bound stems, the first attempt in explication is to explicate to the shortest free stem, or prime. However, if explicating to a prime entails special ad hoc changes that would not be necessary in explicating to a bound stem, then we explicate to the bound stem. For instance, following the first priority to explicate to a free stem, we could explicate *theorist* to a prime, *theory:* (theory̸)ist). This explication is consistent with known general processes, for there is a tactical rule that prescribes the regular deletion of stem-final *y* when adding a derivational suffix that starts with an *i*. (See 3.4.3.2 for details.) But words such as *theorem* and *theoretical* would then have to be explicated to (theory̸)em) and (theory̸)etic)al), and there is no general process to justify these deletions of *y* before *e*. Thus, the first-priority explication to a free stem, or prime, gives way to one involving the bound stem *theor* + , which makes possible such simple, though somewhat more abstract, explications as (theor + ist), (theor + em), (theor + etic)al)—and (theor + y).

2.2.7 Terminative and Nonterminative Elements

When elements are written out, they are italicized. When bound bases are written out, they have a plus sign either before or after them—for instance, + *sume* and *sumpt* + . The plus sign in front means that + *sume* can have a right-hand word boundary immediately following it, as in *resume*. The plus sign at the back of *sumpt* + means that it cannot have a right-hand word boundary immediately after it; it must have elements added at the plus sign before a word boundary can occur—as in *resumption*.

Since elements or stems that can have a right-hand word boundary immediately after them can terminate words, they are called **terminative elements,** or just **terminatives.** Not too surprisingly, elements and stems that cannot terminate words are called **nonterminatives.**

What is being said here is that a terminative element *can* have a word boundary after it, not that it *must* have one in a given word. For instance, the bound element + *pete* can be followed by a word boundary—as in words like *compete*—but in some words it does not have a word boundary after it: *impetus* (in̸ + m + pete̸ + us), for instance, or *impetuous* (in̸ + m + pete̸ + u + ous). In these cases + *pete* is not followed immediately by a word boundary, since there are no recorded words spelled *impete* within *impetus* or *impetuous*. The analyses show this by putting a plus sign rather than a close parenthesis after + *pete*. Compare these analyses with *competing*, which explicates to (com + pete̸)ing) and with *competition* (com + pet*é*)it*é* + ion). The close parentheses after +*pete* in these last two analyses indicate that in these instances +*pete* is followed by a right-hand word boundary, even though in *competing* and *competition* elements have been added beyond the boundary.

Thus, saying that an element is terminative is not the same as saying that it must always have a right-hand word boundary immediately after it. Rather, a terminative is an element that is followed by such a boundary in at least one word in which it occurs. And even when it is followed by a right-hand word boundary, it need not necessarily be the last element in the word. A word can contain two or more right-hand word boundaries as suffixes or other bases are added, as in *painted* (paint)ed) and *paintbrush* (paint)(brush).

This distinction between terminative and nonterminative elements is important in orthography because final -*e* deletion and final consonant twinning (see chapters 8 and 9) apply only to terminative elements and not to nonterminatives. For instance, the final *e* is deleted in a word such as *competing* (com + pet*é*)ing) because +*pete* is a terminative base. On the other hand, in *velleity* (velle + ity) there is no final -*e* deletion, because the base *velle* + is nonterminative.

The distinction is also important orthographically because of the existence of bound, nonterminative bases such as *metall* + , which is a coelement to the free, and therefore terminative, *metal*. The bound, nonterminative *metall* + must be assumed in order to explicate such complexes as *metalloid, metallic,* and *metallurgy,* none of which can explicate handily to the prime *metal:* the stress is wrong to invoke the Twinning Rule to account for the double *l*'s in each. Actually, the terminative *metal* is a simplification of the earlier Latin source *metallum* with two *l*'s, English tending in general to avoid ending polysyllables with *ll* (see 3.2.4). The bound, nonterminative *metall* + is in this sense more "conservative" and tends to occur in words common to more formal or technical registers. (For more examples see 9.4.1.)

The orthographic importance of a word such as *metalloid* is the at-first-sight nonregular *ll,* but once we recognize that it contains the bound, nonterminative *metall* + , which retains the Latin *ll,* the explication of the word becomes straightforward enough, the major problem then being to describe the choice between *metal* and *metall* + . The selection rule—or at least *a* workable selection rule—is again quite straightforward: when the base is followed by a derivational suffix, choose *metall* + ; everywhere else, choose *metal*. That formulation of the rule will always produce either *the* correct spelling or at least *a* correct variant.

To summarize, then: A terminative element does not have to have a word boundary immediately after it in every word in which it occurs. And when a terminative element does have a right-hand word boundary after it, that is not necessarily the last word boundary in the word.

2.3   The Explication of Sets

Elements often come in sets, as with the suffixes [-*s, -es*] or the bases [*metal, metall* +]. A set is a group of elements—or, more precisely, **co-elements**—that differ from one another in written form, may or may not differ in spoken form, contribute essentially the same content to a word, usually share a common ancestry, and are functionally parallel. For instance, in the two words *remit* and *remission,* (re + mit) and (re + miss)ion), it is clear that the two bases +*mit* and +*miss* are in a certain sense two different forms of the "same" element. They are members of a set, coelements with the same semantic content; with the same basic etymology (deriving, as is often the case, from different inflected forms of the same Latin verb); with similar but not identical spellings; and with a distribution and functional parallelism that render them orthographic partners. The notion of sets provides a way of describing in orthography many of the things that in phonology are described by the notion of morphophonemics.

Describing the distribution for a set of coelements like +*mit* and +*miss* is made difficult by the richness of word formation in English, but for now it is enough to say that +*mit* tends to occur in verb-final position (as in *remit*), while +*miss* tends to occur in noun-medial position before *-ion* (as in *remission*) and in adjective-final or adjective-medial position (as in *remiss* and *remissive*). But the important point is that these two elements are formally and functionally parallel so that they can be called coelements and treated as members of a single set.

2.3.1   The Set [+*sume, sumpt* +]

The terminative base +*sume* occurs in verb-final position, as in *resume;* *sumpt* + does not—ever. On the other hand, *sumpt* + occurs in noun-medial position before *-ion*, as in *resumption*, which +*sume* never does. *Sumpt* + occurs in other positions as well, as in *sumptuous* and *presumptive*, positions in which +*sume* never occurs. Their distribution can be displayed as follows:

(Array 2-1)

Stems with *sumpt +*	Before -*ion*	Before -*ive*	Word-Final	Other Cases
assumpt +	x	x	x	assumptious
consumpt +	x	x	x	consumpted, consumptible
presumpt +	x	x		presumptuous
resumpt +	x	x		
subsumpt +	x	x		
sumpt +	x	x		sumptuous

Stems with +*sume*	Before -*s*	Before -*ed*	Before -*ing*	Before -*er*	Before -*able*
assume	x	x	x	x	x
consume	x	x	x	x	x
presume	x	x	x	x	x
resume	x	x	x	x	x
subsume	x	x	x		x

Array 2-1 shows that there is nearly perfect complementary distribution between +*sume* and *sumpt +*. There are blurrings, to be sure, but they appear finally to confirm the pattern, even to suggest that it is continuing to become stronger. For instance, *consumpted* might at first seem to blur the distribution since in it the stem *consumpt +* takes the inflectional suffix -*ed*, which is normally reserved for stems with the terminative +*sume*. However, it seems likely that the suffix in *consumpted* is not the verb past tense inflection at all, but rather the -*ed* that is used to form adjectives out of nouns, as in *moneyed, fanged, cultured*. The forms *assumpt* and *consumpt*, also both listed in *W3*, might at first seem to blur the nonterminative status of *sumpt +*. However, *assumpt* is listed as obsolete, and *consumpt* is listed as Scots. In fact, the *OED* shows other obsolete misfits to the distribution described above: *consumpt, consumptibility, consumptible, assumpt, assumpted, assumpting, sumpt*. The fact that so many forms with *sumpt +* in a terminative position have gone obsolete, or have been restricted to dialect status (including *consumpted*), suggests strongly that they are peripheral elements within the language, somehow outside the main system. The system, rather than reorganizing itself in order to integrate them more fully, follows instead the strategy of self-regulation via negative feedback: the misfit forms are slowly removed from the lexicon. Thus the complementary distribution between the terminative +*sume* and the nonterminative *sumpt +* is rendered tighter and more reliable. The one word in the array that does in fact blur the distribution is *consumptible*, which contains a coform of the suffix -*able*, usually reserved for stems with +*sume* (see array 2-1). *Consumptible* appears to be very recent and to fill some felt need in the register of economics for a fine distinction between goods that are consumptible and those that are simply consumable.

2.3.2   The Set [*tend, tense, tent*]

The existence of sets of coelements has both a positive and a negative importance to orthography. Positively, they represent strands of simplicity and unity that affirm the existence of pattern and design in what may at first appear to be rather unruly stuff. Negatively, however, they can and do create instances in which two items may sound and act alike while being spelled with slight but important differences. So long as the coelements both sound and are spelled differently, they pose few special problems, as with [+ *sume, sumpt* +]. But problems arise when the two sound the same but are spelled differently. One instance involves the set [*tend, tense, tent*].

A number of verbs with *tend* form abstract nouns by adding *-ion*. The problem can be illustrated as follows:

(Array 2-2)

Verb	Noun
attend	attention
contend	contention
distend	distention, distension
intend ("plan")	intention
extend	extension
intend ("mean")	intension
ostend	ostension
pretend	pretension
protend	protension

The problem, of course, is that in general the stems + *tention* and *tension* are exactly the same in function, content, and sound. They are also very similar in spelling. But that slight difference—*t* versus *s*—is crucial in the binary attitude that prevails in correct spelling.

The history of the spelling of words containing the stems + *tention* and *tension* suggests that an initial divergence was followed by a somewhat confused and incomplete reconvergence. Except for *protension*, which was spelled with an *s* in Latin, all of these words were in Latin originally spelled with a *t*. Some, however, developed variant spellings with *s* in later Latin. Some came into English from Latin by way of French, where more *s* spellings had developed. These *s* and *t* spellings occurred in Middle English, where a *c* spelling also developed. For instance, Chaucer's spelling of *attention* was *attencioun*. Some deliberately Latinate respellings appear to have occurred during the English Renaissance. *Contention,* for example, was spelled with a *t* in Latin and French, with an earlier *c* in Old French. Its earliest spelling in English, in the fourteenth century, was with a *c*. Then, in the sixteenth century, it was respelled with a *t,* in line with the Latin original.

Although array 2-2 contains four forms with *+tention* and six with *tension,* the evidence is that a reconvergence to the *t* spelling has taken place. For one thing, the only common words now spelled with *s* are *extension* and *pretension;* the others are quite technical and rare. (There is, by the way, at least one sign-painter in Ellensburg, Washington, who continues the reconvergence, insisting on *extention.*)

Another bit of evidence for the reconvergence to *t* is found in the variant spellings *distention, distension.* The spelling was originally *t* in Latin, then *s* in later Latin and in French. It has been both *s* and *t* in English since the word's adoption in the seventeenth century. The *OED* gives the *s* spelling as the first form, the *t* spelling as a variant. But, except for the Merriam-Webster dictionaries, American dictionaries consistently give the spelling with *t* as the first, or more common, spelling. If we assume that American English tends to be less conservative than British, then this American tendency to use *distention* can be seen as evidence of the continued convergence—or reconvergence—to *+tention.* And the Ellensburg sign-painter may have his day after all.

But convergence or no, minimal contrasts such as those between *+tention* and *tension* are the stuff of orthographic problems. In array 2-2 the one justifiable contrast is that between *intention* and *intension.* Here is a case where the written language makes a distinction that the spoken language does not. The two homophones are distinguished orthographically, a kind of distinguishing that has long been recognized as an advantage in the English spelling system (Bradley 1970a, 167–68; Bradley 1970b, 174–76; Klima 1972). But again notice that although it may be an advantage for readers, it is a disadvantage for spellers, in that it provides them with one more slight but important contrast to keep straight.

2.3.3   The Set [*verse, vert*]

The set [*verse, vert*] illustrates the complex relationships that are possible in even a simple set of only two coelements. The complexes formed out of this set cluster into several groups. One group consists of verbs with word-final *vert,* adjectives with word-final *verse,* and nouns with *verse* plus *-ion:*

(Array 2-3)

Verb	Adjective	Noun
avert	averse	aversion
convert	converse	conversion
divert	diverse	diversion
invert	inverse	inversion
obvert	obverse	obversion
pervert	perverse	perversion

These complexes are then free to form extended complexes: for instance, the nouns *averseness, perverseness, perversity;* the adjectives *conversionary* and *invertible;* the noun *converter;* the adjective *diverting;* the noun *pervertedness.* There is also the opportunity for verb-to-noun conversions, as in *pervert, convert, invert.*

Very close to the words in array 2-3 are those in the following array, which consists of verbs with word-final *vert,* adjectives with word-medial *verse,* and nouns with word-medial *verse:*

(Array 2-4)

Verb	Adjective	Noun
controvert	controversial	controversion, controversy
evert	eversible	eversion
extrovert	extroversive	extroversion
introvert	introversive	introversion
subvert	subversive	subversion

Here, as in array 2-3, there is also the opportunity for extended complexes: *introversively, subversivism, controversialist.*

After these two fairly regular groups, things grow more unsymmetrical with words that contain *verse* and *vert:*

(Array 2-5)

Verb	Adjective	Noun
adverse	adverse	adversity, adverseness
advert	advertent	advertence
advertise	advertised, -ing	advertisement, -ing
diversify	diverse, divers	diversity
reverse	reverse, -ed, -ing	reverse, -al
revert	revertive	reversion
transverse	transverse, -ed, -ing	transverse, -al, -ness

A description of the selection rules for *vert* and *verse* would obviously be long, involving the prefix, the suffix, and the part of speech of the word. However, from the standpoint of the speller, there are no real problems. The phonetic contrast between the two coelements in, say, *invert* and *inverse* is so great that one is not so likely to confuse the spelling of one for the other as not to notice that they are coelements in the first place. A sharp phonetic contrast is lacking only in those cases where palatalization has occurred before *-ion*, as in *aversion*, or before *-ial*, as in *controversial*. And here the selection rule is simple: whenever the last consonant of the base has palatalized to /sh/ or /zh/, choose *verse*.

2.3.4   Immediate and Mediate Explicata

The notion of sets of coelements leads to the distinction between **immediate** and **mediate explicata**. The term *explicatum* (pl. *explicata*) will be used here to refer to the elements, primes, particles, and processes into which a given word explicates.

The distinction between immediate and mediate explicata can be illustrated with the nouns *interception* and *reception*. The explication of *interception* into prime and suffix is straightforward enough: (intercept)ion). In this it is analogous to many English nouns that are formed by adding the derivational suffix *-ion* to a verb—*prediction* (predict)ion), *audition* (audit)ion), *inflation* (inflate)ion), and so on.

The explication of *reception*, however, is not quite so straightforward. Immediately it would appear to be (recept)ion). But the proposed prime *recept* is a noun, not a verb, a fact which destroys the analogy with *interception* and the others. The verb within *reception* must be *receive*, the terminatives +*ceive* and +*cept* being coelements in a set. This explication, with *receive* as the verb prime of the derived noun *reception*, fills out the analogy: *interception* is to *intercept* as *reception* is to *receive*.

Receive is an explicatum of *reception* in a way quite different from the way *intercept* is an explicatum of *interception*. *Interception* equals *intercept* plus *-ion* clearly and obviously. The case of *reception* is more complex: on the surface *reception* equals *recept* plus *-ion*, but further down, at the level of the semantic and syntactic relationships involved in the controlling analogy, *reception* equals *receive* plus *-ion* via a process that replaces the terminative +*ceive* with its coform +*cept*. This process mediates between *reception* and its verb prime *receive*. Thus we can say that while *interception* has only the immediate verb prime *intercept*, *reception* has two primes: the immediate noun *recept* and the mediate verb *receive*.

The processes involved here are similar to those involved in the explication of words containing assimilated forms of a prefix. For example, *appear* explicates to (ad + p + pear). An immediate explicatum of *appear* is the assimilated prefix *ap-,* but a mediate explicatum is the basic form of the prefix, *ad-.*

In this study, except for cases of prefix assimilation, we will only rarely show the mediate explication. When it is shown, it will be similar to the display used for assimilated prefixes. For instance, *reception* would explicate to (re + c̶e̶i̶v̶e̶)cept)ion). Usually, rather than show this mediating process, the explications will simply show the immediate explicata.

What is here being called a distinction between mediate and immediate explicata is much like the transformationalists' distinction between deep and surface structure. The mediate-immediate distinction uncovers certain ambiguities, as, for example, in the homonym *induction. Induction* (as in "induction into the army") explicates to the immediate verb prime *induct:* (induct)ion). However, *induction* (with the sense "to arrive at a general conclusion from specific instances") must explicate to the mediate verb prime *induce:* (in + d̶u̶c̶e̶)duct)ion). (This distinction is blurred somewhat by the fact that physicists have come to use *induce* and *induct* synonymously.) The disambiguating force represented here is similar to the way in which the distinction between surface and deep structure can help disambiguate such sentences as "The shooting of the hunters was terrible."

Immediate explicata have to do with the visual and phonetic shape of the word—that is, its spelling and pronunciation—while mediate explicata have less to say about spelling and pronunciation and more to say about semantic and syntactic relationships—and about sets. Obviously, the structure of words in which there is no distinction between mediate and immediate explicata is more accessible than the structure of a word such as *reception,* where such a distinction is made.

2.3.5 Sets and Connate Groups

Sets are distinct from a somewhat similar but essentially different entity that we will call the **connate group.** The members of a set are related by equivalence of semantic content, by similarity in their written form, and most importantly by patterns of distribution and selection that allow them to replace one another in systematic ways. They are also, of course, related by their common etymological source, but etymology is just one of a number of shared features, and a fairly weak one at that. The members of a connate group, on the other hand, are related primarily by common etymology. This commonality often leads to a discernible similarity of semantic content and similarity of form, but merely connate elements are never the tactical replacements for one another that coelements like + *mit* and *+miss* are. A striking example of a connate group consists of all of the bases that descend from the many different inflected forms of the Latin verb *facere* 'make or do':

(Array 2-6)

fac+ (*faculty*)	feas+ (*feasible*)	fett+ (*confetti*)
face (*surface*)	feat (*defeat*)	+fex (*pontifex*)
fair (*affair*)	+fect (*perfect*)	+fice (*sufficient*)
fact (*factor*)	+feit (*surfeit*)	+fit (*profit*)
far+ (*multifarious*)	fet+ (*fetish*)	+fy (*rectify*)

The list of bases in this connate group goes on to include the bases found in words like *fazenda* and *fashion*. They all derive from the Latin *facere;* nearly all retain at least an echo of the original sense of "make or do"; there is at least some similarity of written form (primarily the initial *f* followed by a vowel), but none of them replaces any other the way *+mit* and *+miss* do. They are not in complementary distribution in any systematic or useful sense of the phrase. Thus they are not coforms; they are simply connate forms.

However, within this great sprawl of connate bases there is one small, tight set of cobases: [*+fy, +fic*], as in *beatify* and *beatific, modify* and *modification*. So we have a small set within a much larger and looser connate group. Such, in fact, is most often the case.

Although connate groups are of less direct interest to orthography than are sets, they do have their interest. Because they often do have a certain commonality of form and sense running through them, they can provide strands of unity through the written language. And since a perceived unity makes possible certain simplifications that can enhance comprehension, even these modest strands deserve some attention.

2.3.6 Nonterminative Suffixes

The distinction between terminative and nonterminative elements usually involves bases. Prefixes, by definition, can never be terminative. When a prefix is clipped and used as a free element—for instance, when *pro-* was clipped from *professional* to form the free element *pro*—the one-time prefix becomes a free base, and thus, though terminative, is no longer a prefix. But though the obverse would seem to hold with suffixes—that is, that by definition they would always be terminative—things are not quite so simple. Most suffixes are indeed terminative, but there are at least four that are not. Compare, for instance, the adjective and the derived noun *intractable* (in(tract)able) and *intractability* (in(tract)abil+ity). The suffix *-abil+*, a coform of *-able*, occurs only in nonterminative settings. In this sense the suffix *-abil+* is like the nonterminative bound base *abil+*, as in *able* and *ability* (abil + ity). A parallel case involves the suffix set [*-ible,* *-ibil +*], as in *possible* and *possibility.* A third nonterminative suffix, *-ionn +*, occurs in French adoptions like *questionnaire* and *legionnaire,* (quest)ionn + aire) and (leg + ionn + aire). A fourth, *-os +*, a coform of *-ous,* occurs in words like *fabulosity* and *generosity;* compare the stems *fabulous* and *generous.*

2.4 The Explication of Particles

A particle is a letter inserted into the spelling of a word between elements. Unlike elements, particles do not contribute to the semantic or syntactic content of the word. Some particles, however, do have a tactical function. Thus, for instance, particles like the *b* inserted into *robber* (rob)b + er) because of the Twinning Rule function tactically by avoiding the VCV string in *rober,* the spelling that would result if the particle *b* were not inserted. (For more on the Twinning Rule see chapter 9.) Similarly, the particle *k,* inserted into *panicked* (panic)k + ed), functions tactically by avoiding the look of a soft *c:* *paniced (see 27.3.3.13). In a more complicated way the particles *i* and *u,* inserted into *partial* and *gradual,* (part)i + al) and (gradé)u + al), function tactically by marking the palatalization of the sounds spelled by the *t* and *d* to /sh/ and /j/; compare *partible* and *gradate,* where there is no palatalization and no particle insertion, (part)ible) and (gradé)ate). (For more on palatalization see chapter 30.)

In each of the foregoing cases the insertion of the particle was well motivated by sound and tactics. Some particles have no tactical function but do still enter into the sound of the word. Examples are the particles *i* and *u* in words like *tutorial* and *conspicuous,* (tutor)i + al) and (conń + n + spic + u + ous). In addition to responding to the phonetic demand, these particles can also be seen as responding to the etymological demand. The *i* is in the Latin sources of *tutorial* and *partial: tutorious* and *partiālis.* The *u* is in the Latin *conspicuous* and *graduālis.*

2.4.1 The Linking Particles

Particles that have both phonetic and etymological motivation are the linking *i* and the linking *o* in words such as *omnivorous* and *speedometer,* (omn + i + voré)ous) and (speed)o(meter). The linking *o,* by and large, was adopted from the Greek; the linking *i,* from the Latin.

Dictionaries often treat these linking particles as part of the preceding element. Thus, *W3* lists *hydro +* and *hydr +* as variants of the same bound base. However, it is not necessary to multiply all of these coforms, for the linking *o* and linking *i* can be treated as inserted particles. Thus we will consistently explicate the "variant" *hydro* to an element plus a particle: (hydr + o).

The linking particles *o* and *i* occur in many words. Some other examples are *philosophy* (philé + o + soph + y), *geography* (ge + o(graph)y), *beautify* (beaut)i + fy), and *modification* (modé)i + fic + até + ion).

The linking particle *i* has tended to assimilate other forms to it. For instance, *handicraft* (hand)i(craft) derives from Middle English *handiecraft,* which was a variant of *handcraft.* And *handiwork* (hand)i(work) derives from Old English *handgeweorc.* Also, *handicap* is a simplification of the phrase "hand in cap"—apparently with somewhat the same sense as the modern phrase "with one hand tied behind my back."

2.4.2   The Initial Particle

Particles usually occur between elements, which means that they usually occur in word-medial position. It is rare for particles to occur at the beginning of a word. However, one type of word-initial particle is the so-called euphonic *e* added at the front of French or Spanish words before the clusters *sc, sp,* or *st.* When Latin words starting with these consonant clusters were taken into French and Spanish, the *e* was added to ease pronunciation. These languages still resist initial *s* clusters, as can be verified by anyone who has taught English to a Spanish-speaking person. Although Partridge lists this *e* as a prefix, it does not fit our definition of prefix, since it has no semantic content. We could say that it does carry a certain amount of etymological information, since it marks the word's language of origin, much like the *rh* and *ps* in Greek words. But this etymological information is not truly semantic content, and thus according to our definitions of prefix and particle, the "euphonic *e*" must be treated as a particle.

Two examples are *espy* (e(spy) and *escrow* (e + scrow). Other known instances are:

(Array 2-7)

escalade	escolar	especial	establish
escalate	escritoire	esperance	estancia
escalator	escudo	espial	estate
escallop	escutcheon	espionage	estop
escarp	espadrille	espouse	estoppel
escarpment	espalier	esprit	estray
eschallot	esparto	esquire	

Esplanade is a circular example. It comes from French, which adopted it from the Italian *spianala,* which looks like a case of the French initial particle *e*. But the Latin source of the Italian *spianala* was *explānāre*, which suggests that the *es* could be treated as an assimilated form of *ex-*, which is the explication preferred here: (ex + s(planè)ade). (For more on the assimilation of *ex-* to *es-*, see 10.3.2.)

2.5 Explication versus Other Lexical Analyses

Although its desiderata include concreteness and accessibility, explication does not claim to duplicate the way people go about spelling words. For one thing, different people go about spelling in different ways, and in fact the same person will go about spelling in different ways in different situations. To spell a word that is known to the point of automaticity—for most adult literates, words like *cat* and *the,* for instance—is itself an automatic act. Where a spelling is known but has momentarily escaped, it is not unusual for a person to write the word down and check to see if it "looks right," clearly a matching of a visual or auditory-visual image against the spelling on the page. Sometimes when typing such an automatic word—especially the very common *the*—two or three words later in the line the typist will get a sense that "something did not feel right back there," clearly a warning from some sort of kinesthetic memory. Scanning back in the line more often than not reveals that the *h* and *e* have been reversed—again an appeal to a visual memory.

In more difficult situations more elaborate strategies are invoked. Faced with indecision about whether it should be *ence* or *ance* at the end of *existence*, a speller with considerable morphological sophistication may call up the related word *existential*, thus getting the stress shifted to the vowel in front of the *n* and thus releasing the color of /e/. Through a complex kind of analogical reasoning such a speller will decide on *ence*. More than once at spelling bees—the finals for the western half of Washington State, and thus a showcase for far better than average young spellers—I have given contestants words that they clearly have never heard or seen before. They routinely gather all the information they can, apparently trying to confirm their intuitions concerning sound-to-spelling correspondences and clearing up ambiguous ones. For instance, a young speller faced with the word *monostich,* thought for a few seconds and then asked for a definition ("a single verse") and the language of origin (Greek). The definition apparently confirmed that the /män/ sound was in fact the element that contributed the content "one, single" and thus was spelled *mon*. The Greek source apparently cleared up the medial schwa: it was the linking particle *o* common to Greek words. The Greek origin, together with the formality and technicality of the word, also cleared up the ambiguous final /k/ sound. The rest of the word, the *sti,* was fairly straightforward after that.

As can be seen from this example, spelling is a diverse process, running from a nearly automatic act to a very rich bringing-to-bear of all sorts of knowledge—phonological, semantic, etymological—together with a certain amount of faith that the cords of analogy within the system are going to remain consistent and predictable for this case. Explication does not try to duplicate the actual process that a speller might use in the act of spelling, but it does try to analyze the spelling system in a way that unfolds as much as possible of the information that is there in the system, waiting to be brought to bear in various spelling situations. It does not attempt to describe the spelling act, but it does attempt to provide information that is the most concrete and accessible for spellers.

2.5.1   Explication versus Etymological Analysis

The criteria and guidelines for explication differ from the criteria and guidelines for other lexical analyses that have other purposes. For instance, etymologists like Skeat, Onions, and Partridge had as their goal the reconstruction of historical processes. Their major criterion was historical accuracy; their major guidelines were designed to assure that accuracy, as seen in Skeat's "Canons for Etymology" ([1891] 1970, 452–62).

The goal of explication is not historical reconstruction; rather, it is increased rationality, concreteness, and accessibility. The etymological demand must be acknowledged, but it is just one of the four major, and often contending, forces: the phonetic, the semantic, the etymological, and the systemic. History and etymology are sources of insight, but they are not the major criteria for deciding a given issue. For instance, etymologically the verb *annoy* does not deserve its second *n.* The Middle English spelling was *anoien* from the Old French *anoier* from the Latin *in odio.* But during the late Middle Ages the power of analogy caused this verb to be treated as one of a number of other verbs that came from Latin and that contained a form of the prefix *ad-* in which the *d* had changed to *n* before a stem that started with *n: annex, annihilate, annotate, announce.* These and many other verbs earned their second *n*'s through the process of assimilation. The *d* in the prefix assimilated to the *n* in the stem: (ad + n + nex). (For more details see 10.6.) What is written today as *annoy* was given that second *n* to make it fit with that large group of *ann* words, and today it explicates to (ad + n + noy). Even though such an analysis does violence to the French and Latin etymology of the word, it does make the word more rational and accessible as a member of a large and systematic English group. And at one level it is also historically accurate, for the effects of analogy and folk etymology are also legitimate parts of its history.

The role of history, then, is quite different in explication from what it is in etymology. Although etymology is one of the four major demands made on the orthographic system, and although etymology is a rich and important source of insight, etymological accuracy is not the sole criterion of the explications offered here. We will contradict etymology very cautiously, but we will on occasion do just that as we offer a non-etymological explication in the name of rationality and accessibility.

2.5.2 Explication versus Generative Analysis

By the same token the analyses of modern scientific linguists—those of the generativists, for instance—also differ from explication, having different goals, methods, and criteria. Because of its quest for concreteness and accessibility, explication characteristically eschews the large abstractions typical of much of modern linguistics. In this respect it is somewhat old-fashioned in its orientation, more philological than transformational.

The differences between explication and generative analysis are perhaps most starkly illustrated by Mark Aronoff's *Word Formation in Generative Grammar* (1981). Basically, the generativist is concerned to describe the rules and information that a speaker must have in order to generate all and only the words of his language. The major concern is synthesis, and the generative morphologist has difficulty with all of those complex and compound words in the language whose contents do not appear to equal directly the sum of the contents of their constituent parts. Thus, the generativist has particular difficulty with older words, most of which must finally be listed as separate and essentially unanalyzable items in the lexicon.

The major concern of explication, on the other hand, is quite different. It is less concerned with the synthesis of new words, more concerned with the understanding of given words. Many of the problems that pester the generativist are accounted for as far as explication is concerned by treating the content of a word as being a disjunctive set of conjunctive subsets. Many more are accounted for by the willing acceptance of diachronic, or historical, knowledge. Our concern is not so much to know exactly what is necessary and sufficient to generate words; it is more to know what potential knowledge is folded into written words. It is to unfold knowledge that can help the speller analyze those words and better understand their written structure. This is not an insignificant distinction.

Further, a work such as Chomsky and Halle's *Sound Pattern of English* has as its major goals those that are most often associated with scientific analysis: consistency, rigor, simplicity, symmetry, conciseness—conciseness carried at times to a soaring abstractness and terse abbreviation. Some of these goals overlap with those of explication, but at some point the abbreviation and abstraction begin to run counter to the accessibility and concreteness for which explication strives. Thus, for instance, unlike generative grammar, explication does not invoke the notion of abstract underlying forms. In this respect explication might be described as more Aristotelian than Platonic.

On the other hand, the analyses of some modern linguists seem closer to the goals of explication. For instance, Per Linell, especially in his *Psychological Reality in Phonology* (1979), argues against the abstraction of the generativist analysis with its highly abstract underlying forms. He argues instead for the primacy of the concrete word, and in this eschewal of high abstraction for greater concretion his analysis comes closer to that which is offered here. Also, Larry Nessly (1975), who has reservations about the highly general and abstract rules of Chomsky and Halle and who argues in favor of more local and concretely based rules, is close in some ways to the spirit of the analysis offered here.

All in all, our position toward modern scientific linguists is much like that toward the etymologists: There are shared goals and methods; we try to learn from them; we contradict them with caution; but at some point their analyses and ours will more than likely begin to pull in different directions.

Orthographic explication is explication in the older sense of the word: it is a folding out, an unfolding of the simpler written forms and processes that are folded into a more complex word. Just as it does not attempt to describe the actual spelling process, it does not attempt to record the actual historical development of written words over the centuries. Nor does it attempt to record the development of semantic relationships among clusters of words. What it does attempt to record is the way in which written words can be explicated, or unfolded, to reveal the simpler written words, elements, and processes they contain.

2.6 On Orthographic Concepts

Part of the question of how orthographic explication relates to other kinds of linguistic analysis involves what might be called "orthographic concepts." By this phrase we mean not just those concepts that have to do with orthography, but more precisely those concepts that have to do with orthography and at first seem inconsistent with concepts from other linguistic realms, especially those from phonology. The concept of "long vowels versus short vowels" is just such a concept. In spite of the name "long" and in spite of certain areas of coincidence, the notion of a long vowel is not a phonological concept; it is an orthographic one. It combines certain phonological, etymological, and systemic features. That is one reason, apparently, why modern phonologists' attempts to revise the concept of a long vowel have not been very effective. When, for instance, Richard Venezky tries to replace the long/short distinction with Hans Kurath's free/checked distinction, he is not simply fighting against the tug of pedagogical conservatism. He is also attempting to impose, too energetically, the structures and distinctions of phonology onto those of orthography (1970, 14, 35–36).

To take a specific instance: The notion of long *a*, /ā/, the sound in *bait*, is not simply a notion based on the phonological distinction between free and checked or between tense and lax. It is also a distinction that reflects the centuries of custom and usage in the evolution of the English orthographic system. Brengelman mentions the role of seventeenth-century orthographers in rationalizing this distinction (1980, 346–49). It is a concept as much defined by the tactics of orthography as by those of phonology. In fact, the sound that we symbolize as /ā/ is phonologically a diphthong. A speaker of, say, Norwegian will hear this not as a single sound but rather as a diphthong, much as we hear /ȯi/ or /au̇/. The same is true of /ō/ and /ī/, which also can be analyzed as diphthongs rather than as simple vowel sounds. The point here is that in spite of the phonological analysis, in terms of the development of orthographic structures and distinctions, these are now best treated, in orthographic theory, as simple sounds, no longer as diphthongs, because of the way they function in terms of English orthographic tactics.

The phrase used earlier, "long *a*," may seem odd to a reader used to thinking in phonological rather than orthographic terms. But such a phrase offers a convenient way to say, in effect, "the letter *a* spelling a long vowel sound." Such a phrase is especially convenient when referring to vowels in Old, Middle, and Early Modern English, when the actual vowel sounds being spelled were often different from their Modern English descendants. Thus, for instance, an Old English long *a* was quite different phonologically from the Modern English long *a*, or /ā/. Also, phrases such as "long *u*," "short *o*," and "short *u*" are convenient to the present analysis, which recognizes two long *u*'s (/ū/ and /yū/), two short *o*'s (/ä/ and /ȯ/), and two short *u*'s (/u/ and /u̇/) (see 11.1.2). Besides being convenient to such generic reference, phrases like "long *a*" are another

reminder that in spite of their close and complex interdependence, orthographic concepts are different from phonological ones.

This distinction between orthographic and phonological concepts
arises in other realms as well. For instance, Aronoff, in a brief study of the
connate set of suffixes, *-our, -or,* and *-er,* describes their development and
function in British and American English as an example of the way
"spelling can be sensitive to subtle linguistic generalizations that are
neither phonetic nor phonological" (1978, 302). The distinction between
orthographic and phonological concepts also arises in the definition of
vowels and consonants (see 11.3). The distinction between orthographic
and etymological concepts arises repeatedly, as when our orthographic
explications contradict the evidence of etymology and we offer counter-
etymological explications—for instance, the explication of *annoy* to
(ad + n + noy).

2.6.1 Silent Letters

Another example of an orthographic concept that seems to contend with,
say, phonological theory is the notion of the "silent" letter, such as the
silent final *e* in words like *like* and *mouse.* In a phonological sense the
notion of a "silent" letter is empty, for no letters are "unsilent"; letters do
not have sounds, and to act as if they do is to confuse letters with sounds.
However, in orthographic theory the concept of silent letters is not at all
empty, nor is it contradictory. Some letters are pronounced and some are
not. Letters that are not pronounced are silent; you do not hear any
evidence of them in the spoken word. The concept of silent letters is very
useful in orthographic theory in describing certain tactical issues.

A major issue concerns silent consonants that occur in clusters whose
pronunciation has simplified from an earlier stage when all the letters
were pronounced. For instance, should we say that the /m/ in *bomb* is
spelled *mb?* Or *m* with the *b* not entering in? The latter approach leads to a
somewhat awkward problem in accounting for the final *b.* We would
apparently have to posit a unit of silence as part of the catalog of English
sounds, perhaps symbolizing it as /∅/. Then the final *mb* of *bomb* would
analyze to /m/ = *m* and /∅/ = *b.* Further study may argue more convincingly for such an analysis, but at this time it seems needlessly awkward.
The notion of an orthographically significant unit of silence floating
around in our words seems odd. We will speak very little of silent letters in
this sense—that is, as letters spelling a unit of silence.

The approach adopted in this study may prove to be as odd as the one
just rejected, but it does underlie the sound-to-spelling analysis presented
in subsequent chapters. Rather than positing a unit of silence, it posits an

evolutionary process in which in certain contexts certain consonant letters are not pronounced as separate units and instead enter into the sound-to-spelling correspondences of the adjacent consonants. It posits, that is, a type of orthographic merging that reflects a usually earlier process of phonological simplification. Thus, it analyzes the /m/ in *bomb* as being spelled *mb*. It groups *bomb* with all other known instances of this correspondence and describes the distribution, behavior, and sources of this minor correspondence in the English spelling system. Thus, it groups *bomb* with *lamb, climb,* and *tomb.* The /m/ = *mb* correspondence, occurring only in word-final position, reflects the simplification of an old cluster in which the *b* was pronounced. (For more details on this correspondence see 31.2.1.1.) In short, this analysis treats most silent consonants as the unpronounced members of clusters whose behavior can be understood in terms of the total system, reflecting historical and contemporary tactical demands and processes.

2.7 Problems and Questions

2.7.1 The Explication of Form and Content

Explication is concerned with the unfolding of contained written forms, but obviously there must be some sort of semantic concern—an element, after all, is in part defined in terms of its semantic content. In any explication a semantic relationship must still exist, or at least must have existed (since the semantics of words change faster than their spellings), between any two adjacent concentric free stems in the explication.

Usually the semantic relationships are very close and obvious. For instance, the semantic content of *zebra* in the singular noun *zebra* is identical with its content as the prime in the plural *zebras.* By and large the semantic content of *mother* in the base noun *mother* is the same as its content as the prime in the derived nouns *motherhood* and *motherliness.*

But at times the semantic relationships in an explication are more distant. For instance, they are not all immediately apparent in the word *statistician,* which explicates to (state)ist)ic)ian). The innermost pair of parentheses marks the prime, *state* (which in this case also happens to be the base). Among the disjunctive senses that make up the content of *state,* one, "nation," relates directly to the next-larger free stem in the explication—*statist* (state)ist) 'politician, diplomat'. *Statist* in turn relates directly to the next-larger free stem, the adjective *statistic* (statist)ic), which originally meant "pertaining to statists and state matters," then specialized and nominalized to "facts and information about states and their citizens," then generalized again to "facts in general, especially quantifiable, mathematical facts." Once the more "mathematical" sense of *statistic* was established, it was a logical step to progress to the derived form *statistician* (statistic)ian) 'one skilled in the use of statistics'.

It is important to remember here that the contents of words are disjunctive, not conjunctive. The various senses of a word are joined with *or*'s, not with *and*'s, which allows for the sometimes rather far-reaching strings of different senses that may unfold in the explication of a complicated word like *statistician*. (For more on the disjunction of semantic content see 2.2.3.)

Similar lines of thought are involved in the explication of the types of words discussed by Aronoff (1981). Aronoff is dealing with the nature of morphemes in generative terms, and he is concerned with the fact that it is hard to find a general meaning that can be said to be shared by, for instance, the *straw* in *strawberry* and the free stem *straw*. Similar problems are posed by the first elements in *blueberry, blackberry,* and *gooseberry* and by Latinate bound bases such as +*fer,* +*ceive,* +*mit,* and the like. Within the theory of explication, recognizing that the contents of words and elements are disjunctive rather than conjunctive, and recognizing, too, the salience of the etymological demand, we can account for such troublesome elements. For instance, the *straw* in *strawberry* seems quite plausibly to reflect some earlier metaphoric or metonymic connection: Strawberries do look a bit as if they are sprinkled with short pieces of straw; or the runners, when dry, look like straw; or the plants are often protected in a mulch of straw. By the same token, it seems plausible that some early metaphoric or metonymic connection is involved in *gooseberry.* A Latinate bound base such as +*ceive* will develop disjunctive and slightly different contents as it occurs in different words. The base +*ceive* does not contribute exactly the same content to *conceive* that it contributes to, say, *perceive,* but still its contributions to the various words in which it occurs can be explicated to a cluster of disjunctive contents. They all contain echoes—perhaps slight and difficult at times to recover—of the earlier etymological sense.

2.7.2   Element and Particle Boundaries

In the explication of words most boundaries tend to be very clear and easy to determine, but some can be obscure and difficult. In general, for instance, the boundaries between primes in a compound word are clear: *blackbird* (black)(bird), *dogfight* (dog)(fight), even the *blackberry* and *gooseberry* that trouble Aronoff. Compounds tend to explicate easily even when they contain a linking particle in addition to their primes: *speedome-*

ter, (speed)o(meter). Such explications are straightforward, the primes easy to recognize, the element boundaries clear and obvious.

The boundaries between prefix and stem are only slightly less easy to determine. Usually a recognizable prefix simply adds to a recognizable prime, as in *restring* (re(string), or to a longer stem that includes a prime, as in *unseeing* (un(see)ing) or *reinstate* (re(in(state). Even when a prefix is being added to a bound stem or a unique prime, the boundaries are usually quite clear, as in *repeated* (re + peat)ed) and *unkempt* (un + kempt). These, too, are straightforward, even though the base +*peat* is not only bound but also unique to this word and its derivatives, and even though the base *kempt* is now archaic.

In general the boundaries between prefix and stem become most obscure when assimilation occurs and the semantic contribution of prefix and stem is not immediately apparent. For instance, is *suspend* to be explicated (sub + spend) or (sub + s + pend)? *Suspend* parallels etymologically, semantically, and formally words like *depend, impend, expend,* even *pending.* Confronted with such a list, we can invoke something like the orthographic equivalent of arithmetic's principle of the largest common denominator. Briefly, this Principle of the Longest Common String is that in a given sample of words one should examine closely the longest string of letters common to all words in the sample, on the grounds that that string is likely to be a common stem. As with any inductive sampling method, the reliability of this one depends on the nature of the sample— its size, its representativeness, its "tightness" or parallelism in terms of semantic relationships, and the like. So the Principle of the Longest Common String never proves anything; it just provides nudges and hints. In this case the principle suggests that the base is +*pend* and that *suspend* thus must be explicated as (sub + s + pend), an unusual assimilation of the prefix *sub-* to *sus-,* but not a unique one, since it occurs also in words like *sustain* and *susceptible,* (sub + s + tain) and (sub + s + cept + ible). (For more on the assimilation of *sub-* see 10.4.)

Usually the boundary between stem and suffix is quite accessible, too. Words like *haltingly* (halt)ing)ly) and *formalities* (form)al)ity)i + es) pose no problems. But there can be problems and questions at certain stem-suffix boundaries. For instance, does *patience* explicate to (pat + ience) or to (pati + ence) or to (pat + i + ence)? Is the *i* a part of the suffix *-ience,* which would appear to be a coform of *-ence?* Or is the *i* a part of the base? Or is it, as in the third explication, a particle inserted between the base and suffix?

Actually, an *i* appears in this position in many words. These *i*'s are of some importance, especially when palatalization occurs (see chapter 30). And these *i*'s do in fact come from each of the three sources suggested in the three proposed explications of *patience:*

First, in a relatively small number of cases the *i* is part of the base, as in *society* and *social,* (soci + ety) and (soci + al). Other examples:

(Array 2-8)

acrimony	connubial	glacial	propriety
amiable	crucial	glacier	sentient
appropriate	excruciating	inebriated	sentiment

We describe a base as ending in *i* only if doing so allows us to account for all of the words derived from that base. If there are derivatives that do not contain *i* or in which the absence of the *i* cannot be explicated through some systematic deletion, we choose to say that the base does not end in *i* and that the *i* in any derivative is part of the suffix or is an inserted particle. The number of bases that end in *i* is quite small.

A much more productive source of these presuffixal *i*'s is the terminative base or stem that ends in a *y* that is replaced by *i* when the suffix is added, as in *burial* and *colloquial,* (bur*y̸*)i + al) and (colloqu*y̸*)i + al). Other examples:

(Array 2-9)

carrier	faculties	marriage	stories
dreariest	industrial	primarily	wateriness
drowsier	luxurious	scurried	worrisome

Third, in several cases the *i* is a particle. Sometimes a particle *i* is inserted to mark palatalization, as in *partial* and *sufficient,* (part)i + al) and (suffic*e̸*)i + ent). Other examples:

(Array 2-10)

captious	conscientious	glazier	officiate
circumstantial	differentiate	gracious	provincial
commercial	facial	hosiery	satiate

In some instances the *i* is a particle that is pronounced but that does not serve any diacritical function, such as marking palatalization. Some examples are:

(Array 2-11)

adverbial (adverb)i + al)	censorious (censor)i + ous)
censorial (censor)i + al)	tutorial (tutor)i + al)

This last type of particle *i* is a problem. It would be possible to treat it as not a particle at all but as simply a part of the suffix—(adverb)ial), (censor)ious), and so on. Thus we could posit sets containing variant

forms of the suffixes involved: [-*al*, -*ial*], [-*ous*, -*ious*]. Since the *i* is always
pronounced in these instances, the selection rule would be fairly straightforward: pick the coform that matches the pronunciation. The problem
with this otherwise attractive approach is that it would require many such
sets. We would need, for instance, to accommodate -*ual*, -*uous*, -*uity*,
-*ience*, -*ient*, -*uent*, and so on. To multiply sets in this way would be to
head in the wrong direction. We would still feel the cut of Occam's razor
in such matters. It seems better to keep the number of different entities to
a minimum, listing sets only when necessary, and otherwise trying as
often as possible to describe the general process that generates the various forms, the process in this case being particle insertion. On the other
side of the argument, however, is the admission that this "process" is at
best weakly motivated. The matter is not at all settled, but for now we will
treat such *i*'s as particles, eschewing the solution that multiplies sets.

There is a basic indeterminacy in such matters, and our choices are
molded as much by the assumptions informing our descriptions as by the
nature of the material we are describing. Different assumptions lead to
different descriptions, and different descriptions lead to different insights
into the material. In such matters a given description is not necessarily
right or wrong relative to another; there is instead an element of complementarity among contending descriptions.

2.7.3 The Rule of Syllabicity

Studied from a rigorously etymological point of view, the words *cost* and
rest would have to be explicated as each consisting of a prefix plus the
base +*st*: (com + st) and (re + st). Words such as *distant* and *substance*
would be explicated as a prefix plus the base +*st* plus a suffix: (dis +
st + ant) and (sub + st + ance). This alleged base +*st* is connate with a
number of other, more recognizable bases, all of which descend from the
Latin verb *stāre* 'stand'—for instance, the +*stice* of *solstice* and *armistice*
or the *stit* + of *substitute* and *superstitious*. In words like *cost* and *rest* we
find the fossils of historical prefixes, just as in *distant* and *substance* we
find the fossils of historical suffixes. But it seems quite unconvincing to
analyze such words so as to explicate those fossils. Not only have the
prefixes and suffixes lost nearly all of their original identity, but the base
proposed in such explications is troubling: +*st* just does not make a very
convincing base.

Elements that are less than a full syllable long are quite rare. The most
common ones are the -*s* suffixes that mark noun plurals and third person
singular present tense verbs. But these subsyllabic suffixes are always
added to free stems and are thus recognized immediately as being some-

thing separate unto themselves. The *st* in a word like *rest* or *distant* is quite different. Common sense tells us that *rest* is an unanalyzable single element and that *distant* analyzes into prefix and base, (dis + stant), not into prefix plus base plus suffix. Common sense tells us that the historical base spelled *st* has absorbed prefixes and suffixes to form newer, fully syllabic bases such as *rest, cost,* and the + *stant* and *stance* of *distant* and *distance.*

What emerges here is a Rule of Syllabicity, which urges that an element be at least a syllable in length. Such a rule is not as arbitrary as it may at first appear to be. The syllable plays an immediate and concrete role in spoken language; it seems only natural and efficient to expect the elements to follow the seams and boundaries set down by the syllables. Doing so lends to the element the concreteness and immediacy of the syllable.

Elements are much more accessible in words where their boundaries coincide with syllable boundaries, as compared with words whose elements cut across syllable boundaries and vice versa. In a word such as *restitute,* for instance, there is little parallelism between syllable and element, and the elements can be quite inaccessible: The syllabication of *restitute* is /'res tə ˌt(y)ūt/; its explication into elements is (re + stit + ute). Compare this with a word in which syllable and element boundaries coincide—for instance, *rebroadcast:* /rē 'bròd ˌkast/, (re(broad)(cast). It is germane here that folk etymology tends to work toward "elements" that are a syllable long, as in the development of *crayfish,* and that learned mistakes often do the same, as in *ptarmigan.*

This Rule of Syllabicity can be formulated even more stringently: The element tends to be no less and no more than a syllable long; indeed, the length of most elements is exactly one syllable. And often when elements contain two or more syllables, the extra syllables tend to "feel" like prefixes and suffixes—that is, like additional elements—even though upon closer inspection it is clear that the words must be treated as single, multisyllabic elements. Consider, for instance, the disyllabic elements *mother, father, brother, sister.* Since the suffix *-er* is a common noun ending, these words have a common noun look and sound. But in these four cases the *er* endings are not suffixes at all; each word is a single, disyllabic element with an ending that looks and sounds like a suffix but is not. Sisters do not *sist, nor do fathers *fath. Nor, looking at the other common suffix spelled *er,* are brothers "more broth." The evolution of the endings of these words toward "pseudosuffixes" can be seen as an attempt to accommodate these disyllabic elements to the Rule of Syllabicity: elements should be one and only one syllable long, or at least they should look and feel as if they might be.

2.7.3.1 Lexical Simplification

Further support for such a rule can be found among the many words that have been simplified over the centuries from two or more syllables to just one. For instance, the word *lord* was in Old English *hlāfweard,* which meant, literally, "loaf-warden"—that is, "keeper of the bread"—which would equal at least two elements and syllables. Over the centuries the sense of the word moved away from the original bread-image, the word becoming in time a single element and gradually shortening to one syllable: *hlāfweard* to *hlāford* to *loverd* to *lord.*

The shortening of older, longer words to modern, monosyllabic simplexes is extremely common. Some random examples: *twit* from Old English *ætwītan, sport* from Middle English *disporten, dirge* from Middle English *dirige, king* from Old English *cyning, yet* from Old English *gieta,* and *death* from Old English *dēath,* which was disyllabic. The more recognizable clippings also tend to follow syllable boundaries: *van* from *caravan, gym* from *gymnasium, bus* from *omnibus.* Sometimes the syllable boundaries cut through old elements, as in *bike* from *bicycle* (bi(cycle); *mike* from *microphone* (micr + o(phone); *bra* from *brassiere,* apparently (brass + iere). The result of these clippings is the creation of new monosyllabic elements.

2.7.4 Merging

It is not at all uncommon for a sound and a letter that were once part of an element to move across a boundary and merge with a different element. For instance, a number of English verb bases contain a *t* that has merged from a Latin inflectional ending. English verbs were often adapted from Latin past participles. For instance, *corrupt* is adapted from *corruptus,* the past participle of *corrumpere.* The *t* in *corrupt,* then, echoes the Latin past participle inflection; more accurately, it echoes the supine stem on which the past participle was formed. It has lost that force in English, however, as is attested by the fact that we now form the past participle with the regular *-ed.* We would not now analyze *corrupt* as *(com + r + rup + t) or *(com + r + ru + pt). We explicate it as (com + r + rupt), treating the *t* as part of the terminative bound base +*rupt.* Thus the *t* in *corrupt* is an instance of part of a suffix or inflection merging with a base.

Skeat listed the following as other verbs that contain similar final *t*'s that have merged from the Latin inflection: *abduct, abstract, addict, affect, afflict, assert, attract, bisect, circumvent, concoct, conduct, confect, conflict, contort, contract, contradict, convict, correct,* and so on ([1891] 1970, 260–62). This list was compiled from just the letters *a* to *c* in the alphabet (and Skeat could have mentioned several others, such as *accept*).

The size of the sample and the fact that some of the bases involved are very productive make it clear that there are many such verbs in English, all of which illustrate this merging of elements into single-syllable bases.

2.7.4.1 Subelemental Patterning

This merging of elements leads to some interesting patterning at the subelemental level. For instance, we have the interrogative adverb *where,* which can be defined, or paraphrased, as "at what place?" Legitimate answers to *where* are *here* and *there.* We also have the somewhat dated but closely related adverb *whither,* which can be paraphrased as "in what place or direction?"—to which legitimate answers would be *hither* ("this way") and *thither* ("that way"). So a pattern emerges:

(Array 2-12)

Where?	Here	There
(What place?)	(This place)	(That place)
Whither?	Hither	Thither
(What place or direction?)	(This way)	(That way)
Whence?	Hence	Thence
When?	Now	Then
(At what time?)	(At this time)	(At that time)

The overall pattern is this: The left column consists of interrogatives of direction, place, and time—all with the initial cluster *wh.* The middle and right columns represent answers to the interrogatives. The middle column always gives an answer that contains a sense of something like "toward or nearer the speaker," while the right column always gives an answer that contains "away from or farther from the speaker." Looking at the patterning within array 2-12, it is possible to assign apparent semantic content to subsyllabic strings. Running across the rows, initial *wh,* "interrogation"; initial *h,* "nearer the speaker"; initial *th,* "farther from the speaker." Running down the columns, final *ere,* "place"; final *ither,* "place or direction." The final *ence* would be less clear since the *ence* adverbs have a number of different definitions, but it is fairly accurate to describe the apparent semantic content of final *ence* in these words as "from . . . place, time, source." The final *en* in the bottom row contains "point in time," though *now* breaks the pattern, which would call for **hen* at this point. Interestingly enough, the *OED* records *hen, henne,* as common English words up through the middle of the fifteenth century, with a sense that could easily have evolved into the *now*-sense, thereby filling out the pattern.

A similar patterning occurs among the interrogative and demonstrative pronouns:

(Array 2-13)

What? (singular)	This	That
What? (plural)	These	Those

Such patterning is the product of historical developments and change, like the *t*'s at the end of all of those verb bases. The recurrent initial *wh* echoes the Proto-Indo-European root *kwo-, kwi-*, which was a stem for relative and interrogative pronouns and which underlies all of the interrogative *wh* words in Modern English, including also *what, who, which, why*. The recurrent final strings—*ere, ither, ence,* and *en*—echo some Old English and even some Middle English inflections. The *ce* in *whence, hence,* and *thence,* for instance, derives from the early Middle English genitive suffix used to form adverbs. Clearly, however, all of these old stems and suffixes have lost their separate identities by now. They have merged into the usually monosyllabic adverbs and pronouns in arrays 2-12 and 2-13, each of which is now a simplex, with a subsyllabic and subelemental patterning standing as a reminder of the way things once were in the language.

2.7.5 Two Examples of Explication

Some of the problems and questions involved in explication can be illustrated with two fairly complex examples. The first involves the group of words *gym, gymnasium, gymnasia, gymnast, gymnastic, gymnastics, gymnasial, gymnasiarch, gymkhana, gymnosophist, gymnosperm*. The second involves *analyze, analysis, analyst, analytic; catalyze, catalysis, catalyst, catalytic; lyse, lysis, lytic, lysin; paralyze, paralysis, paralytic*.

2.7.5.1 The Set [*gym, gymn +, gymnasi +*]

The first group of words—*gym,* and so on—all derive from the Greek *gumnos* 'naked', which leads to the first difficulty, the semantic contribution of the bases in these words. Most of them have evolved semantically away from the etymological sense "naked," though once the sense is indicated, it is not hard to see the relevance of that etymological sense to each word. At this time it seems best to stay with the etymology, to say that the base in these words still contains the sense "naked," which forms the basis for the various analogical extensions the words in the group have undergone. We can then rely on historical information to explain the underlying relevance—namely, that in ancient Greece gymnasia were places where athletes performed naked.

The second difficulty with this example has to do with deciding how many cobases there are among these words, and what those bases are. First, we must posit the free base *gym*, which historically was clipped from the older and longer *gymnasium*. The free base *gym* also occurs in the very recent formation *gymkhana* (gym)khana), +*khana* being a Hindi adoption with the content "house."

But the base *gym* cannot be an explicatum of *gymnast; nast* is not a recognizable element, and it obscures the more likely suffix in the word— namely, *-ast*, an agent-noun suffix similar to *-ist* which occurs in *enthusiast, scholiast, fantast, dynast, encomiast, elegiast, pederast,* and a few others. Thus, we must posit a bound base *gymn+*, leading to (gymn+ ast). The base *gymn+*, which proves to be nonterminative, is also an explicatum of four other members of the group:

(Array 2-14)

gymnastic (gymn+ast)ic)   gymnosophist (gymn+o(soph+ist)
gymnastics (gymn+ast)ic)s)   gymnosperm (gymn+o(sperm)

This leaves the following words, still unexplicated: *gymnasium, gymnasia, gymnasial, gymnasiarch, gymnasiast.* Neither of the bases posited so far, *gym* or *gymn+*, can help here, for each leads to unlikely terminations such as *asium* or *nasium, asia* or *nasia,* and the like. If we look first for recognizable suffixes, we find the old Latin singular *-um* and its plural *-a* in *gymnasium* and *gymnasia.* We also find a possible *-al* in *gymnasial; -ast* again in *gymnasiast;* and the bound base +*arch* in *gymnasiarch.* The presence of these final elements suggests either a very long bound base spelled *gymnasi* or the somewhat shorter *gymnas* plus the connective particle *i* (see 2.4.1). Future analysis may suggest a better way of accounting for the *asi* string in these words, a way that will allow the base to come closer to the single-syllable ideal, but for now it seems better to posit a third, bound base for our set, *gymnasi+*. The remaining explications, then, would be these:

(Array 2-15)

gymnasia (gymnasi+a)   gymnasiast (gymnasi+ast)
gymnasial (gymnasi+al)   gymnasium (gymnasi+um)
gymnasiarch (gymnasi+arch)

2.7.5.2 The Set [*ly+, lyse, +lyte*]

Some of the same issues are involved in the second set of example words: *analyze, analysis, analyst, analytic; catalyze, catalysis, catalyst, catalytic; lyse, lysis, lytic, lysin; paralyze, paralysis, paralytic.* Etymologically all of these words derive from the Greek verb *luein*, 'to loose, set free'. The group contains three fairly straightforward prefixes: *ana-, cata-,* and *para-. Analysis, catalysis, lysis,* and *paralysis* all clearly contain the suffix *-sis,* which contributes the content "condition, state." Thus we get the following explications:

(Array 2-16)

analysis (ana + ly + sis)	lysis (ly + sis)
catalysis (cata + ly + sis)	paralysis (para + ly + sis)

This, of course, means that we have posited a first base for our set: the nonterminative bound base *ly +* .

Analyst and *catalyst* are somewhat unusual words. Although the prefixes are straightforward enough, and it is reasonable to posit *ly +* as an explicatum of each, our sense of the language urges that somehow they must contain the agent-noun suffix *-ist*. But *ana-* plus *ly +* plus *-ist* would, in the normal course of events, lead to a *y* deletion, producing the unaccepted spelling *analist*. (For more on this *y* deletion see 3.4.3.2.) Three possible explanations suggest themselves: (1) We can assume a nonregular *i*-deletion, (ana + ly + *i*st); or (2) we can posit a coform for the suffix *-ist,* one spelled *yst,* which, due to a tactical constraint against double *y,* would produce (ana + lyⱥ + yst); or (3) we can posit a subsyllabic coform spelled *st:* (ana + ly + st). For now the third option seems most desirable: Although it does violence to the rule of syllabicity, it does avoid the nonregular deletion in (1), and it produces an explication based on simple addition rather than the deletion required in (2), without positing any more coforms than does (2).

Catalyst explicates similarly: (cata + ly + st). So, too, *analyze, catalyze,* and *paralyze,* involving a coform of the suffix *-ize:* (ana + ly + ze), (cata + ly + ze), and (para + ly + ze). (All three of these words have British variants in *se.* The *ze* in the American spellings parallels the American tendency to choose *-ize* rather than the more typically British *-ise.*)

The free base *lyse* is historically a back-formation from *lysis,* which means that (ly + sis) was clipped to (ly + s), with a final *e* added to insulate an otherwise free-base-final *s.* (For more on this insulative function of final *e* see 8.1.4.) *Lyse* thus represents another instance of the merging discussed in 2.7.4. The free base *lyse* is an explicatum of *lysin* (lysⱥ)in), *lysine* (lysⱥ)ine), *lysogenesis* (lysⱥ)o(genesis), and the like.

The remaining words—*analytic, catalytic, lytic,* and *paralytic*—are not quite so difficult. The suffix in each case is clearly the adjective-forming *-ic,* which suggests *lyt* as the base. However, the related terminative bound base *+ lyte,* as in *electrolyte,* can serve as well:

(Array 2-17)

analytic (ana + lytⱥ + ic)	lytic (lytⱥ + ic)
catalytic (cata + lytⱥ + ic)	paralytic (para + lytⱥ + ic)

2.8   Summary

There are a number of indeterminacies and problems in the practice of explication: Drawing some boundaries between elements and particles remains quite problematical. And the goals and strategies of explication sometimes contend markedly with the goals and strategies of other forms of lexical analysis—those of the etymologists and the generativists, for instance. Nevertheless, we can offer the following summary description of explication.

The two fundamental entities in the explication of written words are elements and particles. Elements are the smallest parts of written words that contribute semantic content. Thus, explicating a word into its elements involves an awareness of both the word's formal and its semantic structure. Even though elements and syllables are quite different things, the formation and evolution of elements tends to be governed by a principle of syllabicity that constrains elements to be no more or no less than one syllable long. Elements are either bound or free, and either terminative or nonterminative. There are three types of elements: prefixes, bases, and suffixes. All prefixes and suffixes are bound. Some bases are bound, some are free. A string of elements that contains at least one base is called a stem. Stems can also be either bound or free, terminative or not. Coelements come in sets of two or more and can replace one another, following careful tactical rules. Connate elements are bound primarily by a common etymology and cannot serve as tactical replacements for one another—unless, of course, they are also coelements. Particles are letters inserted usually between elements in a word without contributing semantic content to it.

TACTICS

3 Sequences and Distributions

3.1 Tactics and Tactical Patterns

The word *tactics* comes from a Greek word meaning "to arrange," and tactics deal with the ways in which things in a language do and do not arrange themselves. The stem *tactic* occurs in *syntactic,* and its coform *tax* occurs in *syntax,* which is the study of the way in which words do and do not arrange themselves into phrases, clauses, and sentences. The tactical patterns discussed in chapters 3–7 deal with sounds and their spellings, with which arrangements of sounds and spellings are normal, allowable—expectable—in American English, and which are not.

The study of the arrangements of sounds is called **phonotactics,** and the study of the arrangement of spellings, or letters, is called **graphotactics.** But for the orthographer the two keep mixing together, and since we are most concerned with the interaction between the two, we will speak simply in terms of *tactics,* making it clear when we are talking about the tactics of sounds, about the tactics of spellings, and about the interaction between the two.

Learning the tactics of a language is a large part, although a surprisingly "hidden" part, of learning a language. Any native speaker of English has mastered an immense amount of tactical knowledge, even though for the most part it was mastered unintentionally, more or less along the way. For instance, speakers of English may not be sure immediately whether or not the string of letters *larp* spells an English word (it does not), but they recognize immediately that it *could.* There is nothing non-English about the arrangement of letters and sounds in it. It fits the English tactical patterns. Analogies such as *carp* and *lark* demonstrate that the tactics in the spelling *larp* are in fact English.

On the other hand, native speakers of English also immediately recognize that a string of letters such as *ngabc* not only does not spell an English word but never could. The tactics are all wrong. It looks "funny."

And it would sound funny, too—if you could pronounce it—for it does not readily fit the English-speaking tongue. English tactics constrain against words beginning with the letters *ng* (or the sound /ŋ/). The tactics of other languages—Vietnamese and Rarotongan Maori, for instance—do allow word-initial *ng* and /ŋ/, which is one reason why English-speaking persons have trouble with Vietnamese and Rarotongan names such as Nguyen and Ngatangia. That is also why the very few recent and still minimally integrated words with initial *ng*, such as *ngaio* and *ngege*, look so odd and are adapted in pronunciation to something less formidable, the initial /ŋ/ being replaced by either /n/ or /ən/. By the same token, the tactics of English do not allow words to end in the string *bc* (as in our *ngabc*). We do find *bc* in concatenations where certain word elements come together, as in *abcoulomb*, which equals the prefix *ab-* plus the stem *coulomb*. But *bc* is extremely rare in English words, and it cannot occur in word-final position. Native English-speaking persons know such things about English tactics, even though they probably have never thought of them consciously and almost certainly have never had to learn them deliberately.

Tactical patterns are especially important in spelling (and reading) English because English does not use accent marks and other diacritical signs to help spell sounds. Just as English sentences rely on word order to show syntactic relationships, English words rely on tactical patterns to show orthographic relationships. For instance, orthographic tactics indicate whether the letter *c* is "soft," spelling the sound /s/ as in *cent*, or "hard," spelling the sound /k/ as in *cant*. Tactics also indicate that the well-formed spelling is *manageable*, not *managable*. In a more complex way tactical patterns determine whether the sound /k/ at the end of a monosyllabic word should be spelled *k* or *ck*. The tactical rule is that if the /k/ has a long vowel, a consonant, or a vowel digraph right in front of it, it is spelled *k*, as in *bake, bike, bulk, bark, bank, book*. But if it has a short vowel sound spelled with a unigraph right in front of it, it is spelled *ck*, as in *lack, lick, lock, luck*. We are talking here just about the question of when to choose *k* and when to choose *ck*; if we take into account other ways of spelling word-final /k/—for instance, the *c* in *magic* versus the *ch* in *stomach* or *ache*—the tactics become more complicated. We will discuss these complications in 27.3.

In chapters 4–7 we will deal with some of the more important tactical patterns and rules of American English. But first, in the remainder of this chapter, we will discuss miscellaneous rules concerning the sequencing of consonants and vowels, as well as where certain letters do and do not occur in American words.

3.2   Consonant Sequence Rules

3.2.1   Digraphs, Clusters, and Concatenations

American orthographic tactics place a number of constraints on what and how and where consonant letters may occur in sequences of two or more, constraints that we have usually learned so naturally and thoroughly that we don't even notice them. The following analysis distinguishes among three different kinds of consonant letter sequences: **digraphs, clusters,** and **concatenations.** Though there are complications, the distinctions rest on two factors: whether or not the sequence of letters spells sounds in the same syllable, and whether or not it spells sounds in the same element, as summarized below.

(Array 3-1)

Sequence	Same Syllable	Same Element
Digraph	+	+
Cluster	+/−	+
Concatenation	+/−	−

3.2.1.1   Digraphs

To all intents and purposes, consonant digraphs are single orthographic units. Venezky, for instance, calls them "simple relation units" and groups them with consonant unigraphs (1970, 54). Thus it is not surprising that they necessarily always occur in a single syllable and in a single element. The consonant digraphs are *ch, gh, ph, sh,* and *th.* These five digraphs typically spell single sounds that are different from what either of the constituent letters typically spells in isolation. However, there are complications. The distinction between digraph and cluster, which reflects historical change, is more of a polarity than a dichotomy. Thus, for instance, the *ch* in *chill* is clearly a digraph, but the *ch* in, say, *school,* spelling not /ch/ but /k/, could just as well be treated as a cluster similar to *ck,* since it is no longer spelling a sound different from what the constituent *c* typically spells in isolation. For *sc* see 29.2.2.1.

Further complications occur with the parallel sequences *rh* and *wh.* In English, *rh* always spells /r/, the sound typically spelled by one of its constituents, and is thus not like the other five digraphs listed above. The sequence *wh* is even more complicated: sometimes it spells /w/ or /h/, as in the most common pronunciation of *whale* and in *whole;* but sometimes it spells a metathesized /hw/, as in some pronunciations of words like *whale.* In short, *wh* always spells either a single sound typically spelled by one of its constituents or the two sounds typically spelled by both its constituents, but reversed.

Because of these complications, and recognizing the polarity of the distinction between digraph and cluster, we will treat *rh* and *wh* not as digraphs but as clusters.

Consonant digraphs, then, are essentially single units that spell what we think of as single sounds that are different from what either of the constituent letters normally spells in isolation. Consonant digraphs must occur in the same syllable and in the same element. (For more on the historical development of the consonant digraphs see 11.2.2.)

3.2.1.2 Clusters

A consonant cluster is a sequence of two or more consonant letters that spells (1) either the same sound that one or both of the constituent letters normally spell in isolation or (2) two or more sounds that are the sum of the sounds the constituent letters normally spell in isolation. Consonant clusters occur only within a single element, but they can spell sounds that are spread over two syllables. For instance, the cluster *gn* spells /n/ in the element and syllable *sign*, but in the derived form *signal*, which explicates to (sign)al) and syllabicates to /sig/ + /nəl/, though the cluster is still in the single element, the /gn/ is split by a syllable boundary.

The term *cluster* covers four different types of letter sequences. The most straightforward type spells the sounds typically spelled by the constituent letters. Examples of this type, which we will call **cumulations,** are the *ct* in *act,* the *spr* in *spring,* and the *mps* in *glimpse.* Cumulations can contain digraphs, as in *harsh, throw, ranch.*

A second type of cluster is the **doublet,** like the *gg* in *egg* or the *tt* in *otter.* Closely related are **doublet equivalents,** such as the *ck* (equivalent of double *k*) in *pick,* the *dg* (equivalent of double soft *g*) in *dodge,* and the *tch* (double *ch*) in *ditch.*

A fourth type of cluster involves sequences in which one or more of the constituent letters are not pronounced, such as the *mb* in *bomb* or the *lf* in *half.* In some cases these **simplifications** become cumulations when the addition of a suffix forces a syllable break in the midst of the cluster, as, for instance, in the *sign/signal* example given earlier.

Consonant clusters are obviously a somewhat freer group than consonant digraphs, but they are governed by a number of clustering constraints, some of which lead to the clustering rules to be discussed below. (For more on consonant clusters see Zettersten 1969; Hultzen 1965; Whorf 1956; Roberts 1965, 60–61, 398–427.)

3.2.1.3 Concatenations

Concatenations consist of two or more consonant letters that are juxtaposed when elements are combined. Practically no constraints are imposed on the formation of concatenations, beyond those that control the occurrence of consonant letters at the beginning and end of elements. Especially in compound words, concatenations can get very elaborate, even a bit startling when taken out of context—for instance, the *mbpr* in *bombproof* or the *ckstr* in *blackstrap*. To get some sense of the diversity that is possible in concatenations, consider the following sample, taken from just the compounds beginning with *a* and *b* in Alice Morton Ball's alphabetical list in her *Compounding in the English Language* (1941, 103–21):

(Array 3-2)

aitchbone	*tchb*	bleachground	*chgr*
almshouse	*lmsh*	blindstitch	*ndst*
alongshore	*ngsh*	blockship	*cksh*
archpriest	*rchpr*	boardcloth	*rdcl*
armplate	*rmpl*	boltsmith	*ltsm*
artcraft	*rtcr*	bondslave	*ndsl*
athwartships	*rtsh*	breastwheel	*stwh*
backcast	*ckc*	breechcloth	*chcl*
bandwheel	*ndwh*	brightwork	*ghtw*
beechdrops	*chdr*	buckskin	*cksk*
birthstone	*rthst*	bunkchain	*nkch*
blackbreast	*ckbr*	buntwhip	*ntwh*
blastplate	*stpl*	bushwacker	*shw*

Concatenations are less constrained tactically than clusters, but as the following discussion will show, they often tend to evolve toward the same constraints imposed on clusters. For instance, the assimilation of the final consonants in certain prefixes can be understood as a response to the pressure of certain sequence rules, rules that in other settings are not operative with concatenations.

3.2.2 The Mixed Voicing Rule

In American English there are nine voiceless consonants, eight of which have a voiced partner. A voiceless consonant is pronounced without vibrating the vocal cords. A voiced consonant is pronounced with the vocal cords vibrating. The voiceless and voiced pairs are:

(Array 3-3)

Voiceless Consonants		Voiced Consonants	
/p/	pat	/b/	bat
/t/	tot	/d/	dot
/f/	fine	/v/	vine
/s/	sip	/z/	zip
/k/	cod	/g/	god
/th/	thin	/th/	then
/ch/	chin	/j/	gin
/sh/	dasher	/zh/	azure
/h/	hat		

All of the remaining consonants are voiced: the nasals, /m/, /n/, and /ŋ/; the liquids, /l/ and /r/; and the semivowels, /w/ and /y/. All of the vowels also are voiced.

3.2.2.1 Voicing in Clusters

Voiceless consonants can cluster with other voiceless consonants in the left column of array 3-3, but they cannot cluster with voiced consonants in the right column. Thus we get voiceless clusters like /sk/, /st/, /sp/, /ft/, /kt/, or /pt/, as in *scare, stare, spare, soft, act, apt,* but we do not get mixed clusters like */sg/, */sd/, */sb/, */vt/, */fd/, */kd/, */gt/, */pd/,* or */bt/. The letter *x,* which usually spells a sound cluster, never spells a mixed cluster. That is, *x* spells either /ks/ or /gz/ but never */kz/ or */gs/.

Even though nasals, liquids, and semivowels are normally voiced, they can cluster with voiceless consonants. Thus we get clusters such as /kl/ and /kr/ in *climb* and *crime,* /fl/ and /fr/ in *flee* and *free,* /sm/ and /sn/ in *smack* and *snack,* /sw/ and /tw/ in *swill* and *twill.* Peter Ladefoged points out that liquids and semivowels regularly devoice after voiceless stops (1975, 77), which may be a factor in this larger pattern.

Voiced consonants in the right column of array 3-3 can cluster with nasals, liquids, and semivowels, as in the /nd/ in *and,* /mb/ in *amber,* /ŋg/ in *anger,* /lb/ in *album,* /rg/ in *argon,* /dw/ in *dwindle.* In theory, at least, they can also cluster with other voiced consonants in the right column, though there are very few such voiced clusters—two examples being the /dz/ in *adze* and the /gd/ in *smaragd.*

Thus, a full statement of the Mixed Voicing Rule as it applies to clusters would be as follows: Voiceless consonants in the left column can cluster with one another or with nasals, liquids, and semivowels; voiced consonants in the right column can also cluster with one another or with nasals, liquids, and semivowels; but voiceless consonants in the left column cannot cluster with voiced consonants in the right column.

Mixed clusters—that is, holdouts to the Mixed Voicing Rule—are very rare. One is the /fg/ in *afghan.* The /kd/ in *anecdote* could also be treated as a holdout, although a rigorously historical explication of *anecdote* would be (an + ec + dote), which makes the /kd/ a concatenation rather than a cluster.

3.2.2.2   Voicing in Concatenations

The constraint against mixed voicing applies in a more complex way to concatenations. On the one hand, it accounts for the variation in the pronunciation of the noun plural suffix: /s/ after voiceless consonants, as in /kats/, but /z/ after voiced consonants, /dȯgz/. It also accounts for much of the assimilation of prefixes; for instance, instead of the mixed concatenation in **adpear,* full assimilation produces the letter cluster *pp,* spelling the single sound /p/ in *appear.*

However, there are several instances in which voiced and voiceless consonants concatenate, both in complexes and in compounds. The major pressure for these holdouts is obviously conservative analogy, with its tendency to keep the spelling and pronunciation of a given element consistent from word to word. (For more on conservative analogy see 1.4 and 7.4.) Conservative analogy is particularly potent in compounds and in recently formed complexes, especially complexes in which a prefix or suffix has been added to a free stem.

Mixed concatenations are common at the boundaries between stems and prefixes that end with the letter *b,* as the following sample illustrates:

(Array 3-4)

abfarad	lordship	subcellar	subquality
abhor	needful	subchapter	subshock
abscond	obclude	subclass	subsidiary
absolute	obsequious	subfreezing	substance
dabster	obtrude	subkingdom	subterfuge

These holdouts to the Mixed Voicing Rule usually involve the addition of a prefix or suffix to a free stem. Usually the word in question is a recent formation, formed either in or since the eighteenth century. Both of these factors are conducive to conservative analogy, which works to keep the spelling and pronunciation of elements consistent, even if it creates concatenations with mixed voicing.

The complexity of the Mixed Voicing Rule for concatenations is further illustrated by the fairly large number of words that contain concatenations with variant pronunciations, one with mixed voicing, one without. A sample of such variants is given in array 3-5. According to *W3* a common shift of syllable boundary is made in these words to avoid mixed concatenations in a single syllable. Thus *substyle* is /'subz₁tīl/ or /'sub₁stīl/, and *disgust* is /dəs'gust/ or /də'skust/. Other variants include:

(Array 3-5)

absorb	disbar	obstipate	subsequent
absquatulate	disdain	obstreperous	subsidize
abstain	lobster	obstruct	substantial
abstention	obscure	obstupefy	substitute
abstract	obstacle	presbyter	substract
abstruse	obstetric	subscribe	substruct
asbestos	obstinate	subscription	subsume

3.2.3 The Initial Doublet Rule

Although consonant doublets are quite common in word-medial position (*apple, lettuce*), or in word-final position (*stiff, all*), or at the juncture of free stems and suffixes due to the Twinning Rule—as in *robber* and *running*, (rob)b + er) and (run)n + ing)—they do not regularly occur in word-initial or even in element-initial position. Other than an occasional proper name such as *Lloyd* or *Llewelyn*, the only common holdouts to the rule against word-initial doublets are the recent Spanish adoptions *llama* and *llano* (see also 32.2.2.3).

The only known holdouts to the rule against element-initial doublets are a few terminative bound bases from medicine and anatomy that start with *rrh* and never occur in word-initial position. This *rrh* spelling of the sound /r/ is the English adaptation of Greek double rho, single rho usually being adapted to *rh*. These elements usually have a variant spelling with the more regular *rh*. Some examples are + *rrhage* and its derivatives + *rrhagia*, + *rrhagy*, + *rrhagic*, as in *hemorrhage*, and so on; + *rrhea* as in *diarrhea*; + *rrhaphy* as in *laparorrhaphy*; + *rrheuma* as in *acrorrheuma*; + *rrhexis* as in *hepatorrhexis*; and + *rrhinia* as in *cacorrhinia*.

3.2.4 Final Doublet Constraints

The only final consonant doublets that are common are *ff* (*staff, stiff, stuff*), *ll* (*ball, bell, bill, boll, bull*), and *ss* (*mass, mess, miss, moss, muss*). Up through the sixteenth and seventeenth centuries words that now end in *ss* or *ff* were commonly spelled *sse* or *ffe*. There are also the doublet equivalents mentioned in 3.2.1.2: *ck, tch*, and *dge*. But certain consonant doublets never occur in word-final position: *cc, hh, jj, kk, mm, pp, qq, vv, xx, yy*. The doublets *bb, dd, gg, nn, rr, tt, zz*, are very rare in word-final position, and they often occur only to avoid two-letter words in accordance with the Short Word Rule (see 3.5), as in *ebb, odd, egg, inn, err*.

Also, except for the doublet equivalent *tch,* consonant digraphs never double; there is no *shsh, *thth, *phph, or the like in word-final position, or anywhere else, for that matter.

Although the doublet *ll* is common in word-final position, it is common only in monosyllables. In polysyllables there is a strong constraint against final *ll,* unless the word is a complex that consists of a prefix plus a monosyllabic free base, such as *unwell* or *recall,* (un(well) and (re(call), or is a compound, such as *blackball* or *spoonbill.* The reduction of the base *full* to the suffix *-ful* is an instance of the constraint against final *ll* in polysyllables. The word *excel* was respelled in the eighteenth or nineteenth century from the earlier *excell,* apparently in response to this constraint.

The variants *fulfill* and *fulfil* show some indecision as to whether or not the word consists of a prefix and a free base. Partridge ([1958] 1983) does not show a prefix *ful-.* Etymologically *fulfill* is not a complex at all but rather a compound consisting of *ful* (an Old English variant of *full*) plus *fill.*

3.2.5 The Triplet Rule

English orthographic tactics constrain against consonant triplets—for instance, *ppp and *mmm. This constraint holds for both clusters and concatenations, explaining such unusual deletions as those in *shrilly* (shrill̸)ly) and *fully* (full̸)ly). Actual examples are rare, but if you had a small boat filled with fish, you would have, apparently, a *skifful* (skiff)ful), not a *skiffful. Someone with a very thin face might appear *skulllike* (skull̸)like) rather than *skulllike, though the suffix *-like* is sometimes affixed with a hyphen, *skull-like,* the hyphen serving to break up the triplet *lll.* Similar to this is *hill-less* and *bell-less.*

Offal contains an instance of the Triplet Rule at work. It is a compound of *off* and *fall,* with two deletions: A final *l* is deleted in accordance with the tendency to avoid final *ll* in words of two or more syllables, and an *f* is deleted to avoid the triplet *fff:* (off)(fall̸) rather than *offfall.

3.2.6 Doublets within Larger Clusters and Concatenations

American English orthography contains a weak constraint against clusters or concatenations of three or more consonants that include a doublet. The explication of words such as *eighth* and *chilblain* reflect this constraint: it is (eight̸)th) rather than *eightth, (chill̸)blain) rather than *chillblain.

The constraint is most common, however, at the boundary between certain prefixes and their stems. For instance, it is *ascend* (ad + scend) rather than the normal assimilation of *ad-* to *as-* before *s,* which would produce a doublet within a larger concatenation: *(ad + s + scend), *asscend. (For more on the regular assimilation of *ad-* see 10.6.) Other examples involving the suffix *ad-* include:

(Array 3-6)

ascribe	(ad(scribe), not *asscribe
ascription	(ad(scription), not *asscription
aspect	(ad + spect), not *asspect
asperse	(ad + sperse), not *assperse
aspirate	(ad + spirate), not *asspirate
astringent	(ad(stringent), not *asstringent

There is also *agnate* (ad + gnate) rather than the normal assimilation of *ad-* to *ag-* before *g*, *(ad + g + gnate), which would produce *aggnate. Similarly there is *agnomen* (ad + gnomen) rather than *aggnomen.

Explications that reflect this constraint with the prefix *dis-* include:

(Array 3-7)

discission	(dis + scission), not *disscission
disperse	(dis + sperse), not *dissperse
dispirit	(dis(spirit), not *disspirit
dispread	(dis(spread), not *disspread
distant	(dis + stant), not *disstant
distinct	(dis + stinct), not *disstinct
distinguish	(dis + stinguish), not *disstinguish
distrain	(dis(strain), not *disstrain
distress	(dis(stress), not *disstress
district	(dis(strict), not *disstrict

The prefix *trans-* also produces some instances of *s*-deletion in line with this constraint. Thus, rather than *transscribe we have *transcribe* (trans(scribe). Other instances:

(Array 3-8)

transcend, not *transscend	transpire
transcription, not *transscription	transponder
transection, not *transsection	transubstantiate
transilience	transude
transistor	transumption

There are variants and holdouts, however: The regular *transonic* has the variant *trans-sonic,* the hyphen serving to break up the concatenation. *Transhape* and *tranship* have less regular variants with *ssh.* And *transsegmental* and *transsubjective* are clear holdouts.

There are a few assimilations of the prefix *sub-* that also reflect this constraint. For instance, it is *suspect* (sub + spect) rather than the more expected assimilation of *sub-* to *sus-* before *s* (as in *sussultatory*), which would lead to **susspect*. Also, it is *suspicious* (suƀ + spicious) rather than **susspicious*; and *suspire* (suƀ + spire) rather than **susspire*.

3.2.6.1 Holdouts

The suffixes *-ness* and *-ful* illustrate nicely the weakness of this Doublet Constraint in concatenations. On the one hand, the variants *dulness, fulness, skilful,* and *wilful* reflect the constraint, though always with an *l*-deletion: (dulɫ)ness), (fulɫ)ness), and so on. But the more common variants *dullness, fullness, skillful,* and *willful* are holdouts. Further, *-ness* and *-ful* are involved in a few other holdouts:

(Array 3-9)

allness	glassful	stiffness	wellness
blissful	grossness	stillness	
distressful	illness	successful	

Other suffixes, when added to free stems, sometimes produce holdouts, sometimes not: Thus there is *welfare* but *illfare*. Some other miscellaneous holdouts: *crosswise, hellward, offward, stiffly*. The suffix *-ment* produces a number of holdouts:

(Array 3-10)

amassment	embossment	engrossment	impressment
assessment	enfeoffment	harassment	

For reasons that are not clear the prefix *mis-* also is a regular and systematic holdout to the Doublet Constraint, as in:

(Array 3-11)

misspeak	misspend	misstep
misspell	misstate	misstrike

The exemption of *mis-* from this constraint may reflect the joint facts that it is consistently added to free stems, thus encouraging the pressures of conservative analogy, and that in the past it was often spelled *miss-*. It is worth noticing, too, that spellings such as *mispell* and *mispend*, reflecting the constraint, were common up through the eighteenth century.

Several other holdouts to this constraint involve clusters and concatenations that contain a doublet plus the liquid /l/ or /r/. The liquids are often exempt from rules that apply to other consonants. In 3.2.2, for instance, they are exempt from the Mixed Voicing Rule. Examples of clusters and concatenations containing a doublet and a final liquid are:

(Array 3-12)

abbreviate	agglomerate	effluerage	oppress
acclimate	aggravate	effraction	riffle
accrue	apply	fettle	stiffly
addle	approach	grassless	subbrachial
address	attract	grossly	suppress
affluent	dazzle	mattress	tattle
affricate	ecclesiastic	oddly	wiggle

Addle, fettle, and the like illustrate the important VC'C'*le#* subpattern discussed in 26.2.3.9, 26.3.3.8, 26.4.3.8, 26.5.3.8, 27.2.4.8, 27.3.3.10, 28.2.3.10, 29.1.3.3, and 29.2.3.9.

The inflectional suffix *-s* also is regularly exempt from this constraint, so there are concatenations in such words as *ebbs, odds, doffs, eggs, ills, inns.*

A number of holdouts to the Doublet Constraint involve clusters that occur at the boundary between free stems in compound words. A few examples are:

(Array 3-13)

allspice	buffware	dampproof	millwright
ballflower	bullhead	fishhook	offstage
billsticker	burrknot	grasshopper	passport
bottstick	crosscurrent	hellcat	stillhouse

This group of holdouts is completely regular, however, since a more general tactical rule exempts the boundaries between free stems in compounds from all changes. With very few exceptions, all compounds are formed via conservative analogy and simple addition; the free stems simply add together with no deletions, additions, or changes of spelling. The only known holdout to this general rule is *pastime,* which has the anomalous explication (pas*t*)(time).

The many holdouts to the Doublet Constraint can be brought into some sort of order by stating the rule as follows: Doublets do not occur in clusters of three or more consonants unless the consonant following the doublet is a liquid; and they do not usually occur in concatenations of three or more consonants unless the concatenation is at a boundary between free stems in a compound or at the boundary at the affixes *mis-, -ment, -ness* and *-s,* or unless the consonant following the doublet is a liquid. The Doublet Constraint is weak and ragged at best, yet it still seems important in explaining many otherwise anomalous deletions.

3.3 Vowel Sequence Rules

3.3.1 The Vowel Doublet Rule

The only tactical constraint on vowel sequences that is of any moment to orthography is the Vowel Doublet Rule. The doublet clusters *ee* and *oo* are quite common, but other vowel doublets are avoided, in clusters and to a lesser extent in concatenations.

The doublet cluster *aa* does occur in the imitative *baa* and in a few peripheral and usually quite recent adoptions, but it is clearly odd and unintegrated. The only known examples are:

(Array 3-14)

aardvark	bazaar	praam
aardwolf	kraal	salaam
advocaat	laager	taal

The doublet *uu* also is avoided. There was good reason for this avoidance in the Middle Ages. The *uu* could easily be confused with the fairly new letter *w*, which was originally written *uu*, just as its name suggests. Also, since *u* was used to spell vowel sounds and the consonant /v/, and since *u* followed by a vowel was regularly /v/, *uu* would have been interpreted as /vu/. Often, in places where a *uu* may have been justified phonetically to mark a long *u*, the French-influenced digraphs *ou* and *ow* were used. The only known modern instances of *uu* are in concatenations: in the unintegrated and rare Latin adoption *duumvir* and in the more common *vacuum, continuum,* and *residuum.*

The doublet *ii* also is avoided in both clusters and concatenations. This avoidance is exemplified by words like *society* (soci + ety), in which the coform *-ety* rather than the more common *-ity* operates when the stem ends in *i*, thus avoiding *ii*. Other instances:

(Array 3-15)

anxiety (anxi + ety)	propriety (propri + ety)
contrariety (contrar*y*)i + ety)	sobriety (sobri + ety)
notoriety (notori + ety)	variety (var*y*)i + ety)
piety (pi + ety)	

Related, too, are the unusual words like *analyze, analyst, catalyze,* and *catalyst* discussed in 2.7.5.2; instances of the effects of the constraint against *ii* are discussed in 3.4.3.2, which deals with the replacement of *y* with *i*.

The only known instances of *ii* occur in concatenations: in the technical term *gobiid* (gobi + id), in the Latin plural *radii* (radi + i), which is being replaced by the more integrated *radiuses,* and in *skiing,* the present participle inflection of the very recent Norwegian adoption *ski.*

3.4 Distribution Rules

The preceding two sections discussed the tactics of consonant and vowel clusters and concatenations in English. The present section will deal with distribution rules—that is, the description of those patterns and constraints that control where certain letters do and do not regularly occur within elements and words.

3.4.1 The Final *s* Rule

The fact that final *ss* is such a common final doublet is due in large part to a tactical constraint in English against ending terminative bases with a single *s.* The noun plural suffix -*s* and the verb third person singular -*s* are so common that the tactics appear to try to avoid ending terminative bases with a single *s* so as to avoid the look of one of the -*s* suffixes. The Final *s* Rule is very straightforward: In a terminative base that would otherwise end with *s,* if there is a consonant or a vowel digraph immediately in front of the *s,* add a final *e,* as in *lapse, else, dense, goose, house, noise.* Without the final *e,* these words would have the look of plurals: *laps, els, dens, goos.* If there is a short vowel unigraph immediately in front of the *s,* double the *s,* as in *crass, mess, kiss, gloss, fuss, abyss.* If the *s* has a long vowel unigraph immediately in front of it, the final *e* must be added as well, to mark the long vowel: *erase, franchise, close, ruse.*

The Final *s* Rule applies only to terminative bases. It does not apply to nonterminative bound bases or to prefixes or suffixes. It is strongest when the final syllable of the word is stressed and the *s* is preceded by a consonant. It is weakest when the final syllable is unstressed and the *s* is preceded by a vowel, as in *fracas,* for in such cases the *s* has less of the look of a suffix attached to a singular free stem: **fraca* does not look like an English free stem.

3.4.1.1 Holdouts

Although an immense number of final *e*'s and final *ss*'s exist because of the Final *s* Rule, there are several holdouts. One important, though small, group of holdouts consists of the short function words *is, was, has, us, this, as, yes, thus.* All of these words are of the form that most weakens the Final *s* Rule—that is, a vowel preceding the *s*—and these words are often unstressed in the sentences in which they occur. In *his, hers, ours, yours, theirs,* also apparent holdouts, the final *s* is actually an old genitive inflectional suffix.

As noted earlier, the Final *s* Rule is weakest when the *s* is preceded by an unstressed vowel. In such cases the more regular final *ss* is avoided, apparently because unstressed, reduced vowels are normally not followed by a doublet consonant. For instance, we have *iris* rather than **iriss* in part because the latter suggests stress on the second rather than the first vowel. Other *iris*-type holdouts are:

(Array 3-16)

alias	camus	haggis	morris
ananas	challis	kermes	oasis
atlas	chaos	lammas	omnibus
axis	clevis	lampas	orris
balas	copperas	lewis	pancreas
bathos	dais	lias	pathos
bias	dowlas	litmus	tennis
caddis	eyas	molasses	trellis

Also in this group is *canvas,* though curiously one of its variant spellings, *canvass,* has become distinguished as a separate word, with *ss.* The holdout *bus* is clipped from the older holdout *omnibus,* in which *bus* is actually a Latin dative plural suffix, *omnibus* meaning originally "for all." Harder to explain are *plus, surplus,* which explicates to (sur(plus), *gas* (related to *chaos*), *lens,* and *divers,* a variant spelling of *diverse* that has become distinguished as a separate word and that has a strongly plural feel to it. Also difficult to explain are the rarer and less integrated forms *blewits, bis, kris, os, scops, harquebus.*

3.4.2 The Final *z* Rule

The letter *z* is something of a latecomer to the English alphabet and remains rather rare in English spelling, even though the sound /z/ is very common. More often than not, /z/ is spelled *s,* and thus a close parallelism developed between *s* and *z* in English orthography. An instance of this parallelism is the alternation of *-ize* and *-ise*—for instance, *exercise* and *chastise* versus *criticize* and *fraternize.* British English often has *-ise* where American English has *-ize,* as in American *civilization* versus British *civilisation.* This parallelism appears to have encouraged the Final *s* Rule to carry over by analogy to *z.* For although there is no intrinsic reason why single *z* should be avoided at the end of terminative bases (*z* not being a suffix), double *z* and a final *e* are used to avoid base-final *z* in a way that is perfectly parallel to base-final *s.*

When a consonant or a vowel digraph precedes the *z,* a final *e* is added:

(Array 3-17)

adze	breeze	furze	sneeze
baize	bronze	gauze	squeeze
bonze	freeze	maize	tweeze
booze	frieze	seize	wheeze

When a long vowel unigraph precedes the *z*, a final *e* must be added anyhow, to mark the long vowel: *raze, size, froze.*

When a short vowel unigraph precedes the *z*, the *z* is doubled:

(Array 3-18)

buzz	frizz	huzz
fizz	fuzz	jazz

There are very few holdouts to the Final *z* Rule, no doubt due in part to the fact that *z* is so rare in general. *Phiz* and *coz* are nearly obsolete slang clippings, from *physiognomy* and *cousin*. *Quiz* is of obscure origin and structure, though it, too, may be a clipping, from *inquisition* or *inquisitive*. *Topaz* was spelled with a *c* in Middle English, but in Early Modern English it was respelled to bring it in line with its Latin source, *topazus*, from Greek *topazos*. The final cluster *tz* occurs in *batz, waltz, chintz,* and *wootz,* in all of which the *z* spells the sound /s/. *Fez* is a recent Egyptian adoption.

The use of final *e* to insulate otherwise-final single *s* and *z* is similar to its use to insulate otherwise-final *u* and *v* (see 8.1.4).

3.4.3   The Tactics of *y* and *i*

By the late seventeenth century the convention had been established that *i* and the vowel *y* would work as a tactical team—*i* in word-initial and word-medial positions, *y* in word-final position. Since this is a fairly late convention in the English spelling system, it is not too surprising that there are a number of holdouts and complications.

Normally, a word-initial *y* will be the consonant, not the vowel—as in *year, young, yard*. In a few words, however, the initial *y* is clearly a vowel and is followed by a consonant:

(Array 3-19)

yclept	The archaic past participle of *cleopian*, Old English for "speak, call," and used to mean "known as." The *y* is the simplified modern version of the Old English past participle prefix *ge-*, the *g* in Old English having been pronounced much like /y/.
ylang-ylang	A recent Tagalog adoption.
yttria	Also *ytterbia, ytterbium, yttric, yttrium;* chemical terms, all recent formations, all after *Ytterby,* the Swedish town where ytterbium and yttria were discovered.

Normally, a word-medial /i/ or /ī/ will be spelled in English with *i* rather than *y*. The most important set of holdouts to this pattern are words adopted from Greek in which the *y* represents the Greek letter upsilon—for instance, *typhoid* and *symbol* (see 20.2.2 and 14.3.2).

A word-final vowel sound is regularly spelled with *y* rather than *i*. There are a number of holdouts to this pattern, but by and large they tend to be quite peripheral and rare. The most common instances are:

(Array 3-20)

alibi	From Latin, meaning "elsewhere."
alkali	Apparently a learned respelling of the more regular ME *alkaly*, from L *alcali*, from Arabic *al-galiy*, meaning "the ashes."
ennui	French, finally from L *in odio*, which also gave English the more regular, more integrated *annoy*.
khaki	From the Urdu word *khākī*.
martini	Of obscure origin, though with clear enough effect.
pi	The name of the Greek letter, used in geometry.
rabbi	From a Hebrew word meaning "my master," in which the *i* is a genitive suffix.
spermacetti	From L *spermacēti*, *cēti* in Latin being the genitive of *cētus* ("whale").
taxi	Clipped from *taxicab*, short for *taximeter cab*; in *taximeter*, (tax)i(meter), the *i* is a linking particle.

Fairly common, too, are the Italian food plurals *broccoli*, *macaroni*, *vermicelli*, *spaghetti*, *zucchini*, *rigatoni*, *fettucini*. Less common are the Greek letter names *chi*, *phi*, *psi*, and the Italian musical term *mi*.

Less common and less integrated are the following, several of which have more regular variants:

(Array 3-21)

agouti, agouty	litchi, lichee, lychee
assagai	lori, loris
bouilli	maki
capivi	marconi
charivari, chivaree, shivaree	mufti
chilli, chili, chile	nilgai
coati	okapi
doni	ouakari
elemi	paroli
étui, etwee	patchouli, patchouly
garibaldi	peri
kauri	piccalilli
lazuli	poi

rani, ranee   shanghai
saki, sake   tripoli
salmi, salmis   wistiti

3.4.3.1 The y-to-i Rule

Because of the above tactical distribution of y and i, when a stem ending in y preceded by a consonant takes on a suffix, thus moving the y to medial position, the y is regularly replaced by i, as in:

(Array 3-22)

carried (carry)i + ed)   marriage (marry)i + age)
dandies (dandy)i + es)   merrily (merry)i + ly)

When the y is preceded by a vowel, the replacement does not occur:

(Array 3-23)

boys, not *bois   employed, not *emploied
drayage, not *draiage   haying, not *haiing

The replacement does not occur after a vowel, for in such cases the y is always part of a digraph, and digraphs are exempt from tactical rules of this kind (see 4.1). The apparent holdout to this subrule, gaiety, (gay)i + ety), in which the replacement does occur in a digraph, has the more regular variant gayety. Very old replacements before vowels occur in the past participles laid, paid, said, and, more distantly, staid. There are, in fact, a number of words with medial ai in which the i echoes an Old English g, which in final position evolves to y: main (from Old English mægen) versus may (from mæg), and lair (from leger) versus lay (from lecgan).

3.4.3.2 Holdouts

The holdouts to this y-to-i replacement rule are few and for the most part systematic. If the suffix begins with an i, the y does not change, in order to avoid a double i (see 3.3.1). It is carrying, not *carriing, and it is burying, not *buriing. Since so many verbs end in y, this is a large group.

We choose to explicate words such as jurist to primes—in this case to jury—rather than to bound bases such as jur+ whenever not positing a bound base allows us to explicate all the known forms. Thus, we must treat the following large group as systematic holdouts to the y-to-i replacement rule. The regular replacement would lead to the avoided ii: *(jury)i + ist) = *juriist. Simply adding the stem and suffix together would produce a medial y: *juryist. And so the y is regularly deleted in such words: (jury)ist) = jurist. Other instances:

(Array 3-24)

alchemist	eulogist	prosodist
biologist	ironist	psalmodist
botanist	liturgist	summarist
colonist	melodist	
elegist	parodist	

Many of the words in array 3-24 also have parallel forms in -*ize: ironize, eulogize, colonize, summarize.* The explication of the words in 3-24 parallels that of words such as *analyze* and *analyst* (see 2.7.5.2).

The only known holdout to this subpattern is *copyist,* (copy)ist).

The *y*-to-*i* rule applies to complex words where a stem ending in a *y* preceded by a consonant takes on a suffix. Following the normal exemption of compound words from such tactical changes, the rule does not apply to compounds. Thus *dairymaid,* not **dairimaid.* Other compounds that retain the medial *y* are:

(Array 3-25)

crybaby   (cry)(baby); cf. crier (crÿ)i + er)
plywood   (ply)(wood); cf. pliable (plÿ)i + able)
spyglass   (spy)(glass); cf. espial (e(spÿ)i + al)
tryout   (try)(out); cf. trial (trÿ)i + al)

Handyman is a simple compound, (handy)(man); *handiwork* is a compound with a linking particle *i,* (hand)i(work). The one known exception to the compound word's exemption from the *y*-to-*i* rule is *holiday* (holÿ)i(day). Another unusual set of holdouts to the *y*-to-*i* rule are complexes formed with *lady: ladylike* (lady)like), *ladyship* (lady)ship), *ladyhood* (lady)hood). There is also the late (eighteenth-century) formation *babyhood.*

Among complexes the only other holdout found so far is the plural noun *whys.*

3.5   The Short Word Rule

There are questions to be raised about such words as *odd, egg, ill,* and the like—that is, words ending with a double consonant when a single consonant would have sufficed, and **od, *eg,* and **il* would have been tactically and phonetically adequate spellings. These and similar instances can be understood in terms of what is called the Short Word Rule. Craigie suggests that in such words "the double consonant is retained . . . to preserve the word from the insignificant appearance it would have if written" with only two letters ([1927] 1974, 12). Jespersen, too, notes that "people dislike writing heavy (stressed, significant) words with two letters only" ([1909] 1954, 1:70). Elsewhere he says: "Another orthographic rule was the tendency to avoid too short words. Words of one or two letters were not allowed, except a few constantly recurring (chiefly grammatical) words: *a, I, am. . . .* To all other words that would regularly have been written with two letters, a third was added, either a consonant, as in *ebb . . .* or else an *e*" (ibid., 149).

Whether or not the motivation was as psychological as Craigie and Jespersen suggest, the fact remains that very few words in English are only one or two letters long, and those that are are almost without exception not what Jespersen describes as "heavy." They tend to be unstressed and weak semantically. They tend to be function words: prepositions like *in, on, at,* or conjunctions like *or, as, if,* or pronouns like *I, us, we,* or copulas like *is* and *am.*

The Short Word Rule can be stated as follows: Words that are not function words tend to be three or more letters long; to avoid two-letter words of the VC# pattern, the final consonant is doubled. Instances of the rule:

(Array 3-26)

| abb | egg | err | inn |
| ebb | ell | ill | odd |

The Short Word Rule also affects spellings of the CV pattern. Since the CV# pattern normally involves a long final vowel—as in *so, by,* and *be*—a legitimate question might be why such words as *woe, lye,* and *fee* are not *wo, *ly, and *fe. Again the answer seems to be the strong constraint in the language to reserve two-letter spellings for very common, usually unstressed, semantically weak function words. So if a word not of this type fits the CV# pattern and thus would have only two letters, the convention is to add a final *e.* Other instances:

(Array 3-27)

bee	gee	pie	vie
bye	hie	rye	wee
die	lee	see	zee
dye	lie	tee	
fie	pee	tie	

Since monosyllables ending in *o* sometimes have /ō/ as in *so,* and sometimes /ū/ as in *to,* the addition of a final *e* in words such as *hoe, joe, doe,* and *toe* may have been motivated by the desire to obtain an unambiguous /ō/ sound (though we still have *shoe* and *canoe,* in which the final *oe* spells /ū/).

Closely related to the words in array 3-27 are the few VV*e#* words, such as *aye, eye, owe, ewe,* and *awe.*

3.5.1 Holdouts

Of the apparent holdouts to the Short Word Rule, some have variants that bring them into regularity: *ax, axe; bo, boe* 'hobo'; *pi, pie* 'a confusion of print'. Consider also the letter names ce, cee; de, dee; ef, eff; el, ell; es, ess. The other unintegrated holdouts include some that do not offer a way to apply the Short Word Rule: *oe, ti* 'tropical plant', and the musical notes *do, re, mi, fa, so, la, ti,* all of which are clipped from the words in a medieval hymn to which the notes were sung. Closely related are the baby-talk clippings *ma* and *pa,* which also do not offer a way to apply the strategies of the Short Word Rule. Two other recent clippings are *bo* 'bozo' and *el* 'elevated train'. True holdouts appear to be *os, id;* the letter names em, en, ar; the Greek letter pi; and the Senghalese word *bo* 'a tree'. Another technical holdout is *ox,* although the letter *x* is in many ways a one-letter cluster, regularly spelling a sound-cluster, either /ks/ or /gz/, and having been treated as a double letter by some orthographers. For instance, the anonymous author of *Thesaurarium Trilingue Publicum* analyzed it as a ligature, arguing that it is "not a single but double Consonant, and is no more than Two *c*'s turn'd Back to Back" (1689, 6–7). Admittedly, this author was something of a spelling reformer, wanting, among other things, to remove seven letters from the alphabet, including *x,* but his argument speaks to the perceived duality of the letter. If a single sound spelled with two letters is a digraph or cluster, then a single letter like *x,* which spells two sounds, might be thought of as a "diphone."

3.6 Summary

The area of orthographic tactics discussed in this chapter includes five consonant sequence rules, one vowel sequence rule, three distribution rules, and the Short Word Rule. The five consonant sequence rules set constraints against the mixing of voiceless and voiced consonants in clusters and, less reliably, in concatenations; against initial consonant doublets; against certain final consonant doublets; against consonant triplets; and, in a weak and less than elegant way, against consonant doublets in larger clusters and concatenations. The only vowel sequence rule constrains against vowel doublets other than *ee* and *oo.* The first two of the three distribution rules constrain against final single *s* or *z* in terminative bases. The third describes the distribution of *y* and *i.* The Short Word Rule limits words of one or two letters to a small group of function words.

4 String Patterns and Rules

4.1 On the Term *String*

For the speller (and the reader) probably the most important tactical patterns have to do with sequences of vowel and consonant letters and what those sequences imply about the length of the vowel at the head of the sequence. Using V to represent "vowel letter" and C to represent "consonant letter," we can illustrate the two most important of these sequences in

latter with /a/ and *later* with /ā/.
vcc   vcv

Sequences of letters of this kind are called **strings.** The two in *latter* and *later* are the VCC and VCV strings. Two restrictions apply to the formation of strings: one has to do with the distinction between vowel digraphs and vowel unigraphs; the other has to do with stress. A vowel digraph is a combination of two vowel letters spelling a single sound, like the *ee* and *ea* in *meet* and *meat*. A vowel unigraph is a single vowel letter spelling a single vowel sound, like the *e* and *a* in *met* and *mat*. Since vowel digraphs behave tactically in ways different from vowel unigraphs, the term *string* will be used to refer only to sequences in which the **head vowel,** or **head,** is a unigraph.

Further, usually for a sequence of letters to qualify as a string, the head vowel must bear either primary or secondary stress. This restriction is necessary because, as was pointed out in the preface, the sound-to-spelling correspondences for unstressed vowels are very complex and relatively unpredictable, due to the tendency of unstressed vowels to reduce, losing their regular color and value. This reduction so complicates the description of sound-to-spelling correspondences for unstressed vowels that the term *string* will usually be restricted as well to letter sequences in which the head vowel is stressed.

The one sequence that is recognized as a string even when its head vowel is unstressed is the V.V string, which consists of two vowel unigraphs in hiatus, or divided by a syllable boundary, as in *lion*. As will be seen below, the head vowel in a V.V string is regularly long, even when it is unstressed.

A string, then, is a sequence of letters that starts with a vowel unigraph spelling a vowel sound that is usually stressed. The tactical patterns that are based on what the sequence of vowel and consonant letters implies about the length of the head vowel are known as **string patterns,** and description of the more reliable and uncluttered patterns produces **string rules.** The following section describes the three minor string patterns: V.V, VC#, and V*e*#. Section 4.3 describes the two major patterns: the VCC and VCV strings illustrated earlier in *latter* and *later.*

4.2   The Minor Strings

4.2.1   The V.V Rule

Jespersen describes the V.V pattern as follows: "A stressed vowel immediately preceding another vowel is long" ([1909] 1954, 1:138). But in American English the head of a V.V string is regularly long, even when it is unstressed. One complication here involves V.V strings in which the first vowel, either *e* or *i*, spells an unstressed vowel sound. Kenyon and Knott (1944) often show such cases as /i/ rather than /ē/, as in *create* and *radio*. They do point out, however, that in V.V strings this alleged /i/ is close to /ē/ and that their transcription as /i/ is in large part no more than a graphic expedient (xxxviii). *W3* consistently records such cases as /ē/. In this discussion the head vowel in V.V strings will consistently be treated as long, even when unstressed. (Oswalt [1973] discusses the V.V pattern on pages 13–16.)

Disyllabic instances of the V.V Rule in which the primary stress is on the first syllable are listed in array 4-1. Sometimes an *i* has the value of the English long *i,* as in *quiet,* and sometimes it has the value of the Continental long *i,* as in *fiat.* Other instances:

(Array 4-1)

bias	doer	liar	rhea
boa	dyad	lion	skiey
bruit	flier	lying	skua
chaos	fluent	pious	stoic
creole	fuel	poet	theist
cruel	giant	prior	trio
dais	goer	psoas	triune

Disyllabic instances of the V.V Rule in which the primary stress is on the second syllable are:

(Array 4-2)

coerce	duet	react	triage

The trisyllabic instances of the V.V Rule have been sorted to show the location of the V.V string within the word and relative to the stress: o = syllables; ´ and ` = primary and secondary stress, respectively; and vv = the position of the V.V string in the word.

The **radiance** group, with the pattern óoo:
$$\text{vv}$$

(Array 4-3)

aguish	cambium	foliage	odious
alien	casual	hideous	pantheist
arduous	chariot	linear	radium
axiom	egoist	meteor	scorpion

The **violence** group, with the pattern oóo:
$$\text{vv}$$

(Array 4-4)

diamond*	laity	pianist	prioress
hyacinth	myosin	piety	realist
kaolin	peony	poetess	truancy

The **zodiac** group, with the pattern óoò:
$$\text{vv}$$

(Array 4-5)

aureole	demiurge	grandiose*	mediate
cardiac	fluctuate	ileac	oriole

The **diatribe** group, with the pattern óoò:
$$\text{vv}$$

(Array 4-6)

creosote	dualize	kyanite	reify
deicide	hierarch	neophyte	suicide
diadem	iodize	realize	zoophyte

The **playgoer** group, with antepenultimate primary stress and secondary stress on the penult—that is, the pattern óòo:
$$\text{vv}$$

(Array 4-7)

outgoer	snowshoer	tiptoeing

The **heroic** group, with the pattern oóo:
$$\text{vv}$$

(Array 4-8)

appliance	congruent	lyceum	subdual
archaic	idea	pursuer	supplier

The **hyena** group, with the pattern óó:

vv

(Array 4-9)

chaotic	diurnal	hiatus	piazza
coactive	druidic	iota	sienna
deific	fiasco	noetic	theatric

The **minuet** group, with the pattern òóó:

vv

(Array 4-10)

acquiesce	grandiose*	statuette

The **coincide** group, with the pattern òóó:

vv

(Array 4-11)

coalesce	reabsorb	reinforce	reunite
pioneer	reascend	reinvest	violin

The only known holdout to the V.V Rule is *naive*. The metathesized *geoduck,* though odd, actually satisfies the letter of the rule.

4.2.2 The VC# Rule

The VC# string consists of a stressed vowel unigraph followed by a word-final consonant (the # represents the end of the word). In the VC# string the vowel is regularly short. Array 4-12 displays the variety of vowel and final consonant combinations in monosyllables, the most common kind of word in which the VC# string occurs. The blank slots in the array are due to certain tactical facts. For instance, word-final f is rare after a vowel unigraph. The same is true of k, s, v, and z. Word-final c is rare after a stressed vowel. Word-final l is rare in monosyllables. Word-final j is rare anywhere. And word-final q does not occur.

(Array 4-12)

scab	crib	knob	shrub
lac	sec	tic	roc
shad	skid	clod	scud
	ef	if	of
scrag	dreg	sprig	snug
raj			
yak	lek		
sal	gel	mil	

clam	stem	tom	gum	gym
plan	hen	thin	stun	
snap	step	stop	pup	gyp
gas	yes	his	bus	
flat	whet	clot	glut	
rev	shiv			
tax	sex	phlox	flux	
fez	quiz			

The VC# string is relatively rare in disyllables in which the stress is on the second vowel:

(Array 4-13)

abed	bewig	equip	relax
akin	cravat	kabob	sedan
bedim	embag	rattan	shellac*

The only known holdouts to the VC# Rule are in disyllables ending in *ol*, which usually have a long vowel: *control, patrol, extol, enrol (enroll)*. This group of holdouts is related to the larger fact that *o* is often long when followed by *l* plus another consonant (see 4.3.3.1). *Phenol* has the regular short *o*. So do polysyllables ending in *ol: protocol, alcohol, folderol, parasol, methanol.*

4.2.3 The V*e*# Rule

A stressed vowel immediately followed by a silent final *e* will regularly be long. The following paragraphs present instances of the V*e*# Rule, grouping them around the six vowels (*a, e, i, o, u, y*).

ae#. Words ending in *ae* are quite rare. The only known instances of word-final *ae* spelling /ā/ are in the chiefly Scottish *ae* and the more common *sundae*, which also has a variant pronunciation with /ē/. In *algae* and *alumnae*, two Latin plurals, *ae* also spells /ē/. (For more on the spelling *ae*, see 18.3.6 and 19.3.3.)

ee#. Words ending in *ee* are much more common, the largest single group being complexes with the recipient suffix *-ee*—for instance, *employee, payee, internee*. Final *ee* consistently spells /ē/, even when it is only lightly stressed:

(Array 4-14)

agree	coulee	free	jubilee
banshee	decree	fricassee	pedigree
chimpanzee	degree	guarantee	perigee
coffee	filigree	jamboree	tepee

(For more on the spelling *ee*, see 19.2.4, 18.3.5, and 14.4.4.)

ie#. In word-final position the spelling *ie* regularly spells /ī/ in words that are, or explicate to, monosyllables ending in *ie.* In other cases final *ie* regularly spells /ē/, even when it is only lightly stressed. Instances of both follow:

(Array 4-15)

die	tie	belie (be(lie)	
lie	vie	magpie (mag)(pie)	
pie		outvie (out)(vie)	
aerie	coterie	genie	reverie
collie	diablerie	movie	specie
coolie	eerie	prairie	

oe#. Although in *shoe* and *canoe oe* spells /ū/, in word-final position it regularly spells /ō/:

(Array 4-16)

aloe	mistletoe	pekoe	throe
floe	oboe	sloe	toe
hoe			

ue#. Word-final *ue* is very common, regularly spelling one of the long *u* sounds, /ū/ or /yū/:

(Array 4-17)

accrue	construe	issue	retinue
argue	continue	pursue	subdue
avenue	glue	queue	tissue
barbecue	imbue	residue	venue

Except for *ague* and *argue,* word-final *ue* following *g* or *q* is regularly silent, as in *plague* and *plaque.* In *plague* the *u* is tactically motivated, being used to insulate the *g* from the *e,* thus avoiding the appearance of a soft *g,* or /j/, sound (see 8.1.2). In *plaque* the *u* is again tactically motivated, due to the tactical requirement that all *q*'s be followed by a *u.* The *e* in *plaque* also is tactical, due to the constraint against word-final *u* (see 8.1.4). Other instances of silent word-final *ue* after *q* and *g* are:

(Array 4-18)

antique	caique	macaque	pique
barque	calque	masque	sacque
basique	casque	mosque	statuesque
basque	cazique	oblique	technique
bisque	cirque	opaque	toque
brusque	clique	perique	torque
burlesque	critique	physique	unique
brogue	fatigue	pirogue	togue
drogue	intrigue	rogue	vogue

The following instances, though analogous to the preceding, are different in that the final *e* is less easy to account for:

(Array 4-19)

cangue	dengue	gangue	league
catalogue	dialogue	harangue	tongue
colleague	eclogue	langue	

Dialogue, cangue, gangue, and *catalogue* have more regular spellings without the final *ue*.

ye#.   Word-final *ye* is quite rare, but it always spells /ī/:

(Array 4-20)

bye	dye	lye	rye

In summary, although there is sometimes some indecision about which long vowel sound is being spelled, and although the silent *ue* spelling after some *g*'s and *q*'s introduces a complexity, the V*e*# Rule is quite straightforward: In a V*e*# string the head vowel is long.

4.3   The Major Strings

4.3.1   The VCC/VCV Contrast

The contrast between the VCC string, as in *latter,* and the VCV string, as in *later,* can be stated thus: In the string VCC the stressed head vowel is regularly short; in the string VCV the stressed head vowel is regularly long. (The pattern is also called the Penult Rule; see Oswalt 1973, 9–10, 16.) This initial statement is mightily oversimplified, however; in it immense complexity lurks behind the word *regularly.* Still, it does describe a tendency or disposition in the language; it describes an extremely important and useful pattern. It explains, for instance, the differences that an experienced reader recognizes in two words such as *mating* and *matting.* The VCV string in *mating* cues that the *a* is spelling a long sound, /ā/, while the VCC string in *matting* cues that its *a* is spelling a short sound, /a/. This, in turn, working with conservative analogy, cues that the prime of *mating* is *mate,* the prime of *matting, mat.*

The VCC/VCV contrast also motivates the twinning of the *t* in *matting: mat + ing* cannot simply add together to spell *mating,* because that spelling contains a VCV string, cuing the /ā/ sound rather than the desired short sound, /a/. So the final *t* in *mat* is twinned: *mat + t + ing = matting,* thereby providing the VCC pattern needed to cue the /a/.

Looking just at the stems *mat* and *mate,* it is clear that the VCV pattern is important in cuing the long *a* in *mate.* In fact, the single most important function of the silent final *e* is to mark a long vowel sound by filling out the VCV pattern and avoiding the VC#. Since in words like *mate* the VCV pattern leads to the final *e* in the first place, it is not too surprising that this same pattern also underlies the procedures for keeping or deleting the final *e* when suffixes are added. We delete the final *e* in *mating* (mat*e*)ing), but not in *mates* (mate)s), because in *mating* the upcoming *i* in the suffix fills out the VCV, *mating,* while in *mates* the *e* is still necessary to keep the VCV. (For more on the silent final *e* and its deletion rule, see chapter 8.)

4.3.2 A Short History of the VCC/VCV Contrast

In early Old English the distinction between long and short vowels was not cued so much by tactical context as by diacritical marks (A. Campbell 1959, 12–13). Kim mentions the use of acute accent marks, vowel letter doubling, and, rarely in Old English but more often in Middle English, a postvocalic yogh (1971, 94). Modern editors from the time of Rask and Grimm in the nineteenth century have marked long Old English vowels with macrons (Aarsleff 1983, 197–207).

Long vowels in early Old English could occur in any tactical setting, regardless of syllable structure or what letters followed them. However, in the evolution from Old to Middle English two important developments took place. First, some Old English short vowels lengthened before certain consonant clusters, including *mb, nd,* and *ld.* This lengthening was not entirely consistent; thus *wild, bold,* and the like, developed alongside words like *gild* and *held.* In the thirteenth century more short vowels lengthened in open syllables—that is, in syllables ending with the vowel (Mossé 1952, 16–19; Strang 1970, 181–83, 249–50; Jespersen [1909] 1954, 1:114–20). Since single consonants tend to attach themselves to the vowel following them, anytime there was a VCV string, the first vowel in the string would be in an open syllable, and thus would tend to lengthen. Second, Old English long vowels shortened when they were followed by a doublet consonant or by most consonant clusters, an effect Jespersen calls "the clash of consonants" ([1909] 1954, 1:123 [see also 120–27]; Mossé 1952, 18). Kurath argues convincingly that in early Old English, long consonants, which were phonemically distinct from their short counterparts and were spelled with doublet consonant letters, could occur after either long or short vowels. In time the phonemic contrast between short and long consonants collapsed, and due to the shortening of long vowels in closed syllables, the doublet spellings came to occur only after short vowels. (See also Kim [1973].) As early as the thirteenth century Orm showed vowel shortness by doubling the consonant following it. This development helped lead to the VCC pattern in Modern English.

Though these lengthenings and shortenings did not occur with complete consistency, the general evolution was enough to encourage tactical patterns that would eventually result in the important VCC/VCV contrast that we have today.

The following are some examples of Old English long vowels that were in closed syllables—that is, were followed by a consonant cluster—and were thus shortened in the evolution to Middle English:

(Array 4-21)

Old English	Middle English	American English
āscian, ācsian	asken	ask
cēpte	kepte	kept
hẏdde	hidde	hid
sōfte	softe	soft

The long *i* was shortened in Old English *wīsdōm* to the modern *wisdom,* but not in Old English *wīs, wīse*—modern *wise*—which contained no cluster and in the inflected forms would have had the vowel in an open syllable.

This tendency for Old English long vowels to shorten before clusters also underlies such long-short pairs as *deep* and *depth, wide* and *width, five* and *fifty,* even *goose* and *gosling.*

Old English *cild* and *cildru,* which became the modern *child* and *children,* originally had short *i*'s. As part of the lengthening of some short vowels before clusters like *mb, nd,* and *ld,* the vowel in *cild* lengthened, but that in the plural *cildru* did not, because of the complex *ldr* cluster. Thus the modern contrast between /ī/ in *child* and /i/ in *children.*

The following are examples of Old English short vowels that were in open syllables and thus were lengthened in the evolution to Middle English:

(Array 4-22)

Old English	Middle English	American English
bacan	baken	bacon
etan	eten	eat
hopian	hopen	hope
macian	makien, maken	make
mete	mete	meat
sacu	sake	sake
smoca	smoke	smoke
stelan	stelen	steal

4.3.2.1 The Development of Silent Final *e*

The VCV pattern was encouraged even further by another important development in the evolution from Old to Middle English. Old English was a heavily inflected language, with a complex system of inflectional suffixes. By Middle English times most of these inflectional distinctions had been dropped, and the language came to depend less on inflections to show grammatical relationships and more on word order within the sentence. The old suffixes usually reduced and converged to a common final *e*, which in Middle English was pronounced, making another syllable in the words. Thus, any word that ended with the string VCe#—that is, a stressed vowel plus a single consonant plus a final *e*—would have the head vowel of the string in an open syllable, so that it would tend to be long. Then, in late Middle English and early Early Modern, speakers quit pronouncing the final *e*, which gave rise to a large number of words with a long vowel followed by a single consonant followed by a silent final *e*—in short, the pattern of words such as *bake, mate,* and the like—a special case of the VCV pattern, actually the most reliable case. This development encouraged the evolution of the VCV pattern in Modern English and established the use of final *e* to mark long preceding vowels.

4.3.2.2 Latin "Position" and VCV/VCC

Strong motivation for the VCV/VCC contrast also developed on the Romance side of the English language. In Classical Latin and later in Vulgar Latin there was also a more or less regular tendency for a short vowel to be followed by a consonant cluster, while a long vowel would be followed by a single consonant. The *OED*'s note at *position* is, as usual, informative:

> The situation of a vowel in an open or closed syllable; spec. in Gr. and L. Prosody, the situation of a short vowel before two consonants or their equivalent, i.e., before a consonant in the same syllable, making the syllable metrically long. . . .
>
> In such cases it used to be said that the vowel was "long by position"; but the evidence of Greek and the history of the sounds in Romanic show that the vowel remained short, while the *syllable* was metrically long. When both consonants could be taken to the following syllable, the preceding vowel might be "in position" or not, as in *te-ne-brās* or *te-neb-rās.* In English and the modern languages generally, a long stressed vowel is often shortened by position, as in *weal, wealth; deem, demster; house, husband; Lyne, Lynton.*

What influence the Latin notion of position may have had on the tactical development of Old and Middle English is an interesting but not at all straightforward question. It seems just as likely, perhaps even more so, that the Latin and Old English lengthening and shortening strategies reflected a deep, if somewhat diffuse, tendency in Indo-European syllable structure (Mossé 1952, 12; Kim 1973). Early in the Christian period the phenomenon known as West Germanic gemination (or twinning) seemed to reflect the same sort of tactical tendency (Lass and Anderson 1975, 255–78). Traditionally, West Germanic gemination has been treated as a special kind of assimilation, as a result of certain constraints on syllable structure. Lass and Anderson treat it as the result of certain constraints on the endings of morphemes, constraints that restrict such endings to sequences of either a long vowel plus a consonant or a short vowel plus a long consonant. Like the motivation for the Latin notion of vowel position, however, the motivation for West Germanic gemination, though interesting, leads us somewhat astray. The important point to remember is that it did help lead to that situation in Old English wherein the medial consonant cluster is regularly preceded by a short vowel.

Related to these questions is the observation that Modern English reveals very few instances of VVC'C' strings—that is, strings in which a vowel digraph is followed by twin consonants. Of the few that do exist, some are concatenations resulting from simple addition: *really,* (real)ly). Of the remainder most are adoptions, still quite recent and rather unintegrated. Some examples: *trousseau, caisson, puissant, reconnaissance, questionnaire, guillotine, guerrilla.* With *guillotine* and *guerrilla* it can be argued that the *u* is not part of the vowel spelling at all, but is instead a diacritic, insulating the *g* in order to avoid the soft *g* pronunciation. Also, *guerrilla* has the more integrated variant *guerilla,* with no VVC'C' string. The extent to which such VVC'C' spellings are peripheral to the English orthographic system can be illustrated by contrasting them with other English words that are etymologically related but have been more fully integrated: *trousseau* with *truss; reconnaissance* with *recognize; questionnaire* with *millionaire; puissant* with *possible; caisson* with *case.*

4.3.3 The VCC Pattern

Nearly always in a VCC string—again assuming that the vowel is stressed—the vowel will be short. The VCC pattern is so common and so widespread that it is difficult to give a good and systematic sample of it. The following two arrays simply show the range of vowels and consonant clusters that can be involved—the first in monosyllables, the second in disyllables. Again, the blanks in the monosyllable array are due to certain tactical facts: word-final *m, n, x,* and *z* are rare in clusters.

Instances of the VCC pattern in monosyllables:

(Array 4-23)

ebb	bulb	alb	dumb
talc	zinc	disc	franc
odd	geld	strand	spend
staff	cleft	golf	shelf
hang	egg	sting	thong
much	clash	myth	froth
belch	trench	thatch	crutch
lymph	sylph	fifth	filth
quick	skulk	prank	brisk
swell	swill	doll	dull
phlegm	helm	film	
kiln	damn	inn	
scalp	skimp	cusp	hemp
lens	glass	floss	truss
tract	shaft	stilt	chant
script	crypt	zest	mitt
calx	minx	sphinx	lynx
chintz	batz	fizz	fuzz

Instances of the VCC pattern in disyllables:

(Array 4-24)

/a/	/e/	/i/	/ä/, /ò/	/u/
panda	delta	stigma	dogma	yucca
naphtha	ethics	syndic	rhombus	hubbub
graphic	pentad	limpid	dropsy	rugged
ballad	wretched	riddance	office	husband
transcience	method	distance	commerce	ductile
jasmine	tensile	ginseng	pontiff	juncture
mastiff	welfare	fiftieth	oblong	mustang
brambling	nestling	niblick	snobbish	hundredth
ambush	selfish	cymbal	caldron	mufti
rabbi	hemlock	system	rollick	hummock
shamrock	spectral	sylvan	offal	fungal
scandal	bedlam	fillip	flotsam	mushroom
bantam	gentian	pillar	swallow	sultan
banyan	ketchup	pistol	gossip	vulgar
scallop	cheddar	nimbus	halter	buttress

4.3.3.1 Holdouts

The holdouts to the VCC pattern, though rather numerous and not entirely ruly, do reveal some distinct subpatterns:

1. The letter *o* often spells a long vowel sound in front of the letter *l* plus a consonant, including the *ld* that commonly led to lengthening in Old English:

(Array 4-25)

bold	gold	polder	told
cold	hold	scold	wold
doldrum	mold	sold	
fold	old	soldier	
boll	poll	stroll	wholly
droll	roll	toll	
knoll	scroll	troll	
bolt	dolt	jolt	
colt	holt	volt	
bolster	folk	polka	
dolma	holm	solstice*	
dolman*	holster	yolk	

2. Less often the letter *i* spells a long vowel before the cluster *ld*, as in *wild*, *child*, *mild*, contrasting with the more regular *gild* and *mildew*.

3. The cluster *mb*, another lengthening cluster, occurs after long vowels in a few native and Romance words:

(Array 4-26)

cambric	climb	comber	womb
chamber	comb	tomb	

4. The letter *i* often spells a long sound before *nd*, another of those clusters that sometimes produced lengthening:

(Array 4-27)

behind	find	hind	mind
bind	grind	kind	rind
blind			

Also in this group are the verb *wind* and the adjective *hinder* (both with /ī/), which contrast with the noun *wind* and the verb *hinder* (with /i/). *Pint*, from French and Latin, parallels this group.

5. The letter *i* is regularly long before the digraph *gh* and the cluster *ght*, another feature of the evolution from Old English:

(Array 4-28)

high	nigh	sigh	
bight	fright	plight	wight
blight	knight	right	wright
bright	light	sight	
fight	might	slight	
flight	night	tight	

6. Long vowels sometimes occur before the cluster *gn:*

(Array 4-29)

align	benign	malign	sign
assign	consign	resign	
impugn	oppugn	repugn	

The above *gn* clusters are all word-final. But *gn* has a different tactical force and pronunciation when certain derivational suffixes are added, as is illustrated in the contrast between *sign* and *signal* or *repugn* and *repugnant.* To this general group of words with long vowels before the cluster *gn* can be added the recent French adoptions *champagne* and *cologne.*

The word *cologne* comes, naturally enough, from the name of the city. From the fourteenth through the eighteenth century, many attempts were made to spell it in English, including *coloyne, coleyn, collonge, colleyne.* In the seventeenth and eighteenth centuries a series of spellings appeared that suggested rather thorough integration of the word, complete with the typical English frontshifting of stress: *collen, cullin, cullen, colen, collin.* Then, in the eighteenth and nineteenth centuries, the less integrated spellings *cologn, coulogne,* and *cologne* appeared. Apparently, during the Middle and Early Modern periods the word began to be integrated, but then in the early eighteenth century, when *eau de Cologne* began to be manufactured and marketed, the word came into a new vogue with its more French spelling and pronunciation. *Cologne* thus represents an instance of dis-integration.

7. More than once Jespersen mentions a tendency for the letter *a* to have a long pronunciation, a tendency to "favour long quantity" ([1909] 1954, 1:113, 137, 451). He was speaking of the Early Modern long *a,* more like *ah,* but the tendency remains, for today the letter *a* often spells /ā/ in VCC positions where we would regularly expect a short vowel sound. Words with the spelling *aste* in final position:

(Array 4-30)

baste	chasten	paste	tasty
chaste	haste	taste	waste

To this can be added *pastry,* which has the anomalous explication (past*é*)ry). A holdout is *caste,* a recent Spanish-Portuguese adaptation. More regular nonfinal instances of *aste* occur in *aster, lasted, pastern.* In his discussion of the silent final *e,* Brengelman writes: "Mulcaster believed it should also be used after consonant groups such as *ld, nd,* and *st,* a reasonable suggestion that was followed only in the case of -*ast*. (Because Middle English short *i* and short *o* were almost always lengthened before *ld, nd,* and *mb,* the final *e* was in most instances redundant, Hodges pointed out in 1653.)" (1980, 347–48).

8. The letter *a* also regularly spells a long vowel when it is in the spelling *ange:*

(Array 4-31)

angel	danger	grange	range
arrange	derange	mange	rearrange
change	exchange	manger	strange

A related instance is *ancient*. The only known holdout to this subgroup is *flange. Orange* is only an apparent holdout, since the *ange* is unstressed.

9. There are a few other words with /ā/ = *a* at the head of VCC strings: *Bass* 'low' was spelled *bas* and *base* in Middle English. Historically *bass* and *base* are simply two forms of the same word. Apparently due to the connection with music, *bass* is a respelling via a conservative analogy with Italian *basso,* but it kept its long *a* sound.

10. The letter *o* sometimes spells a long sound when followed by *ss* or *st:*

(Array 4-32)

engross	grossbeak, grosbeak	post
ghost	host	postern*
gross	most	

More regular are *boss, loss, lost,* and *cost.* Jespersen quotes Walker (1791) on the growing tendency in the late eighteenth century to lengthen *o* before *s, ss,* or *s* plus a stop ([1909] 1954, 1:313). Today apparently the only *oss* with /ō/ is *gross,* with many more counterexamples: *moss, toss, cross, dross, floss, gloss.*

11. The correspondence /ō/ = *o* occurs as a VCC head in the word *only.* Historically *only* derives from Old English *ānlic* (ān + lic) 'like one, in the form of one'. *Only* explicates somewhat nonregularly: (oné)ly).

12. The letter *i* spells the Continental long *i* sound, /ē/, in some recent adoptions in which it is followed by consonant clusters:

(Array 4-33)

artiste	batiste	pelisse
bastille	chenille	vanille

The adaptions *vanilla* and *artistic* are more integrated and regular.

13. Other instances of long vowels followed by a consonant cluster are:

(Array 4-34)

buddha	A recent adoption from the Sanskrit *buddha* 'awakened, en-lightened', with the persistent long *u*. (For more on the persistent long *u* see the sections titled "Holdouts" in chapter 5.)
demesne	From ME *demesne*, from OFr *demene*, which also produced the Modern English *domain*. The *s* first appears in Norman French, perhaps via analogy with other French words in which an *s* followed by a nasal would fall silent with a lengthening of the preceding vowel, as in *dime* from *disme*, or *dine* from *disner*, or *blame* from OFr *blasme*.
fuchsia	A New Latin formation from the name of the German botanist Fuchs, also with the persistent long *u*.
indict	A sixteenth- or seventeenth-century respelling of the earlier *enditen*, apparently respelled to make its written form closer to the Latin *indictāre*, with no concomitant change in pronunciation. The Middle English and Early Modern spellings have been retained in *indite*.
island	From ME *eland, ilond, ylond*; from OE *iegland, igland, iland*. For details on the insertion of the *s*, see 32.2.1.1. For *isle* also see 32.2.1.1.

14. VCC strings with long head vowels sometimes occur when prefixes ending in vowels are added to stems starting with clusters, as in:

(Array 4-35)

digram (di(gram)	proscribe (pro(scribe)
duplex (du + plex)	reflex (re(flex)
egress (ex + gress)	reflux (re(flux)

15. A stressed vowel preceding a consonant plus an *l* plus a word-final *e* will regularly be long, as in *rifle*, which contrasts with *riffle*, in which the complex cluster *ffl* is sufficient to mark the short vowel. This VC*le*# string underlies a large and regular subgroup:

(Array 4-36)

able	cycle	noble	staple
bible	disciple	ogle*	stifle
bridle	fable	quadruple	table
bugle	gable	rifle	title
cable	idle	sidle	trifle
coble	ladle	socle*	
cradle	maple	stable	

Related are words like *nucleus* (nucle + us). Holdouts to this important group are *macle* and *debacle*. The apparent holdout *triple* (tri + ple) has an element boundary in the string that could underlie its failure to fit the group, doublets being very rare in element-initial position. A similar case could be made for the related word *treble*. (For the role of boundaries in determining the choice between single and double consonants, see 26.2.3.1.)

The contrast between VC*le*# with a long vowel and VC′C′*le*# with a short—as in *rifle, riffle; gable, gabble; coble, cobble; title, tittle*—is important to the rules for choosing a single consonant letter or a doublet. For more details see, for instance, 26.2.3.1 and 26.2.3.9.

16. A pattern closely related to VC*le*# involves vowels preceding a consonant plus *r*:

(Array 4-37)

acre	hatred	mitral	sacred
apron	hybrid	natron	secret
cedrol	hydrant	negro	theatre
cobra	library	nitrous	tigress
cupreous	matrix	nutrient	tigrine
egret	matron	ochre	vagrant
fibrous	mediocre	patriot	vagrom
flagrant	micron	patron	vibrate
fragrance	migrate	rubric	zebra

This VC*r*V pattern has a number of apparent holdouts, most of which can be explained, and thus brought to regularity, by one of the shortening rules discussed in chapters 5 through 7. Examples are such contrasting pairs as *theater, theatrical; sacred, sacrifice; mediocre, mediocrity; bible, bibliography*.

17. The cluster *qu* sometimes spells the simple consonant sound /k/, as in *opaque*, sometimes the complex sound /kw/, as in *equal*. It is an odd cluster in that it is compulsory within the tactics of English: every *q* must have a *u* immediately following. Actually this cluster falls somewhere between cluster and digraph as they are defined in 3.2.1: It is a cluster rather than a digraph in that its component letters do not combine in it to spell some third sound different from what they would spell in isolation, as, say, the *t* and *h* do in *th;* but it is a digraph rather than a cluster in that it regularly behaves like a single consonant tactically. That is to say, it does not regularly follow a short head vowel. Thus the following:

(Array 4-38)

equal	loquacious	sequel	
frequent	obsequious	sequin	
antique	coquette	perique	toque
baroque	critique	physique	unique
bezique	croquet	piquant	
cazique	oblique	pique	
clique	opaque	technique	

When *qu* does follow a short vowel, it is nearly always a regular instance of one of the shortening rules:

iniquitous	macaque	requiem	ubiquitous
liquid	plaque	requisite	

4.3.4 The VCV Pattern
4.3.4.1 The VCV Pattern in Monosyllables

VCV strings often occur in monosyllables in which the second vowel is a silent final *e,* as in *bake.* This is the VCV pattern at its most reliable. The number of instances is immense; the number of holdouts is quite small and for the most part rational. The following array is presented simply to illustrate the range of these VC*e#* words in terms of different consonants and head vowels in the strings. Blanks indicate that examples cannot be found. The specific string *eCe#* is surprisingly rare. The words with V*re#* are given here, although the values of the head vowel are usually not the simple long vowels the VCV pattern normally calls for. For more details on the effects of *r* on preceding vowels, see chapter 25.

(Array 4-39)

a	*e*	*i*	*o*	*u*	*y*
babe	glebe	scribe	globe	cube	gybe, jibe
space		splice		truce	
blade	cede	guide	code	crude	
chafe		knife			
stage			doge	huge	
quake	eke	strike	yoke	fluke	dyke, dike
shale	hele, heal	smile	hole	rule	chyle
frame	scheme	grime	gnome	flume	rhyme, rime
vane	scene	shrine	zone	rune	
drape		swipe	scope	dupe	type
		pique	toque		
flare	here	mire	snore	pure	lyre
phrase		guise	close	muse	
skate	mete	white	dote	chute	
shave	eve	chive	grove		gyve
daze		size	doze		

Nearly all holdouts to the pattern that calls for a long head vowel in VC*e#* strings in monosyllables involve the consonant *v:*

(Array 4-40)

dove (n.)	glove	live (v.)	shove
give	have	love	

Holdouts such as these can be brought to regularity by treating the final *e* in them as not phonetically motivated. The *e* is present in these words only to insulate an otherwise final *v*, word-final *v* being avoided in English (see 8.1.4). Thus, these holdouts contrast with other words in which the silent final *e* serves double duty, both insulating the final *v* and marking a long vowel, as in *gave, hive, rove,* and the like.

Five other holdouts are less readily regularized: *some, come, one, none, gone.* The first two come from Old English *sum* and *cuman,* with short *u*. The *u*'s were replaced with *o*'s by Norman scribes as part of their tendency to avoid piling up minim letters, especially around *m* and *n* (see 17.1.2 for more details). *One, none,* and *gone* are historically regular enough, but their pronunciations are nonregular. There is a strong tendency for nonsubstantive function words like *one* and *none* to receive weak sentence stress and to have a weak and short vowel sound, which could account for the /u/. However, in *some, come, one, none,* and *gone* the more central question—namely, Why the final *e?*—is less easy to answer. The final *e*'s first appear early in Middle English in all of the words. It is likely that they echo Old English or early Middle English inflectional endings: the final *e* in *none* is first associated with the plural form, for instance. But whatever the historical reasons, these four must be taken as clear holdouts to the otherwise quite reliable VCV pattern in monosyllables.

The force of VCV in disyllabic and longer words will be discussed in chapters 6 and 7.

4.3.4.2 Consonant Digraphs in VCV Strings

The behavior of consonant digraphs in VCV strings is complex. In general we can say that certain digraphs tend to follow certain long vowels in certain conditions, sometimes.

th. The behavior of the digraph *th* is very complex. Usually in V*th*V strings the head vowel will be short, as if the digraph *th* had the tactical force of a cluster. This short vowel occurs in a number of common simplexes, usually with the *th* spelling voiced /<u>th</u>/:

(Array 4-41)

blather	gather	nether	wether
bother	hither	other	whether
brother	lather ("foam")	plethora	whither
father	mether	smother	wither
fathom	mother	tether	zither

Similar, though not simplexes, are *together* and *mathematics.*

The head vowel in a V*th*V string will also regularly be short and the *th* will spell unvoiced /th/ if there is an element boundary immediately in front of or following the *th:*

(Array 4-42)

anathema (ana + thema)	methyl (meth + yl)
apotheosis (apo + the + osis)	monolithic (mon + o + lith)ic)
hypothesis (hyp + o(thesis)	nothing (no)(thing)
lithograph (lith + o(graph)	pathological (path + o(log + ic)al)
metathesis (meta(thesis)	psychopathic (psych + o + path)ic)
methane (meth + ane)	stethoscope (steth + o(scope)

Unusual related cases are *cathode, catholic,* and *method,* all of which historically have had boundaries between the *t* and the *h:* (cat + hode), (cat + holic), (met + hod). Now they should probably be treated as no longer having those boundaries, the old concatenation *t* plus *h* having merged into the digraph *th*.

Practically always when the V*th*V string has a long head vowel, the word either is or explicates to, a prime ending V*the#*. Thus, there is a long *a* in the *lather* that means "lathe worker" and explicates to the V*the#* prime *lathe:* (lathé)er). But there is a short *a* in the *lather* that means "lath worker," (lath)er), with a V*th#* prime. (The third *lather,* meaning "foam," is a simplex and is thus a member of array 4-41 above.) In general *th* will follow a long vowel in words that explicate to primes with V*the#* strings. Other instances:

(Array 4-43)

bathing, from *bathe:* (bathé)ing)
blithen, from *blithe:* (blithé)en), "to make blithe"
lithesome, from *lithe:* (lithe)some)
scatheless, from *scathe:* (scathe)less)
scythestone, from *scythe:* (scythe)(stone)
tither, from *tithe:* (tithé)er)

Included in this group is the prime *kithe, kythe,* with /ī/. Also included is *clothier* (clothé)ier). Historically *clothier* comes from Middle English *clothen,* from Old English *clathian,* which in turn is from Old English *clāth* 'cloth'. The *-ier* suffix came late, apparently due to analogy with other common *-ier* forms. Thus both *clothe* with /ō/ and *cloth* with /ò/ derive from the same Old English word, *clāth.* Normally Old English *ā* evolves into American English /ō/, as it did in *clothe,* but in the VC# pattern, as in *clāth,* the long Old English vowel was shortened, to *cloth.* (For other instances of the shortening of Old English long vowels see 4.3.2.)

Also included in this group are such complexes as *writhingly* from *writhe:* (writhé)ing)ly). This is true in spite of the contrast with *writhen,* with /i/: *writhen* is an adjective formed off of an old past participle marked by the *-n* suffix and the shortened internal vowel. Similar participles (with their infinitive forms) are *bitten, bite; ridden, ride; written, write; risen, rise.* Thus, the /i/ in *writhen* is due to the ablauting of the vowel in the old participle form. This is different from the structure of a word such as *blithen*, with /ī/, in which the suffix *-en*, which forms verbs from adjectives without ablauting the vowel.

Technically the /a/ in *rather* is irregular since it could be explicated to the archaic prime *rathe:* (rathé)er). *Rathe* derives from Old English *hrathe*, with a short *a*. But the explication is at best remote and it is probably better to treat *rather* as a simplex member of array 4-41 above. The /ä/ or /ò/ sound in *swathe* is truly irregular, though there is some consolation in the fact that it comes from Old English *swathian*, with a short *a*.

Long vowels occur unexpectedly in the V*th*V strings in the simplex *python*, and in the complexes *lethal* (leth + al) and *atheism* (a(theism), although the privative *a-* prefix is persistently /ā/ in complexes containing it. Long vowels also occur most unexpectedly before *th*'s at boundaries in such complexes as *ether* (eth[1] + er), *ethos* (eth[2] + os), and *pathos* (path + os). But note the contrast between these and the more regular complexes (with the same three bases) *ethyl, ethic,* and *pathic*.

Except for these few wrinkles, however, the V*th*V pattern is quite straightforward: In words that are, or that explicate to, primes ending with V*the*#, the head vowel will be long; otherwise it will regularly be short.

ch.   The length of vowels preceding the digraph *ch* in V*ch*V strings is less predictable. About half the time such vowels are long:

(Array 4-44)

> Primes in V*che*#:
>
> ache   capuche   croche   loche   psyche
>
> Other primes:
>
> lichen   ocher
>
> Complexes with V*ch*V strings with a long head vowel:
>
> dichotomy (dich + o + tom + y)   trachea (trach + ea)
>
> parochial (par + ochi + al)

More than half the time, however, the vowel preceding *ch* in V*ch*V strings is short:

(Array 4-45)

> Primes in V*che*#:
>
> cache   mustache   niche   panache   tache*
>
> Other primes:
>
> echo
>
> Complexes with V*ch*V strings with a short head vowel:
>
> duchess (duch + ess)   mechanism (mechan + ism)
>
> machination (machiné)ation)   pachyderm (pachy + derm)

ph. The tactical force of *ph* in V*ph*V strings also is quite unpredictable. About half the time the head vowel is long, about half the time short. Usually when the *ph* is element-medial the vowel is long, as in:

(Array 4-46)

aphid	cipher	hyphen	trophy
aphis	gopher	siphon	typhoon

There are some cases of short head vowels preceding medial *ph*— *esophagus, syphilis, staphylococcus, nephew, zephyr*—but all can be seen as instances of one of the shortening rules.

Usually when there is an element boundary directly before or after the *ph,* the head vowel is short, although all of the following instances, at least, fall under one of the shortening rules discussed in chapters 5 through 7:

(Array 4-47)

biographical (bi + o(graph)ic)al)	prophet (pro + phet)
cacophony (cac + o(phoné)y)	sarcophagus (sarc + o + phag + us)
graphite (graph)ite)	seraphic (seraph)ic)
hieroglyphic (hier + o(glyph)ic)	sophistry (soph + ist)ry)
peripheral (peri + pher + al)	sophomore (soph + o + more)
philosophic (philé + o + soph + ic)	typography (typé)o(graph)y)

In two cases long head vowels precede *ph* at an element boundary: *prophylactic* (pro + phylact + ic) and *typhoid* (typh + oid).

sh. The digraph *sh* never occurs with a long head vowel in a V*sh*V string. Words with V*sh*V strings are rather rare, but regularly they have short head vowels:

(Array 4-48)

abashed	bishop	fisher	threshold
ashen	bushel	pasha	usher

gh. Except for *aghast,* in which it follows a reduced vowel, the digraph *gh* that spells the /g/ sound occurs only in word-initial position and does not occur in V*gh*V strings. *Aghast* reflects the Middle English verb *agaste(n)* 'to frighten', and the initial *a* is an intensifying prefix. The digraph *gh* that is silent or that spells /f/ also does not occur in V*gh*V strings.

5 Suffix Rules

5.1 Introduction to the Shortening Rules

Of the tactical patterns exhibited in vowel and consonant strings such as VCC, VCV, V.V, and VC#, the contrast between VCC and VCV is orthographically the most important. It motivates such conventions as the use of silent final *e* to cue long vowels and the use of consonant doublets and clusters to cue short vowels. In the preceding chapter we discussed some of the holdouts to the VCC string and the tactical force of VCV strings in monosyllables. In longer words the VCV pattern suffers an immense number of holdouts, usually in Romance adaptions. But a close examination of these holdouts reveals a rather complex system of subpatterns and subrules. Indeed, there is orderliness beneath the apparent confusion. Many of the holdouts to the VCV pattern can be understood, or rationalized, via the shortening effects of certain suffixes on the vowels immediately preceding them. (For discussion of the effects of some suffixes on word stress and vowel quantity, see Newman 1948, 28–32; Bauer 1983, 112–23.) Others can be understood via their etymologies and the shortening effects of the Stress Frontshift Rule. Others can be rationalized via the shortening effects of the powerful Third Syllable Rule, and still others via the effects of conservative analogy. In chapters 5–7 we will discuss these holdouts to VCV, starting with those suffixes that shorten the vowel preceding it, even if that vowel is the head of a VCV string. (The following discussion covers many of the patterns pointed out by Oswalt in his morphophonemic description of English spelling [1973].)

5.2 The Suffix *-ity* Rule

5.2.1 Introduction to the Rule

The Suffix *-ity* Rule can be stated initially as this: The suffix *-ity* is regularly preceded by a vowel that is stressed and short, as in *rigidity* and *legality*. Since *-ity* is an immensely productive suffix, this rule covers hundreds of words. Since it only complicates the orthography when it preempts other, larger tactical patterns—such as the VCV pattern, for instance—we will restrict our examples to words that involve those preemptions (as in both *rigidity* and *legality*) in which the vowel preceding *-ity,* though stressed and heading a VCV string, is short. The Suffix *-ity* Rule can force a stress shift when *-ity* is added to a word. In the case of *legal* the stress shifts from the *e* to the *a*. Sometimes this stress shift causes changes in vowel length between the stem and the derived word. For instance, in deriving *legality* from *legal* the *a* goes from a reduced schwa in *legal* to a full /a/ in *legality*.

Another kind of shift in vowel length is also common in certain derivations with *-ity*. When *-ity* is added to the stem *sane,* for instance, the stress remains on the *a,* but the vowel length goes from long in the stem to short in the derived word: *sane* /sān/ becomes *sanity* /'sanətē/. Other derivations with *-ity* that contain a shift of long vowel to short in a VCV string:

(Array 5-1)

benign, benignity	grave, gravity	profane, profanity
cave, cavity	inane, inanity	saline, salinity
chaste, chastity	malign, malignity	serene, serenity
divine, divinity	mediocre, mediocrity	sublime, sublimity
extreme, extremity	obscene, obscenity	trine, trinity

Derivations with *-ity* that contain a shift of an unstressed reduced vowel in the stem to a stressed short full vowel in the derived word:

(Array 5-2)

active, activity	ideal, ideality	squalid, squalidity
arid, aridity	local, locality	stupid, stupidity
docile, docility	morbid, morbidity	subjective, subjectivity
facile, facility	positive, positivity	timid, timidity
feminine, femininity	rascal, rascality	utile, utility
feudal, feudality	real, reality	virgin, virginity
frigid, frigidity	solid, solidity	vocal, vocality

All of the instances of the Suffix *-ity* Rule presented so far have involved free stems and preemptions of the VCV pattern. But this rule extends far beyond such instances. It includes, not surprisingly, *-ity* words in which the short presuffixal vowel is in the regular VCC pattern, as in *fecundity,* (fecund)ity), and *solemnity,* (solemn)ity). It also includes *-ity* words formed from bound stems in which the preceding vowel in both VCC and VCV strings is short—as in *indemnity* and *tenacity.*

Other instances in which *-ity* is added to bound stems, thereby leading to preemptions of the VCV pattern:

(Array 5-3)

amenity (amen + ity)	humility (humil + ity)
amity (am*i* + ity)	lenity (len + ity)
atrocity (atroc + ity)	levity (lev + ity)
comity (com + ity)	magnanimity (magn + anim + ity)
equanimity (equ + anim + ity)	proximity (proxim + ity)
equity (equ + ity)	quality (qual + ity)
ferocity (feroc + ity)	unanimity (un + anim + ity)
fidelity (fidel + ity)	velocity (veloc + ity)
frivolity (frivol + ity)	vicinity (vicin + ity)

Also in this group is *reciprocity,* which explicates to (reciproc + ity), though etymologically it has absorbed two earlier Latin prefixes, *re-* and *pro-*, with the sense of "backward and forward."

Derivations with *-ity* that involve the replacement of a terminative base with a nonterminative coform or of the terminative suffix *-ous* with its nonterminative coform *-os +* are listed in array 5-4. Several of the explications are tentative.

(Array 5-4)

ability (able)ity) = (abil + ity)
fabulosity (fabulous)ity) = (fabul + os + ity)
generosity (generous)ity) = (gener + os + ity)
impetuosity (impetuous)ity) = (i*n* + m + pet*é* + u + os + ity)
nebulosity (nebulous)ity) = (nebul + os + ity)
nobility (noble)ity) = (nobil + ity)
numerosity (numerous)ity) = (numer + os + ity)
ponderosity (ponderous)ity) = (ponder + os + ity)
religiosity (religious)ity) = (relig + i + os + ity)
scrupulosity (scrupulous)ity) = (scrupul + os + ity)
stability (stable)ity) = (stabil + ity)
voluminosity (voluminous)ity) = (volumin + os + ity)

5.2.2   Holdouts

The Suffix *-ity* Rule regularly preempts the VCV pattern. But it is itself preempted in two cases: by the persistent long *u* and by the V.V Rule.

5.2.2.1   Long *u*

A long *u* at the head of a VCV string will regularly preempt the Suffix *-ity* Rule. The reason for this is that in such cases Middle and Early Modern English consistently had /iū/, a diphthong, and diphthongs resisted the effects of the shortening rules (Jespersen [1909] 1954, 1:104, 137, 142). Instances of /ū/ before *-ity* in VCV strings:

(Array 5-5)

community	garrulity	jejunity	purity
credulity	immunity	nudity	sedulity
crudity	importunity	opportunity	unity

5.2.2.2 V.V

Some of the instances below contain the persistent long *u*, but the V.V Rule regularly preempts the Suffix *-ity* Rule with other head vowels as well:

(Array 5-6)

acuity	continuity	fortuity	homogeneity
aureity	deity	gaseity	laity
congruity	egoity	gratuity	velleity

Some American dictionaries show *probity* with just one pronunciation, with /ō/, which would make it a holdout to the Suffix *-ity* Rule. However, *W3* and Kenyon and Knott (1944) show variant pronunciations with the more regular short sound, /ä/.

5.2.3 The Final Rule

The Suffix *-ity* Rule can be given this final form: Unless it is long *u* or the head of a V.V string, the vowel preceding the suffix *-ity* will be stressed and short, even if it heads a VCV string.

5.3 The Suffix *-ic* Rule

5.3.1 Introduction to the Rule

The initial statement of the rule for *-ic* is the same as that for *-ity:* The vowel preceding the suffix *-ic* will be stressed and short, even if it heads a VCV string. Relative to length and stress, the behavior of the vowel preceding *-ic* is parallel to that of the vowel preceding *-ity*, and we can use the same sequence of arrays to illustrate it.

Instances with *-ic* that contain a shift of long vowel to short in a VCV string:

(Array 5-7)

aesthete, aesthetic	state, static
athlete, athletic	telephone, telephonic
cone, conic	telescope, telescopic
exile, exilic	theater, theatric
mime, mimic	tone, tonic
parasite, parasitic	type, typic

The following also are members of this group, although each has a variant with the long vowel sound called for by the VCV pattern: *cyclic, domic, tropic. Clinic* can legitimately explicate to (clin*é*)ic), although the semantics of the explication are somewhat distant.

The following are all related to this group. They do not explicate to a free stem with a long vowel, but they are semantically and functionally related to such a stem: *galenic,* with /e/ (compare *galena,* with /ē/); *volcanic* (compare *volcano*); *arthritic* (compare *arthritis*); *narcotic* (compare *narcosis*); *hypnotic* (compare *hypnosis*); *neurotic* (compare *neurosis*).

Derivations with *-ic* that contain a shift of a reduced vowel to a stressed short vowel in a VCV string:

(Array 5-8)

angel, angelic	organ, organic
atom, atomic	patriot, patriotic
carbon, carbonic	period, periodic
dactyl, dactylic	pirate, piratic
demon, demonic	prophet, prophetic
despot, despotic	prosody, prosodic
diameter, diametric	rhapsody, rhapsodic
druid, druidic	satan, satanic
dyad, dyadic	stomach, stomachic
melody, melodic	titan, titanic
ocean, oceanic	vocal, vocalic

Related, though involving coforms, are *messianic* (compare *messiah*), *fantastic* (compare *fantasy*), and *apostolic* (compare *apostle*).

The Suffix *-ic* Rule holds, too, in derivations involving the compound suffixes *-atic* and *-etic:*

(Array 5-9)

aquatic	dogmatic	lymphatic	stigmatic
aromatic	dramatic	operatic	symptomatic
axiomatic	enigmatic	problematic	theorematic
dalmatic	erratic	rheumatic	traumatic
apathetic	dietetic	mimetic	sympathetic

Also a member of this group is *fanatic,* which can explicate to (fan)atic), although historically *fan* is actually a back formation clipped from the earlier *fanatic.* Related, too, are the coforms *splenetic* and *spleen.*

5.3.2 Holdouts

A regular holdout to the persistence of the stress on the vowel and its shortness preceding *-ic* occurs when the suffix *-ity* is added, as in the pair *organic* and *organicity*, in which the primary stress shifts onto the *-ic* with the addition of *-ity*. Other instances:

(Array 5-10)

authentic, authenticity	period, periodic, periodicity
canon, canonic, canonicity	pneumatic, pneumaticity
domestic, domesticity	public, publicity
eccentric, eccentricity	rustic, rusticity
elastic, elasticity	styptic, stypticity
electric, electricity	tone, tonic, tonicity

Clearly, the Suffix *-ity* Rule preempts the Suffix *-ic* Rule. But the *-ic* Rule holds when suffixes other than *-ity* are added after the *-ic:*

(Array 5-11)

aesthetic, aestheticism	neurotic, neuroticism
athletic, athletically	organic, organicist
clinic, clinical	rabbinic, rabbinical
graphic, graphicness	tropic, tropical
hypnotic, hypnotically	typic, typical

There are relatively few other holdouts to the Suffix *-ic* Rule, but they are worth some discussion. In a few cases the stress is not on the penultimate syllable, where the rule would put it. Instances are *heretic, cadaveric, lunatic, arithmetic* (the noun, not the adjective, which does have stress on the penult). The *OED* suggests that the displaced stress in *heretic* is due to the fact that the word was adopted from French rather than directly from Latin or Greek. The same would appear to hold for *cadaveric,* from French *cadaverique,* though *cadaveric* also has a variant pronunciation with three rather than four syllables, the *e* being silent; in this variant the Suffix *-ic* Rule holds. The *-ic* Rule also holds for the apparent holdout *catholic,* since it is usually pronounced with only two syllables, the *o* being silent.

The development of the noun *arithmetic* is remarkably complex, but it, too, was adopted from Old French. That could explain the displaced stress in the noun form, but it leaves open the question of why the stress is where it should be in the adjective form. The *OED,* which marks the adjective form as obsolete, leaves the source open—either French or the Latin *arithmēticus,* which is apparently the unequivocal source of the alternate adjective *arithmetical.* Thus, one way of explaining the difference between the stress in the American English noun and adjective would be to derive the former from French, thus explaining the displaced stress, and to derive the latter from Latin, thus explaining the regular stress placement. *Lunatic* may also come from French, the choice again being open between a French source and a Latin one.

The problem with this otherwise elegant explanation of these holdouts is that some of the words with the regular stress placement also appear to derive from French rather than Latin or Greek—for instance, *arthritic* and a number of others. Perhaps we can simply say that the norm is toward the pattern set down by the Suffix *-ic* Rule—that is, toward a stressed, short penultimate vowel. Adoptions from French tend to counter this norm but are usually regularized to it. A few French adoptions have resisted this regularizing—namely, *heretic, lunatic,* one pronunciation of *cadaveric,* and the noun *arithmetic.* The proper noun *Arabic* is a similar nonregular French adaption. It is perhaps noteworthy that all but one of these words (that one, *cadaveric,* having a more regular variant pronunciation) are used more often as noun than as adjective and that there is a tendency in English to frontshift the stress in nouns, as in stress pairs such as the iambic verb *convict* and the trochaic noun *convict.*

In a few cases the stress placement is correct in words with *-ic,* but the vowel preceding the suffix is long rather than short. Instances are *aphasic, basic,* and *spondaic* with /ā/; *scenic, magnesic, analgesic, strategic,* and *phonemic* with /ē/; *psychic* with /ī/; *aerobic* and *heroic* with /ō/; and *music, cubic, pubic,* and *runic* with long *u*. Clearly the persistent long *u* is the crucial factor in the last group (for other instances of the persistence of long *u* see 5.2.2.1 and 7.2.1). And equally clearly the strong V.V pattern explains the holdouts *heroic* and *spondaic*. The rest—*aphasic, basic, scenic, strategic, phonemic, psychic*—are less readily explained, though in *basic, scenic, phonemic,* and *psychic* conservative analogy seems to play a crucial role.

5.3.3   The Final Rule

The Suffix *-ic* Rule, then, can be given a final form almost identical to that for *-ity:* Unless it is a long *u* or the head of a V.V string, with a few holdouts the vowel preceding the suffix *-ic* will be stressed and short, even if it heads a VCV string. The *-ity* rule preempts the *-ic* rule.

5.4   The Suffix *-ion* Rule

5.4.1   Introduction to the Rule

The vowel preceding *-ion* always bears primary stress. If it heads a VCV string, the vowel will normally be long, unless it is *i*. An *i* preceding *-ion* is regularly short, even if it heads a VCV string.

Instances of long vowels preceding -*ion* in VCV strings, including some words with the compound suffix -*ation:*

(Array 5-12)

causation	contagion	formation	invitation
citation	degradation	foundation	quotation
accretion	completion	deletion	excretion
adhesion	concretion	depletion	lesion
commotion	devotion	erosion	locomotion
corrosion	emotion	explosion	notion
ablution	delusion	illusion	occlusion
communion	diffusion	intrusion	pollution
confusion	dilution	locution	seclusion

Instances of /i/ preceding -*ion* in VCV strings, including some words with the compound suffix -*ition:*

(Array 5-13)

abolition	audition	inhibition	revision
acquisition	collision	partition	sedition
addition	decision	provision	suspicion

The short *i* preceding -*ion* in these words can be seen as a special case of the persistent short *i* in the strong VCVV string (see 7.2.3).

The Suffix -*ion* Rule also holds, though less reliably so, for derivations in which a suffix is added after the -*ion*. Regular instances are *sensational, probationary, invitational, abolitionist, exhibitionist,* and the like.

5.4.2 Holdouts

The only known holdouts to this far-reaching rule are *discretion,* with its unexpected /e/; *companion* and one pronunciation of *ration,* with /a/; and *onion* and *bunion,* with the unexpected /u/. Another holdout is *national,* which involves a shift from the regular long *a* when the -*ion* is the last element in the word, *nation,* to a nonregular short *a* with the addition of the suffix -*al.*

5.4.3 The Final Rule

The final statement of the Suffix -*ion* Rule, then, is as follows: An *i* preceding the suffix -*ion* will be stressed and short, even if it heads a VCV string. All other vowels will, with a few holdouts, be stressed and long.

5.5   The Suffix -*it* Rule

The suffix -*it,* which is used to form nouns, verbs, and adjectives, is
regularly preceded by a stressed, short vowel, even if that vowel heads a
VCV pattern. In the case of the words marked with a question mark in the
following array, there is still some question as to whether the *it* should be
treated as a suffix or simply as an ending.

(Array 5-14)

adit (?)	edit (?)	inhibit	solicit
credit	elicit	licit	tacit
debit (?)	explicit	limit	tipit (?)
decrepit	habit (?)	pipit (?)	visit
deposit	illicit	posit	vomit (?)
digit	implicit	prohibit	

The only known holdouts are *cubit* and *unit* (with the persistent long *u*)
and *deficit* (with the stress frontshifted so that the penult *i* is reduced).

5.6   The Suffix -*id* Rule

The suffix—or, more accurately, the converged set of different suffixes—
spelled *id* is used with nouns and adjectives, as in *acid, liquid,* and the like.
There is a strong tendency for -*id* to be preceded by a short vowel, even in
VCV strings. Other instances:

(Array 5-15)

avid	intrepid	rabid	stolid
frigid	invalid (adj.)	rapid	tepid
gelid	livid	rigid	timid
gravid	olid	sapid	valid
insipid	placid	solid	vapid

5.6.1   Holdouts

A notable set of holdouts involves the persistent long *u:*

(Array 5-16)

druid	humid	pellucid	tumid
fluid	lucid	stupid	

The apparent holdouts *bifid* and *trifid,* with /ī/, actually do not contain -*id,*
explicating instead to (bi + fid) and (tri + fid).

The -*id* rule is rather weak insofar as stress is concerned. In words that
either are, or can explicate to, bisyllabic primes, the stress falls on the
vowel preceding the suffix, naturally enough. But in words of three or

more syllables that do not explicate to bisyllabic primes, the stress can be frontshifted, as in the nouns *invalid* and *pyramid*.

5.6.2 A Second *-id*

The Suffix *-id* Rule is complicated by a second suffix spelled *id* which denotes a member of a zoological family (itself represented by the suffix *-idae*). For instance, a *hominid* (homin + id) is a member of the family *hominidae* (homin + idae). In words formed with this second *id* suffix, the suffix is not regularly preceded by a short vowel. Thus we have *galeid, felid, gobiid, bovid, gadid,* and the like, all with long vowels preceding the suffix. We also have *scolytid,* with a short penultimate vowel; *hominid,* with a schwa; and *geometrid,* with either a schwa or /e/. However, this group poses no telling problems for the Suffix *-id* Rule; the words formed with this second zoological suffix are distinctly technical and rare, quite different from the regular words formed from the first suffix *-id*.

5.6.3 The Final Rule

Thus, despite its weakness insofar as stress placement is concerned, and despite the existence of the second *-id* suffix, the Suffix *-id* Rule can be stated as follows: Except for long *u,* a stressed vowel immediately preceding the suffix *-id* will be short.

5.7 The Suffix *-ish*[2] Rule

Two different suffixes spelled *ish* are recognized in American English. The first, used to form adjectives, occurs in such words as *boyish, fattish, modish,* and the like. It is not tactically preemptive. It is usually added to free stems, and conservative analogy prevails so that it does not affect the placement of stress or the length of the preceding vowel. Thus the above words explicate to (boy)ish, (fat)t + ish), and (modé)ish). Derived from this adjective-forming suffix is the noun-forming suffix in words such as *English, Polish,* and the like. Both forms are treated as essentially the same suffix and are not complex orthographically.

The second *-ish* suffix, however, is quite different. It forms verbs and is regularly added to bound stems. It is tactically preemptive, consistently being preceded by a short, stressed vowel, regardless of the string pattern involved.

Instances of *-ish*[2] in regular VCC strings:

(Array 5-17)

accomplish	burnish	extinguish	languish
anguish	distinguish	furbish	publish
blandish	embellish	furnish	relinquish
brandish	establish	garnish	vanquish

Instances of *-ish²* in preempted VCV strings:

(Array 5-18)

abolish	blemish	finish	ravish
admonish	demolish	lavish	relish
astonish	diminish	polish	replenish
banish	famish	punish	vanish

5.7.1 Holdout

The only known holdout to the *-ish²* rule is *impoverish,* in which the penult does not attract stress in the most common pronunciation. On the other hand, *impoverish* does have a variant pronunciation with only three syllables, the *e* being silent, and in this pronunciation the word follows the rule.

5.7.2 The Final Rule

The Suffix *-ish²* Rule, then, can be stated as follows: The suffix *-ish²* is preceded by a vowel that is stressed and short, regardless of the tactical string involved.

5.8 The Suffix *-ule* Rule

The suffix *-ule* tends to be preceded by a short vowel, regardless of the tactical string involved. Instances:

(Array 5-19)

globule	nebule	schedule
granule	nodule	setule
module	pilule	spicule

This is a small group, to be sure. And there are the expected holdouts due to the persistent long *u; tubule, nucule, plumule,* and *cupule* all have long *u.* Conservative analogy works on at least one other holdout: *spinule,* an eighteenth-century adoption, has /ī/, analogous to its prime, and explicates to (spin*é*)ule).

6 VCV in Disyllables

6.1 Introduction

The VCV pattern, as has been said, is most reliable in monosyllables—that is, in words in which the second vowel in the VCV string is a silent final *e*, as in *rate* or *bite* (see 4.3.4.1). While the VCV string displays much the same reliability in some disyllables as it does in monosyllables, in most disyllables there are complexities.

6.2 Iambs and Trochees

Disyllables that contain VCV strings can be divided into words with stress on the second syllable—a relatively rare type we will call **iambic,** or **iambs**—and words with stress on the first syllable—by far the more common of the two, which we will call **trochaic, or trochees.** Iambs in which the stressed vowel heads a VCV string are exemplified by *alone, confuse, recede, opine.* As far as the VCV pattern is concerned, iambic words enjoy the same regularity and simplicity as do monosyllables.

On the other hand, trochaic words such as *yodel, navel, union, demon, molar, driver,* and *specious* are much more complex tactically. The complexity is illustrated by the fact that although these seven words are all regular in terms of the VCV pattern—that is, all have long head vowels—in each case there is at least one parallel word in which the stressed vowel is short: compare *yodel* to *model, navel* to *gravel, union* to *bunion, demon* to *lemon, molar* to *scholar, driver* to *river,* and *specious* to *precious.*

In fact, in a sample of 872 trochaic words with the VCV pattern (taken from the list of over 10,450 two-syllable words given in Dolby and Resnikoff [1967, 223–75]), 585, or 67 percent, contain long head vowels; 287, or 33 percent, have short head vowels. That constitutes a two-thirds to one-third split. The following effort to describe these two groups will involve us in some of the complexities of English etymology, in some of the processes by which adaptions are integrated into the American English spelling system, and in some curious features of English phonology. Any description must finally contain inconsistencies and question marks, but we will discover that pattern and design control not only the 67 percent with regular, long vowels at the head of the VCV string but also most of the 33 percent with nonregular, short head vowels.

6.3 Regular VCV Trochees

Among the nearly 600 regular instances of the VCV pattern, one of the most accessible groups, as well as the largest (290 instances) consists of complexes that explicate to monosyllabic primes containing a long vowel in the VCV pattern, specifically in the VCe# pattern. Some examples:

(Array 6-1)

dosage (dosé)age)	mulish (mulé)ish)
driver (drivé)er)	pipette (pipé)ette)
famous (famé)ous)	prudence (prudé)ence)
finer (finé)er)	ration* (raté)ion)
gradate (gradé)ate)	scenic (scené)ic)
guidance (guidé)ance)	smoky (smoké)y)
lunar (luné)ar)	tonal (toné)al)
lunette (luné)ette)	typist (typé)ist)

In short, nearly half of the regular instances explicate to monosyllabic primes that are themselves instances of the VCV pattern. In this group of words the regular length effect of the VCV string is reinforced by conservative analogy, working to conserve the sound of the monosyllabic prime in the derived disyllable.

Among the remaining instances of regular VCV strings in our sample there is another highly accessible, though less large, group: words containing the long *u*. As we have seen before and shall see again, long *u* persistently resists shortening (see 5.2.2.1). Some instances with long *u* from our sample:

(Array 6-2)

crucial	julep	pubis	sumac
frugal	junior	puma	super
futile	lupine	rhubarb	tunic
future	mucoid	ruby	tutor
human	mutate	student	unit

Although some words with long *u* were included in array 6-1, none of the words in array 6-2 explicates to a prime.

The next group of trochees in our sample with regular long head vowels in a VCV string is twice as large as the long *u* group, but less easily recognized, less accessible. It consists of nearly one hundred Latin and Greek adoptions, none of which can be further explicated to primes. Included in this group are the following:

(Array 6-3)

agent	crisis	molar	silence
bisect	fetus	pagan	stipend
blatant	focus	potent	suasive
bonus	glacial	precept	talus
bovine	gnomon	prefix	thesis
bromide	halo	private	theta
canine	idyll	rebus	trident
caper	item	recent	tripod
climax	latent	saline	velar
cogent	locate	satyr	venal
colon	major	semen	vocal
crater	minor	senior	zeta

The fourth group of regular instances of VCV consists of native words that had long or short vowels in open syllables in their Old English forms. As noted in 4.3.2, Old English long vowels tended to remain long in open syllables, and often Old English short vowels in open syllables lengthened as they evolved into Middle and Early Modern English. Instances from our sample of trochees:

(Array 6-4)

acorn (OE *æcern*)	ivy (OE *īfig*)
capon (OE *capun*, Fr *capon*)	naked (OE *nacod*)
even (OE *ef[e]n*)	navel (OE *nafela*)
evil (OE *yfel*)	open (OE *open*)
haven (OE *hæfen*)	raven (OE *hræfn, hræfen*)
hazel (OE *hæsel*)	taper (OE *tapor, tapur*)
holy (OE *hālig*)	token (OE *tāc[e]n*)

Three other instances from Old English are *spider* (OE *spīthra*), *clover* (OE *clæfre*), and *lady* (OE *hlæfdige*). The vowels would have remained long in *spīthra* and *clæfre* because consonant clusters with liquids (such as /r/) did not have the regular shortening effect as did other clusters. In Old English *th* was a single letter, so that what we today represent as *thr* in *spīthra* would not have been a shortening cluster. The /ā/ in *lady* (OE *hlæfdige*) probably resisted shortening because the *fd* cluster very early simplified to a single consonant, or was broken with an inserted vowel, putting the *a* into an open syllable. Middle English shows the evolution *lafdi*, then *lavede*, then *ladi*. Other words in our sample that are probably related to this same line of development are *waver* (apparently combining features of ONorse *vafra* 'to be restless' and OE *wæfre* 'restless'), *quaver*

(ME *cwavien,* of vague Germanic origin). Parallel, though later, adoptions from German include *yodel, docent,* and *bromate.*

The group of regular VCV trochees includes some mixed Romance adoptions: From Spanish and Portuguese come *cocoa, nabob, brocade, betal, coco, dido, silo,* and *emu.* From Mexican Spanish comes *sisal,* and from Italian, *solo* and *zany,* the latter from an affectionate version of *Giovanni* 'John'. There are also a number of sometimes peripheral and minimally integrated adoptions: *myna* (Hindi); *tepee, teepee, tipi,* and *totem* (American Indian); *copeck* (Russian); *cosy, cozy,* and *slogan* (Scots); *polo* (Balti); *tapir* (Guarani); *robot* (Czech); *muley* (Irish); *china* (perhaps Sanskrit)—and with a truly impressive pedigree, *shaman* (according to the *AHD,* from German, from Russian, from Tungus, from Tocharian, from Prakrit, from Sanskrit!).

In addition to these there are a number of words of obscure origin: *bogie, bogy; stymie, stymy; kibosh; yokel; mogul; hocus; bogus; tiny; lazy.*

All of the foregoing, from those words that explicate to VCV primes through those that are of obscure origin, constitute nearly all of the regular VCV trochees in our sample. But the remainder, about a hundred words, represent something of an embarrassment. They are French adoptions such as *license, native, regal,* and *motion,* and the embarrassment they represent will become clearer in 6.4.3.1.

6.3.1 Summary

For the most part the regular VCV trochees in our sample sort rather handily into four tight groups plus a fifth that is not so tight. They tend to be words that can be explicated to monosyllabic primes with VCV strings, or they contain long *u* as the head vowel, or they are Latin or Greek adoptions, or they come from Old English words in which the head vowel was in an open syllable. The fifth, looser group contains the miscellaneous adoptions and obscure formations.

To be sure, this is a curiously unparallel and mixed list of groups. Of the four major groups the first is based on orthographic structure, the second on a phonological feature, the third and fourth on etymology. And yet, in spite of this lack of elegance, these four groups do much to help us distinguish the regular VCV trochees from the nonregular ones that will be described next.

6.4 The Nonregular VCV Trochees

Unlike the regular VCV trochees, the nonregular holdouts include very few that explicate to VCV primes—or, for that matter, to primes of any kind. Of these holdouts a few are complexes in which the head vowel of the VCV string is shortened by the Suffix -*ic* Rule:

(Array 6-5)

chemic	cretic	mimic	tonic
chronic	critic	panic	topic
civic	cynic	phonic	tragic
clinic	epic	physic	tropic
conic	magic	static	typic

Indeed, so powerful is the Suffix -*ic* Rule that four words in array 6-5 explicate to VCV primes, the long vowel shortening when -*ic* is added: (coné)ic), (phoné)ic), (typé)ic), (staté)ic).

6.4.1 The Stress Frontshift Rule

Unlike the regular group, in which French adaptions are rather few, French adaptions among the holdouts constitute the largest single type: of the 287 holdouts, 195, or nearly 70 percent, are French adaptions. And unlike the regular group, in which direct Latin adaptions are the second-largest group, among the holdouts there are relatively few Latin adaptions, about 10 percent.

The main stress rule for early French was that words were stressed on the final syllable unless that syllable was a weak *e,* in which case they were stressed on the penult. In time, as early French adoptions were integrated, moving from the periphery to the center of the English spelling system, the stress shifted forward in the words, bringing their intonation more into line with the native English pattern of word stress, which tended to be on the first syllable of the base or in some cases even as far forward as the prefix. Before the stress frontshifting occurred, however, French adoptions would have established pronunciations with the first vowel still unstressed and not long. Then, when the stress moved forward in the word, these first vowels, now stressed, would be unlikely to lengthen. As a result of this Stress Frontshift Rule there are in English hundreds and hundreds of French adaptions that have short, stressed vowels, adaptions in which the VCV pattern would lead us to expect long vowels. Thus, for instance, the seven trochees listed in 6.2 that have short vowels in the VCV pattern all are French adaptions affected by the Stress Frontshift Rule: *model, gravel, bunion, lemon, scholar, river, precious.* Some other instances from our sample of trochees with VCV strings:

(Array 6-6)

agate	flagon	onyx	schedule
balance	govern	pedal	sever
bigot	havoc	pigeon	special
brigand	hazard	pity	spinach
canon	honest	placard	statue
clamor	levee	proverb	tenant
column	lizard	quiver	tenure
cover	madam	ravage	tremor
crevice	medal	refuge	valiant
damage	menace	revel	value
deluge	metal	ribald	venom
dragon	modern	rosin	visage

The sample of trochees also includes a number of French adaptions with VCV strings that fall under one of the suffix rules discussed in chapter 5. Instances:

(Array 6-7)

avid	famish	minion	rapid
banish	fetish	pinion	ravish
blemish	finish	placid	rigid
bunion	habit	polish	solid
credit	lavish	profit	timid
debit	limit	punish	visit

All of the words in arrays 6-6 and 6-7 are French adaptions that were affected by the Stress Frontshift Rule after they were brought into English, the result in each case being that a vowel that had previously been unstressed remained short after the stress was shifted onto it, even though it was the head of a VCV string.

6.4.2   The Consonant *v* in VCV Strings

A small number of holdouts to the VCV pattern in our trochee sample contain short vowels followed by *v*. In Old English both voiceless /f/ and voiced /v/ were spelled *f*, the location of the *f* in the word determining whether it spelled /f/ or /v/. In Middle English the *v* came to be used to spell the voiced /v/ sound. More accurately, in Middle English *u* was used to spell the voiced /v/ sound and the various *u* vowel sounds. In Early Modern English *v* came to be used to spell the consonant sound, while *u* was reserved primarily for the vowels. In Middle English *u* was not doubled, whether it was vowel or consonant. This earlier constraint against double *u* has evolved into a modern constraint against double *v*. Thus a number of Old English words are today spelled with a single *v* after a short vowel. In our sample of trochees we find the following:

(Array 6-8)

clever	grovel	seven	shrivel
cover	hover	seventh	sliver
drivel	never	shiver	snivel
ever	oven	shovel	swivel

This situation constitutes a point of genuine indistinctness in the English spelling system. The constraint against double *v* has for all intents and purposes rendered the VCC/VCV contrast meaningless for vowels that are immediately followed by a lone *v*. Thus, in addition to the nonregular instances shown in array 6-8, there are several regular VCV trochees with a single *v*, among them *clover, navel, mover.*

6.4.3 Further VCV Holdouts

Section 6.3 mentioned an important group of regular VCV trochees that were adopted directly from Latin. There are, unfortunately, also a small number of Latin adaptions that are nonregular, with short head vowels in a VCV string, words such as *atom* and *chemist*. They at first represent a contradiction in the sorting we are striving for here, but most of them can be explained. We will consider the explanation for this apparent contradiction later, in 7.3, in the discussion of the Third Syllable Rule.

Rounding out this group of VCV holdouts in our trochee sample are a number of miscellaneous adoptions, all of which for one reason or another have resisted being adapted to the regular English pattern, which would call for long vowels where these all show short: *khaki* (Urdu); *saki, sake* (Japanese); *shekel* (Hebrew); *slalom* (Norwegian); *tabu* (Tongan); *manage* and *granite* (Italian); *guinea, riata, guano, jaguar, placer* (Spanish and Portuguese).

6.4.3.1 Holdouts to the Stress Frontshift Rule

There is a group of French adaptions that belongs to the regular group in our sample of VCV trochees—that is, that has long head vowels. Since the argument has been that French adaptions are more typical of the holdout group because of the Stress Frontshift Rule, those regular French adaptions complicate the description. It is difficult to account for all of the members of this group. A small number can be explained via the Suffix *-ion* Rule (5.4), which in general says that any vowel immediately before *-ion*, except *i*, will be stressed and long. Thus we get the following French adaptions:

(Array 6-9)

legion	motion	region
lesion	potion	

In addition, some French adaptions with long vowels are due to a spelling change that has occurred in English. For instance, the English word *tiger* is from Old French *tigre*. Since the last syllable of the French *tigre* is a weak *e,* the *i* would be stressed, which leads to today's long *i.* Other instances:

(Array 6-10)

cedar (OFr *cedre*)	miter (OFr *mitre*)
cider (OFr *sidre, cisdre*)	saker ("falcon") (OFr *sacre*)
liter (Fr *litre*)	sober (OFr *sobre*)
meter (OFr, Fr *metre;* OE *meter*)	wafer (NormFr *wafre*)

6.5 Summary

The tactical force of the VCV pattern is much more complicated in disyllables than it is in monosyllables. Although VCV strings in iambic words, with stress on the second vowel, enjoy much the same regularity as do those in monosyllables, things are much more complex in trochees, the more common type of disyllable. About two-thirds of the time trochaic strings are regular. This is especially true in words that explicate to monosyllabic primes with the string VC*e#*. It is also especially true when the head of the VCV string is *u* or in Latin adaptions. Finally, it is also true in native words that derive from Old English words in which today's head vowel was in an open syllable.

The nonregular holdouts, about one-third of our sample, seldom explicate to primes in VC*e#* strings—or to any kind of prime at all. They also occur when the VCV string is preempted by a shortening rule, such as the Suffix *-ic* Rule, and very often when the consonant in the string is *v.* Most of the holdouts are French adaptions that have been affected by the Stress Frontshift Rule.

7 The Third Syllable Rule

7.1 Instances of the Rule

The preceding three chapters have discussed how the VCV string, though a strong and important pattern in the American English spelling system, can be preempted by several less general shortening patterns and rules. This chapter examines more complications in and preemptions of the VCV pattern—in this case, in words of three or more syllables. The most general of all the preemptors of VCV is the Third Syllable Rule.

Jespersen states the Third Syllable Rule clearly and concisely. Speaking of Romance adaptions, he says, "When the stress is on the third (or fourth) syllable from the end of the word, the vowel is short" ([1909] 1954, 1:139). This rule preempts the VCV pattern, thus shortening the head vowels in VCV strings. It is related to the trisyllabic laxing rule described by Chomsky and Halle (1968, 52–53, 178–83, and passim). See also Oswalt's Antepenult Rule and his notion of the missing syllable (1973, 9, 28–29).

The Third Syllable Rule reflects the early English school pronunciation of Latin and of Latin words adopted into English, and thus there are hundreds and hundreds of words that express it—such as *agitate,* in which the VCV string spelled *agi* has a shortened head, and *monument,* in which the head vowel of the VCV string *onu* also is shortened. A very small sampling of other instances includes:

(Array 7-1)

agony	emigrate	medicine	remedy
analysis	eminent	mitigate	salary
anatomist	esophagus	monogram	sanitary
animal	family	national	satellite
cabinet	gratitude	penitent	specify
celery	idiot	policy	tenement
citizen	iterate	president	tragedy
comedy	legacy	probably	unanimous
definite	liberal	propagate	visible

The Third Syllable Rule can be extended to words such as *opinion, vicious,* and *special*—words that are now stressed on the second rather than the third syllable owing to syllable reduction. In Middle and Early Modern English the stress in these words fell on the third syllable back, for at that time a word like *opinion* had four syllables (the *-ion* suffix being pronounced as two syllables), and *vicious* and *special* had three syllables each (the presuffixal *i* in each being pronounced as a separate vowel). As late as Revolutionary times in America, echoes of the old, multisyllabic pronunciations of these words were still heard. One of the many objections raised to Noah Webster's treatment of sounds and syllables in his speller was his realistic treatment of *-ion* as one syllable rather than the by-then-archaic two syllables. The older pronunciations were still heard in formal usage, such as in church services, and some people found Webster's realistic description offensive (Monaghan 1983, 36–40). (Today, the older pronunciations are still heard in some old hymns.) Other instances:

(Array 7-2)

artificial	judicial	resilience
condition	precious	vision

This extension of the meaning of *third* raises problems with the Suffix *-ion* Rule, which calls for a short *i* before *-ion* but for other vowels to be long, as in *nation, secretion, potion, pollution,* and the like. There is obviously a circularity in the description here, but for now it seems better to accept the circularity and to hope for some sort of straightening out later, when the processes are perhaps better understood.

The Third Syllable Rule explains not only many preemptions of the VCV pattern but also several apparently inconsistent word pairs, such as *gratitude* and *grateful.* The two are related semantically and formally, explicating to (grate + itude) and (grate + ful). But in *gratitude* the *a* spells a short vowel because the Third Syllable Rule preempts the VCV pattern, while in *grateful* the *a* spells a long vowel, since the head of the VCV string is not in the third syllable. (Words like *gratefully,* with long third-syllable vowels, will be discussed in 7.4.) Other pairs that show the shortening effects of the Third Syllable Rule on VCV strings:

(Array 7-3)

competitor, compete	penalty, penal
criminal, crime	precedent, precede
defamatory, defame	sacrilege, sacred
fabulous, fable	satisfy, sate
legacy, legal	situate, site
mediocrity, mediocre	solitude, solo
natural, nature	stipulate, stipend
navigate, navy	supremacy, supreme

Closely related instances:

credulous, creed	derision, deride
decision, decide	explanatory, explain
declamatory, declaim	granular, grain

According to the Suffix *-ity* Rule (see 5.2), the vowel preceding the suffix *-ity* is regularly stressed and short. Since this vowel is normally the third syllable from the end of the word, the Suffix *-ity* Rule can be seen as a special and stronger case of the more general Third Syllable Rule, stronger because it declares not only that the vowel in question will be short but also that it will be stressed, while the Third Syllable Rule declares only that the vowel will be short if it is stressed.

7.1.1   The Old English Third Syllable Rule

The Third Syllable Rule applies primarily to Romance adaptions, but it parallels another important development in Old English. Whereas primary stress in Romance words tended to be toward the end of the word, in Old English it tended to be toward the front. Old English regularly stressed the first syllable of the base; in nouns and adjectives it often stressed the prefix. When the stress fell on either the third or the fourth syllable back, there was a strong tendency to shorten the stressed syllable if it was originally long, or to keep it short if already so, regardless of the string it was heading (Jespersen [1909] 1954, 1:122–23; Mossé 1952, 18).

This "Old English Third Syllable Rule" affected the modern form of a few Old English words that have remained with us. Perhaps the most straightforward example is *holiday* (holẏ)i(day), from Old English *hāligdæg* (with a long vowel). Compare this with one of *holiday*'s primes, *holy*. In their Old English forms, *knowledge, breakfast,* and *husband* all had three syllables, were stressed on the third, and the stressed vowel of each was long. Compare *knowledge* with its prime *know, breakfast* with *break, husband* with *house* (in Old English, *hūs*), with a spelling change that reflects the shortening of the vowel. Such is also the case with *shepherd* (OE *scēaphyrde* and ME *sheepherde,* again with three syllables), and with *utter* (OE *ūtera*). There are also such related pairs as *white* and *Whitaker.* Other instances are *hover* (ME *hoveren*), *shadow* (ME *shadowe, schadewe;* OE *sceadue*), *widow* (ME *widewe;* OE *widuwe, weoduwe, wuduwe*), *lily* (ME *lilie,* OE *lilie,* Lat. *līlium*), *southern* (ME *southerne,* OE *sūtherne*), *thirteen* (ME *thrittene,* OE *thrēotīne*).

7.2 Preemptors of the Third Syllable Rule

Although the Third Syllable Rule preempts the VCV pattern, it can itself be preempted. Three of the important preemptors are the persistent long *u,* the V.V pattern, and the strong VCVV string.

7.2.1 Long *u*

The Third Syllable Rule will practically never produce an antepenultimate short *u* since, as has been pointed out (see 5.2.2.1), modern long *u*'s usually derive from earlier diphthongs that routinely resisted shortening. Among the dozens of instances of the long *u*'s preemption of the Third Syllable Rule are the following:

(Array 7-5)

ablution	duteous	luminous	ruminate
alluvial	enthusiast	mutilate	scrutiny
communion	fiducial	numeral	stupefy
connubial	fumigate	plutarchy	unicorn
cumulate	jubilee	protrusion	usual
cupola	junior	pugilist	uterine
cuticle	juniper	punitive	utilize
diffusion	locution	repudiate	uvular

All of the instances in array 7-5 can be explicated into bound stem plus suffix, such as (rudi + ment). Not too surprisingly, the long *u* is also persistent in words that explicate into free stems with a long *u*. A brief sample of instances:

(Array 7-6)

confusion (confus*é*)ion)	futurist (futur*é*)ist)
consumable (consum*é*)able)	humanness (human)ness)
crudity (crud*é*)ity)	humorist (humor)ist)
cubism (cub*é*)ism)	musical (music)al)
disputable (disput*é*)able)	pollution (pollut*é*)ion)
dutiable (dut*ý*)i + able)	usable (us*é*)able)

The only known holdouts to this pattern are *bunion, jugular, truculence, culinary, sugary,* and the quasi-compound *bugaboo.* Of these holdouts, *bugaboo* is obviously being affected by analogy with *bug,* which would appear to be its first element, or quasi-element. The complex *sugary* explicates to (sugar)y), although then the *u* spelling of /ù/ in the prime, *sugar,* raises questions. *Culinary* has variants, one with regular long *u,* one with short. The remaining three instances are clear-cut holdouts: *bunion, jugular,* and *truculence.*

7.2.2   V.V

The V.V Rule (4.2.1) states that when two adjacent vowels are separated by a syllable boundary, the first vowel will be long, as in *diet, chaos,* and *hiatus.* As Jespersen notes ([1909], 1954, 1:138), the V.V. Rule regularly preempts the Third Syllable Rule. Examples:

(**Array 7-7**)

dialect	leviathan	notoriety	psychiatrist
dietary	liable	parietal	quietude
friable	lioness	piety	reliable
iodine	maniacal	propriety	violate

7.2.3   The Strong VCVV String

The VCVV string tends to be tactically stronger than the VCVC string and is less likely to be preempted—as, for instance, by the Third Syllable Rule (Jespersen [1909] 1954, 1:140–41; Oswalt 1973, 12–14, 22).

In section 7.4 we will discuss the interplay between the Third Syllable Rule and conservative analogy. Here it might be useful to look at the interplay between conservative analogy and the VCVV string, with special emphasis on the impact of this interplay on the way the VCVV string preempts the Third Syllable Rule. Generally, conservative analogy is most potent in derivatives that explicate to free stems plus suffixes. In such derivatives the length of the vowel in the stem determines whether the head vowel in a VCVV string is long or short. If a derivative with a VCVV string explicates to a free stem in which the head vowel is short, then the head will remain short in the derivative, in spite of the strong VCVV string. Some instances:

(**Array 7-8**)

busiest (busy̸)i + est)	pitiable (pity̸)i + able)
copier (copy̸)i + er)	statuette (statue̸)ette)
gaseous (gas)eous)	studying (study)ing)
leviable (levy̸)i + able)	valuable (value̸)able)

The instances in array 7-8 support the pattern of the Third Syllable Rule and thus involve preemptions of the VCVV pattern. However, if a derivative with a VCVV string explicates to a free stem in which the head vowel is long, then the vowel will remain long in the derivative. Instances of this pattern:

(Array 7-9)

glazier (glaz*é* + ier)	savior (sav*é*)ior)
gracious (grac*é*)i + ous)	smokier (smok*y*)i + er)
hosier (hos*é*)ier)	spacious (spac*é*)i + ous)
notion (not*é*)ion)	traceable (trace)able)

In these instances the Third Syllable Rule has itself been preempted, by the strong VCVV string and conservative analogy.

In VCVV strings that do not explicate to a free stem, the head vowel is usually long, regardless of the demands of the Third Syllable Rule. The situation here depends on what letter the head vowel is: If it is *o* or (not too surprisingly) *u,* it will regularly be long. If it is *i,* it will regularly be short. If it is *a* or *e,* it will sometimes be long, sometimes short.

Instances of antepenultimate long *o* in VCVV strings that have pre-empted the Third Syllable Rule:

(Array 7-10)

ammonia	jovial	oleander	potion
commodious	linoleum	oleo	protean
erosion	motion	opiate	spoliate
euphonious	negotiable	opium	symposium
explosion	ocean	petroleum	utopia
ferocious	odious	phobia	zodiac

The only known holdout to this pattern is *innocuous,* perhaps via analogy with the related *noxious,* with its VCC string (*x* being tactically equivalent to CC).

The vowel *i* regularly resists the lengthening effect of the VCVV string, yielding instead to the shortening effects of the Third Syllable Rule:

(Array 7-11)

affiliate	filial	militia	religion
ambiguous	habitual	mimeograph	reptilian
ambition	hideous	miniature	resilience
amphibious	humiliate	minion	simian
bilious	idiom	minuet	sinuous
conciliate	incipient	opinion	trivial
condition	initial	pavilion	vicious
conspicuous	insidious	pigeon	vision
dominion	magician	piteous	vizier

The only known true holdout to this pattern is *piceous,* with a long *i.*

The situation with *e* and *a* as head vowels in VCVV strings is more complex than that for *o, u,* and *i.* Most words show antepenultimate long *a* or long *e* in VCVV strings; very few show the shortening effects of the Third Syllable Rule. Instances of antepenultimate long *a* in VCVV strings:

(Array 7-12)

alias	cranial	occasion	ration*
alien	crustacean	patience	salient
amiable	geranium	persuasion	sapience
audacious	glacial	plagiarize	satiate
avian	herbaceous	radiant	spontaneous
brazier	labial	radio	station
contagion	maniac	rapier	vocation

The words in array 7-12 sample a very large group that includes hundreds of words ending in *ation, acean, aceous,* and *acious.*

Instances of antepenultimate long *e* in VCVV strings that preempt the Third Syllable Rule:

(Array 7-13)

allegiance	deviate	lenience	premium
appreciable	ecclesiast	lesion	region
chameleon	expedient	magnesia	senior
cohesion	gardenia	median	specious
collegiate	genius	menial	tedium
comedian	ingredient	meteor	tragedian
convenient	legion	obedience	venial

Instances of antepenultimate short *a* and short *e* in VCVV strings that do not preempt the Third Syllable Rule:

(Array 7-14)

battalion	evacuate	jaguar	spaniel
cameo	evaluate	laniard*	tapioca
casual	fatuous	manioc	vacuole
caviar	flageolet	manual	vacuous
companion	gradual	retaliate	valiant
epaulet	ingenuous	precious	special
genuine	perpetual	renaissance	tenuous

Although the lists in array 7-12 through array 7-14 are far from exhaustive, they are representative, which means that words with long *a* and long *e* are more common than those with short *a* and *e*. This distribution illustrates the extra ability of the VCVV string to resist preemption by the Third Syllable Rule.

When they are added to stems that end with VC, certain suffixes regularly produce VCVV strings that preempt the Third Syllable Rule. A sampling of instances follows, with the suffixes *-ia, -ium, -ian:*

(Array 7-15)

ambrosia	aphasia	hyperemia	paraphernalia
amnesia	aphonia	hyperopia	paraplegia
analgesia	apologia	hypoglycemia	regalia
alluvium	epithalamium	paramecium	symposium
contagium	eulogium	pericranium	trapezium
effluvium	euphonium	proscenium	
antediluvian	bacchanalian	Jeffersonian	subclavian

Instances of the Third Syllable Rule's being preempted by the VCVV string in derivations that end in *i* plus the suffix *-al:*

(Array 7-16)

alluvial	diluvial	epithelial	monopodial
binomial	eluvial	interglacial	pericranial
connubial	epicranial	interstadial	remedial

Relative to arrays 7-15 and 7-16, persistent short *i*'s occur in the following preemptions of the VCVV string: *condominium, beneficial, prejudicial, superficial*. Persistent short *i*'s also occur in the compound suffixes *-ician* and *-itious:*

(Array 7-17)

academician	electrician	musician	phonetician
beautician	metaphysician	obstetrician	politician
clinician	mortician	pediatrician	technician
adventitious	nutritious	propitious	superstitious

7.3   A Special Instance of the Third Syllable Rule

In 6.3 it was argued that among trochaic words with VCV strings, direct Latin adaptions regularly have the long head vowel called for by the VCV pattern. However, there are a few Latin adaptions that pose some problems—namely, Latin trochees with nonregular short vowels in VCV strings that appear not to be affected by any shortening rule. Known instances:

(Array 7-18)

atom (L *atomus*)	monarch (L *monarcha*)
chemist (L *chimista*)	pageant (L *pagina*)
damask (L *damasco*)	promise (L *prōmissum*)
epoch (L *epocha*)	squalor (L *squālēre*)
minim (L *minimus*)	vacuum (L *vacuum*)

Jespersen puzzled over such words and suggested that the vowels in them may be short because of the action of the Third Syllable Rule on their Latin source words ([1909] 1954, 1:142). Each one has a trisyllabic Latin source, and the English school pronunciation of these source words would have led to stressed short antepenultimate vowels, owing to the Third Syllable Rule. Then, when the final syllables were removed in adapting the Latin words to English, they would all become English trochees with short, stressed vowels.

All in all, these few words are a troublesome lot: They complicate an otherwise useful distinction between French adaptions with short vowels in VCV trochees and Latin adaptions with long vowels. Jespersen's rationale for them—even if convincing—surely falls short of the ideal of accessibility. But for now it seems that we must accept it, and hope that further study will eventually lead to a better and more accessible explanation.

7.4   The Third Syllable Rule and Conservative Analogy

The last few chapters have dealt with tactics, which, like any part of a linguistic code, are the residue of history. They reveal the decisions and agreements that have been made, consciously and unconsciously, by the users of the language. These decisions and agreements become part of the abstract code of the language, which is conservative and relatively unchanging. But language is a human system. As people use the language, they must deal innovatively with new situations and problems. Thus, a major contention arises between the conservative code, which is resistant to change, and innovative performance, which encourages change. As a result of this contention, changes are made—in the code slowly, in the performance much more rapidly.

One of the major devices used by the performers of language is **analogy,** the quest for strands of sameness and unity within the ever-changing flow of performed language. Analogy can and does become fixed as part of the code, but it is in the flow and tumble of performed language that analogy is richest.

One kind of analogy that does become fixed in the code—especially in the orthographic code—is conservative analogy, that tendency not simply to treat certain elements as if they were alike but actually to attempt to make them more alike. Conservative analogy works toward that state of affairs in which functionally and semantically equivalent elements are spelled the same.

The influence of conservative analogy was included in the earlier discussion of regular VCV strings in trochaic words (6.3). The length of the vowel in a prime largely determines the length of the vowel in derivatives formed from that prime. This same influence was also discussed in terms of the interplay between the strong VCVV string and the Third Syllable Rule (7.2.3): The *a* in *laciest* is long in part because it is long in the prime *lace;* and the *o* in *copier* is short, in spite of the strong VCVV string, because the *o* in the prime *copy* is short. What is involved here is conservative analogy, which strives to keep the spelling and the pronunciation of functionally equivalent elements the same. (Compare this discussion with Oswalt's distinction between "Environmental Rules," which describe shortening and stress shifts, and "Basal Patterns," which follow the vowel quantity and stress pattern of the stem form and can be seen to result from conservative analogy [1973, 6].)

The Third Syllable Rule, like other tactical rules, is a product of historical demands, reflecting as it does, patterns from Old English and Latin. Its own contribution is variety, because of the changes it renders in vowel length. In *nation* and *national,* for instance, the additional phonological form with /a/ adds the variety. Thus, tactical features like the Third Syllable Rule, with their tendency toward variety, counter the tendency of conservative analogy toward sameness and simplicity.

As demonstrated earlier, contentions can and do arise between the demand of conservative analogy for simplicity and sameness and the demands of tactics to sustain the vowel lengths prescribed by patterns like VCC, VCV, VC#, and V.V. For instance, the *e* in the word *red* spells /e/, a short sound that is consistent with the VC# string. But if we add the suffix -*er,* a conflict arises between conservative analogy and the VCV rule: Via simple addition, *red* plus -*er* would be *reder, with a VCV pattern that makes the first *e* look as if it should be long.

At this point, however, conservative analogy is preempted by tactics. The spelling is complicated (by the insertion of a particle) in order to uphold the tactical VCC pattern: (red)d + er), *redder.* The insertion of the particle *d* here is an instance of a highly systematic process called twinning, which will be described in detail in chapter 9.

In the above example, the spelling is complicated in the service of tactical patterns. Tactics preempt conservative analogy. However, this is not always the case. There is a complex priority of preemption at work in the American English spelling system. Sometimes conservative analogy is preempted and sometimes it does the preempting.

For instance, conservative analogy preempts the Third Syllable Rule in words like *blamable, primary,* and *bravery,* all of which explicate to primes with long vowels: *blame, prime, brave.* The longer derived words retain—or conserve—the pronunciation of their primes, thus preempting the Third Syllable Rule. Other instances, including a full sampling from just one suffix, *-ery:*

(Array 7-19)

abidingly, abide	fatalism, fatal	notable, note
definable, define	favorite, favor	paganism, pagan
equalize, equal	nicety, nice	penalize, penal
apery, ape	finery, fine	popery, pope
bravery, brave	housewifery, housewife	roguery, rogue
bribery, bribe	knavery, knave	ropery, rope
cajolery, cajole	lacery, lace	scenery, scene
chicanery, chicane	machinery, machine	slavery, slave
drapery, drape	napery, nape	tracery, trace

It is difficult to predict whether the Third Syllable Rule or conservative analogy will prevail in a word, or exactly why. For instance, though the prime *penal* produces *penalize* with a variant pronunciation with long *e* via conservative analogy, it also produces *penalty* with a short *e* via the Third Syllable Rule. Compare also *prime, primary,* but *primitive; nation, nationwide,* but *national;* and *vine, vinery,* but *vinegar, vineyard.* In general, however, conservative analogy is most likely to be the controlling factor only if the immediate stem is free (especially a prime) and is a fairly common and well-established word. The Third Syllable Rule is most likely to be preemptive if the immediate stem is bound.

7.5   Some Tentative Conclusions

According to the Third Syllable Rule, if a word is stressed on the third or fourth (or, in certain instances of syllable reduction, the second) syllable from the end, the stressed vowel will be short, even if it heads a VCV string. This is especially true of Romance adaptions. Conservative analogy is a complicating factor here, but more or less regular holdouts to this general and important rule are long *u* and the heads of V.V and strong VCVV strings.

PROCEDURES

8 Silent Final *e* and Its Deletion Rule

8.1 The Functions of Silent Final *e*

The most general and reliable deletion rule in English spelling concerns the deletion of silent final *e*'s when adding suffixes that start with vowels. But in order to understand thoroughly the rule for deleting the final *e*, we need first to summarize the various functions served by silent final *e*'s in the American English spelling system.

8.1.1 Marking Long Vowels

The most common function of silent final *e* is to mark the long head vowel in a VC*e*# string, as illustrated in such pairs as *hat* and *hate, met* and *mete, rip* and *ripe, tom* and *tome, run* and *rune*. In this function the final *e* actually fills out a very special and reliable case of the more general VCV pattern (see 4.3.4.1). This use of final *e* was recognized and encouraged by sixteenth- and seventeenth-century orthographers such as Peter Levins, Richard Mulcaster, Edmund Coote, Christopher Cooper, Guy Miege, and John Evans (Brengelman 1980, 347–48).

Silent final *e* also marks a long head vowel in the less common, V*e*# string, as in *die, tee, roe, glue, dye* (see 4.2.3).

In general, a silent final *e* in a VC*e*# string *may* mark the preceding vowel as long. However, not all VC*e*# strings have long head vowels, for silent final *e* has six other functions, any one of which it may serve without marking a long vowel. As the arrays in this chapter show, a silent final *e* may serve two functions at once: marking a long vowel and serving one of the other six functions as well, as it does in words like *lace, huge,* and *bathe,* which contrast in both vowel and consonant sound with their counterparts without final *e: lac, hug,* and *bath.*

Two of the remaining six functions of silent final *e* are phonetic in nature, three are responses to tactical constraints, and one is a reflection of the etymological pressures at work in the American English spelling system.

8.1.2   Marking Soft *c* and Soft *g*

In word-final position the letters *c* and *g* have a hard sound—that is, /k/ and /g/ respectively, as in *lac* and *rag*. But when *c* and *g* are followed by a final *e,* they have a soft sound—that is, /s/ and /j/, as in *lace* or *rage*. Sixteenth- and seventeenth-century orthographers also encouraged this diacritical use of silent final *e* (Brengelman 1980, 348).

A final *e* marks an immediately preceding *c* as soft, whether the *c* is itself preceded by a vowel unigraph, a vowel digraph, or a consonant. Vowel unigraphs immediately preceding the *c* are regularly long if stressed, short or reduced if not stressed. Instances of silent final *e* marking soft *c:*

(Array 8-1)

acquiesce	choice	fleece	peace
advice	coerce	juice	resource
allegiance	deuce	mantelpiece	sauce
auspice	dulce	niece	science
caprice	efface	ounce	seduce

A final *e* also marks an immediately preceding *g* as soft, regardless of whether the *g* is preceded by a vowel unigraph, a vowel digraph, or a consonant. Though the pattern is not completely sharp (see, for instance, *allege*), a vowel unigraph immediately preceding the *g* is regularly long if stressed, short or reduced if not stressed:

(Array 8-2)

avenge	college	gauge	liege
bilge	deluge	gouge	prestige
bridge	derange	indulge	submerge
cage	disparage	knowledge	syringe

A variation of the final *ge* = /j/, or soft *g*, correspondence occurs in a small number of recent French adoptions, in which the *g* spells the French fricative /zh/:

(Array 8-3)

beige	fuselage	montage	rouge
cortege	massage	persiflage	sabotage

The contrast between regular English /j/ and the French /zh/ is shown in the two words *barrage* 'barrier', in which the /j/ is in an unstressed syllable, and *barrage* 'artillery fire', in which the /zh/ is stressed. Actually /zh/ and /j/ often vary as pronunciations of *g,* as in the variant pronunciations of words like *garage, prestige, camouflage*.

There are two known holdouts to the *ge* = /j/ correspondence. The first is *renege*, with a final /g/. There is a less common but more regular variant, *renig*. The second is *gamboge, camboge*, in which the *oge* is pronounced /ō/.

8.1.3 Marking Voiced *th*

Voiced and voiceless *th*, represented symbolically as /th̲/ and /th/ respectively, occur in *then* /th̲en/ and *thin* /thin/, or in *bathe* /bāth̲/ and *bath* /bath/. (For details on the voiced/voiceless distinction, see 3.2.2.) A final *e* will regularly mark an immediately preceding *th* as voiced, whether the *th* itself is preceded by a vowel unigraph or a vowel digraph. The preceding vowel is always long. Some examples:

(Array 8-4)

breathe	loathe	sheathe	wreathe
clothe	scathe	soothe	writhe
kithe	scythe	teethe	
lathe	seethe	tithe	

Because of the Principle of Preferred Regularity (see 1.6), this rule holds even for those few words that have variant pronunciations with voiced and voiceless *th: lithe, blithe, withe, enswathe*.

8.1.4 Insulating Nonterminative Letters

Silent final *e* is regularly used to insulate certain word endings because of constraints against ending free bases with a single *s* or *z* (see 3.4.1 and 3.4.2) and against ending words with *u* or *v*.

Silent final *e* is regularly used to insulate an otherwise final *u*, whether it is pronounced or silent:

(Array 8-5)

avenue	glue	plaque	statue
barbecue	misconstrue	pursue	tissue
clique	plague	queue	tongue

Silent final *e* is regularly used to insulate an otherwise final *v*, whether it is preceded by a long vowel, a short or reduced vowel, or a consonant. Words with short vowels in the VCe# string—for instance, *love* and *above*—exemplify again the tactical indeterminacy of *v* (see 6.4.2). Instances of final *e* insulating otherwise final *v*:

(Array 8-6)

achieve	cleave	groove	move
active	cove	gyve	naïve
calve	curve	have	shove
carve	evolve	live	sleeve
chive	gave	mauve	waive

As noted in 3.4.1, silent final *e* is regularly used to avoid ending a terminative base with a single *s* that is immediately preceded by a consonant, a vowel digraph, or an unstressed vowel unigraph. Some instances:

(Array 8-7)

bruise	douse	mortise	purpose
cheese	drowse	please	raise
clause	false	poise	sparse
corpse	goose	purchase	tense

The Final *z* Rule states that silent final *e* is also regularly used to avoid ending a free stem with a single *z*, whether it is immediately preceded by a consonant, a vowel digraph, or a long vowel digraph, as in *adze, gauze, gaze*. (For other examples see 3.4.2.)

8.1.5   Silent Final *e* and the Short Word Rule

In a few instances the presence of a silent final *e* can be explained in terms of the Short Word Rule, which constrains against words of less than three letters (for examples see 3.5). In such words the final *e* serves no other tactical function, nor does it mark any vowel or consonant sounds.

8.1.6   Fossil *e*'s

All of the silent final *e*'s discussed so far serve some phonetic or tactical purpose. There are, however, many silent final *e*'s that serve no such function at all and that are a part of words only for etymological reasons, echoing a foreign ending or a final *e* once, but no longer, pronounced. These fossils constitute a large and diverse group. But some useful subgroupings are possible.

8.1.6.1   French Fossil *e*'s

Among the thousands of French adoptions there are hundreds with silent final *e*'s that serve no phonetic or tactical purpose in American English spelling. In many cases they echo the French feminine marker, and since in French one does not pronounce most final consonants, the feminine final *e* often affects the pronunciation of the French words in which it occurs. For instance, French *tout* 'all' (masculine, without a final *e*) is pronounced /tù/. But *toute,* as in *toute-science* 'omniscience' (feminine, with a final *e* in effect insulating the otherwise final *t*), is pronounced /tùt/. Many French words adopted into English retain their French spellings even though the final *e* does not retain its French function and very often does not serve any normal English function. In Middle English most of these final *e*'s were regularly pronounced, but that is no longer the case.

Such final *e*'s, again, are motivated not by English tactics or phonetics but by etymological demand. The following is a small sample of the many different silent French final *e*'s in English:

(Array 8-8)

avalanche	comrade	grille	millionaire
bizarre	debutante	impasse	nocturne
brassiere	demitasse	lacrosse	romaine
cigarette	finesse	madame	troupe
clientele	gazelle	medicine	vaudeville

8.1.6.2 Native Fossil *e*'s

Old English was a heavily inflected language, with a complex system of inflectional suffixes. In the evolution from Old English to Middle English most of these inflections were sloughed off, in many cases simplifying and converging to a final *e* that in Middle English was regularly pronounced /ə/. In the evolution from Middle to Early Modern English this final *e* in most cases remained in the spelling, though it fell completely silent. The few native fossils left in English are:

(Array 8-9)

are	done	none	some
bade	forbade	one	
come	gone	shoe	

8.1.7 Some Special Cases
8.1.7.1 The Ending *le*

The sound cluster /əl/ in word-final position is quite common and has a number of different spellings, as in *able, yodel, modal, basil, missile, wishful, capitol*. About three-fourths of the time it is spelled *le*. In words in which the *l* is immediately preceded by a /t/ or /d/, the *le* spells not /əl/, but rather the syllabic *l*, a single sound symbolized as /ᵊl/ in *W3*, as in *gentle, riddle, rattle*—respectively /'jentᵊl/, /'ridᵊl/, /'ratᵊl/—without a full schwa sound.

The *le* ending is sometimes one of several different recognizable suffixes so spelled (Partridge [1958] 1983, 855). But *le* represents a large and complex historical process, as many different spellings and pronunciations of unstressed final syllables have converged toward the spelling *le* and the two simplified pronunciations /əl/ and /ᵊl/.

The largest single group of modern *le* words derives historically from words that in Middle English ended in an *le* that was usually pronounced /lə/. Today these *le* endings are pronounced either /əl/ or /ᵊl/. Examples include:

(Array 8-10)

article	couple	feeble	soluble
bible	disciple	obstacle	table
cable	double	particle	title
circle	example	probable	uncle

In Old and Middle English the suffix *-le* was used to form frequentive verbs, showing repeated action. Some instances:

(Array 8-11)

crumble (crumb)le)   sniffle (sniff)le)
crumple (crump)le)   snuggle (snug)le) = (snugg + le)
dazzle (daze)le) = (dazz + le)   sparkle (spark)le)
dribble (drib)le) = (dribb + le)   twinkle (twink)le)
joggle (jog)le) = (jogg + le)

The explications of the words in array 8-11 raise some questions. The *le* ending is involved in one of the strong, consistent complications to the VCV/VCC contrast, as seen in words like *rifle* and *riffle,* both of which technically have VCC strings, but contrast in terms of the length of the head vowel. (See, for example, 26.2.3.1 and 26.2.3.9 for more details.) The spellings in array 8-11 are all quite old, and it seems possible that because the VC*le*# string is tactically equivalent to a VCV string, the double consonants in words like *joggle* could explicate to some specialized application of the twinning rule—that is, (jog)g + le). However, in the explications offered in array 8-11 the choice was not to invoke a special use of twinning but rather to posit this small set of coforms: [*daze, dazz* +], [*snug, snugg* +], [*jog, jogg* +].

In Middle English the infinitive forms of verbs regularly ended in *-en,* as in *resemblen* and *anglen.* During the fourteenth century in the London dialect, which was to have much influence on the English Written Standard, the *n* disappeared in the pronunciation, and later in the spelling, of infinitives. This *n* deletion led to a number of modern verbs ending in *le:*

(Array 8-12)

angle	handle	sprinkle	tangle
assemble	muffle	strangle	tingle
bubble	resemble	struggle	tremble

Words that were spelled *le* and pronounced /lə/ in Middle English, including those with the frequentive suffix *-le* and infinitive verbs that were to lose their final *n*'s, provide a norm or target for other, more diverse analogical forms. Thus, other Middle English words with spellings other than *le* and with quite different final pronunciations often converged via analogy to the *le* group. The change to the *le* spelling was normally preceded by a change in which fuller vowels converged and reduced to /ə/; then, in time, the spelling also changed. Instances include the following:

(Array 8-13)

gentle (ME *gentil*)	pebble (ME *pibbil, puble*)
icicle (ME *isikel*)	puddle (ME *podel, pothel*)
idle (ME *idel*)	saddle (ME *sadel*)
little (ME *litel, lutel*)	testicle (ME *testicule*)
middle (ME *middel*)	thimble (ME *thymbyl*)

Certain back-formations and imitative formations show a similar convergence to the *le* ending:

(Array 8-14)

fondle (from *fondling*)	peddle (from *peddler*)
giggle (imitative)	swindle (from *swindler*)

Thus, the fossil final *e* in the ending *le* reflects a spelling that in Middle English would normally have been pronounced /lə/. When the final *e* fell silent in late Middle and Early Modern English words, the final *e* remained in the spellings as a fossil. Also, due to the pressures of analogy, certain modern words end in an *le* that quite likely developed late enough that the *e* was never pronounced at all.

8.1.7.2 The Suffix *-ate* and De-stressing

The description of final *e*'s that at first appear to have no phonetic or tactical function, and thus seem to be fossils, involves us in a widespread and normal process in English which might be called the **de-stressing** of regular VCV strings. Thus, the suffix *-ate* in the verb *approximate* receives at least secondary stress and is pronounced /āt/, consistent with the VCe# pattern. However, in the adjective *approximate* the suffix receives no stress, and its vowel thus reduces, at least partially, to /i/. This apparently nonregular pronunciation of *-ate* is related systematically to its regular /āt/ pronunciation in the verb *approximate*. The process of de-stressing, with its concomitant vowel reduction, accounts for the apparent nonregularity. *Approximate* exemplifies a sizable group of words that can be either verb or adjective-noun and that end in *-ate*:

(Array 8-15)

alternate	certificate	consummate	desolate
appropriate	confederate	degenerate	intimate
approximate	conglomerate	deliberate	mediate

This process of de-stressing and vowel reduction also accounts for the following adjectives and nouns with *-ate*, even though they do not have verb forms with the stressed long *a*:

(Array 8-16)

accurate	delicate	inaccurate	pomegranate
affectionate	fortunate	inordinate	private
commensurate	importunate	literate	senate

8.1.7.3 The Suffix *-ile*

Adjectives and nouns with the suffix *-ile* reveal the same effects of de-stressing and vowel reduction. Compare *virile, ductile,* and *fertile,* in which the suffix is pronounced, respectively, /il/, /əl/, and /ᵊl/.

Thus there is the following range of pronunciations of the suffix *-ile,* showing various degrees of reduction from the long *i* called for by the VCe# pattern when stressed. The pronunciation of the short and reduced vowels is given after each word. The words marked with an asterisk are more regularly pronounced with a long *i:*

(Array 8-17)

agile* /ə/	gracile /i/	projectile* /ə/	stabile* /i/
ductile /i/	habile /ə/	puerile* /i/	subtile /ᵊl/
facile /ə/, /i/	imbecile /ə/, /i/	reptile* /i/	tactile* /ə/
fertile /ᵊl/	infantile* /i/	sensile* /ə/	tensile* /ə/
fragile* /ə/	juvenile* /ə/	servile* /ə/	textile* /i/
futile* /ᵊl/	nubile* /i/	sessile* /ə/	virile /ə/

British English often has /ī/ where American English has /i/ or /ə/: *docile, febrile, sterile, missile, hostile, versatile. Mobile* and *labile* have variant pronunciations with the Continental long *i,* being pronounced /ə/, /ī/, /ē/.

8.1.7.4 The Suffix *-ine*

In American English there is a cluster of suffixes—and nonsuffix endings—spelled *ine* that sometimes contain seemingly anomalous final *e*'s because of the effects of de-stressing and vowel reduction. We can trace a gradation from regular long vowels in stressed *-ine*'s down through short *i*'s and schwas.

In stressed position—that is, with either primary or secondary stress on the *i*—the regular value of the *i* in *-ine* is either the English long *i,* as in *divine,* or the Continental long *i,* as in *machine.* Other instances (with /ī/ in the words at the top of the array, /ē/ in those in the middle, and variants with either sound in those at the bottom) include:

(Array 8-18)

alpine	calcine	concubine	supine
asinine	canine	feline	turpentine

benzine	latrine	marine	pristine
figurine	libertine	mezzanine	routine
grenadine	magazine	nicotine	vaccine
opaline	piscine	saline	

The pronunciation of *quinine* with /ē/ is chiefly British.

In many cases, de-stressing and vowel reduction lead to pronunciations with short *i*. The words below all have this short *i*, although those followed by asterisks have variant pronunciations with one of the two more regular long vowels:

(Array 8-19)

adamantine*	engine	lupine	sanguine
alkaline*	famine	margarine	turbine*
carmine*	feminine	masculine	urine
crystalline	genuine	medicine	uterine*
discipline	heroine	rapine	vulpine*

Full reduction to schwa in *-ine* words, as in *clandestine* and *intestine*, is quite rare. The *i* in the suffix combines with the *a* in the stem *coca* in *cocaine* to spell /ā/, and with the *e* in the stem *caffe+* in *caffeine* to spell /ē/.

8.1.7.5   The Suffix *-ure*

The suffix *-ure* usually derives from the French or Old French *-ure*, which in turn derives from the Latin *-ura*. Some English words were adapted directly from the Latin words with *-ura*. The suffix *-ure* has become an active English suffix, with several nouns formed in English by adding *-ure* to English verbs.

A number of words with endings other than the French *-ure* or the Latin *-ura* have converged via analogy to *-ure*. Examples of this convergence are *failure*, from an earlier *failer*, from Norman French *failer*; *pleasure*, from Old French *plesir, plaisir*; *treasure*, from Old French *tresor*; and *vulture*, from Old French *voltour*.

In all cases the final *e* in *-ure* is a fossil, serving no current phonetic or tactical function. For those words that came into English early enough, it was pronounced in earlier Middle English. But many *-ure* words were adopted into English late enough that the final *e* was no longer pronounced regularly. And, of course, in words like *composure* and *erasure*, English formations of the sixteenth and eighteenth centuries respectively, the final *e*'s were never pronounced.

Nouns ending with *-ure* consistently have penultimate stress, so that the suffix, unstressed, is reduced to /ər/, as in the instances presented so far, though there is an occasional variant pronunciation with /yŭr/—*tenure* being an example.

8.1.7.6 The Suffix -*ite*

Some instances of the suffix -*ite* illustrate the complicating effects of destressing and reduction on the role of final *e*. In some adjectives with sufficient stress on the final vowel, the regular long *i* occurs in the VCe# string:

(Array 8-20)

| erudite | finite | polite | tripartite |

But in most adjectives the *i* is de-stressed so that the vowel reduces to short *i*, as in:

(Array 8-21)

| apposite | definite | favorite | opposite |
| composite | exquisite | infinite | perquisite |

A suffix -*ite* also occurs in two kinds of nouns. First there are a large number of chemical and technical terms, all with the regular long *i*:

(Array 8-22)

anthracite	dynamite	lyddite	theodolite
Bakelite	ebonite	meteorite	thermite
bauxite	graphite	satellite	vulcanite

Second, there are a few personal nouns with the sense of "one from," again with the regular long *i*:

(Array 8-23)

| Chicagoite | cosmopolite | eremite | muscovite |

In these -*ite* nouns the pronunciation of the suffix is quite regular. The only known holdout to this group is the noun *granite,* with a short *i*. In *preterite* the +*ite* is a bound base, not a suffix—(preter + ite)—and there is a more regular spelling, *preterit.*

8.2 Silent Final *e* Deletion

In spite of the complexity of the functions performed by silent final *e*, the rule for deleting it when adding suffixes to stems is quite straightforward. Consider this combination:

make + ing = (maké)ing) = *making*

Simple addition here would lead to *makeing.* Since both the unaccepted
*makeing and the accepted *making* have the desired VCV pattern to mark
the long *a,* the deletion of the final *e* in the accepted spelling must be due
to something other than the demands of the VCV string. It appears to be
due to the systemic demand for economy; the only function of the silent
final *e* in *make* is to mark the long *a* by filling out the VCV pattern.
However, with the addition of the suffix *-ing,* the *e* is no longer needed; the
i can fill out the pattern. (It is relevant here that in *makes* the *e* is still
necessary to the VCV, so no *e* deletion takes place.) In a word like
making—and the thousands of others involving silent final *e* deletion—the
demand for systemic economy preempts conservative analogy and simple
addition. By the early seventeenth century British orthographers were
encouraging this deletion of the silent final *e* (Brengelman 1980, 348).

In thousands of other instances, and with very, very few holdouts, this
same procedure holds, so a preliminary statement of the final *e* deletion
rule can be made: A silent final *e* that marks a long vowel that heads a
VC*e*# string is deleted when a suffix is added that starts with a vowel.

This same rule covers nearly all other kinds of silent final *e.* For
instance, the final *e* that marks a voiced *th* is also deleted before a vowel:
tithing (tith*e*)ing) and *wreathing* (wreath*e*)ing), but *tithes* (tithe)s) and
wreathes (wreathe)s). The same is true of the final *e*'s that insulate otherwise final *s, z, u,* and *v: traipsing* (traips*e*)ing), but *traipses* (traipse)s);
bronzed (bronz*e*)ed), but *bronzes* (bronze)s); *plagued* (plagu*e*)ed), but
plagues (plague)s); *shelving* (shelv*e*)ing), but *shelves* (shelve)s). Even fossil *e*'s follow this same rule, being deleted before vowels but not before
consonants: *femininity* (feminin*e*)ity), but *femininely* (feminine)ly); *coming,* but *comes; doubling,* but *doubles.*

The one type of silent final *e* that occurs in VC*e*# strings and does not
quite fit the procedure described so far is the final *e* that marks a soft *c* or
soft *g.* There is *managing* and *manager,* with *e* deletion, but there is also
manageable, with no deletion. Similarly, there is *peaceable,* with no *e*
deletion, rather than *peacable,* with it. The reason here is easy to find.
Soft *c* and *g* can be marked only by a following *e, i,* or *y.* No other vowel
will do. Therefore, in words like *manageable* and *peaceable* the final *e* of
the stem is necessary to continue to mark the soft sound, since the suffix
in each case starts with an *a;* but in *manager* and *managing,* since the
suffixes start with *e* and *i,* vowels that mark soft sounds, the final *e* is no
longer needed and is thus, again following the demands of systemic
economy, deleted.

This complication is systematic and orderly and can be written into the
final *e* deletion rule: Delete a silent final *e* that marks a soft *g* or *c* only

when adding a suffix that starts with *e, i,* or *y;* but delete silent final *e*'s that mark long vowels in VC*e*# strings, or that mark voiced *th,* or that insulate *s, z, u,* and *v,* or that are fossils when adding a suffix that starts with any vowel.

8.2.1 Holdouts

This rule holds for thousands of words. The number of holdouts is extremely small. The only known cases of a failure to delete where the rule calls for deletion are the following:

(Array 8-24)

acreage	Since VC*r*V can be seen as more or less equivalent to VCV, *acreage,* (acre)age), rather than *acrage with deletion, is treated as a holdout to the general deletion rule.
clarkeite	After Frank W. Clarke; explicates to (clarke)ite).
jadeite	From French; explicates to (jade)ite).
lineage	Meaning "line of descent." Pronounced /'linēij/, it must explicate to (line)age), with no *e* deletion; compare *linage* (meaning "number of lines"), /'līnij/, with *e* deletion, which explicates to (lin*é*)age).
matey	Meaning "sociable, friendly." Explicates to (mate)y). Also a holdout, though *W3* calls it "chiefly British."
mileage	Would also be a holdout, (mile)age), although it has a less common but more regular variant spelling: *milage* (mil*é*)age).
pineal	The gland. Pronounced /'pinēəl/ or /'pīnēəl/, it explicates to (pine)al).
roseate	Pronounced /'rōzēət/ or /'rōzē,āt/, it explicates to (rose)ate).
singeing	Explicates to (singe)ing). Apparently departs from the rule due to a felt need to distinguish it from *singing* (sing)ing). Notice that in *hinging* (hing*é*)ing) there is *e* deletion according to the rule, apparently because there is no *(hing)ing) formation from which it needs to be distinguished. The present participle of *tinge* has variant spellings—*tinging* and *tingeing*—apparently because of an indistinct felt need to contrast that word with the rare participial form of *ting: tinging.*

Perhaps because it is identical in spelling and content to the free base *able,* the suffix *-able* is involved in a number of variant spellings—one with, one without, *e* deletion. If *able* is taken to be a free base, then words formed with it are considered to be compounds rather than complexes, and since compounds are regularly controlled by simple addition, the final *e* deletion rule does not apply. But if the *able* is taken to be a suffix, then the final *e* deletion rule does apply in the complexes formed thereby. In this study *able* is treated as a suffix. Thus, in the following list of variant spellings the Principle of Preferred Regularity (see 1.6) causes us to prefer the first form in each case as the more regular:

(Array 8-25)

hatable, hateable	movable, moveable	salable, saleable
likable, likeable	namable, nameable	sizable, sizeable
linable, lineable	ratable, rateable	tastable, tasteable
livable, liveable		

8.3   Silent Final *e* Deletion in Ve# Strings

The rule for deleting silent final *e* in stems that end with Ve# is more complex than that for the kinds of stems discussed so far. Again, deletion occurs only when the suffix starts with a vowel, but there are special cases that vary from the regular final *e* deletion.

In most cases when the stem ends with *ie* and a suffix is being added that starts with *i,* the *e* is deleted and the *i* in the stem is changed to *y* to avoid *ii* (see 3.3.1), as in:

(Array 8-26)

belying (beli̸e̸)y + ing)	tying (ti̸e̸)y + ing)
dying (di̸e̸)y + ing)	vying (vi̸e̸)y + ing)
lying (li̸e̸)y + ing)	

Hying also has the variant *hieing.* The verb *stymie, stymy,* has the variants *stymieing, stymying.* The rare verbs *sortie* and *birdie* have the nonregular *-ing* forms *sortieing* and *birdieing. Die,* meaning "to form or stamp, as with a die," has the form *dieing,* apparently out of the felt need to distinguish it from *dying.*

When a stem ends with *ue* and adds the suffix *-y* plus another suffix, the *e* is deleted and the *y* is changed to *i: gluier* (glu̸e̸)y̸)i + er) and *plaguily* (plagu̸e̸)y̸)i + ly). Notice that *gluey* is formed via simple addition rather than *e* deletion. *Plague* and *tongue,* however, have the variant adjective forms *plaguey* and *tonguey* via simple addition, and the more regular *plaguy* and *tonguy* via *e* deletion.

In addition to the few instances noted above, simple addition occurs somewhat nonregularly in the following limited cases involving stems ending with Ve#. When a stem ends with *ee* and adds a suffix beginning with *i* or *a,* the integrity of the digraph is maintained and there is no *e* deletion: (tree)ing), *treeing,* rather than *treing.* Other instances:

(Array 8-27)

absenteeism	fleeing	kneeing	seeing
agreeing	guaranteeing	refereeing	teeing
agreeable	foreseeable		

However, when the suffix starts with *e*, final *e* deletion occurs, to avoid the triplet *eee* (see 3.2.5): *agreed* rather than **agreeed*. Other instances: *freest* (free̸est), *foreseer* (foresee̸er), *teed* (tee̸ed).

When a stem ends with *oe* and a suffix starting with *i* is being added, the final *e* is not deleted:

(Array 8-28)

canoeist	hoeing	shoeing	toeing

Tiptoe has the participle *tiptoeing*. Normally, the reason for not deleting the *e* in these cases would appear to be the desire to avoid the potentially misleading sequence *oi*, which could be mistaken for the *oi* digraph spelling the diphthong /oi/, as it would in **hoing* or **toing*. Related variants: *bluing, blueing; bluish, blueish; truing, trueing*.

In all other instances stems ending with V*e#* delete the final *e* when adding a suffix that starts with any vowel:

(Array 8-29)

arguable (argue̸able)	lying (lye̸ing)
barbecuing (barbecue̸ing)	piquant (pique̸ant)
belied (belie̸ed)	prologuize (prologue̸ize)
bluest (blue̸est)	queuing (queue̸ing)
canoed (canoe̸ed)	residuum (residue̸um)
construable (construe̸able)	roguery (rogue̸ery)
continuous (continue̸ous)	shoed (shoe̸ed)
dyer (dye̸er)	subduable (subdue̸able)
fatigued (fatigue̸ed)	tier (tie̸er)
hoer (hoe̸er)	virtuous (virtue̸ous)

The foregoing, somewhat complex examples can be summarized as follows: When adding a suffix that starts with a vowel to a stem ending with V*e#*, cases of *ee* + *i*, *ee* + *a*, *oe* + *i*, or *ue* + *y* combine through simple addition; in all other cases the silent final *e* is deleted.

8.4 Suffixes Starting with Consonants

The rules for silent final *e* deletion apply only to cases in which the suffix starts with a vowel. If the suffix starts with a consonant, there is regularly no deletion. There are very, very few known holdouts to this condition:

(Array 8-30)

argument (argue̸)ment)	duly (due̸)ly)
awful (awe̸)ful)	truly (true̸)ly)

Compare with the nonregular *awful* the regular *awesome*.

In general, a final *e* that marks a soft *g* that is spelled *dg* is deleted before consonants, though there are always more regular, if less common, variants in which *e* deletion does not occur. For instance:

(Array 8-31)

abridg(e)ment	fledg(e)ling
acknowledg(e)ment	judg(e)ment

8.5   The Logic of Silent Final *e* Deletion

The deletion pattern for silent final *e*'s that mark long vowels in VC*e*# strings is clearly the analog that motivates the deletion patterns for silent final *e*'s serving all other functions. Thus the final *e*'s that mark the voiced *th* and those that insulate otherwise final *s, z, u,* and *v* all follow this same pattern, even though the logic for doing so is not immediately apparent. For instance, final *e*'s that insulate *u* and *v* are no longer needed when a suffix that starts with a vowel is added, since the *u* and *v* are no longer at word's end. So the final *e* can be deleted. However, the insulating final *e* is not needed when the suffix starts with a consonant either, so why is it not deleted? Why not *shelvs as well as *shelving?* Or *festivness as well as *festivity?* The answer appears to be the power of analogy working to converge the behavior of final *e*'s around the pattern set down by the final *e* that marks long vowels in VC*e*# strings.

Thus, too, the deletion rule for final *e*'s that mark soft *c* and soft *g* comes as close as it can to that for the long vowel marker in VC*e*# strings—within, that is, the constraints imposed by the tactical distribution rules for soft *c* and soft *g*. And thus, too, the deletion rule for final *e*'s that mark long vowels in V*e*# strings comes as close to the analog as it can, short of violating local constraints on certain potentially confusing pseudodigraphs. Thus, too, fossil *e*'s are deleted in the same way that silent final *e*'s marking long vowels in VC*e*# strings are deleted, even though there is no phonetic or tactical motivation intrinsic to fossil *e* deletion. Again the reason seems to be the power of analogy and the demand for unity and simplicity in the spelling system.

The development of the rule for deleting silent final *e*'s is an interesting example of how changes in a language—especially changes that occur in the sound system and in the spelling system, mismatched as they are in speed—put certain pressures on the language. These pressures lead to certain expectations in the users of the language, expectations about how the language will look and sound. In time, persistent expectations, realized and satisfied with a fair degree of reliability, become what we call **conventions.** A tactical rule is a convention carefully described. A procedural rule, such as that controlling the deletion of silent final *e*'s, is a means of maintaining a convention. In each case, expectation becomes convention, which leads to rule.

9 The Twinning Rule

9.1 Introduction to Twinning

When a suffix that starts with a vowel is added to a free stem that ends in a VC# string, if the stress stays on the VC# string after the suffix is added, the final consonant of the stem is regularly twinned:

occur + *ence* = *occur* + *r* + *ence* = *occurrence*, (occur)r + ence)

Although there are variant spellings with twinning in some polysyllabic stems that end in unstressed vowels, the regular pattern calls for twinning only if the final vowel of the stem is stressed both before and after the suffix is added. Some apparent cases of unstressed twinning—for instance, in *tonsillitis*, which might first seem to explicate to *(tonsil)l + itis)—are actually not twinnings at all, but rather instances of simple addition involving cosets that contain one free form that ends with a single consonant and one nonterminative that ends with two, as in [*tonsil, tonsill +*] (see 2.2.7). Thus, the proper explication of *tonsillitis* is (tonsil + itis)—via simple addition rather than twinning. Some apparent cases of nonregular nontwinning—for instance, *alcoholic*, which might legitimately be considered to be more regularly spelled *alcohollic, or *octopuses*, which might be thought to be more regularly spelled *octopusses, are brought to regularity by way of two subrules, or actually by two clauses added to the main Twinning Rule: (1) the Twinning Rule does not apply if the suffix involved is one of the shortening suffixes, such as -*ic* or -*ity* (see chapter 5); and (2) the Twinning Rule does not apply if there are accepted variant pronunciations in which the final vowel of the stem is not stressed. Thus, *alcoholic* is not affected by the Twinning Rule because of the suffix -*ic*, nor is *octopuses*, which has a variant pronunciation in which the final vowel of the stem is not stressed. There are in fact very few true holdouts to the Twinning Rule, holdouts of either type: twinnings where we would not expect them (a very, very small group) and nontwinnings where the rule would prescribe twinnings (a somewhat larger group).

In chapters 1 and 7 we discussed cases in which orthographic processes must resolve sometimes contending demands within the spelling system, especially contentions between the demands of tactics and those of conservative analogy. The process of twinning is a product of the expectations set up in English by tactical strings, patterns, and rules. In a word that ends with a single consonant preceded by a stressed single vowel, the vowel will be short, because of the VC# pattern (see 4.2.2). But when a suffix that begins with a vowel is added to such a word, the vowel in the suffix creates a VCV string that makes the stem vowel look as if it should be long. For instance, *rat* has a short vowel because of the VC# string, but simply adding *rat* and *-ed* creates *rated, with the *a* now the head of a VCV string and thus looking as if it should be long. *Rated* spells /'rātid/, not /'ratid/. In order for the stem vowel to continue looking short, two consonants must follow it before the upcoming suffixal vowel. Thus the final consonant of the stem is twinned, creating a VCC string:

$$rat + ed = rat + t + ed = \underset{\text{vcc}}{ratted} \ (\text{rat})\text{t} + \text{ed})$$

But although the process of twinning is motivated by the cuing of short and long vowels by the VCC and VCV strings, there are problems with describing twinning in terms of vowel sounds. For instance, a word such as *controller* obviously entails twinning: (control)l + er). But the final vowel in the stem is not short. Similarly, *occurrence* involves twinning—(occur)r + ence)—but it is not clear how we can say that the *u* in *occur* and *occurrence* spells a short vowel. So although the initial motivation for twinning is to maintain a clear graphic representation of a short vowel, the process has grown beyond this basic motivation. Therefore, in the following discussion we will describe the process of twinning insofar as possible without appealing to the idea of short and long vowels.

9.2   Instances of the Rule

Initially, we can describe the twinning process, or state the Twinning Rule, as follows: The final consonant of a stem is twinned when a suffix is added that starts with a vowel, and the stem ends with VC, and there is stress on the final vowel of the stem before and after the suffix is added. This description sets down three conditions, all of which must be satisfied if twinning is to occur: first, the suffix being added must start with a vowel; second, the stem must end in the string VC; third, there must be stress on the final vowel of the stem before the suffix is added, and the stress must stay on that same vowel after the suffix has been added.

The first condition explains such contrasting pairs as those shown in array 9-1. In these pairs the suffix of the first word starts with a vowel and twinning does occur, but the suffix of the second word starts with a consonant and there is no twinning:

(Array 9-1)

droppings, droplet	inner, inward	sunny, sunless
fatten, fats	reddish, redness	twinning, twinship
goddess, godling	shipper, shipment	wedded, wedlock
hottest, hotly	sinned, sinful	whippy, whipster

The second condition, that the stem must end with VC, must be interpreted to mean that the stem must end with a single vowel letter followed by a single consonant letter. It cannot end in VVC. Words that end in VVC do not undergo twinning. For instance:

(Array 9-2)

bloody, not *blooddy	deadest, not *deaddest
broadest, not *broaddest	deafen, not *deaffen
dauber, not *daubber	fraudulent, not *frauddulent

It is also important to note that the stem must end in a single consonant letter. It cannot end in two or more consonant letters, even though only one of the letters is pronounced. Thus, it is:

(Array 9-3)

bomber, not *bombber or *bombmber
calmative, not *calmmative or *calmlmative
talking, not *talkking or *talklking
yachting, not *yachtting or *yachtchting

Also, the stem cannot end in a consonant digraph spelling a single sound:

(Array 9-4)

graphic, not *graphhic or *graphphic
rocky, not *rockky or *rockcky
wished, not *wishhed or *wishshed

By the same token the single consonant letter that ends the stem must spell a single sound. The letter x is the only consonant letter that spells a sound cluster—/ks/ or /gz/. In a way x is the mirror image of di- and trigraphs like *sh* in *fishing* or *cht* in *yachting,* in which one sound is represented by a string of two or more letters. Thus, a final x is never twinned, not even when all other conditions for twinning are satisfied:

(Array 9-5)

boxer, not *boxxer	foxy, not *foxxy	sexes, not *sexxes
fixed, not *fixxed	oxen, not *oxxen	taxing, not *taxxing

The third condition that must be met in order for twinning to occur states that there must be stress on the final vowel of the stem both before and after the suffix is added. In the following words twinning does not occur, because the stress is not on the final vowel of the stem either before or after the suffix is added:

(Array 9-6)

final, finalist	profit, profiting	syndic, syndicate
limit, limited	symbol, symbolism	system, systemize

In the following words twinning does not occur, because although the stress is on the final vowel of the stem after the suffix is added, it was not there before the suffix was added:

(Array 9-7)

eccentric, eccentricity	inhibit, inhibition	solid, solidify
final, finality	magnet, magnetic	symbol, symbolic

In the following words twinning does not occur, because although the stress is on the final vowel of the stem before the suffix is added, when the suffix is added, the stress shifts off of that vowel:

(Array 9-8)

antiphon, antiphony	eponym, eponymy	refer, referee
defer, deference	prolog, prologize	synonym, synonymize

Prologize explicates to (prolog)ize). If we assume the variant term *prologue,* we confront an anomalous *u-* deletion: (prologuė)ize).

Twinning does occur in words such as the following because all three of the above conditions are met:

(Array 9-9)

abhor, abhorrent	control, controller	recur, recurrence
annul, annulled	defer, deferral	refer, referring

If the stem has only one sounded vowel—only one syllable—the assumption is that it has stress, so if the other two conditions are met, the final consonants of monosyllabic stems will twin:

(Array 9-10)

bat, batter	gab, gabbed	in, inning
cad, caddish	hot, hotter	job, jobber
dog, dogged	if, iffy	lob, lobbing

The Twinning Rule does not hold when another free stem, rather than a suffix, is added to a free stem, making a compound word. As usual, compounds are formed through simple addition. Compounds in which the first constituent ends with VC# and the second begins with a vowel are quite rare, but nonhyphenated examples include:

(Array 9-11)

bigeye	(big)(eye); cf. complexes involving twinning, such as *biggish.*
dropout	(drop)(out); cf. complexes like *dropping.*
redeye	(red)(eye), "a fish"; cf. complexes like *reddest.* The other compound *red-eye* (meaning "whiskey") has the hyphen.
runaway	(run)(away); cf. complexes like *runner.*
stopover	(stop)(over); cf. complexes like *stopper.*
sunup	(sun)(up); cf. complexes like *sunny.*

Other instances of compounds without twinning are *forever, whatever, whenever,* and the like.

The Twinning Rule applies to free stems. It does not apply to stems that are bound. Thus it does not apply to stems that end with nonterminative bases. Some instances:

(Array 9-12)

condominium	(condomin + ium), not *condominnium
conspicuous	(conspic + u + ous), not *conspiccuous
critic	(crit + ic), not *crittic
deficient	(defic + i + ent), not *deficcient
ligament	(lig + a + ment), not *liggament
predicament	(predic + a + ment), not *prediccament
recidivism	(recid + ivism), not *reciddivism
speculate	(spec + ulate), not *specculate

In stems that carry secondary stress on the final vowel, variant spellings are quite common, one with twinning, one without. For instance, for the stem *diagram,* with secondary stress on the final vowel, there are the variant inflected forms *diagrammed* and *diagramed.* Since the initial motivation for twinning was to cue short vowels, and since secondary stress is enough to maintain a full short vowel sound (the final vowel in *diagram* spells short *a,* not schwa), the more regular form is that with twinning. Thus, we can restate the Twinning Rule to specify "at least secondary stress on the final vowel of the stem, both before and after the suffix is added."

The Principle of Preferred Regularity leads us to prefer the variant with twinning when suffixes that start with vowels are added to stems that end with VC# and have secondary stress on their final vowels, such as *combat, program, kidnap.* Thus we prefer *combatted* to *combated, programmer* to *programer, kidnapping* to *kidnaping.*

In dozens of cases when the inflectional suffixes *-ed* and *-ing* are added to verb stems that end with an unstressed syllable, there are variant spellings, one with twinning, one without. In nearly every case the final consonant involved is *l*. Dictionaries show the past participle of *apparel* as either *appareled* or *apparelled*. Emery's *Variant Spellings in Modern American Dictionaries* (1973) lists the following verb stems with unstressed final vowels and the kind of variant spellings represented by the verb *apparel:*

(Array 9-13)

barrel	flannel	metal	sentinel
bedevil	frivol	model	shovel
bevel	funnel	nickel	shrivel
cancel	gambol	panel	signal
carol	gavel	parcel	snivel
cavil	gospel	pedal	spiral
channel	gravel	pedestal	squirrel
chisel	grovel	pencil	stencil
corbel	impanel	peril	swivel
counsel	kennel	petal	symbol
cudgel	label	pistol	tassel
devil	laurel	pommel, pummel	tinsel
dishevel	level	quarrel	total
drivel	libel	ravel	trammel
emperil	marshal	revel	travel
enamel	marvel	rival	tunnel
equal	medal	sandal	yodel

Verb stems that end in something other than *l* but that have similar variants with *-ed* and *-ing* are:

(Array 9-14)

benefit	chorus	focus	hocus-pocus
brevet	facet	gossip	worship

The Principle of Preferred Regularity leads us to prefer the variants in *-ed* and *-ing* for the verbs in arrays 9-13 and 9-14 that do *not* exhibit twinning. Thus *barreled* is preferred to *barrelled,* since *barreled* is more regular, the requirement for stem-final stress not being satisfied in this and similar words.

Many verbs with unstressed final syllables also have variants when the derivational suffix *-er* 'one that does' is added, as in *beveler* and *beveller.* Again the Principle of Preferred Regularity leads one to prefer the variant without twinning when *-er* is added to such verbs, as in the following, all of which, like *beveler,* have recorded variants with twinning:

(Array 9-15)

caroler	gaveler	metaler	sniveler
caviler	gospeler	modeler	stenciler
channeler	groveler	quarreler	teetotaler
chiseler	labeler	raveler	traveler
deviler	leveler	reveler	worshiper
driveler	libeler	shoveler	yodeler
focuser	marshaler	signaler	

Related to this group are *pistoleer, counselor,* and *councilor.* Other words that have variants with unstressed twinning:

(Array 9-16)

chancelor	eviler	petaled	tranquilize
corbeling	evilest	portaled	turbaned
crenelated	medalist	sequined	

All of the words in arrays 9-13 through 9-16, though they have nonregular variant spellings exhibiting twinning, also have more regular ones involving simple addition, so we can invoke the Principle of Preferred Regularity to bring them into pattern. It is pertinent here that when suffixes other than the inflections *-ed, -ing, -er, -est,* and the derivational suffix *-er* are added to these stems, the words thus derived are nearly always regular, which is to say that they are formed through simple addition rather than through twinning. Thus we have the following derivatives, all of which are formed from the stems listed in arrays 9-13 through 9-16, and all of which involve regular simple addition:

(Array 9-17)

barrelage	gospelize	panelist	stencilize
channelize	gossipy	parallelism	symbolist
equalize	gravelish	perilous	teetotalism
flannelette	modelist	petaloid	totalitarian
focusable	nickeliferous	signalize	worshipable
frivolous	nickeline	spiralium	

The condition requiring stress on the final syllable of the stem distinguishes the Twinning Rule as it works in American English from its counterpart in British English. Unstressed twinnings are typical of British English but not of American. Some American English dictionaries mark such unstressed twinnings as "chiefly British." But many do not make such a national distinction, and in a few cases the dictionaries give as a first entry a form that exhibits unstressed twinning. It is worth noting that American English dictionaries do not always agree about the ordering of variant spellings, nor do they agree on the use of the "chiefly British" label (Emery 1973, 3–5, 16–21).

All such instances of unstressed twinning, even those in which the nonregular unstressed twinning appears in the first or most frequent variant given in the dictionaries, still have more regular variants without twinning, and thus can be brought into pattern by invoking the Principle of Preferred Regularity.

9.3   An Extended Example: +*fer* Words

The Twinning Rule can be clearly illustrated using the group of words that contain the bound terminative base +*fer* 'carry'. The group contains eleven two-syllable verb stems—six with stress on the final vowel: *confer, defer*[1], *defer*[2], *infer, prefer, refer.* But in four the stress is on the prefix: *differ, offer, proffer, suffer.* These four are unusual since two-syllable verbs regularly stress the final syllable, as, for example, in the noun-verb stress pairs—that is, pairs in which the noun is stressed early, the verb late: *cónvict* the noun versus *convíct* the verb; also *próduce, prodúce; óverrun, overrún.* There is a strong tendency in English for the vowel before a doublet consonant, such as the *ff* in *differ, offer, proffer,* and *suffer,* to be short and stressed. The unstressed schwa normally does not precede a doublet consonant. The chapters of this book that deal with sound-to-spelling correspondences recurrently illustrate the pattern in which a doublet consonant follows immediately a stressed, short vowel, but not schwa, while a single consonant very often follows a schwa. Thus it seems likely that the pressure of this pattern encourages the rather unusual prefix stressing in the above four verbs.

Since the Twinning Rule holds that stress must fall on the final vowel of the stem before and after the suffix is added, we would expect that none of these four would ever undergo twinning, which proves to be the case:

(Array 9-18)

differ	offer	proffer	suffer
differed	offered	proffered	suffered
differing	offering	proffering	suffering
difference	offerer	profferer	sufferer
different	offeror		sufferable
differential			sufferance
differentiate			
differentia			

Because of the lack of stress on the final vowel of the stem, none of the words in array 9-18 should have involved twinning, and the rule held with perfect regularity. However, in the following three verbs (upper half of the array) we would expect twinning, since in each the stress is on the final vowel:

(Array 9-19)

defer[1]	defer[2]	prefer
deferred	deferred	preferred
deferring	deferring	preferring
deferrer		preferrer
deferrable		
deferent	deferent	preferable
	deference	preference
	deferential	preferential

But twinning does not occur when the stress shifts off of the final vowel of the stem when the suffix is added, as in the words in the lower half of the array. The fairly common, but unrecognized, pronunciation of *preferable* with stress on the +*fer* produces a nonregular spelling. With that pronunciation the *r* should twin, as it does in *deferrable*.

The base +*fer* also occurs in medial position in complexes that do not contain free stems: *afferent, efferent, vociferous*. In these and similar cases the *r* does not twin even when a suffix beginning with a vowel is added, because the stems are not free and there is no stress on the +*fer*.

So far all of the +*fer* words and derivatives that have been discussed have been completely regular as far as the Twinning Rule is concerned. The following three verbs also usually add on suffixes in a regular fashion, but there are some complications:

(Array 9-20)

confer	infer	refer
conferred	inferred	referred
conferring	inferring	referring
conferral		referral
conferrer		referrer
conferrable		
conference	inference	reference
conferential	inferential	referential
		referendum

The words in this array are all regular as far as twinning is concerned. There are, in addition, the nonregular variants *conferree,* and *inferable* and *inferably,* both with stress on +*fer. Conferree* has the regular variant *conferee,* and *W3* shows a more regular variant of *inferable—inferrible—* though no *inferribly.* Both *referable* and *referent* have variant pronunciations with stress on the +*fer* rather than on *re-*, which would imply twinning and thus two *r*'s. Each of the lapses from the regular pattern described by the Twinning Rule has involved variant pronunciations or spellings. The Principle of Preferred Regularity brings all such cases into pattern.

The one remaining +*fer* verb poses more serious problems and illustrates some of the complexities of the interplay between sound and spelling. The verb is *transfer*, and the problems with it flow from the fact that its noun and verb forms have two accepted pronunciations—one with stress on the first vowel, one with stress on the final. Obviously this can be expected to cause some indecision about twinning, and this indecision is reflected in the word's derivatives. The inflected forms are regular if we assume that the verb is being stressed on the final syllable: *transferred, transferring*. In some cases the stress is not on the final syllable of the stem after the suffix is added, and no twinning occurs. Again, the pattern is regular: *transferee, transferential*.

However, in some cases the stress remains on the final vowel of the stem, and we get nonregular variant spellings: regular *transferral*, but nonregular *transferal; transferrer* and *transferer*. When pronounced to stress the first syllable, *transference* is regular, but when pronounced to stress the +*fer*, it becomes nonregular. And finally, both *transferable* and *transferability* are nonregular, having at least secondary stress on the +*fer*. *W3* shows the more regular variant *transferrable*.

Again, each case of an apparent lapse from the regular pattern of the Twinning Rule involves either variant pronunciations or variant spellings—one of which is nonregular, one regular. And again the Principle of Preferred Regularity brings things into pattern—resulting in a regular array of twinnings and nontwinnings among these +*fer* words.

9.4   Apparent Nonregular Twinnings

9.4.1   Nonterminative Bound Bases

Because of the stress condition in the Twinning Rule, words like *metalloid* and *medallion* would at first appear to contain nonregular instances of twinning. However, it seems better to explicate these words as not involving twinning at all, but rather as containing nonterminative coforms with final *ll:* (metall + oid) and (medall + ion), thus positing the cosets [*metal, metall*+] and [*medal, medall*+] (see 2.2.7). In such cases the *ll* in the bound form reflects the Latin source, while the single *l* in the free form reflects the simplifying influence of the English constraint against ending polysyllabic simplexes and complexes with *ll*. Other such cosets are [*crystal, crystall+*], [*cancel, cancell+*], [*chancel, chancell+*], [*excel, excell+*], [*tonsil, tonsill+*], [*coral, corall+*], [*pencil, pencill+*], [*pistil, pistill+*]. Related sets include [*pen, penn+*], [*gem, gemm+*], [*tan, tann+*], [*sac, sacc+*]. In general, the bound forms in these sets are more conservative, reflecting their Romance ancestry. The free forms have been more integrated to the English spelling system. The historical progression appears to have been one of eliminating the word-final *ll*'s, in keeping with English tactics. The longer derived forms would tend to keep the Latin *ll* since it is not in actual word-final position.

As might be expected, the free forms tend to be used in a fairly wide range of registers while the less integrated, bound forms tend to be used primarily in words that belong to more formal and technical registers (see Brengelman 1971). Positing these nonterminative coforms makes it possible to explicate such words as the following, which would all be anomalous if explicated to the free form:

(Array 9-21)

cancellate (cancell + ate)	pencilliform (pencill + i + form)
cancellous (cancell + ous)	pennatularian (penn + atularian)
coralloid (corall + oid)	pistillate (pistill + ate)
crystallic (crystall + ic)	saccular (sacc + ular)
crystalliferous (crystall + i + ferous)	tannic (tann + ic)
excellency (excell + ency)	tannometer (tann + o(meter)
excellent (excell + ent)	tonsillectomy (tonsill + ectomy)
gemmiparous (gemm + i + parous)	tonsillitis (tonsill + itis)

The *ll* in *excellent* reflects an earlier stage in English spelling: *excel* was consistently spelled *excell* up to the nineteenth century, when it was simplified to *excel* in keeping with the constraint against ending polysyllables with double *l*. Thus, historically, the spelling *excellent* is an instance of simple addition, as is recognized in the set [*excel, excell+*]. The set [*parcel, parcell+*], necessary to explicate *parcellation*, has a similar historical source: *parcel* was commonly spelled with *ll* up through the eighteenth century. The nineteenth-century formation *parcellation* can be seen as reflecting earlier English spelling, or it can be seen as a very conservative instance of British twinning, parallel to, say, *cancellation*, so rare that there has been no pressure to recognize a more regular variant spelling. This explanation would hold, too, for the anomalous *ll* in *penciller*, which is without a more regular variant. There appears to be no direct Latin source for *penciller;* it was an eighteenth-century English formation from *pencil* and *-er*. Curiously, the *OED*, but not *W3*, shows the more regular variant *penciler*.

A similar set is [+ *glot, glott* +], as in *polyglot*, but *glottal* and *polyglot-*

tic. Closely related is [*flock, flocc +*], as in *flocculent.* Also related are cosets that contain a terminative bound base ending *r* and a nonterminative ending *rr,* as in the following:

(Array 9-22)

> [+ cur, curr +], as in *concur* (but *current*)
> [+ hor, horr +], as in *abhor* (but *horrible*)
> [+ ter¹, terr + ¹], as in *inter* (but *terrace*)
> [+ ter², terr + ²], as in *deter* (but *terror*)

Some apparent unstressed twinnings in unintegrated foreign spellings can also be brought to pattern by positing cosets in this way, although there are some real questions to be asked about how far one should go in setting up these ad hoc solutions to sticky problems. In any case, the *nn's* in such French adoptions as *questionnaire, legionnaire,* and *personnel* cannot be accounted for by the Twinning Rule. They require either cosets or the simple admission that they do not follow the rule. For now it seems best to posit the cosets. Thus we get such instances as the following:

(Array 9-23)

> duello   (duell + o) [*duel, duell +*]
> personnel   (personn + el) [*person, personn +*]
> raillery   (raill + ery) [*rail, raill +*]

The related words *mayonnaise* and *surveillance* explicate to bound bases: (mayonn + aise) and (surveill + ance). For *questionnaire* and *legionnaire* see 2.3.6.

9.4.2 Suffix Rules

In chapter 5 we discussed the group of suffixes that are regularly preceded by a stressed short vowel regardless of whether the tactical string VCV is involved. Such is the strength of this vowel-shortening effect that these suffix rules regularly preempt the Twinning Rule. For instance, when the suffix *-ic* is added to a free stem ending in a stressed VC#, the Twinning Rule is preempted, as in the following instances:

(Array 9-24)

> acrobatic   (acrobat)ic), not *acrobattic
> alcoholic   (alcohol)ic), not *alcohollic
> alphabetic   (alphabet)ic), not *alphabettic
> antiphonic   (antiphon)ic), not *antiphonnic
> democratic   (democrat)ic), not *democrattic
> diplomatic   (diplomat)ic), not *diplomattic
> epithetic   (epithet)ic), not *epithettic
> homonymic   (homonym)ic), not *homonymmic
> panic   (pan)ic), not *pannic
> photostatic   (photostat)ic), not *photostattic

In a few words -*ic* is preceded by a doublet consonant, but in no case is it produced by twinning. Words like *metallic*, as we have seen, explicate via simple addition to (metall + ic). *Witticism*, which formally appears to explicate to *(wit)t + ic + ism), actually is a nonce formation that consists of *witty* (which earns its twin *tt*'s honestly) plus the nonce ending *cism*, as if clipped from words like *criticism*. Thus *witticism* explicates to (wit)t + y̸)i + cism).

There are fewer instances of the -*ity* suffix preempting the Twinning Rule than there are of -*ic* doing so, but it still appears to be a regular subgroup: *homonymity, infidelity, synonymity,* which explicate to (homonym)ity), (infidel)ity), (synonym)ity).

Beyond this there are few instances of stems that meet the conditions of twinning that affix one of the other shortening suffixes. The only known remaining instance is *banish,* (ban)ish), which involves the suffix -*ish²* rule.

The preemption of the Twinning Rules by -*ic* and -*ity* can be seen to be a result of conservative analogy. (For more on conservative analogy see 1.4 and 7.4.) These suffixes draw the primary stress to the immediately preceding vowel, as in *symbolic* and *totality.* When either of these suffixes is added to a stem that ends in an unstressed VC# string, the addition of the suffix shifts the stress onto the VC# string in the stem, as in *symbol* versus *symbolic.* This stress-shifting creates a relatively large number of words in which -*ic* and -*ity* especially are preceded by stressed final vowels in stems ending with VC but without twinning, since the stem-final VC# string was not stressed before the suffix was added. Historically, this fact may have led to a regular expectation of nontwinning before these two suffixes, an expectation that affected the formation of words in which the stress placement was such that twinning should have occurred but did not, as in *antiphonic* and *synonymity.*

9.4.3 Stress-waver

The role of stress-waver was touched on in earlier discussions of variant pronunciations and spellings and their effects on the Twinning Rule. The derivatives of stem verbs that contain the base +*fer* are a case in point (see 9.3). Another example involves the verb *benefit.* The *AHD* shows no stress on the final vowel in *benefit,* and thus spells the inflected forms *benefited* and *benefiting,* without twinning. But *W3* shows variant pronunciations—one with no stress on the final vowel, one with secondary stress. And, consistently enough, *W3* also shows, variant spellings, one without twinning (appropriate to the first pronunciation), the other with twinning (appropriate to the second pronunciation).

Program offers a similar example. Its two variant pronunciations, one with and one without stress on the final VC# string, lead to a complete set of variant spellings of its derivatives, one set with single *m*, one with *mm: programed, programmed; programing, programming; programistic, programmistic; programatic, programmatic; programer, programmer.*

In some instances stress-waver results in a spelling without twinning where the rule would normally call for at least a variant with twinning. An example is *violinist*, (violin)ist), without twinning. One rare pronunciation of *violin* has no stress on the final VC# and is thus consistent with the spelling of *violinist*. But the more common pronunciation, with the VC# bearing secondary stress, is inconsistent with the spelling. The unaccepted *violinnist would actually be more regular in terms of the Twinning Rule, given the more common pronunciation. Another example is *octopuses*, one pronunciation of which would support the spelling *octopusses. *Quadrupedal*, (quadruped)al), is another example; it has four pronunciations, two with stress on the *e*, two without. The two stressed pronunciations would support the spelling *quadrupeddal. It would be possible to plead the effects of a conservative analogy here with *pedal*. *Epithetize* and *surplusage* both have variant pronunciations that stress the final VC# in the stem and thus could support the unaccepted spellings *epithettize and *surplussage.

9.5 Holdouts to the Twinning Rule

9.5.1 Nonregular Twinnings

If we posit co-stems such as [*person, personn +*], [*gram, gramm +*] and [*question, questionn +*] (see 2.2.7 and 9.4.1), then words such as *personnel, diagrammatic,* and *questionnaire* can be explicated via simple addition rather than nonregular twinnings. Granted that strategy, there are no known cases of nonregular twinnings. *Quizzical* is odd in that it has twinning before the suffix -*ic*, which usually preempts the twinning rule.

9.5.2 Nonregular Nontwinnings

There are more nonregular nontwinnings than there are nonregular twinnings. Some instances:

Combatant (combat)ant) satisfies all of the conditions for twinning, but *combattant* is recognized only in a rare British variant dealing with heraldry.

Although it has the regular inflected forms *guitarred* and *guitarring*, *guitar* has the derived form *guitarist*, without twinning.

Although regular twinning occurs in words like *gassy* and *gassing*, there is no twinning in *gasify, gaseous, gaselier,* or *gasoline*. In general, free bases like *gas* and *bus* tend to cause indecision about twinning, perhaps because such bases are quite rare due to the constraint against ending terminative bases with a single *s*. There is still disagreement over whether the spelling should be *bussing* (the regular variant) or *busing* (probably the more common variant). It would be comforting if we could explain the lack of twinning in, say, *gaseous* or *gaselier* by invoking the Third Syllable Rule. We could say that since the suffix *-eous* originally had two syllables, and still does in one variant pronunciation, the stressed vowel is the third from the end, thus being shortened by the Third Syllable Rule, preempting the Twinning Rule. However, though comforting, such an argument would not fit the facts. It is contradicted by too many other words—for instance, *barrable, gettable, flippancy, stoppable,* even the pseudoword *hippity-hoppity.*

Dictionaries imply that the plural of *sassafras* is *sassafrases*, without twinning. But the Twinning Rule calls for *sassafrasses, with twinning—a hardcore, but certainly rare, holdout. Other hardcore holdouts are not so rare:

(Array 9-25)

acrobatism (acrobat)ism)	gastropodous (gastropod)ous)
alcoholism (alcohol)ism)	mandolinist (mandolin)ist)
alphabetist (alphabet)ist)	marathoned (marathon)ed)
cataloged (catalog)ed)	marathoner (marathon)er)
cataloger (catalog)er)	marathoning (marathon)ing)
cataloging (catalog)ing)	Octopodidae (octopod)idae)
combative (combat)ive)	protocolar (protocol)ar)
czarism, tsarism (czar)ism),	protocolist (protocol)ist)
(tsar)ism)	pyramider (pyramid)er)

To avoid an anomalous *u*-deletion, *cataloged, cataloger,* and *cataloging* all imply the stem *catalog,* not *catalogue.*

Crocheted (crochet)ed), *debuting* (debut)ing), and *picoted* (picot)ed) are only apparent holdouts. Since in each case the final *t* is not pronounced, the words do not satisfy the condition that the stem must end with a single vowel letter followed by a single consonant letter that spells a single consonant sound. *Ricocheted,* also pronounced with the correspondence *et* = /ā/, is a regular instance of simple addition as well. But *ricochet* has a variant pronunciation in which the final *t* is pronounced and the concomitant variant spelling *ricochetted* is a regular instance of the Twinning Rule.

9.6 The Final Form of the Twinning Rule

The final consonant letter of a stem is twinned only when all of the following conditions are met:

1. The stem must be free.
2. The stem must end in VC#—that is, with a single vowel letter that is followed by a single consonant letter that spells a single consonant sound.
3. The VC# string in the stem must bear primary or secondary stress both before and after the suffix is added.
4. A suffix is being added that starts with a vowel.
5. The suffix must not be one of the shortening suffixes, such as *-ic, -ity.*

With these conditions there are very few true holdouts to the Twinning Rule and there are thousands of instances. The true holdouts tend to be rarely used words and to involve nonregular nontwinning rather than nonregular twinning.

10 Assimilated Prefixes

10.1 Introduction to Assimilation

In linguistics, when something assimilates, it grows more similar to something else. The base of *assimilate* is *simil +*, which is also the base of *similar.* Assimilation usually occurs as part of the tendency to simplify pronunciation. The kind of assimilation discussed in this chapter involves the final consonants in certain prefixes when they are added to certain stems. Especially in very old assimilations, after the sounds assimilated, the spelling also changed so as to bring the written form of the word more into line with its pronunciation. Thus, for instance, in early Latin there were words such as *adfectio* and *adnotātio,* but in time assimilation caused the *d* in the prefix *ad-* to fall silent, a fact represented in the later spellings *affection* and *annotation.*

When a prefix such as *com-* assimilates to *col-, cor-,* or *con-* in words like *collect, correct,* or *connect,* we are actually presented with a set of coforms, [*com-, col-, cor-, con-*], just as in 2.3 we were given a list of coforms for a set of bases. In the case of prefixes, however, the different assimilated forms can usually be predicted because of the patterned context in which the assimilations occur. And describing the patterns in this case rather than simply listing the different coforms is more economical—and more accurately portrays the system at work in American English orthography.

The existence of the various assimilated coforms of a prefix such as *com-* complicates and even weakens the identity of the prefix itself. One of the things that makes prefixes like *re-* and *un-* so easy to recognize is the constancy of their separate forms; they do not change through assimilation. One of the things that makes prefixes like *com-* or *ob-* harder to recognize in a word is the variety of forms assimilation produces.

Assimilation occurs in the following eleven prefixes in American English: *com-, ex-, sub-, in-*[1] (meaning "not"), *in-*[2] (meaning "in"), *en-, ad-, dis-, ob-, ab-,* and *syn-.*

10.2 The Prefix *com-*

10.2.1 The Assimilations

The assimilation patterns for the prefix *com-* are as follows:

1. *com-* remains *com* before the bilabials, /b/, /p/, and /m/, which means before the letters *b, p,* and *m;*
2. *com-* deletes the *m* to become *co* before vowel letters and *h;*
3. *com-* assimilates fully to *col, con,* and *cor* before, respectively, *l, n,* and *r;*
4. *com-* assimilates partially—to *con*—everywhere else. *Con* constitutes a partial assimilation in that the /n/ is more similar to the upcoming consonant sound than the original /m/ would have been in terms of manner and place of articulation.

The following groups of words exemplify the four patterns.

Words formed by simple addition, in which *com-* before *b, m,* and *p* remains *com:*

(Array 10-1)

accommodate	command	commute	complacent
accompany	commerce	companion	component
accomplish	committee	compensate	comprehend
combat	commodity	compile	compulsion

Words formed with the deletion of *m* before vowels and *h,* so that *com-* assimilates to *co:*

(Array 10-2)

coagulate	coefficient	cohabit	coitus
coalesce	coerce	cohere	cooperate
coalition	coeval	coincide	coordinate

Partridge would also put *cohort* in this group ([1958] 1983, 109). In these words the *co* is regularly pronounced /kō/, usually owing to the effects of the V.V string produced when *co* is added to a stem that starts with a vowel. Out of this *co* = /kō/ form has arisen the currently productive prefix *co-* in English. This prefix and some of its instances are discussed in 10.2.2.

Words in which *com-* assimilates fully to *col, con,* and *cor:*

(Array 10-3)

collapse	collusion	connoisseur	corrigible
colleague	connate	connubial	corrosion
colloquial	connect	correspond	corrupt

Partridge would include *connive* in this group ([1958] 1983, 116).

Words in which *com-* assimilates partially to *con* constitute the largest single group among the various types containing the prefix *com-:*

(Array 10-4)

concatenate	conduct	conjecture	contact
conciliate	confederate	conquer	contemporary
conclude	confiscate	conscious	continent
concomitant	conflation	consent	contort
concrete	conform	consist	contribute
concubine	confront	consonant	contusion
condescend	congestion	conspicuous	convenient
condiment	conglomerate	constituent	convince
condominium	congruent	consummate	convoy

Coun, a very restricted coform of *com-,* occurs in *council, counsel,* and *countenance.* The first two explicate to (coun + cil) and (coun + sel). *Countenance,* related to *contain, continent,* and *incontinence,* explicates to (coun + ten + ance).

10.2.2   The Productive Prefix *co-*

The form of *com-* assumed before vowels and *h*—namely, *co* pronounced /kō/—continues to be productive in English. It can, in theory, be added to stems beginning with any letter or sound and remain *co* = /kō/. Instances of its being added to stems beginning with letters other than vowels or *h* (which are illustrated in array 10-2) include:

(Array 10-5)

cobelligerent	cojuror	copartner	cotangent
coconscious	colatitude	corecreation	covariance
cofeature	comonomer	cosine	coworship

Sometimes, though seldom in American English, the suffix *co-* is attached to its stem with a hyphen. Usage is not at all settled here. The trend seems to be that the hyphen is used as little as possible in American English. The major guideline appears to be to use a hyphen only when the combination of *o* plus the first letter of the stem could lead to confusing letter sequences. Thus, for instance, in American (and British) English, *co-worker* always gets the hyphen, to avoid the *ow* digraph, which could tempt the reader to *cow/orker* or some such. To my eye *coworship* in array 10-5 also would be well served by a hyphen: *co-worship.* Usage is unsettled. We are reminded of the words of the grammarian, rhetorician, teacher, and gentleman Porter Perrin, who in class one day told a concerned student, "He who takes the hyphen seriously shall surely go mad."

10.2.3 Holdouts

The holdouts to the assimilation pattern for *com-* are few. They fall handily into three groups: (1) words containing anomalous *com-* forms, (2) words containing anomalous *co-* forms, (3) words containing anomalous *con-* forms.

1. The most important word with anomalous *com-* is *comfort,* which together with *comfit* and *comfrey* has an *m* where the pattern calls for *n.* According to the *OED* these three had *n*'s in Latin and Old French. The *OED* says that the change of *n* to *m* was English, and Jespersen points out that the sound /m/ when followed by /f/ or /v/ is frequently not pronounced as a bilabial, as it normally would be ([1909] 1954, 1:395). Instead of pressing his or her lips together, the English-speaking person frequently presses the lower lip against the upper teeth to form the /m/, thus preparing the mouth for the pronunciation of the labiodental /f/ or /v/. This change is a special kind of assimilation that contends with the normal assimilation process that works to remove or replace /m/ before any sound that is not a bilabial. The result of this local contention appears to be the holdouts *comfit, comfrey,* and *comfort.*

Other anomalous *com-*'s occur in *comestible* and the related *comedo,* (com + est + ible) and (com + edo), which would regularly be spelled *co-estible and *coedo. The rare singular *comes* 'a Roman legal and military adviser' also is technically a holdout. Though it is probably best treated as a simplex, historically it could explicate to (com + es). This explication is a bit more convincing in the plural form of the word, *comites:* either (com + ites) or (com + it + es). The *comit +* stem is also found in the more common *concomitant* (coṁ + n + com + it + ant), which contains both an assimilated and an unassimilated form of the prefix *com-*. Another technical holdout is *comunidad,* from Spanish, from Latin *communitas.* The *mm* was simplified in Spanish to *m,* and now it is not clear whether the resulting American English word should explicate to the nonregular (com + unidad) or the more regular (co + munidad).

2. Unusual *co-*'s occur in words containing stems that start with the cluster *gn.* In these words the *m* is regularly deleted: *cognate* (coṁ + gnate), *cognition* (coṁ + gnition), *cognizance* (coṁ + gnizance). Also in this group are *recognize, cognoscente,* and *cognomen,* the last having an anomalous explication: (coṁ + g(nomen), the *g* apparently having been inserted via analogy with *cognizance.* The affixation of *com-* to stems that start with *gn* poses some interesting tactical problems: Simple addition would have led to the unusual concatenation *mgn,* a partial assimilation to *ngn.* Full assimilation would have led to *ggn,* which would violate the

constraint against doublets within larger clusters and concatenations (see 3.2.6). The deletion of *m* appears to have provided tactically and phonetically the most efficient solution. An anomalous *co-* occurs in *conusable*, which underwent considerable alteration in its evolution through Old French from the Latin *cognōscere* and would have to explicate to (com̸ + nusable).

3. Anomalous *con-*'s occur in *conurbation* (com̸ + n + urbation), *conalbumin* (com̸ + n(albumin), and *conelrad* (from the phrase "*con*trol of *el*ectromagnetic *rad*iation"). *Constable*, ultimately from the Latin *comes stabuli*, if not treated as a simplex, would have to explicate to (con(stable), the *con* being a development from *comes* that is probably in part due to a felt analogy with the *com-* to *con-* assimilation.

4. A very small fourth group contains words with absorbed, or at least nearly absorbed, *com-* prefixes. *Copula, copulate,* and *couple* are remote instances of *com-* simplified to *co* or *cou*. The first two, if not treated as simplexes, would have to explicate, on a strictly etymological basis, to (com̸ + pula) and (com̸ + pulate). *Couple* comes from Old French, from the same Latin *copula,* which would force an explication to (com̸ + u + ple). All in all, it seems best to treat the historical *com-* in these words as having merged with the base, making *copula* and *couple* connate simplexes, with *copulate* explicating to (copulá + ate). Similarly absorbed *com-*'s occur in *coil, couch, cousin, count, custom,* and the verb *curry* (as a horse), all of which are probably best now treated as simplexes.

10.3 The Prefix *ex-*

10.3.1 The Assimilations

The assimilation patterns for *ex-* are complicated by cases in which the stem begins with the letter *c*, but a reasonable description is as follows:

1. *Ex-* assimilates fully to *ef* before *f*, as in *effect* (ex̸ + f + fect).
2. *Ex-* remains *ex* before all other voiceless consonants and before all vowels, as in *exceed* (ex + ceed) and *exact* (ex(act).
3. *Ex-* assimilates partially to *e* before voiced consonants, as in *evolve* (ex̸ + volve).

Words in which *ex-* assimilates fully to *ef*:

(Array 10-6)

effable	effervesce	effloresce	effort
efface	effete	effluent	effrontery
effect	efficient	effluvium	effulgent
effeminate	effigy	efflux	effuse

Words in which *ex-* affixes by simple addition before voiceless consonants other than *f* and before vowels:

(Array 10-7)

examine	excrescence	experience	exsanguinate
excaudate	exculpate	expiate	exstipulate
except	exercise	explicate	extemporaneous
exchange	exhilarate	export	extinguish
excite	exit	expropriate	extort
exclude	exorbitant	expulsion	extricate
excoriate	expand	exquisite	exult

Words in which *ex-* assimilates partially to *e* before voiced consonants:

(Array 10-8)

ebractate	elapse	emigrate	erode
ebullition	elegant	emotion	erudite
edict	eligible	emulsion	evaporate
educate	eloquent	enervate	event
egest	elucidate	enumerate	evince
egress	emanate	eradicate	evoke
eject	emeritus	erect	evulsion

10.3.2   Holdouts

The patterns laid out in arrays 10-6 through 10-8 are simple and reliable, but they do involve some complications. When *ex-* is affixed to stems that start with the letter *c*, there are some holdouts to the regular pattern. In a few cases *x* assimilates fully to a *c* before *c*: *eccentric* (ex + c(centric), *ecchymosis*, *ecclesiastic*, and *eccrine*. In the French adoptions *éclair* and *ecru* the *x* is deleted, and the words explicate to (ex + clair) and (ex + cru).

In the French adoptions *escambio*, *escape*, *escort*, *estreat*, and *escheat* the *x* assimilates partially to *s*: (ex + s + cambio), (ex + s(cape), and so on. In the French and Italian adoptions *esplanade* and *espresso* the *x* also assimilates to *s*. The same is true of *essay*.

In a very few cases the *x* assimilates partially to *c* before letters other than *c*: *ecdysis* (ex + c + dysis), *eclampsia* (ex + c + lampsia). Also in this group are *eclipse*, *eclectic*, *eclogue*, *ecstasy*, *ectype*, and *eczema*.

In a few recent and technical formations the *x* does not assimilate at all before *f*: *exfiltration*, *exflagellate*, *exfoliate*.

10.3.3   Some "Converted" *ex-*'s

In a few words the normal assimilation process took place only to be followed by a change of *e* to *a* as the words moved from Old French to

English. They are *amend, avoid, award, astonish, astound,* and *affray.* The first three follow the regular pattern for words in array 10-8, with the addition of the *e*-to-*a* change. For instance:

(ex̸(mend) = (e̸ + a(mend) = (a(mend), *amend*

Astonish and *astound* involve partial assimilations of *x* to *s* before *t* with the additional *e*-to-*a* change:

(ex̸ + s + tonish) = (e̸ + a + s + tonish) = (as + tonish), *astonish*
(ex̸ + s + tound) = (e̸ + a + s + tound) = (as + tound), *astound*

Affray, though it follows the normal assimilation of *x* to *f* before *f,* ends up looking more like an *ad*- than an *ex*- word:

(ex̸ + f(fray) = (e̸ + a + f(fray) = (af(fray), *affray*

Excise 'tax' did not start out as an *ex*- word. In Latin it was *ad*-. The Modern English form reflects changes that occurred in Dutch, changes away from the *acc* opening the word had both in Latin and in Old French. In a way, then, *affray* and *excise* are a complementary pair. In this analysis *excise* is explicated counter to its Latin sources, as (ex + cise).

An *ex*- that appears to have been completely lost occurs in *issue,* which was *exita* in Latin, *eissue* and *issue* in Old French. It seems better now to treat *issue* as a simplex.

10.4   The Prefix *sub-*

10.4.1   The Assimilations

The assimilation patterns for the prefix *sub*- are complicated by the fact that in addition to patterns of partial and full assimilation that reflect the Latin sources, in a number of formations, especially recent ones, *sub*- can be added by simple addition to stems beginning with any letter. *Sub*- is still an active and productive prefix in English, and in modern formations the old assimilation patterns are preempted by simple addition. The following description begins with the older assimilations and their patterns.

Words in which *sub*- assimilates fully before *c, f, g, m, p,* and *r,* producing the assimilated spellings *suc, suf, sug, sum, sup,* and *sur,* include:

(Array 10-9)

succeed	sufficient	suggest	suppress
succinct	suffocate	summon	suppurate
succubus	suffrage	supplement	surreptitious
suffer	suffuse	suppose	surrogate

The situation with the *sur* form of *sub-* is complicated by the existence of an entirely separate prefix, also spelled *sur,* with the meaning "over, above." Semantically *sur-* is nearly an opposite of *sub-*, a fact readily apparent in some words that contain *sur-* rather than the assimilated *sur* form of *sub-: surrealism, surrebut, surrejoin, surroyal.* In *surrender,* however, the semantic contribution of the prefix is obscure enough to cause some momentary indecision: Is it a form of *sub-*? Or is it *sur-*? It is *sur-*, its etymological sense being "to deliver over, to render over."

A related complication involves *surround,* the prefix of which is historically neither a form of *sub-* nor the prefix *sur-*. It is, rather, a simplified form of the Latin prefix *super-*. However, since *sur-* itself is a simplified form deriving ultimately from *super-*, *surround* explicates to (sur(round). Etymologically the base of *surround* is not *round;* it is rather *+ound,* from the Latin verb *undāre* 'to rise in waves', as in *abound,* (ab + ound). The spelling with *rr* appears in Early Modern English in the fifteenth and sixteenth centuries. As the *OED* points out, a felt analogy with the word *round* led to the *rr* spelling, and thus to the explication (sur(round) rather than the historically prior (sur + r + ound), with its anomalous *r*-insertion.

A similar problem characterizes the word *sudden.* During Middle English times it was spelled many different ways, but always with a single *d.* The *dd* began to occur in the sixteenth century, and the modern spelling was fixed very late, in the eighteenth century. The Latin source was *subitānus,* which became *sodein, sudein,* in Norman French, from which it was adopted into English. We could invoke analogy to explicate *sudden* to (suƀ + d + den), but the *+den* base is rather unconvincing. It is probably best to treat the word as a simplex.

The prefix *sub-* assimilates fully to *sus* before *s* and partially to *sus* before *c, p,* and *t:*

(Array 10-10)

resuscitate	susception	sussultatory	sustentacular
suscept	suspend	sustain	sustention
susceptible	suspense	sustenance	sustentor

The prefix *sub-* assimilates partially to *su* before *sp,* as in *suspect, suspicion, suspire:* (suƀ + spect), (suƀ + spicion), (suƀ + spire). This partial assimilation is due to the doublet rule (3.2.6), constraining as it does against clusters that contain doublets. The regular partial assimilation to *sus,* as in array 10-10, would produce nonregular clusters in these words—namely, *suspect, *susspicion, and *susspire. (However, compare such words as *subscribe* and *substitute* in array 10-12 below, which do not assimilate to *susscribe or *suscribe, *susstitute or *sustitute.)

The assimilations in arrays 10-9 and 10-10 involve stems that begin with *c, f, g, m, p, r, s, sp,* and *t. Sub-* affixes via simple addition to stems beginning with any other letter:

(Array 10-11)

subalpine	subjacent	sublimate	suburb
subatomic	subject	sublime	subvariety
subbasement	subjoin	subliminal	subversion
subdivide	subjugate	subnormal	subway
subdue	subjunctive	suborder	subxerophilous
subequatorial	subkingdom	subordinate	subzone
subhuman	sublease	subquadrate	
subirrigate	sublet	subquality	

10.4.2 Simple Addition in Recent *sub-* Words

The assimilation patterns illustrated in arrays 10-9 through 10-11 are regular and consistent within themselves, but they exist side by side with scores of other words in which *sub-* is added via simple addition to stems beginning with letters and sounds that normally lead to assimilation. Instances:

(Array 10-12)

subcaliber	subgroup	subpoena	substitute
subclass	submarine	subregion	subsume
subconscious	submerge	subscribe	subterranean
subfamily	submerge	subsequent	subtitle
subgenus	subplot	subside	subtract

From the orthographic point of view, this poses no real problems, for the pronunciation of these words practically always cues the /b/ = *b* correspondence. That is, the *b* is nearly always heard clearly in the pronunciation. In array 10-12 the only instance without the /b/ sound is *subpoena*, and in this case the *b* is silent because of the effects of a very localized tactical constraint: when *b* and *p* come together, the first tends not to be pronounced, as in *raspberry* and *cupboard*.

Stems that begin with *p* are unpredictable: sometimes they involve full assimilation (as in *suppose*), sometimes partial assimilation (as in *suspend*), and sometimes simple addition (as in *subplot* or, even more elusively, *subpoena*). This complexity is heightened by the cluster *sp:* whereas *suspect* is formed via partial assimilation, *subspecies* is formed via simple addition.

A lesser instance of this unpredictability is the assimilation that takes place before *c:* sometimes it is full, as in *succeed*, and sometimes it is partial, as in *susceptible*. A useful distinction here is that the partial assimilation occurs only before soft *c*, while the full assimilation occurs before both soft and hard *c*, as in *success* and *succubus*.

10.4.3 Two Unusual *sub-*'s

In *suttle* and *sojourn* etymological *sub-*'s have been altered and simplified in nonregular ways. *Suttle* 'net weight' is a phonetic respelling of *subtle* and explicates to (sub + t + tle). *Sojourn*, ultimately from the Latin *sub-diurnāre*, reflects simplifications that took place in Old French. The base *+journ* occurs in *journey, journal,* and *adjourn*. Since *+journ* does have this fairly important occurrence, it seems best to recognize the unique *so* as a coform of *sub-*: (so + journ).

10.5 The Prefixes *in-*[1] and *in-*[2]

There are two prefixes in English spelled *in*. The more common one, *in-*[1], adds the semantic content "no, not." The second one, *in-*[2], adds the content "in." Both have the same assimilation pattern. In the arrays that follow, words with *in-*[1] are listed at the top; words with *in-*[2] appear at the bottom.

In- assimilates fully before the liquids *l* and *r:*

(Array 10-13)

illaborate	irreceptive	irreducible	irremediable
illegible	irreclaimed	irrefusable	irreparable
illiterate	irreconcilable	irregular	irresponsible
illogical	irrecuperable	irrelevant	irreverent
illative	illocutionary	irradiate	irritate
illecebraceae	illuminate	irreption	irrogate
illighten	illusion	irrigate	irrupt

In- partially assimilates to *im* before *b, m,* and *p*, letters that spell bilabial sounds:

(Array 10-14)

imbecile	immitigable	impalatable	impotence
immaculate	immortal	impertinent	improvise
immediate	immusical	implausible	impunity
imbase	imbroglio	immure	implicate
imbibe	imbue	impair	impoverish
imbosom	imminent	impetuous	improve

Most often, however, *in-* affixes by simple addition. The following list is just a brief sample:

(Array 10-15)

inarticulate	infamous	innocent	inurbane
incapable	inharmonious	inoperable	inutile
indecent	iniquity	inquietude	invisible
inaugurate	inessive	initial	inspect
incense	inference	inoculate	intend
induce	inhabit	insist	invent

The prefixes *in-* do not affix via simple addition to stems that begin with *b, m,* and *p,* except in *inbalance,* a variant of *imbalance.*

10.5.1 The Coform *en*

In-[2] has coforms spelled *en* (usually) and *em* (sometimes before *b, m,* and *p*). Though some instances come from the Greek *en-,* most often this *en* form reflects a change undergone by Latin *in-* in French. The *i* and *e* forms have competed over the centuries, with words that were earlier *in* being changed to *en,* and vice versa. As the *OED* says, "Nearly every word, of long standing in the language, which is formed with *en-* has at some period been written also with *in-*" (at *En-*). The result of this competition between forms is that today we have some words beginning with *en,* more beginning with *in,* and several with variants in each spelling. The *i* form is much more common than the *e,* but beyond that there is little that can be said by way of selection rules. The *OED* again (at *In-*): "The general tendency (though with numerous exceptions) has been to establish *in-, im-,* in words evidently derived from Latin, reserving *en-, em-,* for words formed in French and not having a Latin type, or in which the Latin type is distinguished by phonetic change, and for words formed in English on the analogy of these." That is, words that are clearly Latinate tend to be spelled with an *i;* those that are not are more likely to be spelled with an *e*—a soft rule at best, and as the *OED* says, one with numerous exceptions.

Array 10-16 contains the *en-, em-,* words given as first entries in *W3* that are not marked "British," "obsolete," or "archaic." The sample includes just those *em-* and *en-* words with stems starting with *a, b,* and *c.* Words followed by an asterisk have variants in *in-, im-* in *W3.* Since the *i* forms are the more common, it seems reasonable to prefer them to the *e* forms, in the name of centering and simplicity. Therefore, words for which *in-* and *im-* are the first entries and for which *en-* and *em-* are variants are not included in this list. In short, this list contains only current words for which *en, em,* is either the only or the first listed form:

(Array 10-16)

embalm	emboss	enarched	encipher
embank	embouchure	enarme	encircle
embarcadero	embound*	enarthrosis	enclasp*
embargo	embowed	encaenia	enclave
embark	embowel	encage	enclitic
embarrass	embower*	encamp	enclose*
embathe	embox	encapsulate	enclothe
embatholithic	embrace	encarnalize	encode
embattle	embrail	encarpus	encoffin
embay	embranchment	encase*	encoignure
embed*	embrangle*	encastage	encolpion
embelif	embrasure	encastre	encolure
embellish	embreathe	encaustic	encomienda
embezzle	embrighten	encave	encomiologic
embiaria	embrittle	enceinte	encomium
embitter*	embrocate	encephalitis	encompass
emblaze	embroider	enchain	encopresis
emblazon	embroil	enchant	encorbelment
emblem	embrown	encharge	encounter
emblossom	embryo	enchase	encourage
embody	embus	enchilada	encroach
embog	embusque	enchiridion	encrust*
embolden	enable	enchondral	encrypt
embolism	enact	enchondroma	enculturation
embolite	enalid	enchorial	encumber
embolium	enamel	enchylema	encyclical
embonpoint	enamor	enchymatous	encyclopedia
embosk	enantiomorph	encincture	encyst

10.6   The Prefix *ad-*

The prefix *ad-* has the most complex and widespread assimilation patterns of all English prefixes.

Ad- regularly undergoes full assimilation before *c, f, g, l, n, p, r, s,* and *t:*

(Array 10-17)

accelerate	affluent	annex	arrive
accident	affricate	annotate	assault
acclaim	affusion	apparatus	assemble
accompany	agglomerate	appetite	assist
accrue	aggression	appliance	assonance
accurate	alleviate	appoint	assure
affair	alloy	appreciate	attack
affect	allusion	appulse	attempt
affidavit	ally	arrest	attract

A somewhat unusual form of partial assimilation occurs when *ad-* is affixed to stems that start with *qu*. Since English tactics constrain against *qq*, requiring instead a *u* after each *q*, *aqqu* is not a viable sequence, and *aququ* would do violence to phonetics. Thus, since the *q* spells a /k/ sound, a hard *c* is inserted to replace the *d* in *ad-*. An example is *acquaint* (ad + c(quaint). Other instances of *ad-* assimilating to *ac* before *q:*

(Array 10-18)

acquest	acquire	acquist
acquiesce	acquisition	acquit

Ad- regularly affixes by simple addition before *a, d, e, h, i, j, m, o, u,* and *v:*

(Array 10-19)

adapt	adequate	adjudicate	adult
addict	adhere	administer	advertise
address	adit	admonition	advise
adduce	adjacent	adolescent	advocate

Consistent with the doublet rule (see 3.2.6), *ad-* affixes via simple addition rather than full assimilation before *sc* and *st*. Full assimilation, normally called for before *s*, would produce the nonregular clusters *ssc* and *sst*. Thus we have *adscititious, adscript,* and *adstipulate* rather than **asscititious, *asscript,* and **asstipulate*. For *ascribe, aspect,* and similar words, see array 3-6.

In a number of words to which the prefix *ad-* was added by simple addition in Latin, the *d* was deleted in Old French and Middle English, only to be returned in Early Modern English. Examples are *adventure, adverse, advice, adjoin, admeasure*.

The large and somewhat sprawling patterns of full and partial assimilation illustrated in arrays 10-17 and 10-18 are complicated by the existence of words formed via simple addition when *ad-* precedes stems beginning with letters before which *ad-* regularly assimilates. The following are instances of this simple addition (words marked with an asterisk have assimilated variants):

(Array 10-20)

adlittoral	adpressed*	adrenal	adsorption
adnate	adpromissor	adrenergen	
adnexa*	adradius	adsessor*	
adnominal	adrectal	adsorb	

Partial assimilation is relatively rare with *ad-*. Two types, however, do occur: the simple *d*-deletion, as in *avenue*, practically always due to the persistence of Old French spellings; and the replacement of *d* with *g*, as in *agnate* (ad + g + nate). It seems likely that the *d*-to-*g* change was affected by the tendency for *d* to be deleted before *gn*, as in *agnition* (ad + gnition) and the archaic *agnize* (ad + gnize). The *d*-to-*g* change re-creates this same *agn* sequence, though in a very limited range. In addition to *agnate* there are *agnomen* (ad + g + nomen) and its more integrated synonym *agname*. Interestingly, the obsolete and rare *agnomination* has variants *annomination* and *adnomination,* so this one word has variants that show full assimilation, partial assimilation, and simple addition!

A few French adoptions retain partial assimilation via nonregular *d*-deletion where there would regularly be simple addition or full assimilation. In some cases the *d*'s were there in Latin but were deleted in French. In other cases the words were formed in French, using the preposition *à,* which was the French simplification of the Latin preposition *ad.* Examples in American English are *aplomb,* from French *aplomb,* from the Old French phrase *à plomb.* Similar instances of *d* deletion:

(Array 10-21)

abandon	adroit	apace	avale
adieu	align	apart	avenge
adret	amerce	apartheid	await

Apartment had *pp* in Latin and French, but its spelling was probably simplified by a felt analogy with *apart.* First recorded in English in the mid-seventeenth century, it was sometimes spelled *pp* through the seventeenth and eighteenth centuries.

The expected *d* is still missing in a few other French adoptions, especially those with stems beginning with *v, b,* and *m:*

(Array 10-22)

abase	amass	amount	avouch
abate	ameliorate	amuse	avow
abet	amenable	avenue	
abeyance	amortize	aver	

In Early Modern English attempts were made to bring at least some of these holdouts into line with the dominant patterns for *ad-: avouch* was sometimes *advouch* in the sixteenth and seventeenth centuries; *abase* was both *abbase* and *adbass* in the sixteenth century, and *amount* was *admount.*

Similar *d*-deletions occur in some Spanish adoptions: *adios* (ad + dios), actually the Spanish translation of *adieu;* also in *alumbrado* (ad + lumbrado), from Spanish, in turn from Latin *alluminare; ayuntamiento,* descending finally from Latin *ad-* plus *junctus.* A distant *d*-deletion occurs in *amontillado,* from *vino amontillado* 'wine made in Montilla', in which the Spanish initial *a* answers to the Latin *ad-*. There is also a distant *d*-deletion in the American-Spanish adoption *aparejo* 'packsaddle', from Spanish *aparejar*, from Latin *appariculare*, with the fully assimilated *ad-*.

10.6.1 The Influence of the Full Assimilation of *ad-*

The pattern for full assimilation of *ad-* is a very strong one, and it has produced a number of regularizing respellings. In a number of cases words with *ad-* when they were adopted from French were spelled in the French fashion, which was to simplify the cluster at the boundary between prefix and stem by deleting one of the double consonants in words that had undergone full assimilation in Latin. In most cases the double consonants were put back into the English spellings, usually during the period of great Latinization in the fifteenth, sixteenth, and seventeenth centuries. The following is just a brief sample of words that had double consonants in Latin, were simplified to single consonants in French and early Middle English, only to have their consonants doubled again in Early Modern English: *account, address, affirm, aggrieve, allege, announce, appease, arrive, attach.*

A number of words have modern spellings that reflect the pressure of analogy to bring older spellings more in line with the strong, full assimilation pattern for *ad-*. Though none of these words historically contained the *ad-*, they are spelled and pronounced as if they did, and since the semantic contribution of the prefix in each case is at best obscure, it seems best to recognize the power of analogy and to treat them all as instances of the full assimilation of *ad-*.

With *abbreviate* there is a question as to whether the prefix in the original was *ab-* or an assimilated form of *ad-*. It is explicated here as the latter: (ad + b + breviate). The Latin source of *allege* was *exlītigāre*, which in Norman French had become *aligier, alegier,* which in turn was taken into Anglo-Latin as *adlēgiāre*. From then on the power of the full assimilation pattern for *ad-* led to *allege* (ad + l + lege).

Assoil represents a probable analogizing to *ad-*, deriving from the Latin *absolvere*, which also produced the English word *absolve*. *Assoil* can thus be explicated to (ad + s + soil). Similar instances are *advance* and *advantage*, the Latin original of *advance* being *abantiare*, while *advantage* comes from the Latin *abante*, which contained *ab-*. Both can now be explicated via analogy to *ad-*: (ad + vance) and (ad(vantage). The rare *accidia* and *accidie* are actually just variants of *acedia* 'sloth', in which the original prefix, the privative *a-*, has analogized to *ad-*.

The obsolete *accloy* 'cloy' and *appeach* 'impeach' both involve analogizing of the Latin prefix *in-* to *ad-*.

Two words that contain altered forms of what was originally in Latin the prefix *ex-* are *assay,* from the earlier *essay,* from Latin *exagiāre;* and *affray,* from Latin *exsartum.* Recognizing the power of analogy, we explicate both now to full assimilations of *ad-* to *as* and *af.*

Acknow and *acknowledge* come from Old English rather than Latin, from the verb *oncnāwan.* But the power of analogy merged the words with the Latin *ad-* set: (ad + c(know) and (ad + c(knowledge). Compare this *d*-to-*c* change with that before /k/ spelled *q* in *acquaint. Afford* is from the Old English *geforthian.* The effect of analogy and convergence is revealed in the explication (ad + f + ford). *Accurse* and *allegiance* are somewhat similar: the former comes from Old English *ācursian,* with the prefix *a-;* the latter comes from Middle English *legiance,* the *al* being added by an apparent analogy with *allegiance,* a legal term derived from *allege.* Both can be explicated as analogical convergences: (ad + c(curse) and (ad + l + legiance). For *annoy* see 2.5.1.

Other Old English words that converged to Latin *ad-* are *affright,* now (ad + f(fright), but originally from Old English *āfyrhted; allay,* now (ad + l(lay), but originally from Old English *ālecgan;* and *anneal,* now (ad + n + neal), originally from *onǣlan.*

In *accomplice* and *accouche,* prepositions spelled *à* or *a* converged analogically to the prefix *ad-,* as in the phrases *a complice* in Middle English and *à coucher* in French: (ad + c + complice) and (ad + c + couche).

10.6.2   Some Only Apparent *ad-*'s

Accipiter 'hawk' reflects Latin folk etymology at work on the Old Latin word *acupeter,* meaning literally "fast flier." Latin folk etymology altered this form apparently due to a felt analogy with *accipere* 'take'. Though the modern spelling appears to contain an assimilated form of *ad-,* perhaps the best explication, true to the ancient history of the word, would be to treat *acci* + as a coform of the historical base, which is *acu-* 'fast', and then treat + *piter* as a coform of the base + *pter* (referring to wings and flight), to which it was originally related. That would lead to the explication (acci + piter).

Arrant also looks like an assimilation of *ad-,* but is instead a variant of *errant,* with the base *err. Arr* + can be treated as a coform of *err;* hence the explication (arr + ant).

Attitude reflects an assimilation that took place in Italian. It comes from the Italian *attitudine,* which in turn comes from the Latin *aptitudo,* the direct source of the English words *aptitude* and *apt*. Treating *att +* as a coform of *apt, attitude* explicates to (att + itude).

10.6.3 Lost *ad-*'s

Alarm and *alert*, both of which came through Italian and then French on their way to English from Latin, could be explicated via the remains of very old Latin prefixes *ad-*. They derive ultimately from the Latin phrases *ad illam arme* 'to arms' and *ad illam erta* 'on the watch'. However, it seems best to treat both as simplexes today: (alarm) and (alert).

    Add is from Latin *addere*, which is *ad-* plus the verb stem *dere* 'to put'. However, the modern explication (ad + d) would be quite unconvincing, so we treat *add* as a simplex. *Aid* is from Latin *adjūtāre*, with the prefix *ad-*, but we treat it as a simplex: (aid).

10.6.4 Summary

This sprawling and untidy pattern for *ad-* actually has at its foundation the same logic and rationale that informs other patterns of assimilation and simple addition. *Ad-* ends with a voiced sound, /d/, so it tends to assimilate fully before letters that spell voiceless sounds, as per the Mixed Voicing Rule: *c, f, k, p, qu, s,* and *t*. To this core are added the liquids, *l* and *r*. It is significant that the list of words formed by simple addition with *ad-* also contains some stems that start with *l* and *r*, which, as was seen in 3.2.2, are often exempt from normal sequence rules. The two true anomalies in the group representing full assimilation are *b*, with only a single instance, *abbreviate*, and *g*. At the core of the simple-addition group are the voiced vowels, the voiced consonants *d, j, m, n*, plus the liquids, *l* and *r*, again. The two anomalies here involve the voiceless *s* and *p*, both of which are quite rare and limited to technical terms that are essentially part of the written technical register.

10.7 The Prefix *dis-*

Dis- assimilates fully to *dif* before *f:*

(Array 10-23)

diffareation	difficult	diffluent	diffract
differ	diffidation	difflugia	diffuse

Dis- partially assimilates via *d*-deletion to *di*—rarely before *d, g, j, sc,* and *sp*, more commonly before *l, m, r, st,* and *v:*

(Array 10-24)

diduce	dilute	disperse	divaricate
digest	dimension	distant	diverse
dijudicate	diminish	distinguish	division
dilapidated	direct	distress	divorce
diligent	discission	district	individual

The *s*-deletion in words like *discission, disperse, distant,* and *distress*—
(dis̸ + scission), (dis̸ + sperse), (dis̸ + stant), and (dis̸(stress)—is consistent
with the demands of the doublet rule (see 3.2.6).

In most cases *dis-* affixes to stems via simple addition. Since *dis-* is such
a productive prefix, the list given in array 10-25 is merely a brief sample. It
illustrates that the Rule of Simple Addition sometimes prevails before
letters that lead to full or partial assimilation in arrays 10-23 and 10-24.

(Array 10-25)

disarray	disgrace	dismember	dissension
disburse	dishonor	disnature	distort
discern	disinter	disobey	distribute
disdain	disjunctive	disparage	disunite
disease	dislocate	disquieting	disvalue
disfigure	dismay	disregard	disweapon

A number of words originally contained the prefix *de-* in Latin, though
the *de-* converged via analogy to *dis-,* in some cases in Latin, in other
cases later. The explications of these words reflect this analogical
convergence:

(Array 10-26)

dilettante (dis̸ + lettante)	diversory (dis̸ + versory)
diminution (dis̸ + minution)	diverticulum (dis̸ + verticulum)
distill (dis̸(still)	divest (dis̸(vest)

10.7.1 Lost and Apparent *dis-*'s

Dine, dinner, and *dirge,* which today are probably best treated as simplexes, contain lost *dis-*'s. *Dine* and *dinner* both derive ultimately from the
Latin *disjējūnāre. Dirge* derives from the Latin *dirige,* which in turn
derives from a complex of *dis-* plus *regere.*

Distaff, from Old English rather than Latin, is a compound that closely
parallels the structure of complexes with *dis-.* It contains the words *dis*
'bunch of flax' and *staff,* with the *s*-deletion called for by the doublet rule
(see 3.2.6). It explicates to the Old English compound (dis̸)(staff), though
the semantics involved are at best remote.

10.8 The Prefix *ob-*

The prefix *ob-* assimilates fully when affixed to stems that begin with *c, f,* and *p:*

(Array 10-27)

occasion	occult	offer	opportune
occident	occupy	oppignorate	opposite
occlude	offend	opponent	oppugn

Ob- assimilates partially before *m* and *t*. It assimilates to *o* before *m:* *omission* (ob(mission) and *omit* (ob + mit). *Ob-* assimilates to *os* before *t*, or more specifically before the set [*tend, tent, tense*]: *ostend* (ob + s + tend), *ostensible* (ob + s + tensible), *ostentatious* (ob + s + tentatious).

Ob- also assimilates fully before *g* in the rare and obsolete *ogganition* 'snarling, grumbling, growling'. The *OED* treats *office* as containing a full assimilation: (ob + f + fice). But more recent dictionaries derive it from a Latin compound of *opus* and *facere* (positing the unconfirmed *opifacium*), which assimilated in Latin to *officium*. We explicate it to another case of convergence via analogy: (ob + f + fice).

Ob- always affixes via simple addition to stems beginning with *a, d, e, i, j, l, n, o, r, s, u,* and *v*—all of which spell vowels or consonants that are usually voiced:

(Array 10-28)

obambulate	oblate	obscure	obstreperous
obdurate	oblivion	observe	obstupefy
obey	obnoxious	obsidious	obumbrate
obituary	obovate	obsolete	obverse
object	obrotund	obstacle	obvious

Obscene is of obscure structure, but Partridge suggests that it explicates to (ob(scene) ([1958] 1983, 446). *Obstruse,* now obsolete, is an analogical variant of *abstruse*. The nonregular *obbligato* is a direct adoption from the past participle of the Italian *obbligare,* which itself is from the Latin *obligāre*. *Obbligato* has a more integrated and regular, though less common, variant *obligato,* which explicates via simple addition like the related *oblige* and *obligation*. Similarly, *ostinato* is a direct adoption of Italian *ostinato* from Latin *obstinatus*. Its relative *obstinate* explicates to (ob + stinate), via regular simple addition, but *ostinato,* reflecting its Italian source, explicates to (ob + stinato), via nonregular partial assimilation.

The assimilation patterns illustrated so far for *ob-* are for the most part consistent with the Mixed Voicing Rule (see 3.2.2): the full and partial assimilations before voiceless consonants avoid concatenating voiceless consonants with the voiced /b/ of *ob-*, while simple addition usually prevails when the stem begins with a voiced sound, either vowel or consonant. The above patterns are complicated, however, by the fact that these *ob-* words exist side by side with *ob-* words formed via simple addition, even in contradiction of the Mixed Voicing Rule. The latter tend to be quite recent and technical formations, primarily part of the written rather than the spoken lexicon, and thus are not prone to the smoothing effects of assimilation. Instances of such nonregular simple addition before voiceless sounds include the following:

(Array 10-29)

obcaecation	obconic	obfirm	obpyramidal
obclavate	obcordate	obfuscate	obpyriform
obcompressed	obcuneate	obfusque	obtain

Though *ob-* assimilates partially before *m* in *omit* and *omission*, it affixes by simple addition in one known instance, *obmutescence* (ob + mutescence).

10.9   The Prefix *ab-*

Ab- has a coform *abs-*, as in *abstain*, which may or may not reflect an early Latin assimilation. In this analysis the addition of *s* in *abs-* will be treated as a form of partial assimilation. Given that concession, the assimilation patterns for *ab-* are quite straightforward: (1) in a few cases *ab-* assimilates partially to *abs* before *c* and *t;* (2) in equally few cases it assimilates partially to *a* before *m, p,* and *v;* (3) everywhere else it affixes by simple addition.

Words in which *ab-* has assimilated to *abs* before *c* and *t:*

(Array 10-30)

abscess	abscond	abstemious	abstract
abscise	abstain	abstergent	abstruse

The variants *abscission* and *abscision* actually represent the mixed convergence of two different words. Etymologically *abscission* derives from Latin *abscindere*, which was *ab-* plus *scindere*. *Abscision* derives from Latin *abscīdere*, which was *abs-* plus *cidere*. Thus technically the modern variants should have two different explications: (ab + scission) and (abs + cision). But as the *OED* says, the two "were confused in Latin, and *abscision* can scarcely be separated from *abscission* in English" (at *Abscission*). We follow the implications of the etymology in *W3*, which lists the two as variants, and converge their explications to (ab + scission) and (ab + scision).

Words in which *ab-* assimilates to *a* before *m, p,* and *v:*

(Array 10-31)

amand	ament	averruncate	avocation
amanuensis	amissible	avert	avulse

In far and away the most cases *ab-* affixes via simple addition:

(Array 10-32)

abaxial	abient	abnegate	absence
abdicate	abject	abominate	absolve
abdomen	abjure	aborigine	absquatulate
abduct	ablative	abound	absurd
aberrant	ablution	abrade	abundant
abhor	abmigration	abrupt	abuse

Converging with this Latin *ab-1* is an *ab-2*, from German, which adds the content "down, off, away" and affixes by simple addition, as in:

(Array 10-33)

abgesang	abraum	abseil
ablaut	abreact	

Ab-1 has generated an *ab-3*, clipped from the word *absolute* and used in words designating electromagnetic units:

(Array 10-34)

abampere	abfarad	abohm
abcoulomb	abhenry	abvolt

The word *vantage* contains a lost *ab-*, the *v* being all that is left of the Latin prefix *ab-*. *Vantage* is from *advantage*, which actually contained *ab-* in the Latin *abante,* on which the French *avantage* was formed. Similar lost *ab-*'s occur in *vanguard,* in its clipping *van* 'forefront', and in *vamp* 'part of a shoe'. All of these words involved the French *avant,* from the Latin *abante: ab-* plus *ante.* Their explications reflect the loss of prefix: (van)(guard), (van), (vamp)—and (vant + age).

10.10 The Prefix *syn-*

The prefix *syn-* comes from Greek by way of Latin. It usually contributes the content "with, together, at the same time, like." It occurs in a number of common words, but is most frequent in the technical registers, often the highly technical ones, where it undergoes the normal assimilation, even though many of the words clearly must be more often written than spoken. The arrays that follow present all of the common words but just a sampling of the technical ones. The assimilation patterns of *syn-* can be described as follows: (1) *syn-* assimilates fully to *syl* before *l;* (2) it assimilates to *sym* before the letters that spell bilabial sounds—*b, m, p,* and *ph* (*ph* in Greek having been a bilabial); (3) it sometimes simplifies to *sy* before *st* or *z;* (4) everywhere else it remains *syn-*.

Words in which *syn-* assimilates to *syl,* as in *syllable* (syń + l + lable):

(Array 10-35)

syllepsis	sylleptic	sylloge	syllogism

Words in which *syn-* assimilates to *sym,* as in *symbiosis* (syń + m + biosis):

(Array 10-36)

symballophone	symbranchia	sympathy	symplectic
symbiotic	symmetallic	sympetalous	symposium
symbol	symmetry	symphony	symptom

Words in which *syn-* simplifies to *sy* before *st* and *z:*

(Array 10-37)

systallic	systole	syzygy
system	systyle	

Words in which *syn-* affixes by simple addition:

(Array 10-38)

synaesthesis	synchronize	syndicate	synopsis
synagog(ue)	syncline	syndrome	synsephalous
synapse	syncopate	synecdoche	syntagm
syncategorematic	syncretism	synergism	synthesis

The affixation patterns for *syn-* are firm and reliable, even though there are very few instances in some of the categories. The only known holdouts are the recent technical formations *synbranch* and *synpelmous.* In one known American English word *syn-* assimilates to *sys* before *s: syssarcosis.* The *OED* also records from Greek antiquities *syssitia* (syń + s + sitia), referring to meals eaten together in public.

CORRESPONDENCES

11 The Sounds and Letters of English

11.1 The Sounds

11.1.1 Phones, Phonemes, Morphophones

So far we have spoken of sounds and letters as if there were no questions at all about what the words *sound* and *letter* mean. But as is so often the case, this apparent simplicity can be misleading. When we speak of the sounds of a word, we do not mean the actual physical events that occur when the word is spoken on a specific occasion by an individual speaker. For these physical sounds—or **phones**—vary infinitely from word to word, from speaker to speaker, from time and place to time and place. Obviously, a deep-voiced older man is going to produce quite a different sound for the vowel in, say, *spin,* from that produced by a high-voiced young girl. Not only that, but his vowel sound is going to vary as he says that same word at different times, with his throat in different states, depending on the acoustics of the place where he speaks.

Differences will also be produced by the word setting in which the given sound occurs. For instance, the sound spelled *p* in *spin* is different from the sound spelled *p* in *pin* because of the effect of the preceding /s/ sound in *spin.* Since this difference is not one that marks differences of meaning in English, we might find it hard to detect. But we can feel the differences if we say the two words with the back of our hand held close to our mouth: with *pin* there is a puff of air at the /p/, but not so with *spin.* This difference, called aspiration, is automatic to us. We learn it as we learn to speak English. However, in English, despite the difference, we feel that the sound spelled *p* in the two words is in some important sense the same sound, even though physically it differs a great deal from one situation to the other. A linguist would say that the sounds, though physically different phones, are members of the same **phoneme.** That is, they are members of the same category of sounds that are all taken to be equivalent. The sounds spelled *p* in *spin* and *pin* are members of the same phoneme, and at the phonemic level of description, the differences do not count. (For a discussion of this categorizing as an instance of analogy at work in the language, see 1.4.)

However, just as we cannot identify our notion of sound with the phone, neither can we identify it with the phoneme. Consider, for instance, the word *greasy*. Some speakers pronounce it with an /s/, some with a /z/. The difference is an acceptable variation of dialect—and to a certain extent, of individual differences or individual situation. In the pronunciation of *greasy* the difference between /s/ and /z/ does not count, even though it is a difference in phonemes. In the pronunciation of, say, *sip* and *zip,* however, the difference counts. For the initial sound in *sip* is a member of the /s/ phoneme, but the initial sound in *zip* is a member of the /z/ phoneme. Thus, in the two pronunciations of *greasy,* sounds that are from two different phonemes are used to realize the "same" sound in the same word, and what we are concerned with spelling—that third consonant sound in *greasy*—cannot be identified with a single phoneme.

Henry Lee Smith calls that consonant sound in *greasy* a **morphophone** (1967, 1968, 1976). A morphophone is a category larger than a phoneme, because it can be realized in different dialects by phones that are members of two different phonemes, like the /s/ and /z/ in *greasy.* Smith contends that English spelling does not spell phonemes, as most linguists would claim. Rather, English spelling spells morphophones. Most of the time a morphophone is realized by members of a single phoneme, but sometimes—as with the two pronunciations of *greasy*—a morphophone can be realized by members of two or more phonemes.

The notion of the morphophone makes it possible for us to explain dialect differences. The spelling indicates the morphophonic structure of a word, and then readers (or spellers) flesh out the morphophonic structure with whatever phonemes or phonemic variations their dialects call for.

An example of spelling that tries to represent phonemes rather than morphophones is the dialect spellings often found in fiction. For instance, when we read that Davy Crockett killed a "bar" when he was only three, that spelling of *bear* is definitely trying to represent the vowel phoneme that the people of Davy's time and place apparently used in pronouncing *bear.* This kind of phonetic dialect spelling also occurs in novels that try to represent the speech of New Englanders saying that something is "clevuh" rather than *clever,* or of Westerners saying, "Smile when you say that, podnuh!"

Another, more important example of phonemic spelling is the written language of the Middle English period. During this time there were wide dialect differences in England. Speakers—and to a lesser extent, readers—from the north, say, could not readily understand a dialect, spoken or written, of the south. There was as yet no morphophonic standard to absorb and level the spoken differences in the written language. People tried to write what they heard, which meant phonemically rather than morphophonically.

In fact, Mulcaster was speaking of this period and this confusion in his allegory ([1582] 1970): Early on, he wrote, Sound was the sole determiner for spelling, and this situation quickly led to confusion. In Mulcaster's terms it was the job of Custom and Reason to sophisticate this primitive reliance on Sound and in effect to transform the English spelling system from a phonemic base to a morphophonic one.

It is almost accurate to say that the sounds we are concerned with in this chapter are morphophones. The remaining difficulty arises from the fact that since, like phonemes, morphophones are really ways of categorizing sounds, it is not quite right to say that you hear morphophones. You do not hear morphophones; you hear the phones that realize them. Hearing a speech sound is a complicated affair, involving not just sensing and perceiving but also conceptualizing, as the phones are sorted into their various phonemes and morphophones. Recognizing this complexity, we will nevertheless refer to the morphophones as sounds, more for stylistic ease than for any other reason. We will enclose morphophonic respellings in the slant lines linguists use to symbolize phonemes, even though phonemes and morphophones are not the same.

11.1.2 English Morphophones

Here are the vowel morphophones—or, again, for the sake of stylistic ease, the vowel sounds—with which chapters 12–25 will be concerned.

(Array 11-1)

The Long Vowel Sounds:
/ā/, bait   /ō/, boat
/ē/, beet   /ū/, boot (simple long *u*)
/ī/, bite   /yū/, beaut (complex long *u*)

The Diphthongs:
/òi/, oil   /aù/, owl

The Short Vowel Sounds:
/a/, bat   /ä/, cot (low short *o*)
/e/, bet   /ò/, caught (high short *o*)
/i/, bit   /u/, buck (low short *u*)
                             /ù/, book (high short *u*)

The reduced vowel (schwa), as in the first syllable of *alive,* is represented /ə/. Three special symbols will be used to represent fields of vowels colored by a following /r/: /âr/, /ôr/, and /êr/ (see 25.2, 25.3, and 25.4, for more details).

Orthographically it seems best to treat /u/ and /ù/ as versions of short *u* (see chapters 16 and 17). The high/low distinction is based on the fact that /ù/ is formed considerably higher in the mouth than /u/.

The two vowels called high and low short *o* in array 11-1 simplify some of the problems encountered in analyzing American English vowels. The /ä/ and /ò/ vowels are both pronounced well back in the mouth with the tongue in a low position. Though /ò/ is formed higher in the mouth than /ä/, we still tend to think of both as low back vowels. And the low back vowels have for centuries been difficult for people who have tried to distinguish among them (Jespersen [1909] 1954, 1:305, 311; Dobson 1957, 2:576–82, 671–73).

The difficulty continues, as we see if we compare the treatment of the low back vowels in three widely used modern references. In *A Pronouncing Dictionary of American English,* Kenyon and Knott recognize three low back vowels, symbolized ɒ, a, and ɔ, plus two more that are closely related, symbolized ɔ̈ and a. They describe these five sounds as follows:

> §10. a. This vowel sound, not in general use in America as a whole, is about midway between the vowel of *sang* . . . and the vowel of *ah.* . . .
>
> §11. *a.* This is the "broad *a*" sound in *ah* . . . , *far* . . . , *father* . . . in most of America. It is also used by the majority of Americans in "short *o*" words such as *top* . . . , *got* . . . , *fodder* . . . , in which some speakers pronounce ɒ.
>
> §12. ɒ. The symbol ɒ represents a vowel not in universal American use. It is the historical "short *o*" now generally used in England in words like *top* . . . , *got* . . . , *fodder* . . . , by many Easterners and Southerners, and in certain kinds of words by many speakers in all parts of the country. It is a sound about midway between *a* in *ah* and ɔ in *wall.* . . . As with a, so with ɒ, there is no key word that will convey to all Americans its exact sound. The key word *watch,* here used, frequently is spoken with ɒ in all parts of America, but it is also often pronounced . . . with *a* as in *ah,* and . . . with ɔ as in *wall.* (1944, xviii–xix; see also xl–xli)

In their discussion of ɔ they say this:

> In most of America ɔ appears to be rather unstable. In most positions except before *r* final or *r* plus a consonant (*war, horse*), ɔ varies with many speakers to ɒ or a. . . . In words in which the sound occurs before *l* plus a consonant (*walnut, Waldo, salt*), . . . the variants *a* and ɒ are very common in America. (1944, xxxviii)

The sound they symbolize as ɔ̈ is more remote from the vowel sounds of *cot* and *caught.* They describe it as "a kind of ɔ sound with the tongue pushed farther forward than in *wall*," and they call it "the so-called 'New England short *o*'" (1944, xxiv).

Kenyon and Knott's ɔ̆ is so high in the mouth and their *a* is so far forward that neither really qualifies as a low back vowel. But their similarities and variations with the low back vowels illustrate how difficult it is to categorize these traditionally elusive and unstable vowel sounds. We can say, then, that Kenyon and Knott recognize three main low back vowels, two of which, ɒ and *a,* are very close, and the third of which, ɔ, is higher and more rounded in its pronunciation.

Webster's Third New International Dictionary recognizes the same sound as Kenyon and Knott's *a,* which *W3* symbolizes as /ä/ and describes as between the vowel sounds of *cad* and *cod.* Unlike Kenyon and Knott, however, *W3* recognizes only two main low back vowels, which they symbolize /ä/ and /ȯ/, as in *cot* and *caught,* corresponding to Kenyon and Knott's *a* and ɔ (see Edward Artin's "Guide to Pronunciation," especially 38a–39a, 43a–44a).

The *American Heritage Dictionary (AHD),* a representative popular desk dictionary, also recognizes three main low back vowels: the short *o* of *cot,* which they symbolize as /ŏ/; the broad *a* of *father,* which they symbolize as /ä/; and the higher, rounder vowel of *caught,* corresponding to Kenyon and Knott's ɔ and *W3*'s /ȯ/, which *AHD* symbolizes as /ô/. There appears to be no parallel between *AHD*'s distinction between /ŏ/ and /ä/ and anything in Kenyon and Knott or in *W3.* There is no explanation of it in *AHD*'s pronunciation guide or in the introductory essays by H. L. Smith ("The Dialects of English") and Wayne O'Neil ("The Spelling and Pronunciation of English").

A comparison of the vowel pronunciations offered by Kenyon and Knott, *W3,* and *AHD* for words containing these low back vowels suggests the lack of agreement among them. The analysis offered in this book is closest to that of *W3* in that it recognizes only two major low back vowels, which we will symbolize as /ä/ and /ȯ/ and will refer to as low and high short *o.*

Orthographically it makes sense to treat these as two forms of short *o,* even though doing so violates some facts of phonology. For instance, all of the vowels we have called orthographically short are phonologically lax; those that are orthographically long are phonologically tense—all except /ä/ and /ȯ/, which do not fit this pattern. For instance, Venezky follows Kurath's analysis of free and checked vowels—free vowels being those that can occur at the end of morphemes, checked vowels those that cannot (1970, 14–15, n. 13). Venezky groups /ä/ with the checked—that is, lax, or short—vowels, but /ȯ/ with the free—tense, or long—vowels. And in Ladefoged's analysis both /ä/ and /ò/ would be tense since both can occur in open syllables, which is his criterion for tenseness (1975, 204). Actually, in Ladefoged's scheme /ò/ is ambiguous since it can also occur in a syllable closed with /ŋ/ (as in *long*), which is his criterion for laxness (1975, table 4.3, p. 74). And the picture is muddied even more by the fact that Kenyon and Knott, *W3,* and *AHD* show variant pronunciations of *long* with both /ò/ and /ä/.

Orthographically, calling /ä/ "short *o*" raises no serious problems, for especially the most common correspondence, /ä/ = *o,* parallels the behavior of the other short vowels. But there are problems with calling /ò/ a short vowel. It is at best a tentative classification. And yet it is apparently not too important a problem. For one thing, the regular spellings of /ò/ are with vowel digraphs, and digraphs are not included in the normal tactical patterns and rules. For another, there appears to be enough variation in pronunciation to encourage us to keep tentative and approximate any decisions we might make with regard to the low back vowels.

The consonant sounds pose fewer problems. For the most part the sounds are symbolized by letters that are immediately associated with them:

(Array 11-2)

The Front Stops:
/b/, bat   /p/, pat
/d/, dot   /t/, tot

The Velar Stops:
/g/, gill   /k/, kill

The Simple Fricatives (I):
/v/, vat   /f/, fat
/th/, then   /th/, thin
                                          /h/, hat

The Simple Fricatives (II):
/z/, zip   /s/, sip

The Palatal Sibilants:
/j/, gyp   /ch/, chip
/zh/, azure   /sh/, ashen

The Nasals:
/m/, sum   /ŋ/, sung
/n/, sun

The Liquids:
/l/, lid   /r/, rid

The Semivowels:
/w/, wet   /y/, yet

11.2   The Letters

11.2.1   The English Alphabet

The question of what we mean by the word *letter* need not be fraught with highly technical issues. Recent scholars have dealt with the question more technically, speaking in terms of **graphemes,** a written parallel to the spoken language's phonemes (see, for example, Pulgram 1951; Vachek 1966b; Haas 1970; and Bazell 1966, who questions the parallelism). But from the standpoint of orthographic description there does not appear to be any reason why we cannot use the word *letter* to refer to those twenty-six items that make up the English alphabet and to a short list of consonant digraphs. Earlier we discussed the complexity of the notion of hearing a speech sound. The same complexity applies to the notion of seeing a letter. Just as we speak of a sound as a class of phonic events, a letter is a class of graphic events. Sounds and letters are types, of which the physical events are tokens. Given these assumptions, it is accurate to say that if sounds are things we hear, letters are things we see.

It is easy to assume that the English alphabet has always been around, pretty much intact. But it, like everything having to do with language, has been evolving and changing over the centuries. We could go back to the Phoenicians and their alphabet, and after them the Greeks, and after them the Etruscans, those rather mysterious people who had the misfortune of living in Italy during the rise of the Romans. But we need go back only so far as the Romans, who adapted most of their alphabet from the Etruscans, who had adapted theirs from the Greeks, who had apparently adapted theirs from the Phoenicians. (A detailed history of the English alphabet and digraphs is to be had in the entries for each letter and digraph in the *OED*. See also Fisher 1951; Gelb 1952, 166–89; A. Campbell 1959, 12–29; Mossé 1952, 7–12.)

11.2.1.1   The Roman Influence

The Roman alphabet changed and grew over the centuries of its use, but it is accurate to say that in its early form it had just twenty letters: *A, B, C, D, E, F, H, I, K, L, M, N, O, P, Q, R, S, T, V,* and *X.*

There are no letters there that we are not used to, but there are some missing that we might expect: *G, J, U, W, Y, Z,* plus all of the lower case forms. Early on, the Romans used *C* to represent the sounds /k/ and /g/, but in time they added a horizontal bar to the *C* to spell the /g/ sound, thus making *G.* Originally the Romans used *V* to spell both the /w/ and what we think of as the *u* vowel sounds. In time *U* developed, but it was not until the seventeenth century that the roles of *u* and *v* were clearly settled in

English, the first being used to spell the vowel sounds, the second to spell the consonant /v/. For instance, in the 1580s Mulcaster had this to say about the *u* and *v* in his spelling system; the verbatim version from his *Elementarie* illustrates nicely the way he saw *u* and *v* working together. Of *v* he said that as well as spelling the vowel sounds, "it is vsed consonantlike also as well as *i,* when it leadeth a sounding vowell in the same syllab, as *vantage, reuiue* [*revive*], *deliuer,* or the silent *e* in the end, as *beleue, reproue* [*believe, reprove*]. This duble force of both *i,* and *v,* is set from the latin, and therefor it is neither the vncertaintie of our writing, nor the vnstedfastnesse of our tung, for to vse anie letter to a duble vse" ([1582] 1970, 116). In the spelling of Mulcaster's day, *u* was simply the form of *v* used everywhere except in word-initial position, and the two were used interchangeably within that distribution to spell both the vowel and the consonant sounds.

In early Old English a version of *u* was sometimes used to spell /w/. In early Old English the rune wen, *þ*, also was used to spell /w/ (A. Campbell 1959, 26). In time the wen was dropped from use, and double *v* was developed to represent /w/. The double *v* eventually grew together into a single letter, the "double *u*"*: w.*

The Romans had adopted a form of Greek upsilon, a *y*, to use when they were transliterating Greek words. In time it came to be interchanged in Latin with *i*, both the consonantal /y/ sound and the vowel sounds.

The Romans also adopted a form of the Greek zeta, *z*, to use in transliterating Greek words. The Romans did not actually use the late coming *z* much, nor in fact have we in English, since usually /z/ is spelled *s*, not *z*. Mulcaster describes *z* as "a consonant much heard amongst vs, and seldom sene" ([1582] 1970, 123). The letters *q, v,* and *z* were not used in Old English, but were added to the English alphabet by the Norman scribes.

Originally the Romans used *I* to spell both the consonant and the vowel sounds, but in time they added a tail to the *I* to make the beginnings of *J*, using the *I* for vowel sounds and the *J* for consonant sounds, more or less. But it took many centuries for the *j* to establish itself. From the eleventh century until the seventeenth, in English the letter *i* represented both the vowel sounds and a consonant sound that we today symbolize as /j/. In the twenty-four-letter alphabet that Mulcaster presents, the *j* is still missing. Actually, in Mulcaster's uppercase alphabet there are only twenty-four letters; there is no *J* or *U*. In his lowercase alphabet, there are twenty-seven characters, but that count includes two forms of *v*—namely, *v* and *u*—as well as three forms of *s:* the regular *s,* an *f*-like tall *s,* and an *e*-like *s* that was used in handwriting but not in print. Mulcaster used the *f*-like tall *s* in every position except word-final, in which case he used what we think of as the regular *s*. Apparently the handwritten *e*-like *s* also was used only at word's end. In any case, there is neither *J* nor *j* in Mulcaster's alphabet. The modern use of these letters was not established until the seventeenth century.

11.2.1.2   The Runic Influence

That brings us to the present English alphabet of twenty-six letters. But there were some developments in Old and early Middle English that deserve our attention. At various times and in various ways certain characters from the European runic alphabet were used in writing Old English. Four of these characters were edh, *ð*, and thorn, *þ*, used to spell /th/ and /<u>th</u>/; wen, *ƿ*, used to spell /w/ sounds; and yogh, *ȝ*, used to spell a velar fricative, subsequently spelled *gh* by the Norman scribes. In time the velar fricative dropped out of the language, but we are left with the *gh* spelling in words like *knight, laugh, dough, right,* and the like. The edh died out in the thirteenth century. Over the years the thorn became more and more easily confused with the *y* in handwriting. Also, in the late fifteenth century, when Caxton set up the first English printing press, his type fonts did not include the thorn, so he consistently used *th.* Thus, the thorn also died out. Old English also used the vowel ligature ash, *æ,* which, together with the other four characters, dropped out of the language after the Norman Conquest.

11.2.2   Consonant Digraphs

In addition to the twenty-six letters of the English alphabet, there are five consonant digraphs that deserve special mention. (For a definition of *digraph,* see 3.2.1 and 3.2.1.1.) All five have *h* as a second element.

The digraph *ch* was used in Latin to transliterate Greek words containing the letter chi. A number of Modern English words with *ch* echo that old chi: *chronicle,* for instance, and *Christ.* (In fact, the Greek chi looked like the English letter *X,* which is why we sometimes abbreviate *Christmas* as *Xmas;* the *X* represents the old letter chi.) The digraph *ch* was hardly used at all in Old English to spell the /ch/ sound, which was usually spelled with a *c* followed by an *e.* But the Norman scribes introduced its wider use in English. After long vowels they spelled it *ch;* after short vowels they used a "double" form of the digraph, *cch,* which in time became our quasi-doublet *tch.*

The Norman scribes used *gh* to represent the velar fricative spelled with yogh or, later, *h* in Old English. In the fifteenth century, Caxton often used *gh* to represent the sound /g/. He had apparently learned of it during his stay in the Netherlands, where it was widely used. The only cases of "Caxton's *gh*" in Modern English are the words *ghost, ghastly,* and *aghast.* Of other *gh* words in English, *ghoul* comes from the Arabic *ghūl,* a very new adaption that has probably retained its *gh* because of a felt analogy with the older *ghost* and *ghastly. Gherkin* was adapted from the Dutch *(a)gurkkijn,* and the source of its *gh* (not the simple *g*) is something of a mystery, perhaps reflecting older Netherlands usage. *Ghetto* is a direct adoption from Italian, in which *gh* is always pronounced /g/, as in *spaghetti.* Of the other only partially integrated words with *gh,* all are borrowed from Hindi or some other Near Eastern language.

The digraph *ph* was used in Latin to transliterate the Greek letter phi, and most English words with *ph* are old Greek words: *philosophy,* for instance, and *graph.* Eventually in Latin the distinction collapsed between the sound spelled *f* and that spelled *ph,* which led to some interchanging of spellings. Some English words, for instance, went from *ph* to *f* and then, especially during the Renaissance, back to *ph.* This led to some mixed pairs, such as *phantasm* and *fantasy.*

The digraph *sh* was brought into English by the Norman scribes. The /sh/ sound occurred in Old English, but there it was spelled *sc.* The /sh/ sound was new to the scribes, so they cast about for a standard spelling of it, trying *sc, s, ss, ssh, szh,* and *sch.* The digraph *sh,* probably a simplification of the earlier *sch,* became standard in the fifteenth century.

The Romans used *th* to write the Greek letter theta. In Old English the sound /th/ was usually spelled with the thorn or edh, very rarely with *th.* Under the influence of the Norman scribes the runic thorn and edh died away, being replaced in time by the *th.*

Double consonants, like the double *b*'s in *cabbage* and *rubbing,* might in the loose sense of the term be thought of as digraphs, but in the present analysis they will be treated as clusters (as in *cabbage*) or as concatenations (as in *rubbing*). (For a discussion of clusters, see 3.2.1.2; for concatenations, see 3.2.1.3.) Doublets pose no special problems and are discussed in the chapters on consonant sounds and their spellings. The same is true of doublet equivalents like *ck, dg,* and *tch,* which are treated in the discussions of /k/, /j/, and /ch/, at 27.3.3, 30.4.3, and 30.3.2. For the clusters *rh* and *wh* see 3.2.1.1.

11.3 Vowels and Consonants

The distinction between *vowel* and *consonant* is not an easy or obvious one. For one thing, both terms are applied to two different things: sounds and letters. Spoken English contains vowel and consonant sounds; written English contains vowel and consonant letters. The traditional division of the letters is into *a, e, i, o,* and *u* as vowels, and everything else as consonants, with some indecision about *y*, which clearly behaves differently in words such as *yowl* and *owly*.

There are also some complexities in the linguistic division of sounds into vowels and consonants. Linguists who adhere to the distinctive-feature approach to the analysis of sounds posit two descriptive features, which they call **vocalic** and **consonantal.** In *The Sound Pattern of English*, Chomsky and Halle describe these features as follows:

> Vocalic sounds are produced with an *oral* cavity in which the most radical constriction does not exceed that found in the high vowels [i] and [u] [the equivalents of /ē/ and /ū/ in this volume] and with cords that are positioned so as to allow spontaneous voicing; in producing nonvocalic sounds one or both of these conditions are not satisfied. . . . Consonantal sounds are produced with a radical obstruction in the midsagittal region of the vocal tract; nonconsonantal sounds are produced without such an obstruction. (1968, 302)

In terms of these two features, vowel sounds are defined as those that are vocalic and nonconsonantal, while consonant sounds are those that are nonvocalic and consonantal:

(Array 11-3)

	Vocalic	Consonantal
Vowels	+	−
Consonants	−	+

This is a clear and useful description. But it is complicated by two other groups of sounds. The first, the liquids—/l/ and /r/—are vocalic and consonantal. The second, the **semivowels**—/y/, /w/, and /h/—are nonvocalic and nonconsonantal. Thus there are actually four groups of sounds:

(Array 11-4)

	Vocalic	Consonantal
Vowels	+	−
Consonants	−	+
Liquids	+	+
Semivowels	−	−

The liquids and semivowels have special qualities in English orthography that support this four-way distinction rather than the traditional two-way division into vowels and consonants. Liquids, for instance, are exempt from certain tactical constraints on other consonants (see, for instance, 3.2.2 and 10.6.4). Semivowels are involved with the four letters of the English alphabet that are sometimes vowels, sometimes consonants: (1) the letter *y*, a consonant in *yowl* but a vowel in *owly;* (2) the letter *w*, a consonant in *wed* but a vowel in *dew;* (3) the letter *u*, nearly always a vowel, but considered a consonant when it spells /w/, as in *queen* and *language;* (4) the letter *h*, nearly always a consonant, but considered a vowel in words like *John* and *dahlia.*

In the following discussion we will maintain the distinction between vowel and consonant, both sound and letter, as clearly and cleanly as possible, but we will also attempt to do justice to the complexity of the issue. We will, in short, try to balance the desire for accessibility with the need for descriptive adequacy.

As far as the distinctive-feature analysis into vowels, consonants, liquids, and semivowels is concerned, we will treat the last three—consonants, liquids, semivowels—as consonants. In short, the two consonant features—nonvocalic and consonantal—will be considered disjunctive: a sound is a consonant if it has either or both of these two features.

The letters *a, e, i,* and *o* are in all cases treated as vowels. The letters *u* and *y* are sometimes consonants, though usually vowels. The fact that the letter *u* is a consonant when it spells /w/, as in *quiz,* explains the tactics of words like *quitter* and *quizzes,* in which the *t* and *z* are twinned when the suffixes *-er* and *-es* are added. (For more details on twinning see chapter 9.) The letter *y* is a consonant only when it spells the /y/ sound, which is always in syllable-initial position and precedes a vowel, as in *year* or *beyond.*

The letters *h* and *w* are usually consonants. The letter *w* is a consonant when it spells the /w/ sound (*wile, wait*) and when it is part of the clusters *wh* and *wr* (*while, whole, write, wrong*). It is a vowel only in the digraphs *aw, ew,* and *ow,* as in *awful, few, low.* The letter *h* is almost always a consonant, spelling the /h/ sound, as in *hair* and *ahead,* or as part of the consonant digraphs *ch, gh, ph, sh,* and *th* and the clusters *wh* and *rh.* It is a vowel only when it is the second letter in a vowel digraph, as in *ah, oh, uh, John, ohm, dahlia,* and a few other words.

All other letters of the English alphabet are always consonants. Thus we get the following categories: (1) letters that are always vowels (*a, e, i,* and *o*); (2) letters that are sometimes consonants but usually vowels (*u* and *y*); (3) letters that are sometimes vowels but usually consonants (*h* and *w*); and (4) letters that are always consonants (*b, c, d, f, g, j, k, l, m, n, p, q, r, s, t, v, x,* and *z*).

12 Short *a*, /a/

12.1 Historical Sources

The sound that today we think of as short *a*, the sound in *bat*, is probably very close to a sound that existed in Old English, spelled with the ligature ash, *æ*. There was also a long version of this sound, which was apparently the same sound stretched longer and which was more or less consistently marked with some diacritic. Each of these Old English sounds changed in the evolution to Middle English, so that for all intents and purposes there was no sound in Middle English like the one we today think of as short *a*. In general, Old English *æ* evolved into a Middle English sound closer to what we today think of as short *o*, as in *cot*, while Old English *ǣ* evolved into Middle English sounds like modern long *a* or /r/-colored long *a* (see 25.2), or low back sounds close to modern /ä/ and /ò/.

In the Great Vowel Shift the Middle English low back sound evolved into what we today think of as short *a*. In British English, however, when this vowel occurred before the sounds /s/, /f/, and /th/, its evolution was more complex. The Middle English vowel moved to the front of the mouth, becoming what we think of as short *a*, but then it was stretched to a sound similar to the Old English *ǣ*. In time—probably by the late seventeenth or the eighteenth century—this sound moved to the back of the mouth again, becoming broad /ä/. This led to the broad pronunciation of words like *pass, staff,* and *laugh* in British English, and to a lesser extent in the Northeastern dialects of American English (Jespersen [1909] 1954, 1:79–83, 246–47, 422–23; Dobson 1957, 2:545–57; Prins 1972, 78, 83–85, 144–46; for Webster on the "short" versus the "broad" *a*, see Holmberg 1965, 123–24).

12.2   The Major Spelling of /a/

12.2.1   /a/ = *a*

Close to 100 percent of the time /a/ is spelled *a* (Hanna et al. 1966, 468).
The correspondence /a/ = *a* holds in the regular short vowel strings, VCC
and VC#. Words with /a/ = *a* in VCC strings:

(Array 12-1)

absence	aptitude	grammar	rapture
accurate	asteroid	hatchet	saffron
affable	atlas	oleander	salmon
aggravate	chrysanthemum	quack	vascular
angry	fragment	rampage	wrangle

Words with /a/ = *a* in VC# strings:

(Array 12-2)

ad	at	habitat	maniac
am	canal	jab	wag
as	caravan	kayak	yap

The correspondence /a/ = *a* is also common in VCV strings that have
been preempted by the Third Syllable Rule (see chapter 7), the Stress
Frontshift Rule (see 6.4.1), or one of the suffix rules (see chapter 5).

According to the Third Syllable Rule, if the stress is on the third or
fourth syllable from the end of the word, the stressed vowel will be short,
regardless of the tactical string involved. Words with an antepenultimate
/a/ heading a VCV string because of preemption by the Third Syllable
Rule:

(Array 12-3)

amazon	cataclysm	hexameter	octagonal
asinine	cavalcade	latitude	philately
banister	diagonal	manifold	strategy
beatify	extrapolate	masochism	tabulate
caliber	gratify	metabolism	vernacular

Since the Third Syllable Rule also affects stressed fourth syllables, it
produces several cases of preantepenultimate /a/, either primarily or sec-
ondarily stressed, heading a VCV string:

(Array 12-4)

aborigine	animosity	fatigable	navigable
adolescent	apathetic	haberdasher	panacea
amicable	caterpillar	manufacture	vocabulary

The correspondence /a/ = *a* also holds in a number of VCV strings that
have been preempted by the Stress Frontshift Rule. Hundreds of words

adopted from French, following French stress patterns, were originally stressed on the final syllable, thereby producing a short first vowel. As part of the words' adaption into English, the stress was frontshifted to the first syllable, but the quantity of the first vowel remained the same whatever tactical string it might be heading. Thus, in words like the following French adaptions, a short *a* heads VCV strings:

(Array 12-5)

cabin	facet	panel	statute
chapel	imagine	radish	tavern
enamor	maxim	satire	valor

As noted in chapter 5, words affected by the Suffix *-ity* Rule are also affected by the more general Third Syllable Rule. The following words express the correspondence /a/ = *a* in VCV strings immediately preceding *-ity:*

(Array 12-6)

audacity	fugacity	mordacity	rapacity
calamity	generality	nationality	sequacity
depravity	humanity	opacity	tenacity
duality	individuality	perspicacity	vanity

The following words express the correspondence /a/ = *a* in VCV strings that have been preempted by the Suffix *-ic* Rule:

(Array 12-7)

botanic	emphatic	ischiadic	sciatic
ceramic	galvanic	nomadic	uranic

Instances of /a/ = *a* before *-ic* in strings that contain consonant digraphs or clusters that are regularly headed by long vowels:

(Array 12-8)

antipathic	chemiatric	gnathic	seraphic
cambric	fabric	psychiatric	stomachic

12.3   Holdouts to the /a/ = *a* Correspondence

Actually, as far as /a/ is concerned, the question of how it is spelled, unlike most questions dealing with spelling, is remarkably simple to answer: except for *plaid, laugh, draughts,* and a few words with variant pronunciations, /a/ is spelled *a*.

In *laugh, draughts,* and variant pronunciations of *aunt, sauce,* and *saucy* (also *sassy*), /a/ = *au*. The sources of the broad *a* pronunciation are discussed in 12.1. Although this pronunciation has all but disappeared from American English except in New England, it is significant that five of the seven holdouts to the /a/ = *a* correspondence—namely, *dahlia, laugh, aunt, sauce,* and *draughts*—have variant pronunciations with both short and broad *a*. In the eighteenth century there were more holdouts to the /a/ = *a* correspondence, since other *au* words that today have broad *a* then had short *a*—for instance, *flaunt, gauntlet, jaunt,* and *haunt.* An Appalachian dialect rhymes *haunt* with *ant.*

About *plait* the *OED* says that of the three variant pronunciations—/plāt, plat, plēt/—the third, /plēt/, is the most common with the sense "fold, crease—that is, pleat." But the second pronunciation, with /a/, is the most common with the sense "braid"—in which case the variant *plat* also is available. Thus, for all intents and purposes, *plait* is obsolete as a spoken word, its functions being served by *pleat* and *plat.*

Daiquiri, from Cuban Spanish, has a more common and less anomalous variant pronunciation with /ī/ rather than /a/.

The word *plaid,* apparently of Scottish origin, has a Scottish spelling but not a Scottish pronunciation. Its Scottish pronunciation would be /plād/, but during the sixteenth, seventeenth, and eighteenth centuries it was commonly spelled *plad, pladd, pladde*—spellings that suggest the modern pronunciation. Thus, *plaid* very likely represents an instance of mixed convergence: the pronunciation of one word being attached to the spelling of another. (For further examples of mixed convergence, see *ache* at 27.3.2.3 and *colonel* at 32.3.1.3.)

13 Short *e, /e/*

13.1 Introduction

The spelling of /e/ is more complicated than that of /a/, but it is based on one simple correspondence: more than nine times out of ten, /e/ = *e* (Hanna et al. 1966, 518–19). The second most common spelling of /e/ is *ea*, which occurs less than 4 percent of the time. The remaining 3 percent or so of the instances of /e/ are divided among such minor spellings as *ai* (*again*), *ay* (*says*), *ei* (*heifer*), *eo* (*leopard*), *ie* (*friend*), and *u* (*bury*). The following discussion first illustrates the major correspondences, /e/ = *e* and /e/ = *ea*, and then tries to cast some light on the small tangle of minor spellings.

13.2 Historical Sources

In general nearly all of the instances of the correspondence /e/ = *e* derive from early short vowels spelled *e* in Old English or Scandinavian or Old French. A few such instances derive, via shortening, from Old English long vowels—specifically *ē, ēo,* and even *ǣ*. But excluding these, together with a few other miscellaneous shortenings, American English /e/ spelled *e* can be traced back to sources with the spelling *e* (Jespersen [1909] 1954, 1:72–74, 420; Dobson 1957, 2:565–69; Prins 1972, 78, 150). Specific details from the histories of the less important spellings of /e/ are given in 13.4.

13.3 The Major Spellings of /e/

13.3.1 /e/ = *e*

The /e/ = *e* correspondence occurs regularly in VCC and VC# strings. Examples in VCC strings:

(Array 13-1)

apoplexy	effervescent	extract	project
avenger	effort	fellow	quench
beggar	employ	gremlin	settle
brethren	endorse	hexagon	spaghetti
chevron	engender	kennel	ventilate
eccentric	ethnic	lettuce	zest

Words with /e/ = *e* in VC# strings:

(Array 13-2)

bed	compel	hem	lapel
clarinet	duet	jet	wren

Like the /a/ = *a* correspondence, /e/ = *e* occurs in an immense number of VCV strings that have been preempted by the Third Syllable Rule (see chapter 7). A very small sample of such instances:

(Array 13-3)

acetylene	credulous	desiccate	emanate
archipelago	decimal	desolate	emery
benefit	dedicate	disseminate	emissary
benevolent	defecate	ebony	emulate

Words with /e/ = *e* in VCV strings preempted by the Stress Frontshift Rule (see 6.4.1):

(Array 13-4)

decade	leper	penance	resin
denim	level	prelate	senate
especial	melon	premise	tenor
felon	menace	presence	tenure

There are also a few native words with /e/ = *e* in VCV strings that have been preempted by the ambiguity of the consonant *v*, as in *devil* and *eleven*. For other examples see 6.4.2.

For examples of /e/ = *e* in VCV strings that have been preempted by the Suffix -*ity* Rule, see 5.2.

There are many words in which /e/ = *e* in VCV strings that have been preempted by the Suffix -*ic* Rule. A sample:

(Array 13-5)

alphabetic	diuretic	irenic	relic
bathetic	epic	kinetic	synthetic
cretic	frenetic	peripatetic	theopathetic

A number of the words in this array have variant pronunciations with /ē/, but invoking the Principle of Preferred Regularity (see 1.6) brings them into pattern.

There are just a few words with /e/ = *e* in VCV strings that have been preempted by the other suffix rules. With *-ish: blemish, replenish, relish.* With *-id: intrepid.* With *-it: debit, credit, decrepit. Edit* is historically a back-formation from *editor,* which earns its short *e* via the Third Syllable Rule.

13.3.2   /e/ = *ea*

The *ea* spelling of /e/ resulted from a minor change that is slightly different from a major change that occurred during the Great Vowel Shift. In Middle and Early Modern English there were two long vowel sounds: one similar to the present-day /ā/, as in *mate;* the other similar to a stretched short *e,* as in one pronunciation of *mare* (see 25.2). By the end of the Great Vowel Shift these two vowels had converged, becoming what today we think of as long *e,* as in *streak* and *bead* (see 19.1). However, two small groups of words developed differently: In one group the stretched short *e* sound became long *a,* as in *steak* and *break.* In the second group the stretched short *e* became /e/, as in *bread* and *sweat.* Since the stretched short *e* was rather consistently spelled *ea* in Early Modern English, and since the change to /e/ occurred after the spellings had become fairly well fixed, today we still have a small number of words in which /e/ = *ea* (Jespersen [1909] 1954, 1:72, 242–44; Dobson 1957, 2:502–3, 470–71; Prins 1972, 141–42).

For the most part the correspondence /e/ = *ea* occurs before a limited number of consonant sounds, usually /d/, /t/, /f/, /v/, /th/, /th/, /z/, and /zh/, and before consonant clusters and concatenations.

Words with /e/ = *ea* before /d/, /t/, /v/, /f/, /th/, /th/, /z/, and /zh/:

(Array 13-6)

ahead	endeavor	leaven	spread
bread	feather	meadow	stead
breadth	head	measure	steady
breath	heather	peasant	sweat
dead	heaven	pheasant	thread
deaf	instead	pleasant	threat
death	lead ("metal")	read (past tense)	treasure
dread	leather	ready	weather

Words with /e/ = *ea* before consonant clusters and concatenations:

(Array 13-7)

abreast	cleanliness	dealt	realm
breakfast	cleanly*	health	stealth
breast	cleanse	leapt	wealth

These clusters help explain some long- and short-vowel contrasts between derivational pairs: *break* with /ā/, but *breakfast* with /e/; *clean*, but *cleanliness* and *cleanse; deal*, but *dealt; heal*, but *health; leap*, but *leapt; steal*, but *stealth; weal*, but *wealth.*

A few other words in which /e/ = *ea* do not fit into array 13-6 or array 13-7:

(Array 13-8)

jealous	treachery	weapon	zealot

13.4 The Minor Spellings of /e/

In most cases the minor spellings of /e/ reflect relatively late shortenings of earlier long vowels which were not accompanied by changes in spelling.

13.4.1 /e/ = *ai, ay*

Short *e* is spelled *ai* in *against, again,* and *said*. Probably the original long vowel in *against* was shortened by the *nst* cluster. By conservative analogy, this may have led to the shortening of the vowel in the closely related *again*. Interestingly enough, some people still attempt *again* with /ā/. Jespersen suggests that *said* was probably shortened to /e/ because the verb so often occupies an unstressed position in the sentence, which could also explain why /e/ occurs in *says,* apparently the only word in which /e/ = *ay* ([1909] 1954, 1:324–25). This does not explain why the vowel in *say* remains long, but the fact that the *ay* is in word-final position in *say,* but not in *says,* may be involved here, since there appear to be no cases of word-final /e/ in English (Jespersen [1909] 1954, 1:120–21, 324–25; Dobson 1957, 2:498–99; Prins 1972, 168n).

13.4.2 /e/ = *ie, ei*

The vowel sound in *friend* was originally long and may have been expected to develop parallel to, say, *fiend*. The heavy consonant clusters in common derivatives such as *friendship* and *friendly* may have led to a shortening of the vowel in them, which in time, through conservative analogy, carried over to *friend. Fiend,* which did not shorten, does not have common derivatives with such heavy consonant clusters. The /e/ = *ie* in *hygienic* is probably due to the Suffix *-ic* Rule (also sometimes with an /ē/; *AHD* shows /ē/ only). The first vowel sound in *heifer,* one of the hard-core exceptions to the *i*-before-*e* rule, also was originally long. It derives from the Old English *hēahfore,* and in Middle English times there were two main lines of spelling. The first suggests a long vowel: *hayfre, hayfare, heyghfer, heyffer.* The second suggests a short vowel, perhaps shortened by the consonant cluster that developed from the Old English *hf: hekfore, hefker, heffeker, heffre*. The modern spelling of *heifer* can be seen, then, as another instance of mixed convergence, in this case the converging of the long vowel spelling with the short vowel pronunciation (Jespersen [1909] 1954, 1:121, 124; Dobson 1957, 2:471, 476, 477n, 647; Prins 1972, 169n).

13.4.3   /e/ = u

The /e/ = *u* correspondence in *bury* and *burial* is another example of mixed convergence. The two words stem from Old English words spelled with *y: byrgan* and *byrgels*. In certain southern dialects this Old English *y* was spelled *u*, following the Norman influence. In Kent the Old English *y* was pronounced /e/. In the modern words, then, the southern spelling converges with the Kentish pronunciation (Jespersen [1909] 1954, 1:69, 72–73; Dobson 1957, 2:566–67, 713; Prins 1972, 76–77).

13.4.4   /e/ = eo

Short *e* is spelled *eo* in *leopard* and *jeopardy*, and in a variant pronunciation of *feoff*. Jespersen suggests that these words all involved a rare Middle English vowel sound that was similar to the first vowel sound in the name *Goethe* and was rendered *eo* ([1909] 1954, 1:79). This same sound was probably present in *yeoman* and *people* (see 21.3.3 and 19.3.4). In *leopard* and *jeopardy* the sound unrounded to /e/ (Jespersen [1909] 1954, 1:79; Dobson 1957, 2:474). Compare the names *Leonard* and *Geoffrey*.

13.4.5   /e/ = ae

Short *e* is spelled *ae* in a few Latin adoptions, but always, it seems, there are variants with plain *e: aesthetics, esthetics; aestivate, estivate*.

14 Short *i*, /i/

14.1 Historical Sources

The American English correspondence /i/ = *i* basically derives from older vowel sounds also spelled *i*—in Old English, Old Norse, and Old French. Over time, however, this foundation has been widened by a few convergences, two of which merit our attention. The first involved a number of cases in which /e/ had earlier changed to /i/, often before /ŋ/. The change in sound usually, but not always, led to a concomitant change in spelling, with the earlier *e* becoming *i*, as in *think* (OE *thencan*), *ink* (OFr *enque*, *enke*), and *string* (OE *streng*) (Jespersen [1909] 1954, 1:64–66). This change in both sound and spelling widened the extension of the /i/ = *i* correspondence, but in a number of instances, although the /e/ changed to /i/, the *e* did not change to *i*. This partial change added several instances to the common /i/ = *e* correspondence that occurs in unstressed syllables. The less common /i/ = *e* correspondence that occurs in stressed syllables is discussed in 14.4.1.

The second important convergence stemmed from the fact that in a number of Greek adaptions the Greek vowel sound spelled with upsilon was transliterated into *y*, with either an /ī/ or an /i/ sound, thus leading to several instances of the /i/ = *y* correspondence, which is discussed in 14.3.2 (Jespersen [1909] 1954, 1:62–66, 120, 123–24; Dobson 1957, 2:569–70; Prins 1972, 75, 150).

A number of other less important convergences to /i/ also took place, such as the shortening of earlier long vowels, especially before consonant clusters, and the shortening of earlier diphthongs to simple /i/. The historical details of these convergences are provided later in this chapter.

14.2 Stressed and Unstressed /i/

When discussing /i/ in American English, it is important to recognize the differences between /i/ in a stressed syllable and /i/ in an unstressed syllable. In unstressed syllables there is a strong tendency for /i/, like other vowels, to reduce to schwa, /ə/.

Dictionaries vary in their treatment and advice. Kenyon and Knott say this, for instance:

> The nonfinal unaccented vowel spelt *i* and originally pronounced /i/ shows a tendency in innumerable words of normal conversation to be obscured in the direction of the sound /ə/, as in *possible . . . divide*. As a rule only one pronunciation (/ə/ or /i/) is shown in the vocabulary [that is, their dictionary]. The alternative pronunciation with /i/ is permissible if it does not sound artificial (as it would in *possible*), with /ə/ if it does not sound slovenly (as it would in *sluggish*). But such judgments depend somewhat on habit, and as regional practice varies considerably, only an enlightened judgment and observation can decide. (1944, 212–13)

Thus they show an /i/ for the unstressed second *i* in *crisis,* though as the quote says, there is the possibility of a variant with /ə/.

Following Kenyon and Knott, *W3* uses a combination sound symbol, a dotted schwa, which they describe as "a compound or two-part symbol, the two components being /ə/ and the dot of the symbol /i/. [The dotted schwa] is used when /ə/ occurs in some dialects and /i/ in others, or when the same speaker may have /ə/ in ordinary speech but /i/ in formal speech" (34a).

AHD, however, shows just /i/ for the second vowel in *crisis,* and in general seems to prefer /i/ where *W3* often has the dotted schwa. Given the general decision here not to include correspondences that involve unstressed and reduced vowels, the following discussion will deal only with stressed /i/.

14.3 The Major Spellings of /i/

14.3.1 /i/ = *i*

The spelling of /i/ starts with a major correspondence and then becomes somewhat complicated by several minor correspondences. The major correspondence is that in the vast majority of cases (more than nine times out of ten), /i/ is spelled *i* (Hanna et al. 1966, 588–90). Moreover, this correspondence usually holds in the regular short vowel strings, VCC and VC# (see 4.3.3 and 4.2.2).

Instances of /i/ = *i* in VCC strings:

(Array 14-1)

bacillus	fiction	intersect	omniscience
blister	figment	kindred	scissors
distinct	igneous	listen	stripped

Instances of /i/ = *i* in VC# strings:

(Array 14-2)

amid	clip	dim	remit
chagrin	dig	nib	violin

As we might expect, the correspondence /i/ = *i* also applies to the heads of VCV strings that have been shortened by the Third Syllable Rule (see chapter 7). The number of instances in this group is large, and the following is only a small sample:

(Array 14-3)

aborigine	assiduous	capitulate	centrifugal
administer	assimilate	carboniferous	commiserate
articulate	auxiliary	carnivorous	constituent

The correspondence /i/ = *i* also occurs in VCV strings whose head vowels have been shortened by the effects of the Stress Frontshift Rule (see 6.4.1):

(Array 14-4)

chisel	figure	primer	vicar
city	frigate	prison	vigil
consider	image	rigor	vigor

Many instances of /i/ = *i* occur in VCV strings whose head vowels have been shortened by the Suffix -*ity* Rule. A small sample:

(Array 14-5)

ability	adaptability	elasticity	imbecility
acidity	duplicity	humidity	sensibility

Several instances of /i/ = *i* in VCV strings whose head vowels have been shortened by the Suffix -*ic* Rule:

(Array 14-6)

civic	inimical	neolithic	prolific
critic	monolithic	political	sybaritic

The letter *i* is regularly shortened by the Suffix -*ion* Rule, which leads to several instances of /i/ = *i* at the head of VCV strings:

(Array 14-7)

abolition	definition	ignition	prohibition
admonition	deposition	malnutrition	repetition
ambition	derision	minion	requisition

In a few instances, /i/ = *i* where the head vowels of VCV strings have been shortened by the Suffix -*it* Rule. See 5.5 for examples.

A few instances of /i/ = *i* in VCV strings reflect the tactical constraint against double *v* (see 6.4.2).

(Array 14-8)

divot	driven	liver	trivet

For other examples see 6.4.2.

A small number of words with /i/ = *i* in VCV strings are less easily explained. They include:

(Array 14-9)

chili	linen	spigot	wizard
lily	sinew	widow	wizen

Lily derives from Old English *lilie* (with short *i*), which in turn derives from Latin *līlium*. During its early history the short *i* of Old English *lilie* appears to have resisted lengthening, even though it was in an open syllable, probably owing to the Old English Third Syllable Rule (see 7.1.1). Spellings of the word with double *l* occurred during the fifteenth and sixteenth centuries, which suggests the persistence of the short /i/ sound and the growing salience of the VCV/VCC contrast. But the spelling with the historical single *l* has prevailed.

From its origins in Old English, *linen* had two earlier spellings: one with long *i* and a single *n*, the other with short *i* and double *n*. The *OED* shows instances of both *linen* and *linnen* from the eleventh through the eighteenth century. The modern pronunciation and spelling can be treated, then, as another instance of mixed convergence, probably reinforced by analogy with bisyllables affected by the Stress Frontshift Rule.

The Old English source of *sinew* had a complex vowel sound, which was spelled variously, including *seonowe* and *sionwe*. The variety of Old English spellings not too surprisingly gave way to a tangle of Middle and Early Modern spellings as well. The complex Old English vowel simplified to *i* in one line of early spellings, and variants of the word with *nn* evolved from the fifteenth through the eighteenth century.

Spigot is a fairly late addition to the English lexicon. The *OED*'s first citation is from the fourteenth century. The word's origins are obscure, a fact perhaps reflected in the indecisiveness of its written form. The *OED* gives separate entries for two alternants of *spigot*—the metathesized pair *spicket* and *spiddock*—suggesting that the absence of a straightforward historical source caused people to fall back on phonetic spellings, trying to capture the sounds they heard in their dialects' various pronunciations. *Spigot* was also spelled *spiggot* from the seventeenth through the nineteenth century.

The history of *widow* is quite similar to that of *lily. Widow* derives from Old English *widewe* and is another instance of the Old English Third Syllable Rule (see 7.1.1). From the fifteenth through the eighteenth century, spellings with *dd* did occur, but as in the case of *lily,* the historical VCV spelling has persisted, in spite of the short head vowel.

Wizard is a quite late Middle English formation, ultimately from *wise* plus the suffix *-ard,* as in *drunkard, sluggard,* and the like. The *e* disappeared early and the modern pronunciation likely reflects a felt analogy with the *wis* + in the much older *wisdom,* where the cluster would tend to shorten the *i.* Our analysis posits a coset: [*wise, wis* +, *wiz* +]. Spellings of *wizard* with *ss* and *zz* occurred from the sixteenth through the eighteenth century.

The history of *wizen* is somewhat like that of *lily* and *widow.* It, too, derives from an Old English word with a short vowel: *wisnian.* During the early centuries, the *sn* cluster worked to keep the Old English short vowel short. The *OED* shows only two citations between 1050 and 1787: one in 1450 and another in 1513. In the eighteenth and nineteenth centuries *wizen* was sometimes spelled *wizzen.*

14.3.2   /i/ = *y*

When the Romans transliterated Greek words into Latin, they used *y* to represent the Greek upsilon, eventually giving it the value of a normal *i.* This "Greek *i*" occurs in American English in both short and long form, as in *gyp* and *type.* In practically all cases the words with /i/ = *y* are adapted from Greek. The few exceptions are sometimes clearly, other times probably, formed by analogy with true Greek adaptions. The /i/ = *y* correspondence is common in the different forms of the prefix *syn-* (see 10.10).

In Old English and Old Norse the letter *y* also occurred as a vowel spelling. Actually, there was both a long and a short form, *ȳ* and *y,* but the sound represented by Old English *y* was not /i/. In apparently every instance both the sound and the spelling of this Old English or Old Norse *y* changed. In many cases it changed to an *i,* which came to spell the modern short *i.* In each of the following examples the /i/ spelled as *i* was originally a different vowel sound spelled *y* or (rarely) *ȳ* in Old English or Old Norse:

(Array 14-10)

bridge	filth	kiss	thimble
cripple	giddy	kitchen	think
din	inch	little	trim
fill	king	sister	wish

None of the cases of /i/ = *y* in American English derives from the Old English or Old Norse *y*.

Instances of /i/ = *y* in the regular VCC short vowel pattern in Greek adaptions:

(Array 14-11)

abyss	cymbal	laryngeal	rhythm
amethyst	cyst	lynx	strychnine
apocalypse	gypsum	molybdenum	syllable
calypso	hymn	mystery	symbol
cataclysm	hypnotism	mythical	symmetry
chlorophyll	hyssop	nymph	syndicate
crypt	idiosyncrasy	pharyngeal	synthesis
crystal	idyllic	pygmy	system

Non-Greek words with /i/ = *y* in VCC strings:

(Array 14-12)

lymph	sylvan	syphilis	tryst
lynch			

Greek adaptions with /i/ = *y* in VC# strings:

(Array 14-13)

antonym	gym	gyp	hieroglyph

Instances of /i/ = *y* in VCV strings in which the head vowel has been shortened by the Third Syllable Rule:

(Array 14-14)

chrysalis	glycerin	sybarite	synagogue
cylinder	hypocrite	sycamore	synonym
dysentery	polygamous	sycophant	typify

Instances of /i/ = *y* in VCV strings in which the head vowel has been shortened by the Suffix -*ic* Rule:

(Array 14-15)

analytic	electrolytic	patronymic	physics
cynic	hieroglyphic	physician	salicylic

Synod, though ultimately Greek in origin, came into English via Latin, its Latin source being *synodus*. It can be treated, then, as another of that small group of bisyllables in which the vowel at the head of the VCV string is short due to the effects of the Third Syllable Rule working on the trisyllabic Latin source (see 7.3).

14.4   The Minor Spellings of /i/

14.4.1   /i/ = *e*

According to the dictionaries, the correspondence /i/ = *e* occurs only in *England, English,* and *pretty,* although I believe I hear it fairly often in conversational pronunciations of words like *engine, length,* and *strength. England* and *English* reflect the common change of /eŋ/ to /iŋ/, but without the normal change of *e* to *i.* The pronunciation of *pretty,* like certain issues in its etymology, is somewhat mysterious (see the *OED*).

14.4.2   /i/ = *o*

The correspondence /i/ = *o* occurs only in the word *women.* In Old English the singular form was *wīfmon(n)* or *wīfman(n);* the plural was *wīfmen(n).* In Middle English these became *wimman* and *wimmen* (singular and plural). Beginning in the twelfth and thirteenth centuries the /i/ began to be rounded to /ù/, leading in time to the spellings *womman, wommen,* which in about the fifteenth century became *woman, women,* with /wū/ in the singular, /wi/ in the plural, as today. In short, in spite of the change in spelling, the plural has retained an earlier pronunciation. One explanation for this apparent perversity has to do with the desire to establish a clear spoken contrast between the two forms. Following the model of *man, men,* the singular/plural contrast is marked in the second syllables of the written *woman, women.* But unlike *man, men,* the second syllable of *woman, women,* is weakly stressed, which makes the singular/plural contrast, clear in the written form, quite obscure in speech, since the unstressed *man* and *men* both tend to reduce to /mən/. Retaining the earlier pronunciation of the plural creates a phonetic contrast between the stressed first syllables of the spoken words, thereby making the singular/plural contrast clear. Such a strategy, though it surely complicates the sound-to-spelling correspondences of English, does get the job done (Jespersen [1909] 1954, 1:84, 264; Dobson 1957, 2:478).

14.4.3   /i/ = *u*

The stressed correspondence /i/ = *u* occurs only in *busy,* which derives from Old English *bysig* by way of Middle English *bisy.* The spelling with *u* did not appear until the fifteenth century. It is apparently a southern spelling, which generally rendered Old English *y* with the Norman French *u,* keeping the Old English round vowel sound rather than easing it to the /i/ common elsewhere. The American English pronunciation reflects the more typical easing of the Old English vowel sound, but the American English spelling reflects the uneased southern spelling. *Busy,* then, is another instance of mixed convergence—similar to *bury, colonel,* and *ache.* Where there were earlier two separate pronunciations and spellings, we now have the convergence of one pronunciation with the other spelling (Jespersen [1909] 1954, 1:69; Dobson 1957, 2:572).

14.4.4 /i/ = *ee, ea*

The correspondences /i/ = *ee* and /i/ = *ea* occur only in *been, breeches* 'trousers', and in one pronunciation of *creek* and *teat.* Both *breeches* and *teat* have variants that reflect this /i/ pronunciation, *britches* and *tit.* The vowel in *been* was probably shortened because it is so often unstressed. The reasons for the shortenings in the others are less apparent (Jespersen [1909] 1954, 1:115, 239; Dobson 1957, 2:478–79, 503–4).

14.4.5 /i/ = *ei, ie*

The correspondence /i/ = *ei* occurs in the bound base +*feit.* It is stressed in *counterfeit,* unstressed in *forfeit* and *surfeit.* The base +*feit* is a hard-core holdout to the *i*-before-*e* pattern in English.

Because of the effects of simple addition, in a few words the concatenation *ei* is pronounced /i/, as in:

(Array 14-16)

herein (here)(in)	therein	wherein

The correspondence /i/ = *ie* occurs only in the word *sieve. Sieve* derives from Old English *sife,* by way of Middle English *sive,* though, as usual, in Middle English there were an immense number of variant spellings. It is related in both form and content to *sift.* The modern spelling did not appear until the sixteenth century. Its pronunciation is historically regular; its spelling is anomalous.

14.4.6 /i/ = *ui*

In most cases the correspondence /i/ = *ui* is only apparent, for the *u* is a diacritic, not involved with the spelling of the vowel sound, and the true correspondence is the regular /i/ = *i.* Instances:

(Array 14-17)

guild	guilt	guitar	mannequin

In all of the words of this array the *u* either insulates the *g* from the *i* in order to retain a hard sound, /g/, or it is mandated by the preceding *q.*

The only known true instance of /i/ = *ui* occurs in *build* and its past tense, *built. Build* is from Old English *byldan.* Old English *y* regularly develops into American English /i/, as it does here, but normally the spelling would be *i*. The *ui* spelling is apparently from a southern dialect, in which the Old English *y* retained its Old English rounded sound and was spelled in the Norman French fashion, either *u* or *ui*. *Build* and *built*, then, are further cases of mixed convergence. (Jespersen [1909] 1954, 1:118; Dobson 1957, 2:480, 654).

15 The Short *o*'s, /ä/ and /ȯ/

15.1 Introduction

As we noted in 11.1.2, merely identifying the sounds that can be called "short *o*" is in itself difficult, so we might expect some difficulty in spelling them. However, the patterns sort themselves out fairly well. More than 90 percent of the instances of the main short *o*, symbolized /ä/, are accounted for by two major spellings—the unigraphs *o* and *a*—which are tactically distinct. About two-thirds of the instances of the sound we are also calling short *o*, symbolized /ȯ/, also are accounted for by two major and tactically distinct spellings, the digraphs *au* and *aw* (Hanna et al. 1966, 473, 626–27, 636, 638). Except for the word *broad*, all other instances of /ȯ/ are spelled *o* or *a*, and nearly all occur in recent adoptions or in words in which there is much indecision and variation in the pronunciation of the vowel. (For the complex history of these low back vowels, see Jespersen [1909] 1954, 1:90–91, 99–100, 107–111, 297–317, 427–29, 434–37; and Prins 1972, 80, 99, 146–150, 170–71.)

15.2 The Spellings of /ä/

Clearly, the first step should be to identify the distributions of /ä/ = *o* and /ä/ = *a*. The most important distinctions can be stated straightforwardly. The correspondence /ä/ = *o* is the more common of the two, and is well integrated into the English orthographic system, occurring regularly in the tactical patterns and being affected by the same shortening rules that operate on the other short vowels. The correspondence /ä/ = *a* is restricted in distribution and in general is less well integrated. Many of its occurrences are in relatively unadapted foreign words and many have a variant pronunciation with the more integrated /a/.

15.2.1 The Major Spellings of /ä/
15.2.1.1 /ä/ = *a*

The following array offers examples of /ä/ = *a* in words with variant pronunciations. Asterisked words here and in array 15-2 have variants with the more integrated /a/:

(Array 15-1)

adagio*	bravo*	finale*	plaza*
alcalde*	calf*	half*	salve*
almond*	calves*	halves*	scallop*
andante*	cantata	lava*	suave
behalf*	diorama*	pajamas*	
bravado	drama*	pasha*	

In those words in which the pronunciation is more settled, /ä/ = *a* occurs commonly in adoptions that have retained much of their unintegrated foreign sound and look, often in words with the French pronunciation of the -*age* suffix:

(Array 15-2)

bra	maharaja	persiflage	swastika
camouflage	maharani	raja	toccata
garage	massage	sabotage	wampum
guano	mirage	saga*	wigwam
incommunicado	naïve	schwa	yacht
legato	obbligato	sonata	
llama	padre	staccato	

Sometime during the Early Modern period the short *a* sound began to be rounded after /w/ and before /l/ (Jespersen [1909] 1954, 1:316–17). By late in the seventeenth century this rounding had reached polite speech. There was also a tendency to round the short *a* between /w/ and /r/ or /n/, but not before back consonants. The correspondence /ä/ = *o*, though it is about twice as common as /ä/ = *a*, does not regularly occur after /w/ or before /l/. This historical rounding after /w/ underlies nearly all remaining occurrences of the correspondence /ä/ = *a* in American English:

(Array 15-3)

equality	squab	swaddle	wallop
quadrant	squabble	swallow	wallow
qualify	squad	swamp	wan
quality	squadron	swan	wander
qualm	squalid	swap	wanton
quantify	squalor	wad	watch
quantity	squash	waddle	water
quantum	squat	waffle	watt
quarantine	swab	wallet	

Beyond these three groups, /ä/ = *a* occurs in a few pseudo- and imitative words: *aha, huzza, la, mama, papa.* It occurs, too, in the four parallel words *balm, calm, palm,* and *psalm.* (Jespersen [1909] 1954, 1:297–98 discusses this group.) The only remaining known instances of /ä/ = *a* are *father* and one pronunciation of *rather.* Both of these correspondences are, according to the *OED*, "anomalous." There were two pronunciations of *father* in Middle English—one with short *a*, one with long. The pronunciation with long *a* developed from the uninflected nominative form—*fæder*—owing to the lengthening that was brought on by the open syllable in the VCV string. The pronunciation with the short *a* developed from the genitive form, whose inflections led to a consonant cluster after the vowel, thus forestalling any lengthening. The Middle English short *a* would regularly become American English /a/, as in *lather;* the Middle English long *a* would regularly become American English /ä/, as in *bather.* Apparently the presence of both long and short vowel pronunciations caused *father* not to undergo either of the normal vowel changes in Early Modern English. Thus, the anomaly—at least in *father* (Prins 1972, 146).

15.2.1.2 /ä/ = *o*

The distribution of the more common /ä/ = *o* is quite different from that of /ä/ = *a*. The correspondence /ä/ = *o* holds regularly in VCC and VC# strings, but unlike /ä/ = *a*, never after /w/ and only rarely before /l/, as in the following few instances:

(Array 15-4)

absolve	colloquy	follow	lollipop
collar	devolve	folly	mollusk
colleague	doll	hollow	resolve
collier	dolphin	holly	volley

Instances of /ä/ = *o* in other VCC strings:

(Array 15-5)

accomplish	bronze	expostulate	obviate
across	cobble	fondle	occupy
adopt	cockle	goblin	octopus
apostrophe	cognate	hockey	omnibus
approximate	comma	impromptu	opposite
beyond	compress	joggle	progress
blotch	concrete	jostle	prophet
bonnet	consul	longitude	rhomboid
bother	context	nozzle	toboggan
bottle	convent	obdurate	vodka
bottom	doctrine	object	wobble
broccoli	ensconce	obstetrics	zombi

Instances of /ä/ = *o* in VC# strings:

(Array 15-6)

allot	clog	lollipop	rayon
begot	coupon	neon	snob
blob	drop	ocelot	tripod

Since the /ä/ = *o* correspondence is so common in Old Latin and French adaptions, it, unlike /ä/ = *a,* occurs often in VCV strings in which the head vowel has been shortened by one of the shortening rules. Instances of /ä/ = *o* in VCV strings affected by the Third Syllable Rule:

(Array 15-7)

abdominal	evocative	modulate	positive
abomination	hippopotamus	monument	prodigal
chronicle	holocaust	nominee	solitary
colony	idolatry	novelty	sovereign
cooperate	indomitable	omelet	theosophy
document	jocular	optometry	tolerable
ecology	mahogany	phenomenon	volunteer

Instances of /ä/ = *o* in VCV strings in which the head vowel has been shortened by the Stress Frontshift Rule:

(Array 15-8)

honor	modest	process	solace
melancholy	novice	proper	solemn

Instances of /ä/ = *o* in VCV strings in which the head vowel has been shortened by one of the suffix rules:

(Array 15-9)

comic	laconic	pomposity	topic
harmonic	logic	sardonic	viscosity
hydroponics	microscopic	symbolic	zoological

For other examples see chapter 5.

Jespersen suggests that *body* is an instance of a VCV string in which /ä/ = *o* owing to a consonant cluster that occurred in its earlier inflected form ([1909] 1954, 1:117). In *globule* and the noun *project* the correspondence may be /ä/ = *o* owing to the Third Syllable Rule's working on the English pronunciation of their trisyllabic Latin sources: *globulus* and *prōjectum.* In *hovel* and *grovel* the correspondence /ä/ = *o* is consistent with the constraint against *vv.*

A special instance of /ä/ = *o* is the linking particle *o* that is common in usually technical words from Latin and Greek. By and large the linking *o* works to avoid consonant clusters that jar or that tend to blur element boundaries. The linking *o* is regularly stressed, and, usually consistent with the Third Syllable Rule, the stressed linking *o* is pronounced /ä/. Some instances of this correspondence in VCV strings:

(Array 15-10)

accelerometer (acceler + o(meter)	ontology (ont + o + logy)
acidophilus (acid)o + philus)	philosophy (phil + o + sophy)
anthology (anth + o + logy)	psychology (psyche)o + logy)
aristocracy (arist + o + cracy)	rhinoceros (rhin + o + ceros)

15.2.2   The Minor Spellings of /ä/
15.2.2.1 /ä/ = *ow*

The correspondence /a/ = *ow* occurs only in the complex *knowledge* and the derivative *acknowledge,* which blends Middle English *acknowen* 'to recognize, to acknowledge' with Middle English *knowlege.* These explicate to (know)ledge) and (ad + c(know)ledge) (see 10.6.1). The shortening of the expected /ō/ is a case of the native version of the Third Syllable Rule (see 7.1.1). In the Middle English period, when final *e* was still pronounced, *knowledge* had three syllables; *acknowledge* had four, and in both the stress was on the third syllable from the end. Variations with /ä/ and /ō/ occurred in these words up to the nineteenth century (Jespersen [1909] 1954, 1:126–27; Dobson 1957, 2:486).

15.2.2.2 /ä/ = *ah*

The correspondence /ä/ = *ah* occurs only in the pseudowords *bah* and *ah,* in the Hindi adoption *sahib,* and in one pronunciation of the late eighteenth-century coinage *dahlia,* after Anders Dahl, a Swedish botanist.

15.2.2.3 /ä/ = *e*

The correspondence /ä/ = *e* occurs in some recent French adoptions— *encore, entree, entrepreneur, gendarme*—approximating the normal sound of nasalized *e* before *n* in French. The correspondence /ä/ = *e* also occurs in *sergeant,* where the *er* has retained in American English the pronunciation it often has in British English. This British pronunciation is also reflected in the spelling of the proper name *Clark,* which derives from the British pronunciation of *clerk.* Similar cases involve the pairs *university* and *varsity, person* and *parson.*

15.3   The Spellings of /ò/

Among the six spellings of /ò/ the most important are *aw* and *au,* and *au* is
the more common of the two by about two to one. The four minor
spellings are *a, o, oa,* and *ou.*

15.3.1   The Major Spellings of /ò/
15.3.1.1   /ò/ = *aw*

The correspondence /ò/ = *aw* typically occurs in word-final position or
before C#, specifically before word-final *k, l,* and *n.* It is very rare before
CC and CV. Instances of /ò/ = *aw* in word-final position:

(Array 15-11)

caw	gnaw	mackinaw	squaw
claw	guffaw	maw	straw
coleslaw	haw	paw	thaw
daw	jackdaw	raw	
draw	jaw	saw	
flaw	law	seesaw	

Awe also fits into this group, the final *e* being explainable via the Short
Word Rule (see 3.5).

The only known instances of /ò/ = *aw* in quasi-VCC strings are *awkward* and *tawdry. Awkward* is an old complex of the now-obsolete adjective
awk and the suffix *-ward,* the *aw* being regular before C# in the simplex
awk. Tawdry is from *tawdry lace,* which is a simplification of *Seynt Audries
lace,* an instance of the merging of a sound and letter at the end of one
word with the beginning of the following word. But this bit of lore leaves
unanswered the question of why the spelling changed from the more
regular *au* to the less regular *aw.* There was a common variant spelling
with the older *au* up through the eighteenth century.

Instances of /ò/ = *aw* in quasi-VCV strings can be explicated to patterns that are more regular for the *aw* spelling. Instances include:

(Array 15-12)

bawdy (bawd)y)	hawser (hawsé)er), from
brawny (brawn)y)	*hawse* 'to lift' (obs.)
crawfish (craw(fish)	lawyer (law)yer)
	sawyer (saw)yer)

Tawny is a simplex, from Norman French *taune,* from Old French *tane.*
The *OED* suggests that the *aw* and *au* spellings, both common in Middle
and Early Modern English, may have arisen to duplicate the Old French

pronunciation, which had a nasalized vowel before the *n* (see Jespersen [1909] 1954, 1:108–11). The source of *awning* is uncertain beyond the fact that it was a seventeenth-century adoption, probably of nautical origin.

Instances of /ȯ/ = *aw* before C#:

(Array 15-13)

bawl	fawn	scrawl	tomahawk
brawl	gawk	shawl	yawn
brawn	hawk	spawn	
crawl	lawn	sprawl	
drawn	prawn	squawk	

15.3.1.2 /ȯ/ = *au*

The correspondence /ȯ/ = *au* also occurs before C# with some overlap with /ȯ/ = *aw*, though usually the two correspondences occur before different final consonants. The spelling *aw* occurs only before final *l*, *n*, and *k*, while *au* typically occurs before other consonants:

(Array 15-14)

aeronaut	centaur	dinosaur	laud
applaud	daub	fraud	taut

The separation between *aw* and *au* before C# is marked, but not complete. In the following instances /ȯ/ = *au* before *l* and *n:*

(Array 15-15)

faun	haul	leprechaun	maul

Although /ȯ/ = *aw* regularly occurs in word-final position, /ȯ/ = *au* never does. Both occur before C#. But /ȯ/ = *au*, unlike /ȯ/ = *aw*, is very common before CC and CV. Instances of /ȯ/ = *au* before CC:

(Array 15-16)

assault	author	exhaust	laundry
auction	auxiliary	haunch	maudlin
augment	cauldron	jaundice	saunter
aunt*	caustic	jaunt	somersault
auspice	daunt	laugh*	staunch
austere	debauch	launch	vaunt

A special case of *au* before CC involves the cluster *ght:*

(Array 15-17)

aught	distraught	naught	taught
caught	fraught	onslaught	
daughter	haughty	slaughter	

Since the VCV pattern holds for unigraphs but not for digraphs, and since the digraph *au* does not spell long *o* in any American English words (save for a handful of recent Frenchisms—*gauche* and *chauffeur,* for instance), it is not too surprising that /ȯ/ = *au* occurs quite often before CV, creating a kind of quasi-VCV string:

(Array 15-18)

auburn	cauliflower	gaunt	pauper
audacious	causal	gauntlet	plaudit
audible	cauterize	hydraulic	raucous
augur	caution	inaugural	saucer
august	dauphin*	laudable	sausage
authenticity	faucet	marauder	tarpaulin*
automatic	fauna	mausoleum	tautological
autumn	fraudulent	nausea	trauma
caucus	gaudy	nautical	vaudeville

In some cases of *au* before CV the vowel following the consonant is a final *e* that is simply marking a soft *c* or insulating an otherwise final *s* or *z* and thus technically is not involved with the spelling of the vowel.

(Array 15-19)

applause	clause	pause
cause	gauze	sauce

In summary, then, /ȯ/ = *au* is distinguished from the less common /ȯ/ = *aw* as follows, allowing for some minor holdouts here and there: (1) the correspondence /ȯ/ = *aw* occurs in word-final position and before word-final *l, n,* and *k;* (2) the correspondence /ȯ/ = *au* never occurs in word-final position, and it seldom precedes word-final *l, n,* or *k;* (3) unlike *aw, au* occurs regularly before CC and CV.

15.3.2   The Minor Spellings of /ȯ/
15.3.2.1   /ȯ/ = *o*

As far as the major correspondences are concerned, the spellings of /ȯ/ are nicely distinguished from those of /ä/. But with sounds as unstable and easily confused as these two are, we might expect some overlap in their spelling, and overlap there is, especially with the spellings *a* and *o*, which are major spellings of /ä/ and minor ones of /ȯ/.

Instances of /ȯ/ = *o* behave like a transitional group between /ȯ/ and /ä/, and thus are characterized by much variation in pronunciation. A subset of this group consists of words that end with *ogue.* Some examples:

(Array 15-20)

accost	coffin	gone	soft
alcohol	demagog(ue)	loss	synagog(ue)
alcoholic	dialog(ue)	offal	travelog(ue)
analog(ue)	doggerel	office	wroth
belong	dogma	on	
catalog(ue)	epilog(ue)	parasol	
chocolate	foster	prolog(ue)	

The reason for /ȯ/ = *o* in *gone* is not clear. Coming from Old English *gegān,* in the normal development of vowel changes it should have evolved into /ō/ in American English, as is suggested by its modern spelling. Jespersen suggests that the shortening may have resulted from the vowel's normally occurring with weak stress, like the *e* in *been,* but this is not a convincing argument, for *gone* is a full participle rather than an auxiliary ([1909] 1954, 1:314–15; Dobson 1957, 2:505).

In *chocolate,* a fairly recent Spanish adoption, the correspondence /ȯ/ = *o* may occur by analogical extension of the Third Syllable Rule, especially since the remaining two syllables are weak.

15.3.2.2 /ȯ/ = *a*

In the discussion of the /ä/ = *a* correspondence in 15.2.1.1, we mentioned the Early Modern English rounding of short *a* before /l/ and after /w/. This same rounding leads to all of the known cases of /ȯ/ = *a:* after /w/ in *wash, wasp,* and *water,* all three of which have common variants in /ä/; before /l/ in all remaining instances. Some examples of the latter:

(Array 15-21)

alder	altogether	false	stalk
all	always	falsetto	stalwart
almanac*	asphalt*	falter	talk
almighty	bald	halter	walk
almost	balsa	palfrey	waltz
already	caldron	palsied	withal
also	calk	salt	
altar	falcon*	scald	
alter	fall	small	

15.3.2.3 /ȯ/ = *ou*

The correspondence /ȯ/ = *ou* occurs only before *gh,* usually in word-final *ght:*

(Array 15-22)

bought	cough	ought	thought
brought	fought	sought	wrought

Nought, a variant of *naught,* also has variant pronunciations, one with /ä/, one with /ò/. There is a clear parallel here with the instances of *au* before *ght* in array 15-17 (Jespersen [1909] 1954, 1:99–100; Prins 1972, 99, 170–71).

15.3.2.4   /ò/ = *oa*

The correspondence /ò/ = *oa* occurs only in the word *broad.* Since *broad* is from Old English *brād,* it should have evolved to /brōd/ as the spelling suggests, as in *load* and *goad.* Jespersen suggests that the shortening occurred "possibly . . . on account of a shortened form, now extinct; the shortening would naturally occur before consonant-groups, as in *broadly, broadcloth, broadness,* but would by no means be unparalleled before final *d* (cf. *dead*)" ([1909] 1954, 1:315; see also Dobson 1957, 2:505, 530, 534n.3, 541, 542–43n, 759, 796n.4).

16 High Short *u*, /ù/

16.1 Introduction

The two major spellings of /ù/—*u* and *oo*—account for close to 90 percent of all the instances of /ù/ in Hanna et al., with *u* being about twice as frequent as *oo* (1966, 653). High short *u* is formed higher in the mouth than low short *u*. High short *u* is a rare sound in English, and an elusive one. Especially in polysyllables with the correspondence /ù/ = *u*, variant pronunciations are common, /ù/ varying with /ū/ and /ə/. Dictionaries disagree considerably over whether a given word should be pronounced with /ù/. For instance, most cases of /ù/ = *u* in the *AHD* are /ə/, not /ù/, in *W3*. The same is true of the variant /yù/, which is /yə/ in *W3*. In fact, it would appear that the only absolutely clear-cut case of /ù/ = *u* occurs in the disyllable *sugar.* To a remarkable extent words with the correspondence /ù/ = *oo* are from Old English, and those with /ù/ = *u* are from the Romance languages. Thus, the correspondence /ù/ = *oo* is regular in monosyllables or in complexes and compounds that explicate to monosyllabic primes.

16.2 Historical Sources

Historically, /ù/ derives from both the Middle English short *u*, which in sound was close to the modern /ù/, and the Middle English long *u* (Jespersen [1909] 1954, 1:429). The first major source appears to be early short *u* preceded by a labial sound and followed by /l/, as in *bull* (ibid., 333–34; Dobson 1957, 2:720–22). The second major source is early words with variant pronunciations with short and long *u*. In words like *foot* and *could* the presence of the long variant apparently hindered the normal unrounding of early short *u* to the modern low short *u* (Jespersen [1909] 1954, 1:334–35; Dobson 1957, 2:511–12).

16.3   The Major Spellings of /ù/

16.3.1   /ù/ = *oo*

Instances of /ù/ = *oo:*

(Array 16-1)

book	good	rook	took
brook	hood	shook	wood
cook	hook	soot	woof
foot	look	stood	wool

Also included in this group are the following Old English compounds and complexes that explicate either to monosyllabic primes with /ù/ = *oo* or to the Old English suffix *-hood:*

(Array 16-2)

partook (par(took)	boyhood (boy)hood)
hoodwink (hood)(wink)	neighborhood (neighbor)hood)

Parallel instances with /ù/ = *oo* from a Germanic source other than Old English are *crook* (Old Norse), *nook* (Scandinavian), and *hooker* (Dutch). For *moor, boor,* and other instances of /ùr/ see 25.6. Imitative *oomph, oops,* and *oompah* have variant pronunciations with /ù/. The only known Romance instance of /ù/ = *oo* is the monosyllable *rook* 'chess piece'.

16.3.2   /ù/ = *u*

The correspondence /ù/ = *u,* almost always from a non-Germanic source, tends to be most common in polysyllables that do not explicate to monosyllabic primes. It is also common in the suffix *-ure* and in the nonsuffixal ending *ure,* which are discussed in 25.6.1.1. Instances of /u/ = *u* in stressed VCC strings:

(Array 16-3)

ambush	bulletin	butcher	pulley
buffet (n.)	bullion	pudding	pulpit
bullet	bushel	pullet	push

The correspondence /ù/ = *u* also occurs in weakly stressed VCV or V.V strings, though the number of variant pronunciations encountered in these contexts reveals the contention between, on the one hand, the lack of stress urging reduction to /ə/, and, on the other, the VCV or V.V strings urging long vowels. The asterisked words in array 16-4 are variously pronounced with /yù/, /ə/, /ū/, or a combination of the three:

(Array 16-4)

adjutant*	erudite*	sensual*	superfluous*
conjugal*	quadruped*	sensuous*	
conjugate*	quadruple*	sugar	

Instances of /ù/ = *u* in Old English are *pull, bull, full,* the related suffix *-ful* (as in *handful, cupful*), and *put.* Germanic words other than Old English are *bulwark* (Middle High German), *bush* (Middle Low German), and *kaput* (German). *Hussar* is Hungarian. *Cuckoo* is imitative.

16.4 The Minor Spellings of /ù/

16.4.1 /ù/ = *ou*

The correspondence /ù/ = *ou*, clearly showing the influence of the Norman scribes in Middle English, is most common before *r* in the cluster /ùr/, which is treated in 25.6.2. The other known instances of /ù/ = *ou* are Norman-influenced respellings of Old English words: *could* (Old English *cūthe*), *should* (Old English *sceolde*), and *would* (Old English *wolde*). (See Jespersen [1909] 1954, 1:334–35; Dobson 1957, 2:451–52, 456–57, 462–63.)

16.4.2 /ù/ = *o*

All known instances of the correspondence /ù/ = *o* are from Old English: *bosom* (Old English *bōsm*), *wolf, wolves* (Old English *wulf, wulfas*), and *woman* (Old English *wīfman(n), wīfman(n)*) (see 14.4.2).

16.5 The Spellings of /ù/ Summarized

Although there is some unpredictability about the minor spellings of the high short *u* and about its pronunciation in cases of /ù/ = *u* in lightly stressed VCV and V.V heads, still the major correspondences, which account for nearly nine out of ten instances of /ù/, sort themselves out rather clearly. With very few holdouts, /ù/ = *oo* in monosyllabic primes, especially those from Old English or other Germanic sources, while /ù/ = *u* in polysyllables derived from non-Germanic sources.

17 Low Short *u*, /u/

17.1 The Major Spellings of /u/

The correspondence /u/ = *u* holds nearly 90 percent of the time, while /u/ = *o* holds nearly 10 percent of the time. The remaining few instances of /u/ are accounted for by two minor spellings, *ou* and *oo* (Hanna et al. 719).

17.1.1 /u/ = *u*

The correspondence /u/ = *u* occurs regularly in the short vowel strings VCC and VC#. Instances in the VCC string:

(Array 17-1)

adjudge	industrial	sculptor	umbrella
blush	juggle	suffer	uncle
bucket	luster	suspect	unctuous
construct	publish	triumph	under
custom	pulse	udder	vulnerable
dumbfound	redundant	ultimate	yummy

Instances in the VC# string:

(Array 17-2)

annul	drum	mum	rub
begun	dud	omnibus	shut
club	gut	overrun	slug
cup	homespun	plus	walnut

The correspondence /u/ = *u* is relatively rare in VCV strings, and in those few instances in which it does occur, it is seldom due to the effect of one of the shortening rules. As noted in 5.2.2.1 and 7.2.1, long *u* has a strong tendency to resist the regular shortening rules. Instances of /u/ = *u* in VCV strings whose head vowel is affected by the Stress Frontshift Rule:

(Array 17-3)

| bunion | ducat | pumice | study |

For /u/ = *u* in syllables affected by the Third Syllable Rule, see 7.2.1. Most instances of /u/ = *u* in VCV strings occur in complexes or compounds that explicate to the more regular VC# pattern, as in *bugaboo* (bug)a(boo) (?) and *runaway* (run)(away). The correspondence /u/ = *u* is common in VCV strings created when *un-* or *sub-* is added to a stem starting with a vowel:

(Array 17-4)

| subequatorial | suborbital | unemployed | unorthodox |
| subirrigated | suburb | unintelligent | unusual |

17.1.2 /u/ = *o*

The most common spelling of /u/, *u*, occurs regularly in VC# and VCC strings, but quite rarely in the VCV pattern. The second major spelling, *o*, has almost the reverse distribution: /u/ = *o* also occurs regularly in VCC strings, but is common in VCV strings and rare in the VC# pattern. A number of modern *o* spellings of /u/ evolve from Old English *o* and *ō*, whose sounds became /ù/ in Middle English and then in many instances were lowered to /u/ in the Early Modern period. Instances are *glove, brother,* and *other,* all spelled *ō* in Old English; and *oven* and *shovel,* in Old English spelled *o* (Jespersen [1909] 1954, 1:426–27, 330–33; Prins 1972, 151–52).

The *o* spelling of /u/ arose in large part because of the two different ways in which the French and English writing systems were getting "crowded." First, in the miniscule script used in manuscripts during the Middle English period, many letters—*i, u, n, m, w,* and *v*—were made of combinations of simple downstrokes called **minims.** Since the style was to compress the words, leaving little white space, this led to genuine legibility problems when "minim letters" came in succession. For instance, the word *minim* itself would consist of ten downstrokes arranged in a crowded, more or less undistinguished string. Obviously this led to problems for readers, especially in view of the wide dialect differences in spelling and pronunciation at that time. To help ease this problem, scribes began using *o* for *u* where a *u* would lead to an unbroken series of potentially ambiguous minims—that is, adjacent to other minim letters like *m* and *n* and the still-evolving *u, v,* and *w.* Thus, to a certain extent the present correspondence /u/ = *o* is due to an old bit of spelling reform designed to make things easier for the reader, not the writer (Prins 1972, 79–80).

The second type of crowding that led to the use of *o* for *u* occurred in French during the same period. In French the letter *u* was used to represent the consonant sound /v/ and a number of different vowel sounds produced by various simplifications and convergences in the transition from Latin to French. In English much the same crowding occurred: *u* was used to spell /v/ plus a number of different vowel sounds. One attempt to reduce the workload on *u* again involved using the French spelling *o* in its place (Jespersen [1909] 1954, 1:87–90).

As a result of all this, there is a strong tendency for the correspondence /u/ = *o* to occur before or after minim letters such as *m, n, u, v, w,* and *i.* Instances of /u/ = *o* in the short vowel string VCC and before or after minim letters:

(Array 17-5)

affront	discomfit	month	smother
among	front	mother	spongy
comfort	mongrel*	nothing	tongue
confront	monkey	pommel*	wonder

Instances of /u/ = *o* in VC# strings include *son, ton,* and *won,* all of which were originally spelled with a *u* in Old English and in all of which the *o* is adjacent to a minim letter.

In the majority of cases of /u/ = *o* in VCV strings, the *o* also falls either before or after minim letters. But since many of the words involved are Romance adoptions, they also reveal the effects of the shortening rules. Since *o* was not used to spell long *u* in Middle English, the persistent long *u* was not such an issue with *o,* so the *o* spelling of short *u* seemed to be more commonly affected by shortening rules than did the *u* spelling. Instances of /u/ = *o* in VCV strings in which the head vowel is shortened by the Stress Frontshift Rule:

(Array 17-6)

color	covet	dozen	money
covert*	covey	hovel (?)	stomach

Instances due to the Third Syllable Rule include *onion, covenant,* and *somersault.*

Several instances of /u/ = *o* in VCV strings reflect respellings of words in which *u* was adjacent to minim letters:

(Array 17-7)

above	dove	love	some
come	honey	shove	

Special cases of /u/ = *o* in VCV strings include *none, one,* and *done. One* and *none* belong to the important group that includes *once, only, atone, alone.* At the root of these words is the Old English *ān,* which would normally have evolved into /ōn/, as with *stone* and *bone* from Old English *stān* and *bān.* The only words in the group that followed that normal evolution, however, are *alone* (all)(one), *atone* (at)(one), and *only* (one)ly). In the others the vowel shortened. Old English *ā* developed regularly into a Middle English vowel similar to modern /ò/. During the Great Vowel Shift this Middle English vowel normally evolved into /ō/, as in *home.* This normal evolution explains *alone, only,* and *atone.* But the remaining members of the group went through a shortening process that resulted in /ù/, which then in the seventeenth century was lowered to /u/. Thus we have *none, once, one* (Jespersen [1909] 1954, 1:333). For more on *one* and *once* see 33.2.1.

17.2   The Minor Spellings of /u/

17.2.1   /u/ = *oo*

The correspondence /u/ = *oo* occurs only in *blood* and *flood,* from Old English *blōd* and *flōd,* which in Middle English took on the long *o.* This long *o* was shortened to /ù/ in the sixteenth century, and then was lowered in the seventeenth to /u/, before sounds like /d/, pronounced with the tip of the tongue against the upper alveolar ridge (Jespersen [1909] 1954, 1:332; Prins 1972, 87, 133–34).

17.2.2   /u/ = *ou*

The correspondence /u/ = *ou* occurs in two groups of words—one group from Old French, the other from Old English. Instances of Old French adaptions:

(Array 17-8)

country	cousin	touch
couple	double	trouble

Related is *doubloon* (from Spanish *doblon*), which explicates to (double)oon).

The Old English group consists essentially of words with *ō* or *ū* in Old English, which underwent some version of the shortening and lowering described earlier, usually before *gh* = /f/, representing an Old English velar fricative (Jespersen [1909] 1954, 1:287):

(Array 17-9)

enough (OE *genōg*)   southern (OE *sūtherne*)
rough (OE *ruh*)   tough (OE *tōh*)
southerly (cf. *south,* from OE *sūth*)

Related are *young* (Old English *geong*), *chough* (akin to Old English *cēo*), and *slough* (which rhymes with *rough* but is of obscure structure).

18 Long *a*, /ā/

18.1 Historical Sources

The spellings of /ā/ are complicated in two ways. First, and most important, /ā/ is the product of a historical process that caused several different earlier sounds, and their attendant spellings, to converge. As usual, the changes in sound were more numerous than the changes in spelling, so today we have a number of spellings that represent distinctions that are no longer made. The second complication, closely related to the first, is the fact that we have adopted a number of foreign words that contain sounds we pronounce as /ā/ while keeping the original foreign spellings.

18.1.1 Middle English Long *a*

In Middle English there were at least three sounds that subsequently converged to the modern /ā/. The first, the Middle English long *a*, had a long "ah" sound. During the Great Vowel Shift in the sixteenth and seventeenth centuries this sound shifted forward in the mouth as the tongue was raised a bit in its articulation. The result was a shift to a vowel sound much closer to what we today think of as long *a*, /ā/. The four major sources of Middle English long *a* were as follows (Jespersen [1909] 1954, 1:81–83).

(Array 18-1)

Words with the Old English short vowels *a*, *æ*, and *ea* in open syllables, which evolved into such American English words as:

acre	graze	ladle	shade
ape	hate	name	shame
bathe	hazel	raven	snake

Words with a Scandinavian short vowel in an open syllable:

gate, gait	same	scathe	take

Old French words with a long *a:*

able	blame	danger	nature

Old French words with *au:*

chafe	flame	gauge	save

18.1.2 Two Middle English Diphthongs

Also, in early Middle English two diphthongs were distinguished from each other both in pronunciation and spelling. One was spelled *ai* or *ay*, the other *ei* or *ey*. By the end of the Middle English period these two sounds had converged into one, though at the beginning the two diphthongs had different sources (Jespersen [1909] 1954, 1:96–98; Prins 1972, 167–69):

(Array 18-2)

Old English words with a vowel plus *g* (the Old English *g* here spelling a sound very close to the present-day /y/), which evolved into such Modern English words as:

brain	gray, grey	maiden	nail

Words with a Scandinavian *ei:*

bait	raise	swain	they

Words with Old French *ai* or *ei:*

aid	pray	survey	vein

18.1.3 From Middle to American English

The Middle English distinction between *ai* and *ei* (and between *ay* and *ey*) and the Old French distinction between *ai* and *ei* are only partially still with us, for during the late Middle English and Early Modern periods many words originally spelled with *e* were respelled with *a*. Some examples:

(Array 18-3)

Old French	Middle English	American English
constraindre	constreinen	constrain
deintié	deinte	dainty
desdeign	desdeynen	disdain
despérer	despeiren	despair
estreit	streit	strait
feid, feit	feith, feth	faith
peindre	peynten	paint
peine	paine	pain
preier	preyen	pray
presier	preisen	praise

The pronunciation and spelling of the Early Modern long *a* and the diphthong were kept distinct through the sixteenth century; words like *ail* and *ale, pain* and *pane, sail* and *sale,* were not then homophones. In the seventeenth century the convergence of the two sounds began and by the eighteenth century it was complete. Thus we have sounds and spellings from close to a dozen Old English, Old Scandinavian, and Old French sources converging into three Middle English sounds, which then converged into two Early Modern English sounds, which finally converged into what in American English we perceive as one sound, /ā/, or long *a*. And all of this phonological convergence was accompanied by minimal and inconsistent attempts to adjust the spellings of such words. However, there are patterns at work in the various spellings of long *a*, and these will help clear things up.

18.2   The Major Spellings of /ā/

The words in array 18-1, all of which reflect the Middle and Early Modern English long *a*, express the correspondence /ā/ = *a* at the head of a VCV string. However, in the words in array 18-2, all of which come from the Early Modern diphthong, the /ā/ sound is spelled with a digraph, usually either *ai* or *ay*. The spellings *a*, *ai*, and *ay* are the major spellings of /ā/, accounting for nearly 90 percent of the instances of /ā/ in Hanna et al. (1966, 441–42).

18.2.1   /ā/ = *a*

Of these major spellings *a* is far and away the most important, accounting by itself for about 80 percent of the instances of /ā/.

Instances of /ā/ = *a* in regular VCV strings are fairly rare in word-initial position:

(Array 18-4)

aces	aged	amiable	apiary
aching	alias	apex	atheist
acorn	alien	aphid	aviation

There are no instances of /ā/ = *a* in word-final position, but the correspondence is extremely common in word-medial VCV strings, very often in such suffixes as *-ate*, *-ation*, *-aceous*, *-acean*, *-acious*, *-ane*, *-ative:*

(Array 18-5)

audacious	chicanery	insane	paraphrase
bakery	evasive	kleptomaniac	renegade
basis	exaggeration	marmalade	tornado
became	gracious	mistaken	vacation
capable	hurricane	oasis	vaporize

Words with /ā/ = *a* at the head of VC*l*V and VC*r*V strings (for other examples see 4.3.3.1):

(Array 18-6)

able	atrium	macron	sacroiliac*
apricot*	fragrant	matriarch	sacrum
April	glabrous	sable	satrap*

The correspondence /ā/ = *a* holds at the head of V.V strings. Notice that the V.V pattern preempts the suffix -*ic* and -*ity* rules:

(Array 18-7)

aedes	algebraic	archaic	mosaic
aeneous	aorta	chaotic	phaeton*

The correspondence /ā/ = *a* holds at the head of several VCC strings. For more details see 4.3.3.1.

18.2.2   /ā/ = *ai, ay*

After *a* the most important spellings of /ā/ are the pair *ai* and *ay.* These two spellings bear a clear relationship to each other: almost without exception *ai* is used in word-initial and medial positions, while *ay* is used in word-final position. Words with word-initial or medial /ā/ = *ai:*

(Array 18-8)

afraid	braid	hail	paint
aid	caisson	grain	quail
ail	disdain	liaison	sustain
aim	explain	maintain	travail
attain	faith	maize	waitress

A number of words with word-medial *ai* are closely related to words with word-final *ay: laid, lay; staid, stay; portrait, portray.* Other words with word-final *ay:*

(Array 18-9)

array	caraway	gray	relay
away	dismay	jay	say
bay	display	may	spray
betray	flay	okay	tray

The correspondence /ā/ = *a* does not occur in word-final position, and usually when *ay* appears to be in medial position, the word explicates to a prime with word-final *ay:*

(Array 18-10)

layman (lay)(man)	rayon (ray)on)
mayhap (may)(hap)	waylay (way)(lay)

Always is an old genitive, (al(way)s).

Some instances of nonregular medial *ay* occur in fairly recent adoptions that reflect French spellings: *layette, mayonnaise, bayonet, crayon.* One older word that appears to be a true holdout is *mayhem,* although it does have a more regular but less common variant spelling, *maihem.*

The most common spelling of /ā/, *a,* regularly occurs in some form of the VCV pattern. Although *ai* also occurs sometimes just before CV—as in *traitor* or *raisin*—usually there is an element boundary between the C and the V following the *ai.* Thus, although *raisin* is a single element, *traitor* explicates to (trait + or), with a boundary dividing the quasi-VCV string. This is typical of words in which *ai* precedes the CV:

(Array 18-11)

aileron	(ail + eron), a rare French diminutive
available	(avail)able)
bailiff	(bail)iff); cf. *plaintiff* and *caitiff*
claimant	(claim)ant)
complaisant	(complais + ant)
daily	(day̸)i + ly) (?)
daisy	A distant and obscured compound of *day's eye,* which technically explicates to (day̸)i + s + y), but is probably better treated as a simplex
gaily	(gay̸)i + ly)
jailer	(jail)er)
lackadaisical	From *lackadaisy,* from *lackaday*
maiden	(maid)en)
raiment	(rai + ment); *rai* + is a coform of the + *ray* in *array.*
tailor	(tail)or); the base *tail* is not related to the common noun, as in "tail of the dog," but occurs in *entail, detail, retail,* and the legal term *tail.*

The explication of *liaison* is less certain, and the word may well have to be treated as a holdout to the pattern being described here.

In the following words the final *e* is insulating a *v* or a single *s* or *z* that would otherwise fall at the end of a terminative base. The *e* is not part of the spelling of the /ā/ sound:

(Array 18-12)

appraise	maize	polonaise	waive
braise	malaise	praise	
chaise	mayonnaise	raise	

The following words, with their fossil final *e*'s, must be treated as holdouts to this pattern (see 8.1.6):

(Array 18-13)

aide	moraine	romaine
cocaine	ptomaine	

The only known cases of /ā/ = *ai* in V.V strings are *naiad* and *maieutic*.

18.2.3 Summary

The *ai* spelling of /ā/ occurs regularly in front of C# or CC#, as in *pain* and *paint*. With a very few holdouts, the *ai* spelling does not occur before CV, a setting that is regular for the *a* spelling. In cases where *ai* seems to head a quasi-VCV string, an element boundary almost always intervenes. Thus, there is a fairly distinctive distribution pattern for the three main spellings of /ā/: *a* occurs in VCV strings, in word-initial and medial positions, but not in word-final position; *ai* occurs in front of C#, CC#, or C followed by an element boundary, in initial and medial positions; and *ay* occurs only in word- or element-final position. These three major spellings, ruly and quite predictable, account for nearly 90 percent of the instances of /ā/.

18.3 The Minor Spellings of /ā/

There are eight minor spellings of /ā/, plus three more that occur in only one word each.

18.3.1 /ā/ = *ei, ey*

The most important of these minor spellings are *ei* and *ey*. They are closely related to *ai* and *ay*, coming as they do from different spellings of the same Early Modern English diphthong. The spelling *ei* is medial; *ey* is final. Although it does not seem to be possible to write a tactical description that separates *ai* from *ei* or *ay* from *ey*, some solace is found in the observation that the spellings with *a* are much more common than those with *e*. The following are fairly exhaustive lists for *ei* and *ey*.

Words with /ā/ = *ei*:

(Array 18-14)

beige	feint	obeisance	skein
deign	heinous	reign	surveillant
eight	lei	rein	veil
feign	nisei	reindeer	vein

Like *ai*, *ei* occurs regularly before C# or CC#, as in *rein* and *feint*. Usually, apparent holdouts explicate to the regular pattern:

(Array 18-15)

heinous	(hein + ous)	The base *hein +*, historically related to *hate*, apparently occurs only in this one word, but the suffix is clear enough.
obeisance	(obeis + ance)	The stem *obeis +* is a coform of *obey* and *obed +*, as in *obedient*.

The final *e* in *beige* is not part of the /ā/ spelling; it marks the soft *g*. The final *ei*'s in *lei* and *nisei* are the only known cases of word-final *ei*. Both are very recent, twentieth-century, adoptions—one from Hawaiian, the other from Japanese.

Words with element-final *ey:*

(Array 18-16)

bey	mangabey	survey	whey
convey	obey	they	
fey	prey	trey	
hey	purvey	wey	

Abeyance explicates to (abey + ance), with element-final *ey*.

18.3.2   /ā/ = *eigh, aigh*

The minor spellings *eigh* and *aigh* are special cases of the *ei* and *ai* spellings. Words with *eigh:*

(Array 18-17)

eight	inveigh	neighbor	weigh
freight	neigh	sleigh	weight

Except for *inveigh* and *sleigh,* in each case the *gh* reflects a lost Old English velar fricative, spelled either *g* or *h* in Old English. *Inveigh* comes from the Latin *invehī*, and it seems likely that back in Middle English times the *h* was confused with the Old English velar *h*, thus leading to the *eigh* spelling, with perhaps a conservative analogy to a word like *weigh*. *Sleigh,* an American adoption from the colonial Dutch *slee,* remains more of a mystery.

The only word in which /ā/ = *aigh* is *straight,* whose *gh* reflects the velar fricative in its source, the Old English *streht,* the past participle of *streccan* 'to stretch'. Though the Middle English spelling of this word is quite confused, it can be treated as one of the several cases in which an earlier spelling with *e* was regularized to *a*—or *ai*. In this way the loss of the early velar led to the *aigh* spelling.

18.3.3 /ā/ = *ea*

The sound /ā/ is spelled *ea* in only four words: *break, great, steak,* and *yea.*
In *steak* the pronunciation is historically regular but the spelling is odd. In
the other three the spelling is regular but the pronunciation is /ā/ where
regularly we would expect /ē/. Why these three resisted the regular shift to
/ē/ during the Great Vowel Shift is not at all clear. Jespersen suggests—
though, as he says, "with some doubt"—that *break* may have resisted the
shift because of its tie in, via conservative analogy, with the shortened
base in *breakfast. Great,* he suggests, may have resisted because of an
analogical tie with its comparative and superlative forms; its comparative
form, for instance, was earlier *gretter,* rhyming with *better.* And *yea,*
Jespersen suggests somewhat more assuredly, probably became /ā/ because it was normally paired and contrasted with *nay* ([1909] 1954, 1:338–
39).

18.3.4 /ā/ = *et*

In slightly more than a dozen words /ā/ is spelled *et.* This is the case in
relatively recent French adoptions and in words in which /ā/ is in word-
final position:

(Array 18-18)

ballet	cachet	gourmet	sobriquet
beret	crochet	parquet	valet
bouquet	croquet	piquet, picquet	
buffet	filet	ricochet	
cabriolet	flageolet	sachet	

18.3.5 /ā/ = *e, ee*

Long *a* is spelled *e* in the Italian adoptions *andante* and *allegro* and *e* or *ee*
in a few relatively unintegrated French adoptions:

(Array 18-19)

café, cafe	forte
carburetor	matinee, matinée
crepe, crêpe	melee
elite	negligee, negligée, négligé,
entrée, entree	negligé, neglige
fete, fête	regime, régime

The /ā/ = *e* correspondence is also found in other relatively unintegrated adoptions: the Spanish *mesa* and *alcalde,* and the Hawaiian *ukulele.*

18.3.6 /ā/ = *ae, ao, au*

Long *a* is spelled *ae* in *usquabae, usquebae* 'whiskey'; in *tael;* and in *Gaelic*. It is spelled *ao* in the rather old-fashioned British *gaol,* which is perhaps best considered not a part of American English at all. It is spelled *au* in *gauge,* which has the more regular but less common variant *gage*. In a number of words from French, *au* simplified to *a* pronounced /ā/. Apparently *gauge* made the change in pronunciation but kept the old *u* spelling.

19   Long *e, /ē/*

19.1   Historical Sources

As in the case of all the other long vowel sounds in English, the spelling of /ē/ is complicated by a complex family tree. In Middle English times the vowels still had their Continental sounds, so the Middle English long *e* was closer to what we today would call a long *a*. Actually, there were two Middle English long *e* sounds. One, the so-called close form, sounded like the *a* in American English *mate*, /ā/. The second, the open form, sounded like the *a* in *mare*, which might be described as a "stretched" /e/ (Mossé 1952, 22–23; Prins 1972, 131–32, 138–41). The sounds were distinguished quite carefully in Middle English. For instance, poets did not rhyme one with the other. But the two sounds were spelled rather indiscriminately (Jespersen [1909] 1954, 1:76–79).

The close Middle English long *e*, /ā/, had five major sources, which are described below, together with several representative modern descendants (Jespersen [1909] 1954, 1:74):

(Array 19-1)

Words with Old English *ē*:

| cheese | need | queen | sheep |

Words with Old English *ēo*:

| creep | fiend | knee | seethe |

Words with Old English *œ̄* (the long *o + e* ligature, not the long ash):

| beseech | meet | seek | teeth |

Words with Old English *e*, which lengthened before *ld*:

| field | shield | yield |

French words with long *e*:

| achieve | decree | niece | siege |

The open Middle English long *e*, the stretched /e/, also had five major sources (Jespersen [1909] 1954, 1:74–76):

(Array 19-2)

Words with Old English *ǣ* (the long ash):

| heathen | lead (v.) | mean | sea |

Words with Old English *ēa:*

| beacon | east | flea | leaf |

Words with Old English *e*, lengthened in open syllables:

| bequeath | eat | meal | weave |

French words with *e* in Anglo-Norman:

| eager | increase | lease | plead |

Words adopted directly from Latin and Greek:

| aegis, egis | amoeba, ameba | phoenix, phenix |

Although the spellings of the Middle English /ā/ and stretched /e/ were not carefully distinguished, the beginnings of a pattern are clearly discernible. By and large the modern words that descended through the close Middle English /ā/ tend to be spelled either *ee* or *ie*. The modern words that descended through the open Middle English stretched /e/ tend to be spelled *ea* or *e*, at the heads of VCV strings. In the sixteenth century a more or less careful attempt was made to strengthen and regularize this pattern. The Early Modern English vowel that had come from Middle English /ā/ was spelled *ee, ie,* or *ei,* while that from the stretched /e/ was spelled *ea* or *e,* before CV strings. In fact, however, the *e* spelling tended to be used for both and became the major spelling (Jespersen [1909] 1954, 1:76–79).

During the Great Vowel Shift of the fifteenth and sixteenth centuries, Middle English close long *e* shifted to a sound closer to what we today think of as long *e*, the vowel in *meet*, /ē/. The Middle English stretched /e/ also shifted, becoming /ā/. So in Early Modern English there were still two sounds: /ā/ and /ē/. During the seventeenth and eighteenth centuries the two vowels converged, and by the end of the eighteenth century there was only one sound, the modern long *e*, /ē/ (Jespersen [1909] 1954, 1:238–39, 242–43; Prins 1972, 122–27). Thus, the American English long *e* represents the convergence of two Middle English vowel sounds, which themselves represent the convergence of nearly a dozen major earlier sources. This multiple convergence accounts for much of the diversity in the spellings of /ē/, this plus the fact that adoptions from French and other languages after the Great Vowel Shift often contained vowels that we pronounce /ē/ but spell according to their foreign spellings. Thus, for instance, the many cases in which /ē/ is spelled with the Continental *i*, as in *machine*.

19.2   The Major Spellings of /ē/

The five major spellings of /ē/—*e, y, i, ee,* and *ea*—account for about 97
percent of the instances in Hanna et al. The first three alone account for
more than 80 percent, and *e* alone accounts for about 40 percent (1966,
492–93).

19.2.1   /ē/ = *e*

The major spelling of /ē/, *e,* usually occurs in the regular long vowel strings
VCV or V.V. Words in which /ē/ = *e* in VCV strings, in initial and medial
positions:

(Array 19-3)

athlete	edict	magnesium	supremely
blaspheme	evening	obese	veto
cedar	extremist	senior	zenith
congenial	hyena	species	zoogamete

Words in which /ē/ = *e* in V.V strings, and in which both vowels occur
in the same element:

(Array 19-4)

area	creosote	linoleum	pancreas
beatify	eolian	meander	pleonasm
cameo	eon	oceanic	rodeo
chameleon	galleon	oleander	theater
cornea	genealogy	osteopath	theory

The correspondence /ē/ = *e* often occurs in V.V strings involving
certain prefixes and suffixes:

(Array 19-5)

-ean	epicurean, herculean
-eous	homogeneous, hideous, igneous, instantaneous
-eum	coliseum, lyceum, mausoleum, museum
geo-	geodetic, geographic, geology, geometry
homeo-	homeostasis
neo-	neolithic; neon, (neø + on); neophyte

In V.V strings the correspondence /ē/ = *e* is often the product of simple addition, as in *reappear* (re(appear) and *atheist* (a(the + ist). Other
instances:

(Array 19-6)

albeit (al(be)(it)	create (cre + ate)
being (be)ing)	deism (de + ism)
choreography (chore + o(graph)y)	heterogeneity (heter + o(gene)ity)

linear (line)ar) (see 8.2.1)   pharyngeal (pharynge + al)
nucleus (nucle + us)   phraseology (phrase)o + log + y)
paleontology (pale(ont + o + log + y)   rheostat (rhe + o + stat)
pantheon (pan + the + on)   stereophonic (stere + o(phoné)ic)

The correspondence /ē/ = *e* occurs in final position. Words from Old English:

(Array 19-7)

be	maybe	she	we
he	me	the (stressed)	

Words from Latin or Greek:

(Array 19-8)

aborigine	anemone	epitome	simile
acme	apostrophe	hyperbole	syncope
acne	catastrophe	recipe	synecdoche

Usually the head of a VC# string is short, but there are a number of instances in which the correspondence /ē/ = *e* occurs in *e*C# strings. Most of these are Latin and Greek plurals that are still thought of as plurals in English, including the plurals of the nouns given in array 19-8. Sometimes the correspondences in question are shown as unstressed in the dictionaries, but they still carry the distinct long *e* coloring. Other instances include:

(Array 19-9)

apices	calices	larynges	penates
appendices	codices	matrices	pharynges
apsides	indices	mores*	theses
calces	lares	parentheses	

Also in this group are *bases* (plural of *basis*) and *axes* (plural of *axis*). Many of these noun forms are quite rare, and many have more regular variant plurals, especially those whose singulars end in *x: indexes, calxes, apexes, appendixes, larynxes, matrixes, pharynxes.*

A few instances of /ē/ = *e* in *e*C# strings are not now, strictly speaking, plurals. Some never have been; some were but are now used as singulars:

(Array 19-10)

antipodes	diabetes	isosceles	pyrites
cantharides	feces	manes	tabes

There are a few instances of /ē/ = *e* at the head of VC*r*V strings:

(Array 19-11)

cathedral	egress	febrile*
ebractate	egret*	inebriate

All cases of /ē/ = *e* at the head of VCC strings have an element boundary between the *e* and the CC—specifically with the prefixes *de-*, *pre-*, *re-*, or *se-* added to stems that start with a consonant cluster:

(Array 19-12)

debrief	dethrone	prescript	replant
defrost	preflight	rebroadcast	rewrite
deglutition	preprint	reclaim	secret

This type of simple addition accounts for all cases of /ē/ = *e* at the head of VCC strings found so far.

19.2.2 /ē/ = *y*

Surprisingly, perhaps, /ē/ is spelled *y* almost as often as it is spelled *e*, at least in some pronunciations. The correspondence /ē/ = *y* always occurs in unstressed or very lightly stressed syllables, usually in suffixes like *-ly*, *-ity*, *-ary*, and *-y*. The *AHD* consistently shows /ē/ for such unstressed *y*'s. *W3* also shows this correspondence, often with /i/ as a variant, and in general describes /i/ as "an always-to-be-understood variant of unstressed" /ē/ (41a). Kenyon and Knott show /i/ for these *y* spellings, but explain that, especially with word-final *y*, "very many speakers use the higher vowel approaching" /ē/ (1944, 481, xviii). Because of the earlier decision not to deal with unstressed vowels that involve the complications of reduction, we will say no more here about the /ē/ = *y* correspondence.

19.2.3 /ē/ = *i*

In most languages of the world, including several in continental Europe, the letter *i* is pronounced /ē/, as it was back in Middle English times. This Continental *i* is surprisingly common in English, notably in recent adoptions, but also in many completely integrated and native words.

The unstressed correspondence /ē/ = *i* is common as an inserted particle in words like *burial* (bury̸)i + al) and *enviable* (envy̸)i + able). Like /ē/ = *y*, it also occurs in several affixes, such as *anti-*, *semi-*, *-ior*, *-ion*, *-ious*. Except in V.V strings, the variation that is characteristic of reduced and partially reduced unstressed vowels characterizes these unstressed spellings, and we will therefore restrict the following discussion of /ē/ = *i* to V.V strings and other cases in which the vowel has enough stress to maintain the long *e* coloring and to hold off any signs of reduction.

When a word-final *y* pronounced either /ē/ or /i/ is changed to *i* upon the addition of a suffix that starts with a vowel, the result is a V.V string containing the correspondence /ē/ = *i*:

(Array 19-13)

colonial (colony̸)i + al)	mysterious (mystery̸)i + ous)
fiftieth (fifty̸)i + eth)	subsidiary (subsidy̸)i + ary)
invariable (in(vary̸)i + able)	variance (vary̸)i + ance)
luxuriant (luxury̸)i + ant)	

If a stem ends in *i* and the suffix starts with a vowel and there is no palatalization, then /ē/ = *i* is likely in V.V strings, as in the following words with the suffix *-ary: apiary, aviary, incendiary, intermediary, pecuniary.* (See chapter 30 for more on palatalization.)

The weakly stressed /ē/ = *i* correspondence occurs in words that contain prefixes that end in *i;* sometimes the string involved is VCC, but usually it is V.V or VC. *Anti-* and *semi-* often have variant pronunciations with /ī/. Some instances in V.V strings:

(Array 19-14)

anti-	antiaircraft, antienzyme, antioxidant
demi-	demiurge
semi-	semiannual, semierect, semiofficial

In a few cases the *i* in suffixes is pronounced /ē/—most notably, *-ia, -ian, -ine, -ion, -ior, -ious, -ique,* and *-ium.* Often *-ious, -ian,* and *-ium* produce palatalization of the final consonant of the stem, in which case the *i* is not pronounced /ē/. However, very often there is no palatalization, and so /ē/ = *i* in V.V and some VCV strings:

(Array 19-15)

-ia[1]	anemia, diphtheria, euphoria, hernia, hydrophobia, hysteria, insomnia, kleptomania, mania, myopia, neurasthenia, paraplegia, phobia, schizophrenia, toxemia
-ian	aeolian, comedian (comedy̸)ian), grammarian, gregorian, guardian, historian, mammalian, reptilian, ruffian, stentorian, tragedian
-ine[1]	gabardine, latrine, limousine, mezzanine, quarantine, ravine, routine, tangerine
-ine[2]	benzine, chlorine, gasoline, morphine, nicotine
-ine[3]	figurine, tambourine
-ion	accordion, carrion, clarion, criterion, ganglion, oblivion, perihelion, scorpion
-ior	anterior, exterior, inferior, interior, posterior, superior, ulterior
-ious	abstemious, censorious, commodious, hilarious, ingenious, spurious, uproarious, victorious
-ique	antique, critique, oblique, physique, technique

-ium[1]   aquarium, auditorium, compendium, emporium, planetarium,
          sanitarium, solarium, stadium

-ium[2]   ammonium, calcium, chromium, helium, magnesium, plutonium,
          potassium, radium, sodium, strontium

Other words with /ē/ = *i* in V.V strings:

(Array 19-16)

caviar	piano	sierra	tapioca
chariot	piazza	siesta	
lariat	pistachio	soviet	

In a number of words, usually quite recent adoptions, /ē/ = *i* medially
in the base. Some instances that affect the heads of VCV strings:

(Array 19-17)

caprice	frijoles	liter	petite
diva	intrigue	maraschino	prestige
elite	khedive	nisei	suite
fatigue	kilo	paprika	valise

Also, /ē/ = *i* in a few antitactical contexts: In *chenille, batiste,* and
artiste it occurs in VCC strings; but final *ll* is also usually preceded by long
rather than short *o* (as in *roll;* see 32.2.2.8), and *ste* is preceded by long
rather than short *a* (as in *paste;* see 4.3.3.1). Moreover, *st* is often preceded
by long rather than short *o* (as in *ghost;* again see 4.3.3.1). In these cases,
then, the /ē/ = *i* correspondence parallels specific subpatterns that are at
work in English. The cases of /ē/ = *i* in the VC# strings of *motif* and
massif, however, appear to be unintegrated holdouts.

19.2.4 /ē/ = *ea, ee*

Still to be discussed are the spellings that descend directly from the
Middle and Early Modern English spellings of Middle English /ā/ and the
stretched /e/. Since some changes were made in the spelling of several of
these words during the Middle and Early Modern periods, a closer look at
their historical sources helps but little in distinguishing *ea* from *ee*. Even
tactical patterns are of limited help here, since so many homophones
involve these two spellings: *seem* and *seam, feet* and *feat, reed* and *read,*
and so on. This is clearly an area of weak distinction in the system, a kind
of blurring brought on by all the converging of sounds and spellings over
the centuries. Nevertheless, a closer look at the tactical distributions of *ea*
and *ee* reveals some interesting distinctions between them.

Both *ee* and *ea* occur most often, more than half the time, before C#:

(Array 19-18)

beech	feel	jeep	peel
bleed	genteel	kneel	peep
careen	greet	leek	queen
deep	heed	meet	redeem
esteem	indeed	peek	reef
bleak	feat	jean	peak
conceal	gleam	knead	peal
dean	heap	leak	peat
each	heat	meat	reap
entreat	impeach	ordeal	retreat

The spelling *ee* often occurs in word-final position, *ea* less often. The following list for *ee* is only representative, but that for *ea* is fairly exhaustive:

(Array 19-19)

agree	employee	glee	see
bee	fee	guarantee	tee
chimpanzee	filigree	jubilee	thee
decree	flee	knee	tree
dungaree	free	marquee	wee
flea	pea	sea	
lea	plea	tea	

The following lists of words with *ee* and *ea* before CC also are fairly exhaustive. Notice that *ee* occurs only before C*l*V and that *ea* occurs most commonly before *st:*

(Array 19-20)

beetle	needle	tweedledee
feeble	steeple	wheedle
beagle	east	measles
beast	feast	treacle
eagle	least	yeast

Before CV *ea* is much more common than *ee*. The *ee* list in array 19-24 is fairly exhaustive; the *ea* lists in arrays 19-21 through 19-23 are representative. In most cases the vowel following the consonant in the CV sequence is a diacritical final *e*, either marking or insulating a letter, and the consonant in the CV sequence is a fricative:

(Array 19-21)

appease	decease	heave	pease
bereave	decrease	increase	please
breathe	disease	league	release
cease	easy	lease	tease
cleave	eaves	leave	weave
crease	grease	peace	wreathe

Most other apparent cases of *ea* before CV explicate to an element boundary between the consonant and the vowel in the sequence, which turns them into cases of *ea* before C# and C + —that is, before word- and element-final consonants:

(Array 19-22)

demeanor (demean)or)	heathen (heath)en)
feasible (feas + ible)	malfeasance (mal(feas + ance)
feature (feat)ure)	treaty (treat)y)

Squeamish explicates to (squeam + ish). The suffix is clear enough, and the base, though obscure, is probably related historically to *swim* 'dizziness'. *Creature* explicates to (creatė)ure), an interesting case of orthographic modification with the addition of the -*ure* suffix: in *create* the /ē/ is spelled *e* in the V.V string, but in *creature* the loss of the /ā/ changes the correspondence to /ē/ = *ea*.

The number of cases of *ea* before CV in primes is quite small, and some of them may well prove to explicate to cases of *ea* before C# and C + :

(Array 19-23)

beacon	eager	queasy	weasel
beaver	easel	reason	
deacon	meager	treason	

In nearly all cases of *ee* before CV, the final vowel of the sequence is a final *e* that insulates or marks the penultimate consonant letter:

(Array 19-24)

breeze	geese	sleeve	wheeze
fleece	peeve	sneeze	
freeze	seethe	squeeze	

The somewhat mysterious *tweezers* and *squeegee* can be explicated to (tweezė)er)s) and (squeegė)ee), though questions remain (for *squeegee* see Partridge 1983, 656). The only inexplicable cases of *ee* before CV are *teeter* from an earlier *titter,* and *weevil* from Middle English *wevel.* The change to *ee* may reflect the tactical ambiguity of *v* (see 6.4.2).

Tactically, then, there is little to distinguish *ee* and *ea* from each other.

They occur most commonly in word-final position or before a final consonant, and there are very few true instances of them before CV. Before CC,
ee occurs only before the sequence C*l*V; *ea* occurs there also, but more
commonly before *st,* where *ee* does not occur at all.

19.3 The Minor Spellings of /ē/

19.3.1 /ē/ = *ie, ei*

The most important of the minor spellings of /ē/ are *ie* and *ei,* partly
because of the notorious *i*-before-*e* problem. As far as the spelling of /ē/ is
concerned, the old rhyme is fairly reliable; most of the time /ē/ is spelled *ie*
rather than *ei.* The major subcondition of the rhyme is that after the letter
c it will always be *ei,* never *ie:*

(Array 19-25)

ceiling	conceive	deceive	receipt
conceit	deceit	perceive	receive

Notice that what we have here are mainly the bound bases +*ceit* and
+*ceive.*

There are very few holdouts to the generalization that as far as *ie* and *ei*
are concerned, /ē/ = *ei* after *c,* and that elsewhere /ē/ = *ie.* The majority
of the holdouts have alternative pronunciations with a sound other than
/ē/, as indicated:

(Array 19-26)

either, /ī/	leisure, /e/	sheik, /ā/
inveigle, /ā/	neither, /ī/	

The only other instances found so far in which /ē/ = *ei* without a
preceding *c* are *seize, caffeine, protein,* and the /r/-colored /ē/ in *weir* and
weird. Seize is from Middle English *saisen, seisen,* from Old French *saisir,
seisir.* From the sixteenth through the eighteenth century some people
tried to regularize the spelling to *ie,* but the nonregular historical *ei*
remains. *Caffeine* is a nineteenth-century adoption. Some scholars derive
it from German *Kaffein,* from *kaffee* 'coffee', from French *café* (*AHD,
W3*). Others derive it directly from French *caféine.* In either case, in
American English the *ei* of *caffeine* is split by an element boundary:
(caffe + ine). Though the *e* is difficult, *protein* is probably best explicated
as (prote)in, *-in* being a variant of the same suffix that appears in *caffeine*
(a variant of which is *caffein*).

An unstressed *ie* spelling of /ē/ occurs in many plural nouns whose
singulars end in C*y*# (*cities, puppies*), in some formal plurals that are used

as singulars (*series, caries, species, superficies, rabies*), and in the third-person singular present tense of verbs ending with C*y*# (*busies, hurries*).

Except for some rare, usually Scottish, variants that are of no real concern in American English (*eik, eild, eilding*), the correspondence /ē/ = *ei* occurs in initial position only in *either*. In initial position *ie* never spells /ē/. Neither *ie* nor *ei* occurs in final position spelling /ē/. Notice their much different pronunciations in such words as *lie* and *lei*.

In medial position /ē/ = *ie* or *ei* either before C# or, more often, before C*e*#, with the final *e* marking or insulating the consonant. This is true of nearly all of the *ei* words in arrays 19-25 and 19-26 and of all of the *ie* words in array 19-27. *Receipt*, in array 19-25, is graphically an instance of CC# but phonetically an instance of C#. Instances of /ē/ = *ie* before C# and C*e*# include the following:

(Array 19-27)

achieve	chief	mien	reprieve
aggrieve	fief	niece	retrieve
believe	frieze	piece	shriek
besiege	liege	relief	thief
brief	lien	relieve	thieve

Fossil final *e*'s occur in the variant *caffeine* and in *hygiene*. The only complications to the basic distribution of *ei* and *ie* before C# and C*e*# are expected ones: The correspondence /ē/ = *ie* occurs before CC if the clusters involved are *ld*, *st*, or *nd*, all of which allowed the lengthening of a preceding short Old English vowel. Examples are *field, shield, wield, yield, priest, fiend*.

19.3.2   /ē/ = *ey*

A minor but interesting spelling of /ē/ is *ey*—which is apparently always word-final and most often unstressed, as in *donkey, attorney, skyey, hockey, pulley*, and the like. The one known stressed instance, *key*, is curious. Earlier, *key* rhymed with *grey* and *whey*, whose *ey*'s descended from the Old English spelling *æg*, but the *ey* in *key* descends from *ǣg*. Why *key* now has /ē/ is not clear; the sound may reflect a northern dialect pronunciation.

19.3.3   /ē/ = *ae, oe*

The spellings *ae* and *oe* used to be ligatures and sometimes still are. The ligatures were much more common just a few decades ago than they are now, especially in British English. Their decline is probably due as much to the increased use of the typewriter as to anything else. Back in 1926, when they were more common, Fowler suggested that in the case of words with variant spellings in *e*, the *e* variant should be preferred, and for words that did not have variants, the preferred spelling should be *ae* rather than *æ*, and *oe* rather than *œ*. That is still good advice, and today there are more variants with *e* than there were then (Fowler [1926] 1965, 12).

The *ae* spelling has nothing at all to do with the ash ligature in Old English; it comes, rather, from Latin and Greek. The *oe* spelling is the Latin rendering of Greek *oi*, which in most cases has been simplified to *e*, as in *economy, penal,* and *cemetery.* In more recent adoptions the *oe* and *ae* spellings have tended to stay, especially in classical proper names (*Caesar, Oedipus*), in words that refer to historical antiquities (*oecist*), and in technical terms, even though American English more than British tends to simplify *oe* and *ae* to *e* whenever possible. All of the words in array 19-28 have variant spellings with *e*. Those with asterisks are the more common spellings in American English.

(Array 19-28)

aegis*	daemon	maenad*	praefect
aeon	encyclopaedia	mediaeval	taenia*
aether	faeces	naevus	taeniacide*
aetiology	gastraea	paean	taeniasis*
amoeba*	foetid	oecology	oesophagus
coeliac	foetus	oedema	phoenix*
coenogenesis	oecoid	oenology*	poenology

A number of Latin words carry the plural suffix *-ae,* but most also have more integrated variants. All of the following have variants with the regular *-s* plural suffix:

(Array 19-29)

amoebae	copulae	formulae
caesurae	faunae	hetaerae
cicadae	florae	lacunae

W3 does not record variant spellings with *e* or regular *-s* plural suffixes for the following:

(Array 19-30)

aeciospore	algae	chaeta	paeon
aecium	archaeopteryx	chaetognath	sequelae
aeolian	Caesar	Hominidae	sundae (Fr)
coelacanth	oecist, oekist	Oedipus	oenomel
coenocyte	oedicnemus	oenocyte	onomatopoeia

The /ē/ = *ae* or *oe* correspondence also occurs in technical words with
the affixes *-ineae, -aceae, -idae, aegi-, aego-,* and *-oecia.*

19.3.4 /ē/ = *eo*

The *eo* in *people,* from Middle English *peple,* has been explained in at least
two different ways: Linksz suggests that the *o* was inserted late in Middle
English times or during the Early Modern period to reflect the historical
origin of the word, the Latin *populus*—a happy notion, and one that is
consistent with the several classical respellings that did take place (1973,
78–79). But Linksz's explanation is probably less accurate historically
than Jespersen's suggestion that *eo* was the standard spelling of a rare
Middle English vowel sound (the first vowel sound in the German name
Goethe). Jespersen attributes this same vowel sound to *jeopardy* and
leopard (see 13.4.4) ([1909] 1954, 1:79).

19.3.5 /ē/ = *agh, ah*

The long *e* sound at the end of *shillelagh* is apparently rendered *agh,*
though there is a variant spelling, *shillalah,* with /ē/ apparently spelled *ah,*
and a variant pronunciation with a more integrated, final schwa rather
than a long *e.* It is, after all, an Irish word.

19.3.6 /ē/ = *ay*

Quay, which rhymes with *key,* was earlier spelled like it, too, coming from
the Early Modern English *key,* from the Middle English *kay, key.* From the
fourteenth through the eighteenth century, it was usually spelled *key,* less
often *kay.* The pronunciation of the word changed during those centuries
to make it rhyme with *day.* The *quay* spelling appeared in the eighteenth
century, in imitation of the French *quai.* All three spellings continued up
into the nineteenth century. The modern *key,* as in Key Largo, is actually
from the Spanish *cayo,* the spelling having been influenced by the now-
obsolete *key* variant spelling of *quay.* All in all, the /ē/ = *ay* correspondence in *quay* is another instance of mixed convergence.

20 Long *i*, /ī/

20.1 Historical Sources

The sound and spellings of /ī/ are somewhat unusual. In most of the languages that use the Roman alphabet, the letter *i* is associated with a sound that in our analysis would be described as long *e*, /ē/—the Continental *i*. The letter *i* was also typically associated with this /ē/ sound in Old, Middle, and Early Modern English, for in those earlier forms, by and large the vowels had a Continental value. But during the Great Vowel Shift from about 1500 through 1700, as all of the stressed long vowels shifted from their earlier values, the sound associated with the letter *i* shifted from the earlier /ē/ to the Modern English /ī/. Although phonologically this /ī/ is in fact a diphthong, orthographically it can be treated as a simple vowel.

In most cases the modern English sound /ī/ derives from the Early Modern English sound /ē/. And in most cases the /ē/ sound derives from the Old English long *i*, pronounced /ē/ and usually spelled *i*, often with a diacritic marking the length. However, some Old English short *i*'s were lengthened when followed by the consonant clusters *ld, nd,* or *mb* when these clusters were in final position or were followed by a vowel. This group of short *i*'s is important to the spelling of /ī/, for it explains several holdouts to the VCC pattern, such as *child, wild, blind, climb* (Mossé 1952, 16–18; Prins 1972, 69–73). Also, a velar fricative, usually spelled *h* in Old English and *gh* in Middle English and pronounced like the final sound in the Scots word *loch,* disappeared over the years from the spoken language, though it remained in the spelling. This *gh* lengthened a preceding short *i*, thereby creating the spelling *igh*, as in *thigh* and *sight* (Prins 1972, 75–76).

The spellings of /ī/ are complicated by other historical factors as well: By the end of the seventeenth century it had pretty well been established that the letters *i* and *y* would work together as a team. In most cases the vowel sound would be spelled *i* in word-initial or medial position but *y* in word-final position. Complicating that pattern was a tendency to retain some *y* spellings of medial /ī/ if the *y* was the Roman version of the Greek upsilon, which explains the /ī/ = *y* correspondence in such words as *type* and, via analogy, *typhoon, scythe,* and *rhyme.* Some other complexities come into play as well, but in spite of this minor untidiness, the spelling of /ī/ remains basically regular and straightforward.

20.2   The Major Spellings of /ī/

About 75 percent of the time /ī/ is spelled *i*, usually in the regular long vowel strings, VCV and V.V. About 15 percent of the time /ī/ is spelled *y*. Together, these two major spellings account for about 90 percent of the instances of /ī/. The most important minor spellings are *ie* and *ei*. The other six—*eigh, ai, ay, ey, uy, oy*—usually occur in no more than two or three words each (Hanna et al. 1966, 545–46).

20.2.1   /ī/ = *i*

The most important spelling of /ī/, *i*, usually occurs at the head of VCV and V.V strings. It is common in both word-initial and medial positions. A few examples of /ī/ = *i* at the head of VCV strings:

(Array 20-1)

arrive	ideal	isolate	primary
bride	idol	isotope	quite
homicide	irony	porcupine	whitish

The /ī/ = *i* correspondence occurs in several common suffixes. The asterisked words in array 20-2 have variant pronunciations without the /ī/ sound:

(Array 20-2)

-ide	bromide, chloride, oxide
-ile	infantile*, mercantile*, nubile*, percentile*
-ine	alpine, bovine*, canine, divine, saline*
-ise	advertise, chastise, exercise, franchise
-ite	(adj.) erudite, finite, polite
-ite	(n.) appetite, dynamite, satellite, vulcanite
-itis	arthritis, myelitis, scleritis
-ize	baptize, legalize, moralize, sterilize
-like	deathlike, godlike, warlike, wifelike
-wise	crosswise, lengthwise, likewise

Examples of /ī/ = *i* in V.V strings whose head vowels are in word-initial and medial position, with the *i* and the following vowel located in the same element:

(Array 20-3)

diagram	friar	maniacal	riot
diatom	iodine	miasmus	triumph
diet	lion	phial	viaduct

The *i* spelling of /ī/ often occurs at the head of V.V strings because of simple addition or some other process that concatenates the two vowels:

(Array 20-4)

biennial (bi + enni + al)	friable (fri + able)
biography (bi + o(graph)y)	liar (lie)ar)
dial (di + al)	piety (pi + ety)
diary (di + ary)	science (sci + ence)
diode (di + ode)	symbiosis* (syn + m + bi + osis)
diuretic (dia + ur + etic?)	triangle (tri(angle)

This correspondence is also common before some suffixes—for instance, *-ety.* Some instances in addition to *piety:*

(Array 20-5)

anxiety	propriety	society	variety
notoriety	sobriety		

Another productive suffix is *-able,* which is often added to verbs ending in *y,* which in turn changes to *i,* as in *deniable* (deny)i + able):

(Array 20-6)

classifiable	justifiable	reliable	specifiable

Other examples of /ī/ = *i* when *y* changes to *i:*

(Array 20-7)

amplifier	crier	denial	trial
appliance	defiance	flier	varietal

The /ī/ = *i* correspondence also occurs at the head of V*e*# strings:

(Array 20-8)

belie	fie	lie	tie
die	hie	pie	vie

English words rarely end with *i.* However, in a few words *i* occurs in final position, spelling /ī/. Usually such words are Latin plurals. The asterisked words in array 20-9 have more integrated plurals with the regular *-es* ending rather than *-i,* as in *radius, radii, radiuses:*

(Array 20-9)

alumni	cacti*	fungi*	magi
bacilli	foci*	loci	

In most cases, nonplurals with word-final /ī/ = *i* have simply retained their foreign spellings:

(Array 20-10)

alibi (from L *alibī*)	quasi (from L *quasi*)
anti (from Gk *anti*)	rabbi (from Fr, from L, from Hebr
pi (from Gk *pi*)	*rabbī*)

But some of these words are more difficult to explain. *Alkali* comes from the Latin *alkali,* which explains the *i.* But in Middle and Early Modern English it was spelled, reasonably enough, *alcaly.* The current spelling did not appear until the eighteenth century. Folk etymology may have been at work here, trying to relate the word (which is actually Arabic, like so many English words with word-initial *al*) to some supposed Greek source. Or there may have been a feeling that the *y* at the end of a polysyllable had more of the look of unstressed /ē/ than of /ī/. The word *pi* 'a confusion of type' is of obscure origin, both in meaning and form. Related printing terms have developed a more regular variant spelling, *pie.*

There are a number of cases of /ī/ = *i* at the head of VCC strings. In several cases the irregularity is only apparent, since the CC is really a digraph. For instances of /ī/ before digraphs see 4.3.4.2.

The velar fricative spelled *h* in Old English regularly became *gh* in Middle English. By late Middle and Early Modern English the sound had been dropped in certain contexts and had become /f/ in others. In cases where it was dropped, the preceding vowel routinely became long, whether it had been long or short in Old English. The *gh* is always either in final position, as in *sigh,* or is followed by a final *t,* as in *bright.* The following is a fairly exhaustive list:

(Array 20-11)

alight	fright	nigh	thigh
bight	high	night	wight
bright	knight	plight	wright
fight	light	right	
flight	might	sight	

Analogy produced antietymological *gh*'s in six words. *Sigh* is from Old English, but from a word with a *c* after the *i* rather than an *h*. *Slight* and *tight* are from the Old Norse words *slēttr* and *thēttr. Plight* 'predicament', *delight,* and *sprightly* are from Latin and developed their *gh*'s late, during the Early Modern period. *Sprite,* related to *sprightly,* has a variant, *spright,* also with an antietymological *gh* (Jespersen [1909] 1954, 1:285). *Blight* is of obscure origin.

Examples of /ī/ = *i* before C*l*V:

(Array 20-12)

bible	entitle	isle	stifle
bridle	idle	rifle	title
disciple	island	sidle	trifle

There are some instances of /ī/ = *i* before CrV as well:

(Array 20-13)

digraph	microscope	tigress
library	migrate	titration
microbe	nitrate	vibrate

Vowels that were short in Old English tended to lengthen in Middle and Early Modern English if they were followed by the consonant clusters *gn, ld, mb*, or *nd*. Thus we have the following instances of /ī/ = *i* at the head of VCC strings:

(Array 20-14)

align	child	hind	remind
assign	climb	kind	resign
behind	consign	malign	rind
benign	design	mild	sign
bind	find	mind	wild
blind	grind	pint	wind (v.)

These lengthenings could be preempted, however. For instance, if the consonant cluster was followed by a third consonant (sound or letter), the vowel often remained short, giving us such contrasting pairs as *kind, kindred; behind, hindrance; wild, wilderness; child, children.* Jespersen suggests that the noun *wind* 'movement of air' may have retained the short *i* because of the analogy drawn with such compounds as *windmill*, with its three-consonant cluster (Jespersen [1909] 1954, 1:118). The *i* in *ninth* is probably long (in spite of its three-consonant cluster) because of a strong analogy with *nine*. The long *i* in *viscount* is something of a mystery. The word was adopted from an Anglo-French word with the *sc* spelling. From the fifteenth to the eighteenth century there were two contending spellings in English—one with *s*, one without it. The persistence of the spelling without the *s*—and thus of the open syllable form, *vi-count*—throughout Middle and Early Modern English may have allowed the lengthening of the *i* to occur. The *sc* spelling that we have today is another instance of mixed convergence (see also 27.3.2.9).

The spelling of *indict* is an example of analogy at work. In Middle English it was *enditen*, from Anglo-French *enditer*, from Latin *indictāre*. The modern spelling apparently developed out of the sense that the word should reflect in its spelling (though no longer in its pronunciation) its

Latin origins, through the base +*dict*. Thus its spelling groups it with its Latin origins, but its pronunciation groups it with its French ancestry.

20.2.2 /ī/ = *y*

The correspondence /ī/ = *y* occurs most often in word-final position:

(Array 20-15)

ally	fly	rely	spy
by	fry	reply	thy
cry	ply	satisfy	try
descry	prophesy	shy	why
dry	pry	spry	wry

There are also many verbs with the suffix -*ify*—for instance, *classify, horrify, justify*. The -*efy* form of this suffix occurs in only four common words:

(Array 20-16)

liquefy	putrefy	rarefy	stupefy

In a few cases the Short Word Rule (see 3.5) leads to /ī/ = *y* before final *e:*

(Array 20-17)

bye	dye	lye	rye

Usually /ī/ = *y* in medial position owing to the Greek origins of the word. When Greek words containing the letter upsilon were adopted into Latin, the upsilon was transliterated as *y*. Cases of medial /ī/ = *y* at the head of VCV strings, including some instances involving consonant digraphs:

(Array 20-18)

analyze	gyroscope	papyrus	streptomycin
asylum	hygiene	paralyze	thyme
cybernetics	hyperbole	phylum	thymus
cynosure	hypercritical	proselyte	thyroid
dynamo	hypoglycemia	psyche	type
dynasty	lyceum	pylon	tyrant
electrolyte	lyre	pyromania	zygote
gyrate	neophyte	python	zymurgy

In a few cases of /ī/ = *y* at the head of VCV strings, spellings that etymologically should have been *i* were changed via analogy to the Greek *y*. *Style*, from Latin *stilus*, was probably influenced by the Greek *stulus*, with the *u*-like upsilon and the meaning "pillar, column." *Tyro*, also spelled *tiro*, is from Latin *tīrō*, which is of obscure origin. Medieval Latin scribes often spelled it with a *y* (which led to the Modern English spelling), either because they took it for a Greek adoption or perhaps because it was a Greek adoption and the earlier spelling with *i* was incorrect. It all remains a minor mystery.

The story behind the spelling of *rhyme* is complex and disputed, enough so that it seems best simply to quote the *OED*'s note:

> Down to c. 1560 the original spelling *rime* (*ryme*) continued to prevail in English. About that date the tendency to alter orthography on classical models led to the new spelling *rithme, rhythm(e)*, [apparently with the *th* not pronounced,] which continued to be current till about the close of the 17c. . . . Soon after 1600, probably from a desire to distinguish between "rime" and "rhythm" the intermediate forms *rhime, rhyme* came into use, and the latter finally established itself as the standard form. . . . The original *rime*, however, has never been quite discontinued, and from about 1870 its use has been considerably revived, especially by writers upon the history of the English language or literature. To some extent this revival was due to the belief that the word was of native origin, and represented Old English *rīm*.

It is notable that although the *OED* views the ultimate source of *rhyme* as the Latin *rhythmus,* Jespersen suggests that it is of Old English origin, representing the *rīm* mentioned in the last sentence of the note in the *OED* ([1909] 1954, 1:72).

Tycoon, from Japanese *taikun,* from an Ancient Chinese word meaning "great prince," was originally used in English to refer to the shogun of Japan. It was originally spelled *taikun* in English. The *OED* gives six citations for *tycoon* and its derivatives, the earliest in 1863. In five of them the word is spelled as today, *tycoon.* In the sixth one, from the 1881 edition of the *Encyclopaedia Britannica, tycoon* is branded a common misspelling of *taikun!*

The correspondence /ī/ = *y* is relatively rare at the head of V.V strings:

(Array 20-19)

cyanide	hyacinth	hyena	poliomyelitis

More often the V.V string is due to affixation, as in *dyer,* (dy*é*)er), and *lying,* (li*é*)y + ing).

The correspondence /ī/ = *y* occurs at the head of VCC strings primarily when the CC is tactically an ambiguous digraph or forms a VC*l*V or VC*r*V string:

(Array 20-20)

carbohydrate	dehydrate	hydrochloric	psychology
cycle	encyclopedia	hydrogen	python
cyclone	hybrid	hyphen	typhoid
cyclotron	hydra	psyche	typhus

In both *scythe* and *typhoon* /ī/ = *y* at the head of VCC strings that
reflect the effects of conservative analogy. *Scythe* is from Old English
sīthe. The etymologically correct spelling would be **sithe*. The *y* occurred
early, in the thirteenth century, though it did not displace the *i* till the
seventeenth century. The reason for its appearance is not clear. The *c*
apparently occurred because of the notion, etymologically inaccurate,
that the word was a Latin adoption, descending from *scindere* 'to saw'. It
is possible that the confusion extended to the mistaken notion that *scythe*
was a Greek word adopted by the Romans, which would explain the
nonetymological *y*. The *sci* and *scy* spellings are recorded in the *OED* as
seventeenth-century forms. *Typhoon* is from Cantonese *tai fung* 'great
wind'. The English spelling was apparently influenced by the Greek *Ty-
phon*, the name of the god of winds.

20.3   The Minor Spellings of /ī/

20.3.1   /ī/ = *ie*

Long *i* is often spelled *ie* in words that are formed from stems ending in /ī/
= *y*. These cases are different from the /ī/ = *i* instances at the head of V.V
strings discussed in arrays 20-3 through 20-7 because in the present
instances the vowel following the *i* is not pronounced separately. Notice
the distinction: /ī/ = *i* in *drier* (drȳ)i + er), in which the *e* is pronounced;
but /ī/ = *ie* in *dried* (drȳ)i + ed), in which the *e* is not pronounced separately. Other instances of /ī/ = *ie*: *skies* (skȳ)i + es), *applied* (applȳ)i + ed),
qualifies (qualifȳ)i + es). For *tie* and similar instances, see array 20-8.

20.3.2   /ī/ = *ei*

The following is a fairly exhaustive list of the words in which /ī/ = *ei*.
Notice that the *ei* is always word-initial or medial. Asterisked words have
variant pronunciations with /ē/:

(Array 20-21)

eider	eikon, icon	Fahrenheit	neither*
eidetic	einkorn	feisty	poltergeist
eidolon	einsteinium	gneiss	seismic
eidos	either*	kaleidoscope	stein

20.3.3   /ī/ = *eigh*

Closely related are the few words in which /ī/ = *eigh*. *Height* comes from
an Old English word in which the *h* was later changed to *gh* (see 11.2.2 and
20.2.1). *Sleight* comes from Old Norse *slægth*. *Heigh-ho* is of obscure
origin.

20.3.4 /ī/ = *ai*

Long *i* is spelled *ai* in a few relatively unintegrated adoptions: *assagai, assegai; assai*[1,2]*; kaiser.* It also occurs in *aisle,* which in Middle English was *ile, ele, eile.* In Early Modern English *ile* was confused with *isle,* and was often spelled *isle* from the sixteenth through the eighteenth century. In fifteenth- and sixteenth-century French it was sometimes written *aisle,* apparently in imitation of the Latin word *ascella.* The *aisle* spelling first appeared in English in the eighteenth century, apparently combining the earlier confusion with *isle* and the current French *aile.* (The *OED*'s note at *Aisle* is informative.) Samuel Johnson, in his influential dictionary, entered *aisle* thus spelled with what might be called half-hearted endorsement: "Thus the word is written by Addison, but perhaps improperly; since it seems deducible only from *aile,* a wing, or *allée,* a path; and is therefore to be written *aile*" ([1775] 1983).

20.3.5 /ī/ = *ay*

Long *i* is spelled *ay* in three recent adoptions: *bayou,* from Louisiana French, from Choctaw *bayuk; cayenne,* earlier *kian, chian,* from Tupi *kyinha,* the modern spelling having been influenced by Cayenne Island; and *kayak,* from Eskimo *qajaq,* which poses some interesting integration problems!

20.3.6 /ī/ = *ey*

Long *i* is spelled *ey* in *geyser,* from Icelandic *Geysir,* and in *eye,* the final *e* being attributable to the Short Word Rule (see 3.5). *Eye* comes from Old English *ēage,* and suffered an incredible array of spellings during the late Old to Middle English period. The *OED* lists 49 different spellings, ranging in complexity from *i* to *hyghe.*

20.3.7 /ī/ = *uy*

Long *i* is spelled *uy* in three cases—*buy* and *guy*[1,2]. *Buy* comes from Old English, and though the early spelling was confused, the *uy* had fairly well asserted itself by the early thirteenth century. *Guy*[1] 'rope' is from Old French *gui, guie,* a regular case of integration. *Guy*[2] 'fellow' is apparently from *Guy Fawkes,* and the given name *Guy* is from Old French *Wido, Guido.*

20.3.8 /ī/ = *oy*

Long *i* is spelled *oy* only in *coyote* and its diminutive *coyotillo,* both from Mexican Spanish, ultimately from Nahuatl *coyotl.*

21 Long *o*, /ō/

21.1 Historical Sources

The major single source for modern /ō/ is Old English *ā*, which was pronounced with a broad "ah" sound. In the twelfth century *ā* began to be pronounced with more rounding of the lips, which led to a sound similar to the Modern English /ò/. This change in pronunciation gradually began to be reflected in Middle English spelling as words with *ā* in Old English were respelled with either *a* or *o*, and then only with *o*. During the Great Vowel Shift, Middle and Early Modern English /ò/ changed to the sound that we think of as long *o*, /ō/ (Jespersen [1909] 1954, 1:92; Prins 1972, 85–86, 142–43). Thus the following evolutions were common:

(Array 21-1)

Old English	Middle English	American English
hām	hom(e)	home
stān	stane, stone	stone
sāpe	saip, sope	soap
āth	ooth	oath

Middle and Early Modern /ò/ also descended from sources other than Old English *ā*. In some cases it came from an Old English short *a* that lengthened before the clusters *ld* and *mb*, as in *cold* and *comb*. In other cases it came from an Old English short *o* that lengthened in open syllables, as in *open* and *hope*. In still other cases it came from a stressed *o* in Old French, as in *robe* and *noble*. The modern /ō/'s that evolved from Middle and Early Modern /ò/, regardless of their ultimate source, are always spelled either *o* or *oa*, with *o* being far and away the more common. In the sixteenth century a woefully inconsistent attempt was made to spell /ò/ *oa*, in a move similar to the attempt to use *ea* to spell the open stretched /e/ so as to distinguish it from the close /ā/ (see 19.1) (Jespersen [1909] 1954, 1:92–94).

In Middle and Early Modern English there was a second sound, actually a diphthong close to the vowel in *cow,* which by the seventeenth or eighteenth century had converged into /ō/. Words that descended through this diphthong tend to be spelled *ou* or *ow,* in sharp contrast with those that descended through the /ò/ and are normally spelled *o* and *oa* (Jespersen [1909] 1954, 1:89–90, 99, 325).

In addition to these main sources for modern /ō/, there are also a number of Romance adoptions, old and new, in which /ō/ = *o*, often in word-final position, as in *allegro.* There are also a number of usually recent French adoptions in which /ō/ = *eau* or *au*—for instance, *beau* and *chauffeur.*

21.2   The Major Spellings of /ō/

21.2.1   /ō/ = *o*

Far and away the most important spelling of /ō/ is *o,* which accounts for more than 85 percent of the instances of this sound, usually at the head of a regular long string (Hanna et al., 1966, 608–9).

Examples of /ō/ = *o* at the head of VCV strings:

(Array 21-2)

composer	oboe	opiate	solar
diplomacy	ode	pedagogy	suppose
grotesque	odious	petroleum	viola
obedience	omission	polarity	wrote

In a few cases /ō/ = *o* in V.V strings in which the two vowels are part of the same element:

(Array 21-3)

goa	noel	oasis	stoa

Much more often /ō/ = *o* in V.V strings in which the two vowels are concatenated and are part of different elements:

(Array 21-4)

coalesce (co + al + esce)	inchoate (in(cho + ate)
coed (co + ed)	photoelectric (photo)(electr + ic)
coerce (co + erce)	poem (po + em?)
coordinate (co(ordin + ate)	protozoa (prot + o + zo + a)
going (go)ing)	sacroiliac (sacr + o + ili + ac)
heroic (hero)ic)	zoological (zo + o(log + ic)al)

The correspondence /ō/ = *o* occurs in the regular long V*e#* string:

(Array 21-5)

foe	froe, frow	roe	woe

There are several words with /ō/ = *o* in final position. Word-final vowels, if they are sounded, are usually long, and /ō/ = *o* is the most common correspondence involving a stressed word-final vowel unigraph. Although most of these instances are fairly recent and not thoroughly integrated adoptions, several are native or quite old and well integrated. Words from Old English or Old Norse:

(Array 21-6)

ago	fro	lo	so
for(e)go	go	no	whoso

Old adoptions from French and Latin:

(Array 21-7)

calypso	farrago	kilo	rococo
domino	gigolo	portfolio	torpedo
echo	halo	pro ("for")	tyro
ego	hello	ratio	vertigo

There are also some back-formations and clippings in which word-final /ō/ = *o*, as in *pro* 'professional':

(Array 21-8)

audio	hero	pseudo
curio	magneto	radio
dynamo	photo	video

However, the largest single source of such instances is Italian, and most of the words deal with music and the arts:

(Array 21-9)

adagio	falsetto	manifesto	sirocco
allegro	fiasco (via Fr)	maraschino	solo
alto	fresco	morocco	soprano
archipelago	ghetto	motto	staccato
cameo	grotto	oratorio	stiletto
canto	gusto	piano	stucco
casino	impresario	piccolo	studio
cello	incognito	pistachio	tempo
concerto	inferno	portico	torso
contralto	largo	presto	trio
crescendo	legato	rondo	virtuoso
dado	libretto	salvo	volcano
ditto	maestro	scenario	zero (via Fr)

Another large source is Spanish:

(Array 21-10)

armadillo	fandango	mulatto	pueblo
bolero	guano	patio	rodeo
bravado	incommunicado	peccadillo	tango
burro	indigo	pimento	tobacco
cargo	merino	poncho	tomato
embargo	mosquito	potato	tornado

A few words come from Portuguese:

(Array 21-11)

albino	flamingo (?)	mango
buffalo	lingo	

A few reflect old Latin inflections:

(Array 21-12)

folio	memento	quarto	verso
innuendo	placebo	recto	veto
limbo	proximo	ultimo	

And there are a few miscellaneous adoptions, analogical formations, and words of obscure origin and structure:

(Array 21-13)

banjo	dido	jingo	kimono
calico	dildo	judo	polo
desperado	hobo	jumbo	sumo

All of the foregoing *o* spellings of /ō/ occur in regular tactical strings for long head vowels. But in a few cases /ō/ is spelled *o* at the head of VCC strings. First, there are the normal cases in which the CC is *qu* or a digraph:

(Array 21-14)

baroque	coquetry	gopher	prophylactic
brochure	crochet	ocher	trophy
clothes	croquet	parochial	

A few cases of /ō/ = *o* occur in VC*l*V and VC*r*V strings:

(Array 21-15)

aeroplane	appropriate	mimeograph	program
approbrious	expropriate	ogle	sobriquet

For other instances of /ō/ = *o* before *l* plus another consonant and at the head of other VCC strings, see 4.3.3.1. For instances of /ō/ before word-final *l*, in spite of the VC# string, see 4.2.2.

21.2.2 /ō/ = *oa*

The second major spelling of /ō/, *oa*, occurs in about 5 percent of the instances cited in Hanna et al. (1966, 608). The most common words with initial and medial /ō/ = *oa* are:

(Array 21-16)

approach	croak	groats	oakum	shoal
bloat	encroach	load	oat	soak
boast	float	loaf	oath	soap
boat	foal	loam	poach	stoat
broach	foam	loan	reproach	throat
cloak	gloat	loath	roach	toad
coach	goad	moan	road	toast
coal	goal	moat	roam	
coast	goat	oaf	roan	
coat	groan	oak	roast	

Practically all of these words were spelled either *o* or *oo* in Middle English. The *oa* spelling was extremely rare in that period. In most cases, the words assumed the *oa* spelling during the Early Modern period, especially during the sixteenth-century attempt to use *oa*, more or less consistently, to spell /ō/.

The confusion of *o* and *oa* spellings of /ō/ was the result of a spelling reform that failed—or succeeded only partially—because of the relentless tendency of pronunciation to change and simplify itself.

The only instance of word-final /ō/ = *oa* occurs in *cocoa*, which appears to be a codified mistake: a variation of *cacao*, it was apparently confused, via analogy, with (coco(nut).

21.2.3 /ō/ = *ow*

Long *o* is spelled *ow* about 5 percent of the time (Hanna et al. 1966, 609). The correspondence /ō/ = *ow* almost always occurs in word-final position:

(Array 21-17)

blow	grow	show	throw
bow	know	slow	tow
crow	low	snow	
flow	mow	sow	
glow	row	stow	

The correspondence /ō/ = *ow* is very rare in word-initial or medial position, the only clear-cut instances apparently being *bowl*, *own*, and *owe*. Other instances are actually inflected or derived forms that explicate to a word-final *ow* similar to that in *flown*, (flow)n). Other instances:

(Array 21-18)

bellows	grown	known	sown
gallows	growth	shown	thrown

The *ow* spelling of /ō/ occurs in final position in longer words as well, though in almost all two-syllable words with final /ō/ = *ow* the modern spelling and pronunciation reflect a regular convergence and shift that occurred earlier in English. Old English contained a number of different word endings, including *we, rg, lg, rh,* and *u.* In Middle English all of these endings converged into *we,* which would have been pronounced /wə/ in those days when final *e* was still pronounced. But later, when the final *e* stopped being pronounced, Middle English *we* became similar to the sound /ū/. This, in time, was rounded to /ō/. In most cases, during the fourteenth century the *ow* spelling came to represent this final vowel sound, which in American English is regularly /ō/ (Jespersen [1909] 1954, 1:192). This development is involved in almost all of the following words, many of which have variant pronunciations with /ə/:

(Array 21-19)

arrow	fallow	mellow	swallow
barrow	fellow	minnow	tallow
bellow	follow	morrow	tomorrow
billow	furrow	narrow	wallow
borrow	hallow	pillow	wheelbarrow
bungalow	harrow	sallow	widow
burrow	hollow	shadow	willow
callow	marrow	shallow	window
elbow	marshmallow	sorrow	winnow
escrow	meadow	sparrow	yellow

21.3 The Minor Spellings of /ō/

The three major spellings—*o, oa,* and *ow*—account for more than 95 percent of the instances of /ō/. The remaining few instances are spelled *ou, ough, eau, au, oo, oh, ew,* and *eo.*

21.3.1 /ō/ = *ou, ough*

In Middle English short *u,* spelled either *u* or *ou,* usually lengthened and opened before *ld* or *lt* to become /ō/ (Prins 1972, 153). Thus:

(Array 21-20)

boulder	poultice	shoulder
mould, mold	poultry	

Soul is from Old English *sāwol*. The *OED* cites a great variety of spellings through Old, Middle, and Early Modern English. The modern spelling first appeared in the fifteenth century. Long *o* is also spelled *ou* in the French adoption *cantaloup(e)*, which has the variants *cantalope* and *cantelope*.

Closely related are cases of /ō/ = *ou* before the now-silent *gh*, the remnant of an Old English or Old Norse *g* or *h:*

(Array 21-21)

although	dough	though
borough	thorough	

Related via analogy is *furlough*, a seventeenth-century adaption of the Dutch *verlof.* In the seventeenth and eighteenth centuries it had variant pronunciations: sometimes with /f/, sometimes simply with /ō/. It also had variant spellings that reflect the uncertainty of its pronunciation back then: sometimes it ended with *f, ff, ffe*, sometimes with *o, oe, ow*.

21.3.2   /ō/ = *eau, au*

There are a few words that have resisted integration and retain what might be thought of as French *o*'s: *eau* and *au*. The correspondence /ō/ = *eau* always occurs in final position:

(Array 21-22)

beau	fricandeau,	plateau	tableau
bureau	fricando	portmanteau	trousseau

The correspondence /ō/ = *au* is always either word-initial or medial:

(Array 21-23)

aubade	chaudfroid	chauvinism	hauteur
auberge	chauffeur	gauche	mauve
aubergine	chausses	hautboy	rechauffe

21.3.3   /ō/ = *oo, oh, ew, eo*

Except for the /r/-colored vowel in *door* and *floor,* the correspondence /ō/ = *oo* occurs only in one spelling of *brooch*, which has a variant spelling *broach* and a variant pronunciation with /ū/. Actually *brooch* 'pin' and *broach* (v.) are etymologically the same word, and have only recently been distinguished in spelling and pronunciation.

Three other minor spellings of /ō/ are *oh, ew,* and *eo*. The first occurs only in *oh* and in the recent German adoption *ohm*. The correspondence /ō/ = *ew* occurs only in the archaic *shew* and in *sew*, which actually has a nonregular pronunciation. Historically *sew* should be /sū/. The several spellings cited in the *OED* suggest that in earlier centuries there were variant pronunciations. The correspondence /ō/ = *eo* occurs only in *yeoman,* which was originally spelled with the more regular *o*. The *eo* spelling did not occur until the fifteenth century, and then it was but one of a number of variants. The etymology is not entirely clear, and there were variant pronunciations, one with /ē/ rather than /ō/ surviving into the eighteenth century.

21.4   The Spellings of /ō/ Summarized

To sum up, then, by and large /ō/ is spelled *o,* usually in accordance with the regular tactical patterns for long vowels, but often, too, in front of consonant clusters that more often would follow a short vowel. The *ow* spelling tends overwhelmingly to occur in word-final position, quite unlike the *ou* spelling. There are a few minor spellings, of which the most important are perhaps the two unintegrated French *o*'s, *eau* (always final) and *au* (never final).

22   The Simple Long *u*, /ū/

22.1   Introduction

Long *u* has two forms, the simple /ū/, as in *coot,* and the complex /yū/, as in *cute.* Complex /yū/ is treated in chapter 23. Many words have variant pronunciations with /ū/ and /yū/. Such cases also are treated in the next chapter. The present chapter deals only with simple /ū/.

22.2   Historical Sources

Surprisingly few instances of American English /ū/ derive from Early Modern English /ū/. The major source of the current /ū/ is Early Modern long *o,* a sound similar to the present-day /ō/, but not diphthongized as the modern /ō/ tends to be. The Early Modern long *o* had several sources, the most important being Old English *o* and *ō,* together with *ō* from Old Norse and *o* from Norman or Old French. In Middle English these sounds were most often spelled *o,* but sometimes *oo* to show length (much as today we spell /ē/ *ee*). During the Great Vowel Shift the Early Modern long *o* was pronounced higher in the mouth, becoming /ū/. Thus the many cases in which /ū/ is spelled *o* or *oo*—for instance, *prove* and *proof.*

Early Modern English long *o* is only one of five major sources of American English /ū/. A second source involves a number of sixteenth- and seventeenth-century French adaptions that ended in *on* and became fairly consistently *oon* in English, as in *balloon, platoon, saloon.* These adaptions produce many more cases of /ū/ = *oo.* Indeed, it makes sense to think of *oo* as the distinctively English spelling of /ū/. Few instances of American English /ū/ derive from late Middle English long /ū/, which usually became a diphthong /aù/ in the Great Vowel Shift, as in *house* and *mouse.* However, whenever Early Modern /ū/ occurred before a labial consonant, as in *coop, room, tomb,* it did not diphthongize, thus leading to more cases of /ū/ = *o* and *oo,* the third major source of modern /ū/. Adoptions made after the Great Vowel Shift constitute a fourth source;

any such late adoption of a word containing /ū/ tended to retain the /ū/ in English, as in *routine* and *coup*. Comprising a fifth source were the many words adopted from Latin, either directly or via French, in which /ū/ = *u*, as in *junior, fluid, prudent* (Jespersen [1909] 1954, 1:236–37, 241–42, 340, 430; Prins 1972, 132–33, 130–31).

22.3   The Major Spellings of /ū/

The five major sources begin to suggest the various spellings of /ū/. Those cases that derive from late Middle English /ō/ or /ū/ before a labial, or from the later French *on* adaptions, tend to be spelled *oo* or, less often, *o*. Later adaptions from French tend to be spelled *ou*, though there are a few other typically French /ū/'s, as discussed in 22.4.5 and 22.4.6. And finally, those /ū/'s that were adapted from Latin tend to be spelled *u*. About 75 percent of the time /ū/ is spelled *oo* or *u* (Hanna et al. 1966, 646–47). These two major spellings will be treated first.

22.3.1   /ū/ = *oo*

The spelling *oo* accounts for about 40 percent of the instances of /ū/. About 75 percent of the time the correspondence /ū/ = *oo* occurs before C#. In fact, about 80 percent of the occurrences of /ū/ before C# are spelled *oo:*

(Array 22-1)

aloof	coot	lagoon	proof
baboon	doom	monsoon	school
bloom	droop	moot	scoop
boot	festoon	mushroom	smooth
brood	food	noon	tooth
cartoon	gloom	pool	typhoon

The correspondence /ū/ = *oo* is fairly common in word-final position:

(Array 22-2)

bamboo	cuckoo	kangaroo	tattoo
boo	halloo	kazoo	too
bugaboo	hullabaloo	shampoo	woo
coo	igloo	taboo	zoo

The spelling *oo* is rare before CV—that is, as the head of a quasi-VCV string. The few cases in which *oo* does occur before CV are "odd" words, often looking as if they ought to explicate to *oo* plus a consonant, with the following vowel in a different element:

(Array 22-3)

bazooka	from Bob Burns's musical instrument
booby	from Spanish *bobo*
boomerang	from Native Australian *wo-mur-rāng* or *būmarin*
booty	from Middle English *bottyne*
coolie	from Hindi *kulī*
goober	from Angolese *nguba*
loony, looney	from *lunatic* and with the variant *luny* (possibly folk etymology is at work here, the newer spelling with *oo* suggesting a link with *loon*)
googol	coined by the physicist Edward Kasner

When the vowel in the CV following *oo* is silent final *e*, the *e* always marks or insulates the consonant and is not involved in the spelling of the vowel sound:

(Array 22-4)

behoove	groove	noose	soothe
choose	loose	ooze	
goose	moose	papoose	

Word-initial /ū/ is rare (/yū/, as chapter 23 will show, being much more common), but when it does occur, it is regularly spelled *oo:*

(Array 22-5)

oodles	oofy	oompah*	oops*
ooftish	oolong	oons	ooze

The rare and unintegrated *umiak* and *urali,* both with nonregular initial /ū/ = *u,* have more integrated variant spellings with *oo.*

22.3.2 /ū/ = *u*

While *oo* is very rare before CV, *u* is common in that position, so that the correspondence /ū/ = *u* is very common at the head of VCV strings:

(Array 22-6)

ablution	glucose	lube	rumor
brute	hula	lukewarm	schedule
conclude	inscrutable	obtrusive	scrutiny
conclusion	jejune	parachute	spruce
crusade	jubilant	plumage	truly
elude	junior	plutocrat	tuna
excruciating	juniper	rhubarb	unruly

The spelling *oo* never occurs immediately before a silent final *e,* but *u* does so very often. Instances of /ū/ = *u* at the head of Ve# strings:

(Array 22-7)

blue	ensue	rue	tissue
clue	flue	statue	true
construe	fondue	sue	virtue

In *gruesome* (grue + some) the base *grue* + reflects an obsolete word that means "shiver." The only case of word-final /ū/ = *u* is in the very recent adaption *gnu*.

The digraph *oo* spelling /ū/ never occurs in V.V strings. But *u* occurs there quite often:

(Array 22-8)

| altruistic | congruity | fruition | ruin |
| bruin | congruous | mellifluous | truism |

22.3.2.1   The Correspondence /ū/ = *u* and the Third Syllable Rule

Although the correspondence /ū/ = *u* poses no special problems for the speller, it is important to point out that /ū/ = *u* often occurs in a stressed antepenultimate syllable, thereby preempting the Third Syllable Rule. Some instances:

(Array 22-9)

adjudicate	crucible	inscrutable	plutocrat
agglutinate	excruciate	juvenile	superfluity
community	glutinous	lunacy	unscrupulous

The words listed in array 22-9 confirm Jespersen's point that the Third Syllable Rule does not apply to the /ū/ from French or Latin ([1909] 1954, 1:142).

22.3.3   The Major Spellings of /ū/ Summarized

The tactical distributions of the two major spellings of /ū/—*oo* and *u*—are quite clear and straightforward: in general, *oo* regularly occurs before C# and in word-final and word-initial position, while *u* regularly occurs in VCV (including VC*e*#), V.V, and V*e*# strings.

22.4   The Minor Spellings of /ū/

22.4.1   /ū/ = *o*

The *o* spelling of /ū/ is considerably less common than either *oo* or *u*. The following is an exhaustive list of known words that contain it:

(Array 22-10)

approve	move	tomb	whose
do	prove	two	womb
improve	reprove	who	
lose	to	whom	

Tomb comes ultimately from Latin *tumba*. In Middle English it was spelled sometimes *u*, sometimes *o*, sometimes *ou*. It seems likely that the *o* spelling was an instance of the Norman scribes' using an *o* rather than a *u* in order to break up otherwise confusing strings of minims (see 17.1.2). The *OED* points out that although the present spelling never quite reflected the sound of the word, it became standard in the seventeenth century.

The spellings of *whom* and *womb* reflect the same historical process. When Old English *ā* occurred between *w* and a labial consonant such as *m*, instead of evolving into the regular /ò/ in Middle or Early Modern English, it evolved into /ō/. This Early Modern /ō/ then evolved into the present-day /ū/ (Jespersen [1909] 1954, 1:91). *Whom* is unusual since the /w/ was subsequently dropped, though the *w* lingered in the spelling. The vowel in the Old English *hwām* evolved into Middle English /ò/, then into /ō/, leading to *whom*, /hwōm/. From there it evolved to either /hwūm/ or /hūm/, depending on whether the /w/ disappeared before or after the Great Vowel Shift.

Do and *to* have the /ū/ only when they are fully stressed; otherwise the vowel reduces to schwa or to no sound at all, as in clipped phrases like "He wants t'go." Both *to* and *do* derive from Old English words with *ō*, which became Early Modern /ō/, which after the Great Vowel Shift were /ū/. Both *two* and *who*, however, derive from Old English words with *ā*, which regularly evolved into American English /ō/ rather than /ū/. The reason for their evolution, as with that for *whom* and *womb*, lies with the influence of the preceding *w*. The *OED* suggests that Old English *twā* evolved in a way similar to *whom*. Instead of evolving into the regular /ò/ of Middle and Early Modern English, because of the labializing influence of the preceding /w/ the vowel in *twā* evolved into Middle and Early Modern /ō/. Then, with the loss of the /w/ and the onset of the Great Vowel Shift, /twō/ became /tū/. *Who* and *whose* have much the same history.

Lose comes from Old English *lōsian*, reflecting the regular evolution of Old English *ō* into modern /ū/.

Prove, approve, improve, reprove, and *move* all came into Middle English from French. Jespersen points out that Old French *o*'s near labials such as /p/ and /m/ tended to evolve into Early Modern /ō/ and thus into modern /ū/ ([1909] 1954, 1:92).

22.4.2 /ū/ = *oe*

The correspondence /ū/ = *oe* occurs in *shoe* and *canoe*. *Shoe* also comes from an Old English word with *ō*. The reason for the final *e* is not clear. It did not appear until the sixteenth century, about the same time that the now-standard *oe* spelling first appeared. The *e* may reflect a concern over the spelling of the plural: *shos looks odd to English eyes, and notice the confusion that is still experienced over the plural of nouns ending in *o:* *heros* versus *heroes*, *tomatos* versus *tomatoes*. Of course, why *shoe* did not become *shoo* and *shoos*, which are among the spellings recorded in the *OED*, is not clear. Basically, the final *e* remains a mystery, though the /ū/ = *o* relationship is straightforward enough.

Canoe is a sixteenth-century adaption from Spanish *canoa*. It was spelled *canoa* in English up through the eighteenth century, but in the seventeenth century variants began to appear, such as *canow, canowe, canno, canoo, canoe*. As with *shoe*, the final *e* remains something of a mystery, though most final *e*'s in English reflect simplifications and convergences of earlier suffixes, and the *e* in *canoe* may echo the earlier *a* ending.

22.4.3 /ū/ = *ou*

The *ou* spelling usually occurs before CV, as in the following words:

(Array 22-11)

accouterment	coulee	nougat	routine
agouti	coupon	noumenon	souvenir
boulevard	goulash	r(o)uble	toucan
bouquet	insouciant	rouge	troubadour
cougar	louver	roulette	troupe

It rarely occurs in final position, specifically only in the following instances:

(Array 22-12)

acajou	caribou	roucou, rocou	you
bayou	marabou	sou	

Marabou has a variant spelling, *marabout*, but generally speaking, *ou* is rare before C#. Other instances:

(Array 22-13)

amour	ghoul	uncouth
burnous, burnoose	group	youth
croup	soup	

This *ou* is essentially a French /ū/, for in nearly all cases it comes directly from Old French, French, Louisiana French (*bayou*), or Canadian French (*caribou*, *coulee*). Sometimes it represents the French Norman scribes' respelling of an Old English word originally spelled with *u*, *ū*, or *ēo*, as part of the tendency of the scribes to introduce French orthographic conventions after the Norman Conquest, as in *uncouth*, *wound*, *youth*, *you*. The only cases that are not attributable to French in one way or another are all recent adoptions: *ghoul* (eighteenth century), from Arabic *ghūl; noumenon* (eighteenth century), from German *Noumenon*, from Greek *noumenon; goulash* (twentieth century), from Hungarian *gulyas* (*hus*) 'herdsman's (meat)'; and *acoustics* (seventeenth century), from Greek *akoustikos* (though the seventeenth-century adaption of *acoustic* is attributed to the French *acoustique*).

You is a special case, not only because it is such an important word, but also because historically it is unusual. It is one of a rather large group of words whose /ū/ derives from Old English *ēo* plus *w*; but it is the only one in which /ū/ = *ou*:

(Array 22-14)

Old English	American English
blēow	blew
brēowan	brew
cēowan	chew
ēowu	ewe
gecnēow	knew
nēowe	new
hrēowan	rue
trēowe	true
trēowth	truth
ēow	you

It is not clear why of all the words in this group only *ēow* took on the *ou* spelling. But we might notice these closely related developments: Old English *ēower* evolved into *your*, and Old English *geoguth* evolved into *youth*.

Related to the Gallicized Old English derivatives *youth*, *uncouth*, *wound*, and *you* are *through* and *slough* 'a bog, despair'. Both derive from Old English words and both reflect in their *ou* spellings the influence of the Norman scribes. The *gh* is the now-silent shadow of the Old English velar fricative spelled *h* in Old English, *gh* in Middle English (see 11.2.2 and 20.2.1). But in most cases this French /ū/ occurs in words that retain much of the total French look and feel: *boulevard*, *roulette*, *sou*, *souvenir*, *troubadour*, and so on.

The /ū/ = *ou* correspondence also occurs in some minimally integrated adoptions, such as *caoutchouc; chibouque, chibouk; koumiss.* And except for the Russian *koumiss,* all of these peripheral adoptions, though they originated in other languages, came into English, complete with their *ou* spellings, through French.

22.4.4   /ū/ = *ew*

The correspondence /ū/ = *ew* is, for the most part, an Old English element in the American English spelling system. In the great majority of cases, words spelled with *ew* evolved from Old English words spelled with some kind of vowel-plus-*w* complex vowel, usually *ēow* or *ēaw.* Nearly all of the others come from Norman French or Old French, from words with vowels such as *ieu, eu,* and the like. The following is a fairly exhaustive list of American English words in which /ū/ = *ew* (as usual excluding any that have the variant pronunciation /yū/). Those from French are marked *Fr;* the others are from Old English:

(Array 22-15)

blew	drew	mildew	stew (Fr)
brew	eschew	new	steward
chew	flew	news	strew
clew	grew	screw (Fr)	strewn
crew (Fr)	jewel (Fr)	sewage (Fr)	threw
curlew (Fr)	knew	shrew	yew
dew	lewd	shrewd	

The homographs *sewer* 'liquid wastes' and *sewer* 'servant' also are French. Some special cases are *whew, slew*[1,2,3,4], and *newt. Whew* is an imitative form first recorded from the Early Modern period. *Slew*[1] 'a large number' is from Irish Gaelic *slaugh; slew*[2] 'past tense of *slay*', and *slew*[3], a variant of the *slough* meaning "despair," both come from Old English words spelled *slōh; slew*[4], also *slue,* meaning "twist," is of obscure origin.

Newt is one of those rare cases in which part of one word has merged with another. It derives from Old English *efeta,* which became *evte,* then *ewte,* often occurring in the Middle English phrase "an ewt(e)," which in time was mistakenly construed as "a newt." (Similar cases are *nickname, apron, adder, auger, umpire, eyas, ouch* 'a brooch'—though all of these words, except for *nickname,* lost rather than gained an *n.*)

22.4.5   /ū/ = *eu*

Although *ew* and *eu* at first appear to be closely related, historically they reflect quite different lines of evolution. Again, the correspondence /ū/ = *ew* is distinctly Old English, but /ū/ = *eu* almost without exception comes from French and Greek. Instances of /ū/ = *eu* from French:

(Array 22-16)

| adieu | maneuver | neutron |
| deuce | neuter | rheum |

Cases of /ū/ = *eu* from Greek:

(Array 22-17)

| deuteron | leukemia | pseudonym |
| leucine | pleuston | rheumatism |

The only three cases discovered so far that do not come from French or Greek are *sleuth,* from Old Norse; *reuben,* from Hebrew; and *streusel,* from German.

22.4.6   /ū/ = *ui*

The minor correspondence /ū/ = *ui* usually reflects the spelling of French words adopted into English, as in:

(Array 22-18)

| bruit | nuisance | suit |
| fruit | pursuit | |

Juice and *sluice* also come from French, though they are spelled with *u* rather than *ui* in the French. There appears to have been considerable confusion during the Middle and Early Modern English periods over the spelling of the diphthong that was the source of this particular modern /ū/, and the *i* was probably introduced into *juice* and *sluice* by analogy. *Cruise* is apparently from the Dutch *kruisen.* But *bruise* is a historical misfit: It derives from Old English *brȳsan,* which means that its normal evolution would have been into the modern *brise;* the *OED* suggests that *brȳsan* converged with the Old French *bruisier,* probably as part of the same confusion that led to *juice* and *sluice.*

22.4.7   /ū/ = *uo, uh, w*

Buoy has variant pronunciations, one with /òi/, one with /ū/. In the latter case the correspondence would have to be /ū/ = *uo*. The history here is somewhat confused, but it seems likely that the pronunciation with /ū/, and the *uo* spelling, reflect a more French-like pronunciation with a prevocalic /w/. Early spellings include *bwoy. Buhl* (also *boule* and *boulle*) 'an elaborate furniture style' derives from the name of a French cabinet-maker, André Boulle. The form with *uh* is apparently a Germanized spelling (compare *ohm, John,* and so on). In the unintegrated Welsh adoption *cwm,* /ū/ = *w*!

23   The Complex Long *u*, /yū/

23.1   The Distribution of /yū/ and /ū/

In Old, Middle, and Early Modern English a number of diphthongs and one triphthong gradually converged into /yū/ (Jespersen [1909] 1954, 1:101–7, 260, 340; Prins 1972, 102–4, 173–74). Starting in the eighteenth century, the /y/ began to be dropped when it followed certain sounds (Jespersen [1909] 1954, 1:381–85). There is much variation and ongoing change at work here: British English differs considerably from American in this distribution; certain American dialects differ one from another; and even a given speaker will pronounce the same word differently from time to time, sometimes with /yū/, sometimes with /ū/. At this time we can identify three groups of words with some form of long *u* in American English: (1) those recorded by current dictionaries as always being pronounced with /ū/, (2) those recorded as always being pronounced with /yū/, and (3) those with recorded variants in /ū/ and /yū/.

The first step in the following description is to identify where the complex /yū/ occurs.

23.1.1   Initial /yū/

Complex /yū/ occurs initially:

(Array 23-1)

eulogy	ewe	unicorn	use
euthanasia	ewer	unique	usury

23.1.2   /yū/ after Labials and Velars

Complex /yū/ tends to occur after labials such as /p/, /b/, /f/, /v/, /m/, and /th/, and after velars such as /g/, /k/, and /h/:

(Array 23-2)

ambiguous	compute	human	pewter
askew	execute	imbue	queue
attribute	feud	legume	revue
beauty	fume	mew	thew
commuter	hew	nephew	view

The holdout *hula*, with /ū/ rather than /yū/ after /h/, is a very recent adoption, still reflecting the pronunciation of *u* in Hawaiian.

23.1.3   /ū/ after Liquids

By and large the /y/ sound no longer exists in American English after the liquids /l/ and /r/. It was apparently after /r/ that the /y/ first began to disappear in English, and today in American English it is consistently absent:

(Array 23-3)

crew	gruel	rheumatism	scruple
crucial	gruesome	rhubarb	shrewd
frugal	reuben	ruby	truth

The process is less complete in the case of the liquid /l/. When the /l/ is in initial position or is preceded by a consonant or is spelled *ll*, the /y/ is consistently dropped:

(Array 23-4)

agglutinate	fluid	lubricate	plumage
allude	glue	lukewarm	pollute
blew	inclusion	lute	sleuth
exclude	lewd	pleuston	superfluity

But when the /l/ before the *u* is preceded by a vowel, the situation is less clear-cut. Some words have only /yū/: *deluge, value*. Others, like *prelude*, have variants with both /ū/ and /yū/. Most have only /ū/: *delude, dilute, absolute, salute*.

23.1.4   /ū/ after Fricatives

In general, the /y/ is dropped after the fricatives /s/, /z/, /ch/, /sh/, /zh/, and /j/. A few words still allow variants after /s/—*consume, subsume, suitable* (though not *suit*)—but for the most part the /y/ is consistently dropped after fricatives:

(Array 23-5)

assiduous	jejune	pseudonym	statue
chew	jewel	schedule	sue
chute	junior	sewer	sumac

23.1.5   /yū/ and /ū/ after Dentals

For the rest, which means essentially after the dentals /t/, /d/, and /n/, pronunciations are mixed and varied. Instances of /ū/ only after dentals: *gnu, do, too, toucan*. Instances of /yū/ only after dentals: *continue, extenuate, manual*. In most instances there are variants with /ū/ and /yū/:

(Array 23-6)

adieu	dupe	neuter	residue
amplitude	institute	nude	retinue
costume	knew	nuisance	seduce
deutzia	maneuver	obtuse	steward
duke	mildew	opportune	tuna

23.2   The Spellings of /yū/

In view of the distributions just described, it is not too surprising that the spellings of /yū/ are much the same as those of /ū/. The major difference is actually a simplification: although the most important single spelling of /ū/ is *oo*, *oo* never spells /yū/ (Hanna et al. 1966, 700–701).

23.2.1   /yū/ = *u*

Most of the time /yū/ is spelled *u* within the regular long strings—VCV, V.V, and V*e*#:

(Array 23-7)

acuity	commune	fuselage	pupil
ambiguous	continual	human	rebuke
barbecue	cupid	music	rescue
butane	cute	mutiny	union
circuitous	fuel	peculiar	usual

Bugle has /yū/ = *u* in a VC*le* string; *putrid* has it in a VC*r* string. *Impugn* has it before *gn*, another consonant cluster that often follows long vowels (see 4.3.3.1).

The only cases discovered so far of /yū/ = *u* in VCC strings are *fuchsia*, from the name *Fuchs*, and *butte*, from French *butte*.

23.2.2   /yū/ = *ew*

The second most important spelling of /yū/ is *ew*, though it is much less common than *u*:

(Array 23-8)

askew	few	nephew	sinew
curfew	hewn	pew	skewer
ewe	mew	pewter	spew

23.2.3 /yū/ = *eu*

The correspondence /yū/ = *eu* occurs most often in initial and medial position:

(Array 23-9)

eunuch	euthanasia	maieutic	queue
euphonic	feud	propaedeutic	therapeutic

23.2.4 Other Spellings of /yū/

The minor spellings of /yū/ are *ui* (*nuisance, suitable*), *eau* (*beauty*), *ieu* (*adieu, purlieu*), *iew* (*view*), and *ugh* (the names *Hugh* and *Pugh*).

24 The Diphthongs, /ȯi/ and /au̇/

24.1 On Diphthongs

A diphthong is essentially two vowel sounds that have merged into a single syllable. It is like a V.V string in which the hiatus represented by the period has been eliminated. In some cases the second sound in the diphthong is a true vowel sound; in others it is a glide or semivowel. The analysis used in this study recognizes only two modern diphthongs: /ȯi/, as in *coil,* and /au̇/, as in *cowl.* This decision, an expedient, is intended primarily to keep the orthographic discussion in this book fairly close to the simplified version of American English vowels found in standard textbooks and dictionaries. In fact, other long vowels in American English can be analyzed as diphthongs, although the sounds of the two constituent vowels are less accessible in some cases than in others. For instance, during the Great Vowel Shift, the Middle English long *i,* which had a sound then close to what we think of as /ē/, diphthongized to /äi/ or /äy/. And though this study treats /ī/ as a monophthong, the two constituent vowel sounds can still be heard. To varying degrees among different speakers, /ā/ and /ō/ also can be diphthongized. Again, however, in keeping with the current text and reference book simplifications, this study recognizes only the two diphthongs /ȯi/ and /au̇/, treating the other long vowels as monophthongs.

24.2 The Spellings of /ȯi/

The diphthong /ȯi/ did not occur in Old English. All of the modern instances of /ȯi/ either appear in adopted words or are cases in which a different Old English vowel has evolved into /ȯi/ over the centuries—for instance, *boil* from Old English *bȳle,* or *groin* from *grynde* (Jespersen [1909] 1954, 1:100–101, 330, 439; Prins 1972, 104, 171–73).

24.2.1   The Major Spellings of /ȯi/

Almost all of the instances of /ȯi/ are accounted for by the two major spellings *oi* and *oy* (Hanna et al. 1966, 612). The two major spellings sort themselves one from the other almost perfectly and with rare simplicity: consistent with the general constraint against final *i* and the distribution for *i* and *y* (see 3.4.3), in element-final position /ȯi/ is spelled *oy;* everywhere else it is spelled *oi.*

24.2.1.1   /ȯi/ = *oy* in Final Position

Instances of /ȯi/ = *oy* in word-final position:

(Array 24-1)

alloy	corduroy	enjoy	savoy
annoy	coy	envoy	sepoy
boy	decoy	joy	soy
carboy	deploy	octroy	toy
cloy	destroy	paduasoy	troy
convoy	employ	permalloy	viceroy

Instances of /ȯi/ = *oy* in element-final but word-medial position:

(Array 24-2)

clairvoyant (clair + voy[1] + ant); cf. *voyeur*
flamboyant (flamboy + ant); related to *flambeau, flame*
loyal (loy + al)
voyage (voy[2] + age); cf. *envoy*

24.2.1.2   Initial and Medial /ȯi/ = *oi*

Instances of /ȯi/ = *oi* in initial and medial position:

(Array 24-3)

adjoin	devoid	loin	sequoia
anoint	embroider	moist	soil
appoint	embroil	noise	spoil
boisterous	foible	ointment	turmoil
choice	groin	point	voice

The correspondence /ȯi/ = *oi* is also common in the suffix *-oid,* as in *asteroid, celluloid, trapezoid.* Consistent with the doublet rule, there is a notable deletion of the *o* in the explication of *paranoid:* (para + nø + oid) (see 3.2.6).

24.2.1.3   Holdouts, Apparent and Real

Boycott and *boysenberry* are only apparent holdouts to the distribution pattern for terminative *oy* and nonterminative *oi.* Both come from proper names: Charles Boycott and Rudolph Boysen. The name *Boycott* is likely an old compound of *boy* and the obsolete *cot, cott,* as in *cottage. Boysen* must be a complex of *boy* and the patronymic suffix *-sen* 'son'. Other apparent holdouts, *hoyden* and *sloyd,* have the regular variants *hoiden* and *sloid.*

True holdouts are the unintegrated *poi* (a recent Hawaiian adoption), *oyster,* and *gargoyle. Oyster,* from Old French *oistre, uistre, huistre,* had a common and more regular variant spelling with *oi* up through the eighteenth century. Some folk etymology may have been at work here, leading to the assumption that the *ster* was the suffix *-ster* (*youngster, gangster*), and thus suggesting that the segment pronounced /òi/ was some sort of obscure element which, since the diphthong would be element-final, should be spelled *oy.*

Gargoyle is from Old French *gargouille, gargoule, gargole.* Its Middle and Early Modern English spellings suggest uncertainty as to whether the vowel was /òi/. In the fifteenth century the spellings *oy* and *oi* were recorded; then both dropped out of sight for 300 years, with *oy* returning and becoming standard in the nineteenth century.

Noisome, at first seemingly from *noise,* may appear to be an instance of the distribution pattern for *oi* and *oy.* It is, however, a true holdout: *noi* + is a coform of + *noy,* as in *annoy.* It explicates to (noi + some).

24.2.2   The Minor Spellings of /òi/

The correspondence /òi/ = *eu* occurs only in the less integrated variant pronunciation of the German adoption *streusel.* The correspondence /òi/ = *uoy* occurs in one pronunciation of *buoy.*

24.3   The Spellings of /aù/

24.3.1   The Major Spellings of /aù/

The two major spellings of /aù/, *ou* and *ow,* account for about 99 percent of the instances of /aù/ in Hanna et al. (1966, 617). Of these two spellings, *ou* occurs more than twice as frequently as *ow.* The distribution of the two are fairly predictable, though a bit inelegant to describe. The correspondence /aù/ = *ow* is regular (1) in word-final position, (2) before vowels, and (3) before *l* and word-final *n.* There is overlap between *ou* and *ow* before medial /d/ and before /z/. Everywhere else /aù/ is spelled *ou.* There are some holdouts to this distribution, but the pattern holds in the great majority of cases.

24.3.1.1 /aủ/ = *ow* in Final Position

The use of *ow* rather than *ou* in word-final position is part of the general constraint in American English against ending words with *u*. Much of the force for this constraint arose from the Middle and Early Modern English convention whereby *u* followed by a vowel was read as /v/, in much the same way that today we read *c* followed by *e, i,* and *y* as /s/. Problems arose with words ending in the vowel *u* that could then take suffixes starting with a vowel. The solution was to use word-final *w*, as in *ow:*

(Array 24-4)

allow	chow	mow	row
avow	cow	now	scow
bow	endow	plow	vow
brow	how	prow	wow

The one known holdout to this group is *thou*, which until about the sixteenth century, when its use became rare, had a common variant in *ow*.

24.3.1.2 /aủ/ = *ow* before Vowels

The fact that in Middle and Early Modern English *u* before a vowel was read as /v/ encouraged the use of *ow* rather than *ou* to spell /aủ/ before vowels. This convention actually led to the respelling of some words, changing some *ou*'s to *ow*. For instance, the /r/ in a word like Middle English *shour* began to be pronounced more as a syllabic /ər/. Apparently by the sixteenth century this vowel was felt strongly enough before the /r/ to cause an *e* to be inserted, which in turn would urge the *u*, now followed by a vowel, to be changed to *w*, to keep *shouer* from being read with a /v/ sound. Thus *shower.* Similar instances include the following:

(Array 24-5)

bower	OE *būr,* ME *bour*
cower	Of Scandinavian origin; ME *couren*
flower	OFr *flo(u)r,* ME *flo(u)r.* The modern words *flower* and *flour* were originally one word, with variant spellings. The present distinction was not made until the eighteenth and nineteenth centuries.
glower	Of uncertain origin; ME *glo(u)ren*
lower	'frown'; ME *l(o)uren*
tower	OE *torr;* OFr *tor, tur;* ME *to(u)r*

Other instances of /aủ/ = *ow* before vowels:

(Array 24-6)

bowel	dower	nowadays	towel
coward	however	power	trowel
dowager	howitzer	prowess	vowel

24.3.1.3 /aȯ/ = *ow* before *l* and Final *n*

Instances:

(Array 24-7)

brown	drown	howl	scowl
clown	fowl	jowl	town
cowl	frown	owl	yowl
crown	gown	prowl	
down	growl	renown	

There are two holdouts to this correspondence, *foul* and *noun*, both of which had more regular variant spellings with *ow* up through the seventeenth century.

24.3.1.4 /aȯ/ before /d/ and /z/

The correspondence /aȯ/ = *ow* and /aȯ/ = *ou* both occur before /d/, though *ow* tends to be more frequent before medial /d/, *ou* more frequent before final /d/:

(Array 24-8)

chowder	dowdy	rowdy
crowd	powder	
aloud	loud	shroud
cloud	proud	

There is also overlap between /aȯ/ = *ow* and /aȯ/ = *ou* before /z/ spelled *s*, though *ou* is much more frequent:

(Array 24-9)

blouse*	drowse	lousy	thousand
browse	espouse	mouse (v.)	tousle
carouse	house (v.)	rouse	trousers

The only known instance of /aȯ/ = *ow* before /z/ spelled *z* is *frowzy*.

24.3.1.5 /aȯ/ = *ou*

In all other instances the correspondence /aȯ/ = *ou* holds. Notice that although /aȯ/ is regularly spelled *ow* before word-final /n/ (array 24-7), before medial /n/ it is regularly spelled *ou*:

(Array 24-10)

avouch	crouch	pouch	vouch
couch	grouch	slouch	
gouge			
abound	bounce	flounce	mound
account	bounty	flounder	mountain
aground	compound	foundry	ounce
amount	confound	fountain	profound
announce	council	hound	scoundrel
around	counsel	jounce	sound
astound	dumfound	lounge	wound
devour	flour	our	sour
dour*	hour	scour	
blouse	house (n.)	mouse (n.)	
douse	joust*	oust	
grouse	louse	souse	
bout	drouth	pout	south
clout	flout	redoubt	spout
devout	gout	rout	sprout
doubt	lout	scout	stout
doughty	mouth	shout	tout
drought	out	snout	trout

24.3.2   The Minor Spellings of /au̇/

The minor spellings of /au̇/ are *au*, *aue*, *ao*, *aou*, and *ough*. The *au* and *aue* spellings occur primarily in recent German adoptions: *umlaut*, *ablaut*, *hausfrau*, *sauerkraut*, *sauerbraten*. *Gaur* is from Hindi.

The correspondences /au̇/ = *ao* and /au̇/ = *aou* occur in a few recent, rather unintegrated adoptions: *tao*, *ciao*, *giaour*, *caoutchouc*. *Bough* and one pronunciation of *slough* contain /au̇/ = *ough*.

Although it is questionable whether *compter* should be considered part of American English, the correspondence /au̇/ = *o* does occur in one of its pronunciations.

25 Vowels before /r/

25.1 /r/ Coloring

So far the discussion of tactical strings—VCC, VCV, and the like—has excluded cases in which the consonant letter after the head vowel in the string spells the sound /r/. The reason for this exclusion is that the sound /r/ strongly colors a vowel immediately preceding it, especially if the two sounds are in the same syllable. This coloring probably has been evident throughout the history of the English language. It surely has been evident for the last six hundred years (Jespersen [1909] 1954, 1:68, 78, 318–21, 358–63; Prins 1972, 153–66; Dobson 1957, 2:724–62). The vowel immediately before an /r/ is especially vulnerable to variation and change. And there are wide differences in how these vowels are pronounced, not only from one dialect to another, but also within a dialect—indeed, from utterance to utterance with a given speaker. Thus we will address two major concerns in this chapter. First, we will reclassify vowel sounds that immediately precede /r/ in an attempt to account for the extra variability and diffuseness. Second, we will formulate new tactical patterns for vowels followed by /r/.

The sounds and spellings of vowels before /r/ group in unusual ways (Venezky 1970, 109–12). In general, the vowel sounds that would be /ā/ or /ē/ or /ō/ immediately before, say, /t/, have a wide range of pronunciations, and spellings, when they occur immediately before /r/. Thus it is easier to speak not of specific sounds here but rather of fields of sound having poles that represent the extremes contained within the fields. These fields are somewhat analogous to Henry Lee Smith's morphophones (see 11.1), though they are more diffuse than the entities of which Smith speaks. They may better be thought of as "supermorphophones."

Long *i* and the /ù/ and /yù/ sounds before /r/ are considerably more ruly and can be treated without resorting to the notion of a field or supermorphophones.

Finally, because of the massive convergence of once-distinct vowel sounds before /r/, a convergence in which each vowel sound's distinctive coloring was leeched out, there is a large cluster of neutral vowels plus /r/—represented here as /ur/. These will be analyzed as well.

25.2   The /âr/ Field

Clearly in *mate* and *mare* the *a* spells different sounds, a difference the standard VCV pattern cannot account for. Some people pronounce a word like *mare* with a vowel sound very close to the regular long *a*, /ā/; others pronounce it with a sound very close to short *e*, /e/; others pronounce it with a sound very close to short *a*, /a/. And, of course, there is the inevitable range of variant pronunciations linking the three extremes.

In the analysis that follows we will symbolize the one large field of vowel-plus-/r/ sounds as /âr/, and will use it to cover a range of sounds from /ār/ to /ar/ to /er/. As seen in figure 25-1, this /âr/ field is represented as a triangle, with /âr/ symbolizing all the sounds that fall within that broad and diverse category.

25.2.1   The Major Spellings of /âr/

To make things more manageable, we will then subdivide the triangular field into the six tactical patterns that are at work here. As seen in figure 25-2, there are six major spellings within the /âr/ field. In general, as a sound approaches the /ār/ extreme, it is more likely to be spelled *ar*VV or *ar*V#. As it approaches /ar/, it is more likely to be *arr* or *ar*VC. And as it approaches /er/, it is more likely to be *err* or *er*VC.

25.2.1.1   /âr/ = *ar*V#, *ar*VV

The major spellings of /âr/ near the /ār/ extreme are *ar*V# and *ar*VV. Instances of words with *ar*V#:

(Array 25-1)

aware	declare	hare	scare
blare	dictionary	imaginary	share
canary	flare	legendary	unwary

Instances of words with *ar*VV:

(Array 25-2)

agrarian	barbarian	honorarium	planetarium
antiquarian	calcareous	multifarious	precarious
aquarium	gregarious	nefarious	secretariat

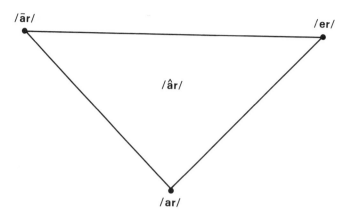

Figure 25-1. The /âr/ Field

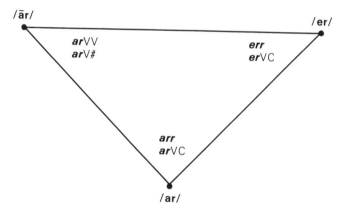

Figure 25-2. The /âr/ Field and Its Major Spellings

25.2.1.2 /âr/ = *ar*VC, *arr*

The major spellings of /âr/ near the /ar/ extreme are *ar*VC and *arr*. Some representative *ar*VC words:

(Array 25-3)

aristocracy	character	guaranty	marathon
baron	disparage	harem	parable
caravan	familiarity	maraschino	parabolic

Some representative *arr* words:

(Array 25-4)

arrant	barracks	carriage	harry
arras	barricade	embarrass	marry
arrogate	barrier	garrison	narrow

25.2.1.3   /âr/ = *err, erVC*

The major spellings of /âr/ near the /er/ extreme are *err* and *erVC*. Some words with *err*:

(Array 25-5)

berry	errand	gerrymander	serrated
cherries	ferret	herring	sherry
derrick	ferry	merry	sierra

Some representative *erVC* words:

(Array 25-6)

austerity	derivation	heritage	serenade
cerebellum	emeritus	imperishable	sheriff
ceremony	erudite	numerical	sterile
cherub	esoteric	peripatetic	therapy
derelict	herald	prosperity	veritable

25.2.1.4   The Major Spellings of /âr/ Summarized

In summary, then, the six major spellings in the /âr/ field are:

(Array 25-7)

Near the /ār/ extreme:	*ar*VV, as in *area*
	*ar*V#, as in *aware*
Near the /ar/ extreme:	*arr,* as in *arrow*
	*ar*VC, as in *arable*
Near the /er/ extreme:	*err,* as in *errand*
	*er*VC, as in *erudite*

Moreover, these six spellings can be reduced to two groups:

(Array 25-8)

1. *ar*V and *arr*   2. *er*VC and *err*

25.2.2   The Minor Spellings of /âr/

After this relatively ruly and elegant beginning for the spellings of /âr/, we should not be surprised to find several complicating minor spellings within the field.

Usually *er*VV spells the sound in the first syllable of *cereal* (see

25.4.1.1), but in some cases *er*VV spells /âr/, as in *hysteria, heroine, heroism.* Usually *er*V# spells the sound in the word *here* (see 25.4.1.1 again), but in a few words it spells /âr/:

(Array 25-9)

confectionery	millinery	there
dysentery	monastery	very
ere	stationery	where

Other *er*V# spellings are *bolero* and *portiere.* Like so many Italian words dealing with music, *concerto* has resisted integration, retaining its /âr/ sound instead of the /ur/ sound normal for *er*C spellings, as in *concert* (see 25.7.2.2).

For a discussion of the unusual /âr/ spelling in *bury* and *burial,* see 13.4.3.

Several vowel digraphs—namely, *ae, ai, ea, ei*—are associated with the /ā/ sound and appear in spellings of /âr/:

(Array 25-10)

aerate	clairvoyant	forbear	repair
aeronaut	corsair	hair	stair
affair	dairy	heir	swear
air	debonair	millionaire	tear (v.)
bear	despair	pear	their
cairn	fair	prairie	wear

A special holdout is *scarce,* with its *ar*C spelling, which normally produces a vowel sound like that in the word *farce.* It is not clear why *scarce* is pronounced the way it is. *W3* shows ten variant pronunciations for it, but only two for the more regular *farce.*

25.3   The /ôr/ Field

The /ôr/ field ranges among the extremes heard in the words *borrow, bore,* and *barn*—that is, respectively, roughly through /ȯr/, /ōr/, and /är/.

25.3.1   The Major Spellings of /ôr/

As seen in figure 25-3, the ten spellings of /ôr/ may at first seem rather chaotic, but they reduce handily, and discussing them in detail reveals the tendency of subpatterns to develop within the field.

25.3.1.1   /ôr/ = *orr, or*VC

These two spellings tend toward the *borrow* extreme of the field. Some *orr* words, including several in which the prefix *com-* is fully assimilated:

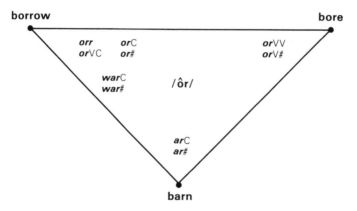

Figure 25-3. The /ôr/ Field and Its Major Spellings

(Array 25-11)

correlate	corrigible	lorry	sorry
correspond	corrugate	porridge	torrent
corridor	horrible	sorrel	torrid

Some *or*VC words:

(Array 25-12)

allegorical	corollary	hydrochloric	orifice
amoral	coronary	inferiority	origin
borax	coronet	meteoric	priority
caloric	florin	moratorium	rhetorical
categorical	forage	mores	seniority
chorister	horizontal	orange	thorax

25.3.1.2 /ôr/ = *or#*, *or*C

These two spellings also tend toward the *borrow* extreme, though some variants tend closer to the *bore* extreme. Some *or#* words:

(Array 25-13)

abhor	furor	matador	or
condor	humidor	mentor	sopor
for	ichor	nor	tor

Some *or*C words:

(Array 25-14)

abort	aorta	divorce	lord
absorption	border	enormity	morgue
accordion	corpse	export	north
afford	distort	fortune	orchestra

order	porch	resort	torpedo
organ	porpoise	sworn	vortex

25.3.1.3 /ôr/ = warC, war#

The spellings warC and war# also tend toward the *borrow* extreme of the field because of the rounding effect the /w/ has on the vowel following it. The warC words:

(Array 25-15)

athwart	sward	ward	warp
award	swarthy	warden	wart
dwarf	thwart	warm	wharf

When the /w/ is spelled *u* rather than *w*, as after *q* in words like *quartz*, the spellings fit into this same pattern:

(Array 25-16)

quarantine	quartan	quartet
quark	quarter	quartic

Although *arr* usually spells /âr/ (see figure 25-2 and array 25-4), after /w/ it spells /ôr/ because of the rounding effect of the preceding /w/:

(Array 25-17)

quarrel	warrant	warrior
quarry	warren	

The only known war# word is *war.*

25.3.1.4 /ôr/ = orVV, orV#

These two spellings tend more toward the *bore* extreme of the field. Some orVV words:

(Array 25-18)

auditorium	equatorial	memorial	porous
canorous	euphoria	meritorious	sartorial
corporeal	excoriate	moratorium	senatorial
dictatorial	foray	orient	storied
disorient	foreign	oriole	valedictorian
editorial	historian	phantasmagoria	victorious

Some orV# words:

(Array 25-19)

adore	deplore	ignore	sophomore
albacore	dory	implore	stevedore
ashore	encore	lore	swore
aurora	explore	ore	sycamore
before	flora	sagamore	yore

25.3.1.5 /ôr/ = arC, ar#

The vast majority of /ôr/ words near the *barn* extreme fall into the *arC* pattern. Some examples:

(Array 25-20)

alarm	carcass	guard	parsley
archetype	carpenter	harbinger	pharmacy
argue	cartography	harness	rhubarb
artery	charlatan	lark	snarl
arthritis	compartment	leotard	tarnish
barbecue	darling	marmalade	varsity

The known *ar#* words are:

(Array 25-21)

afar	commissar	jaguar	sonar
ajar	czar	mar	star
bar	far	par	tar
car	feldspar	radar	
caviar	guitar	scar	
cigar	hussar	seminar	

The adjective *tarry* 'covered with tar' at first looks like a holdout; compare its homograph, the verb *tarry* 'stay, remain'. But the adjective explicates to the regular *ar#* pattern: (tar)r + y).

25.3.1.6 The Major Spellings of /ôr/ Summarized

The ten major spellings listed in figure 25-3 can be reduced to four, more general descriptions:

(Array 25-22)

1. *or*   2. *orr*   3. /w/*arC*   4. /w/*ar#*

25.3.2 The Minor Spellings of /ôr/

Four digraph vowel spellings enter the /ôr/ field near the *bore* extreme: *oar, our, oor,* and *aur.* The *oar* spelling occurs only in the settings *oar#* and *oarC*:

(Array 25-23)

aboard	coarse	hoarse	soar
boar	hoar	oar	uproar
board	hoard	roar	

Apparent *oarV* spellings actually explicate to the *oar#* pattern: *uproarious,* (uproar)i + ous); *soaring,* (soar)ing); and so on.

The *our* spellings also occur only before # or C:

erVV
erV#

irr
irVC

Figure 25-4. The /êr/ Field and Its Major Spellings

(Array 25-24)

concourse	four	pompadour	source
course	gourd	pour	troubadour
court	intercourse	recourse	your
discourse	mourn	resource	

The *oor* spelling apparently occurs only in *door* and *floor.*

The *aur* spelling tends toward the *borrow* extreme of the field and occurs only before V:

(Array 25-25)

aura	auricle	laureate	saury
aural	auricula	laurel	taurine
aureate	aurora	lauric	tauromachy
aureole	aurum	saurel	thesaurus

All of these *aur* words came either from or through Latin.

Another minor spelling of /ôr/ occurs in only one variant pronunciation of *extraordinary,* in which case the /ôr/ vowel is spelled *aor.*

Minor spellings of /ôr/ near the *barn* extreme of the field are the *ear* in *hearken, heart,* and *hearth,* and the *er* in *sergeant,* all of which were caught up in the early change of short *e* plus /r/ to /är/, as in *barn* (see 25.7.3). Some recent borrowings have kept their Continental pronunciations rather than integrate into the more regular /ar/ or /är/ that their spellings suggest: *bizarre, aria, impresario* (see 25.2.1.1 and 25.2.1.2). The auxiliary *are* is another clear holdout from the regular pattern, probably because, like *were* and *was,* it is normally unstressed. Compare the contraction *'re,* in which the vowel sound has been completely eased out of hearing.

25.4   The /êr/ Field

As seen in figure 25-4, the /êr/ field is defined by only two extremes: /ēr/ and /ir/. Because the combination /ēr/ does not seem to occur when the vowel and the /r/ are in the same syllable, we can treat /ēr/ as an extreme that is approached but never reached, at least not in words in which the vowel and the /r/ are in the same syllable.

25.4.1   The Major Spellings of /êr/
25.4.1.1   /êr/ = *er*VV, *er*V#

The major spellings near the /ēr/ extreme are *er*VV and *er*V#. Some *er*VV words:

(Array 25-26)

arterial	ethereal	managerial	serious
bacteria	experience	material	sidereal
cereal	funereal	mysterious	stereophonic
criterion	imperial	period	superior
deleterious	imperious	posterior	ulterior
deteriorate	inferior	serial	venereal

Some *er*V# words:

(Array 25-27)

adhere	cere	interfere	severe
ampere	cohere	mere	sincere
atmosphere	era	persevere	sphere
austere	here	query	stere
cashmere	hero	revere	zero

25.4.1.2   /êr/ = *irr*, *ir*VC, *ir*VV

Some *irr* words, most of which contain the assimilated form of the prefix *in-*:

(Array 25-28)

chirrup*	irresistible	irritate
irrepressible	irresponsible	mirror
irreproachable	irrigate	stirrup*

Some *ir*VC words:

(Array 25-29)

conspiracy	iridescent	spirit
dirigible	miracle	virile
empirical	satirical	virulent

The only known *ir*VV words are *delirious* and *suspirious*. Venezky says that *ir*VV should correspond not to /êr/ but to /īr/, though he gives no examples (1970, 110–11). There appear to be no /īr/ = *ir*VV words in Hanna et al. (1966) or in Dolby and Resnikov (1967). Cases like *desirous* explicate to *ir*V#: (desir€)ous).

25.4.2 The Minor Spellings of /êr/

The most important minor spellings of /êr/ involve vowel digraphs associated with /ē/—*ee, ea, ie,* and *ei.* Some of the variety in these spellings is due to the fact that in Middle and Early Modern English there were two quite distinct long *e* sounds, and in the sixteenth century a fairly serious attempt was made to distinguish between them: one was to be spelled *ee, ie,* and much less often, *ei;* the other, *ea* or *eCe#* (see 19.1).

25.4.2.1 /êr/ = *eer*

Except for *eerie,* the *eer* spelling always occurs in word-final position, often in one of the *-eer* suffixes:

(Array 25-30)

auctioneer	domineer	mountaineer	racketeer
banqueteer	electioneer	mutineer	sonneteer
charioteer	engineer	privateer	volunteer

Less immediately obvious in this group are *pioneer* and *buccaneer. Pioneer* explicates to (pion + eer), the base coming from an Old French word for "foot soldier." *Buccaneer* explicates to (buccan + eer), *buccan +* evolving from French *boucaner* 'to cure meat', which in turn comes from a South American Indian word meaning "barbecue frame." Seventeenth-century pirates learned to cure meat over the barbecue rack from the South American Indians.

Other *eer* words:

(Array 25-31)

beer	cheer	leer	sheer
career	deer	peer	sneer
chanticleer	jeer	queer	veneer

25.4.2.2 /êr/ = *ear*

Except for *beard,* the *ear* spelling always occurs either in word-final position or before *y#*:

(Array 25-32)

appear	dreary	near	spear
arrear	ear	rear	tear (n.)
bleary	fear	sear	weary
clear	gear	shear	year

25.4.2.3 /êr/ = *ier*

Nearly all cases of the *ier* spelling occur in word-final position, usually as the suffix *-ier,* which is closely related in form and content to the suffixes *-er* and *-eer:*

(Array 25-33)

bombardier	chandelier	fusilier, fusileer
brigadier	chevalier	gondolier
cashier	chiffonier	gonfalonier
cavalier	financier	grenadier

Less obviously part of this group are *frontier* and *premier,* the latter of which has a specialized, less integrated form, *premiere.* Also, with the fossilized French final *e, brassiere.*

Other *ier* words:

(Array 25-34)

bier	fierce	pier	tier
denier	kier	pierce	vizier*

25.4.2.4 Other Minor Spellings of /êr/

The *eir* spelling occurs only in *weir, weird,* and the Spanish *Madeira,* a kind of wine, wood, roach, and so on.

The *aer* spelling of /êr/ occurs only in *hetaera,* which has the more regular alternate spelling and pronunciation, *hetaira* with /īr/, and in *chimaera,* which has the more regular alternative *chimera.*

In a few minimally integrated adoptions, the spelling of /êr/ contradicts regular tactical patterns. *Amir, fakir,* and *souvenir* all have /êr/ = *ir* in contexts that would regularly have /ur/. *Lira* has *ir* spelling /êr/ where we would expect /īr/.

The letter *y,* usually in Greek words, often occurs where we would normally expect *i.* The *y* produces some *yr* spellings of /êr/:

(Array 25-35)

lyric	myriad	pyramid	tyranny

The *yr* spelling also occurs in some variant pronunciations: *panegyric,* also with /īr/; *syringe,* also with /ər/; and *syrup, sirup,* also with /ur/.

25.5 The Spellings of /īr/

Compared to the /âr/, /ôr/, and /êr/ fields, /īr/ is phonologically quite simple. Unlike the others, it contains a full vowel sound rather than one that has been leeched out by the following /r/. A following /r/ does not affect the sound of a preceding /ī/ as dramatically as it does other long vowels. So the major spellings remain straightforward.

25.5.1   The Major Spellings of /īr/
25.5.1.1   /īr/ = irV#, irV

The basic tactical pattern for /īr/ is irV#. In simplexes the V is usually silent final *e:*

(Array 25-36)

admire	entire	perspire	tire
afire	esquire	quire	transpire
aspire	expire	require	umpire
attire	fire	retire	vampire
conspire	hire	satire	wire
desire	inquire	shire	

The sound /īr/ also occurs in many complexes in the pattern irV, but normally it explicates to irV#:

(Array 25-37)

admirer (admiré)er)	inquiry (inquiré)y)
aspirant (aspiré)ant)	retiring (retiré)ing)
desirable (desiré)able)	wired (wiré)ed)

25.5.2   The Minor Spellings of /īr/

The Greek *y* occurs in the /īr/ = yr correspondence in *lyre* and *pyre*. The correspondence /īr/ = ier occurs in one variant pronunciation of the element *hier+* (as in *hierarchy* and *hieroglyphic*) and in the word *fiery*. The history of the *ier* spelling in *hier+* is straightforward enough: the spelling comes by way of Middle English, Old French, and Latin from Greek, *hierarkhia,* the base *hier+* having the content "sacred, holy." It is not so clear why *fiery* is spelled as it is instead of in accordance with its most logical explication, (firé)y), which would give us **firy.* Jespersen suggests that it was spelled *fiery* in the sixteenth century, replacing earlier spellings such as *fyry* and *firy,* because by the sixteenth century the glide before the /r/ was being pronounced as a distinct vowel sound and therefore the spelling was changed to show it. He suggests a parallel with such words as *brier* and *frier,* which also grew new *e*'s in the sixteenth century ([1909] 1954, 1:318–19). One learns to argue gingerly with Jespersen's suggestions, but if his argument holds for *fiery,* one wonders why we have *fire* rather than **fier.* A less elegant countersuggestion would be that since there was much indecision and variation in the spelling of both *fire* and *fiery* up through the seventeenth century, it seems possible that the two spellings were standardized more or less independently of each other, with *fiery* being standardized as if the *fier* spelling of *fire* were standard.

25.6 The Spellings of /ùr/ and /yùr/

The distinction between /ùr/ and /yùr/ is essentially the same as the distinction between /ù/ and /yù/ (see 23.1). In certain contexts the sound is pronounced /ùr/; in other contexts it is /yùr/; and in a small number of contexts it can be either one. The sound is /ùr/ after fricatives and after the liquids, /l/ and /r/. Everywhere else it is /yùr/.

25.6.1 The Major Spellings of /ùr/ and /yùr/
25.6.1.1 /ùr/ = *ur*V

The correspondence /ùr/ = *ur*V occurs after fricatives and liquids:

(Array 25-38)

abjure	forfeiture	lurid	sure
allure	injurious	mature	temperature
assure	insure	plural	thurible
brochure	jural	pruritus	thurifer
caricature	jurisdiction	rural	usurious

25.6.1.2 /yùr/ = *ur*V

The correspondence /yùr/ = *ur*V holds after stops and nasals and in word-initial position:

(Array 25-39)

bureau	inure	ordure	spurious
burette	manicure	procure	tenure
burin*	mural	pure	uranium
cure	mure	purine	urethane
demure	murex	purulent	urine
epicure	muricate	secure	uropod

The fact that the pattern of distribution of /ùr/ and /yùr/ is still developing is revealed by some holdouts, especially variant pronunciations. For example, after the stops /d/ and /t/ most words have variant pronunciations, one with /ùr/, one with /yùr/:

(Array 25-40)

centurion	during	endure
durable	duroc	mature*
duration	durum	tureen

When *t* palatalizes to /ch/, the *ur* is pronounced /ùr/, as in *signature*, but when *t* does not palatalize and is pronounced /t/, the *ur* can be pronounced either /yùr/ or /ùr/, as in *mature* and *centurion*. *Manure* also has variants with /ùr/ and /yùr/, and the rather rare *gravure*, as in *rotogravure*, and *hure* have /yùr/ after a fricative.

25.6.2   The Minor Spellings of /ùr/ and /yùr/

The Norman French spelling *ou* occurs in a few words with /ùr/:

(Array 25-41)

contour	detour	paramour	tourmaline
courier	gourmet	tour	

Dour has one pronunciation with /ùr/, one with /aùr/. *Gourd, course, troubadour,* and *your* have variant pronunciations with vowel sounds from the /ôr/ field. *Your,* when unstressed, is /yər/. *Tournament* and *tourniquet* have alternative pronunciations with /ùr/.

The sound /ùr/ is spelled *oor* in *poor, moor* (noun and verb), and *boor.* In each case there is a labial consonant before the /ùr/, as contrasted with *floor* and *door,* in which *oor* spells /ôr/, with no preceding labial. *Poor, boor,* and *moor* come from a variety of etymologies, which makes it difficult to see any historical reason for the /ùr/ sound in them. *Poor's* etymology is especially intriguing: it derives from Middle English *poure, povre,* from Old French *povre,* from Latin *pauper.*

The correspondence /ùr/ = *uor* holds in one pronunciation of words with the element *fluor +,* as in *fluorescent, fluoride, fluorine.*

The correspondence /ùr/ = *eur* holds in words with the element *pleur +,* as in *pleurisy, pleura, pleurotomy.* Words with the element *neur +* have alternate pronunciations with /ùr/ and /yùr/: *neural, neuralgia, neurologist, neuron, neurosis, neurasthenia.* And in *heuristics* the *eur* spells /yùr/. *Heuristics* and the *pleur +* words fit the basic distribution pattern for /ùr/, which calls for /yùr/ after /h/ and for /ùr/ after /l/. The *neur +* words are holdouts to the pattern.

25.7   The /ur/ Convergence

25.7.1   Historical Sources

The next group of spellings involves not so much a field of sounds as a massive historical convergence of several distinct sounds into one: the neutral /ur/ sound of words such as *bird*. There is little, if any, vowel color left in such words; it has all been leeched out over the centuries by the /r/.

Another way of explaining it is to say that the vowel and the /r/ are now pronounced simultaneously, one on top of the other, as it were. The /ur/ convergence is represented nicely by the trio *firm, furl,* and *fern,* in all of which the vowel sound is /ur/. To this group we might add a smaller special group represented by the word *word.*

The /ur/ convergence is in some ways the mirror image of what happens in the speech of *r* droppers, as in Northeastern American English. The *r* dropper basically replaces the /r/ coloring with a schwa sound. Here, in the converged /ur/, the vowel is replaced, in a sense, by the /r/.

It may not be fanciful to suggest that the /ur/ convergence marks a later stage in the evolution of vowels preceding /r/, an earlier stage of which is marked by the existence of the /âr/, /êr/, and /ôr/ fields. The fields represent cases in which vowel distinctions are blurred by change and variation, the final result of which could well be convergence to a single, more or less neutral vowel, as has happened most dramatically with /ur/.

The /ur/ convergence duplicates with stressed vowels a convergence to schwa in /ər/ with unstressed vowels. The parallel cases of /ər/ will not be explored, however, owing to the general decision not to include schwa in this discussion.

The /ur/ convergence began in the sixteenth century (Jespersen [1909] 1954, 1:319–21; Prins 1972, 154–57; Dobson 1957, 2:746–59). Before that time the three sounds spelled *ir, ur, er* (and *or* after *w*) were distinguished one from the other. By about 1600 *ir* and *ur* had converged into a single sound, probably somewhat different from what either had been before. This convergence was most likely the motivation for some late spelling changes. Middle English *chirche* became *church; chirne* or *cherine* became *churn. Sprutten* became first *spirt* in Early Modern English and then *spurt* in Modern English. Other pairs whose differences are probably partly due to this convergence of *ir* and *ur* in Early Modern times include Middle English *hirchon, irchon,* and modern *urchin;* Middle English *mirke* and modern *murk;* Middle English *borow* and modern *burrow;* Middle English *sloor, slore,* and modern *slur.* Later changes are represented by *surly,* which derives from *sir,* and *tureen,* which as late as the eighteenth and nineteenth centuries was often spelled *terrine* and *terrene,* after the French *terrine,* ultimately from Latin *terra* 'earth', a good instance of the etymological demand being overridden by phonology and analogy.

By about 1600, then, *ir* and *ur* had converged in pronunciation, with *er* still held distinct. But by about 1700 the convergence was complete, with all three spellings assuming a pronunciation close to the modern /ur/.

25.7.2 The Major Spellings of /ur/
25.7.2.1 /wur/ = wor

The movement of *wor* toward /wur/ began very early. For instance, from the eleventh through the sixteenth century, the spellings of *word*, from Old English *word*, suggest that the distinctive *o* coloring was fading: *wurd*, *werd*, even *wrd*. The development of other modern *wor* words is complicated by the fact that they derive from Old English words that had some vowel other than simple *o*, but the fact remains that *or* after *w* usually falls into the /ur/ convergence: *world*, *worm*, *worth*, *worse*, *worst*, *worship*. To this group might be added *wort* and *worry*, the first with the variant sound /ôr/, the second with an extra *r*. The holdout *worn* has quite likely been held to the /ôr/ pronunciation by analogy with *wore*. *Whorl* has two pronunciations, one with /ôr/, one with the converged /ur/. The /ur/ pronunciation of *whorl* actually fits the *wor* pattern since, like the other *wh* words, the *w* and *h* metathesize here to /hw/ or simplify to /w/.

25.7.2.2 /ur/ = erC, er#

Some *erC* words:

(Array 25-42)

alert	emerge	jerk	terminate
assert	eternal	lucerne	terse
berserk	expert	pachyderm	tubercular
clergy	fraternity	perquisite	vermin
coerce	herb	perverse	vertigo
desert	hyperbole	sermon	verve

The *er#* words, five of which contain the bound base *+fer:*

(Array 25-43)

aver	deter	inter	refer
confer	her	per	
defer	infer	prefer	

Medial *err* spellings explicate to *er#*: *deferral*, (defer)r + al), and *deterrent*, (deter)r + ent). *Err* has two pronunciations: the more regular one is /âr/, fitting the *err* pattern (see 25.2.1.3); less regular is /ur/. The pronunciation of the verb *were* is completely nonregular. Probably it has eased to the /ur/ sound because it so often occurs in unstressed positions. It can be compared in this respect with *was*, also usually unstressed and also eased from a more demanding vowel color.

25.7.2.3 /ur/ = *ir*C, *ir*#

Some *ir*C words:

(Array 25-44)

affirm	dirk	infirmary	squirt
birch	dirt	irk	swirl
chirp	first	quirk	thirst
circle	gird	sirloin	virgin
confirm	girth	smirk	virtuoso
dirge	hirsute	squirm	whirl

The *ir*# words:

(Array 25-45)

fir	sir	stir	whir

Most cases of /ur/ = *irr* explicate to *ir*#: *firry*, (fir)r + y), and *stirred*, (stir)r + ed). The only true instances of /ur/ = *irr* are *squirrel* and *birr. Stirrup* and *chirrup* have more regular variants with /êr/ (see 25.4.1.2).

25.7.2.4 /ur/ = *ur*C, *ur*#

Some representative *ur*C words, several with the prefix *sur-*:

(Array 25-46)

appurtenance	liturgical	surcharge	taciturn
blurt	murder	surcingle	thaumaturgy
burlesque	nocturne	surface	turbine
curl	purse	surgeon	urchin
curve	scurvy	surly	urge
disburse	sturdy	surname	zymurgy

Some *urr* spellings explicate to *ur*#:

(Array 25-47)

demurrer, (demur)r + er)	occurrence, (occur)r + ence)
furry, (fur)r + y)	recurring, (recur)r + ing)

In most cases, however, the *urr* spelling is primitive:

(Array 25-48)

burr	current (?)	hurricane	scurrilous
burro	curry	hurry	scurry
burrow	flurry	murrain	turret

The *ur*# words are:

(Array 25-49)

blur	demur	larkspur	recur
bur	fur	murmur	slur
cur	incur	occur	spur

25.7.2.5 The Major Spellings of /ur/ Summarized

There are nine major spellings of /ur/:

(Array 25-50)

*er*C	*er#*	*wor*
*ir*C	*ir#*	*irr*
*ur*C	*ur#*	*urr*

25.7.3 The Minor Spellings of /ur/

The correspondence /ur/ = *ear* occurs in a few words:

(Array 25-51)

dearth	earnest	learn	search
earl	earth	pearl	yearn
early	heard	rehearse	
earn	hearse	research	

These few words are part of the residue of an important change that occurred in English pronunciation (and in some cases spelling) in the fourteenth, fifteenth, and sixteenth centuries (Jespersen [1909] 1954, 1:197–99). The old Middle English short-*e*-plus-/r/ sound changed into a broad "ah" plus /r/. This change underlies such varied things as the (to Americans) curious British pronunciation of *clerk* as if it were spelled *clark*. In many cases the spelling, usually *er,* changed to reflect the change in pronunciation, usually becoming *ar.* Thus Middle English *sterre* became *star; werble* became *warble,* and *merke* became *mark.* Thus, too, the Middle English single word *persone* split into two words: *person* and *parson.* Similarly, *vermin* developed the colloquial *varmint,* and *university* developed the clipping *varsity.* Some of the early *ear* spellings did not change, although their pronunciations did: *heart, hearth, hearken.* Finally, some of the early *ear* spellings did not change, nor did their pronunciations. Those *ear* words that resisted change converged to the /ur/ sound, together with the *er, ir,* and *ur* and *wor* spellings discussed earlier. Thus we have words like those in array 25-51, in which /ur/ is spelled *ear.*

Several Early Modern words with short *u* plus /r/ were spelled *our* rather than *ur.* This *our* spelling comes from French. As part of the general convergence already described, in most cases the /ur/ of these words is now spelled *our:*

(Array 25-52)

adjourn	courtesy	journal	nourish
courage	flourish	journey	scourge

Also in this group, *tournament, tourney,* and *tourniquet* have variant pronunciations with /ur/.

The correspondence /ur/ = *eur* occurs in a few recent adoptions that remain relatively unintegrated, closer to their French look and sound: *chauffeur, entrepreneur, hauteur, raconteur, saboteur.* All except *chauffeur* and *entrepreneur* have variant, less integrated pronunciations.

The correspondence /ur/ = *yr* occurs in the Greek adaptions *myrtle* and *myrmidon,* and in the base *myrmec+* 'pertaining to ants'. The unique /ur/ = *yrrh* occurs in *myrrh.*

26   The Front Stops: /b/, /p/, /d/, and /t/

26.1 Introduction

The front stops have much in common, both in the way they are spoken and in the way they are written. They are all produced by closing off, or stopping, the airflow toward the front of the mouth, and then releasing it quickly. With the first two of the four—the **bilabial stops** /b/ and /p/—the lips stop the airflow. With the second two—the **dental stops** /d/ and /t/—the tongue stops the airflow by pressing against the back of the upper tooth ridge. The bilabial stops differ from each other in only one way: with /b/ the vocal cords vibrate; with /p/ they do not. Sounds like /b/, pronounced with the vocal cords vibrating, are called **voiced sounds.** Sounds like /p/ are **voiceless.** The same distinction holds between /d/ and /t/: /d/ is voiced, /t/ is voiceless. (For more on the voiced/voiceless distinction see 3.2.2. For historical sources see Jespersen [1909] 1954, 1:19–21, 208–11, 389–93; Prins 1972, 197–99, 208–9, 226–27.)

This phonological grouping is paralleled by important orthographic similarities. The resemblance among the four front stops extends to the general patterns for their spellings. Most commonly each of them is spelled with the letter used between slant lines to indicate the sound itself. Thus /b/ is usually spelled *b*, /p/ is usually spelled *p*, /d/ is usually *d*, and /t/ is *t*. In each case the second most important spelling is a doubling of the single letter: *bb, pp, dd, tt.* According to Hanna et al., /p/ is spelled either *p* or *pp* 100 percent of the time (1966, 939). Actually, things are more complicated than that, for there are different spellings of /p/ in words such as *hiccough* and in common pronunciations of *diphthong* and *diphtheria.* Also, according to Hanna et al. more than 99 percent of the time /b/ is spelled *b* or *bb*, /t/ is spelled *t* or *tt*, and /d/ is spelled *d* or *dd* (1966, 733, 756, 1068). In the description that follows, which is based on a larger sample than that used by the Hanna group and a slightly different method of analysis, we will find that the figures given by Hanna et al. are high, but not by much. Moreover, we will discover that the spelling of the front stops is tidy and patterned, with just a few special cases that need to be explained and with the strong phonological similarities among the front stops reflected in equally strong orthographic similarities.

What makes the spelling of the front stops particularly elegant is not just that, say, *t* and *tt* account for so many instances of /t/, but also that almost without holdout we can write selection rules that allow us to anticipate when to choose *t* and when to choose *tt*. In each case the *tt* spelling is due to one of the following: twinning, assimilation, the VCC/ VCV contrast, or a special kind of simple addition in which an element beginning with a *t* is added to an element ending in *t*, thus producing a doublet. This special kind of addition is called **duplicative addition.**

26.2   The Spellings of /b/

26.2.1   Overview

More than 99 percent of the time /b/ is spelled either *b* or *bb*—and more than 95 percent of the time it is spelled *b* (Hanna et al. 1966, 733). Though the *b* spelling occurs in all three positions of the word—initial, medial, and final—it is rare in final position. Or, more accurately, the sound /b/ is rare in final position. A silent *b* occurs in the final clusters *mb* and *bt* (*bomb, thumb, doubt, debt*), and in the initial cluster *bd* (*bdelium, bdeloid*, and other technical words). (For more on *mb* see 31.2.1.1; on *bt* see 26.5.2; on *bd* see 26.4.2.) The *bb* spelling occurs only in medial position, except in *ebb*, the one word in which it is final and whose second *b* is an instance of the Short Word Rule at work (see 3.5). The *bb* spelling is never word-initial. In the following discussion we will treat the minor spelling first and then distinguish the major spellings, *b* and *bb*, from each other.

26.2.2   The Minor Spelling of /b/

From a purely sound-to-spelling point of view /b/ is spelled *pb* in the medial concatenations in *cupboard, clapboard, raspberry,* and *Campbell*. From a tactical point of view, however, it could be argued that the basic correspondence /b/ = *b* holds in these words and that when the two stops /p/ and /b/ concatenate, the sound of the first is lost in the pronunciation (compare *subpoena*).

26.2.3   The Major Spellings of /b/
26.2.3.1   The Major Spellings of /b/ Summarized

The following rules govern the selection of the *b* and *bb* spellings:

1. The correspondence /b/ = *bb* holds at element boundaries that are affected by instances of twinning, duplicative addition, or full assimilation.

2. Within elements, unless one of the shortening rules applies (see chapters 5–7), the correspondence /b/ = *bb* also holds between a short stressed vowel and a following vowel or *le*.
3. Everywhere else /b/ is spelled *b*.

These selection rules can be summarized best in the order just given, but another ordering controls their application. The phrase "everywhere else" in rule 3 leads to five specific subrules that describe where the correspondence /b/ = *b* holds, and these take precedence over the situations described in rules 1 and 2:

i. /b/ = *b* at any boundary not described in rule 1;
ii. /b/ = *b* in VCV strings shortened by one of the shortening rules;
iii. /b/ = *b* within consonant clusters and concatenations, but with a systematic complication being posed by a following *le;*
iv. /b/ = *b* after vowel digraphs;
v. /b/ = *b* after long vowels.

In cases of conflict subrules (i) through (v) within rule 3 are applied before and take precedence over rules 1 and 2. For instance, if rule 2 were to apply before subrule (iv) *bauble* would be spelled *baubble.

Also, there is considerable redundancy among the rules. Two or more rules may cover a single spelling. For instance, the *b* spelling in *dauber* is covered by rule 3(i) since an element boundary occurs after the /b/, (daub)er), and by rule 3(iv) since a vowel digraph, *au,* precedes the /b/.

The phrase "everywhere else" in rule 3 leads to a sixth specific setting in which the correspondence /b/ = *b* holds: after reduced vowels. This subrule, however, cannot take precedence over rules 1 and 2. If it did, a word like *abbreviate* would pose problems with its initial reduced vowel, or schwa, followed by the *bb* spelling called for by rule 1.

The discussion of the major spellings of /b/ in 26.2.3.2 through 26.2.3.10 follows the order that controls the application of these rules and subrules. Thus, it treats the major spellings *b* and *bb* in terms of the following nine rules:

1. /b/ = *b* at boundaries not affected by twinning, assimilation, or duplicative addition (what we will call **simple boundaries**).
2. /b/ = *b* in VCV strings shortened by one of the shortening rules.
3. /b/ = *b* within consonant clusters and concatenations, but with a regular complication being posed by a following *le*.
4. /b/ = *b* after vowel digraphs.
5. /b/ = *b* after long vowels.
6. /b/ = *bb* at boundaries affected by twinning, assimilation, or duplicative addition (what we will call **complex boundaries**).

7. /b/ = *bb* between a short stressed vowel and a following vowel if none of the shortening rules apply.
8. /b/ = *bb* between a short stressed vowel and a following *le*.
9. /b/ = *b* after reduced vowels.

26.2.3.2 /b/ = *b* at Simple Boundaries

Except for *ebb,* the correspondence /b/ = *b* holds at all boundaries not affected by twinning, full assimilation, or duplicative addition. A few instances:

(Array 26-1)

abdicate (ab + dic + ate)	imbecile (im + becile)
aboard (a(board)	insubordinate (in + sub + ordin + ate)
abominate (ab + omin + ate)	oblige (ob + lige)
acrobat (acr + o + bat)	reimburse (re + im + burse)
blob (blob)	rhomboid (rhomb + oid)
combustion (com + bust + ion)	sibling (sib)ling)
diabetes (dia + bet + es)	sublimate (sub + lim*é*)ate)
embroider (em + broider)	suburban (sub(urb)an)
hamburger (ham + burger)	thrombosis (thromb + osis)

26.2.3.3 /b/ = *b* in Shortened VCV Strings

The correspondence /b/ = *b* holds in VCV strings affected by one of the shortening rules. Instances with the Third Syllable Rule include:

(Array 26-2)

collaborate	fabulous	nebula	sybarite
debonair	haberdasher	obelisk	tintinnabulation
ebony	labyrinth	probable	vocabulary

Tribute and *tribune* are instances in which the Third Syllable Rule seems to have shortened the trisyllabic Latin sources, *tribūtum* and *tribūnus.*
Instances of the Stress Frontshift Rule include:

(Array 26-3)

cabin	giblet	ribald	tableau

There are not many instances in which a vowel preceding a /b/ is shortened by one of the suffix rules, but some examples are:

(Array 26-4)

biblical	exhibit	habit	public
cannabic*	fabric	inhibit	rabid
debit	globule	prohibit	syllabic

26.2.3.4 /b/ = *b* in Consonant Clusters and Concatenations

The reason for the *bb* spelling between a short stressed vowel and another vowel is obviously the force of the VCC pattern. But if the /b/ is followed or preceded immediately by another consonant, the *bb* is not needed to fill out the VCC string. Even more generally, the tendency for *bb* not to occur adjacent to another consonant is an instance of the constraint against doublets within large clusters and concatenations (see 3.2.6). The correspondence /b/ = *b* occurs in few clusters, and in especially few **tight clusters,** clusters that occur in the same syllable: *br (brush, bring), bl (blush, blood), rb (barb, urban, proverb).* Some other examples of /b/ = *b* in clusters and concatenations:

(Array 26-5)

absinthe	carbonic	jumbo	symbol
albacore	dissemble	lobster	umbrella
bible	husband	molybdenum	vibration

A systematic complication occurs if the /b/ is followed by an *l*. If the vowel preceding the /b/ is stressed and long, as in *bible* or *noble*, /b/ = *b*. But if the vowel is stressed and short, as in *dribble* or *hobble*, /b/ = *bb*. (For more details see 26.2.3.9.)

Due to the characteristic weakness of the doublet constraint with the inflectional suffix *-s,* there is a doublet within a concatenation in *ebbs*.

26.2.3.5 /b/ = *b* after Vowel Digraphs

After any vowel digraph—spelling a diphthong or a long or a short monophthong—/b/ = *b:*

(Array 26-6)

amoeba	double	goober
auberge	feeble	phoebe
auburn	foible	troubadour

26.2.3.6 /b/ = *b* after Long Vowels

Since the *bb* spelling is used primarily to mark a preceding short vowel, it is not surprising that after a long vowel /b/ = *b:*

(Array 26-7)

adobe	exuberant	labor	rabies
baby	fiber	libel	robot
cybernetics	jubilee	oboe	ubiquitous

26.2.3.7 /b/ = *bb* at Complex Boundaries

The correspondence /b/ = *bb* holds at boundaries affected by twinning, duplicative addition, and assimilation. Because the *b* spelling is rare in word-final position, the doublet *bb* due to twinning is rather rare. Two examples:

(Array 26-8)

chubby	(chub)b+y	Apparently the adjective comes from *chub,* a fattish fish.
shabby	(shab)b+y	*Shab* reflects an obsolete word used to refer to a skin disease of sheep and to a low fellow.

Less obscure twinnings:

(Array 26-9)

dubbing	fobbed	robbery	shrubbery
flabby	jobber	rubber	stubby

Very few instances of /b/ = *bb* are due to duplicative addition. In careful speech the two *b*'s are often pronounced separately, thus creating not an instance of /b/ = *bb* but two consecutive instances of /b/ = *b*. In rapid speech, however, the following are usually pronounced with /b/ = *bb*:

(Array 26-10)

dumbbell	subbasement	subbranch
ribband	subboreal	

Even more rare are cases of /b/ = *bb* due to assimilation. The one possible instance, *abbreviate,* is of obscure structure. It could be explicated to (ab+brevi+ate) via duplicative addition with the rare prefix *ab-,* but we choose to explicate it to (ad+b+brevi+ate) via the assimilation of *ad-*.

26.2.3.8 /b/ = *bb* after Short Vowels

Unless one of the shortening rules applies, /b/ = *bb* between a short stressed vowel and a following vowel, thereby fitting the VCC pattern:

(Array 26-11)

abbey	cabbage	hobby	rabbit
blubber	gibberish	hubbub	ribbon
bobbin	gibbous	jabber	rubbish

In addition, this selection rule overlaps with all instances of twinning.

Three holdouts are *baboon, taboo,* and *abalone.* Although *baboon* has endured many different spellings since the fourteenth century, it has never, apparently, been spelled with *bb* after the first vowel. The other two words are very recent adoptions: *taboo* from Tongan in the eighteenth century, *abalone* from American Spanish in the nineteenth century. Both *baboon* and *taboo* have variant pronunciations with schwa preceding the /b/, which would make them regular instances of 26.2.3.10 below. And the nonregular *b* in *abalone* can be seen as an instance of the tendency to shorten a stressed vowel that is followed by two or more weaker syllables. This general tendency, of which the Third Syllable Rule is a more specific instance, seems to underlie the relative shortage of long stressed vowels early in polysyllabic words that do not contain shorter free stems.

26.2.3.9   /b/ = *bb* between Short Vowels and *le*

The correspondence /b/ = *bb* holds between a preceding short stressed vowel and the sequence *le:*

(Array 26-12)

babble	gabble	pebble	squabble
bubble	gobble	quibble	stubble
cobble	hobble	rabble	wobble
dabble	nibble	rubble	
dribble	obbligato (It)	scribble	

The apparent holdouts *double* and *doubloon* are brought into pattern by the prior vowel digraph rule (see 26.2.3.5).

26.2.3.10   /b/ = *b* after Reduced Vowels

Again, since *bb* serves essentially as a marker of short vowels, it is not surprising that after reduced vowels /b/ = *b:*

(Array 26-13)

ability	filibuster	observe	tobacco
cerebellum	habitual	prohibition	toboggan
exhibition	hullabaloo	subdue	vagabond

The holdout *sabbatical* is related to *sabbath,* in which the *bb* is regular after the short stressed vowel. Conservative analogy may be at work in *sabbatical.*

26.3   The Spellings of /p/

26.3.1   Overview

More than nine times out of ten, /p/ is spelled *p* in any position: initial, medial, final. In nearly every case in which /p/ is not spelled *p* it is spelled *pp,* though only in medial position, never in initial or final. The *pp* spelling does occur in final position from the standpoint of pronunciation in the relatively unintegrated seventeenth-century Russian adoption *steppe*. *Steppe* often had the more integrated form *step* up through the nineteenth century; the current spelling, an instance of dis-integration, reflects either German or French.

26.3.2   The Minor Spellings of /p/

The sound /p/ is spelled in some way other than *p* or *pp* only in *diphtheria, diphthong, naphtha, hiccough,* and *subpoena.* Each of the first three words has variant pronunciations, one with *ph* = /p/ and a more regular one with *ph* = /f/. In general the /fth/ cluster seems to be vulnerable in English pronunciation, not only in Greek adoptions such as *phthisic,* with *phth* now simplified to /th/, but even in native words such as *twelfth* and *fifth,* where maintaining the /f/ in /fth/ takes some special attention and care. It seems likely that in *diphtheria, diphthong,* and *naphtha* the variant pronunciations with *ph* = /p/ arose out of that same strain. As we pronounce the words, we can feel a natural enough dissimilation occurring, changing the /f/ to /p/ before /th/, encouraged visually, perhaps, by the letter *p* on the page.

Usually *hiccough* is pronounced with *gh* = /p/. The *hiccough* spelling is the result of some folk etymology. The word had a number of earlier forms, including *hicker, hickop, hickock,* as well as the phonetically regular current variant *hiccup.* The spelling with *cough* is apparently due to the notion that the word must have something to do with coughing. Actually, the sound and spelling of *hiccough* were originally imitative, and there is no semantic or historical connection with *cough.* By now, according to *W3,* a spelling pronunciation with *gh* = /f/ has developed. Smaller modern dictionaries do not record this variant, nor does the *OED,* which suggests dropping the *hiccough* spelling as "a mere error" (at *Hiccup*). Samuel Johnson, on the other hand, preferred the *hiccough* spelling and labeled *hickup* "corrupted from *hiccough,*" though he gave no pronunciation. In a sense, then, the case of /p/ = *gh* in *hiccough* is an instance of mixed convergence.

The correspondence /p/ = *bp* in *subpoena* is the mirror image of the /b/ = *pb* correspondence in *cupboard* and *raspberry,* and it arises from the tendency in English for *pb* and *bp* concatenations to drop the sound of the first stop (see 26.2.2). This dropping is common in older words; in some recent formations both stops are still pronounced, as in *subplot* and *subprinciple.* But though the dictionaries still show /bp/ in the pronunciation of such words, as we say them, we can feel the /b/ slipping away. *W3* and Kenyon and Knott (1944) show rare variant pronunciations of *sub-poena* with /bp/.

Kopje, also *koppie,* from Dutch *kopje,* only seems to have /p/ = *pj*. From the historical point of view the *j* echoes the Dutch glide and is best associated with the vowel *e* rather than the consonant *p,* as the variant spelling *koppie* does by rendering the *j* as *i*.

26.3.3 The Major Spellings of /p/

The sound /p/ is spelled *p* or *pp* more than 99 percent of the time. The rules for selecting between *p* and *pp* are exactly the same as those for selecting between *b* and *bb,* and the following discussion deals with those rules in the order in which they appear in 26.2.3.1.

26.3.3.1 /p/ = *p* at Simple Boundaries

(Array 26-14)

archipelago (arch + i + pelago)	monopoly (mon + o + pol + y)
constipation (con + stip + ation)	replica (re + plica)
deprecate (de + prec + ate)	reprobate (re(prob + ate)
diploma (di + ploma)	separate (se(parè)ate)
encyclopedia (en + cycl + o + ped + ia)	typify (typè)ify)

26.3.3.2 /p/ = *p* in Shortened VCV Strings

Instances involving the Third Syllable Rule:

(Array 26-15)

aperture	epicure	obstreperous	property
cosmopolite	hypocrite	oviparous	telepathy
deputy	manipulate	papillary	trapezoid

Tapioca fits into this group, too, except that it is not a Latin or French early adaption. It is a seventeenth-century adoption from Portuguese or Spanish, from Tupi, a South American Indian language. It, like *abalone,* is an instance of the more generalized effects of the Third Syllable Rule (see chapter 7).

Instances of /p/ = *p* in VCV strings shortened by the Stress Frontshift Rule are less numerous:

(Array 26-16)

chapel	leper	poplin	rapine
copy	poplar	proper	trapeze

Instances due to the suffix rules:

(Array 26-17)

decrepit	microscopic	sapid	topic
epic	philanthropic	scolytid	tropic
insipid	priapic	tepid	vapid

26.3.3.3 /p/ = p in Consonant Clusters and Concatenations

The p spelling occurs in a number of tight clusters: sp (sparkle, aspirin, grasp), pl (plane, steeple), lp (help), mp (bump), pt (script), rp (sharp), pth (depth), mps (glimpse), mpt (prompt). It also occurs in a number of different loose clusters and concatenations. Some instances of /p/ = p adjacent to other consonants:

(Array 26-18)

calypso	hospital	shampoo	split
culprit	rupture	shrapnel	spread
exemption	serpent	soprano	tempt

26.3.3.4 /p/ = p after Vowel Digraphs

(Array 26-19)

couple	people	traipse	weapon

26.3.3.5 /p/ = p after Long Vowels

(Array 26-20)

cupidity	occupy	sepal	utopia
cupola	opal	stipend	vapor
hyperbole	opaque	stupid	viper

26.3.3.6 /p/ = pp at Complex Boundaries

It is rare for the correspondence /p/ = pp to result from duplicative addition, and when pronounced carefully the few instances given below are probably examples of /pp/ rather than /p/:

(Array 26-21)

chappaul	stepparent	upputting (Scot)
lamppost	toppiece	

The correspondence /p/ = pp is much more often due to the full assimilation of the prefixes ad-, ob-, and sub- before stems beginning with p:

(Array 26-22)

appeal	appositive	oppress	supply
appear	approach	opprobrious	support
appendicitis	approve	supplant	suppose

Since many free stems end in a stressed single vowel followed by a final single *p*, the Twinning Rule produces many instances of /p/ = *pp:*

(Array 26-23)

clipping (clip)p + ing)	hopper (hop)p + er)
flippant (flip)p + ant)	slipper (slip)p + er)
gypped (gyp)p + ed)	stripped (strip)p + ed)
happen (hap)p + en)	upper (up)p + er)
happy (hap)p + y)	zipper (zip)p + er)

26.3.3.7 /p/ = *pp* after Short Vowels

(Array 26-24)

copper	guppy	pepper	puppet
dapper	hippopotamus	pippin	puppy
frippery	kipper	poppy	supper

The only known holdout to this rule is *jalopy,* in which /p/ = *p,* even though there is no known shortening rule to account for it. The word is of unknown origin and structure and has a more regular but less common variant *jaloppy.*

26.3.3.8 /p/ = *pp* between Short Vowels and *le*

(Array 26-25)

apple	grapple	ripple	supple
cripple	nipple	scapple	tipple
dapple	popple	stipple	topple

26.3.3.9 /p/ = *p* after Reduced Vowels

(Array 26-26)

apostle	kaput	recapitulate	soprano
epistle	lapel	reciprocity	supremacy
epitome	opinion	sepulchral	trapezium

26.4 The Spellings of /d/

26.4.1 Overview

Parallel with /b/ and /p/, /d/ is spelled either *d* or *dd* more than 99 percent of the time according to Hanna et al., and in the vast majority of instances it is spelled *d* (1966, 756).

One instance of /d/ is worth a special note: when preceded by /n/ or /l/ and followed by a fricative, especially /z/, the /d/ sound is easily lost, leading to pronunciations in which *lends,* for instance, is homophonic with *lens,* or *fields* with *feels.* Other important instances are *grandfather, grind-*

stone, and, without the following fricative, *handkerchief.* Such pronunciations lead to instances of only apparent silent *d*'s.

26.4.1.1 The Flapped *d*

In conversational English the pronunciations of *tt* and *t* in words like *latter* and *later* pick up voicing from the preceding and following vowels and sound more like /d/ than /t/. But actually what is symbolized here as /d/ is less than a full-voiced stop. The /d/ sound in *latter* is so quick that it is technically called a **flap.** The phonological rule involved—the Flap Rule— covers more than the shift of /t/ to a *d* flap. It says that when either of the dental stops, /t/ or /d/, occurs between vowels, only the first of which is stressed, the /d/ or /t/ becomes a *d* flap (Akmajian, Demers, and Harnish 1984, 126).

This complexity has led to a difference between the treatment of flapped-*d* words in desk dictionaries like the *AHD* and that in *W3.* The broader, more morphophonic respellings of the *AHD* record only the pronunciations with /t/ for *latter, matter, litter, butter,* and the like, while the closer, more phonemic respellings in *W3* show pronunciations with both /t/ and /d/.

The Flap Rule describes an automatic phonological process, and since *W3* shows variants with both /d/ and /t/ for such words, from the orthographic point of view we can treat the spellings more broadly, or morphophonically, by treating them as instances of /t/ if they are spelled *t* or *tt* and of /d/ if they are spelled *d* or *dd.*

26.4.2 The Minor Spellings of /d/

The most important spelling of /d/ other than *d* and *dd* involves the past tense or past participle suffix *-ed.* For instance, the past tense of *burn, burned,* is pronounced /burnd/. Though they run counter to our general guideline that consonant letters spell consonant sounds, and vowel letters spell vowel sounds, such cases involve the correspondence /d/ = *ed.* Whenever an infinitive ends in a voiced sound other than /d/, the suffix *-ed* adds the sound /d/:

(Array 26-27)

boomed	freed	played	sighed
filled	mowed	razzed	sinned
filmed	parred	rigged	stewed

If the infinitive ends in the voiced /d/, the *-ed* is pronounced /id/, as in *folded,* and the /d/ = *d.*

The second most important minor spelling is limited to just four words:

/d/ = ld in *could, should, would,* and *solder.* The three modals—*could, should, would*—all come from Old English, and in each case the *l* was pronounced up through Early Modern English. Then, at some point in the seventeenth century, the *l* ceased to be pronounced. *Could* in Old and Middle English was spelled and pronounced without an *l.* In the late Middle English period the *l* spelling and /l/ sound were added, making the word more parallel formally with its workmates *should* and *would,* both of which had the *l* and /l/ from Old English. But then, in the general simplification of the seventeenth century, the newly gained /l/ in *could* was dropped, again keeping it parallel with the others (Jespersen [1909] 1954, 1:293–94; Dobson 1957, 2:451–52, 456–57, 462–63). The only other instance of /d/ = *ld* is in *solder,* which was spelled and pronounced without *l* or /l/ up to the fifteenth century. Then, in that century it was respelled to bring it into line with the Latin source *solidāre.* The *l* is sometimes pronounced in British English. The present spelling became standard in the sixteenth century.

The correspondence /d/ = *dh* or *ddh* is a recent and highly unintegrated form, occurring only in *Buddha, dhow, dhurra, sandhi,* and *kadhi* (which has the somewhat more integrated variant spellings *cadi, kadi, qadi*).

The correspondence /d/ = *bd* holds in *lambda* and *bdellium.*

26.4.3   The Major Spellings of /d/

The rules controlling the choice of *d* and *dd* are exactly like those controlling *b* and *bb, p* and *pp,* as given in 26.2.3.1.

26.4.3.1   /d/ = d at Simple Boundaries

(Array 26-28)

adept (ad + ept)	endorsement (en + dorse)ment)
adequate (ad(equ + ate)	evildoer (evil)(do)er)
admonish (ad + mon + ish)	foundation (found)ation)
ambidextrous (ambi(dextr + ous)	freedom (free)dom)
antedate (ante(date)	subdue (sub + due)
candidate (candid)ate)	taxidermy (taxi + derm + y)
condemn (con + demn)	undid (un(did)
contradiction (contra(dict + ion)	width (wid*é*)th)

The only known holdouts are *odd, redd, rudd,* and *sudd,* of which only the first is of much significance. From a strictly historical point of view, *add* could be explicated to a case of duplicative addition: (ad + d). But this explication is so bizarre and +*d* is such an unconvincing base (see 2.7.3 on the Rule of Syllabicity) that in the present analysis *add* is treated as a simplex, and thus it is a holdout to the constraint against *dd* at simple element boundaries. Similarly, *addition* is explicated to (add)ition). Both *odd* and *add* can be brought into pattern as instances of the Short Word Rule (see 3.5).

26.4.3.2 /d/ = *d* in Shortened VCV Strings

Instances involving the Third Syllable Rule:

(Array 26-29)

adamant	federal	meridian	recidivism
adenoid	hideous	moderate	ridicule
codicil	idiom	pedagog(ue)	sedative
editor	invidious	predilection	video

Instances involving the Stress Frontshift Rule:

(Array 26-30)

medal	modern	pedal	study

Instances involving the suffix rules:

(Array 26-31)

credit	heredity	morbidity	solidity
dyadic	medical	nomadic	sporadic
edit	methodical	periodic	timidity

26.4.3.3 /d/ = *d* in Consonant Clusters and Concatenations

The /d/ = *d* correspondence occurs in several tight clusters: *dr* (*dread, dress*), *nd* (*fiend, friend*), *ld* (*field, weld*), *rd* (*ford, weird*), *rld* (*world*), as well as the more exotic *ldt* (*veldt*), *dz* (*adze*), *dv* (*dvandva, dvi+*), and *sdr* (*sdrucciola*). Other instances involving clusters and concatenations:

(Array 26-32)

beadle	larder	propaganda	tendril
bedspread	madness	redstart	under
breadth	madras	scandal	vodka
didst	meander	smolder	width
headless	molybdenum	sturdy	wonder

Because of the weakness of the constraint against doublets within larger clusters and concatenations with certain suffixes or compounds are involved (see 3.2.6), the inflected forms of three of the holdouts listed in 26.4.3.1 are holdouts here: *adds, redds, odds, oddly, oddness, oddment, oddling*—plus the compound *oddball*.

26.4.3.4 /d/ = *d* after Vowel Digraphs

(Array 26-33)

chowder	meadow	pseudonym	rowdy
embroider	powder	ready	vaudeville

26.4.3.5 /d/ = d after Long Vowels

(Array 26-34)

cadence	code	idea	lading
cathedral	cradle	identify	odometer
cedar	credence	idle	redecorate

26.4.3.6 /d/ = dd at Complex Boundaries

Instances due to twinning:

(Array 26-35)

bidden	goddess	reddest	sadden
daddy	muddy	reddish	wadding
faddist	redden	riddance	wedding

Instances due to duplicative addition, some with /dd/ rather than /d/ when pronounced carefully:

(Array 26-36)

addict (ad + dict)	midday (mid)(day)
address (ad + dress)	reddition (red + dit + ion)
adduce (ad + duce)	reddock (red)(dock)

The only known instance of /d/ = dd due to assimilation is *sudden* (sub + d + den), though a case could be made for treating *sudden* as a simplex, which would then make it an instance of the VCC pattern described in the following section.

26.4.3.7 /d/ = dd after Short Vowels

(Array 26-37)

bladder	haddock	ridden	shudder
caddie	ladder	rudder	udder
eddy	paddock	ruddy	

Among the holdouts to this pattern are *body, bodice, shadow,* and *widow*. All are from Old English. Jespersen suggests that in *body* (and in *bodice,* which was at first simply the plural of *body*) the short vowel is due to the fact that *body* derived from an Old English inflected form in which a consonant cluster occurred after the vowel, thereby shortening it. The same is true of *shadow,* which should be compared to the related *shade,* which derived from an Old English form with no following cluster and thus did not undergo shortening ([1909] 1954, 1:117). The reason for the spelling of *widow* with one *d* is less clear. The vowel was apparently short, or even reduced, very early. Orm spelled the word *widdwe* in the thirteenth century (see also 14.3.1).

Other holdouts to this /d/ = dd pattern are three words that have variant pronunciations with the more regular long vowel: *bade, fusillade, promenade.* The only other known holdouts are relatively unintegrated adoptions, all with the low back /ä/ (asterisked words have variants with the more regular /ā/):

(Array 26-38)

armada*	cadi	desperado*
bravado	cicada	incommunicado

26.4.3.8 /d/ = *dd* between Short Vowels and *le*

(Array 26-39)

coddle	huddle	peddle	saddle
cuddle	meddle	puddle	toddle
fiddle	middle	riddle	waddle

26.4.3.9 /d/ = *d* after Reduced Vowels

(Array 26-40)

accommodate	comedy	peccadillo	subsidy
adore	daffodil	perfidy	tragedy
ambassador	infidel	rhododendron	trepidation

26.5   The Spellings of /t/

26.5.1   Overview

More than 95 percent of the time /t/ is spelled *t,* and about 99 percent of the time it is spelled either *t* or *tt* (Hanna et al. 1966, 1068). But that other 1 percent of the time it is spelled a surprising variety of ways—*ed, th, bt, pt, ct, dt, tw, cht*—and in at least one word, *eighth,* it can be said to have no letter spelling it at all.

The /t/—or, more accurately, a /t/-like flap—is often pronounced in words, even though it is not part of the recorded pronunciations and is not reflected in the accepted spellings. For instance, because of the movements of the vocal organs, it is common for a /t/-like flap to occur between /n/ or /l/ and a following /s/, /sh/, or /th/. This flapped /t/ occurs, for instance, in the middle of words like *sense* (compare it with *cents*) and *mansion.* Because of the flapped /t/ between the /n/ and /sh/ in *mansion,* the /sh/ sounds more like /ch/ (linguistic analyses like that used by Kenyon and Knott treat /ch/ as a complex sound, /tsh/). The same is true of the word *intention,* in which, since the /sh/ is spelled *t,* there is the added inducement to pronounce a /t/, thus rendering what should be /sh/ as /ch/. The distinctions between sounds are very close here. A flapped /t/ also occurs in *ninth* and *tenth.* And *false,* with its flapped /t/, sounds exactly like *faults*. However, since the flapped /t/ occurs automatically, and is not part of the recorded pronunciation or spelling of words, most listeners do not even perceive it. Thus, they are not tempted to spell it with an obtrusive *t*. Orthographically it remains an interesting, but almost subliminal and not too bothersome, phenomenon.

26.5.2 The Minor Spellings of /t/

The most important of the minor spellings of /t/ is the past-tense or past-participle verb suffix *-ed*. When added to an infinitive that ends in a voiceless sound other than /t/—that is, /f/, /s/, /p/, /k/, /ch/, or /sh/—the suffix is pronounced /t/:

(Array 26-41)

ached	compressed	fixed	stopped
advanced	cracked	hoofed	striped
arched	finished	hooked	unbiased

The correspondence /t/ = *th* occurs in very few words: *Thomas* and *Thames, thyme,* and the adoption *thaler.* Instances of /t/ = *th* also occur in variant pronunciations of *posthumous* and *imposthume.* A number of words now spelled with *th* were in Middle and Early Modern English spelled with a *t,* and thus changed both in spelling and in pronunciation: *author* is from Middle English *autor; authentic* is from *autentik; throne* is from Early Modern English *trone,* from Latin *thronus; apothecary* is from *apotecarie,* from Latin *apothēcārius.* Although the spelling of *apothecary* changed in the sixteenth century, the word continued to be pronounced with /t/ up through the eighteenth century (Jespersen [1909] 1954, 1:45–46). Some Old English /th/ sounds have become Modern English /t/, and vice versa: *swarthy* is from Old English *sweart; nostril* is from *nosthryl.* This indecision about /t/ and /th/ is reflected in the /t/ = *th* correspondence in *Thomas, Thames,* and *thyme,* which have changed their spellings while keeping their old pronunciations. *Thaler,* also more regularly *taler,* is an eighteenth-century adoption from the German *thaler,* which earlier gave English the more integrated word *dollar.*

Posthumous and *imposthume* are more commonly pronounced with /ch/, but both have variant pronunciations in which the *th* is pronounced /t/. *Posthumous* today explicates to (post(humous), the *h* having been inserted in Late Latin via a bit of folk etymology that confused the earlier Latin source—*postumus,* the superlative form of "coming after"—with *post + humus, humus* 'earth' suggesting death and burial. Although for the purpose of this analysis we have agreed to speak as little as possible of silent letters, the *h* in *posthumous* and *imposthume* seems to be most convincingly a silent letter. Indeed, the letter *h* often falls silent in the middle of words; compare, for instance, *harmonic* with its clear /h/ and *philharmonic,* usually with none. We will treat the *h* in *posthumous* and *imposthume* as silent, with the correspondence thus being /t/ = *t*.

In the words *doubt, redoubt, debt,* and *subtle* the correspondence is /t/ = *bt*. In all four cases the words were spelled without *b* in Middle English. The *b* was inserted during the Renaissance, with its revival of interest in things classical, including Latin spelling. The present *b* in *debt* (Middle English *det, dette*) reflects the Latin *dēbita. Doubt* (Middle English *duten, douten*) is a respelling closer to the Latin *dubitāre. Redoubt,* both verb and noun, was modeled after *doubt. Subtle,* from Old French *soutil, sotil, sutil,* is a respelling after Latin *subtīlis.* In Early Modern English there was considerable indecision between *subtle* and *subtile;* thus we have today's contrasted pair, *subtle* and *subtile.*

The correspondence /t/ = *pt* occurs at the beginning of a number of words that were adapted from Greek, and at the end of a more native word that has been respelled along the lines of its Latin model. The cluster *pt* is common in Greek, where both the /p/ and the /t/ are pronounced. In an untypical expression of reformism, the *OED* has encouraged the /pt/ pronunciation of such words: "As the *p* is pronounced in French, German, and other languages, as well as by Englishmen reading Greek, and by some scholars in English, the full form is here given as an optional pronunciation often to be preferred" (at *Pt-*). The attempt has not been successful, however. Jones (1956) shows an optional /pt/ for *pterodactyl* and *pterosaur,* but for all other words with initial *pt* in his British English pronouncing dictionary the correspondence is simply /t/. *W3* shows no cases of word-initial /pt/ in American English. *Pt* is pronounced /pt/ in American English only when it is word-final (*apt, slept*) or when a syllable boundary cuts the cluster—as, for instance, in *helicopter,* which explicates to (hel + ic + o + pter), but syllabicates to /hel/ + /ə/ + /käp/ + /tər/. Most of the words in which initial /t/ = *pt* are quite technical and rare. Some examples:

(Array 26-42)

pterodactyl	ptilinal	ptomaine	ptyalin
pteroyl	ptisan	ptosis	ptyxis

For the /t/ = *pt* in *ptarmigan* see 1.4.3.

The correspondence /t/ = *pt* also occurs in *receipt,* from Norman French *receit.* The spelling with *p,* modeled after the original Latin source, *recepta,* began to occur in English and Old French in the fourteenth century and became standard in the Latinization of English in the sixteenth century. *Receipt* is historically and semantically related to *deceit* and *conceit*, both of which had variant spellings with *p* in earlier times but have since dropped them. *Ptisan* has also undergone a learned respelling. In Middle English it was *tisan,* from Old French, from Latin *tisana,* from Greek *ptisanē*.

The correspondence /t/ = *ct* occurs in *indict* for reasons much like those underlying the /t/ = *pt* in *receipt*. In Middle English *indict* was *enditen,* from Norman French *enditer.* In the sixteenth century the *c* was added, with no change in pronunciation, apparently to reflect the Latin source, *indictāre.* In spite of the differences in pronunciation of the base, *indict* is related etymologically, semantically, and orthographically to such words as *dictate* and *predict* (see 20.2.1). The correspondence /t/ = *ct* also occurs in a variant pronunciation of *arctic,* though a case could be made for treating the *c* in that pronunciation as a bona fide silent letter. The same correspondence occurs initially in a few technical words that contain the bound base *cten+* 'comb': *ctene,* for instance, and *ctenidium* and *ctenocyst*. It also occurs in *ctelology*.

The correspondence /t/ = *dt* in *veldt* reflects an obsolete Dutch spelling. In Afrikaans, the immediate source, it was *veld;* in earlier Dutch it was *veldt, veld, velt. Veldt* is ultimately related to such words as *field, feldspar, plane.*

The correspondence /t/ = *ght* holds in certain words involved in the general accommodation of the *gh* spelling of the lost Old English velar fricative. The correspondence /t/ = *ght* occurs only after vowel digraphs ending in *i* or *u* and after /ī/ spelled *i:*

(Array 26-43)

bight	fight	knight	sight	thought
blight	flight	night	slaughter	tight
bought	fought	nought	sleight	weight
bright	fraught	onslaught	slight	wright
caught	freight	ought	sought	wrought
drought	fright	plight	straight	
eight	height	right	taught	

Eighth contains what we will call an "invisible sound." Thus analyzed, it represents an interesting counterpart to those silent consonant letters that mime their way through American English. It explicates to (eight)th), with the *t* deleted consistent with the constraint against doublets in larger clusters, thus avoiding the rather incredible concatenation *ghtth,* as in **eightth.* In terms of sound-to-spelling correspondences, *eighth* could be said to contain /ā/ = *ei* and /th/ = *th,* thus leaving no plausible letter to spell the /t/ there between the /ā/ and the /th/. But then what do we make

of the *gh*? It could be treated as a redundant long-vowel marker, perhaps.
Or we could say that *ght* spells /t/, as in the words in array 26-43 above,
thus leaving the *h* to spell /th/. Or we could say that the *t* serves double
duty—that is, spells both /t/ and /th/ as it participates simultaneously in
the cluster *ght* and the digraph *th*. This may seem like a large fuss over one
small word, but it does involve us in some important matters of theory and
procedure. It involves the larger question, as yet unresolved, of how to
deal with *gh,* which at times is part of vowel spellings, as in *sleigh,* but at
other times is part of consonant spellings, as in *sleight.* It also involves the
larger question of how to decide when a letter should be called silent and
when it should be treated as part of a digraph, cluster, or concatenation.
The question of whether or not the /t/ in *eighth* is an invisible sound will
have to wait, it seems.

The correspondence /t/ = *cht* occurs only in the Dutch adaption *yacht.*
The Dutch spelling was *jaghte,* and in Early Modern English the word was
spelled an immense number of ways, the velar fricative represented by the
gh in Dutch causing problems because of the general shifting about of
similar sounds in English pronunciation and spelling. The *ch* in *yacht* is
there for much the same reason that the *gh* occurs in, say, *taught.* Indeed,
one of the earlier spellings of *yacht* was *yaught.* A few of the other Early
Modern English spellings recorded in the *OED* are *yeagh, yoath, yeaught,*
yaucht, jacht, yatcht.

The correspondence /t/ = *phth* occurs only in variant pronunciations of
phthisic, its derivatives, and a few other technical words.

The correspondence /t/ = *tw* occurs only in *two.* In earlier centuries
the *w* was pronounced, as it still is in related words such as *twice, twin,*
twelve, twenty, twain, twilight, between, betwixt, twist, twine, twig, twill (see
Watkins 1985, at *dwo-*).

26.5.3 The Major Spellings of /t/

After the complex tangle of minor spellings, the two major spellings of
/t/—*t* and *tt*—settle down to the simplicity characteristic of the other front
stops, following the rules set forth in 26.2.3.1.

26.5.3.1 /t/ = *t* at Simple Boundaries

(Array 26-44)

downtown (down)(town)	lieutenant (lieu)(ten + ant)
foretaste (fore(taste)	outlook (out)(look)
fourteen (four)teen)	test (test)

This rule applies in thousands and thousands of instances. The only
holdouts appear to be complexes with the French suffix *-ette* and the
following:

(Array 26-45)

batt	butt	matt	sett
boycott	butte	mitt	watt
brett	gavotte	putt	

Common holdouts with -*ette*:

(Array 26-46)

barrette	layette	rosette
cigarette	palette	roulette
kitchenette	pipette	statuette

The suffix -*ette* is a French feminine diminutive, the masculine form being the (in English) more regular -*et*, as in *cigaret, tablet, midget, cabinet.*

26.5.3.2 /t/ = *t* in Shortened VCV Strings

Instances of the Third Syllable Rule at work:

(Array 26-47)

acetylene	competitive	litany	platinum
anatomist	dichotomy	litigate	ratify
beatify	etymology	mitigate	retina
botany	fatigable	monotony	satellite
cataclysm	fraternize	obliterate	satisfy
compatible	legitimate	philately	veteran

Instances involving the Suffix -*ic* Rule also are common:

(Array 26-48)

analytical	chaotic	geodetic	parasitic
antibiotic	critic	heretical	parenthetic
apathetic	despotic	idiotic	piratical
apologetic	dietetic	kinetic	political
aristocratic	ecstatic	mathematics	static
aromatic	erotic	narcotic	sympathetic

Instances involving the other suffix rules are less common:

(Array 26-49)

carotid	definition	nutrition	tradition
chastity	edition	parotid	tripartition
cognition	nitid	scolytid	vomiturition

Instances involving the Stress Frontshift Rule:

(Array 26-50)

atom	fetish	patent	sateen
city	matin	petal	satin
combatant	metal	pity	satire

There are a few cases of /t/ = *t* in VCV strings that do not fall under any of the shortening rules defined so far. Usually they have variant pronunciations, one with the more regular long vowel, one with the less regular short: *data, datum, gratis, atoll, apparatus*. Some end with old Romance diminutive suffixes, which, unlike the more common French -*ette*, end with a vowel that is pronounced: *cantata, sonata, machete*. Some, dealing with art and music, end with an Italian past-participle inflection: *legato, obbligato, staccato*.

26.5.3.3   /t/ = *t* in Consonant Clusters and Concatenations

The correspondence /t/ = *t* occurs in many different tight clusters: *ct* (*sect, inflict*), *ft* (*daft, tuft*), *lct* (*mulct*), *lft* (*delft*), *lpt* (*sculpt*), *lt* (*salt, colt*), *ltz* (*waltz*), *mpt* (*tempt*), *nct* (*defunct*), *nt* (*tent, bunt*), *ntz* (*chintz*), *pt* (*crypt*), *rst* (*thirst*), *rt* (*dart, court*), *rtz* (*quartz*), *st* (*fast, staff*), *str* (*strain, stress*), *tr* (*train*), *tw* (*twig*), *xt* (*text*). It occurs, too, in some adopted clusters that put a strain on English tactics: initial *ts* (*tsetse, tsuga, tsunami*), initial *tz* (*tzedakah, tzimmes, tzar*), and *rscht* (*borscht*). A few examples of other clusters and concatenations:

(Array 26-51)

aptness	heartbreak	partner	temptress
driftwood	lantern	strictness	trustful

Other than the inflected forms of some of the holdouts in array 26-45—*batts, boycotts, butts, mitts, watts*, and so on—the only known holdouts to this rule are *buttress* and *mattress*. In both, the liquid *r* is the other consonant in the cluster, and liquids often preempt the constraint against doublets within larger clusters and concatenations (see 3.2.2 and 3.2.6).

26.5.3.4   /t/ = *t* after Vowel Digraphs

(Array 26-52)

accouterment	cauterize	praetor	tautological
beauty	exploit	propaedeutic	therapeutic
booty	neuter	route	traitor
caitiff	pewter	routine	treatise

26.5.3.5   /t/ = *t* after Long Vowels

(Array 26-53)

acetic	elite	meningitis	veto
beetle	hiatus	petite	vital
beta	incognito	rotate	white

26.5.3.6 /t/ = *tt* at Complex Boundaries

Instances due to twinning:

(Array 26-54)

admittance	cottage	pottery	setter
battery	flattest	rebuttal	shutter
bettor	knitting	remittance	transmitter
committal	knotted	rotten	witticism

Instances due to duplicative addition, at least some of which have /tt/ in careful pronunciation:

(Array 26-55)

cattail	outtalk	rattrap
outtake	outturn	

Instances due to assimilation:

(Array 26-56)

attack	attend	attest	attribute
attain	attentive	attire	attune

26.5.3.7 /t/ = *tt* after Short Vowels

(Array 26-57)

attic	fritter	motto	regatta
better	glitter	mutter	settee
butter	grotto	operetta	skittish
chatter	jetty	petticoat	sputter
cotton	lettuce	poinsettia	titter
falsetto	matter	puttee	utter

26.5.3.8 /t/ = *tt* between Short Vowels and *le*

(Array 26-58)

battle	kettle	prattle	tattle
bottle	little	rattle	throttle
brittle	mettle	scuttle	whittle
cattle	mottle	settle	
cuttle	nettle	shuttle	

26.5.3.9 /t/ = *t* after Reduced Vowels

(Array 26-59)

amputate	debutante	italic	platoon
arbitrary	despotism	metallic	protect
authoritative	determine	moratorium	retainer
centripetal	digitalis	orator	rickety
cotillion	eternity	pituitary	strategic

27 The Velar Stops, /g/ and /k/

27.1 Introduction

The velar stops—/g/ as in *glue* and /k/ as in *clue*—are formed by stopping the air well back in the mouth, at the soft palate, or velum. The orthography of /g/ is basically like that of the four front stops, with somewhat greater complexity among the minor spellings. But the orthography of /k/ is radically different from that of any of the other stops, owing to the convergence of many different source orthographies into the Modern English /k/.

27.2 The Spellings of /g/

27.2.1 Overview

About 93 percent of the time /g/ is spelled either *g* or *gg*, and about 90 percent of the time it is spelled *g* (Hanna et al. 1966, 778). The spelling of /g/ is complicated somewhat by the ambiguity of the letter *g:* at times it is soft, as in *gym;* at times it is hard, as in *gum.* Because of this ambiguity an insulating *u* is sometimes used to retain the hard *g* spelling. Among the minor spellings, in the sound cluster /gz/, /g/ is sometimes spelled *x,* and a few words contain the correspondence /g/ = *gh.*

27.2.2 Hard and Soft *g*, *gu*, and *gg*

Since the Modern English *g*, like its counterparts in Old French and Middle English, is ambiguous—usually representing the hard /g/ sound but representing the soft /j/ when followed by *e*, *i*, or *y*—the spelling *gu* is used for hard *g* before those three vowels. The *u* is actually an insulator here, standing between the *g* and the *e*, *i*, or *y* that would give it the appearance of being soft. We will treat this *u* as a diacritic, rather like a silent final *e*, so that the correspondence in such cases will remain /g/ = *g*, but with the added diacritic. Instances of /g/ = *g* with the insulating *u* before *e*, *i*, and *y:*

(Array 27-1)

beguile	guernsey	guile	guy
brogue	guess	guillotine	intrigue
disguise	guest	guilt	plague
fatigue	guide	guimp	rogue
fugue	guidon	guinea	vague
gue(r)rilla	guild	guitar	vogue

A few words of this kind end with *e*'s that raise these questions: Is the *u* there to insulate the *g* from the *e*? Or is the *e* there to insulate an otherwise word-final *u*? The instances are few: *league, morgue, analogue,* and all other words with the *+logue* base, which has the more regular variant *+log*.

In French the *gu* spelling was originally pronounced /gw/, in time (at least in Central French) becoming simply /g/. A few Modern English words continue this earlier /g/ = *gu* correspondence as a kind of fossil:

(Array 27-2)

guarantee	guaranty	guard	vanguard

Compare these with instances of the more regular *gu* = /gw/:

(Array 27-3)

anguish	guaiacol	jaguar	penguin
distinguish	guanaco	language	sanguine
extinguish	guano	languish	
guacamole	guava	linguistic	

The doublet *gg* is regularly /g/, even before *e, i,* and *y,* as in words like *ragged, begging, eggy, aggie.* The only known holdouts are four: *suggest* and *suggilation,* both of which are sometimes pronounced with /j/, sometimes with /gj/, and *agger* and *exaggerate,* both pronounced with /j/.

27.2.3 The Minor Spellings of /g/

The sound /g/ occurs fairly often in the correspondence /gz/ = *x,* as in *exact.* Jespersen argues that in earlier English the letter *x* was always pronounced /ks/, but during the fifteenth, sixteenth, and seventeenth centuries English pronunciation changed in many ways, including the voicing of a number of sounds that had earlier been voiceless. In certain tactical contexts the voiceless /ks/ pronunciation of *x* changed to /gz/. For the change to occur, the *x* had to occur between two voiced sounds, the first of which had to be a weakly stressed vowel (Jespersen [1909] 1954, 1:199–200, 205; Prins 1972, 222–24). Dobson disagrees, arguing that /gz/ was the common value of *x* in the medieval pronunciation of Latin words

(1957, 2:934–36). In any case, the following are instances of the correspondence /g/ in /gz/ = *x:*

(Array 27-4)

auxiliary	exasperate	exhaust	exist
exaggerate	executive	exhibit	exonerate
exalt	exemplary	exhilarate	exorbitant
examine	exempt	exhort	exuberance

Instances of the correspondence /g/ = *gh:*

(Array 27-5)

burgher	ghee	ghoul	sorghum
dinghy	gherkin	narghile*	spaghetti
ghastly	ghetto	nilghai*	yataghan
ghat	ghost	ogham*	

Most cases of /g/ = *gh* are due to recent adoptions from foreign languages, but a few—*ghost, ghastly, ghoul*—came into English in the fifteenth century, apparently owing to the influence of William Caxton, who had learned about the *gh* spelling of /g/ during his stay in the Netherlands. (For more on *gh* see 11.2.2.)

Because of the tendency to lose the first stop sound in a sequence of two stops, there are some curious spellings of /g/: In *mortgage* /g/ = *tg.* In *blackguard* /g/ = *ckgu*! And *backgammon* has a variant pronunciation with /g/ = *ckg.* It is not clear whether these correspondences should be as given or whether the *t* and the *ck*'s should be treated as silent letters (see 26.2.2, 26.3.2).

27.2.4   The Major Spellings of /g/

The major spellings of /g/—*g* and *gg*—can be summarized with the same set of selection rules used for the front stops in 26.2.3.1.

27.2.4.1   /g/ = *g* at Simple Boundaries

(Array 27-6)

agape (a(gape)	progressive (pro + gress)ive)
aglow (a(glow)	prolongation (pro(long)ation)
biography (bio(graph)y)	regard (re + gard)
digress (di + gress)	shagrag (shag)(rag)
disgust (dis + gust)	tugboat (tug)(boat)
foregone (fore(gone)	ungoverned (un(govern)ed)
hieroglyphic (hier + o(glyph)ic)	woebegone (woe)(be(gone)
kindergarten (kinder)(garten)	zygoid (zyg + oid)

The only known holdout to this rule is *egg*, whose *gg* can be explained via the Short Word Rule (see 3.5).

27.2.4.2 /g/ = g in Shortened VCV Strings

Instances involving the Third Syllable Rule:

(Array 27-7)

agony	contiguous	legacy	negative
ambiguous	derogatory	ligament	obligatory
antagonist	diagonal	ligature	polygamous
bigamy	exogamy	magazine	prerogative
brigantine	invigorate	megaphone	regular
coagulate	jugular	monogamy	vagabond

The disyllables *pygmy, pigmy,* and *negate* may be instances of the Third Syllable Rule's affecting the English pronunciation of their trisyllabic Latin sources, *pygmæus* and *negatus. Negate* may have been influenced via conservative analogy with *negative.*

Instances involving the Stress Frontshift Rule:

(Array 27-8)

agate	fagot	jaguar	spigot
bigot	figure	legate	sugar
brigand	flagon	legume	vigor
dragon	frigate	rigor	wagon

There are no known instances of /g/ = g in VCV strings shortened by the suffixes *-ity, -ic, -id,* or *-ion*—in part, at least, because the letter g before *i* regularly spells /j/ rather than /g/. There are no known instances of the suffix *-ule* being added to a stem ending in Vg. Thus, there are no known instances of /g/ = g in VCV strings shortened by any of the suffix rules.

27.2.4.3 /g/ = g in Consonant Clusters and Concatenations

The correspondence /g/ = g does not enter into many tight clusters. Most common are *gr* and *gl,* as in *grow* and *glow.* The cluster *rg* also occurs: *erg, burg.* Medially, /g/ = g occurs in loose clusters in which in final position the g is silent: compare *signal* (with /gn/) and *sign* (with /n/), *paradigmatic* (with /gm/) and *paradigm* (with /m/). This pattern is related to the behavior of the digraph *ng:* compare *single* (with /ŋg/) and *singer* 'one who sings' (with /ŋ/). (For more on *ng* see 31.4.) Other examples of /g/ = g in clusters and concatenations:

(Array 27-9)

agree	bagful	dogsled	rugby
amalgamate	bugfish	flagrant	sanguine
angle	dogma	pangolin	smorgasbord

The only known instances of /g/ = *gg* in larger concatenations involve *egg*, the holdout to the constraint against *gg* at simple boundaries: *eggs, eggless,* and various compounds, such as *eggbeater, eggcrate, eggfruit, egghead, eggnog, eggplant, eggshell.*

27.2.4.4   /g/ = *g* after Vowel Digraphs

(Array 27-10)

augment	beagle	eagle	meager
augur	cougar	inaugurate	nougat

27.2.4.5   /g/ = *g* after Long Vowels

(Array 27-11)

bogus	frugal	regal	vagary
ego	hogan	rogue	yogi
egress	legal	slogan	zygote

27.2.4.6   /g/ = *gg* at Complex Boundaries

The correspondence /g/ = *gg* is fairly commonly produced by twinning:

(Array 27-12)

baggy	buggy	logging	sluggard
beggar	digger	luggage	sluggish
braggart	druggist	ragged	wagged

The only prefix that assimilates to instances of /g/ = *gg* is *ad-*, which converts to *ag-*:

(Array 27-13)

agglutinative	aggravate	aggression	aggrieve
aggrandize	aggregate	aggressive	aggroup

Instances of /g/ = *gg* due to duplicative simple addition are very rare. The only known instance is *doggone.*

27.2.4.7   /g/ = *gg* after Short Vowels

(Array 27-14)

dagger	maggot	stagger	toboggan
doggerel	niggard	swagger	trigger

Holdouts are *saga,* an eighteenth-century adoption from Old Norse, and *agar,* from Malay, which actually has a more regular variant pronunciation with /ā/.

27.2.4.8 /g/ = *gg* between Short Vowels and *le*

(Array 27-15)

boggle	haggle	smuggle	wiggle
boondoggle	jiggle	snuggle	wriggle
giggle	joggle	straggle	

27.2.4.9 /g/ = *g* after Reduced Vowels

(Array 27-16)

allegation	brigade	extravaganza	phantasmagoria
allegorical	category	homologous	propaganda
alligator	cigar	interrogate	subjugate
altogether	conjugation	navigate	variegated

The only known instance in which /g/ = *gg* after a reduced vowel is the exotic adoption *baggataway*.

27.3 The Spellings of /k/

27.3.1 Historical Sources

The spellings of /k/ are much more complicated than those of any of the other stops—indeed, more complicated than those for any other consonant. The various spellings of Modern English /k/ represent a historical convergence of quite different spelling strategies. In Old English /k/ was practically always spelled *c*, even before /w/, so that *queen* in Old English was *cwēn*. In Middle English, however, the Norman scribes introduced some Continental spellings. Since *c* was ambiguous in French then, somewhat as it is today, the scribes began to use *k* for /k/ before *i, e*, and *y*, the letters before which *c* was regularly pronounced /ch/ rather than /k/. They also introduced *qu* for /kw/. During the Renaissance some learned respellings emerged, among them the *ch* spelling of /k/, the Latin equivalent of Greek chi, as in *school*. Some *k*'s crept in from German and from the Greek kappa. And since *k* is commonly used when nonliterate languages are written down for the first time—by either professional or amateur anthropologists—in a number of recent adoptions the correspondence /k/ = *k* occurs in places where native English spelling tactics would not normally allow it: *kangaroo, kapok, kayak, kona, skunk,* and others. As a result, the system of /k/ spellings is complicated (Jespersen [1909] 1954, 1:24–28, 394–95; Penzl 1947).

Instead of having one basic simple spelling that accounts for the majority of its instances (as, for instance, /g/ has *g*), plus a doublet to account for another large fraction (like *gg*), /k/ has two basic simple spellings, *c* and *k*, which are more or less clearly distinguished by tactical distributions. The most common "doublet" for /k/ is *ck*. The correspondence /k/ = *cc* does occur, but it is usually the result of assimilation, as in *accord*. The doublet *kk* is even rarer. Thus there are three major spellings to be sorted out: *c*, *k*, and *ck*. There are also quite a number of minor spellings: *cc, kk, ch, qu, q, kh, cch,* and *lk*.

27.3.2   The Minor Spellings of /k/
27.3.2.1   /k/ = *cc*

The correspondence /k/ = *cc* is rare, accounting for less than 2 percent of the instances in Hanna et al. (1966, 820–21). It occurs most often as a result of the assimilation of the prefixes *ad-* to *ac-*, *ob-* to *oc-*, and *sub-* to *suc-*. It also occurs in a few other words, usually in rather unintegrated adoptions, usually after a stressed short vowel, and always with a vowel following it:

(Array 27-17)

accumulate	felucca	occupy	stucco
broccoli	hiccup	peccadillo	succor
buccaneer	impeccable	peccary	succulent
coccus	moccasin	piccolo	tobacco
desiccate	morocco	raccoon	toccata
ecclesiastical	occasion	staccato	yucca

The only known instance in which /k/ = *cc* because of twinning is the verb *sic* 'incite, set'. The past tense can be either *sicced* or the more regular *sicked;* the present participle can be either *siccing* or *sicking*. *Saccate* and *saccule* would at first appear to be instances of twinning, but given the existence of the technical bound base *sacc +*, it seems better to explicate the two complexes from it rather than from the free base: (sacc + ate), (sacc + ule).

27.3.2.2   /k/ = *kk*

The only known instances of /k/ = *kk* are the Hebrew adoption *akkum* and the inflected forms of, and two derivations from, the unusual verb *trek: trekked, trekking, trekker, trekkie*. The verb *yak, yack,* has variant inflected forms with *kk: yakked, yacked; yakking, yacking*.

27.3.2.3   /k/ = *ch, cch*

For the most part, the correspondence /k/ = *ch* comes from Greek, a transliteration of the letter chi. As might be expected, though, this correspondence involves some complications. For one thing, a certain number of words are spelled *ch* for reasons other than an underlying chi: *maraschino* derives from the Italian word *marasca; masochism* comes from the surname Sacher-Masoch, an Austrian novelist whose books describe the behavior; the *ch* in *leprechaun,* from Irish, originally represented a velar fricative. During the last century this velar fricative has eased to the velar stop /k/. (The *OED* shows the older fricative as the current pronunciation.) The anomalous spelling of *ache* is an example of mixed convergence. There used to be two words in English, a related noun and verb pair, *ake* and *ache.* Similar pairs are *bake, batch; break, breech; make, match; speak, speech; stick, stitch; wake, watch; wreak, wretch.* The verb *ake* was pronounced /āk/; the noun *ache* was pronounced /āch/. In time the verb spelling disappeared, as did the noun pronunciation; the pronunciation of the verb converged with the spelling of the noun to give us the Modern English *ache* (Jespersen [1909] 1954, 1:24–25).

Some Modern English words in which /k/ is spelled *c* or *k* historically could have been spelled *ch,* since their sources go back to Greek words with chi. Examples are *card, cartel, cartridge, cartoon, sketch,* and *cord,* which historically is the same word as *chord.* Some other words during the Old French and Middle English periods lost the *h* and were then spelled with the more common *c.* But during the fifteenth and sixteenth centuries these words were respelled in the classical mode, which brought back the *ch:*

(Array 27-18)

chameleon	chord	echo	schedule
character	Christmas	eunuch	scholar
cholera	chronicle	melancholy	stomach

Due to the practice in later Latin of inserting an *h* between *c* and *r,* there are a few words with /k/ = *ch* whose Greek or Latin sources do not have chi: *anchor, lachrymal, pulchritude, sepulchre.*

However, in spite of these complications, by and large the Modern English correspondence /k/ = *ch* reflects Greek chi. Most words with /k/ = *ch* are technical and involve a relatively small number of elements. For instance, the bound base +*arch* 'ruler' is contained in *anarchy, monarch, oligarch, patriarch, matriarch, hierarchy, archon.* Closely related is *arch*+ 'first, ultimate', as in *architect, archives, archipelago, archetype, archangel.* And only slightly less closely related is *archa*+ 'old', as in *archaic, archaeology.* All three *arch* bases have the same Greek source. *Psyche* underlies several words dealing with the mind or spirit: *psychic, psychol-*

ogy, psychiatry, psychopath, psychoanalysis, psychosis. The base *chlor+* (in Greek, "yellowish green") occurs in *chloride, chlorine, chloroform, hydrochloric, chlorophyll. Chor+* occurs in *chorus, choral, choreography. Techn+* occurs in *technical, technique, pyrotechnics, technician. Chrys+* 'golden' occurs in *chrysalis* and *chrysanthemum; chron+* 'time' occurs in *chronic, chronicle, chronology, chronometer, synchronize, anachronism.*

The following is a sample of the remaining, more common words with the correspondence /k/ = *ch*, all of which reflect Greek chi:

(Array 27-19)

alchemy	chrome	machinations	parochial
bronchitis	dichotomy	mechanical	scheme
chaos	epoch	ocher	schizophrenia
chasm	ichthyology	orchestra	strychnine
chimera	inchoate	orchid	synecdoche
chiropractor	lichen	pachyderm	trachea

The correspondence /k/ = *cch* occurs in *saccharin* and *zucchini*.

The most important known instance in which /kw/ is spelled other than *qu* is *choir,* which in Middle English was *quere,* from Old French *cuer,* from Latin *chorus.* The *OED* shows *quire* as an equally viable variant of *choir,* though modern American dictionaries do not. The spelling *choir* arose in the seventeenth century, apparently as a mixed convergence of the English pronunciation with the Latin spelling. For other instances of /kw/ spelled other than *qu* see 33.2.2.1.

27.3.2.4 /k/ = *q, qu*

The *q* and *qu* spellings of /k/ were introduced into English by the Norman scribes to replace Old English *cw* as well as in new French and Latin adoptions. In a word like *antique* the /k/ is spelled by the consonant cluster *qu;* but in, say, *antiquity* the /w/ is spelled by the *u,* which means that the /k/ is spelled by the *q* alone. Thus there are two correspondences to deal with here: /k/ = *qu* and /k/ = *q.* Since whether or not the *u* is pronounced /w/ it must always come after the *q,* this is a complexity more for analysis and display than for the speller.

More often than not, *qu* is pronounced /kw/, so the first correspondence we will look at is /k/ = *q.* It is nearly always either element-initial or element-final. It is particularly common in word-initial position or as part of the initial cluster *squ,* pronounced /skw/:

(Array 27-20)

quack	queasy	quorum	squeal
quadrant	queen	quotient	squeamish
quaff	question	squab	squeeze
quantity	quixotic	squawk	squirrel
quarrel	quiz	squeak	squirt

Instances of /k/ = q at other element boundaries:

(Array 27-21)

adequate (ad(equ + ate)	loquacious (loqu + acious)
antiquarian (antiqué)arian)	obliquity (obliqué)ity)
aquarium (aqu + arium)	obsequious (ob + sequ + ious)
banquet (banqu + et)	propinquity (pro + pinqu + ity)
bequeath (be + queath)	relinquish (re + linqu + ish)
delinquent (de + linqu + ent)	request (re(quest)
equal (equ + al)	sequential (sequ + ent + i + al)
frequent (frequ + ent)	soliloquy (soli + loqu + y)
inquiry (in + quiré)y)	vanquish (vanqu + ish)

Although /k/ = q usually occurs at element boundaries, it does sometimes occur in medial position:

(Array 27-22)

equestrian	harlequin	requisite	sequoia
equip	marquis*	sequester	tranquil
exquisite	perquisite	sequin	ubiquitous

The correspondence /k/ = qu is practically always word-final, where
the /kw/ pronunciation would be awkward. It thus always involves a final e
to insulate the u:

(Array 27-23)

antique	burlesque	marque	pique
baroque	calque	masque	plaque
barque	catafalque	mosque	statuesque
basque	clique	oblique	technique
bezique	critique	opaque	toque
bisque	grotesque	perique	torque
brusque	macaque	physique	unique

When /k/ = qu does occur medially, it is often at the end of an element
followed by a diminutive suffix:

(Array 27-24)

bouquet	mannequin	mosquito	turquoise
coquette	marquee	piquant	
croquet	marquise*	sobriquet	

Word-initial /k/ = *qu* is rare, usually occurring in relatively un-integrated adoptions. Asterisked words have variants with the more regular /kw/:

(Array 27-25)

quatrefoil	quenelle	quiche	quoin*
quay	quetzal	quintar	quoit*
quebracho	queue	quipu	qurush

27.3.2.5   /k/ = *cq, cqu*

In those few words in which the prefix *ad-* is affixed to stems that start with *q*, assimilation leads to the concatenation *cqu*, which in turn leads to the minor correspondence /k/ = *cq:*

(Array 27-26)

acquest	acquire	acquisition	acquit
acquiesce	acquisite	acquist	

Acquaint comes from Old French *acointer,* from Latin *accognitāre,* which explicates to (ad + c + com + gnitāre). The *cq* spelling arose in Middle English in the fourteenth century. The French *coi* would lead to /kw/, which in English is regularly spelled *qu*. We can invoke analogy to explicate *acquaint* to (ad + c + quaint).

The correspondence /k/ = *cqu* occurs only in *sacque, lacquer,* and *lacquey,* the latter of which has a more regular variant, *lackey.*

27.3.2.6   /k/ = *x*

Although the letter *x* usually spells /ks/ or /gz/, when *x* occurs before /s/, as in *exceed* or *exsanguinate*, the blurring and simplification of the /ks/ and the /s/, respectively, produces cases that are best analyzed as containing the correspondence /k/ = *x:*

(Array 27-27)

excel	excerpt	exsect
excelsior	excess	exsert
except	exscind	exsiccate

27.3.2.7   /k/ = *lk*

The correspondence /k/ = *lk* arises from the historical tendency of a once-pronounced /l/ sound to cease being pronounced between a preceding /ō/ or low back vowel and a following /k/ (Dobson 1957, 2:989; Jespersen [1909] 1954, 1:291–92):

(Array 27-28)

balk	chalk	stalk	walk
calk	folk	talk	yolk

27.3.2.8   /k/ = *kh*

The minor correspondence /k/ = *kh* occurs only in recent adoptions, most of which are from the Middle East and are unintegrated:

(Array 27-29)

akh	akhissar	ankh	khan
akha	akhundzada	khaki	khedive

27.3.2.9   /k/ = *sc*

The correspondence /k/ = *sc* occurs only in the compound *viscount,* from Old French *visconte,* from Latin sources that would equal *vice* plus *count.* The *sc* spelling has persisted from the beginning in English, though in the fifteenth century, spellings without the *s* began to appear, which suggests that the *s* was not regularly pronounced at that time (see also 20.2.1).

27.3.2.10   /k/ = *gh, kg*

These correspondences occur only in one variant spelling and pronunciation of *dinghy* and in the variant spelling *gingko* (see 31.4.4).

27.3.3   The Major Spellings of /k/
27.3.3.1   The Major Spellings of /k/ Summarized

Of the two major simple spellings of /k/, *c* is about five times as common as *k*. The correspondence /k/ = *k* tends to be restricted to free bases, in initial or final position. In initial position, either alone or in the *sk* cluster, it regularly precedes *e, i,* and *y*. In final position it regularly follows a long vowel or consonant. The correspondence /k/ = *c* has a wider range of regular settings: it occurs in both free and bound elements, and in initial, final, and medial position. In initial or medial position, either alone or in clusters, it regularly precedes *a, o,* and *u*. It is rare in final position in free bases, but when it does occur there, it is regularly preceded by a short vowel or a consonant. The *c* spelling is more common in words of Romance origin, so /k/ = *c* is regular in VCV strings affected by one of the shortening rules; it is also regular after reduced vowels and in the cluster /kt/. The third major spelling of /k/, the quasi-doublet *ck*, behaves much like any other stop doublet in that the correspondence /k/ = *ck* holds, if no shortening rule applies, between a stressed short vowel spelled with a unigraph and a following vowel or *le*. It also holds in final position in free

bases after a short vowel unigraph and in instances of *k*-insertion, as in
picnicking.

27.3.3.2 /k/ = *k* before *e, i,* and *y,* but *c* before *a, o,* and *u*

The letter *c* is systematically ambiguous—spelling /s/ before *e, i,* and *y,*
but spelling /k/ elsewhere. That distribution forms the first important
distinction in the distribution of *c* and *k*: /k/ = *c* before *a, o,* and *u,* and
/k/ = *k* before *e, i,* and *y.* Though there are some holdouts to this basic
tactical pattern, it is a powerful and useful one, for it establishes many of
the normal expectations about the spellings of /k/ in English and much of
the sense of what "looks English" and what does not. For instance, the
following are all instances of this pattern:

(Array 27-30)

abdicate	discomfort	locust	scream
acorn	eclipse	percussion	sculpture
attract	falcon	scatter	uncle
calculate	local	scold	volcano
baking	cheeky	kidney	sky
blanket	dusky	market	spoke
bookish	kept	pumpkin	whisky

To move away from this distribution is to begin to feel an increasing
exoticism, a decline in integration:

(Array 27-31)

kale	kapok	kona	skate
kangaroo	kaput	paprika	ukase

27.3.3.3 The Regular Settings for /k/ = *k*

The /k/ = *k* correspondence occurs, by and large, in the Old English line
of the American English spelling system, while the /k/ = *c* correspondence occurs in the French and Latin lines. This historical fact bears
heavily on the settings in which the two correspondences tend to occur.
Since Old English did not produce many Modern English bound elements,
/k/ = *k* tends to be set in initial and final position in free bases only; it is
especially rare in bound forms. The correspondence /k/ = *k* usually
precedes *e, i,* and *y,* in either initial or final position or in the initial cluster
sk. In final position it regularly follows a long vowel or a consonant,
especially in the final clusters *nk, rk,* and *sk*. Instances of initial /k/ = *k*
preceding *e, i,* and *y*:

(Array 27-32)

keen	kernel	kipper	kylix
keg	kind	kitchen	kymograph
kelp	kinetic	kyanite	kyphosis

Instances of /k/ = *k* in the initial cluster *sk,* preceding *e, i,* and *y:*

(Array 27-33)

skein	sketch	skimp	skirt
skeleton	skid	skin	skittles
skeptic	skillet	skirmish	sky

Instances of final /k/ = *k* following a long vowel:

(Array 27-34)

artichoke	croak	hike	rebuke
awake	dike	joke	sheik
bake	drake	lukewarm	shriek
beak	duke	mistake	smoke
break	eke	oak	soak
cheek	fluke	peak	streak

The /k/ = *k* correspondence is rare in final position after a short vowel. The only regular cases occur after /ù/ = *oo: book, brook, cook, look, took.* These cases are part of a systematic pattern: the quasi-doublet *ck* is regular after short vowels in word-final position, but doublets do not normally follow vowel digraphs. An apparent holdout, the verb *yak* has the more regular variant *yack. Trek* is a true holdout.

Instances of word-final /k/ = *k* in consonant clusters:

(Array 27-35)

ark	dirk	link	quirk
bask	embark	mask	shrank
berserk	flank	milk	shrink
brisk	frisk	monk	spark
bulwark	honk	murk	task
clerk	irk	pink	yank

The correspondence /k/ = *k* is very rare in bound elements, occurring only in bound bases, not in prefixes or suffixes: *klept+* (*kleptomania*), *kym+* (*kymograph*), *kyph+* (*kyphosis*), *ker+* (*kerosene*), *kal+* (*kaleido-scope*), *mark+* (*market*), *+buke* (*rebuke*), *+voke* (*invoke*). The termina-tive *+voke* has a nonterminative coform, *voc+: revoke, revocation.* The *voc+* form is older. *Revoke* began to be spelled with a *k* in Middle English times, coming from an Old French verb spelled with *qu,* which came from a Latin source spelled with a *c*. The *k* was adopted for the infinitive verb, thus avoiding problems with the ambiguous *c* when adding suffixes such as *-ed* and *-ing:* *revoced and *revocing would be pronounced with a soft *c*, or /s/ sound.

Those rare cases in which /k/ = *k* after reduced vowels, except for words such as *akimbo* and *akin*, with the Old English prefix *a-*, are adoptions that have been only partially integrated:

(Array 27-36)

akala	akeley	hakim	swastika
akela	fakir	manikin	

27.3.3.4   The Regular Settings for /k/ = *c*

The regular and most common settings for /k/ = *k* contrast neatly with those for /k/ = *c*. When *c* or *sc* occur before *e, i,* and *y,* the *c* regularly spells /s/, not /k/, the only known holdouts being *sceptic,* which has the more regular American English variant *skeptic,* and the verb forms *synced* and *syncing.* When a word ends in *ce,* the *c* never spells /k/; it always spells /s/. Although *c* does (very rarely) occur at the end of free bases, when it does, it is never preceded by a long vowel; it is always preceded by either a consonant or a short or reduced vowel:

(Array 27-37)

almanac, almanack	lilac	sumac, sumach
arc	maniac	talc
bivouac	picnic	zinc
bloc	sac	zodiac
disc, disk	sacroiliac	
havoc	shellac, shellack	

Practically always when a word ends with *c*, it does so in the suffix *-ac* or the extremely productive *-ic:*

(Array 27-38)

ammoniac	emphatic	hypnotic	stylistic
elegiac	hydraulic	spasmodic	syllabic

Because of its Latin and French background and the hard/soft *c* contrast, the /k/ = *c* correspondence regularly occurs in settings that are quite unusual for /k/ = *k*. Initial *c* and *sc* regularly occur before *a, o,* and *u* and before the consonants *l* and *r:*

(Array 27-39)

caffeine	clean	climber	clown
clarify	clergy	cloister	clutch

combine	cripple	cry	scorch
crabby	crocodile	curfew	scrape
crawfish	crucial	customer	scrutiny
crevice	cruiser	scarlet	scuttle

Although the /k/ = *k* correspondence is for the most part restricted to free bases, /k/ = *c* is extremely common in Romance bound elements:

(Array 27-40)

abdicate (ab + dic + ate)
accident (a*d* + c + cid*é* + ent)
apocalypse (apo + calypse)
application (a*d* + p + plic + ation)
aristocrat (arist + o + crat)
conspicuous (co*m* + n + spic + uous)
decapitate (de + capit + ate)
declamatory (de + clam + atory)
declare (de + clare)
difficult (di*s* + f + fic + ult)
exclude (ex + clude)
facsimile (fac(simile)

holocaust (hol + o + caust)
indiscreet (in + dis(creet)
intricate (in + tric + ate)
narcosis (narc + osis)
nomenclature (nomen + clat + ure)
percussion (per + cuss + ion)
promiscuous (pro + misc + uous)
recurrence (re + cur)r + ence)
sarcastic (sarc + ast + ic)
seclusion (se + clus*é* + ion)
toxicology (tox + ic)o + logy)
viscosity (visc + os + ity)

27.3.3.5 /k/ = *c* in Shortened VCV Strings

Due to its Romance background, the /k/ = *c* correspondence occurs in many VCV strings that have been shortened by one of the shortening rules. Instances involving the Third Syllable Rule:

(Array 27-41)

articulate	executive	matriculate	recognize
binocular	faculty	meticulous	reticular
conspicuous	immaculate	molecular	secular
decorate	indicative	ocular	sycamore
ecumenical	inoculate	perpendicular	truculent
evacuate	jocular	provocative	vernacular

Instances involving the Stress Frontshift Rule:

(Array 27-42)

decade	fecund	placard	second
ducat	jocund	record (n.)	vicar

Because *c* spells /s/ before *i*, there are no instances of /k/ = *c* in VCV strings shortened by the suffixes *-ity, -ic, -id,* or *-ion.* The Suffix *-ule* Rule does lead to *spicule,* with /i/ in the shortened VCV string.

27.3.3.6 /k/ = c after Reduced Vowels

Unlike /k/ = k, /k/ = c is very common after reduced vowels:

(Array 27-43)

abacus	acuity	barricade	gynecology
abdicate	acumen	cacophony	pecan
acacia	acute	decussate	peculiar
academy	application	delicatessen	pelican
acetic	apricot	eclipse	reciprocate
acoustics	avocation	educate	suffocation

The correspondence /k/ = c after reduced vowels is particularly common in the suffixes -ic, -ical, -icose, -ication, and -ification.

27.3.3.7 /k/ = c in the Cluster /kt/

A very specific remarkable contrast of the k and c spellings of /k/ involves the consonant cluster /kt/, especially when it is in element-final position. The /kt/ cluster is very common in English, but the only known instance of /kt/ = kt is plankton. In all other instances /kt/ is spelled ct. The following list, though long, is just a small sample:

(Array 27-44)

abstract	derelict	galactic	pectin
adjunct	dictator	genuflect	phylactery
bacteria	direct	hectic	precinct
bisect	distinct	inspect	protect
cactus	doctor	invective	rectangle
cataract	effect	lacteal	reluctant
chiropractor	eject	misconduct	restrict
compact	electric	nectar	sacrosanct
concoct	enact	neglect	select
conflict	evict	nocturne	succinct
defunct	expect	obstruct	verdict
depict	fluctuate	octagon	victim

27.3.3.8 The Spellings c and k in Other Consonant Clusters and Concatenations

Both c and k enter into consonant clusters and concatenations within words, especially clusters with the letters l, r, s, and n. Instances of medial lc and lk:

(Array 27-45)

alcalde	alkali	falcon	talcum
alcohol	balcony	fulcrum	volcano
alcove	calculate	polka	welkin

Instances of medial *rc* and *rk:*

(Array 27-46)

altercate	circle	jerky	porcupine
arcade	gherkin	mazurka	sparkle
arkite	herculean	mercantile	tubercular
barcarole	jerkin	mercury	turkey

Instances of medial *sc* and *sk:*

(Array 27-47)

alfresco	biscuit	escalate	musket
ambuscade	brisket	fiasco	obscure
ascot	casket	frisky	rascal
askance	descant	gasket	rescue
askew	descry	masculine	whisker
basket	dusky	muscatel	whisky

The clusters with *c* tend to be element-medial—*calculate* (calcul + ate), *falcon* (a simplex)—or to occur at the boundaries of bound elements, while the clusters with *k* tend to occur at the end of elements that are either free or at least seem as if they must have been free when the word in question was formed: (jerk)y), (frisk)y), (a(skew), (a(skant), (cask)et).

There are other important differences in the way *c* and *k* enter into clusters. For instance, *c* often enters into the *cr* and *scr* clusters within words, but so far there are no known instances of medial *kr* or *skr*. Even in initial position, where the clusters *kr* and *skr* do occur, they are quite rare and occur within recent, relatively unintegrated adoptions: *krypton, skrimshander,* the variant *skreak.* Instances of the medial clusters *cr* and *scr:*

(Array 27-48)

acrid	alacrity	descry	sacred
acrobat	barcarole	fulcrum	sacristan
acropolis	democracy	mediocre	secret

On the other side of the coin, the medial clusters *nk* and *nkl* are quite common, while *nc* and *ncl* are not. Instances of medial *nk* and *nkl:*

(Array 27-49)

anker	crinkle	periwinkle	tinker
ankle	frankfurter	plankton	tinkle
anklong	frankincense	rankle	trinket
bunker	monkey	sprinkle	twinkle

The only known instance of *ncl* is *uncle.*

The correspondence /k/ = c occurs in concatenations involving the prefix *ex-* assimilated to *ec-* in *ecstasy* and *eczema*, (ex̸ + c + stasy) and (ex̸ + c + zema).

27.3.3.9 The Spelling *ck* Summarized

With the other stops we have seen a definite pattern in the use of single and double consonant letters. A similar pattern holds with /k/ except that *c* and *k* share the major single letter duties, while *ck* serves as the doublet form. The selection rules for *ck,* though somewhat weaker, are like those for other stop doublets:

1. If no shortening rule applies, /k/ = *ck* between a stressed short vowel spelled with a unigraph and a following vowel or *le*.
2. In final position in free bases, /k/ = *ck* after a short vowel spelled with a unigraph.
3. The correspondence /k/ = *ck* holds in cases of the *k*-Insertion Rule.
4. Everywhere else the major spelling of /k/ is *c* or *k*.

27.3.3.10 /k/ = *ck* after Short Vowels

Section 27.3.3.5 demonstrates that /k/ = *c* after vowels that have been shortened by one of the shortening rules. When no shortening rule applies, /k/ = *ck* between a preceding short vowel unigraph and a following vowel or *le:*

(Array 27-50)

beckon	docket	lackey	snicker
bracket	hickory	mackerel	sprocket
chicken	hockey	pickerel	ticket
cricket	jackal	pucker	tucker
dicker	lackadaisical	reckon	wicked

The correspondence /k/ = *ck* follows a vowel digraph in the archaic *yoicks,* which in the eighteenth and nineteenth centuries had such variant spellings as *yoics* and *yoix.*

Section 27.3.3.8 illustrates that when /k/ is preceded by another consonant and followed by *le,* the regular spelling is *k*. When /k/ is preceded by a reduced vowel and followed by *le,* the regular spelling is *c*, as in *spectacle, testicle, particle, vehicle, manacle, icicle, miracle, monocle, receptacle* (see 27.3.3.6). But when the /k/ is preceded by a short stressed vowel and followed by *le,* the regular spelling is *ck:*

(Array 27-51)

buckle	crackle	huckleberry	sickle
cackle	freckle	knuckle	speckle
chuckle	hackle	pickle	tackle
cockle	heckle	shackle	tickle

Holdouts to this pattern are *debacle* and *motorcycle,* the latter of which has a variant pronunciation with the more regular /ī/. In a few concatenations *ck* falls between a stressed short vowel and a consonant other than *l*—for instance, in *huckster, hackney,* and *cockney,* which appear to explicate to (huck + ster), (hack)ney), and (cock)ney). In *nickname,* (nick(name), *nick* is a merging of the phrase *an eke.*

27.3.3.11 Word-final /k/ = *ck* after a Stressed Short Vowel

With other stops the VC# pattern prevails, as in *deb, did, dip, dot, dug;* VC'C'# is rare, as in *add, ebb, egg.* However, single *c* and *k* are rather rare in word-final position after short vowels, examples being *sac, tic,* and *trek.* The otherwise powerful VC# pattern for short vowels is not basic and regular when the final consonant sound involved is /k/. In word-final position and after short vowels the regular spelling for /k/ is *ck,* which makes the VCC pattern regular in the final as well as in the normal medial position:

(Array 27-52)

attack	crock	jack	shamrock
bailiwick	duck	knock	shylock
brick	fleck	pack	speck
burdock	geoduck, gweduc	pinchback	tamarack
check	gimcrack	pluck	thick
cossack	hick	ransack	wreck

27.3.3.12 Sometimes Word-final /k/ = *ck* after Reduced Vowels

Although normally polysyllables that end in /k/ preceded by a schwa or an unstressed /i/ end in *c* (*magic, traffic*), a few of them end in *ck.* Often these polysyllables are very old compounds whose constituents have lost their separate identities, leading to the stress reduction in the final element. Sometimes they end with the old diminutive suffix -*ock.* And sometimes they are obviously the result of folk etymology and analogy working as if they were one of the preceding kinds of words. In the past there were many more cases of word-final *ck* where today we have *c*—*magic* and *traffic* being two cases in point. Samuel Johnson ([1775] 1983) cited many instances of word-final *ck* that have since been simplified to *c.* This simplification was a spelling reform introduced by Noah Webster. Webster's argument was from analogy: Since there is no *k* in *magical,* there should be none in *magic.* (Johnson listed *magick,* but *magical; tragick,* but *tragical.*) None of the following instances of word-final *ck* after reduced vowels has derivatives that would encourage the simplification of *ck* to *c:*

(Array 27-53)

arrack*	derrick	hammock	maverick
bannock	dornick	hassock	niblick
barrack	elleck	hillock	paddock
bullock	futtock	hummock	rollick
buttock	gimmick	limerick	splacknuck
cassock	haddock	mattock	tussock

27.3.3.13   /k/ = *ck* and the *k*-Insertion Rule

When a free stem ending in *c* adds a suffix beginning with an *e, i,* or *y,* if the /k/ sound does not shift to /s/ in the derived word, a *k* is inserted after the *c* to insulate it from the *e, i,* or *y,* thus avoiding the look of the soft /s/ sound. Though limited in scope, this *k*-Insertion Rule accounts for such instances of /k/ = *ck* as the following:

(Array 27-54)

bivouacked (bivouac)k + ed)	sicked (sic)k + ed)
panicky (panic)k + y)	trafficking (traffic)k + ing)
picnicker (picnic)k + er)	

Shellacked explicates to either (shellac)k + ed) or (shellack)ed), though it does have the nonregular variant *shellaced.* When the final *c* of a stem does not retain the hard /k/ sound in the derived word, *k*-insertion does not occur: *critic* versus *criticism, magic* versus *magician.*

27.3.3.14   The Cluster /ks/

The cluster /ks/ is often spelled *x.* Section 27.2.3 discusses a small but important group of words that contain the sound /g/ in the correspondence *x* = /gz/—for instance, *exact, exhibit, executive.* Usually, however, *x* spells /ks/—specifically, when it does not have voiced sounds on both sides of it. Since all vowels are voiced and since /ks/ does not occur in initial position, this requirement means that the *x* spelling of /ks/ regularly has a voiceless consonant either before or after it, or a word boundary after it. Thus, one of the most common settings for the correspondence /ks/ = *x* is at word's end:

(Array 27-55)

affix	convex	index	pharynx
apex	crucifix	larynx	relax
ax	equinox	lynx	smallpox
calyx	fox	onyx	vex
climax	helix	ox	vortex
coax	hex	paradox	wax

Consistent with the Mixed Voicing Rule (3.2.2), another common setting for /ks/ = *x* is in front of a voiceless consonant, especially when *x* is part of the prefix *ex-* or its extension *extra-:*

(Array 27-56)

excavate	excruciating	express	extraordinary
exchange	exhalation	exquisite	extrapolate
exclaim	expedite	extant	extraterrestrial

In a number of other cases the /ks/ = *x* correspondence occurs as part of the *xt* clusters, just as it does in *extra-:*

(Array 27-57)

admixture	exterior	extrinsic	sextant
dexterity	external	juxtapose	text
dextrose	extreme	next	textile

The correspondence /ks/ = *x* occurs nonregularly between vowels in the following words, usually in element-final position:

(Array 27-58)

doxology	exude	oxalic	quixote
exit	fixation	plexiglass	taxonomy
exogamy	hexameter	plexus	toxemia
exotic	luxuriant	proximity	

As soon as we recognize the sound cluster /ks/ as a unit of concern, we must recognize that it has other spellings—notably, *cs* (*panics*), *cks* (*slacks*), and *ks* (*forks, brakes*). Further, some homophones involve /ks/: *tacks, tax; sics, six; secs* (short for "seconds"), *sex*. The correspondences /ks/ = *cs, ks,* and *cks* occur most often in word-final position. They are most common when the plural suffix *-s* or the third person singular present tense suffix *-s* is added to a stem ending in *c, k,* or *ck:*

(Array 27-59)

backs	books	bricks	mistakes
blinks	brakes	maniacs	panics
blocks	breaks	mechanics	takes

The correspondence /ks/ = *cs* is also common in the complex suffix *-ics:*

(Array 27-60)

acoustics	dramatics	genetics	obstetrics
ballistics	economics	hysterics	politics
cybernetics	ethics	mathematics	semantics

Though the concatenation is broken by a syllable boundary, the correspondence /ks/ = *cc* occurs in a few assimilations of *ad-, ex-, ob-,* and *sub-* to *ac-, ec-, oc-,* and *suc-:*

(Array 27-61)

accelerate	access	occidental	succeed
accent	accident	occipital	succinct
accept	eccentric	occiput	succinic

The correspondence /ks/ = *cc* also occurs in *flaccid* and *vaccine.*

28 The Simple Fricatives /v/, /f/, /th/, /t͟h/, and /h/

28.1 The Spellings of /v/

28.1.1 Historical Sources

In Old English, /v/ occurred only in word-medial position, and it was almost always spelled *f*, rarely *u*, never *v*. After the Norman Conquest, due to the influence of the Norman scribes and their Continental ways, the correspondence /v/ = *u* became quite common. All through Middle English times and most of the Early Modern period *u* and *v* worked interchangeably, serving double duty as both vowel and consonant. By the late seventeenth century the distinction between *v* and *u* that we are used to had become fairly standard, although lapses of one kind or another continued up through the nineteenth century, at least (Jespersen [1909] 1954, 1:38–39, 41–42, 199–201; Prins 1972, 222–25; see also 11.2.1.1).

Over the centuries several /v/ sounds have been dropped from the English language and even more have been added. The Old English /v/ = *f* correspondence has simply vanished in several words where once it existed, vanished in both letter and sound. For instance, all of the following at one time contained a /v/ spelled *f*: *had, lady, head, woman, poor, curfew, kerchief. Lady,* for example, comes from an Old English compound *hlǣfdige* 'loaf-digger, loaf-kneader'. This tendency to drop /v/ sounds is illustrated in a number of contractions: *o'er* for *over, e'er* for *ever, e'en* for *even, o'* for *of.* A few old /v/ sounds evolved into vowels. Jespersen offers as an example *hawk,* which in Old English was *he(a)foc,* with /v/ = *f.* Apparently the *f* became a *u* (since *u* and *v* were then interchangeable), and in time the pronunciation shifted from consonant /v/ to a vowel sound spelled *au.* The current *w* first appeared in the fifteenth century. Jespersen also mentions *auger* (OE *nafogār*), *launder* (OFr *lavandier*), and *newt* (from the earlier phrase *an evete*), and he speculates that *lord* (OE *hlāfweard* 'loaf-warden') may be an example as well ([1909] 1954, 1:39–41).

Some current words with a *-y* suffix derive from earlier words with the suffix *-if: jolly, hasty, tardy,* for instance. But in most cases Middle English

-if became the current *-ive*, though a few words contain a closer version of the Middle English suffix—for instance, *plaintiff, bailiff, caitiff. Plaintiff,* the legalistic noun, contrasts with *plaintive,* the more general adjective.

However, although a number of /v/ sounds have been lost in one way or another over the centuries, even more have been gained—or, more specifically, even more instances of the correspondence /v/ = *v* have been gained. For one thing, in many words that contained /v/ = *f* in Old English, the *f* has changed to *v.* For another, many older words that once contained /f/ = *f* now contain /v/ = *v.* First the /f/ was voiced as /v/, and then, in time, the spelling *f* was changed to *v* to reflect the new pronunciation. Instances of /v/ = *v* gained in one of these ways are *vat, vixen, vane, give, drive, love, carve, calve, swerve, sieve, starve, hive,* and the common suffix *-ive.*

The tendency of /f/ to be voiced as /v/ and of *f* subsequently to change to *v* is reflected in a few noteworthy features of the English spelling system. In some dialects, and especially in British English, *nephew* is pronounced with a /v/ rather than the more regular /f/. The semantically related words *vial* and *phial* are just two different versions of what was once the same word. The tactical rule in Old English was quite straightforward: in the middle of words *f* = /v/; in initial or final position *f* = /f/. When suffixes were added to stems that ended with *f,* the final /f/ became a medial /v/. This Old English tactical pattern underlies an important relationship between the correspondences /f/ = *f* and /v/ = *v,* as illustrated in the singular noun *calf,* its plural *calves,* and the verb *calve* (remembering that the Old English verb inflectional system was much more elaborate than the one we use today). Thus, Old English tactics underlie the following cluster of more or less systematically arrayed coelements:

(Array 28-1)

Singular Noun	Plural Noun	Related Verb
belief	beliefs	believe
dwarf	dwarves, dwarfs	dwarf
elf	elves	—
half	halves	halve
hoof	hooves, hoofs	hoof
knife	knives	knife
life	lives	live
loaf	loaves	loaf (?)
motif, motive	motifs, motives	motivate
relief	reliefs	relieve
safe	safes	save
scarf	scarves, scarfs	scarf
self	selves	—

Singular Noun	Plural Noun	Related Verb
serf	serfs	serve
sheaf	sheaves	sheave
shelf	shelves	shelve
staff	staves, staffs	staff
strife	strifes (?)	strive (?)
thief	thieves	thieve
wharf	wharves, wharfs	wharf
wife	wives	wive
wolf	wolves	wolf

28.1.2 The Minor Spellings of /v/
28.1.2.1 /v/ = vv

The doublet *vv* is very rare. The constraint against double *v* arose in the Middle English period since it was then interchangeable with *u*. Already a different double *u*, *w*, was becoming more common, so a double *v* posed problems. The constraint against double *u* is still felt in the English spelling system today. Add to that the constraint that arose in Middle and Early Modern English against ending a word with *v*, since that ambiguous letter served as a consonant only when it was followed by a vowel. For example, when /v/ = *u* occurred at word's end, a final *e* was added to provide the vowel that was needed to mark the /v/ = *u* correspondence. For this reason, *v* today seldom stands in word-final position; instead, an insulating final *e* is used, as in *valve, have, serve*. The only known holdouts are very recent additions: *rev*, clipped from *revolution;* and *shiv*, from Romany *chiv*. Since *v* so seldom occurs in word-final position, it is not acted upon by the Twinning Rule, which provides a continuing constraint against double *v*. The only known instances of *vv* due to twinning occur in the inflected forms of *rev: revving* and *revved*.

There are only six other known instances of *vv*, all of which occur in very recent formations. Three of them were formed by clipping longer words and adding -*y* or -*ies: divvy*, from *dividend* or *divide; navvy*, from *navigator;* and *civvies*, also *civies*, from *civilian*. The fourth, *skivvy, scivvy*, 'undershirt', of obscure origin, is possibly a blend of *skin* and *civvies*. The fifth known case is *flivver*, another word of obscure origin. The sixth, *savvy*, is a variation of Spanish *sabe*. All six of these words were formed long after the *u*, *v*, and *w* patterns of usage had been established. At least one of them came into direct conflict with an established word: *navvy* challenged *navy*. Though the VCV/VCC contrast is for all intents and purposes waived for *v* (see 6.4.2), there may have been a feeling that *divy, *fliver, and *skivy looked as if they had long vowels, while the *vv* made their pronunciation unambiguous. All in all, the few instances of *vv* do not appear to be enough to undercut the otherwise very powerful generalization that in English the *v* is not doubled.

28.1.2.2 /v/ = *lv*

The correspondence /v/ = *lv* holds in only three words—*calve, halve, salve*—and their inflected forms. Notice that it occurs only after short *a*, but that another correspondence also occurs there: compare *salvage* and *valve*, in which the *l* before the *v* is pronounced (Dobson 1957, 2:989; Jespersen [1909] 1954, 1:298).

28.1.2.3 /v/ = *f*

The only remaining instance of this once-common correspondence occurs in *of*, in which the older spelling converges with the newer pronunciation (Jespersen [1909] 1954, 1:200; Dobson 1957, 2:937, 455).

28.1.3 The Major Spelling of /v/

In American English /v/ is spelled *v* almost 100 percent of the time (Hanna et al. 1966, 1082). Interestingly, however, the correspondence occurs in only a few clusters:

(Array 28-2)

absolve	elves	kvass	scurvy
canvas	envy	salvage	solvent
carve	harvest	salvo	sylvan
chevron	involve	scarves	twelve

Since the /v/ = *v* correspondence is so powerful, the following descriptions have little real impact on orthographic choice, and thus are brief. The power of the constraint against *vv* is so strong that for vowels immediately preceding *v*, the tactical contrast between VCC and VCV is, as has been said, waived. Nevertheless, some tactical settings are distinguishable. Instances of word-initial /v/ = *v*:

(Array 28-3)

vampire	vehicle	vivacious	vulcanize
vaudeville	viable	vodka	vulnerable

Instances of /v/ = *v* after a long vowel:

(Array 28-4)

abbreviate	graven	loaves	oval
arrival	ivory	louver	over
behavior	jovial	maneuver	peevish
deprive	knives	naval	uvula

Instances of /v/ = *v* after a reduced vowel:

(Array 28-5)

avenge	controversy	elevated	provide
contravene	derivation	innovation	television

Instances of /v/ = *v* in VCV strings affected by the Third Syllable Rule:

(Array 28-6)

avalanche	equivalent	malevolent	ravenous
benevolent	frivolous	navigate	several
carnivorous	javelin	omnivorous	travesty

Instances of /v/ = *v* in VCV strings affected by the Stress Frontshift Rule:

(Array 28-7)

avid	endeavor	novel	ravage
bevel	govern	pivot	sever
cavil	havoc	quiver	tavern

Instances of /v/ = *v* in VCV strings affected by the suffix rules:

(Array 28-8)

brevity	depravity	longevity	objectivity

28.1.4 The Spellings of /v/ Summarized

The spellings of /v/ can be summarized as follows: The sound /v/ is spelled *f* only in *of;* it is spelled *vv* only in *navvy, savvy, skivvy, civvies, divvy, flivver, revved, revving;* it is spelled *lv* in *calve, halve, salve,* and their inflected forms; everywhere else /v/ is spelled *v.*

28.2 The Spellings of /f/

28.2.1 Historical Sources

In Old English and very early Middle English the spelling of /f/ was quite simple: *f.* In Old English the letter *f* was used to spell both /f/ and /v/. In Middle English the doublet *ff* also was common. In the fourteenth century the digraph *ph* began to be used to spell certain learned words. This *ph* was the Latin version of the Greek letter phi, which had in early Latin represented a bilabial fricative. By the fifth century this bilabial sound had converged to the regular labio-dental /f/. In the various languages that descend from Latin the old *ph* digraph tended to be replaced with *f.* Such was the case in Old French and in Middle English. But during the late Middle and Early Modern English periods, especially during the fifteenth,

sixteenth, and seventeenth centuries, many cases of *f* were changed back
to *ph*. In some cases, in fact, the change was made in words that did not
originally have *ph*'s in them. This led to some curious contrasts. For
instance, we have both *phantasy* and *fantasy*, and both *phantasm* and
fantasm, but only *fantastic* (Jespersen [1909] 1954, 1:43–44; Prins 1972,
213, 230).

Further complicating the once-easy question of how to spell /f/, the old
velar fricative usually spelled *h* in Old English and *gh* in Middle English
underwent the complex evolution described in 11.2.2, 20.2.1, and elsewhere. Part of that evolution involved a few native words in which the
correspondence /f/ = *gh* held, as it does in *tough* and *laughter*. Also, about
half a dozen words took on the correspondence /f/ = *ft* (*soften*) or /f/ = *lf*
(*calf*). These minor spellings are described in more detail in the following
section.

28.2.2   The Minor Spellings of /f/
28.2.2.1   /f/ = *ph*

The correspondence /f/ = *ph* usually occurs in words of Greek origin, but
it also occurs in a few from Hebrew. It occurs most commonly in word-
initial position, and there it has much the same distribution as /f/ = *f*—
that is, before any vowel and, though rarely, before the consonants *l* and *r*.
It is also very rare before *u:*

(Array 28-9)

phaeton	pheasant	philology	photograph
phalanx	phenol	phlegm	phrase
phallic	phenomenon	phobia	phrenetic
phantasm	phenotype	phoebe	phugoid
pharmacy	phial	phoenix	phylactery
pharynx	philanthropy	phone	phylum
phase	philately	phosphate	physical

Unlike *f*, *ph* readily clusters with a preceding *s*, especially in element-
initial position:

(Array 28-10)

asphalt	sphere	sphygmomanometer
asphyxiate	sphinx	stratosphere

Instances of element-initial /f/ = *ph:*

(Array 28-11)

aphasia	cellophane	diphthong	hydrophobia
bibliophile	chlorophyll	emphatic	metaphor
blaspheme	diaphragm	euphemism	metaphysics

microphone	paraphrase	prophecy	schizophrenic
neophyte	peripheral	prophylactic	sycophant
paraphernalia	periphrastic	sarcophagus	telephonic

Instances of element-medial /f/ = *ph:*

(Array 28-12)

alphabet	cipher	naphtha	pamphlet
aphid	decipher	nephew	siphon
apostrophe	diphtheria	nephritis	staphylococcus
asphodel	ephah	nuphar	syphilis
camphor	esophagus	ophthalmoscope	typhoon
catastrophe	gopher	orphan	zephyr

Instances of /f/ = *ph* in final position:

(Array 28-13)

amorphous	dolphin	humph	sophomore
amphibian	elephant	lymph	teraphim
bibliography	epitaph	nymph	triumph
caliph	graphite	seraph	trophy
dauphin	hieroglyph	sophisticated	typhoid

As the preceding arrays show, a relatively few very productive elements account for most instances of /f/ = *ph: phot+, phys+, +phile, phone, +phobe, sphere, graph,* and *soph+.*

Because of the indecision about *f* and *ph* in Middle and Early Modern English and because of the general congruence in distribution between the two spellings, a few words have variant spellings of /f/, one with *f* and one with *ph.* In addition to those mentioned earlier:

(Array 28-14)

calif, caliph	frenzy, phrensy
fantasmagoria, phantasmagoria	raffia, raphia
fantom, phantom	sulfur, sulphur
frenetic, phrenetic	telfer, telpher

28.2.2.2   /f/ = *pph*

The minor correspondence /f/ = *pph* occurs only in *sapphic* and *sapphire.*

28.2.2.3   /f/ = *gh*

The correspondence /f/ = *gh* occurs in native words in which the *gh* reflects the Old English velar fricative that is no longer present in the English sound system. This correspondence occurs only after short vowels spelled with a digraph that contains a final *u.* It occurs only in word-final position or in the *ght* cluster:

(Array 28-15)

chough	draughts	laughter	sough*
clough	enough	rough	tough
cough	laugh	slough	trough

28.2.2.4 /f/ = *lf*

This correspondence occurs only in *behalf, calf,* and *half.* It is the voiceless counterpart of the /v/ = *lv* in *calve, halve,* and *salve* (see 28.1.2.2).

28.2.2.5 /f/ = *ft*

This correspondence occurs only in *often* and *soften.* It is related to the /s/ = *st* correspondence in words like *castle* and *hasten* (see 29.2.2.3) (Jespersen [1909] 1954, 1:225; Dobson 1957, 2:968).

28.2.3   The Major Spellings of /f/
28.2.3.1   The Major Spellings of /f/ Summarized

According to Hanna et al., /f/ is spelled either *f* or *ff* nearly 90 percent of the time (1966, 768–69). The rules for selecting between *f* and *ff* are much the same as those governing the selection between singlet and doublet spellings of the stops. The major differences involve the *ff* spelling in word-final position, as described in rule 1 below, and the strong tendency for /f/ to occur at element boundaries, thus making rule 2 unusually powerful and rendering other rules redundant, especially rules 3–6 and rule 10.

1. /f/ = *ff* in word-final position after a stressed short vowel unigraph.
2. /f/ = *f* at all other simple boundaries not affected by twinning, assimilation, or duplicative addition.
3. /f/ = *f* in VCV strings shortened by one of the shortening rules.
4. /f/ = *f* within consonant clusters, but with the regular complication posed by a following *le*.
5. /f/ = *f* after vowel digraphs.
6. /f/ = *f* after long vowels.
7. /f/ = *ff* at complex boundaries affected by twinning, duplicative addition, or assimilation.
8. /f/ = *ff* between a stressed short vowel and a following vowel if none of the shortening rules apply.
9. /f/ = *ff* between a stressed short vowel and a following *le*.
10. /f/ = *f* after reduced vowels.

28.2.3.2 /f/ = *ff* in Word-final Position

Like word-final *ck,* word-final /f/ is regularly exempt from the VC# pattern that is so powerful elsewhere. Word-final /f/ after a stressed vowel spelled with a unigraph is regularly *ff,* not *f:*

(Array 28-16)

bluff	duff	off	sniff
buff	fluff	quaff	snuff
chaff	gaff	rebuff	staff
cliff	gruff	ruff	stiff
cuff	huff	scoff	stuff
distaff	muff	scuff	whiff

The only known holdouts to this correspondence are the French adoptions *chef* and *clef* and the native *if.* In Middle and Early Modern English *if* was at least sometimes pronounced with the /v/ sound, like *of.* Why the *f* in *of* has remained /v/ while the *f* in *if* has devoiced to /f/ is not clear. Nor is it clear why the *f* in *if* did not change to *ff* to mark the devoicing, as was the case in the contrast that developed between *of* and *off* (Jespersen [1909] 1954, 1:200; Dobson 1957, 2:454). The *OED* records a thirteenth-century spelling of *if* from Orm with *ff,* and spellings with *ff* occur up through the seventeenth century.

There are fossil final *e*'s in *gaffe, giraffe,* and *tartuffe,* the last of which has variant pronunciations, one with /u̇/, the other with the less regular /ū/.

28.2.3.3 /f/ = *f* at Simple Boundaries

Although the correspondence /f/ = *ff* is regular in word-final position after stressed short vowel unigraphs, /f/ = *f* is regular and extremely common at initial and medial simple boundaries. It is especially common in word-initial position, and even more so in element-initial position. This Simple Boundary Rule accounts for an immense number of instances in which *f* is chosen rather than *ff.* In initial position *f* occurs before any vowel (though rarely before *y*) and before *l* and *r:*

(Array 28-17)

afield	disinfect	fleece	manufacture
artificial	enfranchise	foam	perfidy
benefactor	fable	frame	portfolio
brimful	feast	friction	profession
defendant	fiat	fudge	sacrifice
disfigure	flank	fyrd	satisfaction

28.2.3.4 /f/ = *f* in Shortened VCV Strings

Because element-medial *f* is rare and element-initial *f* is so very common, the Simple Boundary Rule preempts most instances that would otherwise require invoking one of the shortening rules. Some instances of shortening, most of which involve /f/ at simple boundaries:

(Array 28-18)

cafeteria	deferential	pacific	referee
defamation	definition	profanation	refugee

28.2.3.5 /f/ = *f* in Consonant Clusters and Concatenations

The correspondence /f/ = *f* holds in clusters, but with the usual complication posed by a following *le* (for which see array 28-24 below). Instances of /f/ = *f* in clusters and concatenations:

(Array 28-19)

after	cleft	palfrey	sassafras
alfalfa	draft	pilfer	sulfuric
bereft	mufti	rafter	wrathful

The only known holdout cluster is in *saffron*. For holdout concatenations see 28.2.3.8.

28.2.3.6 /f/ = *f* after Vowel Digraphs

The correspondence /f/ = *f* holds regularly after vowel digraphs, even in word-final position:

(Array 28-20)

camouflage	deaf	roof	woof
coif	heifer	waif	

28.2.3.7 /f/ = *f* after Long Vowels

Consistent with the VCV pattern, /f/ is regularly spelled *f* rather than *ff* after a long vowel:

(Array 28-21)

aloof	fife	reef	stifle
brief	leaf	rifle	trifle
chafe	loaf	sofa	wafer

The only known holdout is the recent French adoption *chauffeur.*

28.2.3.8 /f/ = ff at Complex Boundaries

The correspondence /f/ = ff is only rarely due to twinning or duplicative addition. It is more commonly produced by the assimilation of prefixes. The only known instance due to twinning is in the adjective *iffy* (if)f + y)— and, of course, its inflected forms, *iffier* and *iffiest*. Known instances of /f/ = ff due to duplicative addition are *wolffish*, *shelfful*, and *griefful*, all of which have careful pronunciations with double /f/. Though its development is complicated, *safflower* can best be explicated as a case of duplicative addition: (saf(flower), the bound base *saf+* being related to *saffron*. Although the still-productive suffix *-ful* makes possible such nonce words as *scarfful*, duplicative addition remains a minor source of instances of /f/ = ff. The regular occurrence of word-final /f/ = ff after stressed vowel unigraphs, together with *-ful* and the Triplet Rule (see 3.2.5), makes possible other nonce words containing /f/ = ff: *cufful* (cuff)ful) and *skifful* (skiff)ful), for instance. But should the need for such words arise, the hyphen probably would be put to use: *cuff-ful* and *skiff-ful*.

A much more productive source for /f/ = ff is assimilation. In many words, before stems beginning with *f*, *ad-* assimilates to *af-*, *dis-* assimilates to *dif-*, *ex-* to *ef-*, *ob-* to *of-*, and *sub-* to *suf-*:

(Array 28-22)

affair	differ	effigy	offer
affection	difficult	effort	office
afferent	diffuse	effrontery	sufferance
affiliate	efface	effuse	suffice
afford	effect	ineffable	suffocate
coefficient	efficacy	offend	suffuse

Paraffin, meaning literally "too little affinity to," contains an old assimilation, (par + ad + f + fin). *Proffer* contains an unusual deletion and a somewhat unexpected assimilation, (prø(oʋ + f + fer).

28.2.3.9 /f/ = ff after Short Vowels

Instances of /f/ = ff in regular VCC strings:

(Array 28-23)

buffalo	coffee	muffin	stuffy
buffet (v.)	coffin	offal	taffeta
caffeine	daffodil	offer	toffee
chiffonier	griffin	scaffold	traffic

28.2.3.10 /f/ = *ff* between Short Vowels and *le*

(Array 28-24)

baffle	piffle	riffle	sniffle
muffle	raffle	ruffle	waffle

28.2.3.11 /f/ = *f* after Reduced Vowels

The *f* spelling is regular after schwa and unstressed /i/, often occurring at an element boundary:

(Array 28-25)

afar	café	pacifism	prefer
amplify	conifer	persiflage	profess
benefit	default	pinafore	safari

There are some holdouts to this pattern, most of which involve the suffix -*iff* or endings that appear to have converged to it:

(Array 28-26)

bailiff	mastiff	plaintiff	sheriff
caitiff	midriff	pontiff	tariff

Bailiff, caitiff, and *plaintiff* all contain the suffix -*iff;* the others ending in *iff* are analogical convergences. Other holdouts occur in *buffet* 'a kind of meal', *chiffon,* and *buffoon,* all from French and all with the typical French end-stress. A final holdout, *guffaw,* of obscure origin but probably imitative, has a more regular variant pronunciation with stress on the first syllable.

28.3 Spelling /th/ and /th/

28.3.1 Historical Sources

In American English two *th* sounds are more or less consistently distinguished in pronunciation, but distinguished very little in spelling. The two sounds are the voiceless /th/ heard at the beginning of *thin* and the voiced /th/ heard at the beginning of *this.* The major spelling for both is *th.* Nearly 100 percent of the time /th/ = *th* and /th/ = *th* (Hanna et al. 1966, 1071, 1073).

In Old English two runic characters were used to spell /th/ and /th/: edh, or crossed *d* (ð), and thorn (þ).These two characters did not, however, distinguish between the two sounds. They were simply two different ways of spelling either of two different sounds. In late Old English or very early Middle English, the edh dropped out, being replaced by the thorn. Then, toward the end of the fourteenth century, the thorn was gradually replaced by the digraph *th*, another of the Continental innovations of the Norman scribes (Jespersen [1909] 1954, 1:44–47; Prins 1972, 214, 230; *OED* at *Th-*).

28.3.2 The Minor Spellings

In a few technical words the cluster *phth* occurs in initial position and is pronounced /th/. Instances of the correspondence /th/ = *phth:*

(Array 28-27)

apophthegm*	phthalic	phthiriasis	phthisis*
phthalein	phthiocol	phthirophagous	phthor

The correspondence /th/ = *chth* occurs in *chthonic,* which contrasts with *autochthonic,* in which *ch* = /k/ and /th/ = *th,* because of the syllabication.

The correspondence /th/ = *tth* occurs in the name *Matthew.*

28.3.3 The Major Spelling
28.3.3.1 /th/ = *th*

The correspondence /th/ = *th* occurs freely in initial, medial, and final position:

(Array 28-28)

apotheosis	epithet	oath	thought
authentic	mathematics	pathology	thunder
breath	method	teeth	thyroid
catholic	mouth	theory	wrath
cloth	myth	thirtieth	zenith

Orthographically the most interesting thing about the /th/ = *th* correspondence is the amazing array of consonant clusters and concatenations into which it enters:

(Array 28-29)

aesthetic	depth	hundredth	sixth
anthracite	diphtheria	ichthyology	tenth
arthritis	eighth	illth	thrash
athlete	ethnic	labyrinth	thwack
breadth	fifth	lengthen	twelfth
calisthenics	filthy	orthography	warmth

28.3.3.2 /t͟h/ = *th*

Unlike /th/ = *th,* the correspondence /t͟h/ = *th* occurs in a limited range of settings. The following are the only known instances in which it occurs in a consonant cluster, nearly always clustering with /r/:

(Array 28-30)

| brethren | farthing | northern | swarthy |
| farther | further | rhythm | worthy |

In all other instances the /t̲h̲/ = *th* correspondence is followed by a vowel, usually an *e*. Indeed, one of the functions of silent final *e* is to mark a voiced final /t̲h̲/, as illustrated in the following pairs:

(Array 28-31)

breath (n.)	breathe (v.)
loath (adj.)	loathe (v.)
seeth (?)	seethe (v.)
sheath (n.)	sheathe (v.)
sooth (?)	soothe (v.)
wreath (n.)	wreathe (v.)

The final *e* in the above verbs marks the voiced /t̲h̲/. In other instances the final *e* serves double duty, also marking a long vowel:

(Array 28-32)

bathe	lathe	swathe (?)
blithe	lithe	tithe
clothe	scythe	writhe

The only known holdouts to this pattern for word-final /t̲h̲/ are *bequeath, with, mouth* (v.), and *smooth*. Of these four, the first two have more regular variant pronunciations with voiceless /th/. Also, up through the sixteenth and seventeenth centuries *bequeath* and *smooth* were often spelled with a final *e*. A holdout of a different type is *absinthe*, with voiceless /th/ before the final *e*.

Some singular nouns that end in voiceless /th/ have plurals with voiced /t̲h̲/ and with the plural suffix also voiced, as /z/. Examples are *bath, baths; lath, laths*. Related to this is the way stem-final *th* is sometimes voiced when a vowel suffix is added: *worth, worthy; north, northern*.

28.4   The Spellings of /h/

28.4.1   /h/ = *h*

There are only two spellings of /h/, one very common, the other considerably less so (Hanna et al. 1966, 782, 783). The sound /h/ is most often word-initial, almost always element-initial, and always syllable-initial. The most common spelling of /h/ is *h*. Although the letter *h* occurs in a number of consonant digraphs (*ch, sh, th,* and the like), except for *rh* and the special cluster spelled *wh* and pronounced either /hw/, /w/, or /h/, the correspondence /h/ = *h* does not enter into clusters.

Instances of /h/ = *h* in element-initial position:

(Array 28-33)

abhor	cohere	girlhood	hockey
adhesive	disinherit	halcyon	hustle
apprehend	exhale	hesitate	hyacinth
behavior	exhume	hibernate	mishap
carbohydrate	foolhardy	hobby	rehearsal

The correspondence /h/ = *h* only rarely occurs in element-medial position. Some instances:

(Array 28-34)

alcohol	mahogany	menhaden	vehicular
Jehova	mahout	menhir	
maharaja	mayhem	tomahawk	

Other instances worthy of special comment include *mohair* and *penthouse*. Both are technically simplexes that look like compounds due to the analogizing force of folk etymology. *Mohair* was earlier *moochary* and *mocayare*, fairly close renderings of the Italian-Arabic origins of the word. But the notion of "hair," together with the phonetic similarity to *hair,* led to the present form. Similarly, *penthouse* comes from Middle English *pentis,* from Old French *appentis,* from Latin *appendix.* Again, the combination of apparent semantic relationship and rhyme led to the present form. Due to this evolution, *penthouse* can now be explicated to (pent)(house), "hanging house."

28.4.2   /h/ = *wh*

The second, considerably less common, spelling of /h/ is *wh*. The correspondence /h/ = *wh* occurs in only a few words and always in word-initial position:

(Array 28-35)

who	wholly	whoop	whore
whole	whom	whooping	whose

Whoop and *whooping* both have variant pronunciations with /h/ and /hw/. *Who, whom,* and *whose* come from Old English words spelled *hw* and pronounced /hw/. By the late thirteenth century *hw* had become *wh*, probably via analogy with other consonant digraphs ending in *h: ch, gh, sh, th,* and so on. In most cases the /hw/ pronunciation persisted, but not before /ū/—that is to say, not in *who* and its relatives (Jespersen [1909] 1954, 1:215; *OED* at Wh-). Because of pronunciation changes and some other problems with /h/ that will be discussed later, Middle English spelling was quite unsettled as far as /h/, *h,* and *wh* were concerned. In about the fifteenth century many words that had in Old English been spelled *h* grew an unetymological *w.* By the end of the sixteenth century almost all of these words had lost their unetymological *wh* spellings, reverting back to the more historical *h.* Only *whole, wholly,* and *whore* kept the unetymological correspondence /h/ = *wh.*

28.4.3   /hw/ = *wh*

In most words that had *hw* in Old English, now always spelled *wh,* the old pronunciation, /hw/, has persisted—at least as a variant (Jespersen [1909] 1954, 1:38, 398; Prins 1972, 233; Dobson 1957, 2:974–75). For all of the following words, Kenyon and Knott (1944) give the /hw/ pronunciation and a variant pronunciation with /w/:

(Array 28-36)

awhile	whelk	whey	whisper
overwhelm	whelp	which	whistle
whale	when	while	white
wharf	whence	whilom	whither
what	where	whilst	why
wheat	whet	whine	
wheel	whether	whinny	

Because of the power of the pattern represented in this group of Old English words, together with the general uncertainty surrounding the /h/ sound and *h* spelling in Middle English, a number of other words have come down to Modern English, also with *wh* and also with the variant pronunciations /w/ and /hw/. For some of them there is historical justification for the *w: whangee,* from Chinese *huangli,* for instance; *whir* from Danish *hvirre; whirl* from Old Norse *hvirfla.* But many others have picked up unetymological *w*'s or else are of uncertain origin. Many of these words are clearly imitative—for instance, *whoop* and *whiz,* in which the /h/ was perhaps felt to add to the echoic quality of the pronunciations. Instances of Modern /hw/ = *wh* that do not come from the Old English correspondence /hw/ = *wh:*

(Array 28-37)

whack	whicker	whinstone	whooper
wham	whiff	whip	whoops
whang	whiffle	whisk	whoosh
wheal	whim	whisker	whop
wheedle	whimbrel	whisky, whiskey	whopper
wheeze	whimper	whist	whorl
whelk	whimsy	whit	whort
wherry	whin	whoa	whortleberry
whew	whinchat	whoopee	whydah, whidah

Similar to the words in this group is *whittle,* which in Old English was *thwītan.*

The correspondence /hw/ = *wh* is an instance of mixed convergence: a pronunciation originally associated with the spelling *hw* has converged with a new spelling, *wh.* In technical terms this convergence is an instance of metathesis, the transposition of sounds or letters within a word. The /hw/ pronunciation is in a sense a fossil that is being replaced by the simpler variant /w/. If the correspondence /hw/ = *wh* is treated as a metathesis, it simply becomes another instance of /h/ = *h* transposed with an instance of /w/ = *w.*

28.4.4   The Spellings of /h/ Summarized

The few spellings of /h/ can be summarized as follows: (1) /h/ = *wh* in *who, whole, whore,* and their derivatives; (2) /h/ = *h* everywhere else.

28.4.5   Silent *h*

Though we are not speaking about the sound /h/ in so doing, it seems appropriate here to speak of some cases of silent *h.* The most noticeable instances are these:

(Array 28-38)

hautboy	herb*	honor
heir	honest	hour

Such words illustrate more of the uncertainty that surrounded /h/ and *h* in Old, Middle, and Early Modern English. The specific problem here involved adoptions from French. In many cases English adopted French versions of Latin words in which the original Latin *h* was no longer pronounced in French—indeed, was often not even reflected in the spelling. In Old and Middle English, words such as those listed in array 28-38, and many others, apparently were sometimes pronounced with /h/, sometimes without; that is to say they were sometimes spelled with *h,* sometimes not (Jespersen [1909] 1954, 1:60–62; Dobson 1957, 2:974–75, 991–92; Scragg 1970). Out of this period of uncertainty just about every combination has arisen. Words that have lost both /h/ and *h:*

(Array 28-39)

ability	arbor	ombre	ostler
able	it	ordure	

Words that have picked up unetymological /h/ and *h* include *hermit, hostage, hellebore.* And, of course, with *heir, honest,* and the others above, there are instances of words that have lost the /h/ but have retained the *h.*

    In addition to this problem with Latin *h,* there is the complication that the /h/ sound is in a sense quite vulnerable and easily lost in certain settings. For instance, when it occurs between a preceding stressed vowel and a following unstressed one, it tends to be lost, as in *philharmonic*, which contrasts with *harmonic*, in which the /h/ is intact. Other instances:

(Array 28-40)

annihilate	graham	posthumous	vehement
forehead	nihilism	shepherd	vehicle

Though *h* is usually /h/ before a stressed vowel, it is silent when preceded by *ex-*, as in:

(Array 28-41)

exhaust	exhilarate	exhume
exhibit	exhort	

In rapid speech there is a fairly relentless tendency for an initial /h/ to be dropped if it is followed by a weakly stressed vowel, as in *historical, habitual, hallucination, hereditary, hilarious, hospitable,* and the like. This tendency apparently underlies some speakers' use of *an* rather than *a* before words starting with /h/. Fowler on this point ([1926] 1965, 1):

> *A* is used before all consonants except silent *h* (*a history, an hour*); *an* was formerly usual before an unaccented syllable beginning with *h* and is still often seen and heard (*an historian, an hotel, an hysterical scene, an hereditary title, an habitual offender*). But now that the *h* in such words is pronounced the distinction has become anomalous and will no doubt disappear in time. Meantime speakers who like to say *an* should not try to have it both ways by aspirating the *h*.

In one variant pronunciation of *threshold*, in which both the /sh/ and the /h/ are pronounced, there appears to be just the opposite of a silent letter: an invisible /h/. If the *sh* is spelling /sh/, there is nothing left to spell the /h/. This pronunciation apparently arose from the mistaken notion that *threshold* is a compound of *thresh* and *hold*. Actually the structure is obscure, though the first element clearly appears to be *thresh*, in the sense of "tread." In Old English, *threshold* was spelled variously, according to the *OED: therscold, therscwold, therxold, therxwold, threxold, threxwold.* Whatever that second element might be—or, more accurately, might have been—it is clearly not *hold*. It would therefore be better to treat *threshold* as a simplex, and thus to argue for the pronunciation without /h/.

29   The Simple Fricatives /z/ and /s/

29.1   The Spellings of /z/

29.1.1   Historical Sources

Similar to the pattern for /f/ and /v/, both of which in Old English were spelled *f* and were kept separate by their position in words, Old English /s/ and /z/ were spelled *s,* with /z/ occurring only when preceded and followed by voiced sounds, and /s/ occurring everywhere else. In Old English the letter *z* was used infrequently, and then to spell /ts/, not /z/. The Norman scribes introduced the widespread use of the correspondence /z/ = *z* during the Middle English period. And gradually *z* came into use, not only in new adoptions that already contained it (especially "learned" words), but also to represent the /z/ sound in native words that had once been spelled with *s* (Jespersen [1909] 1954, 1:47–48; *OED* at *Z*). *Freeze,* for instance, was in Old English *frēosan.* Other examples: *dizzy* (Old English *dysig*), *daze* (Old Norse *dasa*), and *amaze* (Old English *āmasian*). Over the centuries there has been a marked tendency for /s/ in voiced settings— that is, /s/ surrounded by vowels and voiced consonants—to be pronounced /z/ (Jespersen [1909] 1954, 1:201–5). Thus, more and more cases have developed in which an *s* that once spelled /s/ now spells /z/, which makes the correspondence /z/ = *s* very important and widespread.

29.1.2   The Minor Spellings of /z/

The only minor spellings of /z/ are as follows: In word-initial position, *x* regularly spells /z/, as in *xylophone.* In *czar* and its derivatives /z/ = *cz.* Since *czar* has the variant spellings *tsar* and *tzar,* we must also recognize *ts* and *tz* as minor spellings of /z/. The correspondence /z/ = *sth* occurs only in *asthma,* much like the case with *isthmus,* in which /s/ = *sth.*

29.1.3   The Major Spellings of /z/

According to Hanna et al., the four major spellings of /z/—*z, zz, s,* and *ss*—account for more than 90 percent of the occurrences of this sound: /z/

is spelled *z* or *zz* about 25 percent of the time, and *s* or *ss* about 65 percent of the time (1966, 1097). Although there is some overlap between *s* and *z*, the four spellings sort themselves out rather well. In the following discussion we will approach this sorting-out in four steps—first, by distinguishing between *z* and *zz;* second, by distinguishing between *s* and *ss;* third, by distinguishing between *zz* and *ss;* and, finally, by distinguishing between *z* and *s*.

29.1.3.1 *z* versus *zz*

The spellings *z* and *zz* can be distinguished by applying a set of ordered rules much like those first described in 26.2.3.1:

1. In those rare cases in which word-final /z/ occurs after a stressed short vowel, the distribution of *z* and *zz* is about fifty-fifty.
2. /z/ = *z* at all other simple boundaries.
3. /z/ = *z* in VCV strings shortened by a shortening rule.
4. /z/ = *z* within consonant clusters, but with the regular complication posed by a following *le*.
5. /z/ = *z* after vowel digraphs.
6. /z/ = *z* after long vowels.
7. /z/ = *zz* at complex boundaries affected by twinning.
8. /z/ = *zz* between a stressed short vowel and a following vowel if none of the shortening rules apply.
9. /z/ = *zz* between a stressed short vowel and a following *le*.
10. /z/ = *z* after reduced vowels.

/z/ = *z and* zz *in Word-final Position.* The situation with word-final /z/ after a stressed short vowel is ambiguous. In English there is a constraint against ending free bases with a single *s*, and so final *e* and *ss* are used to avoid this configuration, as in *purse* and *kiss* (see 3.4.1). Because of the close relationship between *s* and *z*, a fairly consistent tendency to treat *z* like *s* in free-base-final position has evolved, as in words like *buzz* and *bronze*, **buz* and **bronz* being quite adequate from a simple sound-and-spelling point of view (see 3.4.2). However, if a constraint against free-base-final *z* is in fact at work in the English spelling system, it is a weak one, as illustrated by the following two sets of words:

(Array 29-1)

buzz	frizz	huzz
fizz	fuzz	jazz
coz	phiz	topaz
fez	quiz	whiz

/z/ = z at Simple Boundaries. This correspondence usually occurs at element-initial boundaries:

(Array 29-2)

benzine	zebra	zigzag	zone
schizophrenia	zebu	zinc	zoo
zany	zenith	zinnia	zygote

/z/ = z in Shortened VCV Strings. This rule, too, is quite limited, since *z* was so rare in Latin words and thus in Romance adoptions. Instances of the Third Syllable and Stress Frontshift rules:

(Array 29-3)

azimuth	hazard	lozenge
dozen	lizard	vizier

/z/ = z in Consonant Clusters. Instances, almost always in the cluster *nz*:

(Array 29-4)

adze	bronze	furze
bonanza	cadenza	influenza
bonze	frenzy	stanza

/z/ = z after Vowel Digraphs. Instances:

(Array 29-5)

breeze	gauze	seize	tweezers
frieze	maize	sneeze	wheeze
frowzy	ooze	squeeze	woozy

/z/ = z after Long Vowels. Array 29-5 contains a number of instances of */z/ = z* after long vowels spelled with digraphs; instances after long unigraphs include the following:

(Array 29-6)

assize	daze	hazel	razor
capsize	frozen	lazy	suzerain
cozy	gazing	maze	trapeze

/z/ = zz at Complex Boundaries. There are no known cases of */z/ = zz* at complex boundaries due to assimilation or duplicative addition, and very few cases are due to twinning, since word-final *z* is in itself rather rare:

(Array 29-7)

quizzed, quizzing, quizzes, quizzical
whizzed, whizzing, whizzes, whizzer
fezzes
cozzes

W3 calls for the very rare plurals of *phiz* and *wiz, phizes* and *wizes,* apparently, but the regular pattern would involve twinning, as in *fezzes* and *cozzes.*

/z/ = zz in VCC Strings.   Instances of /z/ = *zz* between a stressed short vowel and another vowel:

(Array 29-8)

blizzard	dizzy	mezzotint*	piazza*
buzzard	gizzard	mizzen*	razzia

Apparent holdouts are *plaza, wizen,* and *wizard. Plaza,* a seventeenth-century adoption from Spanish, retains some of the sound of the Spanish *a.* In fact, it has variants in both /a/ and /ä/, and the *OED* shows the *z* as pronounced /th/ or /s/. *Wizen,* with /i/, is from Old English *wisnian.* The early *sn* cluster served to keep the *i* short, aided somewhat, perhaps, by the pressure of the Old English Third Syllable Rule (see 7.1.1). *Wizard* is a late Middle English formation combining *wys* 'wise' and the suffix *-ard.* In Middle English it had variant spellings with *zz* and *ss.* The short *i* and single *z* may be due to a felt analogy with *wisdom.*

/z/ = zz between a Stressed Short Vowel and le.   Instances:

(Array 29-9)

dazzle	frazzle	grizzly	nuzzle
drizzle	frizzle	guzzle	puzzle
embezzle	grizzled	muzzle	sizzle

/z/ = z after Reduced Vowels.   The correspondence /z/ = *z* is very common after schwa in the compound suffix *-ization,* as in *centralization* and *realization.* Other instances:

(Array 29-10)

amazon	citizen	horizontal	metazoan
azalea	cognizance	kazoo	spermatozoan
bizarre	denizen	magazine	trapezoid

29.1.3.2 *s* versus *ss*

The spelling *s* is the most common of the spellings of /z/; *ss* is one of the least common. The first rule for contrasting *s* with *ss* is that word-final /z/ = *s,* though often the *s* is insulated with a final *e.* The remaining eight rules are the same as those for contrasting *z* with *zz* (see 29.1.3.1).

/z/ = s in Word-final Position.   Usually free-base-final /z/ = *s* is insulated by a silent final *e,* which may or may not also be marking a long vowel. In

a few instances uninsulated free-base-final /z/ = s, though usually the *s* echoes a now-lost inflectional suffix. In thousands of instances word-final /z/ = s owing to the use of the noun plural suffixes -*s* and -*es*, the third person singular verb suffixes -*s* and -*es*, and the various forms of the genitive.

(Array 29-11)

as	has	horses'	torch's
dog's	hers	is	torches
dogs'	horse's	lens	was
accuse	despise	malaise	these
applause	disease	noise	whose

Word-final /z/ is never spelled *ss*.

/z/ = s at Other Simple Boundaries. The correspondence /z/ = s occurs at the boundaries, both initial and final, of both free and bound bases:

(Array 29-12)

commiserate	feasible	perquisite	resent
divisible	gymnasium	president	transistor
envisage	observe	proviso	wisdom

/z/ = s in Shortened VCV Strings. Instances of /z/ = s in VCV strings shortened by the Third Syllable Rule, the Stress Frontshift Rule, or one of the suffix rules:

(Array 29-13)

closet	misery	positive	resin
hesitate	physic	repository	visage
inquisitive	physiology	resident	visit

/z/ = s in Consonant Clusters and Concatenations. Instances:

(Array 29-14)

alms	dismal	kismet	palsy
cataclysm	grisly	measles	plasma
clumsy	jasmine	miasma	presbyter
cosmic	jersey	muslin	tongs

Many words with the suffix -*ism* fit this pattern: *anachronism, fascism, rheumatism,* and so on. Also in this category is *raspberry,* which involves an odd voiced concatenation: although adjacent to the *s* there is a *p*, which usually spells a voiceless sound, the sound adjacent to the /z/ is the voiced /b/, and thus the minor correspondence /b/ = *pb* holds here (see 26.2.2).

/z/ = s *after Vowel Digraphs.*   Instances:

(Array 29-15)

browse	easel	lackadaisical	raisin
bruise	easy	limousine	tease
causeway	geyser	mayonnaise	thousand
cousin	hawser	poison	turquoise

Holdouts to this pattern are *reconnaissance* and *renaissance,* both of which have variant pronunciations with /s/ rather than /z/.

/z/ = s *after Long Vowels.*   Instances:

(Array 29-16)

apprise	hosanna	propose	symposium
basil	mosaic	revise	use
divisor	nasal	rosary	visor

/z/ = ss.   The correspondence /z/ = *ss* is very rare. It occurs via duplicative addition in *dissolve, dessert,* and *possess,* the last of which shows the Triplet Rule at work: (poss + sess). The *ss* spelling also occurs in regular VCC strings, as in *hussar, scissors,* and one pronunciation of *hussy.* It is also a holdout to the reduced-vowel rule (see below) in the French adoptions *brassiere* and, again, *reconnaissance* and *renaissance.*

/z/ = s *after Reduced Vowels.*   Instances:

(Array 29-17)

acquisition	deposition	exquisite	orison
artisan	desert (v.)	opposite	partisan

29.1.3.3   *zz* versus *ss*

Distinguishing between these two spellings is quite straightforward: The correspondence /z/ = *zz* occurs (1) via twinning, (2) between a short vowel and *le,* (3) in word-final position after a short vowel, and (4) in VCC strings. The correspondence /z/ = *ss* overlaps with this distribution only in VCC strings, and then only in the words *hussar, scissors,* and *hussy.*

29.1.3.4   *z* versus *s*

Distinguishing between these two spellings is much less clear-cut—and much more important, since these two account for nearly 90 percent of the instances of /z/ in Hanna et al. 1966 (1097). As sections 29.1.3.1 and 29.1.3.2 indicate, the only area of straightforward contrast between them is that the /z/ = *z* correspondence occurs in word-initial position, while the /z/ = *s* correspondence does not, except in some rare and unintegrated recent German adoptions, such as the variant pronunciations of *sitzmark* and *sitzkreig*. Also, the *s* spelling is much more common than the *z*, especially in bound bases.

29.2 The Spellings of /s/

29.2.1 Historical Sources

In Old English, /s/ was always spelled *s*. In Latin and Old French, /s/ was also usually spelled *s*, so the modern correspondence /s/ = *s* reflects both the Germanic and the Romance sides of the language. However, Old French also used *c* to spell /s/. Originally in Old French that *c* spelled /ch/, but gradually the sound eased to /s/, and by the Middle English period both *s* and *c* were widely used to represent the same sound, /s/. Then, as now, the correspondence /s/ = *c* held only in front of the letters *e, i,* and *y;* everywhere else the correspondence was *c* = /k/ (Jespersen [1909] 1954, 1:48–50; *OED* at *S* and *C*). Thus three major spellings of /s/ developed: *s, c,* and, of course, *ss*. The doublet *cc* cannot spell /s/, for the first *c,* since it is not followed by *e, i,* or *y,* must be hard. Thus *cc* is always pronounced /k/, as in *accord,* or /ks/, as in *accede*.

29.2.2 The Minor Spellings of /s/

The most important minor spelling of /s/ is *sc,* as in *scene*. Also of considerable importance is *ps,* as in *psychology,* and *st,* as in *listen*. Of lesser importance are *z, waltz; sw, sword; sch, schism;* and *sth, isthmus*.

29.2.2.1 /s/ = *sc*

The correspondence /s/ = *sc* usually comes from Latin, either directly or by way of French. However, a few cases of *sc* developed in English, either through attempts to distinguish between homophones or simply through incorrect assumptions about words' etymologies. For instance, *scent* is from Middle English *senten,* from Old French *sentir,* from Latin *sentīre*. Jespersen suggests that the present spelling of *scent* is probably an attempt to distinguish it from *sent* and *cent* ([1909] 1954, 1:49). For the *sc* in *scissors* and *scythe* see 1.5.3. Whatever the various reasons for the correspondence /s/ = *sc,* it is quite rare, accounting for only about 1 percent of the instances of /s/ in Hanna et al. (1966, 1015). However, in spite of its relative rarity, it is remarkably widespread in distribution, occurring in initial, medial, and final position.

Tactically *sc* is not a double letter; it does not behave like a double soft *c,* for instance, the way that *ss* is a double *s*. The *sc* sequence can most often be classified as an unusual cluster. But it must be treated as a concatenation when it is a product of assimilation, as in *suscepti-*

ble, resuscitate, and *ascertain*—(suɓ + s + ceptible), (re(suɓ + s + citate), (aɗ + s(certain)—or when it is a product of simple addition, as in the only known instance: *abscess,* (abs + cess).

/s/ = sc *in Word-initial Position.* Instances:

(Array 29-18)

scenario	sciatica	scintillate	scissors
scene	science	sciolism	sciuroid
scepter	scintilla	scissile	scythe

Words with variant spellings include *scend* (*send*) and *scirocco* (*sirocco*). The *sc* spelling, like the simple *c,* spells /s/ only immediately before *e, i,* and *y.* Compare these cases of *sc* = /sk/: *scatter, sclerosis, scofflaw, scold, scratch, sculpture.* There are only three known word-initial holdouts—or, more accurately, near holdouts—to this distribution: *scilicet* and *scirrhus* have variant pronunciations, the more regular one with /s/, the less regular one with /sk/. *Sceptic,* with /sk/, has the more regular variant spelling *skeptic.*

/s/ = sc *in Medial Position.* The following words are treated here as instances of element-medial /s/ = *sc,* though more detailed explication could either move the *sc* to a boundary or split the *s* and *c* between two elements. For instance, *obscene* is of obscure structure, but it could be explicated as (obs + cene). *Miscellaneous, muscle,* and *corpuscle* all contain old Latin diminutives—respectively, "little mix," "little mouse," and "little body"—and they could be explicated as (mis + cell + aneous), (mus + cle), and (corp + us + cle). But for now, at least, we will treat all of the elements involved here as functional simplexes, which explicate to (obscene), (miscell + aneous), and (muscle). Other instances of medial /s/ = *sc:*

(Array 29-19)

ascetic	discipline	fascinate	lascivious
disciple	eviscerate	fasciola	oscillate

/s/ = sc *in Element-final Position.* Instances, many of which contain the suffix *-esce:*

(Array 29-20)

acquiesce	crescent	fluoresce	nascent
adolescence	effervescent	irascible	obsolescence
convalescent	fascicle	miscible	proboscis

29.2.2.2 /s/ = *ps*

Except in a few near-words like *pst!*, the spelling *ps* comes from Greek. It is the Latin rendering of the Greek letter psi, which in Greek was pronounced /ps/. For quite some time in English both the *p* and the *s* were pronounced, or were supposed to be pronounced. The *OED*, in one of its relatively few overt attempts at orthographic engineering, encouraged the /ps/ pronunciation for all such words, except the *psalm* and *psalter* groups, which came from Greek by way of Old English and thus could be taken as more native (at *Ps-*). However, the relentless pressure of simplification has prevailed, and in American English all such words are now pronounced with /s/, except for the Egyptian adoption *pschent*, which is pronounced /skent/ or /pskent/. All of the known instances of /s/ = *ps* are in initial position:

(Array 29-21)

psalliota	psephite	psilanthropy	psoriasis
psalloid	psephology	psilate	psorosis
psammon	psephomancy	psithyrus	psychology
psedera	psettodid	psittacism	psywar
pselaphid	pseudograph	psoas	
pselaphognath	psi*	psocid	
psephism	psicose	psophometer	

Because, as the list shows, /s/ = *ps* is common in technical words, a number of the technical combining forms represented above are used to form many other words. Some of the more productive of these forms are *pseud+*, *psych+*, *psamm+*, *psil+*, *psor+*, and *psychr+*.

29.2.2.3 Other Minor Spellings of /s/

The correspondence /s/ = *z* occurs in the following, most of which are German adoptions:

(Array 29-22)

batz	eczema*	quartz	waltz
chintz, chints	howitzer	sitzmark	wootz

The correspondence /s/ = *st* occurs in several words, but apparently in only two settings, either before *en* or before *le* (Jespersen [1909] 1954, 1:224–25; Dobson 1957, 2:968–69):

(Array 29-23)

chasten	fasten	hasten	moisten
christen	glisten	listen	

apostle	gristle	mistletoe	throstle
bristle	hustle	nestle	trestle
bustle	istle, ixtle	pestle	whistle
castle	jostle, justle	rustle	wrestle
epistle	mistle, missel	thistle	

The correspondence /s/ = *sw* occurs only in *sword* and *answer*. It occurs in *sword* owing to the tendency of /w/ to be dropped in a stressed syllable when it comes between a consonant and certain back vowels. Compare the word *two*, with no /w/, with, say, *twice*. Similarly, compare *sword* and, say, *swerve*. In *answer* the /s/ = *sw* correspondence is due to the tendency of /w/ to be dropped from a weakly stressed syllable when it is between a preceding consonant and a vowel or, more strongly, the liquid /r/. Compare *conquer*, with no /w/, with *conquest*, or *liquor* with *liquid*. For more details see 27.3.2.4.

The correspondence /s/ = *sch* occurs only in the word *schism*, which has a more regular pronunciation with /sk/.

The correspondence /s/ = *cs* occurs only in the proper noun *Tucson*, from American Indian *Stjukshon*.

The correspondence /s/ = *sth* occurs only in *isthmus*, in which the *th* gets caught awkwardly between the two syllables and thus, apparently, has been lost in the pronunciation (Jespersen [1909] 1954, 1:225).

29.2.3   The Major Spellings of /s/

The three major spellings of /s/ are *s, ss,* and *c,* with *s* and *ss* accounting for about 80 percent of the instances of /s/ (Hanna et al. 1966, 1015). The distribution of the *s* and *ss* spellings can be described through the by now familiar list of ordered rules, although toward the end of the list some areas of overlap make the *s* versus *ss* distinction less clear-cut than has been the case with most single and double letter spellings heretofore:

1. Word-final /s/ = *ss* after a stressed short vowel.
2. /s/ = *s* at most other simple boundaries.
3. /s/ = *s* in VCV strings shortened by a shortening rule.
4. /s/ = *s* within voiceless consonant clusters, but with the regular complication posed by a following *le*.
5. /s/ = *s* after vowel digraphs.
6. /s/ = *s* after long vowels.
7. /s/ = *ss* at complex boundaries affected by twinning, duplicative addition, or assimilation.

8. /s/ = *ss* between a stressed short vowel and a following vowel if none of the shortening rules apply.
9. /s/ = *ss* between a stressed short vowel and a following *le*.
10. /s/ = *s* after reduced vowels.

29.2.3.1 /s/ = *ss* in Word-final Position after Short Vowels

As noted in 3.4.1, *ss* is regularly used after a stressed short vowel to avoid ending a free base with a single *s*. A few of the scores of instances of word-final *ss*:

(Array 29-24)

abyss	confess	glass	muss
amass	dismiss	hiss	remiss
caress	fuss	moss	toss

The only known holdouts to this pattern include *bus, plus, sis, gas, sassafras, alas,* and *madras,* the last of which also is pronounced with the more regular /ə/ before the final *s*. Other holdouts are the function words *this, yes,* and *us,* the last of which could be seen as a reverse instance of the Short Word Rule (see 3.5).

The correspondence /s/ = *ss* holds in some cases in which *ss* is followed by a fossil final *e:*

(Array 29-25)

crevasse	finesse	impasse
demitasse	fosse	lacrosse

29.2.3.2 /s/ = *s* at Other Simple Boundaries

This correspondence is very common, especially in initial position:

(Array 29-26)

asylum	heresy	schedule	straight
besiege	hypocrisy	second	suffer
blaspheme	kerosene	sibyl	sustenance
chrysanthemum	minuscule	sieve	swagger
creosote	parasite	smear	trespass
desideratum	parasol	sneeze	unison

There are an immense number of instances of this rule, so it is not too surprising that there are also quite a few holdouts, all involving *ss* in element-final position. The following words contain /s/ = *ss* at simple boundaries. Several are also holdouts to the later rule that calls for *s* after reduced vowels:

(Array 29-27)

admissible	essence	missile	possess
aggressive	essential	narcissism	possible
ambassador	fricassee	narcissus	potassium
colossal	incessant	necessary	predecessor
commissar	lassitude	necessitate	promissory
decussate	massage	osseous	submissive
embassy	message	passenger	vicissitude

That may appear to be a formidable list of holdouts, but just a few productive bound bases account for many of them—*miss +*, for instance, and *cess +* and *mess +*.

29.2.3.3 /s/ = *s* in Shortened VCV Strings

Because of the tendency of /s/ to be voiced as /z/ between vowels, there are relatively few instances of /s/ = *s* in VCV strings that have been affected by one of the shortening rules. However, this correspondence does occur in VCV strings that have been shortened by the Third Syllable Rule or the Suffix *-ity* Rule. Some instances:

(Array 29-28)

animosity	desolate	impetuosity	prosecute
asinine	desultory	infinitesimal	proselyte
chrysalis	disability	misanthrope	prosody
curiosity	dysentery	monstrosity	vesicle

29.2.3.4 /s/ = *s* in Consonant Clusters and Concatenations

Instances:

(Array 29-29)

adjust	atheist	clasp	liverwurst
amnesty	bestial	conquest	taskmaster
apostasy	brusque	desk	tsetse
aspirin	burst	ghastly	waistcoat

As might be expected, in view of the generally more loose nature of concatenations and the large number of bases and suffixes ending in *ss*, the /s/ = *ss* correspondence is fairly common in consonant concatenations, both voiceless and mixed. Some instances:

(Array 29-30)

airlessness	crossbow	glassware	hopelessly
chessboard	dressmaker	grasshopper	stressful

29.2.3.5 /s/ = *s* after Vowel Digraphs

Instances:

(Array 29-31)

jealous	mausoleum	rebellious	tortoise
louse	nuisance	sausage	unloose

The holdouts here, as with /z/, are *reconnaissance* and *renaissance,* both of which have variant pronunciations with /z/ and /s/. Two other known holdouts, also French adoptions, are *trousseau* and *caisson.*

29.2.3.6 /s/ = s after Long Vowels

This correspondence holds, among other places, in word-final position with a silent final *e:*

(Array 29-32)

abstruse	cease	diagnosis	isotope
apotheosis	conclusive	diffuse	masonry
bison	decisive	goose	thesis

Other than *trousseau* and *caisson* again, the only known holdouts to this pattern are the adjectives *bass* 'low' and *gross.*

29.2.3.7 /s/ = ss at Complex Boundaries

Instances of /s/ = ss due to twinning are rare, since so few free bases end in single *s*. The following is probably an exhaustive list:

(Array 29-33)

bussed, bussing, busses
gassed, gassing, gasses, gassy
plussed, plussing, plusses, plussage
yessed, yessing, yesses
krisses
thisses
sissy

For more on the twinning of *s* see 9.5.2.

A number of instances of /s/ = ss result from duplicative addition, usually the addition of a prefix ending in *s* to a stem beginning with *s*. In careful speech a number of these are actually pronounced /ss/, but in ordinary speech they are more often pronounced /s/. The first *s* is voiced as a /z/ in some pronunciations. Some instances of /s/ = ss via duplicative addition:

(Array 29-34)

dissatisfy	dissipate	dyssebacia	lissome
dissect	dissociate	dyssodia	misspeak
dissertation	dissuade	intussuscipiens	transsegmental

The correspondence /s/ = *ss* due to the assimilation of the prefix *ad-* to *as-* before *s* is fairly common:

(Array 29-35)

assail	assess	assign	assonance
assault	assets	assimilate	assort
assemble	asseverate	assist	assuage

Two words that historically contained the prefix *ex-* have undergone an assimilation that reflects the mistaken notion that they contained *ad-*: *assay* and *assart*. In a few instances /s/ = *ss* owing to the assimilation of other prefixes:

(Array 29-36)

assoil	essay	essoin	sussultatory

29.2.3.8   /s/ = *ss* in VCC Strings

After short vowels that are not affected by one of the shortening rules, the correspondence /s/ = *ss* holds:

(Array 29-37)

blossom	gusset	mussel	russet
casserole	hassock	opossum	vassal
cassock	hyssop	pessimism	vessel

29.2.3.9   /s/ = *ss* between Short Vowels and *le*

There are only two known instances of this correspondence: *tussle* and *hassle*. During my boyhood the common term for *wrestle* was /'rasᵊl/, apparently to be spelled *rassle*, although no dictionary records this as a variant.

29.2.3.10   /s/ = *s* after Reduced Vowels

Instances of medial /s/ = *s* after reduced vowels:

(Array 29-38)

argosy	esophagus	jettison	nemesis
basilica	garrison	leprosy	pleurisy
caparison	genesis	moccasin	thesaurus

The only known holdouts to this pattern are the first *ss* in *assassin*, *reconaissance, renaissance,* and the examples included in arrays 29-27 and 29-40.

Also regularly spelled *s* is word-final /s/ after a reduced vowel. There are an immense number of instances involving many suffixes and other endings that have converged in various ways to suffixes. A sampling includes:

(Array 29-39)

abacus	colossus	madras	promise
apparatus	epidermis	oasis	radius
arthritis	fracas	parenthesis	synopsis
asparagus	hippopotamus	phosphorus	tuberculosis
basis	homeostasis	premise	walrus

For other examples see 3.4.1.1.

Again, in view of the hundreds of instances of this pattern, we should not be surprised that there are a number of holdouts, most of which involve the suffixes -*less*, -*ness*, and -*ess:*

(Array 29-40)

abbess	buttress	embarrass	mindless
actress	carcass	faultless	prowess
artiness	compass	faultlessness	tigress
artless	congress	fortress	waitress
baseless	cutlass	harness	wilderness
baseness	cypress	mattress	windlass

29.2.4   /s/ = c

As noted before, the correspondence /s/ = c derives from the Romance side of the English language. And although the correspondence holds only immediately preceding the letters e, i, and y, it still accounts for nearly 20 percent of the instances of /s/ in Hanna et al. (1966, 1015). (The sound /s/ is spelled with a c marked with a cedilla, and thus no following e, i, or y, in, apparently, only the words *curaçao, curaçoa,* and *garçon.*) The correspondence /s/ = c is most common in element-initial and word-final position, marked with a silent final e.

29.2.4.1   /s/ = c in Element-initial Position

Instances:

(Array 29-41)

ceremony	cyanide	disconcert	procedure
cession	cybernetics	egocentric	receipt
cicada	cynic	encyclopedia	recidivism
cinema	cypress	incendiary	recital
cipher	decease	misconception	secession
citizen	deceive	necessary	supercilious

29.2.4.2   /s/ = c in Element-medial Position

The correspondence /s/ = c is relatively rare in element-medial position, and a more detailed explication of some of the instances cited below could well show the c to be either initial or final:

(Array 29-42)

acetic	fancy	mercenary	pincers
ancillary	hyacinth	mucilage	porcelain
bacillus	insouciance	nacelle	recalcitrant
cancel	larceny	ocelot	society
cancer	lucerne	parcel	vicinity
council	lyceum	penicillin	vicissitude

29.2.4.3 /s/ = c in Element-final Position

The correspondence /s/ = c is quite common in element-final position, always, of course, with a following final e in the shortest form to mark the soft c. In derivatives with suffixes that start with e, i, or y, the original final e is deleted. Thus, in the shortest form *juice* there is a final e, while in its derivatives *juiciness* and *juicy* the e has been deleted. During the Middle English period some words ending in *se* were spelled with *ce* to avoid the ambiguity of the *se* ending, which can be pronounced either /s/ or /z/, as in *ruse* and *rose*. This respelling produced some modern variants: *licence, license; offence, offense; defence, defense.* Other instances of element-final /s/ = c:

(Array 29-43)

advance	elasticity	inducement	priceless
audacity	elegance	medicinal	racism
benefice	facet	notice	romance
caprice	felicitate	obedience	solace
docile	icing	pacify	specification
duplicity	implicit	placid	velocipede

29.2.4.4 /s/ = c in Consonant Clusters

Since c must be followed by e, i, or y in order to spell /s/, it can enter into consonant clusters only when it is preceded by a consonant—specifically c, l, n, or r:

(Array 29-44)

agency	farce	force	narcissus
calcium	fence	halcyon	pencil
dulcet	flaccid	larceny	sincere

30 The Palatal Sibilants: /sh/, /ch/, /j/, and /zh/

30.1 Introduction

The palatal sibilants—/sh/, /ch/, /j/, and /zh/—all have a distinct sibilant sound and all are pronounced at the hard palate. The four can be divided into two pairs: the fricatives /sh/ and /zh/, and the affricates /ch/ and /j/. The affricates are complex sounds consisting of a stop plus a fricative; thus /ch/ and /j/ can be, and sometimes are, symbolized as /tsh/ and /dzh/. Orthographically the four palatal sibilants are interesting because they give rise to two kinds of spelling. The first kind, the **simple spelling**, occurs when, for instance, /ch/ is spelled *ch* or *tch*, or when /sh/ is spelled *sh*. The second kind, the **palatalized spelling**, occurs when the sound is spelled by letters that normally spell nonpalatal sounds, as, for instance, when /ch/ is spelled *t* in *question*, /sh/ is spelled *c* in *social*, or /j/ is spelled *d* in *residual*. This distinction between simple and palatalized spellings is clear-cut and useful in the case of /sh/, /ch/, and /j/; it is less clear-cut in the case of /zh/, the rarest sound in English and one that remains somewhat unintegrated into the overall orthographic system.

30.2 The Spellings of /sh/

Although we tend to associate the digraph *sh* with the sound of /sh/, the simple correspondence /sh/ = *sh* holds only about 25 percent of the time; the most common spelling of /sh/ is the palatalized *t*, as in *nation* (Hanna et al. 1966, 1028–29). In the following subsections we will discuss, first, the minor simple spellings, *ch* and *sch;* second, the major spelling, *sh;* and, third, the palatalized spellings, *t, s, x, ss, sc,* and *c.*

30.2.1 The Minor Simple Spellings of /sh/: *ch* and *sch*

The correspondence /sh/ = *ch* occurs in usually rather recent French adoptions that have retained quite a bit of their French pronunciation. For instance, the English word *chef,* a nineteenth-century adoption, has the

French correspondence *ch* = /sh/, while the more integrated word *chief,* borrowed from the same French source (but in the late thirteenth century), has the regular correspondence *ch* = /ch/. Other instances of the French /sh/ = *ch:*

(Array 30-1)

brochure	chaise	crochet	mustache
cache	champagne	echelon	nonchalance
cachet	charlatan	gauche	parachute
chagrin	chevron	machine	ricochet

Although this study is not much concerned with proper names, it may be worthwhile to note that the *ch* = /sh/ in many Midwestern place-names—*Chicago* and *Michigan,* for instance—reflects the early French influence in that part of the country.

The correspondence /sh/ = *ch* also holds in *pistachio,* which was adapted from the Italian *pistacchio.*

The minor correspondence /sh/ = *sch* usually occurs in German and Yiddish adoptions, including an amazing set of Yiddish pejoratives.

(Array 30-2)

schlemiel	schmaltz	schnauzer	schnozzle
schlep	schmo	schnitzel	schottische
schlimazel	schmuck	schnook	schuss
schlock	schnapps	schnorrer	schwa

Although the *sch* spelling regularly occurs in initial position, it does occur medially in *seneschal,* from Old French.

For the record, in the botanical term *eschscholtzia* /sh/ is spelled *schsch.*

30.2.2 The Major Simple Spelling of /sh/: *sh*

In Old English, /sh/ was spelled *sc,* which caused problems for the Norman scribes. In the first place, the sound /sh/ did not exist in early Old French, so the scribes were quite unfamiliar with both sound and spelling. For another thing, the letter *c* was already doing double duty in their orthography, rather as it does today. They tried many different ways of rendering /sh/: the *OED* records *s, ss, ssh, szsh, szh, sg, ch,* and *x* (at *Sh-*). But from roughly the twelfth through the fourteenth century the most common spelling was *sch,* especially in initial position. By the fourteenth century *sh* had become the most common spelling around London, probably as a simplification of the earlier *sch.* After the fifteenth century, in part due to the influence of Caxton, *sh* became the "native" spelling of /sh/.

Thus it may be thought of as the English /sh/, late in coming though it was (Jespersen [1909] 1954, 1:52–54; Prins 1972, 215, 231).

The correspondence /sh/ = sh occurs nearly always in initial or final position. Because its source is commonly Germanic, it occurs almost exclusively in free bases; the only important bound elements in which it occurs are the suffixes -ship and -ish. Instances of initial and final /sh/ = sh:

(Array 30-3)

abash	galosh	rubbish	shoulder
bashful	hardship	shambles	shroud
courtship	harsh	sheaf	shush
devilish	makeshift	sheik	shy
fresh	nourish	shingle	vanish

The correspondence /sh/ = sh is very rare in medial position. Known instances are:

(Array 30-4)

bishop	marshal	pasha
bushel	mushroom	usher

30.2.3 The Palatalized Spellings of /sh/

There are six palatalized spellings of /sh/: t, s, ss, sc, c, and x, as in *nation, extension, mission, conscience, social,* and *sexual.* In the first five cases the /sh/ always occurs between a preceding stressed vowel and two following unstressed vowels, *i* plus some other. When *t, s, ss, sc,* or *c* occur in that context, the sounds they spell are palatalized to /sh/ (see Chomsky and Halle, 1968, 230–31 and passim; Venezky 1970, 42, 92–93).

In general, the palatalization process started in English sometime after 1600. The *i* in a word such as *nation* or *tension* eased from full vowel sound to /y/-like glide, and then finally more or less merged with the preceding consonant, leading to the palatalization. A number of instances of the "native" correspondence /sh/ = sh are actually respellings of words that in Old French contained palatalized *s*'s. For instance, *anguish* comes from Old French *angoisse,* in which the *ss* spelling palatalized. In Middle English the word was spelled with *s* or *ss;* the *sh* spelling did not appear until the fourteenth century. Similar instances are *nourish, bushel, cushion, brush, crush, finish, radish.* Such words represent very old palatalizations that led to spelling changes. The palatalizations we are dealing with here, as in *nation* and *social,* however, came much later—in the seventeenth century—and thus did not affect the spelling, which was already for the most part firmly established (Jespersen [1909] 1954, 1:341–44; Dobson 1957, 2:957–58).

30.2.3.1 /sh/ = *t*

Most dictionaries, including Kenyon and Knott's, show the correspondence *t* = /sh/ for all of the following words. *W3*, however, shows *t* = /ch/ for the five asterisked words, in which the *t* is preceded by an *n* (see *W3* 40a, at \ch\).

(Array 30-5)

abbreviation	dietitian	initial	partial
abduction	differential*	insatiable	pretentious*
circumstantial*	differentiate*	junction	quotient
consentient	impatience	nasturtium	ratio
description	inertia	notion	reception
detention*	infectious	palatial	tertiary

In all of these words the *t* is the last letter in the stem. The following *i* is either the first letter of the suffix—*nation* (nat + ion)—or it is a particle inserted between the stem and the suffix, providing the necessary pattern to mark the palatalization—as in *captious* (capt + i + ous) (see 2.4).

30.2.3.2 /sh/ = *s*

The correspondence /sh/ = *s* raises some complexities that are not encountered with /sh/ = *t*. There tends to be considerable variation in the pronunciation of words containing a palatalized *s* spelling. Some words have variant pronunciations, one with the *s* palatalized, one without palatalization. Normally, if a vowel precedes the *s*, the palatalization leads to /zh/ rather than /sh/, as in *abrasion, lesion, vision, explosion, fusion*. If there is an *r* in front of the *s*, the palatalization regularly produces two variant pronunciations, one with /zh/, one with /sh/. If an *l* or *n* precedes the *s*, the palatalization is regularly to /sh/. Among the following instances of /sh/ = *s*, asterisked words have variant pronunciations of the *s*, and in those cases in which *s* is preceded by an *n*, *W3* consistently shows *s* = /ch/ rather than /sh/:

(Array 30-6)

apprehension	dyspepsia*	intension	revulsion
condescension	emulsion	magnesium*	subversion*
dimension	expansion	mansion	suspension
dispersion*	immersion*	propulsion	transient*

Although the pronunciation of *nausea* is far from settled, the *e* following the *s* can lead to palatalization of the *s*, which is variously pronounced /z/, /zh/, /s/, and /sh/. *Nauseous* has variants with /z/ and /sh/, and although the stress pattern is not normal for palatalization, *nauseate,* with secondary stress on the second *a,* has variants in which the *s* is pronounced /z/, /zh/, /s/, and /sh/. Apparently the unsettled pronunciation plus the power of conservative analogy encourage the anomalous palatalizations.

The correspondence /sh/ = *s* occurs in *sensual* and *sensuous,* with *u* rather than *i* triggering the palatalization. A similar palatalization occurs in *sexual.*

In a few cases the /sh/ = *s* correspondence holds before a *u* that is stressed and followed by a consonant, usually *r.* The only known instances are:

(Array 30-7)

censure	insure	sumac*
commensurate*	mensuration*	sure
ensure	sugar	tonsure

The palatalization in *sugar* and *sure* stems from the fact that in earlier English many vowels that now have simple vowel sounds had complex vowel sounds with an initial /y/-like glide. In certain contexts this glide was lost, and the modern simple vowel sounds emerged. In the seventeenth century the words *sugar* and *sure,* which then would still have been pronounced with the /y/-glide, appear to have palatalized rather than simply shedding the glide. Thus we have the modern palatalized /sh/ pronunciations (Jespersen [1909] 1954, 1:368). The cases in which *sur* palatalized to /shùr/ and /shər/ probably did so via conservative analogy.

A similar palatalization occurs in one pronunciation of *luxury.*

30.2.3.3   /sh/ = *ss*

The pattern for this spelling is as it was regularly for /sh/ = *s* and /sh/ = *t:* the *ss* occurs at the end of the stem and is followed by an unstressed *i* followed by another unstressed vowel. Instances:

(Array 30-8)

accession	congressional	fission	percussion
commission	digression	intermission	session
confession	expression	passion	succession

The following instances of /sh/ = *ss* are related to the *sur* group mentioned in the preceding section: *assurance, fissure, pressure, issue, tissue.*

30.2.3.4   /sh/ = *sc*

In a few Latin adoptions (usually with the base *sci +*) *sc* palatalizes, again before an unstressed *i* followed by another unstressed vowel:

(Array 30-9)

conscience	luscious	prescient
conscientious	omniscience	unconscious

The correspondence /sh/ = *sc* also occurs in the Italian adoptions *fascist, cognoscenti,* and *crescendo**. These, however, are adopted simple spellings rather than palatalizations of the type discussed earlier in this section.

30.2.3.5 /sh/ = *c*

Instances:

(Array 30-10)

ancient	coercion	glacier	specialty
appreciate	commercial	judiciary	species
associate	efficacious	liquefacient	specious
beneficiary	financial*	provincial*	suspicion

W3 has *c* = /ch/ for the two asterisked words in this array.

The palatalized correspondence /sh/ = *c* also occurs in *ocean* and in words with the suffixes *-acean* and *-aceous,* such as *crustacean* and *curvaceous.* In these instances the basic pattern for palatalization is satisfied by the presence of an *e*, rather than an *i*, after the *c*.

30.3   The Spellings of /ch/

The sound /ch/ has two simple major spellings: *ch* and the quasi-doublet *tch*. It has three simple minor spellings: two from Italian words, *c* and *cc;* one from German, *tsch*. And it has one important palatalized spelling—*t*—plus two others, *s* and *c*, after *n*, according to *W3*.

30.3.1   The Minor Simple Spellings of /ch/

In Italian, *c* followed by *e* or *i* is pronounced /ch/, which leads to the few cases of /ch/ = *c* in English: *cello, cicerone, vermicelli,* and *concerto.* (Compare *concert*, which was adopted from French rather than from Italian.) Closely related to the four instances of /ch/ = *c* is the Italian adoption *capriccio,* in which /ch/ = *cc*.

The minor correspondence /ch/ = *tsch* occurs in the German adoptions *kitsch* and *putsch,* and in the technical terms *tscheffkinite* and *tschermigite,* both also from German.

30.3.2   The Major Simple Spellings of /ch/: *ch* and *tch*

Two-thirds of the time /ch/ is spelled either *ch* or *tch*, with *ch* being the more common of the two by a ratio of 5:1 (Hanna et al. 1966, 738). The

Romans used the digraph *ch,* but only to transliterate Greek words containing the letter chi. Throughout the Middle Ages *ch* was used in various languages on the Continent and expressed different phonetic values. In Old English it was not used—or, at most, was used very rarely—the sound /ch/ being in Old English spelled *c* or *cc.* Thus, for instance, *ditch* comes from Old English *dīc, fetch* from Old English *feccan, choose* from *cēosan.* The Norman scribes, however, introduced *ch* into English to spell both French adoptions with *ch* and to respell native words with *c.* During the early Middle English period, in words that had been spelled *cc* in Old English or that had a short vowel before the /ch/, *cch* was used as a double *ch.* But in time *tch* became the standard doublet spelling (Jespersen [1909] 1954, 1:52–55, 346–47; *OED* at *Ch-*). This Middle English usage underlies the contemporary distinction between *ch* and *tch,* which can be sorted out using essentially the same set of ordered rules used earlier to distinguish between single and double consonant spellings, although the contrast between *ch* and *tch* is blurred here and there:

1. Word-final /ch/ after a stressed short vowel is regularly spelled *tch,* though there are a few instances of *ch.*
2. /ch/ = *ch* at all other simple boundaries.
3. /ch/ = *ch* in VCV strings shortened by a shortening rule.
4. /ch/ = *ch* within consonant clusters.
5. /ch/ = *ch* after vowel digraphs.
6. /ch/ = *tch* between a stressed short vowel and a following vowel.
7. /ch/ = *ch* after reduced vowels.

30.3.2.1 /ch/ = *tch* Regularly in Word-final Position

The correspondence /ch/ = *tch* regularly holds in word-final position after a short vowel spelled with a unigraph:

(Array 30-11)

batch	dispatch	hutch	scratch
blotch	etch	itch	thatch
clutch	fetch	notch	watch
crotch	hitch	pitch	wretch

There are, however, some instances of /ch/ = *ch* in this position. For instance, words with the bound base +*tach,* such as *attach* and *detach,* are spelled in accordance with their Old French source words, and pretty much always have been. Other holdouts, derived from Old English words, have more complex histories: *much* (Old English *mycel, micel*), *rich* (Old English *rice*), and *such* (Old English *swelc, swilc, swylc*) all were spelled with *c* or *cc* in early Middle English, but normally with *ch* after the Norman Conquest. In the sixteenth and seventeenth centuries, during the spate of interest in spelling reform, attempts were made to spell each of these words with *tch,* in line with the patterns described above. But in each case the less regular, but traditional, *ch* spelling prevailed. *Which* (Old English *hwelc, hwilc, hwylc*) underwent the same development from *c* in early Middle English to *ch* in Middle English, though, especially in the north, it was often spelled with a *k.* The *OED* does not record a *tch* spelling for *which* in the sixteenth and seventeenth centuries, perhaps because of a conflict with *witch,* which during the sixteenth century was sometimes spelled *whitch.*

30.3.2.2   /ch/ = *ch* at Other Simple Boundaries

This correspondence is common in initial and terminal position in free bases, but less so in bound bases:

(Array 30-12)

achieve	chortle	gulch	merchant
archer	church	henchman	mischief
challenge	drench	interchange	purchase
cheese	duchess	kerchief	surcharge
cherish	enchant	larch	treachery
chief	escheat	lecher	trenchant

There are a few holdouts to this pattern. The correspondence /ch/ = *tch* occurs at the simple boundaries of what are today bound bases in *crotchet, hatchet,* and *satchel.* All three are old diminutives. *Crotch+* is a coform of the obsolete *croche* 'a hook'. *Hatch+* derives from the now-obsolete *hatch.* And *satch+* is a coform of *sack.*

The correspondence /ch/ = *tch* occurs in initial position only in three Russian adoptions: *tchaviche, tchetvert,* and *tchervonets,* the last two of which have more regular variant spellings with *ch.*

30.3.2.3   /ch/ = *ch* in Shortened VCV Strings

Actually, the only clear-cut instance of /ch/ = *ch* in a VCV string shortened by a shortening rule is *bachelor.* The palatalized correspondence /ch/ = *t,* however, is quite common in such a setting, see 30.3.3.

30.3.2.4   /ch/ = *ch* in Consonant Clusters and Concatenations

Instances:

(Array 30-13)

anchovy	filch	mulch	porch
belch	hunchback	orchard	puncheon
birch	launch	parchment	starch
blanch	lynch	poncho	torchlight

Avalanche has *ch* in a word-final cluster with a fossil final *e*. Because word-final *tch* is common, it occurs in several concatenations, such as *pitchstone, scratchproof, watchful.*

30.3.2.5 /ch/ = *ch* after Vowel Digraphs

All known instances are in final position:

(Array 30-14)

avouch	beseech	debauch	leech
beach	coach	grouch	treachery

Except for these cases, in which the vowel is spelled with a digraph, there are no known instances of /ch/ spelled either *ch* or *tch* after a long vowel.

30.3.2.6 /ch/ = *tch* in VCC Strings

Since /ch/ tends in general to be rare in medial position, this rule is not too extensive. Known instances include the following:

(Array 30-15)

butcher	hatchel	ratchet
escutcheon	kitchen	satchel

30.3.2.7 /ch/ = *ch* after Reduced Vowels

Though rather rare in this position, the correspondence /ch/ = *ch* holds after a schwa or unstressed /i/:

(Array 30-16)

artichoke	ostrich	spinach
machete*	sandwich	

30.3.3 The Palatalized Spelling of /ch/: *t*

The most common setting for /ch/ = *t* is parallel to that for /sh/ = *t*: when *t* is followed by an unstressed *u* followed by another usually unstressed vowel, the *u* tends to simplify into a /y/-like glide that merges with the /t/ sound, pulling the point of articulation back in the mouth and giving the sound a palatal sibilant quality. The result is the palatalized correspondence /ch/ = *t*:

(Array 30-17)

accentuate	habitual	situate	tortuous
actual	impetuosity	spirituous	tumultuary
constituency	mortuary	statuesque	unctuous
contemptuous	mutual	sumptuary	virtual
estuary	obituary	tempestuous	virtuosity

Section 30.2.3.1 illustrates how *t* followed by *-ion* regularly palatalizes to /sh/. One complication to this highly regular and reliable pattern is that when the *t* is in an *st* cluster, the *t* palatalizes not to /sh/ but to /ch/. Since /ch/ can be analyzed to the complex sound /tsh/, in this palatalization to /ch/, rather than being replaced by the palatal /sh/, the simple /t/ sound remains and the /sh/ is added on:

(Array 30-18)

bastion	congestion	exhaustion	question
combustion	digestion	ingestion	suggestion

The same correspondence holds, though more rarely, before other instances of *st* followed by unstressed *i* followed by another unstressed vowel: *celestial, fustian, bestial.*

A second complication involves the starred words in 30.2.3.1, 30.2.3.2, and 30.2.3.5, in which *W3* transcribes cases of *t, s,* and *c* before *n*—shown as /sh/ in Kenyon and Knott—as instances of /ch/.

In 30.2.3.2 we saw how *s* followed by *ur* sometimes palatalizes to /sh/. A parallel palatalization occurs with *tur,* especially when it is lightly stressed, as in *feature.* Again, this palatalization, which apparently arose in the eighteenth century, depended upon the earlier existence of a /y/-glide before the /u/ sound that in time merged with the *t:*

(Array 30-19)

adventure	century	fixture	suture
aperture	conjecture	miniature	tincture
armature	creature	moisture	torture
capture	discomfiture	portraiture	vulture

The palatalized correspondence /ch/ = *t* also occurs, though more rarely, before *ul* and *un:*

(Array 30-20)

botulism	congratulatory	fortune	spatula
capitulate	expostulate	importunate	tarantula
congratulate	flatulent	petulant	titular

Posthumous, amateur, and *righteous* contain unusual cases of /ch/ = *t.* In *posthumous,* since the *h* is not pronounced (see 28.4.5), the palatalization occurs in a way parallel to that illustrated in arrays 30-19 and 30-20 (see 26.5.2 for more on *posthumous*). *Amateur* has a variant pronunciation with /ch/, in a palatalization similar to that illustrated in array 30-19. The palatalization in *righteous* is a type that was much more common in the eighteenth century, when it occurred also in words like *courteous, piteous,* and *plenteous.* Apparently the return to the nonpalatalized pronunciations that are now standard was due to the influence of the spelling and increased literacy.

30.4 The Spellings of /j/

30.4.1 Historical Sources

In Old English, /j/ was spelled *cg* and *g:* for instance, *ridge* derives from Old English *hrycg; singe* from *sencgan*. In Old French, /j/ was spelled *j*, especially in initial position, and *g*, before the front vowel sounds spelled by the letters *e, i,* and *y.* In Middle English the doublet *gg* was often used to spell /j/ after a stressed short vowel, but that spelling was ambiguous, as it is today: notice the three different pronunciations of *gg* in *exaggerate, suggest,* and *beggar.* By the fifteenth century, perhaps due to Caxton's influence, *dg* had become the regular quasi-doublet for *j.* The doublet *jj* does not occur in English.

In Middle and Early Modern English, *i* and *j* were two different forms of the same letter, each having both a consonant and a vowel value. The form *j* tended to be used in initial and final position, *i* in medial. The modern distinction between the two—*i* as vowel, *j* as consonant—began to be asserted in the sixteenth century and had become fairly standard by the end of the seventeenth, although Samuel Johnson, like other lexicographers, intermixed words starting with the two letters into a single listing in his dictionary of the late eighteenth century ([1775] 1983). This old functional identity of *i* and *j* is reflected in the spelling and pronunciation of the variants *hallelujah, halleluia,* in which the *j* has the old vowel value (see 11.2.1.1 above; see also Jespersen [1909] 1954, 1:50–52, 347–49; Dobson 1957, 2:959–60; *OED* at *J*).

The upshot of this is that today we have three major spellings of /j/: from Old English *g* and *dg,* and from French and Latin *j* and *g* again, before *e, i,* and *y.* The Romance convention that /j/ = *g* only before *e, i,* and *y* has been extended by analogical respelling to some words from Old English. For instance, from Old English *sencgan* we have *singe,* with a final *e* added. On the other hand, there are still some Old English derivatives with *g* = /g/ before *e* and *i*: *give, girl,* and *get,* for instance.

There is some overlap between the occurrences of *g* and *j* in spelling /j/, as exemplified by such variant spellings as *gibe, jibe; jennet, genet; sergeant, serjeant; gill, jill; jinni, genie,* and even *djinni!* The overlap is exemplified, too, by such related heterographs as *jelly* and *gelatine, jell* and *gel;* and by such unrelated homophones as *gene* and *jean, Jim* and *gym.*

In the following discussion we will look first at the two minor simple spellings, *dj* and *gg.* We will then discuss the three major simple spellings, distinguishing the occurrence of *g* from the quasi-doublet *dg* and then illustrating the regular distribution of /j/ = *j*. Finally, we will describe the occurrences of the palatalized correspondence /j/ = *d*.

30.4.2 The Minor Simple Spellings of /j/: *dj* and *gg*

The correspondence /j/ = *dj* due to simple addition occurs in the following complexes:

(Array 30-21)

adjacent	adjourn	adjunct	adjutage, ajutage
adjective	adjudge	adjure	adjutant
adjoin	adjudicate	adjust	adjuvant

The correspondence /j/ = *dj* also occurs in the recent adoptions *adjag* (from Javanese) and *adjab* (an African word).

The correspondence /j/ = *gg* apparently occurs only in *agger, exaggerate,* and one pronunciation of *suggilation*.

30.4.3 The Major Simple Spellings of /j/

The three major simple spellings of /j/—*g*, *dg*, and *j*—account for about 98 percent of all instances of /j/ (Hanna et al. 1966, 792–93). The spellings *g* and *dg* can be fairly well distinguished using essentially the same set of ordered rules that has been applied to other single and double consonant spellings:

1. Word-final /j/ after a stressed short vowel spelled with a unigraph is regularly spelled *dg*—that is, *dge*.
2. /j/ = *g* at all other simple boundaries.
3. /j/ = *g* in VCV strings shortened by a shortening rule.
4. /j/ = *g* within consonant clusters.
5. /j/ = *g* after vowel digraphs.
6. /j/ = *g* after long vowels.
7. /j/ = *dg* between a stressed short vowel and a following vowel.
8. /j/ = *g* after reduced vowels.

30.4.3.1   /j/ = *dg* in Word-final Position

The correspondence /j/ = *dg* is regular in word-final position after a stressed short vowel spelled with a unigraph:

(Array 30-22)

abridge	dodge	grudge	pledge
badge	dredge	lodge	smudge
cadge	fudge	midge	wedge

The only known holdout to this pattern is *allege.*

30.4.3.2   /j/ = g at Other Simple Boundaries

Instances:

(Array 30-23)

apogee	fragile	gyroscope	photogenic
cogitate	genuine	image	plunge
congeal	giblet	longitude	primogeniture
digestion	gypsum	monogynous	suggest

A small but important set of holdouts to this pattern includes words with word-final *dge* after a reduced vowel: *knowledge, partridge, porridge, cartridge.*

30.4.3.3   /j/ = g in Shortened VCV Strings

There are many instances of /j/ = g in VCV strings shortened by the Third Syllable Rule, the Stress Frontshift Rule, or one of the suffix rules, although in many cases the /g/ is at a simple boundary and thus is covered also by the Simple Boundary Rule:

(Array 30-24)

aborigine	legend	pageant	register
agitate	legerdemain	pigeon	religion
belligerent	legislate	prestidigitation	rigid
exigency	logic	prodigious	tragedy
flagellate	magic	regimen	vegetarian
illegible	menagerie	regiment	vigil

30.4.3.4   /j/ = g in Consonant Clusters and Concatenations

The correspondence /j/ = g is particularly common in the clusters *lg, ng,* and *rg,* although again in many instances the /g/ is already covered by the Simple Boundary Rule:

(Array 30-25)

algebra	dingy	forge	orgy
allergy	divulge	ginger	suggest
angelica	dungeon	manger	ungenerous
clergy	engine	nostalgia	virgin

The correspondence /j/ = g also holds in the clusters in *margarine* and *algae,* even though it is not in either case immediately followed by *e, i,* or *y. Margarine* is related to *margaric,* an example of the regular g = /g/ correspondence. Why assibilation has occurred in the pronunciation of *margarine* is not clear. In *algae* the *ae* spells a front vowel sound, as *e, i,* and *y* normally do.

30.4.3.5 /j/ = g after Vowel Digraphs

Instances:

(Array 30-26)

augelite	besiege	liege
augend	gauge	scrouge, scrooge
augite	gouge	squeegee

30.4.3.6 /j/ = g after Long Vowels

Instances:

(Array 30-27)

agency	doge	hygiene	plagiarism
allegiance	egregious	oblige	pugilist
assuage	fugitive	ogive	refuge

30.4.3.7 /j/ = dg in VCC Strings

Since *dg* developed in Middle English as the spelling for double soft *g,* it is not surprising that it occurs in native VCC strings:

(Array 30-28)

bludgeon	cudgel	fidget	ledger
budget	curmudgeon	gadget	stodgy

30.4.3.8 /j/ = g after Reduced Vowels

The correspondence /j/ = g is very common after reduced vowels, although often the /j/ occurs at an element boundary and is thus already covered by the Simple Boundary Rule:

(Array 30-29)

agenda	eligible	image	origin
agility	hegemony	integer	panegyric
dowager	illegitimate	magenta	syllogism

Many, many instances of this pattern occur in words with the suffix *-age,* as in *voyage* and *carriage.* Important holdouts are words like *knowledge* and *porridge,* which are also listed as holdouts to the Simple Boundary Rule in 30.4.3.2.

30.4.3.9 The Correspondence /j/ = j

The major simple spelling *j* occurs nearly always in initial position, very rarely in medial, and, except for the recent and relatively unintegrated adoption *raj,* never in word-final position. It occurs in element-final position in *major* and *majesty.* With the exception of *banjo,* it does not occur in consonant clusters. In contrast with /j/ = *g*, the correspondence /j/ = *j* regularly occurs before *a, o,* and *u,* and it also occurs before *e* and *i.* Apparently it occurs before *y* only in *jynx* and its derivative *jyngine, jynx* being a kind of woodpecker and the probable source of the word *jinx.*

/j/ = j in Initial Position.   Instances:

(Array 30-30)

abjure	disjointed	jackal	jubilant
ajar	ejaculate	jealous	rejoice
conjecture	enjoy	jiggle	rejuvenate
conjugal	injunction	jockey	sojourn

/j/ = j in Medial Position.   The very rare instances of this correspondence include the following:

(Array 30-31)

banjo	cajole	pajama	raja
cajeput	maharaja	pejorative	

30.4.4   The Palatalized Correspondence /j/ = *d*

The palatalized spelling *d* occurs in settings that usually parallel the settings for the more common palatalized spellings of /sh/ and /ch/. Most often the *d* is followed by an unstressed *u* that is in turn followed by another vowel, as in *arduous,* or by a consonant (usually *l* or *r*), as in *glandular* and *verdure.* In *educate* the following consonant is a *c.* In *cordial, grandeur,* and *soldier* there is no *u* after the *d.* Other instances:

(Array 30-32)

assiduous	graduate	pendulum	schedule
deciduous	incredulous	procedure	sedulous
fraudulent	individual	residual	undulate
gradual	modulate	residuum	

30.5   The Spellings of /zh/

30.5.1   Historical Sources

The /zh/ sound is in many ways more typical of French than of English. It did not exist in Old or Middle English as a separate, recognized sound, though of course the very similar /j/ sound did. (Some linguistic analyses treat the /j/ sound as an affricate analyzable to /d/ plus /zh/.) The first known recognition of /zh/ in English was in 1688 in Miege's *Great French Dictionary* (Jespersen [1909] 1954, 1:345). In Modern English there is a tendency for /zh/ to vary to /j/, so that variants in /zh/ and /j/ are quite common, probably more so than dictionaries indicate. There are also contrasts between /zh/ and /j/ in closely related pairs such as *negligee* with /zh/ and *negligent* with /j/.

In modern English /zh/ has a pair of simple spellings, *g* and *j*, both of which are found in French adoptions, and a more important pair of palatalized spellings, *s* and *z*, which reflect the development of Early Modern English /zi/ to /z/ plus /y/-glide, and the subsequent merging and palatalization.

30.5.2   The Simple Spellings of /zh/
30.5.2.1   /zh/ = *g*

The correspondence /zh/ = *g* occurs in relatively unintegrated French adoptions:

(Array 30-33)

barrage	garage	menage	regime
beige	gendarme	mirage	rouge
camouflage	genre	montage	sabotage
cortege	gigue	persiflage	
fuselage	massage	prestige	

Prestige, garage, and *camouflage* have variant pronunciations with /j/.

30.5.2.2   /zh/ = *j*

The *j* spelling of /zh/ is less common than the *g,* and it is also restricted to fairly recent French adoptions: *acajou, carcajou, bijou. Julienne* and *jongleur* have variants with /j/. The correspondence /zh/ = *j* also occurs in a few unintegrated French phrases, such as *joie de vivre* and *au jus.*

30.5.3   The Palatalized Spellings of /zh/: *s, z,* and *t*

The settings for the fairly common palatalized correspondence /zh/ = *s* are similar to the settings for /sh/, /ch/, and /j/:

(Array 30-34)

anesthesia	elysium	hosier	seclusion
aphasia	embrasure	leisure	transfusion
casual	enclosure	lesion	usual
cohesion	erosion	measure	usury
collision	excursion	persuasion	visual

The palatalized correspondence /zh/ = *z* occurs in *seizure, azure, glazier, brazier.*

Though *t* before *ion* regularly palatalizes to /sh/, as in *nation,* the nonregular correspondence /zh/ = *t* occurs in *equation.*

31 The Nasals: /m/, /n/, and /ŋ/

31.1 Introduction

The three nasal sounds have in common the fact that they are all pronounced using the nasal cavity as part of the resonating chamber. That feature sets them off from all other speech sounds, which are nonnasal, or oral. The three nasals differ among themselves in that they are pronounced by closing off the mouth in different positions. The /m/ is formed when closure occurs at the lips, as in the case of the bilabial oral sounds /p/, /b/, and /w/. The /n/ is formed when closure takes place farther back in the mouth, behind the dental ridge, as it does for /t/ and /d/. The /ŋ/ is formed when closure occurs well back in the mouth, at the velum, as it does for /k/ and /g/. These facts, as we will see, are important to the spelling of /m/ and /ŋ/.

31.2 The Spellings of /m/

The spellings of /m/ fall into two familiar groups. First, there are a small number of minor spellings, the most important of which are *mb, lm, mn,* and *gm.* Second, there are the two major spellings: the single *m* and the doublet *mm.*

31.2.1 The Minor Spellings of /m/

The minor correspondences tend to be of two types: fossils, which reflect spellings of older pronunciations, and miscellaneous odd spellings.

31.2.1.1 /m/ = *mb*

The most important of the fossil correspondences is /m/ = *mb,* which always occurs in word-final position. Most of the instances of this correspondence derive from Old English or Romance words that also contained *mb,* which was originally pronounced /mb/:

(Array 31-1)

aplomb	comb	jamb	rhomb*
bomb	comber	lamb	succumb
catacombs	coxcomb	lambkin	tomb
climb	dumb	plumb	womb

Over the centuries the /b/ following the /m/ in word-final position was gradually dropped (Jespersen [1909] 1954, 1:216–17; Dobson 1957, 2:960). Since both /m/ and /b/ are bilabials, it is easy for the second sound in the cluster to be lost if there is no vowel sound after it to force the syllable break. The /b/ is still heard in derivatives like *bombardier, rhomboid,* and the somewhat more remote *plumbago* and *plumbism.*

There is some evidence that in earlier centuries the /b/ continued to be heard in inflected forms such as *climbing* and *bomber* even after it had fallen silent in the uninflected stem forms, but today the /b/ is not pronounced in inflected or in most derived forms—probably owing to conservative analogy. This fact leads to some unusual homographs. For instance, something that is not rigid or stiff is *limber* (with /b/), but a person who removes limbs from trees is a *limber* (without /b/). And 7 is a *number* (with /b/), but if something grows more numb, it gets *number* (without /b/).

In a few words the *b* as well as the /b/ has disappeared. An old example is *oakum,* from Old English *ācumba.* More recent are *dummy* from *dumb,* and *plummet* from *plumb.*

As might be expected, given the confusion surrounding the *b* and /b/ in such words in earlier centuries, people began to put *b*'s into words where they were not justified etymologically. Some instances: *limb* (from Old English *lim*), *numb* (from Old English *niman*), *thumb* (from Old English *thūma*), and *crumb* (from Old English *cruma*). *Crumb* then lost the *b* again in the derivative *crummy,* which is probably best explicated to (crumm + y), with *crumm+* being treated as a nonterminative coform of *crumb.*

In new adoptions and more technical words containing the cluster *mb,* the /b/ tends to be pronounced. For instance, dictionaries show a /b/ in the pronunciation of *iamb,* a fairly rare and technical word, but among people who use it quite often, the /b/ is usually lost.

31.2.1.2   /m/ = *lm*

The correspondence /m/ = *lm* also is a fossil, since the *lm* spelling reflects a simplified pronunciation (Jespersen [1909] 1954, 1:297–98; Dobson 1957, 2:989). In all of the following words, the /l/ was heard in earlier centuries:

(Array 31-2)

almond	calm	palm	qualm
alms	holm	psalm	

The correspondence /m/ = *lm* also occurs in *balm* and *salmon,* but we are less sure that the /l/ was ever pronounced in them. *Balm* was *basme, bame* in Middle English, coming from Old French *basme,* which in turn derives from Latin *balsamum,* also the source of *balsam.* The *l* began to appear in English spellings in the fifteenth century, and it is not clear whether it reflected an actual pronunciation or was simply another instance of the Early Modern period's enthusiasm for Latinate respellings (Dobson 1957, 2:990, n. 5). *Salmon* derives from Anglo-French *saumon, salmun,* and was spelled both with and without the *l* in English from the time of its adoption, in the fourteenth century. The Latin source is *salmō.* It seems likely that the /l/ was heard in Middle English pronunciation, at least in some areas of England.

31.2.1.3   /m/ = *mn*

The correspondence /m/ = *mn* occurs in the following words (see Jespersen [1909] 1954, 1:215–16; Dobson 1957, 2:960–61):

(Array 31-3)

autumn	condemn	damn	limn
column	contemn	hymn	solemn

In these words the *n* was earlier pronounced, as it still is when a derivational suffix with an initial vowel is added, as in *condemnation, damnable, hymnal, autumnal, columnar, solemnity.* The *n* is not pronounced, however, when an inflectional suffix is added, as in *condemned* and *damning*—again probably because of conservative analogy.

Actually an even greater simplification has occurred in the spelling of many of these words. Several of them had variant Middle English spellings with the cluster *mpn.* For instance, *contemn* was often spelled *contempnen* in Middle English, reflecting the Old French *contempner.* (Old French also had the spelling *contemner.*) The now-missing *p* remains in the related word *contempt.* Thus, in the development from early Middle to American English there has been a simplification, from a cluster of three letters and sounds to only two letters and a single sound. The same pattern holds for *condemn, damn, hymn, autumn, column,* and *solemn.*

31.2.1.4   /m/ = *gm*

This correspondence occurs in just a few words:

(Array 31-4)

apothegm*	paradigm	syntagm
diaphragm	phlegm	

All of these words represent Latin spellings. The *g* is pronounced in English when a derivational suffix that starts with a vowel is added, as in *phlegmatic* and *paradigmatic* (Jespersen [1909] 1954, 1:231).

31.2.1.5   Other Minor Spellings of /m/

There are some recognized variant pronunciations of words in which the correspondence /m/ = *mp* holds—for instance, *symptom* and *pumpkin,* both of which involve complex clusters that are being simplified (Dobson 1957, 2:967–68). Though dictionaries do not record these variants, we can feel the *p* evading pronunciation in words with complex clusters—for instance, *contemptible, redemption,* and *sumptuous.*

In *drachm* and *disme,* pronounced /dram/ and /dīm/, /m/ is spelled *chm* and *sm.* The first comes from the Latin *drachma;* the second is related to *dime* and comes from Latin *decima,* by way of French *disme, dime.*

Mhorr and *mho* contain the only known instances of /m/ = *mh. Mhorr* (usually *mohr*) is a recent Arabic adoption. *Mho* is a recent formation, simply *ohm* spelled backward. (*Ohm* and *mho* raise an interesting analytical wrinkle: in *ohm* the /ō/ is spelled *oh,* making *h* a vowel letter; but in *mho* it seems better to say that /m/ = *mh,* in which case *h* is a consonant letter. Fortunately there is not much of this sort of thing going on in the American English spelling system.)

One variant pronunciation of *tmesis* contains the correspondence /m/ = *tm,* but more often the pronunciation is /tm/ rather than /m/.

31.2.2   The Major Spellings of /m/

In Hanna et al., /m/ is spelled *m* about 94 percent of the time, and *mm* about 4 percent of the time. Thus these two major spellings account for all but 2 percent of the instances of /m/ (1966, 878, 879). The *m* and *mm* spellings can be sorted out quite handily via the now-familiar list of selection rules presented in 26.2.3.1.

31.2.2.1   /m/ = *m* at Simple Boundaries

Instances:

(Array 31-5)

admire	geometry	locomotive	mucous
demand	glum	mackerel	myriad
demonstrate	gym	measure	omission
dismay	intermittent	mighty	prim
emasculate	jam	mom	promiscuous
gem	kleptomania	monument	remains

Five holdouts to this otherwise very powerful pattern are the non-terminative bound bases *flamm +*, *gramm +*, *mamm +*, *plumm +*, and *summ +*. Four of the five are members of cosets containing terminative forms without the *mm*: *flamm +*, as in *flammable*, is a coform of *flame;* *gramm +*, as in *grammar*, is a coform of *gram; plumm +*, as in *plummet*, is a coform of *plumb;* and *summ +*, as in *summary*, is a coform of *sum*. These are clearly instances of the limited tendency for cosets to contain a nonterminative form with a final consonant doublet and a terminative form with a final single consonant (see 2.2.7 and 9.4.1). The nonterminative *mamm +* does not appear to have any coforms that would place it with the other four holdouts, although it is remotely connate with *mom* and *mama*.

31.2.2.2 /m/ = *m* in Shortened VCV Strings

Words in which the correspondence /m/ = *m* occurs in VCV strings shortened by the Third Syllable Rule:

(Array 31-6)

abdominal	cemetery	family	phenomenon
amatory	comatose	hegemony	pomegranate
amazon	democrat	memory	scimitar
amethyst	dominant	mimeograph	seminar
bicameral	dromedary	nemesis	stamina
cameo	emerald	nominate	stimulate
camouflage	facsimile	omelet	timorous

Instances involving the Stress Frontshift Rule:

(Array 31-7)

camel	enamel	lemon	tumult
damage	homage	tremor	

Instances due to the suffix rules:

(Array 31-8)

academic	calamity	limit	vomit
amity	dynamic	patronymic	
anatomical	endemic	polemic	
blemish	extremity	timid	

31.2.2.3 /m/ = *m* in Consonant Clusters and Concatenations

The correspondence /m/ = *m* enters into an immense number of consonant clusters—initial, medial, and final. The following is just a sampling:

(Array 31-9)

acme	drachma	lamprey	rhythm
atmosphere	embryo	member	sigma
badminton	glimpse	nimble	small
cashmere	gremlin	omnivorous	triumph
chasm	hamster	pimple	umpire
crimson	impromptu	pygmy	Xmas

31.2.2.4 /m/ = m after Vowel Digraphs and Long Vowels

There are no known instances of m following a vowel digraph that spells any sound other than a long vowel. Instances of /m/ = m after long vowels:

(Array 31-10)

accumulate	bituminous	enumerate	omen
aim	bromide	heirloom	ptomaine
aluminum	climate	luminous	romaine
amiable	coma	nomadic	steam
binomial	demon	numerical	toxemia

31.2.2.5 /m/ = mm at Complex Boundaries

The correspondence /m/ = mm holds at boundaries affected by duplicative addition, twinning, and assimilation. Duplicative addition most often involves the prefix com-, as in:

(Array 31-11)

command	commerce	commodity	communism
commensurate	commission	communal	noncommittal

Cases in which compounding produces /m/ = mm are quite rare, and in careful speech such words are often pronounced with /mm/ rather than /m/: *roommate, teammate, ohmmeter.*

Twinning produces many instances of /m/ = mm. Some examples:

(Array 31-12)

clammy	dimmest	humming	slimmer
dammed	drummer	rummy	stemmed

The correspondence /m/ = mm also occurs when the prefix in- assimilates to im-, or syn- assimilates to sym-, before stems starting with m:

(Array 31-13)

immaculate	immediate	imminent	immure
immanent	immense	immolate	symmetalism*
immature	immerse	immortal	symmetrical
immeasurable	immigrant	immune	symmetry

31.2.2.6 /m/ = *mm* in VCC Strings

This correspondence is particularly common in words from Old English. Instances, from both Old English and the Romance languages:

(Array 31-14)

ammunition	gimmick	hummock	plummet
backgammon	glimmer	mammon	pommel
comma	grommet	mammoth	simmer
dilemma	hammer	mummy	stammer
dummy	hammock	persimmon	summer

There are several holdouts to this pattern. *Gamut* is a contraction of the Latin phrase *gamma ut,* so it comes by its /a/ honestly. But why it has *m* instead of *mm* (like, say, *gamma*) is not clear. Up through the eighteenth century, variant spellings with *mm* did occur, but now *m* is standard. *Glamor* is a Scots words, actually a variant of *grammar,* introduced into English late, in the eighteenth and nineteenth centuries, and affected in sound, though not in spelling, by its source word, *grammar. Tomahawk* is from Virginian Algonquian *tomahaac* or *tamohake.* The short vowel in front of the *m* could be due to the general tendency to shorten stressed vowels that come early in polysyllables (see 7.1.1). Or there could be some folk etymology and conservative analogy at work via *Tom.*

31.2.2.7 /m/ = *m* after Reduced Vowels

Instances:

(Array 31-15)

adamantine	comedian	imagine	temerity
alimentary	diminish	kimono	testimony
cement	element	legerdemain	timidity
chameleon	familiar	pimento	vehement

Two holdouts to this pattern are *ammonia* and *mammalian. Ammonia* derives from the Greek *Ammon,* a location in Turkey. *Mammalian* contains *mammal,* and via conservative analogy retains the *mm* even after the stress shift reduces the /a/ of *mammal* to the schwa of *mammalian.*

31.3 The Spellings of /n/

The spellings of /n/ divide, as usual, into minor and major correspondences. The minor spellings—*kn, gn, pn,* and *mn*—account for about 1 percent of the instances of /n/. The major correspondences —*n* and *nn*—account for the other 99 percent, with *n* being more common than *nn* by a ratio of about 50:1. (See Hanna et al. 1966, 915.)

31.3.1   The Minor Spellings of /n/
31.3.1.1   /n/ = kn

This correspondence occurs in a small number of Germanic words, always in word-initial position:

(Array 31-16)

knack	kneel	knight	knoll
knapsack	knell	knit	knot
knave	knew	knives	know
knead	knickerbocker	knob	knuckle
knee	knife	knock	knurl

Originally the *k* was pronounced in these words, but in the seventeenth century the sound /k/ before /n/ began to drop out of standard English pronunciation.

31.3.1.2   /n/ = gn

This correspondence occurs in two positions: word-initial, as in *gnash;* and word-final, as in *sign*. Most of the cases of initial *gn*, like *kn*, come from the Germanic side of the English language family, and in them the /g/ sound, like /k/, dropped out before /n/ during the seventeenth century:

(Array 31-17)

gnar	gnash	gnaw	gnome
gnarl	gnat	gneiss	

A few instances of initial /n/ = *gn* come from Greek: *gnomon, gnosis, gnostic*. This Greek *gn* is related to the Germanic *kn* by a common ancestor in Proto-Indo-European. That common ancestry underlies the semantic similarity between, say, *know* and *gnosis,* each of which contains the sense of "knowledge, learning" (Jespersen [1909] 1954, 1:352; Dobson 1957, 2:977–79).

Most instances of /n/ = *gn* in final position come from French adoptions in which the *gn* spelled (in French) a palatalized /n/ sound, like the /ny/ in *canyon* and *onion*. Often the *gn* spelling was borrowed from French, but with a more integrated /n/ pronunciation. Sometimes the French spelling was changed to *n,* and then changed back, in order to parallel either the French source or, more likely, the Latin one (Jespersen [1909] 1954, 1:24, 30–31; Dobson 1957, 2:897). Today, if the vowel preceding this word-final *gn* is stressed, it is pronounced long. Instances are:

(Array 31-18)

align	condign	ensign	reign
assign	deign	impugn	repugn
benign	design	malign	sign

Oppugn comes directly from Latin rather than through French. A few words had *gn* in French but not in Latin, for the Latin spelling was usually with a simple *n: campaign, champaign, poignant,* the last of which has a variant pronunciation with a /y/-glide after the /n/. The recent, and unintegrated, adoptions *champagne* and *cologne* still retain their final *e*'s from French.

In a few cases *g* was added to words that had been spelled without *g* in both French and Latin:

(Array 31-19)

arraign	from OFr *araisner,* from L *adrationāre*
feign	from OFr *faindre, feindre,* from L *fingere*
foreign	from OFr *forein, forain,* from L *forānus*
sovereign	from OFr *souverein,* from L *superānus*

The unetymological *g*'s in *foreign* and *sovereign* seem pretty clearly to have come about via analogy with *reign.*

The correspondence /n/ = *gn* also occurs in the rare *coign,* which is really just an earlier spelling of *coin* that is used in very specialized senses.

31.3.1.3   /n/ = *pn*

This correspondence occurs only in the two closely related nonterminative bases *pneum +* [1] 'wind, air', from Greek *pneûma,* and *pneum +* [2] 'lung', ultimately from Greek *pleúmōn.* As close in meaning as the two are, and because they have become identical in form, we can treat them as a single element, a convergence of two source words. The convergence actually began back in Greek as the original transliterated *pl* was changed to *pn.* Some instances: *pneumatic, pneumonia, pneumococcus, pneuma.*

Although it is likely that the *p* in these words has probably never been widely pronounced, the *OED,* in one of its rare overt forays into linguistic reform, has spoken out in favor of a /pn/ pronunciation:

> The *p* is pronounced in French, Spanish, Italian, German, Dutch, and other European languages; also by Englishmen in reading Greek. It is to be desired that it were sounded in English also, at least in scientific and learned words; since the reduction of *pneo-* to *neo-, pneu-* to *new-, pnyx-* to *nix-,* is a loss to etymology and intelligibility, and a weakening of the resources of the language. (at *Pn-*)

31.3.1.4   Other Minor Spellings of /n/

The correspondence /n/ = *mn* occurs only in the Greek adoption *mnemonic* and its derivatives, from the Greek *mnēmonikós.* Compare the name *Mnemosyne,* goddess of memory and mother of the Muses. The correspondence /n/ = *cn* occurs in the very rare and technical *cne-*

midocoptes, cnemis, cnida, cnidaria, and *cnidoblast.* The correspondence /n/ = *ng* occurs in the recent and unintegrated adoption *ngaio,* /nīō/.

31.3.2 The Major Spellings of /n/

The contrast between the two major spellings, *n* and *nn,* can be described fairly cleanly using the set of ordered rules presented in 26.2.3.1.

31.3.2.1 /n/ = *n* at Simple Boundaries

Instances:

(Array 31-20)

abnormal	deny	nipple	pernicious
admonish	economy	nocturne	pronounce
beneath	enumerate	nutrient	renewal
bun	ignoble	nylon	shin
cloudiness	naughty	paranoia	tan
coconut	neither	pen	won

This pattern is quite reliable in initial position. In word-final position there are some holdouts: *inn, sunn, linn* (related to *linden*), *cann* (related to *can*), and *jinn, djinn,* which also has the variants *jinni, jinnee, djin,* and the closely related and more integrated synonym *genie.* Other holdouts are the two French adoptions *cretonne* and *comedienne,* which retain their French final *e*'s, and *cayenne,* which is either French or is at least modeled after French orthography. The correspondence /n/ = *nn* occurs in final position in a few nonterminative bases: *ann+* and the closely related *enn+,* as in *annual* and *centennial; antenn+,* as in *antenna; sonn+,* only in *sonnet,* with the closely related *son+,* as in *sonant;* and *tyrann+,* as in *tyranny,* which is closely related to *tyrant.* There are also two nonterminative bases with terminative coforms that have *n* rather than *nn: [penn+, pen],* as in *pennant* and *pen;* and *[mann+, man],* as in *mannequin* and *man.*

31.3.2.2 /n/ = *n* in Shortened VCV Strings

Instances involving the Third Syllable Rule:

(Array 31-21)

animate	genuine	janitor	sinuous
banister	ignominious	lanolin	tenement
enemy	impenetrable	manacle	venerate
general	itinerant	penitent	vinegar

Instances involving the Stress Frontshift Rule include *honor* and *panel.* Instances due to the suffix rules:

(Array 31-22)

affinity	electronic	histrionic	serenity
calisthenics	finish	laconic	vanish
divinity	harmonic	onion	vanity

31.3.2.3 /n/ = n in Consonant Clusters

The correspondence /n/ = n occurs in only two initial clusters, *sn* and *schn,* but in a wide array of medial and final clusters, especially those starting with *n:*

(Array 31-23)

ancient	canyon	frenzy	landscape
answer	chintz	gentle	monstrous
anthropology	cleanse	gondola	pencil
banjo	dungeon	hunch	ransom
barn	dwindle	hundred	schnitzel
canvas	enchantress	labyrinth	turnscrew

31.3.2.4 /n/ = n after Long Vowels and Vowel Digraphs

Instances:

(Array 31-24)

abstain	chicanery	gene	phone
adjoin	dune	jaundice	queen
brawny	encounter	launder	raccoon
brownie	faun	moan	vein

31.3.2.5 /n/ = nn at Complex Boundaries

Instances of /n/ = nn due to the assimilation of *ad-* to *an-,* or of *com-* to *con-,* before stems starting with *n:*

(Array 31-25)

annex	announce	connect	connotation
annihilate	annul	connive	connubial
annotate	connatural	connoisseur	reconnaissance

Instances due to twinning:

(Array 31-26)

beginning	funny	inner	thinnest
cannery	gunner	sunned	tonnage

Instances of /n/ = nn owing to duplicative addition usually involve a prefix ending in *n* or the suffix *-ness,* which produces instances in which the *nn* in careful speech is /nn/ but in quick conversation is probably /n/:

(Array 31-27)

ennoble	innervate	innocuous	innumerable
greenness	inness	innovation	leanness
innate	innocent	innuendo	thinness

31.3.2.6 /n/ = *nn* in VCC Strings

Instances:

(Array 31-28)

bonnet	channel	kennel	tennis
bonny	cranny	minnow	tunnel
cannibal	fennel	penny	tunny

Three holdouts to this pattern are *guinea, piano,* and *banana.* These three cannot be treated as instances of the Stress Frontshift Rule, since they are not French adoptions, but come instead, respectively, from Portuguese (probably), Italian, and Portuguese or Spanish. However, their resistance to the regular English *nn* spelling may be due to some felt analogy with the hundreds of other words that have undergone stress frontshifting. A fourth holdout is *honey,* which derives from Old English *hunig.* It is not clear why the *u* in the open syllable resisted lengthening, or, conversely, why the *n* resisted changing to *nn* after the short vowel. This resistance may owe something to the fact that the Norman scribes changed the Old English *u* to *o* in keeping with their practice of using *o* for *u* in the presence of letters made up of minims, such as *n* and *i.* Some attempts to use the tactically more regular *nn* were made in the sixteenth and seventeenth centuries, but the original *n* has prevailed.

31.3.2.7 /n/ = *n* after Reduced Vowels

This pattern is most common in a number of suffixes: *-ion, -ment, -ent, -ence, -ency, -ant, -ance, -ancy,* and so on. Other instances:

(Array 31-29)

canary	grenade	luminescent	nightingale
emanate	kinetic	magnanimity	reminisce
frenetic	linoleum	monogamy	souvenir

The relatively few, but important, holdouts to this pattern can be divided into two groups. The first group consists of words in which a bound base ending in *nn* has had a suffix affixed that causes the stress to shift off of the vowel preceding the *nn,* thereby reducing that vowel. Thus we have *colonnade* (colonn + ade), *tyranny* (tyrann + y), and *tintinnabula-*

tion (tintinn + abul + ation). The second group consists of French adoptions that contain *nn*'s from French orthography: *mayonnaise, personnel, questionnaire, legionnaire*. (For more on these words see 9.5.1.)

31.4 The Spellings of /ŋ/, "eng"

31.4.1 Historical Sources

The rule for spelling /ŋ/ can be stated simply and powerfully: The sound /ŋ/ is spelled *n* in front of the sounds /g/ and /k/; everywhere else it is spelled *ng*. This rule reflects an important historical development. In Old English, /ŋ/ was simply a variant of the sound /n/, a variant that occurred in front of the velars /k/ and /g/. The tactical rule was that *n* spelled the velar sound /ŋ/ when it was followed by *c* or *g;* otherwise it spelled /n/. The cluster *ng* was pronounced /ŋg/. Thus, a word like *sing* was pronounced /siŋg/, just as the first four letters of *single* still are (Jespersen [1909] 1954, 1:36–37, 217–18, 357–58; Dobson 1957, 2:971–73). But today when the *ng* occurs in a single syllable such as *sing* or the suffix *-ing,* the *g* is no longer pronounced, serving instead simply to fill out the old pattern that *n* followed by the velar *g* spells /ŋ/. This simplification is due to the fact that both /ŋ/ and /g/ are velar sounds. When two similar sounds come at word's end, the final one is often dropped, to ease pronunciation. The process is like that which caused *comb,* originally /kōmb/, to simplify to /kōm/. The bilabial cluster /mb/ simplified to /m/, just as the velar cluster /ŋg/ in, say, *sing* simplified to /ŋ/.

Thus, Old English words that ended in *ng* simplified from /ŋg/ to /ŋ/. In words with medial *ng* the /g/ sound was not dropped (for example, from *single*), because the syllable boundary preserved it. There is evidence that earlier, in inflected and derived forms of stems ending in *ng,* the *g* continued for a while to be pronounced. For instance, *sing* was pronounced /siŋ/, while *singer* was pronounced /'siŋgər/, following the pattern whereby the syllable boundary preserved the /g/. However, in time, it appears, the tendency toward conservative analogy grew stronger, and the pronunciation of *sing* in *singer* became the same as that of the stem *sing* in order to heighten the sense of unity and reduce the number of phonetic distinctions. On the other hand, some inflected forms still retain the old /ŋg/ pronunciation, as in the contrast between *strong* and *stronger,* for instance.

The contemporary result of these historical developments is the rule presented at the beginning of this section.

31.4.2 /ŋ/ = n
31.4.2.1 /ŋ/ = n before /k/ = k

(Array 31-30)

ankle	donkey	ink	plankton
blank	drunk	junket	tinker
debunk	honk	monkey	winkle

Related to this group is *handkerchief,* in which /k/ = *dk*. The alveolar cluster /nd/ simplifies to /n/, which sets up the correspondence /ŋ/ = *n* before /k/. Also related is the /ˈpuŋkin/ pronunciation of *pumpkin,* in which, oddly, we would have to say that /k/ = *pk* and /ŋ/ = *m*. The process seems to involve two steps: first, the bilabial cluster /mp/ simplifies to /m/; second, the bilabial /m/ assimilates to the velar /k/, becoming the velar /ŋ/.

31.4.2.2 /ŋ/ = n before /k/ = c

(Array 31-31)

defunct	precinct	sanctuary	uncle
distinct	punctual	syncopation	unction
idiosyncrasy	rancor	tincture	zinc

31.4.2.3 /ŋ/ = n before /g/ = g

(Array 31-32)

anger	dengue*	ganglion	manganese
bungalow	dungarees	hunger	mongrel
commingle	elongate	ingot	sanguine
congress	fungus	linger	tango

Although neither *ng* nor /ŋ/ occurs in initial position in integrated English words, there are some recent and unintegrated adoptions with initial *ng.* In *ngai* and *ngege,* pronounced respectively /əŋˈgī/ and /əŋˈgāgē/, the initial *ng* is rendered /əŋ/, consistent with the native English-speaking person's difficulty in pronouncing initial /ŋ/. In the similar-looking *ngaio,* pronounced /ˈnīō/, the correspondence /n/ = *ng* holds.

31.4.2.4 /ŋ/ = n before /k/ = ch

This correspondence is quite rare, but some instances are *anchor, synchronize,* and *bronchitis.*

31.4.2.5 /ŋ/ = n before x

(Array 31-33)

larynx	minx	pharynx
lynx	phalanx	sphinx

The correspondence /ŋ/ = *n* holds before *x* in *anxious* and *anxiety*, even though in *anxious* *x* = /sh/ in one pronunciation and in *anxiety* *x* = /z/. These two spellings probably reflect earlier pronunciations of *x* as /ks/.

31.4.2.6 /ŋ/ = *n* before *qu*

Instances of this correspondence include *banquet* and *propinquity.*

31.4.3 /ŋ/ = *ng*

The correspondence /ŋ/ = *ng* holds about 60 percent of the time (Hanna et al. 1966, 920)—that is, everywhere except before /k/ and /g/. Usually this correspondence occurs in word-final position, especially in the suffix *-ing.* Instances not involving *-ing:*

(Array 31-34)

along	bring	ringlet	tongs
among	cling	slang	wringer
amongst	dreng, drengh	slung	wrung
bang	kreng	sting	young

The spellings *harangue, gangue* (also *gang*), and *tongue* deserve mention. The first two are French adoptions in which the *ngue* reflects French orthography. *Tongue* is harder to explain. It comes from Old English *tunge,* and in the words of the *OED:*

> The natural modern English representation of OE *tunge* would be *tung,* as in *lung, rung, sung* (and as the word is actually pronounced); but the ME device of writing *on* for *un* brought in the alternative *tonge* with variants *tounge, townge;* apparently the effort to show that the pronunciation was not (tundʒ(e) led to the later *tounghe, toungue, tongue,* although it is true that these hardly appeared before final *e* was becoming mute, so that its simple omission would have been equally effective. The spelling *tongue* is thus neither etymological nor phonetic, and is only in a very small degree historical. (at *Tongue*)

Occasionally the correspondence /ŋ/ = *ng* occurs at the end of nonterminative bases, as in *strength* (streng + th) and *length* (leng + th), which are related to their terminative coforms *strong* and *long.*

Other instances of medial /ŋ/ = *ng* are *hangar* and *orangutan.* The structure of *hangar* is obscure, but its contemporary sense and form lend to it the explication (hang)ar), which is possible historically. Partridge suggests that *hangar* comes from Latin *angārium,* a shed where horses were shod, which further supports the possibility that the root is *hang,* since in Roman times horses were hung in slings to make shoeing easier ([1958] 1983, 278). *Orangutan* is a Malay adoption, from the phrase *ōrang ūtan* 'man of the forest'.

31.4.4   Two Complications to the /ŋ/ Rule

Dinghy poses a minor complication to the /ŋ/ rule. In its most common pronunciation, /'diŋē/, it appears to contain the minor correspondence /ŋ/ = *ngh*. However, *dinghy* has the more regular variant spellings *dingy* and *dingey*. It also has variant pronunciations with /ŋg/ and /ŋk/. All of these variants move in the direction of greater regularity, though the minor pronunciation with /ŋk/ admittedly complicates the sound-and-spelling correspondences for /k/.

The tree that is spelled variously *ginkgo, gingko,* and *ginko* poses somewhat the same complication. All three spellings are regular enough as far as the /ŋ/ rule is concerned, but *ginkgo* does violence to the /k/ correspondence.

32 The Liquids, /l/ and /r/

32.1 Introduction

The liquids are of special orthographic interest for a number of reasons. As noted in 3.2.2, the liquids, /l/ and /r/, are unlike most other consonants in that they are exempt from the normal tactical constraints on mixed voicing. The effect of both sounds on preceding vowels is unlike that of the other consonants, the most dramatic case being /r/ (see chapter 25). But /l/, too, has some unusual effects on preceding vowels, as evidenced by words like *roll*, with its unusual /ō/ before a doublet consonant, and by the contrast between words like *stall* and *stallion* (see 4.3.3.1 and 32.2.2.4 for details). In the present chapter we will discuss another interesting feature of /l/—namely, the indecision about when to use *l* and when to use *ll*. This indecision is of interest in part because it represents a clear case of change at work in the spelling system as variant spellings develop and in time lead to greater order and ruliness.

32.2 The Spellings of /l/

There are two very minor spellings of /l/: *sl* and *ln*. The two major spellings, the regular single and doublet spellings *l* and *ll*, account for more than 99 percent of the instances of this sound (Hanna et al. 1966, 855, 858).

32.2.1 The Minor Spellings of /l/
32.2.1.1 /l/ = *sl*

The correspondence /l/ = *sl* occurs only in *island, isle, aisle,* and *lisle*. *Island* derives from Old English *īland, ī(e)gland,* a compound of *īeg* 'isle' and *land* 'land'. In Middle and Early Modern English it was most often spelled *yland, iland,* but in the fifteenth century it came under the influence of the synonymous French word *isle*. In French the /z/ sound before /l/ was regularly dropped (thus, in modern French *ile* no longer has /z/ or *s*). During the fifteenth and sixteenth centuries the English word was respelled to fit the French model, with perhaps also some pressure from the Latin *īnsula*. Thus we have *island*, in which the *s* has never been pronounced in English. The English *isle* comes directly from the French. For *aisle* see 20.3.4. *Lisle* is a straightforward adoption from the French place-name. (Some other English words that come from Old French words in which /z/ = *s*, but that have dropped both the /z/ and the *s*, are *dinner*, from Old French *disner; blame* from *blasme; emerald* from *esmeraude;* and *male* from *masle*. All of these words also lack both the /z/ and the *s* in their Modern French forms.)

32.2.1.2 /l/ = *ln*

The correspondence /l/ = *ln* occurs only in a variant pronunciation of *kiln* (see Dobson 1957, 2:961, 989).

32.2.2 The Major Spellings of /l/
32.2.2.1 American Variants and the Emerging Pattern

The process of distinguishing between major spellings is less straightforward with *l* and *ll* than with other consonants. The pattern is neither clear nor settled. It is still working itself out, as is suggested by the many variants in American English and the marked differences that exist between American and British orthography as far as *l* and *ll* are concerned. By and large, British spelling tends to be more conservative than American. American pronunciation tends to be more influenced by spelling than does British. The fluid and still-evolving state of the /l/ = *l* and /l/ = *ll* correspondences can be discerned in the lists of variant spellings in American English that are presented below. Each variant is listed in at least one reputable American dictionary, though many *ll* variants bear labels such as "British" or "Chiefly British."

The most common point of variation involves the inflection of two- and three-syllable verbs that end in an unstressed *l*. Thus we have *traveled* and *travelled, traveling* and *travelling*. Since the Twinning Rule for American English, as stated in 9.6, requires stress on the final syllable of the stem both before and after adding the suffix, twinning is not called for in these cases and the *l* is more regular than the *ll*. However, the wide presence of variants with the nonregular *ll* speaks to the indecision here. For Donald Emery's list of verb stems with variant inflected forms in *l* and *ll,* see 9.2. Variation between *l* and *ll* is also common when /l/ is word-final in polysyllables, following a stressed vowel, either short or long. The variants in arrays 32-1, 32-2, and 32-3 are listed with the more common spelling first:

(Array 32-1)

appall, appal	enthrall, enthral
barcarole, barcarolle	extol, extoll
bastille, bastile	install, instal
chlorophyll, chlorophyl	instill, instil
distill, distil	pastille, pastil
enroll, enrol	

There are also variants involving the suffix *-ful, -full* (from *full*), and elements that normally end in *ll* when another element is added to them:

(Array 32-2)

brimful, brimfull	skulduggery, skullduggery
bulrush, bullrush	thralldom, thraldom
dullness, dulness	topfull, topful
fulfill, fulfil	willful, wilful
skillful, skilful	

Other instances of *l* and *ll* variation are taken from a much longer list from Emery (1973):

(Array 32-3)

allodium, alodium	gerbil, gerbille
buhl, boulle, boule	halyard, halliard
caliper, calliper	hullabaloo, hullaballoo
calisthenics, callisthenics	idyll, idyl
camellia, camelia	manila, manilla
carrel, carrell	palette, pallet
chili, chilli	porcelaneous, porcellaneous
coolly, cooly	postilion, postillion
filigree, fillagree, filagree	tonsillar, tonsilar
fontanel, fontanelle	vermilion, vermillion
gallivant, galivant	woolen, woollen

The distribution of *l* and *ll*, still unsettled, continues to sort itself out as variants occur and as gradually more regular variants displace less regular ones. In the following sections we will describe the pattern that is now emerging. Considerable overlapping and blurring will occur, but such a description can at least suggest bases for choosing among allowed variants. The rule of thumb, again, would be the Principle of Preferred Regularity (see 1.6): when given a choice, choose the variant that fits the emerging pattern.

32.2.2.2 The Spellings *l* versus *ll* Summarized

1. /l/ = *l* in initial position.
2. Word-final /l/ = *ll* in monosyllables with a short vowel, and in disyllables with a short vowel if the second syllable is a free base.

3. Word-final /l/ = *l* elsewhere (generally).
4. /l/ = *l* in VCV strings shortened by one of the shortening rules (generally).
5. /l/ = *l* within consonant clusters.
6. /l/ = *l* after long vowels (generally) and vowel digraphs.
7. /l/ = *ll* at complex boundaries affected by twinning, assimilation, or duplicative addition.
8. /l/ = *ll* between a stressed short vowel and a following vowel if none of the shortening rules apply.
9. After reduced vowels the distribution is ambiguous.

32.2.2.3   /l/ = *l* in Initial Position

This correspondence holds in both word- and element-initial position:

(Array 32-4)

alongside	forlorn	liquid	oblation
analysis	geological	lounge	preliminary
believe	interlocutor	luncheon	reliable
chronology	knowledge	lymph	sublimation
delusion	larynx	monolithic	translator
elicit	levitate	neglect	unrelenting

The only known instances of word-initial *ll* are the recent Spanish adoptions *llama, llano, llanero,* and *llautu,* and three geologic terms (usually capitalized) that come from Welsh place names: *Llandeilo, Llandoverian,* and *Llandvirn.*

32.2.2.4   /l/ = *ll* in Word-final Position

In monosyllables with a short vowel, final /l/ = *ll:*

(Array 32-5)

cell	gall	loll	shrill
doll	ghyll	quell	twill
fall	hull	scull	yell

The only known holdouts to this pattern are *sal, el, gel, mil,* and *nil.*

Monosyllables that end in *all* have a short vowel sound, but it is /ò/ rather than /a/. This is due to a change that began in the fifteenth century. The Middle English short *a,* which was more like the modern /ò/ than the modern /a/, began to change to more of a front sound—that is, to the vowel sound we now symbolize as /a/. This change was completed by the end of the sixteenth century and the sound has remained essentially the same ever since. More accurately, the change occurred everywhere except before word-final /l/ or /l/ followed by a consonant. When /l/

was followed by a vowel, the change to /a/ occurred (Jespersen [1909] 1954, 1:289–91; Prins 1972, 147). This explains such contrasts as the following:

(Array 32-6)

all (with /ò/)	alley (with /a/)
ball	ballot
call	callow
fall	fallow
gall	gallows
hall	hallow
mall	mallard
pall	pallor
stall	stallion
tall	tallow

The contrast illustrated in array 32-6 does not occur when the *a* follows /w/: *wall* (also *wallet* and *wallow*).

The only known instance in which *all* in final position in a monosyllable is pronounced /al/ is *shall*.

The correspondence /l/ = *ll* in word-final position after a stressed short vowel also holds in polysyllables if the final syllable is a free base (though the asterisked instances in the following array do have variants with *l*):

(Array 32-7)

appall*	freewill	instill*	resell
distill*	fulfill*	misspell	unwell
enthrall*	install*	refill	whippoorwill

Earlier we noted the variation in forms that end in *ll* when they combine with other elements, leading to such spellings as *skillful* and *skilful*, *fulfill* and *fulfil*. Related to these words are the following holdouts to the pattern illustrated in array 32-7:

(Array 32-8)

therewithal, (there)(with)(all)
until, (un(till)
wherewithal, (where)(with)(all)
withal, (with)(all)

These four holdouts appear to be cases in which the constraint against ending polysyllables with *ll* runs counter to the tendency under discussion here—namely, for the correspondence /l/ = *ll* to hold in word-final position after short vowels in polysyllables if the final syllable is a free base.

32.2.2.5 /l/ = *l* in Word-final Position

In polysyllables whose final syllable is not a free base, word-final /l/ is spelled *l*, and a final *e* is added if the /l/ is preceded by a long vowel unigraph or if the French fossil *e* is involved:

(Array 32-9)

annul	fossil	morale	pistol
cabal	hotel	motel	rebel
canal	impel	muscatel	role
cartel	locale	noel	sibyl
corral	marcel	pale	smile
expel	mogul	pastel	spiral

32.2.2.6 /l/ = *l* in Shortened VCV Strings

Instances involving the Third Syllable Rule:

(Array 32-10)

accelerate	element	malady	salamander
basilica	exhilarate	molecule	silicon
caliber	facilitate	oligarchy	skeleton
celery	gelatin	rehabilitate	tolerable
delicate	kilogram	relative	valentine

Instances due to the Stress Frontshift Rule:

(Array 32-11)

balance	melancholy	palace
color	olive	pavilion

Talent comes from Old English and Old French, both of which adopted it from Latin *talentum*. The Old English form, *talente,* with short *a,* probably resisted lengthening because of the native version of the Third Syllable Rule (see 7.1.1). The Old French form, *talent,* which entered the English language in the thirteenth century, was stressed on the final syllable and thus was an instance of the Stress Frontshift Rule.

Instances of /l/ = *l* owing to one of the suffix rules:

(Array 32-12)

ability	nobility	quality	squalid
abolish	oxalic	relic	utility
apostolic	parabolic	salicylic	valid
demolish	qualify	solid	vilify

Frolic is a Dutch adoption, from *vrolijk,* which consists of the base *vro* 'happy' plus the suffix *-lijk* '-ly'. The *ic* ending in *frolic,* then, is not the suffix *-ic* but rather an example of analogy and convergence. The spelling *frolique* occurred from the sixteenth through the nineteenth century. Since *-ique* is the French source for *-ic* in several English words, there is reason to suspect that it was treated like a French adoption, which would have encouraged its evolution as an instance of the Stress Frontshift Rule.

The shortening rules—especially the Third Syllable Rule—are less reliable with the liquids, /r/ and /l/, than with other consonants. A number of Romance nonterminative bases that end in *ll*'s do not simplify to *l* via any of the shortening rules. And a number of Romance words with medial *ll*'s do not simplify to *l* via the Third Syllable Rule. Some instances of these holdouts:

(Array 32-13)

allegory	billiards	fallible	million	stellar
alley	callous	idyllic	mollusk	tally
appellate	cellar	jelly	palliative	trellis
artillery	cellophane	mallard	pallid	umbrella
bacillus	cerebellum	malleable	pellet	valley
ballad	challenge	mallet	penicillin	vanilla
bellicose	embellish	medallion	portcullis	vellum
billet	fallacy	metallic	sally	villain

32.2.2.7 /l/ = *l* in Consonant Clusters

Since the liquid /l/ enters into an immense variety of consonant clusters, the correspondence /l/ = *l* is widespread in clusters in initial, medial, and final position:

(Array 32-14)

albatross	chloride	galvanize	pilgrim	title
alfalfa	cleaver	gentle	polka	tousle
alpine	culminate	glacier	raffle	ulcer
amble	cultch	grapple	sample	uncle
angle	cyclone	hassle	schmaltz	veldt
axle	delft	jilt	sclerosis	vulgar
balcony	dolphin	juggle	sepulchral	vulnerable
balsa	eagle	kleptomania	sludge	walrus
bilge	feeble	mulct	snarl	whistle
blister	fiddle	myrtle	splash	wield
bolster	flaccid	nibble	sprinkle	world
bottle	foozle	nozzle	staple	zloty
cauldron	fulcrum	phlegm	tackle	zoogler

32.2.2.8 /l/ = *l* after Long Vowels and Vowel Digraphs

(Array 32-15)

alien	ceiling	genteel	prowl	spool
azalea	gale	ghoul	role	tile
broil	gargoyle	jealous	sailor	zealot

The statement that /l/ = *l* after long vowels is a strong and useful one, but there are several holdouts, mainly involving the letter *o* and some French adoptions with unexpected *ll*'s. There is a strong tendency for *o* to be long in the string *olC*: *bolt, cold, holm, folk, holster.* The same is true when the consonant in the string is another *l*: *roll, boll, scroll.* This lengthening does not occur when the *ll* is followed by a vowel: *rollicking, bollix, pollen.* (For more details see 4.3.3.1.) The French adoption *chenille* also has an unexpected long vowel before *ll*.

Known holdouts to the statement that /l/ = *l* after vowel digraphs are less numerous and all are from French—for instance, *raillery, surveillance.*

32.2.2.9   /l/ = *ll* at Complex Boundaries

Instances due to twinning are relatively rare:

(Array 32-16)

compelling	dispelled	impeller	propellant
controller	expellable	patrolling	rebellion

Instances of /l/ = *ll* owing to assimilation usually involve the prefixes *ad-*, *com-*, and *in-*, which assimilate, respectively, to *al-*, *col-*, and *il-*:

(Array 32-17)

allege	alloy	collect	illative
alliterate	collapse	colligate	illogical
allocate	collateral	colloquial	illusion

Less common assimilations include:

(Array 32-18)

ellipse (eń + l + lipse)	pollute (poŕ + l + lute)
intellectual (inteŕ + l + lectual)	syllable (syń + l + lable)
intelligent (inteŕ + l + ligent)	syllogism (syń + l + logism)

In some cases /l/ = *ll* owing to analogy and convergence. The following words are spelled analogically, with *ad-* assimilated to *al-*, although historically they contain other prefixes: *allegiance*, an English formation from Old French *legance, legiance,* perhaps confused in Middle English with *allegeance* (from *allege*), an entirely different word that contains an assimilated *ad-* (see 10.6.1); *allegro*, from Italian *allegro,* from Latin *alacer,* the analogical respelling occurring in Italian before the word's adoption into English; and *allay*, from Old English *alecgan,* which joins *a-* with *lecgan* 'lay'.

The most common cases of /l/ = *ll* owing to duplicative addition involve one of the *-ly* suffixes or *-less* added to a stem ending in *l*: *actually, soulless.*

In a few instances, *ll* and *l* come together, and a deletion must occur to avoid the triplet *lll,* which is disallowed by English tactics (see 3.2.5):

(Array 32-19)

dully (dul*l*)ly)	fully (full)ly)	shellac (shell)(lac)

32.2.2.10 /l/ = *ll* in VCC Strings

In native words especially, and consistent with the VCC pattern, /l/ = *ll* between a preceding short vowel and a following vowel.

(Array 32-20)

ballad	follow	millet	swallow
belly	gallop	pulley	valley
bullet	holler	rally	wallet
collar	lullaby	scallop	willow
fellow	mallard	silly	yellow

For Romance instances of this correspondence see array 32-13.

32.2.2.11 /l/ = *l* after Reduced Vowels

The situation here is rather ambiguous for the same reasons that the situation of /l/ relative to the shortening rules is ambiguous. However, the basic pattern is that after reduced vowels /l/ = *l.* And although there are a number of holdouts with *ll,* it is important to remember that in Hanna et al. (1966) the instances of *l* outnumber the instances of *ll* by a ratio of 10:1. Thus, even with the holdouts, the basic pattern is a broad and useful one. Instances of /l/ = *l* after reduced vowels:

(Array 32-21)

abalone	colossal	formulation	pantaloon
belief	delinquent	hilarity	resolution
celebrity	equilibrium	molecular	ukulele

The holdouts usually involve Romance *ll*'s that are either element-medial or that fall at the end of nonterminative bases:

(Array 32-22)

ancillary	calligraphy	mellifluous	parallel
ballistics	flagellate	miscellaneous	pusillanimous
belligerent	hallucination	oscillation	satellite

32.3 The Spellings of /r/

The important minor spellings of /r/ are *wr,* as in *written,* and *rh,* as in *rhythm.* According to Hanna et al., of the two major spellings, *r* and *rr,* the correspondence /r/ = *rr* occurs only 2 percent of the time, while /r/ = *r* occurs 97 percent of the time. Obviously, then, the minor spellings are quite minor indeed, accounting for only 1 percent of the instances of /r/ overall (Hanna et al. 1966, 982).

32.3.1   The Minor Spellings of /r/
32.3.1.1   /r/ = *wr*

In a few native English words the correspondence /r/ = *wr* holds, always in word-initial position. Originally the *w* was pronounced, but by the middle of the seventeenth century the /wr/ had simplified to /r/. The known instances are:

(Array 32-23)

wrack	wreath	wretch	writhe
wraith	wreck	wriggle	written
wrangle	wren	wring	wrong
wrap	wrench	wrinkle	wrote
wrath	wrest	wrist	wrought
wreak	wrestle	write	wry

Most of the instances of /r/ = *wr* convey a sense of "twisting, turning," which reflects the fact that most of them derive from six closely related Proto-Indo-European roots with definitions dealing with twisting and turning. From Indo-European *wreit-* 'turn': *wreath, wreathe, writhe, wrath, wroth;* from *wergh-* 'turn': *wring, wrong, wrangle;* from *werg-* 'turn': *wrench, wrinkle;* from *wreik-* 'turn': *wry, wriggle, wrist;* from *wrizd-* 'turn, bend': *wrest, wrestle;* from *werp-* 'turn, wind': *wrap.* Four of the *wr* words come from Indo-European *wreg-* 'push, drive, shove, track down': *wreak, wreck, wrack, wretch.*

32.3.1.2   /r/ = *rh, rrh*

The cluster *rh* was used in Latin to transliterate the Greek letter rho when it was aspirated. In English, *rh* did not continue to indicate aspiration, but came to have the same pronunciation as *r.* The words with *rh* are few in number, usually rather technical and rare, and almost always from Greek:

(Array 32-24)

rhabdomancy	rhesus	rho
rhabdomyoma	rhetoric	rhodamine
rhapsody	rheumatic	rhodium
rhatany	rhinal	rhododendron
rhea	rhinencephalon	rhodora
rhematic	rhinoceros	rhombencephalon
rhenium	rhizobium	rhomboid
rheostat	rhizome	rhonchus

rhubarb   rhyolite   rhythm
rhynchoceph

A non-Greek instance is *rhinestone*, which comes from *Rhine*, from Latin *Rhēmus*, from German *Rhein*, from Gaulish *Rēnos*. Another is *rhumba*, which has the more straightforward variant *rumba*.

When Greek words were transliterated into Latin, double rho was rendered *rrh*. The correspondence /r/ = *rrh* occurs in a few, usually technical, words, and usually in initial position:

(Array 32-25)

acrorrheuma	catarrh	hemorrhage	myrrh
arrhythmia	diarrhea	hepatorrhexis	scirrhus
cacorrhinia	gonorrhea	logorrhea	

Historically *catarrh* would explicate to (cata + rrh), which technically puts the *rrh* in the usual, initial position, but the conflict between the proposed base there, * + rrh, and the Syllabicity Rule (see 2.7.3) suggests that it would be better to treat the word as an instance of merging (see 2.7.4) and leave it as a simplex. For more on *rrh* see 3.2.3.

32.3.1.3   Other Minor Spellings of /r/

The correspondence /r/ = *rps* occurs in *corps*. The correspondence /r/ = *l* occurs in *colonel*, though it is not clear what should be done with the second *o*. Etymologists do not agree completely on *colonel*, but whatever the historical dynamics of the word, it is a clear case of mixed convergence, the pronunciation of one, apparently earlier, form, *coronel*, having become attached to the spelling of another.

Because of dissimilation, the process by which sounds change to make them less similar to other sounds, some /r/'s are dropped in a few words. Dissimilation leads to the tendency to drop an /r/ in one syllable of a word if there is another /r/ in another syllable of the word. Though this dissimilative /r/-dropping does not lead to separate minor spellings, this may be a good place to illustrate it:

(Array 32-26)

caterpillar /ˈkadə‚pilər/	reservoir /ˈrezəv‚wär/
governor /ˈguvnər/	surprise /səˈprīz/
paraphernalia /‚parəfəˈnälyə/	

Dictionaries show /r/'s in places where they have been deleted in the words in array 32-26, but in daily speech, pronunciations like those given above are quite common. And obviously if one grows accustomed to neither saying nor hearing the /r/ in such words, the spelling of /r/ becomes even more complicated.

32.3.2 The Major Spellings of /r/

As in the case of the liquid /l/, distinguishing between the single and doublet spellings of /r/ is rather ambiguous and still unsettled. Chapter 25 discussed vowels that occur before the /r/ sound and reveals clearly the complicating effect /r/ can have on preceding vowel sounds. This effect is marked enough that that chapter analyzes the /r/-colored vowels in terms of five fields—or clusters of correspondences—three of which are sprawling and diffuse. The result is that the normal patterns for tactical strings— VCC, VCV, VC#, and the like—are very different when the consonant following the head vowel in the string is /r/. For that reason and because of the unsettled state of the distribution pattern for *r* and *rr,* the following discussion, like that for *l* and *ll,* is highly tentative and describes not so much a controlling pattern as an emerging one.

32.3.2.1 Variant Spellings with *r* and *rr*

As in the case of *l* and *ll,* the unsettled state of the distribution of *r* and *rr* produces a number of variant spellings. The following is a small sampling taken from Donald Emery's list and follows his order for variant spellings:

(Array 32-27)

> begorra, begorah, begorrah
> biretta, birretta, beretta, berretta
> carom, carrom
> carotene, carrotene, carotin, carrotin
> carousel, carrousel
> conferee, conferree
> correlation, corelation
> deferrable, deferable
> garrote, garotte, garrotte, garote
> guerrilla, guerilla
> parakeet, parrakeet, paroquet, parroquet, parroket, paraquet
> transferal, transferral

32.3.2.2 The Spellings *r* versus *rr* Summarized

1. /r/ = *r* in initial position.
2. /r/ = *r* in word-final position.
3. /r/ = *r* in VCV strings shortened by one of the shortening rules, though there are many holdouts with /r/ = *rr.*
4. /r/ = *r* within consonant clusters.
5. /r/ = *r* after long vowels and vowel digraphs.
6. /r/ = *rr* at complex boundaries affected by twinning, assimilation, or duplicative addition.

7. /r/ = *rr* between a stressed short vowel and a following vowel
   if none of the shortening rules apply.
8. After reduced vowels the distribution is ambiguous.

32.3.2.3 /r/ = *r* in Initial Position

Instances of /r/ = *r* in element- and word-initial position:

(Array 32-28)

abrogate	cataract	rabbit	rudder
arisen	derivation	readily	ruinous
bankruptcy	direction	ribald	rye
bereave	erupt	rivalry	unreality
bigotry	kindred	roach	uproarious

Although the minor spelling *rrh* occurs initially in a few highly technical
bound bases (see array 32-25), there are no known instances of initial *rr.*

32.3.2.4 /r/ = *r* in Word-final Position

This correspondence is extremely common in word-final position. In
Dolby and Resnikoff (1967) more than 3,000 instances are listed. A few
examples:

(Array 32-29)

beggar	cheer	lawyer	scar
caviar	doctor	or	spur
cedar	her	player	stir

Though it is very rare, /r/ = *rr* does occur in word-final position. Dolby
and Resnikoff list the following 11 instances. Asterisked words have
variants with the more regular *r:*

(Array 32-30)

birr	chirr, churr	err	skirr
bizarre	curr	mhorr*	whirr*
burr*	dorr	purr*	

Among these holdouts the only common ones are *err* and *bizarre*. The *rr* in
err was in both its French and Latin ancestors. It is also important to note
that *er* would violate the Short Word Rule (see 3.5). *Bizarre* is French and
has retained its French ending.

32.3.2.5 /r/ = *r* in Shortened VCV Strings

There are relatively few cases of /r/ in VCV strings of any kind since /r/
tends to occur such a high percentage of the time in consonant clusters.
Also, as in the case of the spellings of the liquid /l/, the distinction between

r and *rr* is not clear-cut. Nevertheless, in VCV strings shortened by one of the shortening rules the basic pattern is /r/ = *r*. Because of the effects of /r/ on the vowel preceding it, the shortening effects are not always clear, but the following are instances of /r/ = *r* in VCV strings shortened by the Third Syllable Rule:

(Array 32-31)

aquarium	derelict	imperative	miracle
arable	erudite	kerosene	oracle
asparagus	ethereal	lariat	parable
bacterial	funereal	marathon	parasite
carillon	gregarious	marinate	vicarious

Instances involving the Stress Frontshift Rule:

(Array 32-32)

apparel	carol	moral	peril
apparent	herald	orange	tariff
baron	heron	parish	zero

Instances due to the suffix rules:

(Array 32-33)

arid	cherish	hilarity	perish
atmospheric	cleric	lyric	satyric
authority	empirical	merit	severity
charity	florid	parity	verity

A number of Romance bases end in *rr* or contain medial *rr*. These bases lead to a number of holdouts to the Shortening Rule pattern. Some examples:

(Array 32-34)

arrant	embarrass	garret	narrative
barracks	errant	garrulous	quarrel
carrousel	ferric	horrid	terrace
cherry	ferrule	mirror	terrify

32.3.2.6 /r/ = *r* in Consonant Clusters

This rule is probably the most useful of the set, since /r/ appears in consonant clusters—an immense variety of them—a very high percentage of the time. Some instances:

(Array 32-35)

acre	anthropology	burst	corpse
algebra	arthritis	chrome	curtsy
angry	barnacle	circle	darling
antarctic	borscht	control	dervish

dextrose	krill	phrenology	sherbet
doldrums	lustrous	pilgrim	shrapnel
electric	marshal	polyandry	sorghum
embargo	migrate	portrait	sparkle
empress	minstrel	poultry	sprawl
fierce	morsel	purfle	squirm
frail	myrtle	purple	swarthy
fulcrum	orchard	quartz	threnody
furze	ordnance	sarcasm	torque
garble	paprika	scorpion	truculent
gargle	parsley	scrutiny	turkey
girdle	parsnip	sepulchral	umbrella
hydraulic	partner	sergeant	world

32.3.2.7 /r/ = r after Long Vowels and Vowel Digraphs

Although pure long vowels are rare before /r/, vowel digraphs are not, and the regular correspondence /r/ = r holds for both:

(Array 32-36)

aerial	fairy	heuristic	papyrus
aurora	fiery	iris	plagiarism
courage	fluorescent	irony	pleurisy
dowry	gory	marguerite	spirochete
eerie	gyrate	mores	theory
eyrie	heirloom	oriole	thyroid

32.3.2.8 /r/ = rr at Complex Boundaries

Instances involving twinning:

(Array 32-37)

abhorrence	concurring	marrer	starry
barrable	deterrent	occurred	stirring
barrier	furry	recurrent	warrior

Instances due to the assimilation of *ad-*, *com-*, *in-*, and *sub-* to *ar-*, *cor-*, *ir-*, and *sur-:*

(Array 32-38)

arraign	correct	irradiate	irreverent
arrive	corrugate	irrepressible	surreptitious
arrogance	corrupt	irresponsible	surrogate

Instances involving duplicative addition:

(Array 32-39)

barroom	interrogate	surrealism	surrender
earring	interrupt	surrejoinder	surround

32.3.2.9 /r/ = *rr* in VCC Strings

The pressure toward VCC strings and that toward shortened VCV strings contend directly when the consonant following the head vowel is one of the liquids. There are a number of Romance words in which the shortening rules might cause us to expect VCV, with *r*, but in which we get VCC, with the doublet *rr*. The following discussion, which highlights both Romance and native words, is based on the three vowel fields described in chapter 25.

VCC Strings with Head Vowels in the /âr/ Field. The /âr/ field has been described as a triangle whose corners represent the sounds /er/, /ar/, and /är/ (see 25.2). The doublet *rr* occurs among the spellings typical of this field only at the two corners that involve definitely short vowels, /ar/ and /er/. For examples see 25.2.1.2 and 25.2.1.3.

VCC Strings with Head Vowels in the /ôr/ Field. The /ôr/ field has two extremes that involve short vowels, /är/ and /ȯr/; the third extreme involves a long vowel, /ōr/ (see 25.3). The doublet *rr* never enters into the spelling of /ōr/. For instances of *rr* in /ôr/ see 25.3.1.1 and 25.3.1.3.

VCC Strings with Head Vowels in the /êr/ Field. The two extremes of the /êr/ field are /ēr/ and /ir/. Again, the *rr* spelling is associated with the extreme involving the short vowel. For examples see 25.4.1.2.

VCC Strings with Head Vowels in the /ur/ Convergence. Section 25.7 discusses the convergence of once-contrasted vowel-plus-/r/ sounds to the neutral /ur/, as in the words *firm, furl, fern, word*. The *rr* spelling occurs in the /ur/ field regularly in the correspondence /ur/ = *urr*:

(Array 32-40)

burro	current	hurricane	scurrilous
burrow	flurry	hurry	scurry
currant	furrow	murrain	turret

The *rr* spelling also occurs in the correspondence /ur/ = *orr*, as in *worry*, the effect of the /w/ here being similar to that in words like *word, worm, world, work*. *Squirrel, stirrup,* and *chirrup* have variant pronunciations with /ur/.

32.3.2.10 /r/ = *r* after Reduced Vowels

As in the case of /l/, the distribution of the spellings of /r/ after reduced vowels is somewhat unreliable, but the basic pattern is that after schwa and unstressed /i/, /r/ = *r*:

(Array 32-41)

aborigine	exhilaration	inspiration	natural
baroque	ferocity	kangaroo	porphyry
calorie	giraffe	labyrinth	saccharin
diorama	heredity	mercury	sclerotic

Indeed, in the great majority of cases after reduced vowels /r/ = r, but the following are important holdouts to that pattern:

(Array 32-42)

aberration	curriculum	gue(r)rilla	subterranean
barrage	erratic	horrendous	terrain
barrette	erroneous	insurrection	terrestrial
corral	garrotte	narration	terrific

33 The Semivowels, /w/ and /y/

33.1 Introduction

In chapter 11 the /w/ and /y/ sounds are classified as semivowels because they are the only two sounds in English that are neither vocalic nor consonantal (see 11.3). But the letters *w* and *y* also have features that make the name *semivowel* appropriate: each can function as either vowel or consonant. The first *w* in *wow,* for instance, is a consonant, but the second is a vowel, part of the vowel digraph *ow.* Similarly, the first *y* in *yearly* is a consonant, but the second is a vowel.

33.2 The Spellings of /w/

The sound /w/ is relatively uncommon in English, accounting for less than 1 percent of the consonants listed in Hanna et al. (1966). The spellings of /w/ are relatively clear-cut. The two major spellings are *u* and *w.* The correspondence /w/ = *w* is about twelve times more common than /w/ = *u,* and the distribution of the two is, with one minor holdout, cleanly distinguished (ibid., 1086–87). Double *w* does not occur (it is, after all, historically already a doublet, a double *u*). In a few compounds apparent *ww* concatenations do occur—as in *yellowwood* and *cowwheat*—but they are only visual concatenations since in each case the first *w* is a vowel and the second is a consonant. There are three minor spellings of /w/.

33.2.1 The Minor Spellings of /w/

In one pronunciation of the French adaption *bivouac* /w/ = *ou,* presenting an interesting case of the problems sometimes encountered when trying to sort out vowels from consonants. In the pronunciation of *marihuana, marijuana,* that drops the /h/, /w/ must be spelled *hu* and *ju,* though in the pronunciation that keeps the /h/ the /w/ is spelled with the major spelling *u.* In *choir* we apparently must say that /w/ = *o* (see 27.3.2.3).

The /w/ heard at the beginning of *one* and *once* is another instance of mixed convergence. *One* and *once* are members of a sprawling connate group that includes *only, alone, atone, lonely, none, nonce, anon,* and *any.* By the fifteenth century in the southwest and west of England the vowel at the beginning of *one* had evolved from /ō/ through /ūō/ to /wō/. Thus *one* and *once* have retained a once-dialectical pronunciation, even though a concomitant respelling has never taken place (Jespersen [1909] 1954, 1:321; Dobson 1957, 2:993–95). The vowel at the front of *one* and *once* is structurally like the complex vowels with an initial /y/-glide.

33.2.2 The Major Spellings of /w/
33.2.2.1 /w/ = *u*

The correspondence /w/ = *u* occurs only after *q*, as in *queen;* after *g*, as in *language;* and much more rarely after *s*, as in *suede*, and *p*, as in *pueblo.* The *qu* spelling was introduced by the Norman scribes to replace *cw*, the standard Old English spelling of /kw/. Now, in American English, /kw/ is regularly spelled *qu*. Known holdouts are *choir* (see 27.3.2.3), *coif,* and the rare *couac.* The /kw/ sound is spelled *cu* in a number of other relatively unintegrated adoptions: *cuica, cuichunchuli, cui bono, cuiejo, cuir, cuirass, cuir-bouilli, cuisine, cuisse, cuivré.*

The correspondence /w/ = *u* is not widespread after *g*, for the *u* must always be followed by a vowel. However, except in proper names like *Gwen* and *Gwynne* and the Welsh adoption *gwyniad, gwyniard,* the /gw/ sound is always spelled *gu* in English:

(Array 33-1)

anguish	guaiacum*	iguana	languish
consanguinity	guanaco*	jaguar	linguistic
distinguish	guano	language	penguin
extinguish	guarana	languid	sanguine

Instances of /w/ = *u* after *s:*

(Array 33-2)

assuage	persuasive	suave	suerte
dissuade	suasive	suede	suite

The correspondence /w/ = *u* occurs after *p* only in *pueblo* and in variant pronunciations of *puerile* and *puissant.* Again, the *u* is always followed by a vowel. Except in the very rare and unintegrated Burmese adoption *pwe*, the sound /pw/ is never spelled *pw* in English.

33.2.2.2 /w/ = w

The spelling of /w/ as w in /sw/ is not clearly distinguished from its spelling
as u in the same sound, for both occur, and always in initial position. The
sw combination is much more common, however:

(Array 33-3)

swan	sweet	swindle	swoon
swarthy	swerve	swing	swung

The correspondence /w/ = w occurs in other initial clusters as well:

(Array 33-4)

athwart	dwindle	schwa	tweak
dwarf	kwacha	thwack	twenty
dwell	kwashiokor	twain	twice

The correspondence /w/ = w is also common in initial position in free
bases and suffixes:

(Array 33-5)

archway	clockwise	seaweed	weight
award	heavyweight	toward	wisdom
beware	kilowatt	unwieldy	wooden
breakwater	likewise	waitress	wounded

The cluster wh is an inversion, a kind of institutionalized mistake. In
Old English several words began with the cluster hw: hwæl 'whale', hwæt
'what', hwēol 'wheel', and so on. These words are often still pronounced
as if the spelling were hw rather than wh: /hwāl/, /hwut/, /hwēl/. In Middle
English hw became wh, perhaps because the scribes found the /hw/ sound
strange to their ears, perhaps by analogy with the other consonant digraphs ending in h. In addition, pushing the analogy further, during this
same period a few words that had been spelled with w in early Middle
English were changed to wh: whip (early Middle English wippen), whit
(early Middle English wiht or wight). Also, a certain number of words that
had been spelled with h in Old English were changed to wh in Middle
English: whole (Old English hāl), whore (Old English hōre). Thus the
latecoming wh actually had three different sources: Old English hw and h
and some early Middle English words spelled with w (Jespersen [1909]
1954, 1:38, 215, 374–75; Dobson 1957, 2:974–75). For more on wh see 11.2.2
and 28.4.3.

Words with initial wh—whale, wheel, while, whorl, why—are usually
officially pronounced with /hw/ and unofficially pronounced with the
simplified /w/. In their pronouncing dictionary Kenyon and Knott say that

"only the sound *hw* is given for the spelling 'wh', but it is to be understood that in all such cases many speakers replace *hw* with plain *w*" (1944, 473). Thus, depending on the individual pronunciation, such words instance either /w/ = *wh* or /w/ = *w*, metathesized in the cluster /hw/ = *wh*.

33.3 The Spellings of /y/

There are actually three different /y/, or at least /y/-like, sounds. First, there is the consonant /y/ that occurs only in initial position and that is nearly always spelled *y*, as in *yeast*. Second, there is the glide /y/ that never occurs in word- or element-initial position but that is always syllable-initial. It is nearly always spelled *i*, as in *onion* and *billiards*. Third, there is the /y/ that can occur in word-initial, element-initial, or syllable-initial position, but that most often occurs medially. This /y/ is part of the complex vowel sounds /yū/, /yu̇/, and /yə/, as in *cure, euphoria, failure, grandeur.* These complex vowel sounds are usually spelled *u* and less often *eu* (see chapter 23).

33.3.1 The Consonantal /y/

Consonantal /y/ occurs only in initial position and is regularly spelled *y:*

(Array 33-6)

beyond	yawn	yesterday	youth
farmyard	yearn	yield	yucca
yacht	yellow	yodel	yule

Halyard and *lanyard* can be included here, even though their origins have nothing to do with *yard,* and the elements *hal-* and *lan-* are somewhat odd. In Middle English *halyard* was *halier* and *lanyard* was *lanyer.* Still, the explications (hal(yard) and (lan(yard) are justified by the obvious analogy with the nautical term *yard.* The very unusual correspondence /y/ = *ll* occurs in the Spanish adoption *llareta,* which has the more regular variant *yareta.*

33.3.2 The Glide /y/

The glide /y/ never occurs in word-initial position. It is, however, routinely syllable-initial. It is usually spelled *i*, rarely *y* or *e*. It is spelled *e* in *azalea.* It is spelled *y* in *banyan, canyon,* in one pronunciation of *buoyant,* and in the old suffix *-yer,* as in *bowyer, lawyer*,* and *sawyer*.*

The word *capercaillie* 'grouse' has the variant spelling *capercailzie,* which has the variant pronunciation /ˌkapər'kālyē/. The *z* is the Scottish representation of the Middle English letter yogh, which looked much like a cursive *z:* 3. Yogh was used to represent the /y/ in Middle English up through the thirteenth century, when it was replaced by *y* (see 11.2.1.2). Thus the *z* in *capercailzie* is the Scottish printers' version of yogh, with its old value of /y/.

In the great majority of cases the glide /y/ = *i*. The *i* is always preceded by a consonant and followed by a vowel, which is nearly always unstressed (as is the *i*). In most cases the preceding consonant is *l* or *n*. The most common instance of this correspondence is with the suffix -*ion* or analogous *ion* endings:

(**Array 33-7**)

alien	billion	congenial	opinion
ameliorate	brilliant	convenience	pavilion
auxiliary	civilian	dahlia	rebellion
bestial*	collier	dominion	savior
bilious	companion	onion	spaniel

Cases of /y/ = *i* before a stressed vowel occur in *portiere,* and in words like those in array 33-7 to which a suffix such as -*ity* is added, thereby producing a stress shift: *congeniality, bestiality, peculiarity, seniority.* Often when the stress shifts, the /y/ disappears: *familiar* (with /y/), but *familiarity* (with or without); *genial* (with or without /y/), but *geniality* (without).

The correspondence /y/ = *j* occurs in *fjord,* which has a more integrated variant, *fiord.*

34 Conclusion

This study began with the assertion that American English spelling is a self-regulating, self-reorganizing system that works to reconcile—or in the Gestaltists' sense of the term, to "articulate"—the often contending demands made upon it. The first of these demands, the phonetic, urges that sounds be spelled consistently from word to word. This is one of the two basic, or at least chronologically prior, demands, stemming as it does from the invention of alphabetic literacy in ancient Greece (Havelock 1963, 1976; Ong 1982). On the other hand, since written language exists to convey human meanings, equally basic is the semantic demand, which urges that units of semantic content be spelled consistently from word to word. Because language was used before the invention of alphabetic literacy and because there were several well-developed prealphabetic writing systems, the semantic demand is obviously older than the phonetic. The often closely parallel etymological, or, more generally and accurately, historical, demand urges that words be spelled in such a way as to reflect their users' notion of their etymology and historical development. In addition, a number of sociolinguistic demands are made upon the system, demands that change as the social uses and expectations of writing change. Because spelling is systematic, it makes demands that are common to any system—the demands for regularity, predictability, order. Moreover, it strives for simplicity, but in the case of American English spelling, which is worked upon by so many contending forces, such simplicity is best thought of as the careful articulation of these forces and demands, the Gestaltists' maximum simplicity. It is, if the oxymoron be allowed, an intricate simplicity.

The preceding chapters, though numerous, do not begin to do justice to that intricacy of contending demands. Chapters 1 and 2 argue for the systematic nature of American English spelling and thus describe in general terms the interplay of systemic demands. Chapters 3–7, on tactics, and chapters 8–10, on procedures, provide examples of that systematicity at work. Chapters 11–33, which deal with the correspondences between the sounds and letters of American English, speak primarily to the system's phonetic demand, though they acknowledge the underlying contention of phonetic, semantic, systemic, sociolinguistic, and historical demands.

Much more needs to be done. The discussion of elements, particles, and sets in chapter 2 just touches on the semantic demand, which still raises more questions than answers. At the very least we need a systematic catalog of the elements of American English. Bound bases in particular remain undescribed in any useful way. We need a systematic catalog of them, just as we need a thorough catalog of the functioning sets of coelements in the language. It would be interesting and useful to have full explications of a large sample of the American English lexicon. The distinction between terminative and nonterminative bases also remains essentially unexplored. It would be interesting and useful as well to see to what extent the patterns and rules described informally here lend themselves to the formal rigor that characterizes modern linguistic science.

As far as the historical demand is concerned, it seems unlikely that any great surprises await us in English etymology. The work of the philologists and etymologists of the last two hundred years or so has been remarkably thorough and fruitful. But we still do not have a very detailed picture of the more recent history of the language—that is, the changes that have occurred since English began to be written down. Brengelman's convincing and informative argument for the efficacy of the early orthoepists and orthographers in rationalizing English spelling is an important work in this area. But the whole question of sustained literacy in English and its sociolinguistic effects, as well as the obverse question of the effects sociolinguistic change has had on literacy—these questions, discussed by Stubbs in *Language and Literacy* (1980) and more remotely by people like Goody and Watt (1968), Havelock (1976, 1982) and Ong (1982)—remain open to investigation. For instance, Stubbs raises the question of the effects of writing on speech, effects that have largely gone unexplored.

Another question, vast and open to further study, concerns what the increase in orthographic knowledge implies about how best to teach reading and spelling. As Stubbs and others have pointed out, we still do not have a true theory of reading, nor do we have a theory of spelling. What we have are a number of studies, mostly psycholinguistic in focus, that do not always articulate very well, either with one another or with the din and roar of the reading and spelling classroom. It seems probable that a better understanding of the American English orthographic system would lead us toward a better teaching of literacy, even though the evidence to date remains inconclusive.

During the first five or six decades of this century English orthography did not receive much attention. Such has not always been the case. During the Renaissance, for instance, as part of the effort to widen literacy, orthoepists and orthographers like Mulcaster worked hard to describe the rules and regularities of written English. As recently as the nineteenth century philologists emphasized written texts—and thus the written word. But in the early twentieth century the emphasis shifted to the spoken language. Speech was viewed as the "real" language; writing was at best a secondary shadow. In the past two decades, however, attention has shifted back to the written language and its orthography. The orthographic discipline appears to be experiencing a reawakening. If *American English Spelling* plays a part in that reawakening, it will have served its purpose.

Bibliography

Aarsleff, Hans. *The Study of Language in England, 1780–1860.* Minneapolis: University of Minnesota Press, 1983.

Akmajian, Adrian, Richard A. Demers, and Robert M. Harnish. *Linguistics: An Introduction to Language and Communication.* 2nd ed. Cambridge: MIT Press, 1984.

Albrow, K. H. *The English Writing System: Notes Towards a Description.* Schools Council Program in Linguistics and English Teaching, Papers Series II, no. 2. London: Longmans, for the Schools Council, 1972.

Anderson-Inman, Lynne, Robert Dixon, and Wesley Becker. *Morphographs: An Alphabetical List with Exemplars.* Technical Report 1981-1, University of Oregon Follow-Through Project. Eugene: College of Education, University of Oregon, 1981.

Aristotle. *On Interpretation.* Translated by E. M. Eghill. Chicago: Encyclopaedia Britannica, 1952.

Aronoff, Mark. "An English Spelling Convention." *Linguistic Inquiry* 9 (1978): 299–303.

———. *Word Formation in Generative Grammar.* Cambridge: MIT Press, 1981.

Artin, Edward. "Guide to Pronunciation." In *Webster's Third New International Dictionary of the English Language Unabridged,* edited by Philip Gove, 33a–46a. Springfield, Mass.: G. & C. Merriam, 1971.

Ashby, W. Ross. "Principles of the Self-Organizing System." In *Modern Systems Research for the Behavioral Scientist,* edited by Walter Buckley, 108–18. Chicago: Aldine, 1968.

Ball, Alice Morton. *Compounding in the English Language.* New York: H. W. Wilson, 1941.

Balmuth, Miriam. *The Roots of Phonics: A Historical Introduction.* New York: McGraw-Hill, 1982.

Barber, Charles. *Early Modern English.* London: Andre Deutsch, 1976.

Baron, Naomi S. *Speech, Writing, and Sign: A Functional View of Linguistic Representation.* Bloomington: Indiana University Press, 1981.

Bauer, Laurie. *English Word-Formation.* Cambridge: Cambridge University Press, 1983.

Baugh, Albert C., and Thomas Cable. *A History of the English Language.* 3rd ed. Englewood Cliffs, N.J.: Prentice-Hall, 1978.

Bazell, Charles E. "The Grapheme." In *Readings in Linguistics, II,* edited by Eric

Hamp, Fred Householder, and Robert Austerlitz, 359–61. Chicago: University of Chicago Press, 1966.

Berry, Jack. "The Making of Alphabets." In *Readings in the Sociology of Language,* edited by Joshua Fishman, 737–53. The Hague: Mouton, 1968.

——. " 'The Making of Alphabets' Revisited." In *Advances in the Creation and Revision of Writing Systems,* edited by Joshua Fishman, 3–16. The Hague: Mouton, 1977.

Bissex, G. L. *GNYS AT WRK: A Child Learns to Write and Read.* Cambridge: Harvard University Press, 1980.

Black, Max. "The Analysis of Rules." *Models and Metaphors: Studies in Language and Philosophy,* 95–139. Ithaca: Cornell University Press, 1962.

Bloomfield, Leonard. *Language.* New York: Henry Holt, 1933.

Bloomfield, Morton W. "Final Root-Forming Morphemes." *Essays and Explorations: Studies in Ideas, Language, and Literature,* 233–40. Cambridge: Harvard University Press, 1970.

Bolinger, Dwight. "Rime, Assonance, and Morpheme Analysis" (1950), "Visual Morphemes" (1946), and "Word Affinities" (1940). *Forms of English: Accent, Morpheme, Order,* 203–26, 267–76, 191–202. Cambridge: Harvard University Press, 1965.

Bolinger, Dwight, and Donald Sears. *Aspects of Language.* 3rd ed. New York: Harcourt Brace Jovanovich, 1981.

Bowman, Wayne. *"Busses* versus *Buses." American Speech* 40 (1966): 299–300.

Bradley, Henry. "Spelling." *The Collected Papers of Henry Bradley,* 164–68. College Park, Md.: McGrath, 1970a.

——. "Spoken and Written English." *The Collected Papers of Henry Bradley,* 168–88. College Park, Md.: McGrath, 1970b. (Originally published in *Proceedings of the British Academy* 6 [1914]: 211–32.)

Brengelman, Fred H. "Sounds and Letters in American English." *The English Language: An Introduction for Teachers,* 77–98. Englewood Cliffs, N.J.: Prentice-Hall, 1970.

——. "English Spelling as a Marker of Register and Style." *English Studies* 52 (1971): 201–9.

——. "Orthoepists, Printers, and the Rationalization of English Spelling." *Journal of English and Germanic Philology* 79 (1980): 332–54.

Brook, G. L. "Spelling." *A History of the English Language,* 100–114. London: Andre Deutsch, 1958.

Buckley, Walter. *Modern Systems Research for the Behavioral Scientist.* Chicago: Aldine, 1968.

Campbell, A. *Old English Grammar.* Oxford: Oxford University Press, 1959. See especially "Writing, Orthography, and Pronunciation," 12–29.

Campbell, Jeremy. *Grammatical Man: Information, Entropy, Language, and Life.* New York: Simon & Schuster, 1982.

Carroll, John B., Peter Davies, and Barry Richman. *The American Heritage Word Frequency Book.* Boston: Houghton Mifflin, 1971.

Cercignani, Fausto. *Shakespeare's Works and Elizabethan Pronunciation.* Oxford: Clarendon Press, 1981.

Chaytor, H. J. *From Script to Print: An Introduction to Medieval Vernacular Literature.* Cambridge: W. Heffer & Sons, 1950.

Chomsky, Carol. "Reading, Writing, and Phonology." *Harvard Educational Review* 40 (1970): 287–309.

Chomsky, Noam, and Morris Halle. *The Sound Pattern of English.* New York: Harper & Row, 1968.

Clanchy, M. T. *From Memory to Written Record: England, 1066–1307.* Cambridge: Harvard University Press, 1979.

Craigie, William A. *English Spelling: Its Rules and Reasons.* 1927. Reprint. Folcroft, Pa.: Folcroft Library Editions, 1974.

———. *Some Anomalies of Spelling.* Society of Pure English Tract no. 59. 1942. Reprint. Folcroft, Pa.: Folcroft Press, 1969.

———, ed. *The Critique of Pure English, from Caxton to Smollett.* Society of Pure English Tract no. 65. 1946. Reprint. Folcroft, Pa.: Folcroft Press, 1969.

Daneš, Frantisek. "The Relation of Centre and Periphery as a Language Universal." *Travaux Linguistiques de Prague,* 2: 9–21. University: University of Alabama Press, 1966.

Dewey, Godfrey. *Relative Frequency of English Spellings.* New York: Teachers College Press, Columbia University, 1970.

Dickerson, Wayne B. "Decomposition of Orthographic Word Classes." *Linguistics* 163 (1975): 19–34.

Dixon, Robert. *Morphographic Spelling Program.* Eugene, Oreg.: Engelman-Becker Press, 1977. See also Anderson-Inman, Dixon, and Becker 1981.

Dobson, E. J. *English Pronunciation, 1500–1700.* 2 vols. Oxford: Oxford University Press, 1957.

Dolby, J. L., and H. L. Resnikoff. *The English Word Speculum.* Vol. 4, Pt. 2, *The Double Standard Reverse Word List.* The Hague: Mouton, 1967.

Edgerton, William F. "Ideograms in English Writing." *Language* 17 (1941): 148–50.

Emery, Donald W. *Variant Spellings in Modern American Dictionaries.* Urbana, Ill.: National Council of Teachers of English, 1973.

Ewert, Alfred. "Orthography." *The French Language,* 109–22. London: Faber & Faber, 1961.

Fisher, John Hurt. "The Ancestry of the English Alphabet." *Archaeology* (1951): 232–42.

———. "Chancery and the Emergence of Standard Written English in the Fifteenth Century." *Speculum* (1977): 870–99.

Fisher, John Hurt, Malcolm Richardson, and Jane L. Fisher, eds. *An Anthology of Chancery English.* Knoxville: University of Tennessee Press, 1984. See especially "Orthography," 26–35.

Fishman, Joshua, ed. *Advances in the Creation and Revision of Writing Systems.* The Hague: Mouton, 1977.

Fowler, H. W. *A Dictionary of Modern English Usage.* 1926. Revised edition by Sir Ernest Gowers. New York: Oxford University Press, 1965.

Francis, W. Nelson. *The Structure of American English.* New York: Ronald, 1958. See especially "Writing It Down: Graphics," 430–79.

Fried, Vilem. "The Notion of Diacritics in Modern English Graphology." *Brno Studies in English* 8 (1969): 61–67.

Frith, Uta, ed. *Cognitive Processes in Spelling.* New York: Academic Press, 1980.

Fu, Yi-Chin. "Cover Symbols for Morphophonic Alternations in English Orthography." *Studies in Linguistics* 20 (1968): 1–5.

Ganz, Joan Safran. *Rules: A Systematic Study.* Janua Linguarum, Series Minor, no. 96. The Hague: Mouton, 1971.

Gelb, I. J. *A Study of Writing.* Rev. ed. Chicago: University of Chicago Press, 1952.

Gleason, H. A. *An Introduction to Descriptive Linguistics.* New York: Holt, Rinehart & Winston, 1958. See especially 408–39.

Goody, Jack. *The Domestication of the Savage Mind.* Cambridge: Cambridge University Press, 1977.

Goody, Jack, and Ian Watt. "The Consequences of Literacy." In *Literacy in Traditional Societies,* edited by Jack Goody, 27–68. Cambridge: Cambridge University Press, 1968.

Gould, Stephen Jay. "Losing the Edge" and "Reducing Riddles." *The Flamingo's Smile,* 215–29, 245–60. New York: W. W. Norton, 1985.

Gove, Philip, ed. *Webster's Third New International Dictionary of the English Language Unabridged.* Springfield, Mass.: G. & C. Merriam, 1971.

Greenough, James Bradstreet, and George Lyman Kittredge. "Folk-Etymology." *Words and Their Ways in English Speech,* 330–44. New York: Macmillan, 1906.

Gumb, Raymond D. *Rule-Governed Linguistic Behavior.* Janua Linguarum, Series Minor, no. 141. The Hague: Mouton, 1972.

Haas, William. *Phono-Graphic Translation.* Mont Follick Series, no. 2. Manchester: Manchester University Press, 1970.

———. "Writing: The Basic Options." In *Writing without Letters,* edited by W. Haas, 131–208. Mont Follick Series, no. 4. Manchester: Manchester University Press, 1976a.

———, ed. *Alphabets for English.* Mont Follick Series, no. 1. Manchester: Manchester University Press, 1969.

———. *Writing without Letters.* Mont Follick Series, no. 4. Manchester: Manchester University Press, 1976b.

Hall, John R. Clark. *A Concise Anglo-Saxon Dictionary.* 4th ed. Cambridge: Cambridge University Press, 1975.

Hall, Robert A., Jr. Review of *Written Language: General Problems of English,* by Josef Vachek. *Language* 51 (1975): 461–65.

Hamp, Eric, Fred Householder, and Robert Austerlitz, eds. *Readings in Linguistics, II.* Chicago: University of Chicago Press, 1966.

Hanna, Paul R., Jean S. Hanna, Richard E. Hodges, and Erwin H. Rudorf, Jr. *Phoneme-Grapheme Correspondences as Cues to Spelling Improvement.* Washington, D.C.: GPO, 1966.

Hansen, Klaus. "Foreign Graphemes and Grapheme-Phoneme Correspondence in Modern English." *Brno Studies in English* 8 (1969): 89–93.

Havelock, Eric A. *A Preface to Plato.* Cambridge: Harvard University Press, 1963.

———. *Origins of Western Literacy.* Toronto: Ontario Institute for Studies in Education, 1976.

———. *The Literate Revolution in Greece and Its Cultural Consequences.* Princeton: Princeton University Press, 1982.

Heller, Louis G., and James Macris. "A Typology of Shortening Devices." *American Speech* 43 (1968): 201–8.

Hill, Kenneth, and Larry Nessly. Review of *The Sound Pattern of English,* by Noam Chomsky and Morris Halle. *Linguistics* 106 (1973): 57–121.

Hockett, Charles F. *A Course in Modern Linguistics.* New York: Macmillan, 1958.

Hodges, R. E. "The Language Base of Spelling." In *Research in the Language Arts: Language and Schooling,* edited by Victor Froese and Stanley B. Straw, 203–26. Baltimore: University Park Press, 1981.

————. "Theoretical Frameworks of English Orthography." *Elementary English* 49 (1972): 1089–97.

Holmberg, Borje. "Noah Webster and American Pronunciation." *English Studies* 46 (1965): 118–29.

Horn, E. "Spelling." In *Encyclopedia of Educational Research,* edited by C. W. Harris, 1337–54. 3rd ed. New York: Macmillan, 1960.

Horn, T. D. "Spelling." In *Encyclopedia of Educational Research,* edited by R. L. Ebel, 1282–99. 4th ed. New York: Macmillan, 1969.

Hospers, J. H. "Graphemics and the History of Phonology." *Historiographia Linguistica* 7 (1980): 351–59.

Householder, Fred. "The Primacy of Writing" and "Sameness, Similarity, Analogy, Rules, and Features." *Linguistic Speculations,* 244–64, 61–81. Cambridge: Cambridge University Press, 1971.

Hultzen, Lee S. "Consonant Clusters in English." *American Speech* 40 (1965): 5–19.

Jespersen, Otto. *A Modern English Grammar on Historical Principles.* Part 1, *Sounds and Spellings.* 1909. Reprint. London and Copenhagen: Allen & Unwin and Munksgaard, 1954.

————. *A Modern English Grammar.* Part 6, *Morphology.* London: Allen & Unwin, 1946.

Johnson, Samuel. *A Dictionary of the English Language.* 1775. Reprint. London: Times Books, 1983.

Jones, Daniel. *Everyman's English Pronouncing Dictionary.* 11th ed. New York: E. P. Dutton, 1956.

————. *The Phoneme: Its Nature and Use.* 3rd ed. Cambridge: W. Heffer & Sons, 1967. See especially "Further Remarks on Phonetic Writing," 219–33.

Katz, David. *Gestalt Psychology: Its Nature and Significance.* Translated by Robert Tyson. New York: Ronald, 1950.

Kavanagh, James F., and I. G. Mattingly, eds. *Language by Ear and by Eye.* Cambridge: MIT Press, 1972.

Kavanagh, James F., and Richard L. Venezky, eds. *Orthography, Reading, and Dyslexia.* Baltimore: University Park Press, 1980.

Kenyon, John S., and Thomas Knott. *A Pronouncing Dictionary of American English.* Springfield, Mass.: G. & C. Merriam, 1944.

Kerek, Andrew. "The Phonological Relevance of Spelling Pronunciation." *Visible Language* 10 (1976): 323–38.

Kim, Suksan. "Diacritical Functions of the Letter [ʒ] in Middle English." *Journal of English Linguistics* 5 (1971): 94–100.

————. "Long Consonants in Old English." *Linguistics* 102 (1973): 83–90.

King, Robert D. *Historical Linguistics and Generative Grammar.* Englewood Cliffs, N.J.: Prentice-Hall, 1969.

Klima, Edward. "How Alphabets Might Reflect Language." In *Language by Ear and by Eye,* edited by James F. Kavanagh and I. G. Mattingly, 57–80. Cambridge: MIT Press, 1972.

Koffka, Kurt. *Principles of Gestalt Psychology.* New York: Harcourt, Brace, 1935.

Kohler, Wolfgang. *Gestalt Psychology: An Introduction to New Concepts in Modern Psychology.* New York: New American Library, 1959.

Kokeritz, Helge. *Shakespeare's Pronunciation.* New Haven: Yale University Press, 1953.

Kreidler, Charles W. "English Orthography: A Generative Approach." In *Studies in Honor of Albert H. Marckwardt,* edited by James E. Alatis, 81–91. Washington, D.C.: Teachers of English to Speakers of Other Languages, 1972.

Kurath, Hans. "The Loss of Long Consonants and the Rise of Voiced Fricatives in Middle English." *Language* 32 (1956): 433–45.

Ladefoged, Peter. *A Course in Phonetics.* New York: Harcourt Brace Jovanovich, 1975.

Lass, Roger. *On Explaining Language Change.* New York: Cambridge University Press, 1980.

Lass, Roger, and John Anderson. *Old English Phonology.* Cambridge: Cambridge University Press, 1975.

Laszlo, Ervin. *Introduction to Systems Philosophy.* New York: Harper & Row, 1972.

Lehmann, Winfred P. *Historical Linguistics: An Introduction.* 2nd ed. New York: Holt, 1973. See especially "Change in Grammatical Systems: Analogical Change," 177–92, and "Change in Phonological Systems," 147–75.

Levitt, Jesse. "The Influence of Orthography on Phonology: A Comparative Study." *Linguistics* 208 (1978): 43–67.

Linell, Per. *Psychological Reality in Phonology.* Cambridge: Cambridge University Press, 1979.

Linksz, Arthur. *On Writing, Reading, and Dyslexia.* New York: Grune & Stratton, 1973.

Lotz, John. "How Language is Conveyed by Script." In *Language by Ear and by Eye,* edited by James F. Kavanagh and I. G. Mattingly, 117–24. Cambridge: MIT Press, 1972.

Lucas, Peter J. "Consistency and Correctness in the Orthographic Usage of John Capsgrave's *Chronicle.*" *Studia Neophilologica* 45 (1973): 325–55.

McIntosh, Angus. "The Analysis of Written Middle English." *Transactions of the Philological Society* (1956): 26–55.

———. "Graphology and Meaning." In *Patterns of Language,* by M. A. K. Halliday and Angus McIntosh, 98–110. Bloomington: Indiana University Press, 1967.

———. "A New Approach to Middle English Dialectology." *English Studies* 44 (1963): 1–11.

McKnight, George H. *English Words and Their Backgrounds.* New York: D. Appleton, 1923. See especially "Folk Etymology," 180–90.

McLuhan, Marshall. "The Effect of the Printed Book on Language in the Sixteenth Century." In *Explorations in Communication,* edited by Edmund Carpenter and Marshall McLuhan, 125–35. Boston: Beacon Press, 1960.

Marchand, Hans. *The Categories and Types of Present-day English Word-Formation.* 2nd ed. Munich: C. H. Beck'sche, 1969.

Mencken, H. L. *The American Language.* Edited by Raven McDavid, Jr. Abr. ed. New York: Knopf, 1963. See especially "American Spelling," 479–508.

Monaghan, E. Jennifer. *A Common Heritage: Noah Webster's Blue-back Speller.*

Hamden, Ct.: Archon Books, 1983. See especially "Orthography and Pronunciation," 109–30.

Morris, William, ed. *The American Heritage Dictionary of the English Language.* Boston: Houghton Mifflin, 1976.

Mossé, Fernand. *A Handbook of Middle English.* Translated by James A. Walker. Baltimore: Johns Hopkins Press, 1952.

Mulcaster, Richard. *The First Part of the Elementarie.* 1582. Reprint. Menston, Eng.: Scolar Press, 1970.

Murray, James A. H., Henry Bradley, W. A. Craigie, and C. T. Onions, eds. *The Oxford English Dictionary.* 12 vols. Corrected reissue (originally published 1884–1921). Oxford: Clarendon Press, 1933.

Nessly, Larry. *English Stress and Synchronic Descriptions* (Ph. D. diss., University of Michigan, 1974). Ann Arbor: Xerox University Microfilms, 1975.

———. "Nativization and Variation in English Phonology." In *New Ways of Analyzing Variation in English,* edited by C. J. N. Bailey and R. W. Shuy, 253–64. Washington, D.C.: Georgetown University Press, 1973.

Newman, Stanley S. "English Suffixation: A Descriptive Approach." *Word* 4 (1948): 24–36.

Ney, James. *Elitism, Racism, and Some Contemporary Views of English Spelling.* Tempe, Ariz.: Sancho Educational Enterprises, 1974.

———. "Old English Vowel Digraph Spellings." *Linguistics* 45 (1968): 36–49.

Nist, John. "In Defense of English Spelling." *Linguistics* 23 (1966): 81–89.

O'Donnell, W. R., and Loreto Todd. "Speech and Writing." *Variety in Contemporary English,* 2–15. London: Allen & Unwin, 1980.

O'Neil, Wayne. "The Spelling and Pronunciation of English." In *The American Heritage Dictionary of the English Language,* edited by William Morris, xxxv–xxxvii. Boston: Houghton Mifflin, 1976.

———. "English Orthography." In *Standards and Dialects in English,* edited by Timothy Shopen and Joseph M. Williams, 63–83. Cambridge: Winthrop, 1980.

Ong, Walter J. *Orality and Literacy: The Technologizing of the Word.* London: Methuen, 1982.

Onions, C. T., ed. *The Oxford Dictionary of English Etymology.* New York: Oxford University Press, 1966.

Oswalt, Robert L. "English Orthography as a Morphophonemic System: Stressed Vowels." *Linguistics* 102 (1973): 5–40.

Parsons, Talcott. "Social Systems." In *Encyclopedia of the Social Sciences,* edited by David L. Sills, 15: 458–73. New York: Macmillan, 1968.

Partridge, Eric. *Origins: A Short Etymological Dictionary of Modern English.* 1958. Reprint. New York: Greenwich House, 1983.

Penzl, Herbert. "The Phonemic Split of Germanic 'K' in Old English." *Language* 23 (1947): 33–42.

Pilch, H. "The Phonemic Interpretation of Old English Spelling Evidence." *Acta Linguistica Hafniensia* 12 (1969): 29–44.

Pope, Mildred K. *From Latin to Modern French, with Especial Consideration of Anglo-Norman.* 1934. Reprint. Manchester: Manchester University Press, 1974.

Prins, A. A. *A History of English Phonemes.* Leiden: Leiden University Press, 1972.

Pulgram, Ernst. "Phoneme and Grapheme: A Parallel." *Word* 7 (1951): 15–20.

———. "Graphic and Phonic Systems: Figurae and Signs." *Word* 21 (1965): 208–24.

———. "The Typologies of Writing Systems." In *Writing without Letters,* edited by William Haas, 1–28. Manchester: Manchester University Press, 1976.

Quirk, Randolph, Sidney Greenbaum, Geoffrey Leech, and Jan Svartvik. *A Comprehensive Grammar of the English Language.* London: Longmans, 1985.

Rapaport, Anatol. "General Systems Theory." In *Encyclopedia of the Social Sciences,* edited by David L. Sills, 15: 452–58. New York: Macmillan, 1968.

Read, Charles. *Children's Categorization of Speech Sounds in English.* Urbana, Ill.: NCTE, 1975.

———. "Orthography." In *The Psychology of Written Language: Developmental and Educational Perspectives,* edited by Margaret Martlew, 143–61. Chichester, Eng.: Wiley, 1983.

Read, Charles, and Richard E. Hodges. "Spelling." In *Encyclopedia of Educational Research.* 5th ed., 1758–67. New York: Macmillan, 1982.

Reed, David. "A Theory of Language, Speech, and Writing." In *Readings in Applied Transformational Grammar,* edited by Mark Lester, 284–304. New York: Holt, Rinehart & Winston, 1970.

Richardson, Malcolm. "Henry V, the English Chancery, and Chancery English." *Speculum* 55 (1980): 726–50.

Roberts, A. Hood. *A Statistical Linguistic Analysis of American English.* The Hague: Mouton, 1965.

Rohlfs, Gerhard. "From Vulgar Latin to Old French." *The Old French Language.* Translated by Vincent Almazan and Lillian McCarthy, 70–72. Detroit: Wayne State University Press, 1970.

Šaljapina, Z., and V. Ševoroškin. Review of *The Structure of English Orthography,* by Richard L. Venezky. *Linguistics* 84 (1972): 89–100.

Samuels, Michael. "Some Applications of Middle English Dialectology." *English Studies* 44 (1963): 81–94.

———. *Linguistic Evolution with Special Reference to English.* Cambridge: Cambridge University Press, 1972.

Sapir, Edward. *Language: An Introduction to the Study of Speech.* 1921. Reprint. New York: Harcourt, Brace & World, 1949.

Saussure, Ferdinand de. *Course in General Linguistics.* Edited by Charles Bally and Albert Sechehaye, with Albert Reidlinger. Translated by Wade Baskin. 1915. Reprint. New York: Philosophical Library, 1959.

Scragg, D. G. *A History of English Spelling.* Manchester: Manchester University Press, 1974.

———. "Initial *h* in Old English." *Anglia* 88 (1970): 165–96.

Shipley, Joseph T. *The Origins of English Words: A Discursive Dictionary of Indo-European Roots.* Baltimore: Johns Hopkins University Press, 1984.

Skeat, Walter W. *A Concise Etymological Dictionary of the English Language.* 1882. Reprint. New York: Capricorn Books, 1963.

———. *Principles of English Etymology: Second Series, The Foreign Element.* 1891. Reprint. College Park, Md.: McGrath, 1970.

Skousen, Royal. "English Spelling and Phonemic Representation." *Visible Language* 16 (1982): 28–38.

Smith, Henry Lee, Jr. "The Concept of the Morphophone." *Language* 43 (1967): 306–41.

———. *English Morphophonics: Implications for the Teaching of Literacy.* Monograph no. 10. Oswego: New York State English Council, 1968.

———. "The Dialects of English." In *The American Heritage Dictionary of the English Language,* edited by William Morris, xxv–xxx. Boston: Houghton Mifflin, 1976.

Smith, Philip T. "In Defense of Conservatism in English Orthography." *Visible Language* 14 (1980): 122–36.

Smith, Philip T., and R. G. Baker. "The Influence of English Spelling Patterns on Pronunciation." *Journal of Verbal Learning and Verbal Behavior* 15 (1976): 267–85.

Strang, Barbara M. H. *A History of English.* London: Methuen, 1970.

Stubbs, Michael. *Language and Literacy: The Sociolinguistics of Reading and Writing.* London and Boston: Routledge & Kegan Paul, 1980.

Tauli, Valter. "Speech and Spelling." In *Advances in the Creation and Revision of Writing Systems,* edited by Joshua Fishman, 17–36. The Hague: Mouton, 1977.

Thesarium Trilinguae Publicum. 1689. Reprint. Menston, Eng.: Scolar Press, 1971.

Trager, George. "Writing and Writing Systems." In *Current Trends in Linguistics, XII: Linguistics and Adjacent Arts and Sciences,* edited by Thomas Sebeok, 1: 373–496. 4 vols. The Hague: Mouton, 1974.

Trager, George, and Henry Lee Smith, Jr. *An Outline of English Structure.* Studies in Linguistics: Occasional Papers, no. 3. Washington, D.C.: American Council of Learned Societies, 1957.

Uldall, H. J. "Speech and Writing." In *Readings in Linguistics, II,* edited by Eric Hamp, Fred Householder, and Robert Austerlitz, 147–51. Chicago: University of Chicago Press, 1966.

Vachek, Josef. "On Peripheral Phonemes of Modern English." *Brno Studies in English* 4 (1965): 7–109.

———. "On the Integration of the Peripheral Elements into the System of Language." *Travaux Linguistiques de Prague,* 2:23–37. University: University of Alabama Press, 1966a.

———. "Some Remarks on Writing and Phonetic Transcription." In *Readings in Linguistics, II,* edited by Eric Hamp, Fred Householder, and Robert Austerlitz, 152–57. Chicago: University of Chicago Press, 1966b.

———. Review of *The Structure of English Orthography,* by Richard L. Venezky. *Language* 47 (1971): 212–16.

———. *Written Language: General Problems and Problems of English.* Janua Linguarum, Series Critica, no. 14. The Hague: Mouton, 1973.

Vallins, G. H. *Spelling.* Rev. ed. The Language Library. London: Andre Deutsch, 1965.

Venezky, Richard L. *The Structure of English Orthography.* The Hague: Mouton, 1970.

———. "Notes on the History of English Spelling." *Visible Language* 10 (1976): 351–65.

———. "Principles for the Design of Practical Writing Systems." In *Advances in the Creation and Revision of Writing Systems,* edited by Joshua Fishman, 37–54. The Hague: Mouton, 1977.

———. "Overview: From Sumer to Leipzig to Bethesda." In *Orthography, Reading, and Dyslexia,* edited by James F. Kavanagh and Richard L. Venezky, 1–11. Baltimore: University Park Press, 1980a.

———. "From Webster to Rice to Roosevelt." In *Cognitive Processes in Spelling,*
   edited by Uta Frith, 9–30. New York: Academic Press, 1980b.
Vising, Johan. *Anglo-Norman Language and Literature.* London: Oxford Univer-
   sity Press, 1923. See especially "The Character of Anglo-Norman," 27–33.
Watkins, Calvert, ed. *The American Heritage Dictionary of Indo-European Roots.*
   Boston: Houghton Mifflin, 1985. A revision of the appendix of Indo-European
   roots in *AHD,* (1st ed.), 1496–1550.
Webster, Noah. *A Grammatical Institute of the English Language, Part 1.* 1783.
   Reprint. Menston, Eng.: Scolar Press, 1968.
———. "Dissertation I." *Dissertations on the English Language.* 1789. Reprint.
   Menston, Eng.: Scolar Press, 1967.
———. Introduction to *An American Dictionary of the English Language.* 2 vols.
   1828. Reprint. New York and London: Johnson Reprint Corp., 1970.
Weinreich, Uriel, William Labov, and Marvin I. Herzog. "Empirical Foundations
   for a Theory of Language Change." In *Directions for Historical Linguistics,*
   edited by W. P. Lehmann and Y. Malkiel, 95–195. Austin: University of Texas
   Press, 1968.
Weir, Ruth H. "Some Thoughts on Spelling." In *Papers in Linguistics in Honor of
   Leon Dostert,* edited by William M. Austin, 169–77. Janua Linguarum, Series
   Major, no. 25. The Hague: Mouton, 1967.
Wertheimer, Max. "Laws of Organization in Perceptual Forms." In *A Source Book
   of Gestalt Psychology,* edited by Willis Ellis, 71–88. New York: Humanities
   Press, 1950.
Whitford, Harold C. *A Dictionary of American Homophones and Homographs.*
   New York: Teachers College Press, 1966.
Whorf, Benjamin Lee. "Linguistics as an Exact Science." In *Language, Thought,
   and Reality: Selected Writings of Benjamin Lee Whorf,* edited by John B.
   Carroll, 220–32. Cambridge: MIT Press, 1956.
Woodbine, George E. "The Language of English Law." *Speculum* 18 (1943): 395–
   437.
Wyld, Henry Cecil. *A History of Modern Colloquial English.* 3rd ed. Oxford:
   Oxford University Press, 1936.
———. *A Short History of English.* 3rd ed. London: John Murray, 1957.
Zettersten, Arne. *A Statistical Study of the Graphic System of Present-day Ameri-
   can English.* Lund: Studentlitt, 1969.

Index of Words

Where possible, inflected and derived forms are clustered with their prime or with the shortest free stem cited in the text. Compound words are clustered with their first prime. Some of the explications are quite tentative, and clusters have been avoided that would entail highly questionable explications. For any given word, a page number is cited only once, even though the word may appear on that page several times, in one or more sections of the text. For clustered forms that appear on the same page, the page number is given only once, at the end of the cluster.

a, 88, 390
aardvark, 81
aardwolf, 81
abacus, 366, 405
abalone, 332, 333, 335, 447
abampere, 197
abandon, 190
abase, 190
abash, 409; -ed, 111
abate, 190
abaxial, 197
abb, 88
abbess, 405
abbey, 332
abbreviate, 80, 191, 193, 329, 332, 376; -ion, 410
abcoulomb, 70, 197
abdicate, 197, 330, 362, 365, 366
abdomen, 197
abdominal, 234, 427
abduct, 61, 197; -ion, 410
abed, 94
aberrant, 197

aberration, 455
abet, 190
abeyance, 190, 255
abfarad, 75, 197
abgesang, 197
abhenry, 197
abhor, 75, 164, 172, 197, 312, 387; -ence, 453; -ent, 164
abide, -ingly, 141
abient, 197
ability, 47, 114, 224, 333, 389, 444
abject, 197
abjure, 197, 320, 421
ablative, 197
ablaut, 197, 306
able, 47, 105, 149, 249, 252, 389
ablution, 119, 134, 197, 290
abmigration, 197
abnegate, 197
abnormal, 432
aboard, 314, 330
abohm, 197
abolish, 122, 444

abolition, 119, 224; -ist, 119
abominate, 197, 330; -ion, 234
aborigine, 197, 214, 224, 261, 419, 455
abort, 312
abound, 184, 197, 306
above, 147, 246
abrade, 197
abrasion, 410
abraum, 197
abreact, 197
abreast, 219
abridge, 418; -ment, 159
abrogate, 451
abrupt, 197
abscess, 196, 398
abscise, 196
absci(s)sion, 196–97
abscond, 75, 196
abseil, 197
absence, 197, 214
absenteeism, 158
absinthe, 331, 386
absolute, 75, 298

absolve, 191, 197, 233, 376
absorb, 76
absorption, 312
absquatulate, 76, 197
abstain, 76, 196, 433
abstemious, 196, 263
abstention, 76
abstergent, 196
abstract, 61, 76, 196, 366
abstruse, 76, 195, 196, 403
absurd, 197
abundant, 197
abuse, 197
abvolt, 197
abyss, 82, 227, 401
acacia, 366
academy, 366; -ic, 427; -ician, 138
acajou, 293, 422
accede, 397
accelerate, 188, 372, 444
accelerometer, 235
accent, 372; -uate, 415
accept, 61, 372
access, 372; -ion, 411
accident, 188, 365, 372
accidia, accidie. See acedia
accipiter, 192
acclaim, 188
acclimate, 80
accloy, 191
accommodate, 178, 342
accompany, 178, 188
accomplice, 192
accomplish, 122, 178, 233
accord, 397
accordion, 263, 312
accost, 239
accouche, 192
account, 191, 306
accouterment, 293, 348
accretion, 119
accrue, 80, 95, 188
accumulate, 356, 428
accurate, 152, 188, 214
accurse, 192
accuse, 395
acedia, accidia, accidie, 191
aces, 251
acetic, 348, 366, 406
acetylene, 218, 347
ache, 70, 110, 229, 357; -ed, 343; -ing, 251

achieve, 147, 258, 268, 414
acid, 120; -ity, 224; -ophilus, 235
acknow, 192; -ledge, 192, 235; -ledg(e)ment, 159
acme, 261, 428
acne, 261
acorn, 125, 251, 362
acoustic, -s, 294, 366, 372
acquaint, 189, 192, 360
acquest, 189, 360
acquiesce, 93, 146, 189, 360, 398
acquire, 189, 360
acquisite, 360; -ion, 119, 189, 360, 396
acquist, 189, 360
acquit, 189, 360
acre, 106, 249, 452; -age, 156
acrid, 367
acrimony, 58
acrobat, 330, 367; -ic, 172; -ism, 175
acropolis, 367
acrorrheuma, 76, 449
across, 233
act, 72, 74; -ive, 113, 147; -ivity, 113; -ress, 405; -ual, 415; -ually, 446
acuity, 115, 299, 366
acumen, 366
acute, 366
ad, 214
adagio, 232, 282
adamant, 340; -ine, 153, 429
adapt, 189; -ability, 224
add, 193, 339, 369; -ition, 119, 340; -s, 340
adder, 295
addict, 61, 189, 341
addle, 80
address, 80, 189, 191, 341
adduce, 189, 341
adenoid, 340
adept, 339
adequate, 189, 339, 359
adhere, 189, 316
adhesion, 119
adhesive, 387
adieu, 190, 296, 299, 300
adios, 190
adit, 120, 189
adjab, 418

adjacent, 189, 418
adjag, 418
adjective, 418
adjoin, 189, 302, 418, 433
adjourn, 186, 325, 418
adjudge, 244, 418
adjudicate, 189, 291, 418
adjunct, 366, 418
adjure, 418
adjust, 402, 418
a(d)jutage, 418
adjutant, 243, 418
adjuvant, 418
adlittoral, 189
admeasure, 189
administer, 189, 224
admire, 319, 426; -er, 319
admissible, 402
admittance, 349
admixture, 371
admonish, 122, 339, 432
admonition, 189, 224
adnate, 189
adnexa, 189
adnominal, 189
adnomination. See agnomination
adobe, 331
adolescence, 398
adolescent, 189, 214
adopt, 233
adore, 313, 342
adpressed, 189
adpromissor, 189
adradius, 189
adrectal, 189
adrenal, 189
adrenergen, 189
adret, 190
adroit, 190
adscititious, 189
adscript, 189
adsessor, 189
adsorb, 189
adsorption, 189
adstipulate, 189
adult, 189
advance, 191, 406; -ed, 343
advantage, 191, 197
adventitious, 138
adventure, 189, 416
adverbial, 58

adverse, 43, 189; -ity, -ness, 43
advert, -ence, -ent, -ised, -isement, -ising, 43; -ise, 43, 189, 272
advice, 146, 189
advise, 189
advocaat, 81
advocate, 189
adze, 74, 84, 148, 340, 393
ae, 94
aeciospore, 269
aecium, 269
aedes, 252
(a)egis, 259, 269
(a)eneous, 252
(a)eolian, 263, 269
(a)eon. *See* eon
aerate, 311
aerial, 453
aerie, aery, eyrie, 95, 453
aerobic, 118
aeronaut, 237, 311
aeroplane, 283
(a)esthete, 115; -ic, 115, 117, 385; -icism, 117; -ics, 221
(a)estivate, 221
(a)ether. *See* ether
(a)etiology. *See* etiology
afar, 314, 384
affable, 214
affair, 46, 188, 311, 383
affect, 61, 188; -ion, 177, 383; -ionate, 152
afferent, 169, 383
affidavit, 188
affiliate, 136, 383
affinity, 433
affirm, 191, 324
affix, 371
afflict, 61
affluent, 80, 188
afford, 192, 312, 383
affray, 183, 192
affricate, 80, 188
affright, 192
affront, 246
affusion, 188
afghan, 75
afield, 381
afire, 319
afraid, 252
after, 382

again, 217, 220; -st, 220
agape, 352
agar, 354
agate, 128, 353
aged, 251
agency, 406, 420
agenda, 420
agent, 125
agger, 351, 418
aggie, 351
agglomerate, 80, 188
agglutinate, 291, 298; -ive, 354
aggrandize, 354
aggravate, 80, 214, 354
aggregate, 354
aggression, 188, 354
aggressive, 354, 402
aggrieve, 191, 268, 354
aggroup, 354
aghast, 111, 210
agile, 152; -ity, 420
agitate, 131, 419
aglow, 352
agname, 190
agnate, 78, 190
agnition, 190
agnize, 190
agnomen, 78, 190
agnomination, annomina-tion, adnomination, 190
ago, 282
agony, 131, 353
agouti, agouty, 85, 293
agrarian, 308
agree, 94, 265, 353; -able, -ed, -ing, 158
aground, 306
ague, 95; -ish, 92
ah, 204, 212, 235
aha, 233
ahead, 212, 219
aid, 193, 250, 252
aide, 254
ail, 250, 252
aileron, 253
aim, 252, 428
air, 27, 311; -lessness, 402
aisle, 279, 439
aitchbone, 73
ajar, 314, 421
ajutage. *See* a(d)jutage
akala, 364

akela, 364
akeley, 364
akh, 361
akha, 361
akhissar, 361
akhundzada, 361
akimbo, 364
akin, 94, 364
akkum, 356
alacrity, 367
alarm, 193, 314
alas, 401
alb, 101
albacore, 313, 331
albatross, 445
albeit, 260
albino, 283
album, 74
alcalde, 232, 256, 366
alchemist, 87
alchemy, 358
alcohol, 94, 239, 366, 387; -ic, 161, 172, 239; -ism, 175
alcove, 366
alder, 239
ale, 250
alert, 193, 323
alfalfa, 382, 445
alfresco, 367
algae, 94, 269, 419
algebra, 419, 452; -ic, 252
alias, 83, 137, 251
alibi, 85, 274
alien, 92, 137, 251, 445, 460
alight, 274
align, 103, 190, 275, 430
alimentary, 429
alive, 203
alkali, 85, 274, 366; -ine, 153
all, 76, 239, 443; -ness, 79; -spice, 80
allay, 192, 446
allege, 146, 191, 192, 418, 446; -ation, 355; -eance, 192, 446; -iance, 137, 146, 420, 446
allegory, 445; -ical, 312, 355
allegretto, 20
allegro, 256, 281, 282, 446
allergy, 419
alleviate, 188
alley, 443, 445

alligator, 355
alliterate, 446
allocate, 446
al(l)odium, 441
allot, 234
allow, 304
alloy, 188, 302, 446
allude, 298
allure, 320
allusion, 188
alluvial, 134, 138
alluvium, 138
ally, 188, 276
almanac(k), 239, 364
almighty, 239
almond, 232, 424
almost, 239
alms, 395, 424; -house, 73
alodium. See al(l)odium
aloe, 95
alone, 123, 247, 457
along, 437; -shore, 73;
 -side, 442
aloof, 289, 382
aloud, 305
alphabet, 379; -ic, 172, 218;
 -ist, 175
alpine, 152, 272, 445
already, 239
also, 239
altar, 23, 239
alter, 239
altercate, 367
alternate, 151
although, 286
alto, 282
altogether, 239, 355
altruistic, 291
alumbrado, 190
aluminum, 428
alumnae, 94
alumni, 273
always, 239, 252
am, 88, 214
amalgamate, 353
amand, 197
amanuensis, 197
amass, 190, 401; -ment, 79
amateur, 416
amatory, 427
amaze, 391
amazon, 214, 394, 427
ambassador, 342, 402

amber, 74
ambidextrous, 339
ambiguous, 136, 298, 299,
 353
ambition, 136, 224
amble, 445
ambrosia, 138
ambuscade, 367
ambush, 101, 242
ameba. See am(o)eba
ameliorate, 190, 460
amenable, 190
amend, 183
amenity, 114
ament, 197
amerce, 190
amethyst, 227, 427
amiable, 58, 137, 251, 428
amicable, 214
amid, 224
amir, 318
amissible, 197
amity, 114, 427
ammonia, 136, 429
ammoniac, 364
ammonium, 264
ammunition, 429
amnesia, 138
amnesty, 402
am(o)eba, 259, 269, 331; -ae,
 269
among, 246, 437; -st, 437
amontillado, 190
amoral, 312
amorphous, 379
amortize, 190
amount, 190, 306
amour, 293
ampere, 316
amphibian, 379
amphibious, 136
amplify, 384; -er, 273
amplitude, 299
amputate, 349
amuse, 190
an, 390
anachronism, 358, 395
analgesia, 138
analgesic, 118
analog(ue), 239, 351
analysis, 63, 64–65, 131,
 442
analyst, 63, 64–65, 81

analytic, 63, 64–65, 227; -al,
 347
analyze, 63, 64–65, 81, 276
ananas, 83
anarchy, 357
anathema, 109
anatomical, 427
anatomist, 131, 347
anchor, 357, 436
anchovy, 414
ancient, 104, 412, 433
ancillary, 406, 447
and, 74
andante, 232, 256
anecdote, 75
anemia, 263
anemone, 261
anesthesia, 422
angel, 104, 116; -ic, 116; -ica,
 419
anger, 74, 436
angle, 150, 353, 445
angry, 214, 452
anguish, 122, 351, 409, 457
animal, 131
animate, 432
animosity, 214, 402
anker, 367
ankh, 361
ankle, 367, 436
anklong, 367
anneal, 192
annex, 50, 188, 433
annihilate, 50, 390, 433
annomination. See
 agnomination
annotate, 50, 188, 433; -ion,
 177
announce, 50, 191, 306, 433
annoy, 50–51, 54, 302, 303
annual, 432
annul, 164, 244, 433, 444;
 -ed, 164
anoint, 302
anon, 457
answer, 400, 433
ant, 216
antagonist, 353
antarctic, 452
antedate, 339
antediluvian, 138
antenna, 432
anterior, 263

anthology, 235
anthracite, 154, 385
anthropology, 433, 452
anti, 274
antiaircraft, 263
antibiotic, 347
antienzyme, 263
antioxidant, 263
antipathic, 215
antiphon, 164; -ic, 172; -y, 164
antipodes, 261
antique, 95, 106, 263, 358, 359; -arian, 308, 359; -ity, 358
antonym, 227
anxiety, 81, 273, 437
anxious, 437
any, 457
aorta, 252, 312
apace, 190
aparejo, 191
apart, -heid, -ment, 190
apathetic, 116, 214, 347
ape, 141, 249; -ery, 141
aperture, 335, 416
apex, 251, 371; -es, 261
aphasia, 138, 378, 422
aphasic, 118
aphid, 111, 251, 379
aphis, 111
aphonia, 138
apiary, 251, 263
apices, 261
aplomb, 190, 424
apocalypse, 227, 365
apogee, 419
apologetic, 347
apologia, 138
apo(ph)thegm, 385, 425
apoplexy, 218
apostasy, 402
apostle, 116, 337, 400
apostolic, 116, 444
apostrophe, 233, 261, 379
apothecary, 23, 343
apothegm. See apo(ph)thegm
apotheosis, 109, 385, 403
appal(l), 441, 443
apparatus, 27, 188, 348, 405
apparel, 27, 166, 452; -ed, 166

apparent, 452
appeach, 191
appeal, 336
appear, 44–45, 75, 317, 336
appease, 191, 266
appellate, 445
appendices, 261
appendicitis, 336
appendixes, 261
appetite, 188, 272
applaud, 237
applause, 238, 395
apple, 76, 337
application, 365, 366
apply, 80; -ance, 93, 188, 273; -ed, 278
appoint, 188, 302
apposite, 154; -ive, 336
appraise, 253
appreciable, 137
appreciate, 188, 412
apprehend, 387
apprehension, 410
apprise, 396
approach, 80, 284, 336
approbrious, 283
appropriate, 58, 151, 283
approve, 292, 336
approximate, 151, 233
appulse, 188
appurtenance, 324
apricot, 252, 366
April, 252
apron, 106, 295
apsides, 261
apt, 74, 193, 344; -itude, 192–93, 214; -ness, 348
aquarium, 264, 308, 359, 452
aquatic, 116
ar, 89
Arabic, 118
arable, 310, 452
arbitrary, 349
arbor, 389
arc, 364; -ade, 367
archaeology, 357
archaeopteryx, 269
archaic, 93, 252, 357
archangel, 357
arched, 343
archer, 414
archetype, 314, 357

archipelago, 218, 282, 335, 357
architect, 357
archives, 357
archon, 357
archpriest, 73
archway, 458
arctic, 345
arduous, 92, 421
are, 149, 315
area, 260, 310
argon, 74
argosy, 404
argue, 95, 314; -able, 158; -ment, 159
aria, 315
arid, 113, 452; -ity, 113
arisen, 451
aristocracy, 235, 309
aristocrat, 365
aristocratic, 347
arithmetic, 117–18
ark, 363
arkite, 367
armada, 342
armadillo, 283
armature, 416
armistice, 59
armplate, 73
aromatic, 116, 347
around, 306
arrack, 370
arraign, 431, 453
arrange, 104
arrant, 192, 310, 452
arras, 310
array, 252, 253
arrear, 317
arrest, 188
arrhythmia, 449
arrive, 188, 191, 272, 453; -al, 376
arrogance, 453
arrogate, 310
arrow, 285, 310
artcraft, 73
artery, 314; -al, 316
arthritic, 116, 118
arthritis, 116, 272, 314, 385, 405, 452
artichoke, 363, 415
article, 150
articulate, 224, 365

artificial, 132, 381
artillery, 445
artiness, 405
artisan, 396
artiste, 104, 264
artistic, 104
artless, 405
as, 82, 88, 214, 395
asbestos, 76
ascend, 77–78
ascertain, 398
ascetic, 398
ascot, 367
ascribe, 78
ascription, 78
ashen, 111, 206
ashore, 313
asinine, 152, 214, 402
ask, 98
askance, 367
askant, 367
askew, 298, 299, 367
asparagus, 405, 452
aspect, 78
asperse, 78
asphalt, 239, 378
asphodel, 379
asphyxiate, 378
aspire, -ant, 319; -ate, 78
aspirin, 336, 402
assagai. See assegai
assai, 279
assail, 404
assart, 404
assassin, 404
assault, 23, 188, 237, 404
assay, 192, 404
assegai, assagai, 85, 279
assemble, 150, 188, 404
assert, 61, 323
assess, 404; -ment, 79
assets, 404
asseverate, 404
assiduous, 224, 298, 421
assign, 103, 275, 404, 430
assimilate, 224, 404
assist, 188, 404
assize, 393
associate, 412
assoil, 23, 191, 404
assonance, 188, 404
assort, 404
assuage, 404, 420, 457

assume, 36, 40; -able, -ed,
    -er, -ing, -s, 40
assumpt, -ious, -ive, 40;
    -ion, 36, 40
assure, 188, 320; -ance, 411
aster, 103; -oid, 214, 302
asthma, 391
astonish, 122, 183
astound, 183, 306
astringent, 78
asylum, 276, 401
at, 88, 214
atheism, 110
atheist, 251, 260, 402
athlete, 115, 260, 385; -ic,
    115, 117; -ically, 117
athwart, 313, 458; -ships, 73
atlas, 83, 214
atmosphere, 316, 428; -ic,
    452
atoll, 348
atom, 116, 129, 138, 347; -ic,
    116
atone, 247, 457
atrium, 252
atrocity, 114
attach, 191, 413
attack, 188, 349, 369
attain, 252, 349
attempt, 188
attend, 41, 349
attention, 41
attentive, 349
attest, 349
attic, 349
attire, 319, 349
attitude, 192–93
attorney, 268
attract, 61, 80, 188, 362
attribute, 298, 349
attune, 349
aubade, 286
auberge, 286, 331
aubergine, 286
auburn, 238, 331
auction, 237; -eer, 317
audacious, 137, 238, 251
audacity, 215, 406
audible, 238
audio, 282
audition, 119
auditorium, 264, 313
augelite, 420

augend, 420
auger, 295, 373
aught, 237
augite, 420
augment, 237, 354
augur, 238, 354
august, 238
au jus, 422
aunt, 215–16, 237
aura, 315
aural, 315
aureate, 315
aureity, 115
aureole, 92, 315
auricle, 315
auricula, 315
aurora, 313, 315, 453
aurum, 315
auspice, 146, 237
austere, 237, 316; -ity, 310
authentic, 117, 343, 385; -ity,
    117, 238
author, 23, 237, 343; -itative,
    349; -ity, 452
autochthonic, 385
automatic, 238
autumn, 238, 425; -al, 425
auxiliary, 224, 237, 352, 460
available, 253
avalanche, 149, 377, 415
avale, 190
avenge, 146, 190, 377; -er,
    218
avenue, 95, 147, 190
aver, 190, 323
averruncate, 197
averse, 43; -ion, 43–44;
    -ness, 43
avert, 43, 197
avian, 137
aviary, 263
aviation, 251
avid, 120, 128, 377
avocation, 197, 366
avoid, 183
avouch, 190, 306, 415
avow, 190, 304
avulse, 197
await, 190
awake, 363
award, 183, 313, 458
aware, 308, 310
away, 252

awe, 88, 236; -ful, 159, 212;
  -some, 159
awhile, 388
awkward, 236
awning, 237
ax(e), 89, 371
axes (pl. of axis), 261
axiom, 92; -atic, 116
axis, 83, 261
axle, 445
aye, 88
ayuntamiento, 190
azalea, 394, 445, 459
azimuth, 393
azure, 74, 206, 422

baa, 81
babble, 333
babe, 107
baboon, 289, 332–33
baby, 331; -hood, 87
bacchanalian, 138
bachelor, 414
bacilli, 273
bacillus, 223, 406, 445
backcast, 73
backgammon, 352, 429
backs, 371
bacon, 98
bacteria, 316, 366; -al, 452
bade, 149, 342
badge, 418
badminton, 428
baffle, 384
bagful, 353
baggataway, 355
baggy, 354
bah, 235
bailiff, 253, 374, 384
bailiwick, 369
bait, 53, 203, 250
baize, 84
bake, 70, 99, 107, 357, 363;
  -ery, 251; -ing, 362
Bakelite, 154
balance, 128, 444
balas, 83
balcony, 366, 445
bald, 239
baldric, 23
balk, 361
ball, 76, 443
ballad, 101, 445, 447

ballet, 20, 256
ballflower, 80
ballistics, 372, 447
balloon, 288
ballot, 443
balm, 233, 425
balsa, 239, 445
balsam, 425
bamboo, 289
banana, 434
bandwheel, 73
bang, 437
banish, 122, 128, 173
banister, 214, 432
banjo, 283, 420, 421, 433
bank, 70; -ruptcy, 451
bannock, 370
banquet, 359, 437; -eer, 317
banshee, 94
bantam, 101
banyan, 101, 459
baptize, 272
bar, 314; -able, 175, 453;
  -age, 146; -ette, 347, 455;
  -ier, 310, 453; -room, 453
barb, 331
barbarian, 308
barbecue, 95, 147, 299, 314;
  -ing, 158
barcarol(l)e, 367, 441
bark, 70
barn, 311, 314, 315, 433
barnacle, 452
baron, 309, 452
baroque, 106, 283, 359, 455
barque, 95, 359
barrack, 370; -s, 310, 452
barrage, 146, 422, 455. *See
  also* bar
barrel, -ed, 166; -age, 167
barricade, 310, 366
barrow, 285
base, 104; -less, -ness, 405
bases (pl. of basis), 261
bashful, 409
basic, 118
basil, 149, 396
basilica, 404, 444
basique, 95
basis, 251, 261, 405
bask, 363
basket, 367
basque, 95, 359

bass, 104, 403
baste, 103
bastil(l)e, 104, 441
bastion, 416
bat, 74, 164, 203, 206, 213;
  -er, 164; -ery, 349
batch, 357, 413
bath, 145, 147, 386; -s, 386
bathe, 145, 147, 249, 386; -er,
  233; -ing, 109
bathetic, 218
bathos, 83
batiste, 104, 264
batt, 347; -s, 348
battalion, 137
battle, 349
batz, 84, 101, 399
bauble, 329
bauxite, 154
bawdy, 236
bawl, 237
bay, 252
bayonet, 253
bayou, 279, 293, 294
bazaar, 81
bazooka, 290
bdelium, 328, 339
bdeloid, 328
be, 88, 261; -ing, 260
beach, 415
beacon, 259, 266
bead, 219
beadle, 340
beagle, 265, 354
beak, 363
bear, 202, 311
beard, 317
beast, 265
beatific, 46
beatify, 46, 214, 260, 347
beau, 281, 286
beaut, 203
beauty, 298, 300, 348; -ician,
  138; -ify, 48
beaver, 266
became, 251
beckon, 368
bed, 218; -spread, 340
bedevil, 166
bedim, 94
bedlam, 101
bee, 88, 265
beech, 265; -drops, 73

been, 229, 239
beer, 317
beet, 203
beetle, 265, 348
before, 313
beggar, 218, 354, 417, 451
begging, 351
beginning, 433
begorra, begor(r)ah, 450
begot, 234
beguile, 351
begun, 244
behalf, 232, 380
behavior, 376, 387
behind, 102, 275
behoove, 290
beige, 146, 254, 255, 422
belch, 101, 414
belie, 95, 273; -ed, 158; -ing,
   157
belief, 374, 447; -s, 374
believe, 208, 268, 374, 442
bell, 76; -less, 77
bellicose, 445
belligerent, 419, 447
bellow, -s, 285
belly, 447
belong, 239
belying, 157
beneath, 432
benefactor, 381
benefice, 406; -ial, 138;
   -iary, 412
benefit, 166, 173, 218, 384;
   -ed, -ing, 173
benevolent, 218, 377
benign, 103, 113, 275, 430;
   -ity, 113
benzine, 153, 263, 393
bequeath, 259, 359, 386
bereave, 266, 451
bereft, 382
beret, 256
ber(r)etta. See bir(r)etta
berry, 310
berserk, 323, 363
beseech, 258, 415
besiege, 268, 401, 420
bestial, 402, 416, 460; -ity,
   460
bet, 203; -or, 349
beta, 348
betal, 126

betray, 252
better, 256, 349
between, 346
betwixt, 346
bevel, 166, 377; -er, 166
beware, 458
bewig, 94
bey, 255
beyond, 212, 233, 459
bezique, 106, 359
bias, 83, 91
bible, 105, 106, 150, 275, 331;
   -ical, 330
bibliography, 106, 379
bibliophile, 378
bicameral, 427
bicycle, 61
bidden, 341
biennial, 273
bier, 318
bifid, 120
bigamy, 353
bigeye, 165
biggish, 165
bight, 102, 274, 345
bigot, 128, 353; -ry, 451
bijou, 422
bike, 61, 70
bilge, 146, 445
bilious, 136, 460
bill, 76
billet, 445
billiards, 445, 459
billion, 460
billow, 285
billsticker, 80
bind, 102, 275
binocular, 365
binomial, 138, 428
biographical, 111
biography, 273, 352
biologist, 87
birch, 324, 414
bird, 321
birdie, -ing, 157
birr, 324, 451
bir(r)etta, ber(r)etta, 450
birthstone, 73
bis, 20, 83
biscuit, 367
bisect, 61, 125, 366
bisexual, 34
bishop, 111, 409

bison, 403
bisque, 95, 359
bit, 203
bite, 110, 123, 203
bitten, 110
bituminous, 428
bivouac, 364, 456; -ed, 370
bizarre, 149, 315, 394, 451
blackball, 77
blackberry, 56
blackbird, 56
blackbreast, 73
blackguard, 352
blackstrap, 73
bladder, 341
blade, 107
blame, 105, 141, 249, 440;
   -able, 140–41
blanch, 414
blandish, 122
blank, 436
blanket, 362
blare, 308
blaspheme, 260, 378, 401
blastplate, 73
blatant, 125
blather, 108
bleachground, 73
bleak, 265
bleary, 317
bleed, 265
blemish, 122, 128, 219, 427
blew, 294, 295, 298
blewits, 83
blight, 102, 274, 345
blind, 102, 271, 275; -stitch,
   73
blinks, 371
blissful, 79
blister, 223, 445
blithe, 147, 386; -en, 109, 110
blizzard, 394
bloat, 284
blob, 234, 330
bloc, 364
blocks, 371
blockship, 73
blood, 247, 331; -y, 163
bloom, 289
blossom, 404
blotch, 233, 413
blouse, 305, 306
blow, 284

blubber, 332
bludgeon, 420
blue, 291; -berry, 56; -est,
    -ing, -ish, 158
bluff, 381
blur, 324
blurt, 324
blush, 244, 331
bo (bozo), 89
bo (hobo). *See* bo(e)
bo (tree), 89
boa, 91
boar, 314
board, 314; -cloth, 73
boast, 284
boat, 203, 284
bobbin, 332
bodice, 341
body, 234, 341
bo(e) (hobo), 89
bog(e)y, bogie, 126
bog(e)yman. *See*
    bo(o)g(e)yman
boggle, 355
bogus, 126, 354
boil, 301
boisterous, 302
bold, 97, 102
bolero, 283, 311
boll, 76, 102, 446
bollix, 446
bolster, 102, 445
bolt, 102, 446; -smith, 73
bomb, 23, 54–55, 72, 328,
    424; -ardier, 318, 424; -er,
    163, 424; -proof, 73
bonanza, 393
bondslave, 73
bone, 247
bonnet, 233, 434
bonny, 434
bonus, 125
bonze, 84, 394
boo, 289
booby, 290
bo(o)g(e)yman, boogieman,
    26
book, 70, 203, 242, 363;
    -ish, 362; -s, 371
boomed, 338
boomerang, 290
boondoggle, 355
boor, 321

boot, 203, 289
booty, 290, 348
booze, 84
borax, 312
border, 312
bore, 311, 312, 313, 314
borough, 286
borrow, 284, 311, 312, 313,
    315
borscht, 348, 452
bosom, 243
boss, 104
botany, 347; -ic, 215; -ist, 87
bother, 108, 233
bottle, 233, 349, 445
bottom, 233
bottstick, 80
botulism, 416
bough, 306
bought, 240, 345
bouilli, 85
boulder, 285
boulevard, 293, 294
boul(l)e, buhl, 296, 441
bounce, 306
bounty, 306
bouquet, 256, 293, 359
bout, 306
bovid, 121
bovine, 125, 272
bow /baù/, 304
bow /bō/, 284; -yer, 459
bowel, 305
bower, 304
bowl, 284
boxer, 163
boy, 302, 303; -cott, 302–3,
    347; -cotts, 348; -hood,
    242; -ish, 121; -s, 86;
    -senberry, 302–3
bra, 61, 232
bracket, 368
braggart, 354
braid, 252
brain, 250
braise, 253
brakes, 371
brambling, 101
brandish, 122
brassiere, 61, 149, 318, 396
bravado, 232, 283, 342
brave, 141; -ery, 140–41
bravo, 232

brawl, 237
brawn, 237; -y, 236, 433
brazier, 137, 422
bread, 219
breadth, 219, 340, 385
break, 219, 220, 256, 357,
    363; -fast, 133, 219, 220,
    256; -s, 371; -water, 458
breast, 219; -wheel, 73
breath, 219, 385, 386
breathe, 147, 266, 386
breech, 357; -cloth, 73; -es,
    229
breeze, 84, 266, 393
brethren, 218, 386
brett, 347
brevet, 166
brevity, 377
brew, 294, 295
bribe, -ery, 141
brick, 369; -s, 371
bride, 272
bridge, 146, 226
bridle, 105, 275
brief, 268, 382
brier, 319
brigade, 355; -ier, 318
brigand, 128, 353
brigantine, 353
bright, 102, 274, 345; -work, 73
brilliant, 460
brimful(l), 381, 441
bring, 331, 437
brisk, 101, 363
brisket, 367
bristle, 400
britches, 229
brittle, 349
broach, 284, 286. *See also*
    brooch
broad, 231, 240; -cloth, -ly,
    -ness, 240; -est, 163
brocade, 126
broccoli, 85, 233, 356
brochure, 283, 320, 408
brogue, 95, 351
broil, 445
broke, 9
bromate, 126
bromide, 125, 272, 428
bronchitis, 358, 436
bronze, 84, 233, 392, 393;
    -ed, -es, 155

brooch, broach, 286
brood, 289
brook, 242, 363
brother, 60, 108, 245
brought, 240
brow, 304
brown, 305; -ie, 433
browse, 305, 396
bruin, 291
bruise, 148, 296, 396
bruit /'brūē/, 91
bruit /brūt/, 296
brush, 331, 409
brusque, 95, 359, 402
brute, 290
bubble, 150, 333
buccaneer, 317, 356
buck, 203; -skin, 73
bucket, 244
buckle, 369
buddha, 105, 339
budget, 420
buff, 381
buffalo, 283, 383
buffet /bə'fā/, 242, 256, 384
buffet /'bufət/, 383
buffoon, 384
buffware, 80
bugaboo, 134, 245, 289
bugfish, 353
buggy, 354
bugle, 105, 299
buhl. See boul(l)e
build, 229–30
built, 229–30
bulb, 101
bulk, 70
bull, 76, 241, 243; -head, 80
bullet, 242, 447
bulletin, 242
bullion, 242
bullock, 370
bul(l)rush, 441
bulwark, 243, 363
bump, 336
bun, 432
bungalow, 285, 436
bunion, 119, 123, 127, 128, 134–35, 245
bunkchain, 73
bunker, 367
bunt, 348
buntwhip, 73

buoy, 296, 303; -ant, 459
bur, 324
burdock, 369
bureau, 286, 320
burette, 320
burg, 353
burgher, 352
burin, 320
burlesque, 95, 324, 359
burn, -ed, 338
burnish, 122
burnous, burnoose, 293
bur(r), 324, 451; -knot, 80
burro, 283, 324, 454
burrow, 285, 322, 324, 454
burst, 402, 452
bury, 217, 221, 229, 311; -al, 58, 221, 262, 311; -ing, 86
bus, 25, 61, 83, 94, 175, 401; -ed, -es, 25, 403; -ing, 25, 175, 403
bush, 243; -wacker, 73
bushel, 111, 242, 409
bustle, 400
busy, 228–29; -es, 268; -est, 135
butane, 299
butcher, 242, 415
butt, 347; -s, 348
butte, 299, 347
butter, 338, 349
buttock, 370
buttress, 101, 348, 405
buy, 279
buzz, 84, 392
buzzard, 394
by, 88, 276
bye, 88, 96, 276

cabal, 444
cabbage, 210, 332
cabin, 215, 330
cabinet, 131, 347
cable, 105, 150
cabriolet, 256
cacao, 284
cache, 110, 408
cachet, 256, 408
cackle, 369
cacophony, 111, 366
cacorrhinia, 76, 449
cacti, 273
cactus, 366; -es, 273

cad, 164, 205; -ish, 164
cadaveric, 117
caddie, 341
caddis, 83
caddy, 19
cadence, 341
cadenza, 393
cadge, 418
cadi. See qadi
Caesar, 269
caesurae, 269
cafe, café, 256, 384; -teria, 382
caffein(e), 153, 267, 268, 364, 383
cage, 146
caique, 95
cairn, 311
caisson, 100, 252, 403
caitiff, 348, 374, 384
cajeput, 421
cajole, 141, 421; -ery, 141
calamity, 215, 427
calcareous, 308
calces. See calx
calcine, 152
calcium, 264, 406
calculate, 362, 366
caldron, 101, 239
calf, 232, 374, 378, 380
caliber, 214, 444
calico, 283
caliph, calif, 379
calices, 261
calk, 239, 361
call, 443
calligraphy, 447
cal(l)iper, 441
cal(l)isthenics, 385, 433, 441
callous, 445
callow, 285, 443
calm, 233, 424; -ative, 163; -est, 34
caloric, 312
calorie, 455
calque, 95, 359
calve, 147, 374, 376, 377, 380; -s, 232, 374
calx, 101; -es, 261
calypso, 227, 282, 336
calyx, 371
cambium, 92
camboge. See gamboge

cambric, 102, 215
camel, 427
camel(l)ia, 441
cameo, 137, 260, 282, 427
camouflage, 146, 232, 382, 422, 427
campaign, 431
Campbell, 328
camphor, 379
camus, 83
can, 432
canal, 214, 444
canary, 308, 434
cancel, 166, 406; -ation, 26, 171
cancellate, 171
cancellous, 171
cancer, 406
candidate, 339
cang(ue), 96
canine, 125, 152, 272
cann, 432
cannabic, 330
cannery, 433
cannibal, 434
canoe, 88, 95, 293; -ed, -ist, 158
canon, 117, 128; -ic, -icity, 117
canorous, 313
cant, 70
cantaloup(e), cantalope, cantelope, 286
cantata, 232, 348
cantharides, 261
canto, 282
canvas, 83, 376, 433
canvass, 83
canyon, 430, 433, 459
caoutchouc, 295, 306
capable, 251
caparison, 404
caper, 125
capercaillie, capercailzie, 459–60
capitol, 149
capitulate, 224, 416
capivi, 85
capon, 125
capriccio, 412
caprice, 146, 264, 406
capsize, 393
captious, 58, 410

capture, 416
capuche, 110
car, 314
caravan, 61, 214, 309
caraway, 252
carbohydrate, 277, 387
carbon, 116; -ic, 116, 331; -iferous, 224
carboy, 19, 302
carburetor, 256
carcajou, 422
carcass, 314, 405
card, 357
cardiac, 92
careen, 265
career, 317
caress, 401
cargo, 283
caribou, 293, 294
caricature, 320
caries, 268
carillon, 452
carmine, 153
carnivorous, 224, 377
carol, 166, 452; -er, 167
carom. See car(r)om
carotene, carotin. See car(r)otene
carotid, 347
carouse, 305
carousel. See car(r)ousel
carp, 69
carpenter, 314
carrel(l), 441
carriage, 310, 420
carried, 86
carrier, 58
carrion, 263
car(r)om, 450
car(r)otene, car(r)otin, 450
car(r)ousel, 450, 452
carrying, 86
cartel, 357, 444
cartography, 314
cartoon, 289, 357
cartridge, 357, 419
carve, 147, 374, 376
case, 100; -ual, 92, 137, 422
cashier, 318
cashmere, 316, 428
casino, 282
casket, 367
casque, 95

casserole, 404
cassock, 370, 404
caste, 103
castle, 380, 400
casual. See case
cat, 14–15, 21, 49; -fish, -s, 14–15; -tail, 349
cataclysm, 214, 227, 347, 395
catacombs, 424
catafalque, 359
catalog(ue), 96, 239; -ed, -er, -ing, 175
catalysis, 63, 64–65
catalyst, 63, 64–65, 81
catalytic, 63, 64–65
catalyze, 63, 64–65, 81
cataract, 366, 451
catarrh, 449
catastrophe, 261, 379
category, 355; -ical, 312
caterpillar, 214, 449
cathedral, 261, 341
cathode, 109
catholic, 23, 109, 117, 385
catsup, catchup, ketchup, katsup, 19, 101
cattle, 349
caucus, 238
caught, 203, 205, 237, 345
cauldron, 23, 237, 445
cauliflower, 238
cause, -al, 238; -ation, 119
causeway, 396
caustic, 237
cauterize, 238, 348
caution, 238
cavalcade, 214
cavalier, 318
cave, 113
caviar, 137, 264, 314, 451
cavil, 166, 377; -er, 167
cavity, 113
caw, 236
cayenne, 279, 432
cazique, 95, 106
cease, 266, 403
cedar, 130, 260, 341, 451
cede, 107
cedrol, 106
ce(e), 89
ceiling, 267, 445
celebrity, 447
celery, 131, 444

celestial, 416
celiac. *See* c(o)eliac
cell, 442
cellar, 445
cello, 282, 412
cellophane, 378, 445
celluloid, 302
cement, 429
cemetery, 269, 427
cenogenesis. *See*
  c(o)enogenesis
censorial, 58
censorious, 58, 263
censure, 411
cent, 70, 397; -ennial, 432;
  -s, 342; -urion, 320, 321;
  -ury, 416
centaur, 237
centralization, 394
centrifugal, 224
centripetal, 349
ceramic, 215
cere, 316
cereal, 310, 316
cerebellum, 310, 333, 445
ceremony, 310, 405
certain, 23
certificate, 151
cession, 405
chaeta, 269
chaetognath, 269
chafe, 107, 249, 382
chaff, 381
chagrin, 224, 408
chair, 27
chaise, 253, 408
chalk, 361
challenge, 414, 445
challis, 83
chamber, 102
chameleon, 137, 260, 357,
  429
champagne, 103, 408, 431
champaign, 431
chancel(l)or, 167
chandelier, 318
change, 104
channel, 166, 434; -er, -ize,
  167
chant, 101
chanticleer, 317
chaos, 83, 91, 135, 358
chaotic, 93, 252, 347

chapel, 215, 335
chappaul, 336
character, 309, 357
chariot, 92, 264; -eer, 317
charity, 452
charivari, chivaree, chivari,
  shivaree, 85
charlatan, 314, 408
chasm, 358, 428
chaste, 103, 113; -en, 103,
  399; -ise, 83, 272; -ity, 113,
  347
chatter, 349
chaudfroid, 286
chauffeur, 238, 281, 286,
  326, 382
chausses, 286
chauvinism, 286
check, 369
cheddar, 101
cheek, 363; -y, 362
cheer, 317, 451
cheese, 148, 258, 414
chef, 381, 407–8
chemiatric, 215
chemic, 127
chemist, 129, 138
chenille, 104, 264, 446
cherish, 414, 452
cherry, 452; -es, 310
cherub, 310
chervonets, tchervonets,
  414
chessboard, 402
chetvert, tchetvert, 414
chevalier, 318
chevron, 218, 376, 408
chew, 294, 295, 298
chi, 85
chibouk, chibouque, 295
Chicago, 408; -ite, 154
chicane, 141; -ery, 141, 251,
  433
chicken, 368
chief, 268, 408, 414
chiffon, 384; -ier, 318, 383
chilblain, 77
child, 98, 102, 271, 275;
  -ren, 98, 275
chil(l)i, chile, 85, 225, 441
chill, 71
chim(a)era, 318, 358
chimpanzee, 94, 265

chin, 74
china, 126
chintz, chints, 84, 101, 348,
  399, 433
chip, 206
chiropractor, 358, 366
chirp, 324
chirrup, 316, 324, 454
chirr, churr, 451
chisel, 166, 224; -er, 167
chivari. *See* charivari
chive, 107, 147
chloride, 20, 272, 358, 445
chlorine, 263, 358
chloroform, 358
chlorophyl(l), 227, 358, 378,
  441
chocolate, 239
choice, 146, 302
choir, 10, 358, 456, 457
cholera, 357
choose, 290, 413
choral, 358
chord, 357
choreography, 260, 358
chorister, 312
chortle, 414
chorus, 166, 358
chough, 248, 380
chow, 304
chowder, 305, 340
Christ, 209; -en, 399; -mas,
  209, 357
chrome, 358, 452; -ium, 264
chronic, 127, 358
chronicle, 18, 209, 234, 357,
  358
chronology, 358, 442
chronometer, 358
chrysalis, 226, 358, 402
chrysanthemum, 214, 358,
  401
chthonic, 385
chub, -y, 332
chuckle, 369
church, 322, 414
churn, 322
churr. *See* chirr
chute, 107, 298
chyle, 107
ciao, 306
cicada, 342, 405; -ae, 269
cicerone, 412

cider, 130
cigar, 314, 355; -et(te), 149, 347
cinema, 405
cipher, 111, 379, 405
circle, 150, 324, 367, 452
circuitous, 299
circumstantial, 58, 410
circumvent, 61
cirque, 95
citation, 119
citizen, 131, 394, 405
city, 224, 347; -es, 267
civic, 127, 224
civilian, 375, 460
civilization, 83
civ(v)ies, 375, 377
claimant, 253
clairvoyant, 302, 311
clam, 94; -y, 428
clamor, 128
clandestine, 153
clapboard, 328
clarify, 364
clarinet, 218
clarion, 263
Clark, 235
clarkeite, 156
clash, 101
clasp, 402
class, -ic, -ical, -icalization, -icalize, -ically, 34; -ifiable, 273; -ify, 276
clause, 148, 238
claw, 236
clean, 220, 364; -liness, 219, 220; -ly, 219; -se, 219, 220, 433
clear, 317
cleave, 147, 266; -er, 445
clef, 381
cleft, 382
clergy, 323, 364, 419
cleric, 452
clerk, 235, 325, 363
clever, 129, 202
clevis, 83
clew, 295
clientele, 149
cliff, 381
climate, 428
climax, 125, 371

climb, 55, 74, 102, 271, 275, 424; -er, 364; -ing, 424
cling, 437
clinic, 116, 117, 127; -al, 117; -ian, 138
clip, 224; -ing, 337
clique, 95, 106, 147, 359
cloak, 284
clockwise, 458
clod, 93
clog, 234
cloister, 364
close, 82, 107; -et, 395
clot, 94
cloth, 109, 385; -es, 283; -ier, 109
clothe, 109, 147, 386
cloud, 305; -iness, 432
clough, 380
clout, 306
clover, 125, 129
clown, 305, 364
cloy, 302
club, 244
clue, 291, 350
clumsy, 395
clutch, 364, 413
cnemidocoptes, 431–32
cnemis, 432
cnida, 20, 432
cnidaria, 432
cnidoblast, 432
coach, 284, 415
coactive, 93
coagulate, 178, 353
coal, 284
coalesce, 93, 178, 281
coalition, 178
coarse, 314
coast, 284
coat, 284
coati, 85
coax, 371
cobble, 106, 233, 333
cobelligerent, 179
coble, 105, 106
cobra, 106
coca, 153; -ine, 153, 254
coccus, 356
cockle, 233, 369
cockney, 369
coco, 126; -nut, 432
cocoa, 126, 284

coconscious, 179
cod, 74, 205
coddle, 342
code, 107, 341
codices, 261
codicil, 340
coed, 281
coefficient, 178, 383
coelacanth, 269
c(o)eliac, 269
coenocyte, 269
c(o)enogenesis, 269
coerce, 92, 146, 178, 281, 323; -ion, 412
coeval, 178
cofeature, 179
coffee, 94, 383
coffin, 239, 383
cogent, 125
cogitate, 419
cognate, 180, 233
cognition, 180, 347
cognizance, 180, 394
cognomen, 180
cognoscente, 180
cognoscenti, 412
cohabit, 178
cohere, 178, 316, 387
cohesion, 137, 422
cohort, 178
coif, 10, 382, 457
coiffure, 10
coign, 431
coil, 181, 301
coin, 431
coincide, 93, 178
coitus, 178
cojuror, 179
colatitude, 179
cold, 102, 280, 446
coleslaw, 236
coliseum, 260
collaborate, 330
collapse, 178, 446
collar, 233, 447
collateral, 446
colleague, 96, 178, 233
collect, 177, 446
college, 146; -iate, 137
collie, 95
collier, 233, 460
colligate, 446
collision, 119, 422

colloquy, 233; -al, 58, 178, 446
collusion, 178
cologne, 103, 431
colon, 125
colonel, 229, 449
colonnade, 434
colony, 234; -al, 263; -ist, -ize, 87
color, 246, 444
colossal, 402, 447
colossus, 405
colt, 102, 348
column, 18, 128, 425; -ar, 425
coma, 428
comatose, 427
comb, 102, 280, 424, 435
combat, 165, 178; -ant, 174, 347; -ed, 165; -ive, 175
comber, 102, 424
combine, 365
combustion, 330, 416
come, 108, 149, 246; -ing, -s, 155
comedo, 180
comedy, 131, 342; -ian, 137, 263, 429; -enne, 432
comes /'kō,mēz/, 180
comestible, 180
comfit, 180
comfort, 180, 246
comfrey, 180
comic, 234
comites, 180
comity, 114
comma, 233, 429
command, 178, 428
commensurate, 152, 411, 428
commerce, 101, 178, 428; -ial, 58, 412
commingle, 436
commiserate, 224, 395
commissar, 314, 402
commission, 411, 428
committal, 349
committee, 178
commodious, 136, 263
commodity, 178, 428
commotion, 119
commune, 299; -al, 428; -ion, 119, 134; -ism, 428; -ity, 115, 291

commute, 178; -er, 298
comonomer, 179
compact, 366
companion, 119, 137, 178, 460
compartment, 314
compass, 405
compatible, 347
compel, 218; -ing, 446
compendium, 264
compensate, 178
compete, 28, 37–38, 132; -ing, -ition, 28, 37–38; -itive, 28, 347; -itor, 132
compile, 178
complacent, 178
complaisant, 253
completion, 119
component, 178
composer, 281
composite, 28, 154; -ion, 28, 34
composure, 153
compound, 306
comprehend, 178
compress, 233; -ed, 343
compter, 306
compulsion, 178
compute, 298
comrade, 149
comunidad, 180
conalbumin, 181
concatenate, 179
conceal, 265
conceit, 267, 345
conceive, 56, 267
concert, 311, 412
concerti, 20
concerto, 282, 311, 412
conch, 23
conciliate, 136, 179
conclude, 179, 290
conclusion, 290
conclusive, 403
concoct, 61, 366
concomitant, 179, 180
concourse, 315
concrete, 179, 233; -ion, 119
concubine, 152, 179
concur, 172; -ing, 453
condemn, 339, 425; -ation, -ed, 425
condescend, 179

condescension, 410
condign, 430
condiment, 179
condition, 132, 136
condominium, 138, 165, 179
condor, 312
conduct, 61, 179
cone, 115; -ic, 115, 127
conelrad, 181
confect, 61; -ionery, 311
confederate, 151, 179
confer, 169, 323; -able, -al, -ed, -ence, -ential, -er, -ing, 169; -ee, 169, 450
confess, 401; -ion, 411
confetti, 46
confirm, 324
confiscate, 179
conflation, 179
conflict, 61, 366
conform, 179
confound, 306
confront, 179, 246
confuse, 123; -ion, 119, 134
congeal, 419
congenial, 260, 460; -ity, 460
congestion, 179, 416
conglomerate, 151, 179
congratulate, -ory, 416
congress, 405, 436; -ional, 411
congruent, 93, 179
congruity, 115, 291
congruous, 291
conic. See cone
conifer, 384
conjecture, 179, 416, 421
conjugal, 243, 421
conjugate, 243; -ion, 355
connate, 178; -ural, 433
connect, 177, 178, 433
connive, 179, 433
connoisseur, 178, 433
connotation, 433
connubial, 58, 134, 138, 178, 433
conquer, 179, 400
conquest, 400, 402
consanguinity, 457
conscience, 409, 412
conscientious, 58, 412
conscious, 179
consent, 179; -ient, 410

consider, 224
consign, 103, 275
consist, 179
consonant, 179
conspicuous, 47, 136, 165, 179, 365
conspire, 319; -acy, 316
constable, 181
constipation, 335
constituency, 415
constituent, 179, 224
constrain, 250
construct, 244
construe, 95, 291; -able, 158
consul, 233
consume, 36, 40, 298; -able, 40, 134; -ed, -er, -ing, -s, 40
consummate, 151, 179
consumpt, -ed, -ible, -ive, 40; -ion, 36, 40
contact, 179
contagion, 119, 137
contagium, 138
contain, 179
contata, 348
contemn, 425
contemporary, 179
contempt, 425; -ible, 426; -uous, 415
contend, 41
contention, 41–42
context, 233
contiguous, 353
continent, 179
continue, 95, 299; -al, 299; -ity, 115; -ous, 158; -um, 81
contort, 61, 179
contour, 321
contract, 61
contradict, 61; -ion, 339
contralto, 282
contrariety, 81
contravene, 377
contribute, 179
control, 94, 164, 452; -er, 162, 164, 446
controversial, 43–44; -ist, 43
controversion, 43
controversy, 43, 377
controvert, 43
contusion, 179

conurbation, 181
conusable, 181
convalescent, 398
convenience, 460
convenient, 137, 179
convent, 233
converse, -ion, -ionary, 43
convert, -er, 43
convex, 371
convey, 255
convict, 61, 118, 168
convince, 179
convoy, 179, 302
coo, 289
cook, 242, 363
coolie, 95, 290
cool(l)y, 441
coop, 288
cooperate, 178, 234
coordinate, 178, 281
coot, 288, 289
copartner, 179
copeck, 126
copper, 337
copperas, 83
copula, -ate, 181; -ae, 269
copy, 140, 335; -er, 135, 140; -ist, 87
coquetry, 283
coquette, 106, 359
coralloid, 171
corbel, 166; -ing, 167
cord, 357
cordial, 421
corduroy, 302
corecreation, 179
corelate. See cor(r)elate
cornea, 260
corollary, 312
coronary, 312
coronel, 449
coronet, 312
corporeal, 313
corps, 449
corpse, 148, 312, 452
corpuscle, 398
corral, 444, 455
correct, 61, 177, 453
cor(r)elate, 312; -ion, 450
correspond, 178, 312
corridor, 312
corrigible, 178, 312
corrosion, 119, 178

corrugate, 312, 453
corrupt, 61, 178, 453
corsair, 311
cortege, 146, 422
cosine, 179
cosmic, 395
cosmopolite, 154, 335
cossack, 369
cost, 59–60, 104
costume, 299
cosy. See cozy
cot, 203, 205, 213
cotangent, 179
coterie, 95
cotillion, 349
cottage, 349
cotton, 349
couac, 457
couch, 181, 306
cougar, 293, 354
cough, 240, 334, 380
could, 7, 8, 241, 243, 339
coulee, 94, 293, 294
council, 179, 306, 406; -or, 167
counsel, 166, 179, 306; -or, 167
count, 181
countenance, 179
counterfeit, 229
country, 247
coup, 289
couple, 150, 181, 247, 336
coupon, 234, 293
courage, 325, 453
courier, 321
course, 315, 321
court, 315, 348; -eous, 416; -esy, 325; -ship, 409
cousin, 181, 247, 396
covariance, 179
cove, 147
covenant, 246
cover, 128, 129
covert, 246
covet, 246
covey, 246
cow, 281, 304
coward, 305
cower, 304
cowl, 301, 305
co-worker, 179
coworship, 179

cowwheat, 456
coxcomb, 424
coy, 302
coyote, -illo, 279
coz, 84, 392; -es, 393, 394
cozy, 126, 393
crabby, 365
cracked, 343
crackle, 369
cradle, 105, 341
cranial, 137
cranny, 434
crass, 82
crater, 125
cravat, 94
crawl, 237
crayfish, crawfish, 19, 60, 236, 365
crayon, 253
crease, 266
create, 91, 260, 266; -ure, 266, 416
credence, 341
credit, 120, 128, 219, 340
credulity, 115
credulous, 133, 218
creed, 133
creek, 229
creep, 258
crenel(l)ated, 167
creole, 91
creosote, 92, 260, 401
crepe, crêpe, 256
crept, 7
crescendo, 282, 412
crescent, 398
cretic, 127, 218
cretonne, 432
crevasse, 401
crevice, 128, 365
crew, 295, 298
crib, 93
cricket, 368
crier. See cry
crime, 74, 132
criminal, 132
crimson, 428
crinkle, 367
cripple, 226, 337, 365
crisis, 125, 223
criterion, 263, 316

critic, 127, 165, 224, 347, 370; -ism, 173, 370; -ize, 83
critique, 95, 106, 263, 359
croak, 284, 363
croche, 110
crochet, 256, 283, 408; -ing, 175
crock, 369
crocodile, 365
crook, 242
croquet, 106, 256, 283, 359
cross, 104; -bow, 402; -current, 80; -wise, 79, 272
crotch, 413
crotchet, 414
crouch, 306
croup, 293
crow, 284
crowd, 305
crown, 305
crucial, 58, 124, 298, 365
crucible, 291
crucifix, 371
crude, 107; -ity, 115, 134
cruel, 91
cruise, 296; -er, 365
crumb, 424; -le, 150
crummy, 424
crumple, 150
crusade, 290
crush, 409
crustacean, 137, 412
crutch, 101
cry, 276, 365; -baby, 87; -er, 87, 273
crypt, 101, 227, 348
crystal, 227
crystallic, 171
crystalliferous, 171
crystalline, 153
ctelology, 345
ctene, 345
ctenidium, 345
ctenocyst, 345
cube, 107; -ic, 118; -ism, 134
cubit, 120
cuckoo, 243, 289
cuddle, 342
cudgel, 166, 420
cuff, 381; -ful, 383
cui bono, 457

cuica, 457
cuichunchuli, 457
cuiejo, 457
cuir, -ass, -builli, 457
cuisine, 457
cuisse, 457
cuivré, 457
culinary, 134–35
culminate, 445
culprit, 336
cultch, 445
cultured, 40
cumulate, 134
cup, 244; -board, 185, 328, 334; -ful, 243
cupid, 299; -ity, 336
cupola, 134, 336
cupreous, 106
cupule, 122
cur, 324
curaçao, curaçoa, 405
cure, 320, 459
curfew, 299, 365, 373
curio, 282
curiosity, 402
curl, 324
curlew, 295
curmudgeon, 420
curr, 451
currant, 454
current, 172, 324, 454
curriculum, 455
curry, 181, 324
curtsy, 452
curve, 147, 324; -aceous, 412
cushion, 409
cusp, 101
custom, 181, 244; -er, 365
cute, 288, 299
cuticle, 134
cutlass, 405
cuttle, 349
cwm, 396
cyanide, 277, 405
cybernetics, 276, 331, 372, 405
cycle, 105, 277; -ic, 116; -one, 277, 445
cyclotron, 277
cylinder, 227
cymbal, 101, 227
cynic, 127, 227, 405
cynosure, 276

cypress, 405
cyst, 227
czar, tsar, tzar, 314, 348, 391; -ism, 175

dabble, 333
dabster, 75
dactyl, -ic, 116
daddy, 341
dado, 282
d(a)emon, 116, 123, 269, 428; -ic, 116
daffodil, 342, 383
daft, 348
dagger, 354
dahlia, 212, 216, 235, 460
daily, 253
dainty, 250
daiquiri, 216
dairy, 311; -maid, 87
dais, 83, 91
daisy, 253
dalmatic, 116
damage, 128, 427
damask, 138
dammed, 428
damn, 101, 425; -able, -ing, 425
dampproof, 80
dandies, 86
danger, 104, 249
dapper, 337
dapple, 337
darling, 314, 452
dart, 348
dasher, 74
data, 348
datum, 348
daub, 237; -er, 163, 329
daughter, 237
daunt, 237
dauphin, 238, 379
daw, 236
day, 270
daze, 107, 391, 393
dazzle, 80, 150, 394
deacon, 266
dead, 219, 240; -est, 163
deaf, 219, 382; -en, 163
deal, 220; -t, 219, 220
dean, 265
dearth, 325
death, 61, 219; -like, 272

deb, 369
debacle, 105, 369
debauch, 237, 415
debit, 120, 128, 219, 330
debonair(e), debonnaire, 20, 28, 311, 330
debrief, 262
debt, 17–18, 31, 328, 344
debunk, 436
debutante, 149, 349
debuting, 175
decade, 218, 365
decapitate, 365
decease, 266, 405
deceit, 267, 345
deceive, 267, 405
decide, 133
deciduous, 421
decimal, 218
decipher, 379
decision, 119, 133
decisive, 403
declaim, 133
declamatory, 133, 365
declare, 308, 365
decorate, 365
decoy, 302
decrease, 265
decree, 94, 258, 265
decrepit, 120, 219, 336
decussate, 366, 402
dedicate, 218
de(e), 89
deem, 99
deep, 98, 265
deer, 317
defamation, 382
defamatory, 132
defame, 132
default, 384
defeat, 46
defecate, 218
defendant, 381
defense, defence, 406
defer, 164, 169, 323; -able, 169, 450; -al, 164, 323; -ed, -ent, -er, -ing, 169; -ence, 164, 169; -ential, 169, 382
defiance, 273
deficient, 165
deficit, 120

define, -able, 141; -ite, 131, 154; -ition, 224, 347, 382
defrost, 262
defunct, 348, 366, 436
degenerate, 151
deglutition, 262
degradation, 119
degree, 94
dehydrate, 277
deicide, 92
deific, 93
deign, 254, 430
deism, 260
deity, 115
deleterious, 316
deletion, 119
delft, 348, 445
deliberate, 151
delicate, 152, 444
delicatessen, 366
delight, 274
delinquent, 359, 447
delirious, 316
deliver, 208
delta, 101
delude, 298
deluge, 128, 146, 298
delusion, 119, 442
demagog(ue), 239
demand, 426
demeanor, 265
demesne, 105
demitasse, 149, 401
demiurge, 92, 263
democracy, 367
democrat, 427; -ic, 172
demolish, 122, 444
demon. See d(a)emon
demonstrate, 426
demster, 99
demur, -er, 324
demure, 320
dengue, 96, 436
denier, 318
denim, 218
denizen, 394
dense, 82
deny, 432; -able, -al, 273
depend, 57
depict, 366
depletion, 119
deplore, 313
deploy, 302

deposit, 120; -ion, 224, 396
depravity, 215, 377
deprecate, 335
deprive, 376
depth, 98, 336, 385
deputy, 335
derange, 104, 146
derelict, 310, 366, 452
deride, 133
derision, 133, 224
derivation, 310, 377, 451
derogatory, 353
derrick, 310, 370
dervish, 19, 452
descant, 367
description, 410
descry, 276, 367
desert (v.), 323, 396
desiccate, 218, 356
desideratum, 401
design, 15–16, 275, 430;
   -ate, 15–16
desire, -able, 319; -ous, 316
desk, 402
desolate, 151, 218, 402
despair, 250, 311
desperado, 283, 342
despise, 395
despot, 116; -ic, 116, 347;
   -ism, 349
dessert, 396
destroy, 302
desultory, 402
detach, 413
detail, 253
detention, 410
deter, 172, 323; -ent, 323,
   453
deteriorate, 316
determine, 349
dethrone, 262
detour, 321
deuce, 146, 296
deuteron, 296
deutzia, 299
deviate, 137
devil, 166, 218; -er, 167; -ish,
   409
devoid, 302
devolve, 233
devotion, 119
devour, 306
devout, 306

dew, 295
dexterity, 371
dextrose, 371, 453
dghaisa, 20
dhow, 339
dhurra, 339
diabetes, 261, 330
diablerie, 95
diadem, 92
diagnosis, 403
diagonal, 214, 353
diagram, 165, 273; -atic, 174;
   -ed, 165
dial, 273
dialect, 135
dialog(ue), 96, 239
diameter, 116
diametric, 116
diamond, 92
diaphragm, 378, 425
diarrhea, 76, 449
diary, 273
diatom, 273
diatribe, 92
dichotomy, 110, 347, 358
dicker, 368
dictate, 345; -or, 366; -orial,
   313
dictionary, 308
did, 369; -st, 340
dido, 126, 283
diduce, 194
die, 88, 95, 145, 273; -ing,
   157
diet, 135, 273; -ary, 135;
   -etic, 116, 347; -itian, 410
diffareation, 193
differ, 168, 193, 383; -ed,
   -ence, -ent, -entia, -ing,
   168; -ential, 168, 410;
   -entiate, 58, 168, 410
difficult, 193, 365, 383
diffidation, 193
diffluent, 193
difflugia, 193
diffract, 193
diffuse, 193, 383, 403; -ion,
   119, 134
dig, 224; -er, 354
digest, 194; -ion, 416, 419
digit, 120; -alis, 349
digram, 105
digraph, 275

digress, 352; -ion, 411
dijudicate, 194
dike, dyke, 107, 363
dilapidated, 194
dildo, 283
dilemma, 429
dilettante, 194
diligent, 194
dilute, 194, 298; -ion, 119
diluvial, 138
dim, 224; -est, 428
dime, 105, 426
dimension, 194, 410
diminish, 122, 194, 429
diminution, 194
din, 226
dine, 105, 194
dinghy, dingy, dingey, 352,
   361, 438
dingy /'dinjē/, 419
dinner, 194, 440
dinosaur, 237
diode, 273
diorama, 232, 455
dip, 369
diphtheria, 23, 263, 327, 334,
   379, 385
diphthong, 23, 327, 334, 378
diploma, 335
diplomacy, 281
diplomatic, 172
direct, 194, 366; -ion, 451
dirge, 61, 194, 324
dirigible, 316
dirk, 324, 363
dirt, 324
disability, 402
disarray, 194
disbar, 76
disburse, 194, 324
disc. See disk
discern, 194
disciple, 105, 150, 275, 398;
   -ine, 153, 398
discission, 78, 194
discomfit, 246; -ure, 416
discomfort, 362
disconcert, 405
discourse, 315
discretion, 119
disdain, 76, 194, 250, 252
disease, 194, 265, 395
disfigure, 194, 381

disgrace, 194
disguise, 351
disgust, 76, 352
dishevel, 166
dishonor, 194
disinfect, 381
disinherit, 387
disinter, 194
disjointed, 421
disjunctive, 194
disk, disc, 101, 364
dislocate, 194
dismal, 395
dismay, 194, 252, 426
disme, 426
dismember, 194
dismiss, 401
disnature, 194
disobey, 194
disorient, 313
disparage, 146, 194, 309
disparate, 27
dispatch, 413
dispelled, 446
disperse, 78, 194; -ion, 410
dispirit, 78
display, 252
dispread, 78
disputable, 134
disquieting, 194
disregard, 194
dissatisfy, 403
dissect, 403
dissemble, 331
disseminate, 218
dissension, 194
dissertation, 403
dissipate, 403
dissociate, 403
dissolve, 396
dissuade, 403, 457
distaff, 194, 381
distance, 101
distant, 59–60, 78, 194
distend, 41
distention, distension, 41–42
distil(l), 194, 441, 443
distinct, 78, 223, 366, 436
distinguish, 78, 122, 194,
    351, 457
distort, 194, 312
distrain, 78
distraught, 237

distress, 78, 194; -ful, 79
distribute, 194
district, 78, 194
disunite, 194
disvalue, 194
disweapon, 194
ditch, 72, 413
ditto, 282
diuretic, 218, 273
diurnal, 93
diva, 264
divaricate, 194
divers, 43, 83
diverse, 43, 83 194; -ify,
    -ion, -ity, -ory, 194
divert, -ing, 43; -iculum, 194
divest, 194
divide, 223, 375; -end, 375
divine, 113, 152, 272; -ity,
    113, 433
divisible, 395
division, 194
divisor, 396
divorce, 194, 312
divot, 225
divulge, 419
divvy, 375, 377
dizzy, 391, 394
djin(n), djinni. See jinn(i)
do /dō/, 89
do /dū/, 292, 299; -er, 91;
    -ne, 149, 247
docent, 126
docile, 113, 152, 406; -ity, 113
docket, 368
doctor, 366, 451
doctrine, 233
document, 233
dodge, 72, 418
doe, 88
doer. See do
doffs, 80
dog, 15, 34, 36, 164; -ed,
    164; -fight, 56; -fish, -s,
    15; -s', 395; -'s, 34, 395;
    -sled, 353
doge, 107, 420
doggerel, 239, 354
doggone, 354
dogma, 101, 239, 353; -atic,
    116
doldrum, 102; -s, 453
doll, 101, 233, 442

dollar, 343
dolma, 102
dolman, 102
dolphin, 233, 379, 445
dolt, 102
domain, 105
domestic, -ity, 117
domic, 116
dominant, 427
domineer, 317
dominion, 136, 460
domino, 282
done. See do
doni, 85
donkey, 268, 436
doom, 289
door, 286, 315, 321
dornick, 370
dorr, 451
dory, 313
dosage, 124
dot, 74, 206, 369
dote, 107
double, 150, 247, 331, 333;
    -ing, -s, 155; -oon, 247,
    333
doubt, 306, 328, 344
dough, 209, 286
doughty, 306
dour, 306, 321
douse, 148, 306
dove /duv/, 107, 246
dowager, 305, 420
dowdy, 305
dower, 305
dowlas, 83
down, 305; -town, 346
dowry, 453
doxology, 371
doze, 107
dozen, 246, 393
drachm, 426
drachma, 428
draft, 382
dragon, 128, 353
drake, 363
drama, 232; -atic, 116;
    -atics, 372
drape, 107, 141; -ery, 141
draught, 23; -s, 215–16, 380
draw, 236; -n, 237
drayage, 86
dread, 219, 340

dreary, 317; -est, 58
dredge, 418
dreg, 93
drench, 414
dreng(h), 437
dress, 340; -maker, 402
drew, 295
dribble, 150, 331, 333
dried, drier. *See* dry
driftwood, 348
drive, 374; -er, 123, 124; -n, 225
drivel, 129, 166; -er, 167
drizzle, 394
drogue, 95
droll, 102
dromedary, 427
droop, 289
drop, 234; -ing, -out, 165; -ings, -let, 163
dropsy, 101
dross, 104
drought, 306, 345
drouth, 306
drown, 305
drowse, 148, 305; -ier, 58
druggist, 354
druid, 116, 120; -ic, 93, 116
drum, 244; -er, 428
drunk, 436; -ard, 226
dry, 276; -ed, -er, 278
duality, 215
dualize, 92
dubbing, 332
ducat, 245, 365
duchess, 110, 414
duck, 369
ductile, 101, 152
dud, 244
duello, 172
duet, 92, 218
duff, 381
dug, 369
duke, 299, 363
dulce, 146; -et, 406
dull, 101; -ly, 447; -ness, 79, 441
duly, 159
dumb, 101, 424; -bell, 332; -found, 244, 306
dummy, 424, 429
dune, 433
dungaree, 265; -s, 436

dungeon, 419, 433
dupe, 107, 299
duplex, 105
duplicity, 224, 406
durable, 320
duration, 320
during, 320
duroc, 320
durum, 320
dusky, 362, 367
duteous, 134
dutiable, 134
duumvir, 81
dvandva, 340
dwarf, 313, 374, 458; -s, 374
dwarves, 374
dwell, 458
dwindle, 74, 433, 458
dyad, 91, 116; -ic, 116, 340
dye, 88, 96, 145, 276; -er, 158, 277
dying, 157
dyke. *See* dike
dynamic, 427
dynamite, 154, 272
dynamo, 276, 282
dynast, 64; -y, 276
dysentery, 227, 311, 402
dyspepsia, 410
dyssebacia, 403
dyssodia, 403

each, 265
eager, 259, 266
eagle, 265, 354, 445
ear, 317; -ring, 453
earl, 325
early, 325
earn, 325
earnest, 325
earth, 325
easel, 266, 396
east, 259, 265
easy, 266, 396
eat, 98, 259
eaves, 266
ebb, 76, 88, 101, 328, 330, 369; -s, 80, 331
ebonite, 154
ebony, 218, 330
ebractate, 182, 261
ebullition, 182

eccentric, 117, 164, 182, 218, 372; -ity, 117, 164
ecchymosis, 182
ecclesiast, 137; -ic, 80, 182; -ical, 356
eccrine, 182
ecdysis, 182
echelon, 408
echo, 110, 282, 357
éclair, 182
eclampsia, 182
eclectic, 182
eclipse, 182, 362, 366
eclogue, 96, 182
ecology, oecology, 234, 269
economy, 269, 432; -ics, 372
ecru, 182
ecstasy, 182, 368
ecstatic, 347
ectype, 182
ecumenical, 365
eczema, 182, 368, 399
edema, oedema, 269
eddy, 341
edict, 182, 260
edit, 120, 219, 340; -ion, 347; -or, 219, 340; -orial, 313
educate, 182, 366, 421
e'en, 373
e'er, 373
eerie, 95, 317, 453
ef(f), 89, 93
effable, 181
efface, 146, 181, 383
effect, 181, 366, 383
effeminate, 181
efferent, 169
effervesce, 181; -ent, 218, 398
effete, 181
efficacy, 383; -ous, 412
efficient, 181
effigy, 181, 383
effloresce, 181
effluent, 181
effluerage, 80
effluvium, 138, 181
efflux, 181
effort, 181, 218, 383
effraction, 80
effrontery, 181, 383
effulgent, 181
effuse, 181, 383

egest, 182
egg, 72, 76, 87, 88, 101, 352, 353, 369; -beater, -crate, -fruit, -head, -less, -nog, -plant, 354; -s, 80, 354; -shell, 354; -y, 351
egis. *See* (a)egis
ego, 282, 354; -centric, 405; -ist, 92; -ity, 115
egregious, 420
egress, 105, 182, 261, 354
egret, 106, 261
eider, 278
eidetic, 278
eidolon, 278
eidos, 278
eight, 254, 255, 345; -th, 77, 342, 345–46, 385
eik, 268
eikon. *See* icon
eild, 268
eilding, 268
einkorn, 278
einsteinium, 278
either, 267, 268, 278
ejaculate, 421
eject, 182, 366
eke, 107, 363
el, 89, 442
elapse, 182
elastic, 117; -ity, 117, 224, 406
elbow, 285
electioneer, 317
electric, 117, 366, 453; -ian, 138; -ity, 117
electrolyte, 65, 276; -ic, 227
electronic, 433
elegance, 406
elegant, 182
elegiac, 364
elegiast, 64
elegist, 87
element, 429, 444
elemi, 85
elephant, 379
elevated, 377
eleven, 218
elf, 374
elicit, 120, 442
eligible, 182, 420
elite, 256, 264, 348
ell, 88

elleck, 370
ellipse, 446
elongate, 436
eloquent, 182
else, 82
elucidate, 182
elude, 290
eluvial, 138
elves, 374, 376
elysium, 422
em, 89
emanate, 182, 218, 434
emasculate, 426
embag, 94
embalm, 188
embank, 188
embarcadero, 188
embargo, 188, 283, 453
embark, 188, 363
embarrass, 188, 310, 405, 452
embassy, 402
embathe, 188
embatholithic, 188
embattle, 188
embay, 188
embed, 188
embelif, 188
embellish, 122, 188, 445
embezzle, 188, 394
embiaria, 188
embitter, 188
emblaze, -on, 188
emblem, 188
emblossom, 188
embody, 188
embog, 188
embolden, 188
embolism, 188
embolite, 188
embolium, 188
embonpoint, 188
embosk, 188
emboss, 188; -ment, 79
embouchure, 188
embound, 188
embowed, 188
embowel, 188
embower, 188
embox, 188
embrace, 188
embrail, 188
embranchment, 188

embrangle, 188
embrasure, 188, 422
embreathe, 188
embrighten, 188
embrittle, 188
embrocate, 188
embroider, 188, 302, 330, 340
embroil, 188, 302
embrown, 188
embryo, 188, 428
embus, 188
embusque, 188
emerald, 23, 427, 440
emerge, 323
emeritus, 182, 310
emery, 218
emigrate, 131, 182
eminent, 131
emissary, 218
emotion, 119, 182
emperil, 166
emphatic, 215, 364, 378
empirical, 316, 452
employ, 218, 302; -ed, 86; -ee, 94, 265
emporium, 264
empress, 453
emu, 126
emulate, 218
emulsion, 182, 410
en, 89
enable, 188
enact, 188, 366
enalid, 188
enamel, 166, 188, 427
enamor, 188, 215
enantiomorph, 188
enarched, 188
enarme, 188
enarthrosis, 188
encaenia, 188
encage, 188
encamp, 188
encapsulate, 188
encarnalize, 188
encarpus, 188
encase, 188
encastage, 188
encastre, 188
encaustic, 188
encave, 188
enceinte, 188

encephalitis, 188
enchain, 188
enchant, 188, 414; -ress, 433
encharge, 188
enchase, 188
enchilada, 188
enchiridion, 188
enchondral, 188
enchondroma, 188
enchorial, 188
enchylema, 188
enchymatous, 188
encincture, 188
encipher, 188
encircle, 188
enclasp, 188
enclave, 188
enclitic, 188
enclose, 188; -ure, 422
enclothe, 188
encode, 188
encoffin, 188
encoignure, 188
encolpion, 188
encolure, 188
encomiast, 64
encomienda, 188
encomiologic, 188
encomium, 188
encompass, 188
encopresis, 188
encorbelment, 188
encore, 235, 313
encounter, 188, 433
encourage, 188
encroach, 188, 284
encrust, 188
encrypt, 188
enculturation, 188
encumber, 188
encyclical, 188
encyclop(a)edia, 188, 269,
    277, 335, 405
encyst, 188
endeavor, 219, 377
endemic, 427
endorse, 218; -ment, 339
endow, 304
endure, 320
enemy, 432
enervate, 182
enfeoffment, 79
enfranchise, 381

engender, 218
engine, 153, 228, 419; -eer,
    317
England, 228
English, 121, 228
engross, 104; -ment, 79
enigmatic, 116
enjoy, 302, 421
ennoble, 434
ennui, 85
enology. See (o)enology
enormity, 312
enough, 248, 380
enrol(l), 94, 441
ensconce, 233
ensign, 430
ensue, 291
ensure, 411
enswathe, 147
entail, 253
enthral(l), 441, 443
enthusiast, 64, 134
entire, 319
entitle, 275
entreat, 265
entree, entrée, 235, 256
entrepreneur, 235, 326
enumerate, 182, 428, 432
envisage, 395
envoy, 302
envy, 376; -able, 262
eolian, 260
eon, aeon, 260, 269
epaulet, 137
ephah, 379
epic, 127, 218, 336
epicranial, 138
epicure, 320, 335; -ean, 260
epidermis, 405
epilog(ue), 239
epistle, 337, 400
epitaph, 379
epithalamium, 138
epithelial, 138
epithet, 385; -ic, 172; -ize,
    174
epitome, 261, 337
epoch, 138, 358
eponym, -y, 164
equal, 106, 141, 166, 359;
    -ity, 232; -ize, 141, 167
equanimity, 114
equation, 422

equatorial, 313
equestrian, 359
equilibrium, 447
equinox, 371
equip, 94, 359
equity, 114
equivalent, 377
era, 316
eradicate, 182
erase, 82; -ure, 153
ere, 311
erect, 182
eremite, 154
erg, 353
erode, 182
erosion, 119, 136, 422
erotic, 347
err, 76, 88, 323, 451
errand, 310
errant, 192, 452
erratic, 116, 455
erroneous, 455
erudite, 154, 182, 243, 272,
    310, 452
erupt, 451
es. See es(s)
escalade, 48
escalate, 48, 367; -or, 48
escallop, 48
escambio, 182
escape, 182
escarp, -ment, 48
eschallot, 48
escheat, 182, 414
eschew, 295
eschscholtzia, 408
escolar, 48
escort, 182
escritoire, 48
escrow, 48, 285
escudo, 48
escutcheon, 48, 415
esophagus, oesophagus, 111,
    131, 269, 379, 405
esoteric, 310
espadrille, 48
espalier, 48
esparto, 48
especial, 48, 218
esperance, 48
espial. See espy
espionage, 48
esplanade, 48–49, 182

espouse, 48, 305
espresso, 182
esprit, 48
espy, 48; -al, 48, 87
esquire, 48, 319
es(s), 89
essay, 182, 192, 404
essence, 402
essential, 402
essoin, 404
establish, 48, 122
estancia, 48
estate, 48
esteem, 265
esthete, -ic, -icism, -ics. *See*
   (a)esthete
estivate. *See* (a)estivate
estop, 48
estoppel, 48
estray, 48
estreat, 182
estuary, 415
etch, 413
eternal, 323
eternity, 349
ether, aether, 110, 269; -eal,
   316, 452
ethic, 110; -s, 101, 372
ethnic, 218, 385
ethos, 110
ethyl, 110
etiology, aetiology, 269
etui, etwee, 85
etymology, 347
eulogy, 297; -ist, 87; -ium,
   138
eunuch, 300, 357
euphemism, 378
euphonic, 300
euphonious, 136
euphonium, 138
euphoria, 263, 313, 459
euthanasia, 297, 300
evacuate, 137, 365
evaluate, 137
evaporate, 182
evasive, 251
eve, 107
even, 125, 373; -ing, 260
event, 182
ever, 129, 373
eversible, 43
eversion, 43

evert, 43
evict, 366
evil, 125; -er, -est, 167;
   -doer, 339
evince, 182
eviscerate, 398
evocative, 234
evoke, 182
evolve, 147, 181
evulsion, 182
ewe, 89, 294, 297, 299
ewer, 297
exact, 181, 351, 370
exaggerate, 351, 352, 417,
   418; -ion, 251
exalt, 352
examine, 182, 352
example, 150
exasperate, 352
excaudate, 182
excavate, 371
exceed, 181, 360
excel, 77, 171, 360
excellency, 171
excellent, 171
excelsior, 360
except, 182, 360
excerpt, 360
excess, 360
exchange, 104, 182, 371
excise, 183
excite, 182
exclaim, 371
exclude, 182, 298, 365
excoriate, 182, 313
excrescence, 182
excretion, 119
excruciate, 291; -ing, 58,
   290, 371
exculpate, 182
excursion, 422
execute, 298; -ive, 352, 365,
   370
exemplary, 352
exempt, 352; -ion, 336
exercise, 83, 182, 272
exfiltration, 182
exflagellate, 182
exfoliate, 182
exhalation, 371
exhale, 387
exhaust, 237, 352, 390; -ion,
   416

exhibit, 330, 352, 370, 390;
   -ion, 333; -ionist, 119
exhilarate, 182, 352, 390,
   444; -ion, 455
exhort, 352, 390
exhume, 387, 390
exigency, 419
exile, -ic, 115
exist, 352; -ence, -ential,
   49
exit, 182, 371
exogamy, 353, 371
exonerate, 352
exorbitant, 182, 352
exotic, 371
expand, 182
expansion, 410
expect, 366
expedient, 137
expedite, 371
expel, 444; -able, 446
expend, 57
experience, 182, 316
expert, 323
expiate, 182
expire, 319
explain, 133, 252
explanatory, 133
explicate, 182
explicit, 120
exploit, 348
explore, 313
explosion, 119, 136
export, 182, 312
expostulate, 233, 416
express, 371; -ion, 411
expropriate, 182, 283
expulsion, 182
exquisite, 154, 182, 359, 371,
   396
exsanguinate, 182, 360
exscind, 360
exsect, 360
exsert, 360
exsiccate, 360
exstipulate, 182
extant, 371
extemporaneous, 182
extend, 41
extension, 41–42, 409
extenuate, 299
exterior, 263, 371
external, 371

extinguish, 122, 182, 351, 457
extol(l), 94, 441
extort, 182
extract, 218
extraordinary, 315, 371
extrapolate, 214, 371
extraterrestrial, 371
extravaganza, 355
extreme, 113, 371; -ist, 260; -ity, 113, 427
extricate, 182
extrinsic, 371
extroversion, 43
extroversive, 43
extrovert, 43
exuberance, 352
exuberant, 331
exude, 371
exult, 182
eyas, 83, 295
eye, 89, 279
eyrie. See aerie

fa, 89
fable, 105, 132, 381
fabric, 215, 330
fabulosity, 47, 114
fabulous, 47, 132, 330
face, 46; -et, 166, 215, 406; -ial, 58
facile, 113, 152; -itate, 444; -ity, 113
facsimile, 365, 427
fact, -or, 46
faculty, 46, 365; -es, 58
faddist, 341
faeces. See feces
fagot, 353
Fahrenheit, 278
failure, 153, 459
fair, 46, 311
fairy, 453
faith, 250, 252
fakir, 318, 364
falcon, 23, 239, 362, 366, 367
fall, 239, 442, 443
fallacy, 445
fallible, 445
fallow, 285, 443
false, 148, 239, 342; -etto, 239, 282, 349

falter, 239
family, 131, 427; -ar, 429, 460; -arity, 309, 460
famine, 153
famish, 122, 128
famous, 124
fan, -atic, 116
fancy, 406
fandango, 283
fanged, 40
fantasm. See phantasm
fantasmagoria. See phantasmagoria
fantast, phantast, 64; -ic, 116, 378
fantasy, phantasy, 116, 210, 378
fantom. See phantom
far, 204, 314
farce, 311, 406
farmyard, 459
farrago, 282
farther, 386
farthing, 386
fascicle, 398
fascinate, 398
fasciola, 398
fascism, 395
fascist, 412
fashion, 46
fast, 348; -en, 399
fat, 206; -en, -s, 163; -ish, 121
fatal, -ism, 141
father, 60, 108, 204, 205, 233
fathom, 108
fatigable, 214, 347
fatigue, 95, 264, 351; -ed, 158
fatuous, 137
faucet, 238
fault, 18, 23; -less, -lessness, 405; -s, 343
faun, 237, 433
fauna, 238; -ae, 269
favor, 141; -ite, 141, 154
fawn, 237
fazenda, 46
fealty, 23
fear, 317
feasible, 46, 266, 395
feast, 265, 381
feat, 46, 264, 265; -ure, 266, 416

feather, 219
febrile, 152
feces, faeces, 261, 269
fecund, 365; -ity, 113
federal, 340
fee, 88, 265
feeble, 150, 265, 331, 445
feel, 265; -s, 337
feet, 264
feign, 254, 431
feint, 254
feisty, 278
feldspar, 314, 345
felicitate, 406
felid, 121
feline, 152
fellow, 218, 285, 447
felon, 218
felucca, 356
feminine, 113, 153; -ly, 155; -ity, 113, 155
fence, 406
fennel, 434
feoff, 221
fern, 322, 454
ferocious, 136
ferocity, 114, 455
ferret, 310
ferric, 452
ferrule, 452
ferry, 310
fertile, 152
festivity, 159
festoon, 289
fetch, 413
fete, fête, 256
fetid, foetid, 269
fetish, 46, 128, 347
fettle, 80
fettucini, 85
fetus, 125, 269
feud, 298, 300
feudal, -ity, 113
few, 212, 299
fey, 255
fez, 84, 94, 392; -es, 393, 394
fiasco, 93, 282, 367
fiat, 91, 381
fiber, 331
fibrous, 106
fiction, 223
fiddle, 342, 445

fidelity, 114
fidget, 420
fiducial, 134
fie, 88, 273
fief, 268
field, 258, 268, 340, 345; -s, 337
fiend, 220, 258, 268, 340
fierce, 318, 453
fiery, 319–20, 453
fife, 382
fifth, 101, 334, 385
fifty, 98; -eth, 101, 263
fight, 102, 274, 345
figment, 223
figure, 224, 353; -ine, 153, 263
filch, 414
filet, 256
filial, 136
filibuster, 333
filigree, fil(l)agree, 94, 265, 441
fill, 226; -ed, 338
fillip, 101
film, 101; -ed, 338
filth, 101, 226; -y, 385
final, -ist, -ity, 164; -e, 232
financial, 412
financier, 318
find, 102, 275
fine, 74, 141; -er, 124; -ery, 141; -esse, 149, 401; -ish, 122, 128, 409, 433; -ished, 343; -ite, 154, 272
fiord. See fjord
fir, -y, 324
fire, 319–20; -arm, 12
firm, 322, 454
first, 324
fish, 19; -er, 111; -hook, 80; -ing, 163
fission, 411
fissure, 411
five, 98
fixation, 371
fixed, 163, 343
fixture, 416
fizz, 84, 101, 392
fjord, fiord, 460
flabby, 332
flaccid, 372, 406, 445
flagellate, 419, 447

flageolet, 137, 256
flagon, 128, 353
flagrant, 106, 353
flambé, 20
flamboyant, 302
flame, 249, 427
flamingo, 283
flammable, 427
flange, 104
flank, 363, 381
flannel, 166; -ette, 167
flare, 107, 308
flat, 94; -est, 349
flatulent, 416
flaunt, 216
flaw, 236
flay, 252
flea, 259, 265
fleck, 369
fledg(e)ling, 159
flee, 74, 265; -ing, 158
fleece, 146, 266, 381
flew, 295
flight, 102, 274, 345
flippancy, 175
flippant, 337
flivver, 375, 377
float, 284
flocculent, 172
floe, 95
flood, 247
floor, 286, 315, 321
flora, 313; -ae, 269
florid, 452
florin, 312
floss, 101, 104
flotsam, 101
flounce, 306
flounder, 306
flour, 304, 306; -ish, 325
flout, 306
flow, -n, 284
flower, 304
fluctuate, 92, 366
flue, 291
fluent, 91
fluff, 381
fluid, 120, 289, 298
fluke, 107, 363
flume, 107
fluoresce, 398; -ent, 321, 453
fluoride, 321

fluorine, 321
flurry, 324, 454
flux, 94
fly, 276; -er, 91, 273
foal, 284
foam, 284, 381
fobbed, 332
foci, 273
focus, 125, 166; -able, -er, 167; -es, 273
fodder, 204
foe, 281
foetid. See fetid
foetus. See fetus
foible, 302, 331
fold, 102; -ed, 338
folderol, 94
foliage, 92
folio, 283
folk, 102, 361, 446
follow, 233, 285, 447
folly, 233
fondle, 151, 233
fondue, 291
fontanel(le), 441
food, 289
foolhardy, 387
foot, 241, 242
foozle, 445
for, 312
forage, 312
foray, 313
forbade, 149
forbear, 311
force, 406
ford, 340
for(e)go, 282; -ne, 352
forehead, 23, 390
foreign, 313, 431
foreseeable, 158
foreseer, 158
foretaste, 346
forever, 165
forfeit, 229; -ure, 320
forge, 419
forks, 371
forlorn, 442
formalities, 57
formation, 119
formulae, 269
formulation, 447
forte, 256
fortress, 405

fortuity, 115
fortune, 312, 416; -ate, 152
forty, 28, 31
fosse, 401
fossil, 444
foster, 239
fought, 240, 345
foul, 305
foundation, 119, 339
foundry, 306
fountain, 306
four, 28, 315; -teen, 28, 346
fowl, 305
fox, 371; -es, 33; -y, 163
fracas, 82, 405
fragile, 152, 419
fragment, 214
fragrance, 106
fragrant, 252
frail, 453
frame, 107, 381
franc, 101
franchise, 82, 272
frankfurter, 367
frankincense, 367
fraternity, 323
fraternize, 83, 347
fraud, 237; -ulent, 163, 238, 421
fraught, 237, 345
frazzle, 394
freckle, 369
free, 36, 74, 94, 265; -dom, 339; -ed, 338; -est, 158; -will, 443
freeze, 84, 266, 391
freight, 255, 345
frenetic, phrenetic, 218, 378, 379, 434
frenzy, phrensy, 379, 393, 433
frequent, 106, 359
fresco, 282
fresh, 409
friable, 135, 273
friar, 273
fricandeau, fricando, 286
fricassee, 95, 402
friction, 381
friend, 217, 220, 340; -ly, -ship, 220
frier, 319
frieze, 84, 268, 393

frigate, 224, 353
fright, 102, 274, 345
frigid, 113, 120; -ity, 113
frijoles, 264
frippery, 337
frisk, 363; -y, 367
fritter, 349
frivol, 166; -ity, 114; -ous, 167, 377
frizz, 84, 392; -le, 394
fro, 282
froe, frow, 281
frolic, 444–45
front, 246; -ier, 318
froth, 101
frow. See froe
frown, 305
frowzy, 305, 393
froze, 84; -en, 393
frugal, 124, 298, 354
fruit, 296; -ion, 291
fry, 276
fuchsia, 105, 299
fudge, 381, 418
fuel, 91, 299
fugacity, 215
fugitive, 420
fugue, 351
fulcrum, 366, 367, 445, 453
fulfil(l), 77, 441, 443
full, 77, 243, 441; -ly, 77, 447; -ness, 79
fume, 298
fumigate, 134
funereal, 316, 452
fungal, 101
fungi, 274
fungus, 436; -es, 274
funnel, 166
funny, 433
fur, 324; -y, 324, 453
furbish, 122
furl, 322, 454
furlough, 286
furnish, 122
furor, 312
furrow, 285, 454
further, 386
furze, 84, 393, 453
fuselage, 146, 299, 422
fusilier, fusileer, 318
fusillade, 342
fusion, 410

fuss, 82, 401
fustian, 416
futile, 124, 152
futtock, 370
future, 124; -ist, 134
fuzz, 84, 101, 392
fyrd, 381

gab, -ed, 164
gabardine, 263
gabble, 106, 333
gable, 105, 106
gadget, 420
gadid, 121
Gaelic, 257
gaff, 381
gaffe, 381
gage. See ga(u)ge
gaiety. See gayety
gaily, 253
gait. See gate
galactic, 366
galavant. See gal(l)ivant
gale, 445
galeid, 121
galena, 116
galenic, 116
gall, 442, 443
galleon, 260
gal(l)ivant, galavant, 441
gallop, 447
gallows, 285, 443
galosh, 409
galvanic, 215
galvanize, 445
gamboge, camboge, 147
gambol, 166
gamma, 429
gamut, 429
ganglion, 263, 436
gangster, 303
gang(ue), 96, 437
gaol, 257
garage, 146, 232, 422
garble, 453
garçon, 405
gardenia, 137
gargle, 453
gargoyle, 303, 445
garibaldi, 85
garnish, 122
garot(t)e. See gar(r)ot(t)e
garret, 452

garrison, 310, 404
gar(r)ot(t)e, 450, 455
garrulity, 115
garrulous, 452
gas, 83, 94, 175, 401; -ed,
 -es, 403; -eity, 115; -elier,
 -ify, 174; -eous, 135, 174;
 -ing, -y, 174, 403; -oline,
 174, 263
gasket, 367
gastr(a)ea, 269
gastropodous, 175
gate, gait, 249
gather, 108
gauche, 238, 286, 408
gaudy, 238
ga(u)ge, 146, 249, 257, 420
gaunt, 238
gauntlet, 216, 238
gaur, 306
gauze, 84, 148, 238, 393
gave, 108, 147
gavel, 166; -er, 167
gavotte, 347
gawk, 237
gayety, gaiety, 86
gaze, 148; -ing, 393
gazelle, 149
gear, 317
gee, 88
geese, 266
gel, 93, 417, 442; -id, 120
gelatin(e), 417, 444
geld, 101
gem, 426
gemmiparous, 171
gendarme, 235, 422
gene, 417, 433; -esis, 404;
 -etics, 372; -ial, -iality,
 460; -ius, 137
genealogy, 260
general, 432; -ity, 215
generosity, 47, 114
generous, 47
genet. See jennet
genie, 95, 432. See also
 jinn(i)
genre, 422
genteel, 265, 445
gentian, 101
gentle, 149, 433, 445
genuflect, 366
genuine, 137, 153, 419, 432

geodetic, 260, 347
geoduck, gweduc, 93, 369
Geoffrey, 221
geography, 48; -ic, 260
geology, 260; -ical, 442
geometry, 260, 426; -id,
 121
geranium, 137
gerbil(le), 441
gerrymander, 310
get, 417; -able, 75
geyser, 279, 396
ghastly, 210, 352, 402
ghat, 352
ghee, 352
gherkin, 210, 352, 367
ghetto, 210, 282, 352
ghost, 104, 210, 264, 352
ghoul, 210, 293, 294, 352,
 445
ghyll, 442
giant, 91
giaour, 306
gibberish, 332
gibbous, 332
gibe, jibe, 417
giblet, 330, 419
giddy, 226
giggle, 151, 355
gigolo, 282
gigue, 422
gild, 97, 102
gill /gil/, 206
gill, jill /jil/, 417
gimcrack, 369
gimmick, 370, 429
gin, 74
ginger, 419
ginkgo, gingko, ginko, 361,
 438
ginseng, 101
Giovanni, 126
giraffe, 381, 455
gird, 324
girdle, 453
girl, 417; -hood, 387
girth, 324
give, 107, 374, 417
gizzard, 394
glabrous, 252
glacial, 58, 125, 137
glacier, 58, 412, 445
glamor, 429

glandular, 421
glass, 101, 401; -ful, 79;
 -ware, 402
glazier, 58, 136, 422
gleam, 265
glebe, 107
glee, 265
glimmer, 429
glimpse, 72, 336, 428
glisten, 399
glitter, 349
gloat, 284
globe, 107; -ule, 122, 234,
 330
gloom, 289
gloss, 82, 104
glottal, 171
glove, 107, 245
glow, 284, 353
glower, 304
glucose, 290
glue, 94, 145, 147, 298, 350;
 -ier, -y, 157
glum, 426
glut, 94
glutinous, 291
glycerin, 227
gnar, 430
gnarl, 430
gnash, 430
gnat, 430
gnathic, 215
gnaw, 236, 430
gneiss, 278, 430
gnome, 107, 430
gnomon, 125, 430
gnosis, 430
gnostic, 430
gnu, 20, 291, 299
go, 282; -er, 91; -ing, 281;
 -ne, 108, 149, 239
goa, 281
goad, 240, 284
goal, 284
goat, 284
gobble, 333
gobiid, 81, 121
goblin, 233
god, 74; -ess, 163, 341; -like,
 272; -ling, 163
Goethe, 221, 270
gold, 23, 102
golf, 101

gondola, 433
gondolier, 318
gone. *See* go
gonfalonier, 318
gonorrhea, 449
goober, 290, 331
good, 242
googol, 290
goose, 81, 98, 148, 290, 403;
    -berry, 56
gopher, 111, 283, 379
gory, 453
gosling, 98
gospel, 166; -er, -ize, 167
gossip, 101, 166; -y, 167
got, 204
gouge, 146, 420
goulash, 293, 294
gourd, 315, 321
gourmet, 256, 321
gout, 306
govern, 128, 377; -or, 449
gown, 305
gracile, 152
gracious, 58, 136, 251
gradate, 47, 124
gradual, 47, 137, 421
graduate, 421
graham, 390
grain, 133, 252
gram, 427; -ar, 214, 427, 429;
    -arian, 263
grandeur, 421, 459
grandfather, 337
grandiose, 92
grange, 104
granite, 129, 154
granule, 122; -ar, 133
graph, 210, 379; -ic, 101, 117,
    163; -icness, 117; -ite, 111,
    154, 379
grapple, 337, 445
grasp, 336
grasshopper, 80, 402
grassless, 80
grateful, -ly, 132
gratify, 214
gratis, 348
gratitude, 131, 132
gratuity, 115
grave, -ity, 113; -id, 120
gravel, 123, 127, 166; -ish,
    167

graven, 376
gravure, 321
gray, grey, 250, 252
graze, 249
grease, 266; -y, 202
great, 256
greenness, 434
greet, 265
gregarious, 308, 452
gregorian, 263
gremlin, 218, 428
grenade, 434; -ier, 318; -ine,
    153
grew, 295
grey, 268. *See also* gray
griefful, 383
griffin, 383
grille, 149
grime, 107
grind, 102, 275; -stone, 337–
    38
grisly, 395
gristle, 400
grizzled, 394
grizzly, 394
groan, 284
groats, 284
groin, 301, 302
grommet, 429
groove, 147, 290
gross, 104, 403; -beak, 104;
    -ly, 80; -ness, 79
grotesque, 281, 359
grotto, 282, 349
grouch, 306, 415
group, 293
grouse, 306
grove, 107
grovel, 129, 166, 234; -er,
    167
grow, 284, 353; -n, -th, 285
growl, 305
grudge, 418
gruel, 298
gruesome, 291, 298
gruff, 381
guacamole, 351
guaiacol, 351
guaiacum, 457
guanaco, 351, 457
guano, 129, 232, 283, 351,
    457
guarana, 457

guarantee, 94, 265, 351;
    -ing, 158
guaranty, 309, 351
guard, 314, 351; -ian, 263
guava, 351
guernsey, 351
guer(r)illa, 100, 351, 450,
    455
guess, 351
guest, 351
guffaw, 236, 384
guide, 107, 351; -ance, 124;
    -on, 351
guild, 229, 351
guile, 351
guillotine, 100, 351
guilt, 229, 351
guimp, 351
guinea, 129, 351, 434
guise, 107
guitar, 174, 229, 314, 351;
    -ed, -ing, -ist, 174
gulch, 414
gum, 94, 350
gunner, 433
guppy, 337
gusset, 404
gusto, 282
gut, 244
guy, 279, 351
guzzle, 394
gweduc. *See* geoduck
Gwen, 457
gwyniad, gwyniard, 457
Gwynne, 457
gybe. *See* jibe (shift sail)
gym, 61, 63–64, 94, 227,
    350, 417, 426; -khana, 63–
    64
gymnasia, 63, 64
gymnasial, 63, 64
gymnasiarch, 63, 64
gymnasium, 61, 63–64, 395
gymnast, -ic, -ics, 63, 64
gymnosophist, 63, 64
gymnosperm, 63, 64
gynecology, 366
gyp, 94, 206, 226, 227; -ed,
    337
gypsum, 227, 419
gyrate, 276, 453
gyroscope, 276, 419
gyve, 107, 147

haberdasher, 214, 330
habile, 152
habit, 120, 128, 330; -at, 214; -ual, 136, 333, 390, 415
hackle, 369
hackney, 369
had, 373
haddock, 341, 370
haggis, 83
haggle, 355
hail, 252
hair, 212, 311
hakim, 364
halcyon, 387, 406
half, 72, 232, 374, 380
hall, 443
hallelujah, halleluia, 417
halliard. See halyard
halloo, 289
hallow, 285, 443
hallucination, 390, 447
halo, 125, 282
halter, 101, 239
haltingly, 57
halve, 374, 376, 377, 380; -s, 232, 374
halyard, halliard, 441, 459
hamburger, 330
hammer, 429
hammock, 370, 429
hamster, 428
handful, 243
handicap, 48
handicraft, 48
handiwork, 48, 87
handkerchief, 338, 436
handle, 150
handyman, 87
hang, 101, 437
hangar, 437
happen, 337
happy, 337
harangue, 96, 437
harass, 23; -ment, 79
harbinger, 314
hardship, 409
hare, 308
harem, 309
harlequin, 359
harmonic, 234, 344, 390, 433
harness, 314, 405
harquebus, 83

harrow, 285
harry, 310
harsh, 72, 409
harvest, 376
has, 82, 395
hassle, 404, 445
hassock, 370, 404
haste, 103; -en, 380, 399; -y, 373
hat, 74, 145, 206
hatchel, 415
hatchet, 214, 414
hate, 145, 249, 255; -able, 157
hatred, 106
haughty, 237
haul, 237
haunch, 237
haunt, 216
hausfrau, 306
hautboy, 286, 389
hauteur, 286, 326
have, 107, 147, 375
haven, 125
havoc, 128, 364, 377
haw, 236
hawk, 237, 373
hawser, 236, 396
haying, 86
hazard, 128, 393
hazel, 125, 249, 393
he, 261
head, 219, 373; -less, 340
heal, 220; -th, 219, 220
heap, 265
heard, 325
hearken, 315, 325
hearse, 325
heart, 315, 325; -break, 348
hearth, 315, 325
heat, 265
heathen, 259, 266
heather, 219
heave, 266
heaven, 219
heavyweight, 458
heckle, 369
hectic, 366
heed, 265
hegemony, 420, 427
heifer, 217, 220–21, 382
heigh-ho, 278
height, 278, 345

heinous, 254, 255
heir, 311, 389; -loom, 428, 453
held, 97
hele, 107
helicopter, 19, 344
helium, 264
helix, 371
hellcat, 80
hellebore, 389
hello, 282
hellward, 79
helm, 101
help, 336
hem, 218
hemlock, 101
hemorrhage, 76, 449
hemp, 101
hen, 94
hence, 62–63
henchman, 414
hepatorrhexis, 76, 449
her, 323, 451; -s, 82–83, 395
herald, 23, 310, 452
herb, 323, 389; -aceous, 137
herculean, 260, 367
here, 62, 107, 311, 316; -in, 229
hereditary, 390
heredity, 340, 455
heresy, 23, 401
heretic, 23, 117, 118; -al, 347
heritage, 23, 310
heritor, 23
hermit, 23, 389
hernia, 263
hero, 282, 316; -es, -s, 293; -ic, 92, 118, 281; -ine, 153, 311; -ism, 311
heron, 452
herring, 310
hesitate, 387, 395
hetaera, hetaira, 318; -ae, 269
heterogeneity, 260
heuristic, 453; -s, 321
hew, 298; -n, 299
hex, 371
hexagon, 218
hexameter, 214, 371
hey, 255
hiatus, 93, 135, 348
hibernate, 387

hiccough, hiccup, 327, 334, 356
hick, 369
hickory, 368
hid, 98
hideous, 92, 136, 260, 340
hie, 88, 273; -ing, 157
hierarch, 92; -y, 319, 357
hieroglyph, 227, 379; -ic, 111, 227, 319, 352
high, 102, 274
hike, 363
hilarious, 263, 390
hilarity, 447, 452
hill-less, 77
hillock, 370
hind, 102, 275
hinder /'hindər/, 102
hinder /'hīndər/, 102
hindrance, 275
hinging, 156
hippity-hoppity, 175
hippopotamus, 234, 337, 405
hire, 319
hirsute, 324
his, 82–83, 94
hiss, 401
historian, 263, 313
historical, 390
histrionic, 433
hitch, 413
hither, 62, 108
hitter, 33
hive, 108, 374
hoar, 314
hoard, 314
hoarse, 314
hobble, 331, 333
hobby, 332, 387
hobo, 283
hockey, 233, 268, 368, 387
hocus, 126; -pocus, 166
hoe, 88, 95; -er, -ing, 158
hogan, 354
hoiden. See hoyden
hold, 102
hole, 107
holiday, 87, 133
holler, 447
hollow, 233, 285
holly, 233
holm, 102, 424, 446
holocaust, 234, 365

holster, 102, 446
holt, 102
holy, 125, 133
homage, 427
home, 280; -ly, 23; -spun, 244
homeostasis, 260, 405
homicide, 272
hominid, 121; -ae, 121, 269
homogeneity, 115
homogeneous, 260
homologous, 355
homonymic, 172
homonymity, 173
honest, 128, 389
honey, 246, 434
honk, 363, 436
honor, 234, 389, 432; -arium, 308
hood, -wink, 242
hoof, -s, 374; -ed, 343
hook, -er, 242; -ed, 343
hooves, 374
hope, 98, 280; -lessly, 402
hopper, 337
horizontal, 312, 394
horrendous, 455
horrible, 172, 312
horrid, 452
horrify, 276
horse, 204; -s', -'s, 395
hosanna, 396
hosier, 136, 422; -y, 58
hospitable, 390
hospital, 23, 336
host, 23, 104; -age, 389; -ile, 152
hot, 164; -er, -est, -ly, 163
hotel, 23, 444
hound, 306
hour, 306, 389
house, 82, 99, 133, 288, 305, 306; -wife, 23, 141; -wifery, 141
hovel, 234, 246
hover, 129, 133
how, 304; -ever, 305
howitzer, 305, 399
howl, 305
hoyden, hoiden, 303
hubbub, 101, 332
huckleberry, 369
huckster, 369

huddle, 342
huff, 381
hug, 145; -s, 33
huge, 107, 145
Hugh, 300
hula, 290, 298
hull, 442
hullabal(l)oo, 289, 333, 441
human, 124, 298, 299; -ity, 215; -ness, 134
humble, 23
humid, 120; -ity, 224; -or, 312
humiliate, 136
humility, 114
humming, 428
hummock, 101, 370, 429
humor, 23; -ist, 134
humph, 379
humus, 343
hunch, 433; -back, 414
hundred, 433; -th, 101, 385
hunger, 436
hure, 321
hurricane, 251, 324, 454
hurry, 324, 454; -es, 268
husband, 21, 99, 101, 133, 331
hussar, 243, 314, 396
hussy, 396
hustle, 387, 400
hutch, 413
huzz, 84, 392
huzza, 233
hyacinth, 92, 277, 387, 406
hybrid, 106, 277
hydra, 277
hydrant, 106
hydraulic, 238, 364, 453
hydrochloric, 277, 312, 358
hydrogen, 277
hydrophobia, 263, 378
hydroponics, 234
hyena, 93, 260, 277
hygiene, 268, 276, 420; -ic, 220
hying. See hie
hymn, 227, 425; -al, 425
hyperbole, 261, 276, 323, 336
hypercritical, 276
hyperemia, 138
hyperopia, 138

hyphen, 111, 277
hypnosis, 116
hypnotic, 116, 117, 364; -ally, 117
hypnotism, 227
hypocrisy, 23, 401
hypocrite, 23, 227, 335
hypoglycemia, 138, 276
hypothesis, 109
hyssop, 227, 404
hysteria, 263, 311
hysterics, 372

I, 88
iamb, 424
ichor, 312
ichthyology, 358, 385
icicle, 151, 368
icing, 406
icon, eikon, 278
id, 89
idea, 93, 341; -al, 113, 272; -ality, 113
identify, 341
idiom, 136, 340
idiosyncrasy, 227, 436
idiot, 131; -ic, 347
idle, 105, 151, 275, 341
idol, 272; -atry, 234
idyl(l), 125, 441; -ic, 227, 445
if, 88, 93, 164, 381; -ier, -iest, 383; -y, 164, 383
igloo, 289
igneous, 223, 260
ignition, 224
ignoble, 432
ignominious, 432
ignore, 313
iguana, 457
ileac, 92
ill, 88; -fare, -ness, 79; -s, 80; -th, 385
illaborate, 186
illative, 186, 446
illecebraceae, 186
illegible, 186, 419
illegitimate, 420
illicit, 120
illighten, 186
illiterate, 186
illocutionary, 186
illogical, 186, 446
illuminate, 186

illusion, 119, 186, 446
image, 224, 419, 420; -inary, 308; -ine, 215, 429
imbalance, inbalance, 187
imbase, 186
imbecile, 152, 186, 330; -ity, 224
imbibe, 186
imbosom, 186
imbroglio, 186
imbue, 95, 186, 298
immaculate, 186, 365, 428
immanent, 428
immature, 428
immeasurable, 428
immediate, 186, 428
immense, 428
immerse, 428; -ion, 410
immigrant, 428
imminent, 186, 428
immitigable, 186
immolate, 428
immortal, 186, 428
immune, 428; -ity, 115
immure, 186, 428
immusical, 186
impair, 186
impalatable, 186
impanel, 166
impasse, 149, 401
impatience, 410
impeach, 265
impeccable, 356
impel, 444; -er, 446
impend, 57
impenetrable, 432
imperative, 452
imperial, 316
imperious, 316
imperishable, 310
impertinent, 186
impetuosity, 114, 402, 415
impetuous, 37, 186
impetus, 37
implausible, 186
implicate, 186
implicit, 120, 406
implore, 313
importunate, 152, 416
importunity, 115
imposthume, 343–44
impotence, 186
impoverish, 122, 186

impresario, 282, 315
impressment, 79
impromptu, 233, 428
improve, 186, 292
improvise, 186
impugn, 103, 299, 430
impunity, 186
in, 88, 164; -er, 163, 433; -ing, 164; -ness, 434; -ward, 163
inaccurate, 152
inane, -ity, 113
inarticulate, 187
inaugural, 238
inaugurate, 187, 354
inbalance. See imbalance
incapable, 187
incendiary, 263, 405
incense, 187
incessant, 402
inch, 226
inchoate, 281, 358
incipient, 136
inclusion, 298
incognito, 282, 348
incommunicado, 232, 283, 342
incontinence, 179
increase, 259, 266
incredulous, 421
incur, 324
indecent, 187
indeed, 265
indemnity, 113
index, 371; -es, 261
indicative, 365
indices, 261
indict, 18, 31, 105, 275–76, 345
indigo, 283
indiscreet, 365
indite, 105
individual, 194, 421; -ity, 215
indomitable, 234
induce, 45, 187; -ment, 406
induct, -ion, 45
indulge, 146
industrial, 58, 244
inebriate, 261; -ed, 58
ineffable, 383
inertia, 410
inessive, 187
infamous, 187

infantile, 152, 272
infectious, 410
infer, 169, 323; -able, -ably, -ed, -ential, -ible, -ing, 169; -ence, 169, 187
inferior, 263, 316; -ity, 312
inferno, 282
infidel, 342; -ity, 173
infinite, 154; -esimal, 402
infirmary, 324
inflict, 348
influenza, 393
ingenious, 263
ingenuous, 137
ingestion, 416
ingot, 436
ingredient, 137
inhabit, 187
inharmonious, 187
inherit, 23
inhibit, 120, 164, 330; -ion, 119, 164
inimical, 224
iniquitous, 107
iniquity, 187
initial, 136, 187, 410
injunction, 421
injurious, 320
ink, 222, 436
inn, 76, 88, 101, 432; -s, 80
innate, 434
inner. *See* in
innervate, 434
inness. *See* in
inning. *See* in
innocent, 187, 434
innocuous, 136, 434
innovation, 377, 434
innuendo, 283, 434
innumerable, 434
inoculate, 187, 365
inoperable, 187
inordinate, 152
inquietude, 187
inquire, 319; -y, 319, 359
inquisitive, 395
insane, 251
insatiable, 410
inscrutable, 290, 291
insidious, 136
insipid, 120, 336
insist, 187
insomnia, 263

insouciance, 406
insouciant, 293
inspect, 187, 366
inspiration, 455
instal(l), 441, 443
instantaneous, 260
instead, 219
instil(l), 441, 443
institute, 299
insubordinate, 330
insufferable, 34
insure, 320, 411
insurrection, 455
integer, 420
intellectual, 446
intelligent, 446
intend, 41, 187
intension, 41–42, 410
intention, 41–42, 342
inter, 172, 323
intercept, -ion, 44
interchange, 414
intercourse, 315
interfere, 316
interglacial, 138
interior, 263
interlocutor, 442
intermediary, 263
intermission, 411
intermittent, 426
internee, 94
interrogate, 355, 453
interrupt, 453
intersect, 223
interstadial, 138
intestine, 153
intimate, 151
intractability, 46
intractable, 46
intrepid, 120, 219
intricate, 365
intrigue, 95, 264, 351
introversion, 43
introversive, -ly, 43
introvert, 43
intrusion, 119
intussuscipiens, 403
inurbane, 187
inure, 320
inutile, 187
invalid (null), 120
invalid (one who is sickly), 121

invariable, 263
invective, 366
inveigh, 255
inveigle, 267
invent, 187
inverse, 43–44; -ion, 43
invert, 43–44; -ible, 43
invidious, 340
invigorate, 353
invisible, 187
invitation, -al, 119
invoke, 363
involve, 376
iodine, 135, 273
iodize, 92
iota, 93
irascible, 398
irenic, 218
iridescent, 316
iris, 83, 453
irk, 324, 363
irony, 272, 453; -ist, 87
irradiate, 186, 453
irreceptive, 186
irreclaimed, 186
irreconcilable, 186
irrecuperable, 186
irreducible, 186
irrefusable, 186
irregular, 186
irrelevant, 186
irremediable, 186
irreparable, 186
irrepressible, 316, 453
irreproachable, 316
irreption, 186
irresistible, 316
irresponsible, 186, 316, 453
irreverent, 186, 453
irrigate, 186, 316
irritate, 186, 316
irrogate, 186
irrupt, 186
is, 82, 88, 395
ischiadic, 215
island, 105, 275, 439–40
isle, 105, 275, 279, 439, 440
isolate, 272
isosceles, 261
isotope, 272, 403
issue, 95, 183, 411
isthmus, 391, 397, 400
istle, ixtle, 400

it, 389
italic, 349
itch, 413
item, 125
iterate, 131
itinerant, 432
ivory, 376
ivy, 125
ixtle. *See* istle

jab, 214
jabber, 332
jack, 369; -daw, 236
jackal, 368, 421
jadeite, 156
jaguar, 129, 137, 314, 351,
    353, 457
jailer, 253
jalop(p)y, jallopy, 337
jam, 426
jamb, 424
jamboree, 94
janitor, 432
jasmine, 101, 395
jaundice, 237, 433
jaunt, 23, 216, 237
javelin, 377
jaw, 236
jay, 252
jazz, 84, 392
jealous, 220, 403, 421, 445
jean, 265, 417
jeep, 265
jeer, 317
Jeffersonian, 138
Jehova, 387
jejune, 290, 298; -ity, 115
jell, 417; -y, 417, 445
jennet, genet, 417
jeopardy, 221, 270
jerk, 323
jerkin, 367
jerky, 367
jersey, 395
jet, 218
jettison, 404
jetty, 349
jewel, 295, 298
jibe, gybe (shift sail), 107
jibe (taunt). *See* gibe
jiggle, 355, 421
jill. *See* gill /jil/
jilt, 445

Jim, 417
jingo, 283
jinn(i), jinnee, djin(n),
    djinni, genie, 417, 432.
    See also genie
jinx, 421
job, 164; -er, 164, 332
jockey, 421
jocular, 234, 365
jocund, 365
joe, 88
joggle, 150, 233, 355
John, 212, 296
joie de vivre, 422
joke, 363
jolly, 373
jolt, 102
jongleur, 422
jostle, justle, 233, 400
jounce, 306
journal, 186, 325
journey, 186, 325
joust, 306
jovial, 136, 376
jowl, 305
joy, 302
jubilant, 290, 421
jubilee, 94, 134, 265,
    331
judg(e)ment, 159
judicial, 132
judiciary, 412
judo, 283
juggle, 244, 445
jugular, 134, 135, 353
juice, 146, 296, 406; -iness,
    -y, 406
julep, 124
julienne, 422
jumbo, 283, 331
junction, 410
juncture, 101
junior, 124, 134, 289, 290,
    298
juniper, 134, 290
junket, 436
jural, 320
jurisdiction, 320
jurist, 86
justify, 276; -able, 273
justle. *See* jostle
juvenile, 152, 291
juxtapose, 371

jyngine, 421
jynx, 421

kabob, 94
kad(h)i. *See* qadi
kaiser, 279
kale, 362
kaleidoscope, 278, 363
kangaroo, 289, 355, 362, 455
kaolin, 92
kapok, 362
kaput, 243, 337, 362
katsup. *See* catsup
kauri, 85
kayak, 214, 279, 355
kazoo, 289, 394
keen, 363
keg, 363
kelp, 363
kempt, 57
kennel, 166, 218, 434
kept, 98, 362
kerchief, 373, 414
kermes, 83
kernel, 363
kerosene, 363, 401, 452
ketchup. *See* catsup
kettle, 349
key, 268, 270
khaki, 85, 129, 361
khan, 361
khedive, 264, 361
kibosh, 126
kidnap, -ing, 165
kidney, 362
kier, 318
kill, 206
kiln, 23, 101, 440
kilo, 264, 282
kilogram, 444
kilowatt, 458
kimono, 283, 429
kind, 102, 275, 363; -red,
    223, 275, 451
kindergarten, 352
kinetic, 218, 347, 363, 434
king, 61, 226
kipper, 337, 363
kismet, 395
kiss, 82, 226, 392; -es, 33
kitchen, 226, 363, 415; -ette,
    347
kithe, kythe, 109, 147

kitsch, 412
kleptomania, 263, 363, 426,
    445; -ac, 251
knack, 430
knapsack, 430
knave, 141, 430; -ery, 141
knead, 265, 430
knee, 258, 265, 430; -ing,
    158
kneel, 265, 430
knell, 430
knew, 294, 295, 299, 430
knickerbocker, 430
knife, 107, 374, 430. See also
    knives
knight, 102, 209, 274, 345,
    430
knit, 430; -ing, 349
knives, 374, 376, 430
knob, 93, 430
knock, 369, 430
knoll, 102, 430
knot, 430; -ed, 349
know, 284, 430; -ledge, 133,
    146, 235, 419, 420, 442; -n,
    285
knuckle, 369, 430
knurl, 430
kona, 355, 362
kopje, koppie, 335
koumiss, 295
kraal, 81
kreng, 437
krill, 453
kris, 83; -es, 403
krypton, 367
kvass, 376
kwacha, 458
kwashiokor, 458
kyanite, 92, 363
kylix, 363
kymograph, 363
kyphosis, 363
kythe. See kithe

la, 89, 233
laager, 81
label, 166; -er, 167
labial, 137
labile, 152
labor, 331
labyrinth, 330, 385, 433, 455
lac, 93, 145, 146

lace, 140, 141, 145, 146; -ery,
    141; -iest, 140
lachrymal, 357
lack, 70
lackadaisical, 253, 368, 396
lackey, lacquey, 360, 368
laconic, 234, 433
lacquer, 360
lacquey. See lackey
lacrosse, 149, 401
lacteal, 366
lacunae, 269
ladder, 341
ladle, 105, 249
lading, 341
lady, 125, 373; -hood, -like,
    -ship, 87
lagoon, 289
laid, 86, 252
lair, 27, 86
laity, 92, 115
lamb, 55, 424; -kin, 424
lambda, 339
lammas, 83
lampas, 83
lamppost, 336
lamprey, 428
landscape, 433
language, 18, 212, 351, 457
langue, 96
languid, 457
languish, 122, 351, 457
laniard. See lanyard
lanolin, 432
lantern, 348
lanyard, laniard, 137, 459
laparorrhaphy, 76
lapel, 218, 337
lapse, 82
larceny, 406
larch, 414
larder, 340
lares, 261
largo, 282
lariat, 264, 452
lark, 69, 314; -spur, 324
laryngeal, 227
larynges, 261
larynx, 371, 436, 442; -es,
    261
lascivious, 398
lassitude, 402
lasted, 103

latent, 125
later, 90, 96, 338
lath, -s, 386; -er, 109
lathe, 147, 386; -er, 109
lather (foam), 108, 109, 233
latitude, 214
latrine, 153, 263
latter, 90, 96, 338
laud, 237; -able, 238
laugh, 209, 213, 215–16, 237,
    380; -ter, 378, 380
launch, 237, 414
launder, 373, 433
laundry, 23, 237
laureate, 315
laurel, 166, 315
lauric, 315
lava, 232
lavish, 122, 128
law, 236; -yer, 236, 451, 459
lawn, 237
lay, 86, 252. See also laid
layette, 253, 347
layman, 252
lazuli, 85
lazy, 126, 393
lea, 265
lead /led/, 219
lead /lēd/, 259
leaf, 259, 382
league, 96, 266, 351
leak, 265
leanness, 434
leap, -t, 7, 219, 220; -ed, 7
learn, 325
lease, 259, 266
least, 265
leather, 219
leave, 266
leaven, 219
lecher, 414
ledger, 420
lee, 88
leech, 415
leechee. See litchi
leek, 265
leer, 317
left, 7
legacy, 131, 132, 353
legal, 113, 132, 354; -ity, 112–
    13; -ize, 272
legate, 353
legato, 232, 282, 348

legend, 419; -ary, 308
legerdemain, 419, 429
legion, 129, 137
legionnaire, 7, 28, 47, 172, 435
legislate, 419
legitimate, 347
legume, 298, 353
lei, 254, 255, 268
leisure, 267, 422
lek, 93
lemon, 123, 127, 427
lends, 337
length, 228, 437; -en, 385; -wise, 272
lenience, 137
lenity, 114
lens, 83, 101, 337, 395
Leonard, 221
leopard, 217, 221, 270
leotard, 314
leper, 218, 335
leprechaun, 237, 357
leprosy, 404
lesion, 119, 129, 137, 410, 422
lethal, 110
lettuce, 76, 218, 349
leucine, 296
leukemia, 296
levee, 128
level, 166, 218; -er, 167
leviable, 135
leviathan, 135
levitate, 442
levity, 114
lewd, 295, 298
lewis, 83
liable, 135
liaison, 252, 253
liar, 91, 273
lias, 83
libel, 166, 331; -er, 167
liberal, 131
libertine, 153
library, 106, 275
libretto, 282
license, licence, 126, 406
lichee. See litchi
lichen, 110, 358
licit, 120
lick, 70
lid, 206

lie, 88, 95, 268, 273; -ing, 91, 157, 277
liege, 146, 268, 420
lien, 268
lieutenant, 346
life, 374
ligament, 165, 353
ligature, 353
light, 102, 274
like, 54; -able, 157; -wise, 272, 458
lilac, 364
lily, 133, 225
limb, -er, 424
limber, 424
limbo, 283
limerick, 370
limit, 120, 128, 164, 427; -ed, 164
limn, 425
limousine, 263, 396
limpid, 101
linage, 157
linden, 432
lin(e)able, 157
lineage, 156
linear, 92, 261
linen, 225
linger, 436
lingo, 283
linguistic, 351, 457
link, 363
linn, 432
linoleum, 136, 260, 434
lion, 91, 273; -ess, 135
liquefacient, 412
liquefy, 276
liquid, 107, 400, 442
liquor, 400
lira, 318
lisle, 439, 440
lissome, 403
listen, 223, 397, 399
litany, 347
litchi, lichee, lychee, 85
liter, 130, 264
literate, 152
lithe, 147, 386; -some, 109
lithograph, 109
litigate, 347
litmus, 83
litter, 338
little, 151, 226, 349

liturgical, 324
liturgist, 87
live, 107, 147, 374; -able, 157; -s, 374
liver, 225; -wurst, 402
livid, 120
lizard, 128, 393
llama, 20, 76, 232, 442
Llandeilo, 442
Llandoverian, 442
llanero, 442
llano, 76, 442
Llanvirn, 442
llareta, yareta, 459
llautu, 442
Llewelyn, 76
Lloyd, 76
lo, 282
load, 240, 284
loaf, 284, 374, 382
loam, 284
loan, 284
loath, 284, 386
loathe, 147, 386
loaves, 374, 376
lob, -ing, 164
lobster, 76, 331
local, 113, 362; -ity, 113
locale, 444
locate, 125
loch, 271
loche, 110
loci, 273
lock, 70
locomotion, 119
locomotive, 426
locust, 362
locution, 119, 134
lodge, 418
logging, 354
logic, 234, 419
logorrhea, 449
loin, 302
loll, 442
lollipop, 233, 234
lonely, 457
long, 206, 437; -evity, 377; -itude, 233, 419
look, 242, 363
loon, 290
loon(e)y, luny, 290
loose, 290
loquacious, 106, 359

lord, 61, 312, 373; -ship, 75
lore, 313
lori(s), 85
lorry, 312
lose, 292
loss, 104, 239
lost, 104
loud, 305
lounge, 306, 442
louse, 306, 403; -y, 305
lout, 306
louver, 293, 376
love, 107, 147, 246, 374
low, 212, 284
lower (frown), 304
loyal, 302
lozenge, 393
lube, 290
lubricate, 298
lucerne, 323, 406
lucid, 120
luck, 70
luggage, 354
lukewarm, 290, 298, 363
lullaby, 447
luminescent, 434
luminous, 134, 428
lunacy, 291
lunar, 124
lunatic, 117, 118, 290
luncheon, 442
lunette, 124
luny. See loon(e)y
lupine, 124, 153
lurid, 320
luscious, 412
luster, 244
lustrous, 453
lute, 298
luxury, 411; -ant, 263, 371;
    -ous, 58
lyceum, 93, 260, 276, 406
lyddite, 154
lye, 88, 96, 276
lying (pres. part. of lye),
    158
lying. See lie
lymph, 101, 227, 379, 442;
    -atic, 116
lynch, 227, 414
Lyne, 99
Lynton, 99
lynx, 101, 227, 371, 436

lyre, 107, 276, 319; -ic, 318, 452
lyse, -in, -is, 63, 64–65;
    -ine, 64–65; -ogenesis, 65
lytic, 63, 64–65

ma, 89
macaque, 95, 107, 359
macaroni, 85
machete, 348, 415
machine, 141, 152, 259, 408;
    -ation, 110; -ations, 358;
    -ery, 141
mackerel, 368, 426
mackinaw, 236
macle, 105
macron, 252
madam(e), 128, 149
Madeira, 318
madness, 340
madras, 340, 401, 405
m(a)enad, 269
maestro, 282
magazine, 153, 353, 394
magenta, 420
maggot, 354
magi, 273
magic, 70, 127, 369–70, 419;
    -al, 370; -ian, 136, 370
magnanimity, 114, 434
magnesia, 137
magnesic, 118
magnesium, 260, 264, 410
magnet, -ic, 164; -o, 282
magpie, 95
maharaja, 232, 387, 421
maharani, 232
mahogany, 234, 387
mahout, 387
maiden, 250, 253
maieutic, 254, 300
maihem. See mayhem
main, 86
maintain, 252
maize, 84, 252, 253, 393
majesty, 420
major, 125, 420
make, 98, 154–55, 357; -ing,
    154–55; -s, 155; -shift, 409
maki, 85
malady, 444
malaise, 253, 395
male, 440
malevolent, 377

malfeasance, 266
malign, 103, 113, 275, 430;
    -ity, 113
mall, 443
mallard, 443, 445, 447
malleable, 445
mallet, 445
malnutrition, 224
mama, 233, 427
mammal, 429; -ian, 263, 429
mammon, 429
mammoth, 429
man, 228, 432
manacle, 368, 432
manage, 129; -able, -er, -ing,
    155; -erial, 316
mandolinist, 175
manes, 261
maneuver, 296, 299, 376
mangabey, 255
manganese, 436
mange, 104
manger, 104, 419
mango, 283
mania, 263; -ac, 137, 214,
    364; -acal, 135, 273; -acs,
    371
manicure, 320
manifesto, 282
manifold, 214
manikin, 364
manil(l)a, 441
manioc, 137
manipulate, 335
mannequin, 229, 359, 432
mansion, 342, 410
mantelpiece, 146
manual, 137, 299
manufacture, 214, 381
manure, 321
maple, 105
mar, 314; -er, 453
marabou(t), 293
maraschino, 264, 282, 309,
    357
marathon, 309, 452; -ed, -er,
    -ing, 175
marauder, 238
marcel, 444
marconi, 85
mare, 219, 258, 308
margaric, 419
margarine, 153, 419

marguerite, 453
marijuana, marihuana, 456
marine, 153; -ate, 452
mark, 325
market, 362, 363
marmalade, 251, 314
marque, 359
marquee, 265, 359
marquis, 359
marquise, 359
marrow, 285
marry, 310; -age, 58, 86
marshal, 166, 409, 453; -er, 167
marshmallow, 285
martini, 85
marvel, 166
masculine, 153, 367
mask, 363
masochism, 214, 357
masonry, 403
masque, 95, 359
mass, 76
massage, 146, 232, 402, 422
massif, 264
mastiff, 101, 384
mat, 90, 96; -ing, 96
matador, 312
match, 357
mate, 96–97, 99, 219, 258, 308; -ing, 96–97; -s, 97; -y, 156
material, 316
mathematics, 108, 347, 372, 385
matin, 347; -ee, -ée, 256
matriarch, 252, 357
matrices, 261
matriculate, 365
matrix, 106; -es, 261
matron, 106
matt, 347
matter, 338, 349
Matthew, 385
mattock, 370
mattress, 80, 348, 405
mature, 320, 321
maudlin, 237
maul, 237
mausoleum, 238, 260, 403
mauve, 147, 286
maverick, 370
maw, 236

maxim, 215
may, 86, 252; -be, 261; -hap, 252
mayhem, maihem, 253, 387
mayonnaise, 7, 172, 253, 396, 435
maze, 393
mazurka, 367
me, 261
meadow, 219, 285, 340
meager, 266, 354
meal, 259
mean, 259
meander, 260, 340
measles, 265, 395
measure, 219, 422, 426
meat, 90, 98, 265
mechanical, 358
mechanics, 371
mechanism, 110
medal, 128, 166, 340
medal(l)ist, 167
medallion, 170, 445
meddle, 342
medi(a)eval, 269
median, 137
mediate, 92, 151
medical, 340
medicine, 131, 149, 153; -al, 406
mediocre, 106, 113, 132, 367; -ity, 106, 113, 132
meet, 90, 258, 259, 265
megaphone, 353
melancholy, 234, 357, 444
melee, 256
mellifluous, 291, 447
mellow, 285
melody, -ic, 116; -ist, 87
melon, 218
member, 428
memento, 283
memory, 427; -al, 313
men, 228
menace, 128, 218
menad. See ma(e)nad
ménage, 422
menagerie, 419
menhaden, 387
menhir, 387
menial, 137
meningitis, 348
mensuration, 411

mentor, 312
mercantile, 272, 367
mercenary, 406
merchant, 414
mercury, 367, 455
mere, 316
meridian, 340
merino, 283
merit, 452; -orious, 313
merry, 310; -ly, 86
mesa, 256
mess, 76, 82
message, 402
messiah, 116
messianic, 116
met, 90, 145
metabolism, 214
metal, 38, 128, 166, 347; -er, 167
metallic, 38, 173, 349, 445
metalloid, 38, 170
metallurgy, 38
metaphor, 378
metaphysician, 138
metaphysics, 378
metathesis, 109
metazoan, 394
mete, 107, 145
meteor, 92, 137; -ic, 312; -ite, 154
meter, 130
methane, 109; -ol, 94
mether, 108
method, 101, 109, 385; -ical, 340
methyl, 109
meticulous, 365
mettle, 349
mew, 298, 299
mezzanine, 153, 263
mezzotint, 394
mho, 426
mhorr. See mohr
mi, 85, 89
miasma, 395
miasmus, 273
Michigan, 408
microbe, 275
micron, 106
microphone, 61, 379
microscope, 275; -ic, 234, 336
midday, 341

middle, 151, 342
midge, 418; -et, 347
midriff, 384
mien, 268
might, 102, 274; -y, 426
migrate, 106, 275, 453
mike, 61
mil, 93, 442
mild, 102, 275
mildew, 102, 295, 299
mil(e)age, 26, 28, 156
militia, 136
milk, 363
millet, 447
millinery, 311
million, 6–7, 445; -aire, 6–7,
    8, 100, 149, 311
millwright, 80
mime, 115; -etic, 116; -ic,
    115, 127; -ograph, 136,
    283, 427
mind, 102, 275; -less, 405
miniature, 136, 416
minim, 138, 245
minion, 128, 136, 224
minnow, 285, 434
minor, 125
minstrel, 453
minuet, 93, 136
minuscule, 401
minx, 101, 436
miracle, 316, 368, 452
mirage, 232, 422
mire, 107
mirror, 316, 452
misanthrope, 402
miscellaneous, 398, 447
mischief, 414
miscible, 398
misconception, 405
misconduct, 366
misconstrue, 147
misery, 395
mishap, 387
miss, 76
missel. See mistle
missile, 149, 152, 402
mission, 409
misspeak, 79, 403
misspell, 79, 443
misspend, 79
misstate, 79
misstep, 79

misstrike, 79
mistake, 363; -en, 251; -s,
    371
mistle, missel, 400; -toe, 95,
    400
miter, 130
mitigate, 131, 347
mitral, 106
mitt, 101, 347; -s, 348
miz(z)en, 394
mnemonic, 431
moan, 284, 433
moat, 284
mobile, 152
moccasin, 356, 404
modal, 149
model, 123, 127, 166; -er,
    -ist, 167
moderate, 340
modern, 128, 340
modest, 234
modification, 46, 48
modify, 46
modish, 121
module, 122; -ate, 234, 421
mogul, 126, 444
mohair, 387
mohr, mhorr, 426, 451
moist, 302; -en, 399; -ure,
    416
molar, 123, 125
molasses, 83
mold. See mo(u)ld
molecule, 444; -ar, 365, 447
mollusk, 233, 445
molybdenum, 227, 331, 340
mom, 426, 427
monarch, 138, 357
monastery, 311
money, 246; -ed, 40
mongrel, 246, 436
monk, 363
monkey, 246, 367, 436
monocle, 368
monogamy, 353, 434
monogram, 131
monogynous, 419
monolithic, 109, 224, 442
monopodial, 138
monopoly, 335
monostich, 49–50
monotony, 347
monsoon, 289

monstrosity, 402
monstrous, 433
montage, 146, 422
month, 246
monument, 131, 234, 426
moor, 321
moose, 19, 290
moot, 289
moraine, 254
moral, 452; -ize, 272
morale, 444
moratorium, 312, 313, 349
morbid, 113; -ity, 113, 340
mordacity, 215
mores, 261, 312, 453
morgue, 312, 351
morocco, 282, 356
morphine, 263
morris, 83
morrow, 285
morsel, 453
mortgage, 352
mortician, 138
mortise, 148
mortuary, 415
mosaic, 252, 396
mosque, 95, 359
mosquito, 283, 359
moss, 76, 104, 401
most, 104
motel, 444
mother, 55, 60, 108, 246;
    -hood, -liness, 55
motif, 264, 374; -s, 374
motion, 126, 129, 136
motive, -ate, -s, 374
motorcycle, 369
mottle, 349
motto, 282, 349
mo(u)ld, 102, 285
moult, 23
mound, 306
mountain, 306; -eer, 317
mourn, 315
mouse, 54, 288, 305, 306
mouth, 306, 385, 386
move, 147, 292; -able, 157;
    -er, 129; -ie, 95
mow /maù/, 304
mow /mō/, 284; -ed, 338
much, 101, 413
mucilage, 406
mucoid, 124

mucous, 426
muddy, 341
muff, 381
muffin, 383
muffle, 150, 384
mufti, 85, 101, 382
mulatto, 283
mulch, 414
mulct, 348, 445
muley, 126
mulish, 124
multifarious, 46, 308
mum, 244
mummy, 429
mural, 320
murder, 324
mure, 320
murex, 320
muricate, 320
murk, 322, 363
murmur, 324
murrain, 324, 454
muscatel, 367, 444
muscle, 398
muscovite, 154
muse, 107; -eum, 260; -ic,
    118, 299; -ical, 134; -ician,
    138
mushroom, 101, 289, 409
musket, 367
muslin, 395
muss, 76, 401
mussel, 404
mustache, 110, 408
mustang, 101
mutate, 124
mutilate, 134
mutineer, 317
mutiny, 299
mutter, 349
mutual, 415
muzzle, 394
myelitis, 272
myna, 126
myopia, 263
myosin, 92
myriad, 318, 426
myrmidon, 326
myrrh, 326, 449
myrtle, 326, 445, 453
mystery, 227; -ous, 263,
    316
myth, 101, 385; -ical, 227

nabob, 126
nacelle, 406
na(e)vus, 269
naiad, 254
nail, 250
naïve, naive, 93, 147, 232
naked, 125
name, 249; -able, 157
nape, -ery, 141
naphtha, 101, 334, 379
narcissism, 402
narcissus, 402, 406
narcosis, 116, 365
narcotic, 116, 347
narghile, 352
narration, 455
narrative, 452
narrow, 285, 310
nasal, 396
nascent, 398
nasturtium, 410
nation, 119, 131, 140, 141,
    407, 409, 410, 422; -al, 119,
    131, 140, 141; -ality, 215;
    -wide, 141
native, 126
natron, 106
nature, 132, 249; -al, 132,
    455
naught, 237, 240; -y, 432
nausea, 238, 410; -ate, 411
nauseous, 410
nautical, 238
naval, 376
navel, 123, 125, 129
navigable, 214
navigate, 132, 355, 377; -or,
    375
navvy, 375, 377
navy, 132, 375
nay, 256
near, 317
nebula, 330
nebulé, 122
nebulosity, 114
necessary, 402, 405
necessitate, 402
nectar, 366
need, 258; -ful, 75
needle, 265
nefarious, 308
negate, -ive, 353
neglect, 366, 442

negligee, negligée, négligé,
    négligé, neglige, 256, 422
negligent, 422
negotiable, 136
negro, 106
neigh, 255
neighbor, 255; -hood, 242
neither, 267, 278, 432
nemesis, 404, 427
neolithic, 224, 260
neon, 234, 260
neophyte, 92, 260, 276, 379
nephew, 23, 111, 298, 299,
    374, 379
nephritis, 379
nestle, 400
nestling, 101
nether, 108
nettle, 349
neural, 321
neuralgia, 321
neurasthenia, 263, 321
neurologist, 321
neuron, 321
neurosis, 116, 321
neurotic, 116, 117; -ism, 117
neuter, 296, 299, 348
neutron, 296
never, 129
nevus. See n(a)evus
new, 294, 295; -s, 295
newt, 295, 373
next, 371
ngai, 436
ngaio, 20, 70, 432, 436
ngege, 70, 436
nib, 224
nibble, 333, 445
niblick, 101, 370
nice, -ty, 141
niche, 110
nickel, 166; -iferous, -ine,
    167
nickname, 295, 369
nicotine, 153, 263
niece, 146, 258, 268
niggard, 354
nigh, 102, 274
night, 102, 274, 345; -ingale,
    434
nihilism, 390
nil, 442
nilg(h)ai, 85, 352

nimble, 428
nimbus, 101
nine, 275; -th, 275, 342
nipple, 337, 432
nisei, 254, 255, 264
nitid, 347
nitrate, 275
nitrous, 106
no, 282; -thing, 109, 246
nobility, 114, 444
noble, 105, 280, 331
nocturne, 149, 324, 366, 432
nodule, 122
noel, 281, 444
noetic, 93
noise, 82, 302, 303, 395
noisome, 303
nomadic, 215, 340, 428
nomenclature, 365
nominate, 427
nominee, 234
nonce, 457
nonchalance, 408
noncommittal, 428
none, 108, 149, 247, 457
nook, 242
noon, 289
noose, 290
nor, 312
north, 312, 386; -ern, 386
nostalgia, 419
nostril, 343
notch, 413
note, -able, 141; -ice, 406;
   -ion, 119, 136, 410
notoriety, 81, 135, 273
nougat, 293, 354
nought, 240, 345
noumenon, 293, 294
noun, 305
nourish, 325, 409
novel, 23, 377; -ty, 234
novice, 234
now, 62, 304; -adays, 305
noxious, 136
nozzle, 233, 445
nubile, 152, 272
nucleus, 105, 261
nucule, 122
nude, 299; -ity, 115
nuisance, 296, 299, 300, 403
numb, -er, 424
number, 424

numeral, 134
numerical, 310, 428
numerosity, 114
nuphar, 379
nutrient, 106, 432
nutrition, 347
nutritious, 138
nuzzle, 394
nylon, 432
nymph, 227, 379

o', 373
oaf, 284
oak, 284, 363
oakum, 284, 424
oar, 314
oasis, 83, 251, 281, 405
oat, 284
oath, 280, 284, 385
obambulate, 195
ob(b)ligato, 195, 232, 333,
   348
obcaecation, 196
obclavate, 196
obclude, 75
obcompressed, 196
obconic, 196
obcordate, 196
obcuneate, 196
obdurate, 195, 233
obedience, 137, 281, 406
obedient, 255
obeisance, 254, 255
obelisk, 330
obese, 260
obey, 195, 255
obfirm, 196
obfuscate, 196
obfusque, 196
obituary, 195, 415
object, 195, 233; -ivity, 377
oblate, 195; -ion, 442
oblige, 195, 330, 420; -ation,
   195; -atory, 353
oblique, 95, 106, 263, 359;
   -ity, 359
obliterate, 347
oblivion, 195, 263
oblong, 101
obmutescence, 196
obnoxious, 195
oboe, 95, 281, 331
obovate, 195

obpyramidal, 196
obpyriform, 196
obrotund, 195
obscene, 113, 195, 398; -ity,
   113
obscure, 76, 195, 367
obsequious, 75, 106, 359
observe, 195, 333, 395
obsidious, 195
obsolescence, 398
obsolete, 195
obstacle, 76, 150, 195
obstetric, 76; -ian, 138; -s,
   233, 372
obstinate, 76, 195
obstipate, 76
obstreperous, 76, 195, 335
obstruct, 76, 366
obstruse, 195
obstupefy, 76, 195
obtain, 196
obtrude, 76
obtrusive, 290
obtuse, 299
obumbrate, 195
obverse, 43, 195; -ion, 43
obvert, 43
obviate, 233
obvious, 195
occasion, 137, 195, 356
occident, 195; -al, 372
occipital, 372
occiput, 372
occlude, 195
occlusion, 119
occult, 195
occupy, 195, 233, 336, 356
occur, 324; -ed, 453; -ence,
   161, 162, 324
ocean, 116, 136, 412; -ic, 116,
   260
ocelot, 234, 406
ocher, ochre, 106, 110, 283,
   358
octagon, 366; -al, 214
Octopodidae, 175
octopus, 233; -es, 161, 174
octroy, 302
ocular, 365
odd, 76, 87, 88, 101, 339;
   -ball, -ling, -ment, -ness,
   340; -ly, -s, 80, 340
ode, 281

odious, 92, 136, 281
odometer, 341
oe, 89
oecist, oekist, 269
oecoid, 269
(o)ecology. *See* ecology
(o)edema. *See* edema
oedicnemus, 269
Oedipus, 269
oekist. *See* oecist
oenocyte, 269
(o)enology, 269
oenomel, 269
o'er, 373
(o)esophagus. *See* esophagus
of, 93, 373, 376, 381
off, 381; -stage, -ward, 80
offal, 77, 101, 239, 383
offend, 195, 383
offense, offence, 406
offer, 168, 195, 383; -ed, -er,
  -ing, -or, 168
office, 101, 195, 239, 383;
  -iate, 58
often, 380
ogganition, 195
ogham, 352
ogive, 420
ogle, 105, 283
oh, 212, 286
ohm, 212, 286, 296, 426;
  -meter, 428
oil, 203
ointment, 302
okapi, 85
okay, 252
old, 102
oleander, 136, 214, 260
oleo, 136
olid, 120
oligarch, 357; -y, 444
olive, 444
ombre, 389
omelet, 234, 427
omen, 428
omission, 195, 196, 281, 426
omit, 195, 196
omnibus, 61, 83, 233, 244
omnidirectional, 34
omniscience, 223, 412
omnivorous, 47, 377, 428
on, 88, 239
once, 247, 457

one, 108, 149, 247, 457
onion, 119, 246, 430, 433,
  459, 460
only, 104, 247, 457
onomatopoeia, 269
onslaught, 237, 345
ontology, 235
onyx, 128, 371
oodles, 290
ooftish, 290
oofy, 290
oolong, 290
oomiak. *See* umiak
oompah, 242, 290
oomph, 242
oons, 290
oops, 242, 290
oorali, urali, 290
ooze, 290, 393
opacity, 215
opal, 336; -ine, 153
opaque, 95, 106, 336, 359
open, 125, 280
operatic, 116
operetta, 349
ophthalmoscope, 379
opiate, 136, 281
opine, 123; -ion, 132, 136,
  337, 460
opium, 136
opossum, 404
oppignorate, 195
opponent, 195
opportune, 195, 299; -ity, 115
opposite, 154, 195, 233, 396
oppress, 80, 336
opprobrious, 336
oppugn, 103, 195, 431
optometry, 234
or, 88, 312, 451
oracle, 452
orange, 104, 312, 452
orangutan, 437
orator, 349
oratorio, 282
orchard, 414, 453
orchestra, 312, 358
orchid, 358
ordeal, 265
order, 313
ordnance, 453
ordure, 320, 389
ore, 313

organ, 116, 313; -ic, 116, 117;
  -icist, -icity, 117
orgy, 419
orient, 313
orifice, 312
origin, 312, 420
oriole, 92, 313, 453
orison, 396
orphan, 379
orris, 83
orthography, 385
os, 83, 89
oscillate, 398; -ion, 447
osseous, 402
ostend, 41, 195
ostensible, 195
ostension, 41
ostentatious, 195
osteopath, 260
ostinato, 195
ostler, 389
ostrich, 415
other, 108, 245
otter, 72
ouakari, 85
ouch, 295
ought, 240, 345
ounce, 146, 306
our, 306; -s, 82–83
oust, 306
out, 306; -goer, 92; -look,
  346; -take, -talk, -turn,
  349; -vie, 95
oval, 376
oven, 129, 245
over, 373, 376; -run, 168,
  244; -whelm, 388
oviparous, 335
owe, 89, 284
owl, 203, 305; -y, 211, 212
own, 284
ox, 89, 371; -en, 163
oxalic, 371, 444
oxide, 272
oyster, 303

pa, 89
pachouli. *See* pa(t)chouli
pachyderm, 110, 323, 358
pacify, 406; -ic, 382; -ism,
  384
pack, 369
paddock, 341, 370

paddy, 19
padre, 232
paduasoy, 302
p(a)ean, 269
paeon, 269
pagan, 125, 141; -ism, 141
pageant, 138, 419
paid, 86
pain, 250, 254
paint, 36, 250, 252, 254;
    -brush, 38; -ed, 38
pajama, 421; -s, 232
palace, 444
palatial, 410
pale, 444
paleontology, 261
palette, pallet, 347, 441
palfrey, 239, 382
pall, 443
pallet. *See* palette
palliative, 445
pallid, 445
pallor, 443
palm, 233, 424
palsy, 395; -ed, 239
pamphlet, 379
panacea, 214
panache, 110
pancreas, 83, 260
panda, 101
pane, 250
panegyric, 318, 420
panel, 166, 215, 432; -ist, 167
pangolin, 353
panic, 127, 172; -ed, 47; -s,
    371; -y, 370
pantaloon, 447
pantheist, 92
pantheon, 261
papa, 233
papillary, 335
papoose, 290
paprika, 264, 362, 453
papyrus, 276, 453
par, 314; -ed, 338
parable, 309, 452
parabolic, 309, 444
parachute, 290, 408
parade, 27
paradigm, 353, 425; -atic,
    353, 426
paradox, 371
paraffin, 383

parakeet. *See* par(r)akeet
parallel, 447; -ism, 167
paralysis, 63, 64–65
paralytic, 63, 64–65
paralyze, 63, 64–65, 276
paramecium, 138
paramour, 321
paranoia, 432
paranoid, 302
paraphernalia, 138, 379, 449
paraphrase, 251, 379
paraplegia, 138, 263
parasite, 115, 401, 452; -ic,
    115, 347
parasol, 94, 239, 401
parcel, 166, 171, 406
parcellation, 171
parchment, 414
pare, 26–27
parentheses, 261
parenthesis, 405
parenthetic, 347
parietal, 135
parish, 452
parity, 452
parochial, 110, 283, 358
parodist, 87
paroli, 85
par(r)oquet. *See* par(r)akeet
parotid, 347
parquet, 256
par(r)akeet, 450
parsley, 314, 453
parsnip, 453
parson, 235, 325
partial, 47, 58, 410
partible, 47
particle, 150, 368
partisan, 396
partition, 119
partner, 348, 453
partook, 242
partridge, 419
pasha, 111, 232, 409
pass, 213; -port, 80
passenger, 402
passion, 411
paste, 103, 264
pastel, 444
pastern, 103
pastil(l)e, 441
pastime, 80
pastry, 103

pat, 74, 206
pa(t)chouli, patchouly, 85
patent, 347
pathic, 110
pathology, 385; -ical, 109
pathos, 83, 110
patience, 57–58, 137
patio, 283
patriarch, 357
patriot, 106, 116; -ic, 116
patrol, 94; -ing, 446
patron, 106
patronymic, 227, 427
pauper, 238
pause, 238
pavilion, 136, 444, 460
paw, 236
payee, 94
pea, 265
peace, 146, 266; -able, 155
peak, 265, 363
peal, 265
pean. *See* p(a)ean
pear, 311
pearl, 325
peasant, 219
pease, 266
peat, 265
pebble, 151, 333
pecan, 366
peccadillo, 283, 342, 356
peccary, 356
pectin, 366
peculiar, 299, 366; -ity, 460
pecuniary, 263
pedagog(ue), 340
pedagogy, 281
pedal, 128, 166, 174, 340
peddle, 151, 342
pederast, 64
pedestal, 166
pediatrician, 138
pedigree, 94
pee, 88
peek, 265
peel, 265
peep, 265
peer, 317
peeve, 266; -ish, 376
pejorative, 421
pekoe, 95
pelican, 366
pelisse, 104

pellet, 445
pellucid, 120
pen, 432
penal, 132, 141, 269; -ize, 141; -ty, 132, 141
penance, 218
penates, 261
pencil, 166, 171, 406, 433; -er, 171
pencilliform, 171
pend, -ing, 57
pendulum, 421
penguin, 351, 457
penicillin, 406, 445
penitent, 131, 432
pennant, 432
pennaturalarian, 171
penny, 434
penology, poenology, 269
pentad, 101
penthouse, 387
peony, 92
people, 221, 270, 336
pepper, 337
per, 323
perceive, 56, 267
percentile, 272
percussion, 362, 365, 411
perfect, 46
perfidy, 342, 381
peri, 85
pericranial, 138
pericranium, 138
perigee, 94
perihelion, 263
peril, 166, 452; -ous, 167
period, 116, 117, 316; -ic, 116, 117, 340; -icity, 117
peripatetic, 218, 310
peripheral, 111, 379
periphrastic, 379
perique, 95, 106, 359
perish, 452
periwig, 23
periwinkle, 367
permalloy, 302
pernicious, 432
perpendicular, 365
perpetual, 137
perquisite, 154, 323, 359, 395
persevere, 316

persiflage, 146, 232, 384, 422
persimmon, 429
person, 235, 325
personnel, 172, 174, 435
perspicacity, 215
perspire, 319
persuasion, 137, 422
persuasive, 457
perverse, 43, 323; -ion, -ity, -ness, 43
pervert, -edness, 43
pessimism, 404
pestle, 400
petal, 166, 347; -ed, -oid, 167
petite, 264, 348
petroleum, 136, 281
petticoat, 349
petulant, 416
pew, 299
pewter, 298, 299, 348
phaeton, 252, 378
phalanx, 378, 436
phallic, 378
phantasm, fantasm, 210, 378; -agoria, 313, 355, 379
phantast. See fantast
phantasy. See fantasy
phantom, fantom, 379
pharmacy, 314, 378
pharyngeal, 227, 261
pharynges, 261
pharynx, 371, 378, 436; -es, 261
phase, 378
pheasant, 219, 378
phebe. See ph(o)ebe
phenix. See ph(o)enix
phenol, 94, 378
phenomenon, 234, 378, 427
phenotype, 378
phi, 85
phial, 273, 374, 378
philanthropy, 378; -ic, 336
philately, 214, 347, 378
philharmonic, 344, 390
philology, 378
philosophic, 111
philosophy, 48, 210, 235
phiz, 84, 392, 394; -es, 394
phlegm, 101, 378, 425, 445; -atic, 426

phlox, 94
phobia, 136, 263, 378
ph(o)ebe, 331, 378
ph(o)enix, 259, 269, 378
phone, 378, 379, 433; -emic, 118; -etician, 138; -ic, 127
phosphate, 378
phosphorus, 405
photo, 282
photoelectric, 281
photogenic, 419
photograph, 378
photostatic, 172
phrase, 107, 378; -ology, 261
phrenetic. See frenetic
phrenology, 453
phrensy. See frenzy
phthalein, 20
phthalic, 385
phthiocol, 385
phthiriasis, 385
phthirophagous, 385
phthisic, 334, 346
phthisis, 385
phthora, 385
phugoid, 378
phylactery, 366, 378
phylum, 276, 378
physic, 127, 395; -al, 378; -ian, 227; -s, 20, 227
physiology, 395
physique, 95, 106, 263, 359
pi, 85, 89, 274
pianissimo, 20
pianist, 92
piano, 264, 282, 434
piazza, 93, 264, 394
pica, 274
piccalilli, 85
piccolo, 282, 356
piceous, 136
pick, 72
pickerel, 368
pickle, 369
picnic, 364; -er, 370; -ing, 31, 362
picoted, 175
pi(c)quet, 256
pi(e) (a confusion of print), 89
pie, 88, 95, 274
piece, 268
pier, 318

pierce, 318
piety, 81, 92, 135, 273
piffle, 384
pigeon, 128, 136, 419
piglet, 35
pigmy. *See* pygmy
pilfer, 382
pilgrim, 445, 453
pillar, 101
pillow, 285
pilule, 122
pimento, 283, 429
pimple, 428
pin, 201–2
pinafore, 384
pincers, 406
pinchback, 369
pineal, 156
pinion, 128
pink, 363
pint, 102, 275
pioneer, 93, 317
pious, 91
pipette, 124, 347
pipit, 120
pippin, 337
pique, 95, 106, 107, 359;
   -ant, 106, 158, 359
pirate, -ic, 116; -ical, 347
pirogue, 95
piscine, 153
pistachio, 264, 282, 408
pistillate, 171
pistol, 101, 166, 444; -eer, 167
pitch, 413; -stone, 415
piteous, 136, 416
pituitary, 349
pity, 128, 347; -able, 135
pivot, 377
placard, 128, 365
placebo, 283
placer, 129
placid, 120, 128, 406
plagiarism, 420, 453
plagiarize, 137
plague, 95, 147, 157, 351; -ed,
   -s, 155; -ily, -y, 157
plaid, 215, 216
plaintiff, 374, 384
plaintive, 374
plait, pl(e)at, 216
plan, 94
plane, 336, 345

planetarium, 264, 308
plankton, 366, 367, 436
plaque, 95, 107, 147, 359
plasma, 395
plat. *See* plait
plateau, 286
platinum, 347
platoon, 288, 349
plaudit, 238
played, 338
player, 451
playgoer, 92
plaza, 232, 394
plea, 265
plead, 259
please, 148, 266; -ant, 219;
   -ure, 153
pleat. *See* plait
pledge, 418
plenteous, 416
pleonasm, 260
plethora, 108
pleura, 321
pleurisy, 321, 404, 453
pleurotomy, 321
pleuston, 296, 298
plexiglass, 371
plexus, 371
plight, 102, 274, 345
plow, 304
pluck, 369
plumage, 290, 298
plumb, 424, 427; -bago,
   -ism, 424
plummet, 424, 427, 429
plumule, 122
plunge, 419
plural, 320
plus, 83, 244, 401; -age, -ed,
   -es, -ing, 403
plutarchy, 134
plutocrat, 290, 291
plutonium, 264
ply, 276; -able, -wood, 87
pneuma, 431
pneumatic, 117, 431; -ity, 117
pneumococcus, 431
pneumonia, 431
poach, 284
poem, 281
p(o)enology. *See* penology
poet, 91; -ess, 92
poi, 20, 85, 303

poignant, 431
poinsettia, 349
point, 302
poise, 148
poison, 396
polarity, 281
polder, 102
polemic, 427
policy, 131
poliomyelitis, 277
polish, 122, 128
Polish, 121
polite, 154, 272
political, 224, 347
politician, 138
politics, 372
polka, 102, 366, 445
poll, 102
pollen, 446
pollute, 298, 446; -ion, 119,
   132, 134
polo, 126, 283
polonaise, 253
poltergeist, 278
polyandry, 453
polygamous, 227, 353
polyglot, 171; -ic, 171–72
pomegranate, 152, 427
pommel, pummel, 166, 246,
   429
pompadour, 315
pomposity, 234
poncho, 283, 414
ponderosity, 114
pontifex, 46
pontiff, 101, 384
pool, 289
poor, 321, 373
pope, -ery, 141
poplar, 335
poplin, 335
popple, 337
poppy, 337
porcelain, 406
porcel(l)aneous, 441
porch, 313, 414
porcupine, 272, 367
porous, 313
porphyry, 455
porpoise, 313
porridge, 312, 419, 420
portal(l)ed, 167
portcullis, 445

portfolio, 282, 381
portico, 282
portiere, 311, 460
portmanteau, 286
portrait, 252, 453; -ure, 416
portray, 252
posit, 120; -ive, 113, 234, 395; -ivity, 113
possess, 396, 402
possibility, 47
possible, 47, 100, 223, 402
post, 104; -humous, 343–44, 390, 416
posterior, 263, 316
postern, 104
postil(l)ion, 441
potassium, 264, 402
potato, 283
potent, 125
potion, 129, 132, 136
pottery, 349
pouch, 306
poultice, 285
poultry, 285, 453
pour, 315
pout, 306
powder, 305, 340
power, 305
praam, 81
pr(a)efect. *See* prefect
praetor, 348
prairie, 95, 311
praise, 250, 253
prank, 101
prattle, 349
prawn, 237
pray, 250
precarious, 308
precede, -ent, 132
precept, 125
precinct, 366, 436
precious, 123, 127, 132, 137
precise, 23
predecessor, 402
predicament, 165
predict, 345
predilection, 340
prefect, praefect, 269
prefer, 169, 323, 384; -able, -ed, -ence, -ential, -er, -ing, 169
prefix, 125
preflight, 262

prejudicial, 138
prelate, 218
preliminary, 442
prelude, 298
premier(e), 318
premise, 218, 405
premium, 137
prepare, 27
preprint, 262
prerogative, 353
presbyter, 76, 395
prescient, 412
prescript, 262
presence, 218
president, 131, 395
pressure, 411
prestidigitation, 419
prestige, 146, 264, 422
presto, 282
presume, -able, -ed, -er, -ing, -s, 40
presumption, 40
presumptive, 39, 40
presumptuous, 40
pretend, 41
pretension, 41–42
pretentious, 410
preterit(e), 154
pretty, 228
prey, 255
priapic, 336
priceless, 406
priest, 268
prim, 426
prime, -itive, 141; -arily, 58; -ary, 140, 141, 272; -er, 224
primogeniture, 419
prior, 91; -ess, 92; -ity, 312
prison, 224
pristine, 153
private, 125, 152; -eer, 317
pro, 36, 46, 282
probable, 150, 330; -ly, 131
probationary, 119
probity, 115
problematic, 116
proboscis, 398
procedure, 405, 421
process, 234
procure, 320
prodigal, 234
prodigious, 419
produce, 168

profane, 113; -ation, 382; -ity, 113
profess, 384; -ion, 381; -ional, 36, 46
proffer, 168, 383; -ed, -er, -ing, 168
profit, 46, 128, 164; -ing, 164
profound, 306
program, 165, 173, 283; -atic, -ed, -ing, -istic, 174; -er, 165, 174
progress, 233; -ive, 352
prohibit, 120, 330; -ion, 224, 333
project, 218, 234; -ile, 152
prolific, 224
prolog(ue), 164, 239; -ize, 158, 164
prolongation, 352
promenade, 342
promiscuous, 365, 426
promise, 138, 405
promissory, 402
prompt, 336
pronounce, 432
proof, 288, 289
propaedeutic, 300, 348
propaganda, 340, 355
propagate, 131
propellant, 446
proper, 234, 335
property, 335
prophecy, 379
prophesy, 276
prophet, 111, 116, 233; -ic, 116
prophylactic, 111, 283, 379
propinquity, 359, 437
propitious, 138
propose, 396
propriety, 58, 81, 135, 273
propulsion, 410
proscenium, 138
proscribe, 105
prosecute, 402
proselyte, 276, 402
prosody, 116, 402; -ic, 116; -ist, 87
prosperity, 310
protean, 136
protect, 349, 366
protein, 267
protend, 41

protension, 41
protocol, 94; -ar, -ist, 175
protozoa, 281
protrusion, 134
proud, 305
prove, 288, 292
proverb, 128, 331
provide, 377
provincial, 58, 412
provision, 119
proviso, 395
provocative, 365
prow, 304
prowess, 305, 405
prowl, 305, 445
proximity, 114, 371
proximo, 283
prudence, 124
prudent, 289
pruritus, 320
pry, 276
psalliota, 399
psalloid, 399
psalm, 233, 399, 424; -odist, 87
psalter, 399
psammon, 399
pschent, 399
psedera, 399
pselaphid, 399
pselaphognath, 399
psephism, 399
psephite, 399
psephology, 399
psephomancy, 399
psettodid, 399
pseudo, 282
pseudograph, 399
pseudonym, 296, 298, 340
psi, 85, 399
psicose, 399
psilanthropy, 399
psilate, 399
psithyrus, 399
psittacism, 399
psoas, 91, 399
psocid, 399
psophometer, 399
psoriasis, 399
psorosis, 399
pst, 399
psyche, 110, 276, 357
psychiatric, 215

psychiatrist, 135
psychiatry, 358
psychic, 118, 357
psychoanalysis, 358
psychology, 235, 277, 357–58, 397, 399
psychopath, 358
psychopathic, 109
psychosis, 358
psywar, 399
ptarmigan, 18–19, 60
pterodactyl, 19, 344
pterosaur, 344
pteroyl, 344
ptilinal, 344
ptisan, 344, 345
ptomaine, 254, 344, 428
ptosis, 344
ptyalin, 344
ptyxis, 344
pubic, 118
pubis, 124
public, 117, 330; -ity, 117
publish, 122, 244
pucker, 368
pudding, 242
puddle, 151, 342
pueblo, 283, 457
puerile, 152, 457
Pugh, 300
pugilist, 134, 420
puissant, 100, 457
pulchritude, 357
pull, 242
pullet, 242
pulley, 242, 268, 447
pulpit, 242
pulse, 244
puma, 124
pumice, 245
pummel. See pommel
pumpkin, 362, 426, 436
puncheon, 414
punctual, 436
punish, 122, 128
punitive, 134
pup, 94
pupil, 299
puppet, 337
puppy, 337; -es, 267
purchase, 148, 414
pure, 107, 320
purfle, 453

purine, 320
purity, 115
purlieu, 300
purple, 453
purpose, 148
purr, 451
purse, 324, 392
pursue, 95, 147; -er, 93
pursuit, 296
purulent, 320
purvey, 255
push, 242
pusillanimus, 447
put, 243
putrefy, 276
putrid, 299
putsch, 412
putt, 347
puttee, 349
puzzle, 394
pwe, 457
pygmy, pigmy, 227, 353, 428
pylon, 276
pyramid, 121, 318; -er, 175
pyre, 319; -ites, 261
pyromania, 276
pyrotechnics, 358
python, 110, 276, 277

qadi, cadi, kad(h)i, 339, 342
quack, 214, 359
quadrant, 232, 359
quadruped, 243; -al, 174
quadruple, 105, 243
quaff, 359, 381
quail, 252
quake, 107
qualify, 232, 444; -es, 278
quality, 114, 232, 444
qualm, 232, 424
quantify, 232
quantity, 232, 359
quantum, 232
quarantine, 232, 263, 313
quark, 313
quarrel, 166, 313, 359, 452; -er, 167
quarry, 313
quartan, 313
quarter, 313
quartet, 313
quartic, 313
quarto, 283

quartz, 313, 348, 399, 453
quasi, 274
quatrefoil, 360
quaver, 125–26
quay, 270, 360
queasy, 266, 359
quebracho, 360
queen, 212, 258, 265, 355,
    359, 433, 457
queer, 317
quell, 442
quench, 218
quenelle, 360
query, 316
question, 359, 407, 416;
    -ingly, 36
questionnaire, 7, 28, 47, 100,
    172, 174, 435
quetzal, 360
queue, 95, 147, 298, 300,
    360; -ing, 158
quibble, 333
quiche, 360
quick, 101
quiet, 91; -ude, 135
quinine, 153
quintar, 360
quipu, 360
quire, 319
quirk, 324, 363
quite, 272
quitter, 212
quiver, 128, 377
quixote, 371; -ic, 359
quiz, 84, 94, 212, 359, 392;
    -ed, -ing, 393; -es, 212,
    393; -ical, 174, 393
quoin, 360
quoit, 360
quorum, 359
quotation, 119
quotient, 359, 410
qurush, 360

rabbi, 85, 101, 274
rabbinic, -al, 117
rabbit, 332, 451
rabble, 333
rabid, 120, 330
rabies, 268, 331
raccoon, 356, 433
racism, 406
racketeer, 317

raconteur, 326
radar, 314
radiance, 92
radiant, 137
radii. See radius
radio, 91, 137, 282
radish, 215, 409
radium, 92, 264
radius, 405; -es, -i, 81–82,
    273
raffia, raphia, 379
raffle, 384, 445
rafter, 382
rag, 146; -ed, 351, 354
rage, 146
raillery, 172, 446
raiment, 253
raise, 148, 250, 253
raisin, 253, 396
raj, 93, 420
raja, 232, 421
rally, 447
rampage, 214
ranch, 72
rancor, 436
ranee. See rani
range, 104
rani, ranee, 86
rankle, 367
ransack, 369
ransom, 433
rapacity, 215
raphia. See raffia
rapid, 120, 128
rapier, 137
rapine, 153, 335
rapture, 214
rarefy, 276
rascal, 113, 367; -ity, 113
raspberry, 185, 328, 334, 395
rat, -ed, 162
ratchet, 415
rate, 123; -able, 157
rather, 110, 233
ratify, 347
ratio, 282, 410
ration, 119, 124, 137
rattan, 94
rattle, 149, 349
rattrap, 349
raucous, 238
ravage, 128, 377
ravel, 166; -er, 167

raven, 125, 249
ravenous, 377
ravine, 263
ravish, 122, 128
raw, 236
rayon, 234, 252
raze, 84; -or, 393
razzed, 338
razzia, 394
re, 89
're, 315
reabsorb, 93
react, 92
read /rĕd/, 219
read /rēd/, 264
ready, 219, 340; -ly, 451
real, 113; -ist, -ize, 92; -ity,
    113; -ization, 394; -ly, 100
realm, 23, 219
reap, 265
rear, 317
rearrange, 104
reascend, 93
reason, 266
rebel, 444; -ion, 446, 460;
    -ious, 403
rebroadcast, 60, 262
rebuff, 381
rebuke, 299, 363
rebus, 125
rebuttal, 349
recalcitrant, 406
recall, 77
recapitulate, 337
recede, 123
receipt, 267, 268, 344–45,
    405
receive, 44, 267
recent, 125
recept, 44; -acle, 368; -ion,
    44–45, 410
rechauffe, 286
recidivism, 165, 340, 405
recipe, 261
reciprocate, 366
reciprocity, 114, 337
recital, 405
reckon, 368
reclaim, 262
recognize, 100, 180, 365
reconnaissance, 100, 396,
    403, 404, 433
record, 365

recourse, 315
rectangle, 366
rectify, 46
recto, 283
recur, 164, 324; -ence, 164, 365; -ent, 453; -ing, 324
red, 140; -en, 341; -er, 140; -est, 165, 341; -eye, 12, 165; -ish, 163, 341; -ness, 163; -start, 340
redd, 339; -s, 340
reddition, 341
reddock, 341
redecorate, 341
redeem, 265
redemption, 426
redoubt, 306, 344
redundant, 244
reed, 264
reef, 265, 382
refer, 164, 169, 323; -able, -al, -ed, -ence, -endum, -ent, -ential, -er, 169; -ee, 164, 382; -eeing, 158; -ing, 164, 169
refill, 443
reflex, 105
reflux, 105
refuge, 128, 420; -ee, 382
regal, 126, 354; -ia, 138
regard, 352
regatta, 349
regime, régime, 256, 422
regimen, 419
regiment, 419
region, 129, 137
register, 419
registrar, 23
regular, 353
rehabilitate, 444
rehearse, 325; -al, 387
reify, 92
reign, 254, 430, 431
reimburse, 330
rein, -deer, 254
reinforce, 93
reinstate, 57
reinvest, 93
rejoice, 421
rejuvenate, 421
relative, 444
relax, 94, 371
relay, 252

release, 266
reliable. See rely
relic, 218, 444
relief, 268, 374; -s, 374
relieve, 268, 374
religion, 136, 419
religiosity, 114
relinquish, 122, 359
relish, 122, 219
reluctant, 366
rely, 276; -able, 135, 273, 442
remains, 426
remedy, 131; -al, 138
remind, 275
reminisce, 434
remiss, 401; -ion, -ive, 39
remit, 39, 224; -ance, 349
renaissance, 137, 396, 403, 404
renegade, 251
renege, renig, 147
renewal, 432
renig. See renege
renown, 305
repainted, 33, 36
repair, 26–27, 29, 311
repeated, 57
repetition, 224
replant, 262
replenish, 122, 219
replica, 335
reply, 276
repository, 395
reprieve, 268
reproach, 284
reprobate, 335
reprove, 208, 292
reptile, 152; -ian, 136, 263
repudiate, 134
repugn, 103, 430; -ant, 103
request, 359
requiem, 107
require, 319
requisite, 107, 359; -ion, 224
rescue, 299, 367
research, 325
reseeded, 12
resell, 443
resemble, 150
resent, 395
reservoir, 449
resident, 395

residue, 95, 299; -al, 407, 421; -um, 81, 158, 421
resign, 103, 275
resilience, 132, 136
resin, 218, 395
resolution, 447
resolve, 233
resort, 313
resource, 146, 315
rest, 59–60
restitute, 60
restrict, 366
restring, 57
resume, 36, 37, 39, 40; -able, -ed, -er, -ing, -s, 40
resumption, 36, 37, 39, 40
resumptive, 40
resuscitate, 184, 398
retail, 253
retainer, 349
retaliate, 137
reticular, 365
retina, 347
retinue, 95, 299
retire, -ing, 319
retreat, 265
retrieve, 268
reuben, 296, 298
reunite, 93
rev, 94, 375; -ed, -ing, 375, 377
revel, 128, 166; -er, 167
revere, 316
reverie, 95
revers, 20
reverse, -al, -ed, -ing, -ion, 43
revert, -ive, 43
revise, 396; -ion, 119
revive, 208
revocation, 363
revoke, 363–64
revolution, 375
revue, 298
revulsion, 410
rewrite, 262
rhabdomancy, 448
rhabdomyoma, 448
rhapsody, 116, 448; -ic, 116
rhatany, 448
rhea, 91, 448
rhematic, 448
rhenium, 448

rheostat, 20, 261, 448
rhesus, 448
rhetoric, 448; -al, 312
rheum, 296; -atic, 116, 448;
    -atism, 296, 298, 395
rhinal, 448
rhinencephalon, 448
rhinestone, 449
rhinoceros, 235, 448
rhizobium, 448
rhizome, 448
rho, 448
rhodamine, 448
rhodium, 448
rhododendron, 342, 448
rhodora, 448
rhomb, 424; -encephalon,
    448; -oid, 233, 330, 424,
    448; -us, 101
rhonchus, 448
rhubarb, 124, 290, 298, 314,
    449
r(h)umba, 449
rhyme, rime, 107, 272, 277
rhynchoceph, 449
rhyolite, 449
rhythm, 227, 386, 428, 447,
    449
riata, 129
ribald, 23, 128, 330, 451
ribband, 332
ribbon, 332
rich, 413
rickety, 349
ricochet, 256, 408; -ed, 175
rid, 206; -ance, 101, 341
ridden, 109, 341
riddle, 149, 342
ride, 109. See also ridden
ridge, 417
ridicule, 340
riffle, 80, 105, 106, 150, 384
rifle, 105, 106, 150, 275, 382
rigatoni, 85
rigged, 338
right, 102, 209, 274, 345;
    -eous, 416
rigid, 120, 128, 419; -ity,
    112–13
rigor, 224, 353
rime. See rhyme
rind, 102, 275
ringlet, 437

riot, 273
rip, 145
ripe, 145
ripple, 337
rise, -en, 109
rival, 166; -ry, 451
river, 123, 127
roach, 284, 451
road, 284
roam, 284
roan, 284
roar, 314
roast, 284
robber, 47, 76; -y, 332
robe, 280
robot, 126, 331
roc, 93
rock, 9; -y, 163
rococo, 282
rocou. See ro(u)cou
rodeo, 260, 283
roe, 145, 281
rogue, 95, 141, 351, 354;
    -ery, 141, 158
role, 444, 445
roll, 102, 264, 439, 446
rollick, 101, 370; -ing, 446
romaine, 149, 254, 428
romance, 406
rondo, 282
roof, 382
rook, 9, 242
room, 288; -mate, 428
rope, -ery, 141
rose, 406; -ary, 396; -ate,
    156; -ette, 347
rosin, 128
rotate, 348
rotogravure, 321
rotten, 349
rouble. See ruble
ro(u)cou, 293
rouge, 146, 293, 422
rough, 248, 380
roulette, 293, 294, 347
round, 184
rouse, 305
rout, 306
route, 348; -ine, 153, 263,
    289, 293, 348
rove, 108
row /raù/, 304
row /rō/, 284

rowdy, 305, 340
rub, 244; -er, 332; -ing, 210;
    -ish, 332, 409
rubble, 333
ruble, rouble, 293
rubric, 106
ruby, 124, 298
rudd, 339
rudder, 341, 451
ruddy, 341
rue, 291, 294
ruff, 381
ruffian, 263
ruffle, 384
rugby, 353
rugged, 101
ruin, 291; -ous, 451
rule, 107
rumba. See r(h)umba
ruminate, 134
rummy, 428
rumor, 290
run, 15, 145; -away, 165, 245;
    -er, 165; -ing, 9, 15, 76
rune, 107, 145; -ic, 118
rupture, 336
rural, 320
ruse, 82, 406
russet, 404
rustic, -ity, 117
rustle, 400
rye, 88, 96, 276, 451

sabbath, 333
sabbatical, 333
sable, 252
sabotage, 146, 232, 422
saboteur, 326
sac, 364, 369
saccate, 356
saccharin, 358, 455
saccule, 356; -ar, 171
sachet, 256
sack, 414
sacque, 95, 360
sacred, 106, 132, 367
sacrifice, 106, 381
sacrilege, 132
sacristan, 367
sacroiliac, 252, 281, 364
sacrosanct, 366
sacrum, 252
sadden, 341

saddle, 151, 342
safari, 384
safe, -s, 374
safflower, 383
saffron, 214, 382, 383
saga, 232, 354
sagamore, 313
sahib, 235
said, 86, 220
sail, 250; -or, 445
sake /sāk/, 98
sake /säkē/. See saki
saker, 130
saki, sake, 86, 129
sal, 93, 442
salaam, 81
salamander, 444
salary, 131
sale, 250; -able, 157
salicylic, 227, 444
salient, 137
saline, 113, 125, 153, 272;
     -ity, 113
sallow, 285
sally, 445
salmi(s), 86
salmon, 214, 425
saloon, 288
salt, 204, 239, 348
salute, 298
salvage, 376
salve, 232, 376, 377, 380
salvo, 282, 376
same, 249
sample, 445
sanctuary, 436
sandal, 166
sandhi, 339
sandwich, 415
sane, 113
sang, 204
sanguine, 153, 351, 353, 436,
     457
sanitarium, 264
sanitary, 131
sanity, 113
sapid, 120, 336
sapience, 137
sapphic, 379
sapphire, 379
sarcasm, 453
sarcastic, 365
sarcophagus, 111, 379

sardonic, 234
sartorial, 313
sassafras, 175, 382, 401; -es,
     175
sassy. See sauce
satan, -ic, 116
satchel, 414, 415
sate, 132
sateen, 347
satellite, 131, 154, 272, 347,
     447
satiate, 58, 137
satin, 347
satire, 215, 319, 347; -ical,
     316
satisfaction, 381
satisfy, 132, 276, 347
satrap, 252
satyr, 125; -ic, 452
sauce, 146, 215–16, 238; -er,
     238; -y (sassy), 215–16
sauerbraten, 306
sauerkraut, 306
saunter, 237
saurel, 315
saury, 315
sausage, 238, 403
save, 249, 374; -ior, 136, 460
savoy, 302
savvy, 375, 377
saw, 236; -yer, 236, 459
say, 220, 252; -s, 217, 220
scab, 93
scaffold, 383
scald, 239
scallop, 101, 232, 447
scalp, 101
scandal, 101, 340
scapple, 337
scar, 314, 451
scarce, 311
scare, 74, 308
scarf, 374; -ful, 383; -s, 374.
     See also scarves
scarlet, 365
scarves, scarfs, 374, 376
scathe, 147, 249; -less, 109
scatter, 362, 398
scenario, 282, 398
s(c)end, 398
scene, 107, 141, 397, 398;
     -ery, 141; -ic, 118, 124
scent, 397

scepter, 398
sceptic. See skeptic
schedule, 122, 128, 290, 298,
     357, 401, 421
scheme, 107, 358
schism, 397, 400
schizophrenia, 263, 358, 393
schizophrenic, 379
schlemiel, 408
schlep, 408
schlimazel, 408
schlock, 408
schmaltz, 408, 445
schmo, 408
schmuck, 408
schnapps, 408
schnauzer, 408
schnitzel, 408, 433
schnook, 408
schnorrer, 408
schnozzle, 408
scholar, 123, 127, 357
scholiast, 64
school, 71, 289, 355
schottische, 408
schuss, 408
schwa, 232, 408, 458
sciatic, 215; -a, 398
science, 146, 273, 398
scilicet, 398
scimitar, 427
scintilla, -ate, 398
sciolism, 398
s(c)irocco. See sirocco
scirrhus, 398, 449
scissile, 398
scissors, 18, 223, 396, 398
sciuroid, 398
scivvy. See skivvy
scleritis, 272
sclerosis, 398, 445
sclerotic, 455
scoff, 381; -law, 398
scold, 102, 362, 398
scolytid, 121, 336, 347
scoop, 289
scope, 107
scops, 83
scorch, 365
scorpion, 92, 263, 453
scoundrel, 306
scour, 306
scourge, 325

scout, 306
scow, 304
scowl, 305
scrag, 93
scrape, 365
scratch, 398, 413; -proof,
    415
scrawl, 237
scream, 362
screw, 295
scribble, 333
scribe, 107
script, 101, 336
scroll, 102, 446
scrooge, scrouge, 420
scruple, 298
scrupulosity, 114
scrutiny, 134, 290, 365, 453
scud, 93
scuff, 381
scull, 442
sculpt, 348; -or, 244; -ure,
    362, 398
scurrilous, 324, 454
scurry, 324, 454; -ed, 58
scurvy, 324, 376
scuttle, 349, 365
scythe, 18, 147, 272, 278,
    386, 398; -stone, 109
sdrucciola, 340
sea, 259, 265; -weed, 458
seam, 264
sear, 317
search, 325
sec, 93; -s, 371
secession, 405
seclusion, 119, 365, 422
second, 23, 365, 401
secret, 106, 262, 367; -ariat,
    308
secretion, 132
sect, 348
secular, 365
secure, 320
sedan, 94
sedative, 340
sedition, 119
seduce, 146, 299
sedulity, 115
sedulous, 421
see, 88, 265; -ing, 158
seek, 258
seem, 264

seesaw, 236
seeth, 386
seethe, 147, 258, 266, 386
seismic, 278
seize, 84, 267, 393; -ure, 422
select, 366
self, 374; -ish, 101
selves, 374
semantics, 372
semen, 125
semiannual, 263
semierect, 263
seminar, 314, 427
semiofficial, 263
senate, 152, 218; -orial, 313
send (of a wave). See
    s(c)end
seneschal, 408
senior, 125, 137, 260; -ity,
    312, 460
sense, 342; -ational, 119;
    -ibility, 224; -ile, 152; -ual,
    -uous, 243, 411
sent, 397
sentient, 58
sentiment, 58
sentinel, 166
sepal, 336
separate, 27, 335
sepoy, 302
sepulchre, 357; -al, 337, 445,
    453
sequacity, 215
sequel, 106; -ae, 269
sequential, 359
sequester, 359
sequin, 106, 359; -ed, 167
sequoia, 302, 359
seraph, 379; -ic, 111, 215
serene, 113; -ade, 310; -ity,
    113, 433
serf, -s, 375
sergeant, serjeant, 235, 315,
    417, 453
serial, 316
series, 268
serious, 316
serjeant. See sergeant
sermon, 323
serpent, 336
serrated, 310
serve, 375; -ile, 152
sessile, 152

session, 411
sett, 347
settee, 349
setter, 349
settle, 218, 349
setule, 122
seven, -th, 129
sever, 128, 377; -al, 377
severe, 316; -ity, 452
sew, 286–87
sewage, 295
sewer, 23, 295, 298
sex, 94, 371; -es, 163; -ual,
    409, 411
sextant, 371
shab, -y, 332
shackle, 369
shad, 93
shade, 249, 341; -ow, 133,
    285, 341
shaft, 101
shagrag, 352
shale, 107
shall, 443
shallow, 285
shaman, 126
shambles, 409
shame, 249
shampoo, 289, 336
shamrock, 101, 369
shanghai, 86
share, 308
sharp, 336
shave, 107
shawl, 237
she, 261
sheaf, 375, 409
shear, 317
sheath, 386
sheathe, 147, 386
sheave, -s, 375
sheep, 258
sheer, 317
sheik, 267, 363, 409
shekel, 129
shelf, 101, 375; -ful, 383
shellac(k), 94, 364, 447; -ed,
    370
shelve, 375; -ing, 155, 159;
    -s, 155, 375
shepherd, 133, 390
sherbet, 453
sheriff, 310, 384

sherry, 310
shew, 286–87
shield, 258, 268
shillela(g)h, 270
shin, 432
shingle, 409
shipment, 163
shipper, 163
shire, 319
shiv, 94, 375
shivaree. *See* charivari
shiver, 129
shoal, 284
shoe, 88, 95, 149, 293; -ed, -ing, 158
shook, 242
should, 7, 8, 243, 339
shoulder, 285, 409
shout, 306
shove, 107, 147, 246
shovel, 129, 166, 245; -er, 167
show, 284; -n, 285
shower, 304
shrank, 363
shrapnel, 336, 453
shrew, 295
shrewd, 295, 298
shriek, 268, 363
shrill, 442; -ly, 77
shrine, 107
shrink, 363
shrivel, 129, 166
shroud, 305, 409
shrub, 93; -ery, 332
shudder, 341
shumac. *See* sumac(h)
shush, 409
shut, 244; -er, 349
shuttle, 349
shy, 276, 409
shylock, 369
sibling, 330
sibyl, 401, 444
sic(k) (incite), -ing, 356; -ed, 356, 370; -s, 371
sickle, 369
sidereal, 316
sidle, 105, 275
siege, 258
sienna, 93
sierra, 264, 310
siesta, 264
sieve, 229, 374, 401

sift, 229
sigh, 102, 274; -ed, 338
sight, 102, 271, 274, 345
sigma, 428
sign, 15–16, 72, 103, 275, 353, 430; -al, 15–16, 72, 103, 166, 353; -aler, -alize, 167; -ature, 321
silence, 125
silicon, 444
silly, 447
silo, 126
simian, 136
simile, 261
simmer, 429
sincere, 316, 406
sinew, 225, 299
sinful, 163
sing, 435; -er, 353, 435; -ing, 156
singe, 417; -ing, 156
single, 353, 435
sinned, 163, 338
sinuous, 136, 432
sip, 74, 202
siphon, 111, 379
sir, 322, 324
sirloin, 324
sirocco, scirocco, 282, 398
sirup. *See* syrup
sis, 401; -y, 403
sisal, 126
sister, 60, 226
site, 132; -uate, 132, 415
sitzkreig, 397
sitzmark, 397, 399
six, 28, 371; -teen, -ty, 28; -th, 385
size, 84, 107; -able, 157
sizzle, 394
skate, 107, 362
skein, 254, 363
skeleton, 363, 444
skeptic, sceptic, 363, 364, 398
sketch, 357, 363
skewer, 299
ski, 20; -ing, 82
skid, 93, 363
skies. *See* sky
skifful, 77, 383
skillet, 363
skil(l)ful, 79, 441, 443

skimp, 101, 363
skin, 363, 375
skirmish, 363
skirr, 451
skirt, 363
skittish, 349
skittles, 363
skivvy, scivvy, 375, 377
skreak, 367
skrimshander, 367
skua, 91
skulk, 101
skul(l)duggery, 441
skullike, skull-like, 77
skunk, 355
sky, 362, 363; -es, 278; -ey, 91, 268
slacks, 371
slalom, 129
slang, 437
slaughter, 237, 345
slave, -ery, 141
sleeve, 147, 266
sleigh, 255, 346
sleight, 278, 345, 346
slept, 7, 344
sleuth, 296, 298
slew, 295
slight, 102, 274, 345
slimmer, 428
slipper, 337
sliver, 129
sloe, 95
slogan, 126, 354
sloid. *See* sloyd
slouch, 306
slough, 248, 294, 295, 306, 380
slow, 284
sloyd, sloid, 303
sludge, 445
slue, 295
slug, 244; -ard, 226, 354; -ish, 223, 354
sluice, 296
slung, 437
slur, 322, 324
smack, 74
small, 239, 428; -pox, 371
smaragd, 74
smear, 401
smile, 107, 444
smirk, 324

smoke, 98, 363; -ier, 136; -y, 124
smolder, 340
smooth, 289, 386
smorgasbord, 353
smother, 108, 246
smudge, 418
smuggle, 355
snack, 74
snake, 249
snap, 94
snarl, 314, 445
sneer, 317
sneeze, 84, 266, 393, 401
snicker, 368
sniff, 381; -le, 150, 384
snivel, 129, 166; -er, 167
snob, 234; -ish, 101
snore, 107
snout, 306
snow, 284; -shoer, 92
snuff, 381
snug, 93
snuggle, 150, 355
so (conj.), 88, 282
so (musical note), 89
soak, 284, 363
soap, 280, 284
soar, -ing, 314
sober, 130
sobriety, 81, 273
sobriquet, 256, 283, 359
social, 58, 407, 409
society, 58, 81, 273, 406
socle, 105
sodium, 264
sofa, 382
soft, 74, 98, 239; -en, 378, 380
soil, 302
sojourn, 186, 421
solace, 234, 406
solar, 281; -ium, 264
sold, 102
solder, 339
soldier, 23, 102, 421
solemn, 18, 234, 425; -ity, 113, 425
solicit, 120
solid, 113, 120, 128, 164, 444; -ify, 164; -ity, 113, 340
soliloquy, 359
solitary, 234

solitude, 132
solo, 126, 132, 282
solstice, 59, 102
soluble, 150
solvent, 376
some, 108, 149, 246
somersault, 237, 246
son, 246
sonant, 432
sonar, 314
sonata, 232, 348
sonnet, 432; -eer, 317
soot, 242
sooth, 386
soothe, 147, 290, 386
sophisticated, 379
sophistry, 111
sophomore, 111, 313, 379
sopor, 312
soprano, 282, 336, 337
sorghum, 352, 453
sorrel, 312
sorrow, 285
sorry, 312
sortie, -ing, 157
sou, 293, 294
sough, 380
sought, 240, 345
soul, 286; -less, 446
sound, 306
soup, 293
sour, 306
source, 315
souse, 306
south, 306; -erly, 248; -ern, 133, 248
souvenir, 293, 294, 318, 434
sovereign, 234, 431
soviet, 264
sow, 284; -n, 285
soy, 19, 302
space, 107; -ious, 136
spaghetti, 85, 210, 218, 352
spaniel, 137, 460
spare, 74
spark, 363; -le, 150, 336, 367, 453
sparrow, 285
sparse, 148
spasmodic, 364
spatula, 416
spawn, 237
speak, 357

spear, 317
special, 128, 132, 137; -ty, 412
specie, 95; -s, 260, 268, 412
specification, 406
specify, 131; -able, 273
specious, 123, 137, 412
speck, -le, 369
spectacle, 368
spectral, 101
speculate, 165
speech, 357
speedometer, 33, 47, 56–57
spend, 101
spermacetti, 85
spermatozoan, 394
spew, 299
sphere, 316, 378, 379
sphinx, 101, 378, 436
sphygmomanometer, 378
spicule, 122, 365
spider, 125
spigot, 225, 353
spin, 201–2
spinach, 128, 415
spinule, 122
spiral, 166, 444; -ium, 167
spirit, 316; -uous, 415
spirochete, 453
splacknuck, 370
splash, 445
spleen, 116
splenetic, 116
splice, 107
split, 336
spoil, 302
spoke, 362
spoliate, 136
spondaic, 118
spongy, 246
spontaneous, 137
spool, 445
spoonbill, 77
sporadic, 340
sport, 61
spout, 306
sprawl, 237, 453
spray, 252
spread, 219, 336
sprig, 93
spright. See sprite
sprightly, 274
spring, 72

sprinkle, 150, 367, 445
sprite, spright, 274
sprocket, 368
sprout, 306
spruce, 290
spry, 276
spur, 324, 451
spurious, 263, 320
spurt, 322
sputter, 349
spy, 276; -glass, 87
squab, 232, 359
squabble, 232, 333
squad, 232
squadron, 232
squalid, 113, 232, 444; -ity, 113
squalor, 138, 232
squash, 232
squat, 232
squaw, 236
squawk, 237, 359
squeak, 359
squeal, 359
squeamish, 266, 359
squeegee, 266, 420
squeeze, 84, 266, 359, 393
squirm, 324, 453
squirrel, 166, 324, 359, 454
squirt, 324, 359
stabile, 152
stability, 114
stable, 105
staccato, 232, 282, 348, 356
stadium, 264
staff, 76, 101, 213, 348, 375, 381; -s, 375. See also staves
stage, 107
stagger, 354
staid, 86, 252
stair, 27, 311
stalk, 239, 361
stall, 439, 443
stallion, 439, 443
stalwart, 239
stamina, 427
stammer, 429
stanza, 393
staphylococcus, 111, 379
staple, 105, 445
star, 314, 325; -y, 453
starch, 414

stare, 74
starve, 374
state, 115; -ic, 115, 127, 347; -ion, 137; -ionery, 311; -istician, 55–56; -ue, 128, 147, 291, 298; -uesque, 95, 359, 415; -uette, 93, 135, 347; -ute, 215
staunch, 237
staves, staffs, 375
stay, 252
stead, -y, 219
steak, 219, 256
steal, 98, 220; -th, 219, 220
steam, 428
steeple, 265, 336
stein, 278
stellar, 445
stem, 94; -ed, 428
stencil, 166; -er, -ize, 167
stentorian, 263
step, 94; -parent, 336
steppe, 334
stere, 316
stereophonic, 261, 316
sterile, 152, 310; -ize, 272
stethoscope, 109
stevedore, 313
stew, 295; -ed, 338
steward, 295, 299
stick, 9, 357
stiff, 76, 381; -ly, -ness, 79
stifle, 105, 275, 382
stigma, 101; -atic, 116
stiletto, 282
stillhouse, 80
stillness, 79
stilt, 101
stimulate, 427
stimy. See stymie
sting, 101, 437
stink, 9
stipend, 125, 132, 336
stipple, 337
stipulate, 132
stir, 324, 451; -ed, 324; -ing, 453
stirrup, 316, 324, 454
stitch, 357
stoa, 281
stoat, 284
stodgy, 420
stoic, 91

stolid, 120
stomach, 70, 116, 246, 357; -ic, 116, 215
stone, 247, 280
stood, 242
stop, 94; -able, 175; -ed, 343; -er, -over, 165
storied, 313
stories, 58
stout, 306
stow, 284
straggle, 355
straight, 255, 345, 401
strain, 348
strait, 250
strand, 101
strange, 104
strangle, 150
strategy, 214; -ic, 118, 349
stratosphere, 378
straw, 56, 236; -berry, 56
streak, 219, 363
strength, 228, 437
streptomycin, 276
stress, 348; -ful, 402
streusel, 296, 303
strew, -n, 295
strictness, 348
strife, -s, 375
strike, 107
string, 222
striped, 343
stripped, 223, 337
strive, 375
stroll, 102
strong, 435, 437; -er, 435
strontium, 264
struggle, 150
strychnine, 227, 358
stubble, 333
stubby, 332
stucco, 282, 356
student, 124
study, 245, 340; -ing, 135; -o, 282
stuff, 76, 381; -y, 383
stun, 94
stupefy, 134, 276
stupid, 113, 120, 336; -ity, 113
sturdy, 324, 340
style, 276; -istic, 364
stymie, stymy, stimy, 126, 157; -ing, 157

styptic, -ity, 118
suasive, 125, 457
suave, 232, 457
subalpine, 185
subatomic, 185
subbasement, 185, 332
subboreal, 332
subbrachial, 80
subbranch, 332
subcaliber, 185
subcellar, 75
subchapter, 75
subclass, 75, 185
subclavian, 138
subconscious, 185
subdivide, 185
subdue, 95, 185, 333, 339;
    -able, 158; -al, 93
subequatorial, 185, 245
subfamily, 185
subfreezing, 75
subgenus, 185
subgroup, 185
subhuman, 34, 185
subirrigate, 185; -ed, 245
subjacent, 185
subject, 185; -ive, -ivity, 113
subjoin, 185
subjugate, 185, 355
subjunctive, 185
subkingdom, 75, 185
sublease, 185
sublet, 185
sublime, 113, 185; -ate, 185,
    330; -ation, 442; -ity, 113
subliminal, 185
submarine, 185
submerge, 146, 185
submission, 185
submissive, 402
subnormal, 185
suborbital, 245
suborder, 185
subordinate, 185
subplot, 185, 334
subpoena, 186, 328, 334–35
subprinciple, 334
subquadrate, 185
subquality, 75, 185
subregion, 186
subscribe, 76, 184, 186
subscription, 76
subsequent, 76, 186

subshock, 75
subside, 186; -iary, 75, 263;
    -ize, 76; -y, 342
subspecies, 185
substance, 59, 75
substantial, 76
substitute, 59, 76, 184,
    185
substract, 76
substruct, 76
substyle, 76
subsume, 40, 76, 185, 298;
    -able, -ed, -ing, -s, 40
subsumption, 40
subsumptive, 40
subterfuge, 75
subterranean, 185, 455
subtile, 152, 344
subtitle, 185
subtle, 186, 344
subtract, 185
suburb, 185, 245; -an, 330
subvariety, 185
subversion, 43, 185, 410
subversive, -ism, 43
subvert, 43
subway, 185
subxerophilous, 185
subzone, 185
succeed, 183, 185, 372
success, 186; -ful, 79; -ion,
    411
succinct, 183, 366, 372
succinic, 372
succor, 356
succubus, 183, 186
succulent, 356
succumb, 424
such, 413
sudd, 339
sudden, 184, 341
sue, 291, 298
suede, 457
suerte, 457
suffer, 168, 183, 244, 401;
    -able, -ed, -er, -ing, 168;
    -ance, 168, 383
suffice, 383; -ient, 46, 58,
    183
suffocate, 183, 383; -ion,
    366
suffrage, 183
suffuse, 183, 383

sugar, 241, 243, 353, 411; -y,
    134
suggest, 183, 351, 417, 419;
    -ion, 416
suggilation, 351, 418
suicide, 92
suit, 296, 298; -able, 298,
    300
suite, 264, 457
sulfur, sulphur, 379; -ic, 382
sultan, 101
sum, 206, 427
sumac(h), shumac, 124, 298,
    364, 411
summary, 427; -ist, -ize, 87
summer, 429
summon, 183
sumo, 283
sumption, 40
sumptive, 40
sumptuary, 415
sumptuous, 36, 39, 40, 426
sun, 206; -ed, 433; -less,
    163; -up, 165; -y, 163, 165
sundae, 94, 269
sung, 206
sunn, 432
super, 124; -man, 34
supercilious, 405
superficial, 138
superficies, 268
superfluity, 291, 298
superfluous, 243
superior, 263, 316
superstitious, 59, 138
supine, 153
supper, 337
supplant, 336
supple, 337
supplement, 183
supply, 336; -er, 93
support, 336
suppose, 183, 185, 281,
    336
suppress, 80, 183
suppurate, 183
supreme, 132; -acy, 132,
    337; -ly, 260
surcharge, 324, 414
surcingle, 324
sure, 320, 411
surface, 46, 324
surfeit, 46, 229

surgeon, 324
surly, 322, 324
surname, 324
surplus, 83; -age, 174
surprise, 449
surrealism, 184, 453
surrebut, 184
surrejoin, 184
surrejoinder, 453
surrender, 184, 453
surreptitious 183, 453
surrogate, 183, 453
surround, 184, 453
surroyal, 184
surveillance, 172, 446
surveillant, 254
survey, 250, 255
suscept, -ion, 184; -ible, 57,
    184, 185, 397–98
suspect, 78–79, 184, 185, 244
suspend, 57, 184, 185
suspense, 184; -ion, 410
suspicion, 119, 184, 412
suspicious, 79
suspire, 79, 184; -ious, 316
sussultatory, 79, 184, 404
sustain, 57, 184, 252
sustenance, 184, 401
sustentacular, 184
sustention, 184
sustentor, 184
suttle, 186
suture, 416
suzerain, 393
swab, 232
swaddle, 232
swagger, 354, 401
swain, 250
swallow, 101, 232, 285, 447
swamp, 232
swan, 232, 458
swap, 232
sward, 313
swarthy, 313, 343, 386, 453,
    458
swastika, 232, 364
swathe, 110, 386
swear, 311
sweat, 219
sweet, 458
swell, 101
swerve, 374, 400, 458
swill, 74, 101

swim, 266
swindle, 151, 458
swing, 458
swipe, 107
swirl, 324
swivel, 129, 166
swoon, 458
sword, 397, 400
swore, 313
sworn, 313
swung, 458
sybarite, 227, 330; -ic, 224
sycamore, 227, 313, 365
sycophant, 227, 379
syllabic, 330, 364
syllable, 198, 227, 446
syllepsis, 198
sylleptic, 198
sylloge, 198
syllogism, 198, 420, 446
sylph, 101
sylvan, 101, 227, 376
symballophone, 198
symbiosis, 198, 273
symbiotic, 198
symbol, 85, 164, 166, 173,
    198, 227, 331; -ic, 164, 173,
    234; -ism, 164; -ist, 167
symbranchia, 198
symmetalism, 428
symmetallic, 198
symmetry, 198, 227, 428;
    -ical, 428
sympathetic, 116, 347
sympathy, 198
sympetalous, 198
symphony, 198
symplectic, 198
symposium, 138, 198, 396
symptom, 198, 426; -atic,
    116
synaesthesis, 198
synagog(ue), 198, 227, 239
synapse, 198
synbranch, 198
syncategorematic, 198
synced, 364
synchronize, 198, 358, 436
syncing, 364
syncline, 198
syncope, 261; -ate, 198;
    -ation, 436
syncretism, 198

syndic, 101, 164; -ate, 164,
    198, 227
syndrome, 198
synecdoche, 198, 261, 358
synergism, 198
synod, 227
synonym, 164, 227; -ity, 173;
    -ize, 164
synopsis, 198, 405
synpelmous, 198
synsephalous, 198
syntagm, 198, 425
synthesis, 198, 227
synthetic, 218
syphilis, 111, 227, 379
syringe, 146, 318
syrup, sirup, 318
syssarcosis, 198
syssitia, 198
systallic, 198
system, 101, 164, 198, 227;
    -ize, 164
systole, 198
systyle, 198
syzygy, 198

taal, 81
tabes, 261
table, 105, 150; -eau, 286,
    330; -et, 347
taboo, tabu, 129, 289, 332,
    333
tabulate, 214
tache, 110
tacit, 120; -urn, 324
tackle, 369, 445
tacks, 371
tactile, 152
tael, 257
t(a)enia, -cide, 269
t(a)eniasis, 269
taffeta, 383
tail, -or, 253
take, 249; -s, 371
talc, 101, 364; -um, 366
talent, 444
taler, thaler, 343
talk, 239, 361; -ing, 163
tall, 443
tallow, 285, 443
tally, 445
talus, 125
tamarack, 369

tambourine, 263
tan, 432
tangerine, 263
tangle, 150
tango, 283, 436
tannic, 171
tannometer, 171
tao, 306
taper, 125
tapioca, 137, 264, 335
tapir, 126
tar, -y, 314
tarantula, 416
tardy, 373
tariff, 384, 452
tarnish, 314
tarpaulin, 238
tarry (remain), 314
tartuff(e), 381
task, 363; -master, 402
tassel, 166
taste, -y, 103; -able, 157
tattle, 80, 349
tat(t)oo, 289
taught, 237, 345
taurine, 315
tauromachy, 315
taut, 237
tautological, 238, 348
tavern, 215, 377
tawdry, 236
tawny, 236–37
tax, 94, 371; -ing, 163
taxi, 85
taxidermy, 339
taxonomy, 371
tchaviche, 414
tchervonets. See chervonets
tchetvert. See chetvert
tea, 265
teammate, 428
tear /târ/, 311
tear /têr/, 317
tease, 266, 396
teat, 229
technical, 358
technician, 138, 358
technique, 95, 106, 263, 358, 359
tedium, 137
tee, 88, 145, 264; -ed, -ing, 158
teepee. See tepee

teeter, 266
teeth, 258, 385
teethe, 147
teetotalism, 167
teetotal(l)er, 167
telepathy, 335
telephone, 115; -ic, 115, 379
telescope, -ic, 115
television, 377
telfer, telpher, 379
temerity, 429
temperature, 320
tempestuous, 415
tempo, 282
tempt, 336, 348; -ress, 348
tenacity, 113, 215
tenant, 128
tend, 41
tendril, 340
tenement, 131, 432
tenia, -cide. See t(a)enia
teniasis. See t(a)eniasis
tennis, 83, 434
tenor, 218
tense, 41, 148; -ile, 101, 152; -ion, 41–42, 409
tent, 41, 348
tenth, 342, 385
tenuous, 137
tenure, 128, 154, 218, 320
tepee, teepee, tipi, 94, 126
tepid, 120, 336
teraphim, 379
terminate, 323
terrace, 172, 452
terrain, 455
terrestrial, 455
terrific, 455
terrify, 452
terror, 172
terse, 323
tertiary, 410
test, 346
testicle, 151, 368
testimony, 429
tether, 108
text, 348, 371; -ile, 152, 371
thaler. See taler
Thames, 343
that, 63
thatch, 101, 413
thaumaturgy, 324
thaw, 236

the, 49, 261
theater, theatre, 23, 106, 115, 260; -ic, 93, 115; -ical, 106
thee, 265
their, 311; -s, 82–83
theist, 91
then, 62, 74, 147, 206
thence, 62–63
theodolite, 154
theopathetic, 218
theorem, 37; -atic, 116
theoretical, 37
theorist, 37
theory, 37, 260, 385, 453
theosophy, 234
therapeutic, 300, 348
therapy, 310
there, 62, 311; -in, 229; -withal, 443
thermite, 154
thesaurus, 315, 404
these, 63, 395
theses, 261
thesis, 125, 403
theta, 125
thew, 298
they, 250, 255
thick, 369
thief, 268, 375
thieve, 268, 375; -s, 375
thigh, 271, 274
thimble, 151, 226
thin, 74, 94, 147, 206, 384; -est, 433; -ness, 434
think, 222, 226
thirst, 324, 348
thirteen, 133
thirtieth, 385
this, 63, 82, 384, 401; -es, 403
thistle, 400
thither, 62
Thomas, 343
thong, 101
thorax, 312
thorough, 286
those, 63
thou, 304
though, 286
thought, 240, 345, 385
thousand, 305, 396
thral(l)dom, 441
thrash, 385

thread, 219
threat, 219
threnody, 453
threshold, 111, 390
threw, 295
throat, 284
throe, 95
thrombosis, 330
throne, 23, 343
throstle, 400
throttle, 349
through, 294
throw, 72, 284; -n, 285
thumb, 328, 424
thunder, 385
thurible, 320
thurifer, 320
thus, 82
thwack, 385, 458
thwart, 313
thy, 276
thyme, 276, 343
thymus, 276
thyroid, 276, 385, 453
ti, 89
tic, 93, 369
ticket, 368
tickle, 369
tie, 88, 95, 273, 278; -er, 158;
   -ing, 157
tier /têr/, 318
tiger, 130
tight, 102, 274, 345
tigress, 106, 275, 405
tigrine, 106
tile, 445
timid, 113, 120, 128, 427; -ity,
   113, 340, 429
timorous, 427
tincture, 416, 436
ting, -ing, 156
ting(e)ing, 156
tingle, 150
tinker, 367, 436
tinkle, 367
tinsel, 166
tintinnabulation, 330, 434–
   35
tiny, 126
tipi. See te(e)pee
tipit, 120
tipple, 337
tiptoe, 158; -ing, 92, 158

tire, 319
tissue, 95, 147, 291, 411
tit, 229
titan, -ic, 116
tithe, 147, 386; -er, 109; -ing,
   -s, 155
title, 105, 106, 150, 275, 445
titration, 275
titter, 349
tittle, 106
titular, 416
tmesis, 426
to, 88, 292; -ward, 458
toad, 284
toast, 284
tobacco, 283, 333, 356
toboggan, 233, 333, 354
toccata, 232, 356
toddle, 342
toe, 88, 95; -ing, 158
toffee, 383
together, 108
togue, 95
token, 125
told, 102
tolerable, 234, 444
toll, 102
tom, 94, 145
tomahawk, 237, 387, 429
tomato, 283; -es, -s, 293
tomb, 55, 102, 288, 292, 424
tome, 145
tomorrow, 285
ton, 246; -age, 433
tone, 115, 117; -al, 124; -ic,
   115, 117, 127; -icity, 117
tongs, 395, 437
tongue, 95, 147, 157, 246,
   437; -y, 157
tonsil(l)ar, 441
tonsillectomy, 171
tonsillitis, 161, 171
tonsure, 411
too, 289, 299
took, 242, 363
tooth, 289
top, 204; -ful(l), 441; -piece,
   336
topaz, 84, 392
topic, 127, 234, 336
topple, 337
toque, 95, 106, 107, 359
tor, 312

torches, 395
torchlight, 414
torch's, 395
tornado, 251, 283
torpedo, 282, 313
torque, 95, 359, 453
torrent, 312
torrid, 312
torso, 282
tortoise, 403
tortuous, 415
torture, 416
toss, 104, 401
tot, 74, 206
total, 166; -itarian, 167; -ity,
   173
totem, 126
toucan, 293, 299
touch, 247
tough, 248, 378, 380
tour, 321
tourmaline, 321
tournament, 321, 325
tourney, 325
tourniquet, 321, 325
tousle, 305, 445
tout, 306
tow, 284
toward. See to
towel, 305
tower, 304
town, 305
toxemia, 263, 371, 428
toxicology, 365
toy, 302
trace, -ery, 141; -able, 136
trachea, 110, 358
tract, 101
tradition, 347
traffic, 369, 383; -er, 31;
   -ing, 370
tragedy, 131, 342, 419; -ian,
   137, 263
tragic, 127; -al, 370
train, 348
traipse, 336; -ing, -s, 155
traitor, 253, 348
trammel, 166
tranquil, 359; -ize, 167
transcend, 78
transcience, 101
transcribe, 78
transcription, 78

transection, 78
transfer, -ability, -able, -ed,
    -ee, -ence, -ential, -er,
    -ing, 170; -al, 170, 450
transfusion, 422
transhape. *See* tran(s)shape
tranship. *See* tran(s)ship
transient, 410
transilience, 78
transistor, 78, 395
translator, 442
transmitter, 349
transoceanic, 34
transonic, 78
transpire, 78, 319
transponder, 78
transsegmental, 78, 403
tran(s)shape, 78
tran(s)ship, 78
trans-sonic, 78
transsubjective, 78
tran(s)substantiate, 78
transude, 78
transumption, 78
transverse, -al, -ed, -ing,
    -ness, 43
trapeze, 335, 393; -ium, 138,
    337; -oid, 302, 335, 394
trauma, 238; -atic, 116
travail, 252
travel, 166; -ed, -ing, 440;
    -er, 167; -og(ue), 239
travesty, 377
tray, 252
treachery, 220, 414, 415
treacle, 265
treason, 266
treasure, 153, 219
treatise, 348
treaty, 266
treble, 106
tree, 265; -ing, 157
trek, 355, 356, 363, 369; -ed,
    -er, -ie, -ing, 356
trellis, 83, 445
tremble, 150
tremor, 128, 427
trench, 101; -ant, 414
trepidation, 342
trespass, 401
trestle, 400
trey, 255
triage, 92

trial. *See* try
triangle, 273
tribune, 330
tribute, 330
trident, 125
trifid, 120
trifle, 105, 275, 382
trigger, 354
trim, 226
trine, -ity, 113
trinket, 367
trio, 91, 282
tripartite, 154; -ion, 347
triple, 105
tripod, 125, 234
tripoli, 86
triumph, 244, 273, 379, 428
triune, 91
trivet, 225
trivial, 136
troll, 102
trophy, 111, 283, 379
tropic, 116, 117, 127, 336; -al,
    117
troubado(u)r, 293, 294, 315,
    321, 331
trouble, 247
trough, 380
troupe, 149, 293
trousers, 305
trousseau, 100, 286, 403
trout, 306
trowel, 305
troy, 302
truancy, 92
truce, 107
truculence, 134, 135
truculent, 365, 453
true, 291, 294; -ing, 158;
    -ism, 291; -ly, 159, 290;
    -th, 294, 298
truss, 100, 101
trustful, 348
truth. *See* true
try, 276; -al, 87, 273; -out, 87
tryst, 227
tsar. *See* czar
tschefffkinite, 412
tschermigite, 412
tsetse, 348, 402
tsuga, 348
tsunami, 348
tubercular, 323, 367

tuberculosis, 405
tubule, 122
tucker, 368
Tucson, 400
tuft, 348
tugboat, 352
tumid, 120
tumult, 427; -uary, 415
tuna, 290, 299
tunic, 124
tunnel, 166, 434
tunny, 434
turba(n)ned, 167
turbine, 153, 324
tureen, 320, 322
turkey, 367, 453
turmoil, 302
turnscrew, 433
turpentine, 152
turquoise, 359, 396
turret, 324, 454
tussle, 404
tussock, 370
tutor, 124; -ial, 47, 58
twain, 346, 458
tweak, 458
tweedledee, 265
tweeze, 84; -ers, 266, 393
twelfth, 334, 385
twelve, 346, 376
twenty, 346, 458
twice, 346, 400, 458
twig, 346, 348
twilight, 346
twill, 74, 346, 442
twin, 346; -ing, -ship, 163
twine, 346
twinkle, 150, 367
twist, 346
twit, 61
two, 292, 346, 400
tycoon, 277
tying. *See* tie
type, 107, 115, 226, 272, 276;
    -ic, 115, 117, 127; -ical, 117;
    -ify, 227, 335; -ist, 124
typhoid, 85, 111, 277, 379
typhoon, 111, 272, 278, 289,
    379
typhus, 277
typography, 111
tyranny, 318, 432, 434
tyrant, 276, 432

tyro, 276–77, 282
tzar. *See* czar
tzedakah, 348
tzimmes, 348

ubiquitous, 107, 331, 359
udder, 244, 341
uh, 212
ukase, 362
ukulele, 256, 447
ulcer, 445
ulterior, 263, 316
ultimate, 244
ultimo, 283
umbrella, 244, 331, 445, 453
umiak, oomiak, 290
umlaut, 306
umpire, 295, 319, 428
unanimity, 114
unanimous, 131
unbiased, 343
unblushingly, 12
uncle, 150, 244, 362, 367,
   436, 445
unconscious, 412
uncouth, 293, 294
unction, 436
unctuous, 244, 415
under, 244, 340; -dog, 15
undid, 339
undulate, 421
unemployed, 245
ungenerous, 419
ungoverned, 352
unicorn, 134, 297
unintelligent, 245
union, 123, 299
unique, 95, 106, 297, 359
unison, 401
unit, 120, 124
unity, 115
university, 235, 325
unkempt, 57
unlace, 34
unloose, 403
unorthodox, 245
unquestioningly, 36
unreality, 451
unrelenting, 442
unruly, 290
unscrupulous, 291
unseeing, 57
until, 443

unusual, 245
unwary, 308
unwell, 77, 443
unwieldy, 458
upper, 337
upputting, 336
uproar, 314; -ious, 263, 314,
   451
urali. *See* oorali
uranic, 215
uranium, 320
urban, 331
urchin, 322, 324
urethane, 320
urge, 324
urine, 153, 320
uropod, 320
us, 82, 88, 401
use, 297, 396; -able, 134;
   -ual, 134, 299, 422
usher, 111, 409
usquabae, usquebae, 257
usury, 297, 422; -ous, 320
uterine, 134, 153
utile, 113; -ity, 113, 444; -ize,
   134
utopia, 136, 336
utter, 133, 349
uvula, 376; -ar, 134

vacation, 251
vaccine, 153, 372
vacuole, 137
vacuous, 137
vacuum, 81, 138
vagabond, 333, 353
vagary, 354
vagrant, 106
vagrom, 106
vague, 351
valedictorian, 313
valentine, 444
valet, 256
valiant, 128, 137
valid, 120, 444
valise, 264
valley, 445, 447
valor, 215
value, 128, 298; -able, 135
valve, 375, 376
vamp, 197
vampire, 319, 376
van, 61, 197

vane, 107, 374
vanguard, 197, 351
vanilla, 104, 445
vanille, 104
vanish, 122, 409, 433
vanity, 215, 433
vanquish, 122, 359
vantage, 197, 208
vapid, 120, 336
vapor, 336; -ize, 251
variance, 263
variegated, 355
varietal, 273
variety, 81, 273
varmint, 325
varsity, 235, 314, 325
vascular, 214
vassal, 404
vat, 206, 374
vaudeville, 149, 238, 340,
   376
vault, 23
vaunt, 237
vegetarian, 419
vehement, 390, 429
vehicle, 368, 376, 390
vehicular, 387
veil, 254
vein, 250, 254, 433
velar, 125
veldt, 340, 345, 445
velleity, 38, 115
vellum, 445
velocipede, 406
velocity, 114
venal, 125
veneer, 317
venerate, 432
venereal, 316
venial, 137
venom, 128
ventilate, 218
venue, 95
verdict, 366
verdure, 421
veritable, 310
verity, 452
vermicelli, 85, 412
vermil(l)ion, 441
vermin, 323, 325
vernacular, 214, 365
versatile, 152
verse, 42–44

verso, 283
vert, 42–44
vertigo, 282, 323
verve, 323
very, 311
vesicle, 402
vessel, 404
veteran, 347
veto, 260, 283, 348
vex, 371
viable, 376
viaduct, 273
vial, 374
vibrate, 106, 275; -ion, 331
vicar, 224, 365; -ious, 452
viceroy, 302
vicinity, 114, 406
vicious, 132, 136
vicissitude, 402, 406
victim, 366
victorious, 263, 313
victuals, 23
video, 282, 340
vie, 88, 95, 273; -ing, 157
view, 298, 300
vigil, 224, 419
vigor, 224, 353
vilify, 444
villain, 445
vinaigrette, 20
vine, 74, 141; -egar, 141, 432;
   -ery, -yard, 141
viola, 281
violate, 135
violence, 92
violin, 93, 174, 224; -ist, 174
viper, 336
virgin, 113, 324, 419; -ity, 113
virile, 152, 316
virtue, 291; -al, -osity, 415;
   -oso, 282, 324; -ous, 158
virulent, 316
visage, 128, 395
viscosity, 234, 365
viscount, 275, 361
visible, 131
vision, 132, 136, 410
visit, 120, 128, 395
visor, 396
visual, 422
vital, 348
vivacious, 376
vixen, 374

vizier, 136, 318, 393
vocabulary, 214, 330
vocal, 113, 116, 125; -ic, 116;
   -ity, 113
vocation, 137
vociferous, 169
vodka, 233, 340, 376
vogue, 95, 351
voice, 302
volcanic, 116
volcano, 116, 282, 362, 366
volley, 233
volt, 102
voluminosity, 114
volunteer, 234, 317
vomit, 120, 427; -urition,
   347
vortex, 313, 371
vouch, 306
vow, 304
vowel, 305
voyage, 302, 420
vulcanite, 154, 272
vulcanize, 376
vulgar, 101, 445
vulnerable, 244, 376, 445
vulpine, 153
vulture, 153, 416
vying. See vie

wad, 232; -ing, 341
waddle, 232, 342
wafer, 130, 382
waffle, 232, 384
wag, 214; -ed, 354
wagon, 353
waif, 382
waistcoat, 402
wait, 212; -ress, 252, 405,
   458
waive, 147, 253
wake, 357
Waldo, 204
walk, 239, 361
wall, 204, 443
wallet, 232, 443, 447
wallop, 232
wallow, 232, 285, 443
walnut, 204, 244
walrus, 405, 445
Walter, 23
waltz, 84, 239, 348, 397, 399
wampum, 232

wan, 232
wander, 232
wanton, 232
war, 204; -ior, 313, 453;
   -like, 272
warble, 325
ward, 313
warden, 313
warm, 313; -th, 385
warp, 313
warrant, 313
warren, 313
wart, 313
was, 82, 315, 323, 395
wash, 239
wasp, 239
wassail, 23
waste, 103
watch, 204, 232, 357, 413;
   -ful, 415
water, 232, 239; -iness, 58
watt, 232, 347; -s, 348
waver, 125
wax, 371
waylay, 252
we, 88, 261
weal, 99, 220; -th, 99, 219,
   220
weapon, 220, 336
wear, 311
weary, 317
weasel, 266
weather, 219
weave, 259, 266
wed, 212; -ed, -lock, 163;
   -ing, 341
wedge, 418
Wednesday, 23
wee, 88, 265
weevil, 266
weigh, 255; -t, 255, 345, 458
weir, 267, 318
weird, 267, 318, 340
weld, 340
welfare, 79, 101
welkin, 366
wellness, 79
were, 315, 323
wet, 206
wether, 108
wey, 255
whack, 388
whale, 23, 71, 388, 458

wham, 388
whang, 388
whangee, 388
wharf, 313, 375, 388; -s, 375
wharves. *See* wharf
what, 63, 388; -ever, 165
wheal, 388
wheat, 388
wheedle, 265, 388
wheel, 388, 458; -barrow,
    285
wheeze, 84, 266, 388, 393
whelk, 388
whelp, 388
when, -ce, 62–63, 388;
    -ever, 165
where, 62–63, 311, 388; -in,
    229; -withal, 443
wherry, 388
whet, 94, 388
whether, 108, 388
whew, 295, 388
whey, 255, 268, 388
which, 23, 63, 388, 414
whicker, 388
whidah. *See* whydah
whiff, 381, 388
whiffle, 388
while, 212, 388, 458; -om,
    -st, 388
whim, 388
whimbrel, 388
whimper, 388
whimsy, 388
whin, -stone, 388
whinchat, 388
whine, 388
whinny, 388
whip, 388, 458; -ster, -y, 163
whippoorwill, 443
whir(r), 324, 388, 451
whirl, 324, 388
whisk, 388; -er, 367, 388
whisk(e)y, 362, 367, 388
whisper, 388
whist, 388
whistle, 388, 400, 445
whit, 388, 458
Whitaker, 133
white, 107, 133, 348, 388;
    -ish, 272
whither, 62–63, 108, 388
whittle, 349, 389

whiz, 388, 392; -ed, -er, -es,
    -ing, 393
who, 63, 292, 387, 389; -m,
    292, 387; -se, 292, 387,
    395; -so, 282
whoa, 388
whole, 71, 212, 387–88, 389,
    458; -ly, 102, 387–88
whom. *See* who
whoop, -ing, 387; -ee, -er,
    -s, 388
whoosh, 388
whop, -er, 388
whore, 387–88, 389, 458
whorl, 323, 388, 458
whort, 388
whortleberry, 388
whose. *See* who
why, 63, 276, 388, 458; -s,
    87
whydah, whidah, 388
wicked, 368
wide, 98; -th, 98, 339, 340
widow, 133, 225, 226, 285,
    341
wield, 268, 445
wife, 375; -like, 272. *See
    also* wives
wiggle, 80, 355
wight, 102, 274
wigwam, 232
wild, 97, 102, 271, 275; -cat,
    15; -erness, 275, 405
wile, 212
wil(l)ful, 79, 441
willow, 285, 447
wind /wind/, 102, 275; -mill,
    275; -ow, 285
wind /wīnd/, 102, 275
windlass, 405
winkle, 436
winnow, 285
wire, -ed, 319
wisdom, 98, 226, 394, 395,
    458
wise, 98, 226
wish, 226; -ed, 163; -ful, 149
wistiti, 86
witch, 414
with, 386; -al, 239, 443
withe, 147
wither, 108
witty, 173; -cism, 173, 349

wive, 375
wives, 375
wiz, -es, 394
wizard, 225, 226, 394
wizen, 225, 226, 394
wobble, 233, 333
woe, 88, 281; -begone, 352
wold, 102
wolf, 243, 375; -fish, 383
wolves, 243, 375
woman, 228, 243, 373
womb, 102, 292, 424
women, 228
won, 246, 432
wonder, 246, 340
woo, 289
wood, 242; -en, 458
woof, 242, 382
wool, 242; -en, 441
wootz, 84, 399
woozy, 393
word, 36, 322, 323, 454
wore, 323
work, 454
world, 323, 340, 445, 453,
    454
worm, 323, 454
worn, 323
worry, 323, 454; -some, 58
worse, 323
worship, 166, 323; -able, -er,
    167
worst, 323
wort, 323
worth, 323, 386; -y, 386
would, 7, 8, 243, 339
wound /waúnd/, 306
wound /wūnd/, 294; -ed, 458
wow, 304, 456
wrack, 448
wraith, 448
wrangle, 214, 448
wrap, 448
wrath, 385, 448; -ful, 382
wreak, 357, 448
wreath, 386, 448
wreathe, 147, 266, 386, 448;
    -ing, -s, 155
wreck, 369, 448
wren, 218, 448
wrench, 448
wrest, 448
wrestle, 400, 404, 448

wretch, 357, 413, 448; -ed, 101
wriggle, 355, 448
wright, 102, 274, 345
wring, 448; -er, 437
wrinkle, 448
wrist, 448
write, 109, 212, 448
writhe, 109–10, 147, 386, 448; -en, 109–10; -ingly, 109
written, 109, 447, 448
wrong, 212, 448
wrote, 281, 448
wroth, 239, 448
wrought, 240, 345, 448
wrung, 437
wry, 276, 448

Xmas, 209, 428
xylophone, 391

yacht, 232, 346, 459; -ing, 163
ya(c)k, 93, 356, 363; -ed, -ing, 356
yank, 363
yap, 214
yard, 84, 459
yareta. See llareta
yataghan, 352
yawn, 237, 459
yclept, 84
yea, 256

year, 84, 212, 317; -ly, 456
yearn, 325, 459
yeast, 265, 459
yell, 442
yellow, 285, 447, 459; -wood, 456
yeoman, 221, 287
yes, 23, 82, 94, 401; -ed, -es, -ing, 403
yesterday, 23, 459
yet, 61, 206
yew, 295
yield, 258, 268, 459
ylang-ylang, 84
yodel, 123, 126, 149, 166, 459; -er, 167
yogi, 354
yoicks, 368
yoke, 107
yokel, 126
yolk, 102, 361
yore, 313
you, 293, 294; -r, 294, 315, 321; -rs, 82–83
young, 84, 248, 437; -ster, 303
youth, 293, 294, 459
yowl, 211, 212, 305
ytterbia, 84
ytterbium, 84
yttria, 84
yttric, 84
yttrium, 84

yucca, 101, 356, 459
yule, 459
yummy, 244

zany, 126, 393
zealot, 220, 445
zebra, 36, 55, 106, 393; -s, 55
zebu, 393
zee, 88
zenith, 260, 385, 393
zephyr, 111, 379
zero, 282, 316, 452
zest, 101, 218
zeta, 125
zigzag, 393
zinc, 101, 364, 393, 430, 436
zinnia, 393
zip, 202, 206; -er, 337
zither, 108
zloty, 445
zodiac, 92, 136, 364
zombi, 233
zone, 107, 393
zoo, 289, 393; -gamete, 260; -ological, 234, 281; -ophyte, 92, 101
zoogler, 445
zucchini, 85, 358
zygoid, 352
zygote, 276, 354, 393
zymurgy, 276, 324

General Index

In addition to regular topics and authors, this index lists references to sounds (enclosed in virgules), letters and spellings (italicized), bound elements (prefixes, bound bases, suffixes) and particles (also all italicized). It also lists sets that contain at least one bound form (the bound form being cited first). Alphabetically, short sounds come first (for instance, /a/), followed in order by short sounds with diacritics (/ä/), long sounds (/ā/), letters (a), and bound elements in the order bases, prefixes (a-), suffixes (-a), and particles. Schwa, /ə/, is alphabetized after /ē/ and before e.

For æ (ash), ð (edh), þ (thorn), ƿ (wen), and ȝ (yogh), see Runes. For IPA equivalents of the sound symbols used here, see pages xxxi–xxxii. For the IPA vowel sounds ɒ, a, ɑ, ɔ, and ö, see pages 204–5.

/a/, 203, 213, 231; = a, 214–15; = ah, 216; = ai, 215, 216; = au, 215–16; history of, 213; shortened VCV and, 214–15; spellings of, 214–16; VC# and, 214; VCC and, 214

/ä/, 203, 204–6, 213, 231; = a, 232–33; = ah, 235; = e, 235; = o, 233–35; = ow, 235; shortened VCV and, 234–35; spellings of, 232–35; v and, 234; VC# and, 233, 234; VCC and, 233. See also /ö/

/ā/, 53, 203; = a, 251–52; = ae, 257; = ai, 252–54; = aigh, 255; = ao, 257; = au, 257; = ay, 252–54; = e, 256; = ea, 256; = ee, 256; = ei, 254–55; = eigh, 255; = et, 256; = ey, 254, 255; history of, 249–51; persistent, 103–4; spellings of, 251–57; VCC and, 103–4; in VClV and VCrV, 251–52; VCV and, 251, 253–54; V.V and, 252, 254

a, 136–37, 207, 211, 212. See also /a/; /ä/; /ā/; /ö/

a- (assimilation of ab-), 196, 197

a- (assimilation of ad-), 190–91

a- (Old English), 111, 192

a- (privative), 110, 191

-a, 64

aa, 81

Aarsleff, Hans, 97

ab-, 70, 177, 191, 196–97

-abil+, 46–47

-able, 40, 46–47, 156–57, 273

abs-, 196

ac-, 188–89, 356, 360, 372

-ac, 364

Accepted spellings, 27–29

Accessibility, 29, 32, 37, 49, 50–52, 124–25, 212

acci+. See [acu+, acci+]

-aceae, 270

-acean, 251, 412

-aceous, 251, 412

-acious, 251

[acu+, acci+], 192

ad-, 44–45, 50–51, 77–78, 177, 183, 188–93, 332, 336, 349, 354, 356, 360, 372, 383, 404, 418, 433, 446, 453

Adaption, and adoption, 17–20. *See also*
    Folk etymology; Integration; Periphery
    vs. center
Addition. *See* Duplicative addition; Simple
    addition
ae, 94. *See also* /ā/; /e/; /ē/
-ae, 269
aegi-, 270
aego-, 270
aer. See /âr/
af-, 188, 383
Affricates, 407, 421. *See also* /ch/; /j/
ag-, 188, 354
-age, 232, 420
agh. See /ē/
ah. See /a/; /ä/; /ē/
ai. See /a/; /ā/; /e/; /ī/
aigh. See /ā/
air. See /âr/
-aire, 6
Akmajian, Adrian, et al., 338
al-, 188, 446
-al, 15, 34, 59, 138
Albrow, K. H., xxv, 4, 17
all, word-final, in monosyllables, 442–43
Alphabet, 207–9. *See also* Consonant
    letters; Runes; Vowel letters
American Heritage Word Frequency Book,
    xxviii
an- (assimilation of *ad-*), 188, 433
ana-, 64
Analogy, 10–12, 25, 50–51, 83, 104, 109, 139–
    41, 150, 153, 159–60, 180, 181, 184, 187,
    190, 191–92, 210, 225, 226, 274, 275, 360,
    370, 387, 444, 446. *See also* Conservative
    analogy
-ance, 434
-ancy, 434
Anderson, John. *See* Lass, Roger
-ane, 251
ann+, 432
-ant, 434
antenn+, 432
anti-, 262, 263
Antiadaption. *See* Dis-integration
ao. See /ā/; /au̇/
aou. See /au̇/
ap-, 188, 336
/âr/ field, 27, 204, 454; = *aer,* 311; = *air,*
    311; = *ar,* 308–9, 311; = *arr,* 309–10;
    = *ear,* 311; = *eir,* 311; = *er,* 310–11;
    = *err,* 310; spellings of, 308–11; = *ur,*
    311

ar. See /âr/; /ôr/
ar-, 188, 453
arch+, 357
+arch, 64, 357
archa+, 357
-ard, 394
Aristotle, 16
Aronoff, Mark, xxvi, 51, 54, 56
arr. See /âr/
[*arr+, err*], 192
Artin, Edward, 205
-ary, 262, 263
as- (assimilation of *ad-*), 188, 404
as- (assimilation of *ex-*), 404
Ash. *See* Runes
Ashby, W. Ross, 9
Assimilation, 44–45, 49, 50–51, 57, 73, 75,
    100, 177–98; /b/ and, 332; /d/ and, 341; /f/
    and, 383; full, 178, 181, 182, 183–84, 185,
    186, 188, 193, 195, 198, 328, 332, 336, 341,
    354, 356, 372, 383, 397–98, 404, 428, 433,
    446, 453; /g/ and, 354; /k/ and, 356, 360;
    /l/ and, 442, 446; /m/ and, 428; /n/ and,
    433; /p/ and, 336; partial, 178, 179, 182,
    184, 185, 186, 189–91, 193–94, 195–97, 198;
    /r/ and, 450, 453; /s/ and, 400, 404; /t/
    and, 349; /z/ and, 393. *See also* *ab-; ad-;*
    com-; dis-; en-; ex-; in-; ob-; sub-; syn-
-ast, 64
at-, 188, 349
-ate, 15, 151–52, 251
-atic, 116
-ation, 34, 119, 251
-ative, 251
[*att+, apt*], 192–93
/au̇/, 203, 301; = *ao,* 306; = *aou,* 306;
    = *au,* 306; = *aue,* 306; = *o,* 306; = *ou,*
    303, 305–6; = *ow,* 303–5; spellings of,
    303–6
au. See /a/; /ā/; /au̇/; /ȯ/; /ō/
aue. See /au̇/
aur. See /ôr/
aw, 212. *See also* /ȯ/
ay. See /ā/; /e/; /ē/; /ī/

/b/, 206, 327; = *b,* 328–31, 333; = *bb,* 327–
    30, 332–33; = *bd,* 339; in clusters and
    concatenations, 329, 331; at complex
    boundaries, 328, 329, 332; after long
    vowels, 329, 331; = *pb,* 328; after
    reduced vowels, 329, 330, 333; after
    short vowels, 329–30, 332–33; shortening
    rules and, 329, 330; at simple bound-

aries, 329, 330; spellings of, 328–33; after vowel digraphs, 329, 331
b, 207; silent, 328. *See also* /b/
Baker, R. G. *See* Smith, Philip
Ball, Alice Morton, 73
Bases, 32–33, 35; nonterminative, 82, 170–72
Bauer, Laurie, 112
Bazell, Charles, 207
bb, 76. *See also* /b/
bd, 328. *See also* /d/
bi-, 34
Bilabial stops, 178, 186, 327. *See also* /b/; /p/
Bissex, G. L., 17
Black, Max, 10
Bloomfield, Leonard, 16
Bolinger, Dwight, 17, 23
Bound elements, 32–33, 36
Boundaries, in explication, 56–63. *See also* Complex boundaries; Simple boundaries; Syllables
Bowman, Wayne, 25
Bradley, Henry, 17, 42
Brengelman, Fred, 4, 8, 12, 20, 53, 103–4, 145, 146, 155, 171, 462
bt, 328. *See also* /t/
buccan +, 317
+ buke, 363
Bullokar, William, 3

c, 93, 207; soft and hard, 70, 146–47, 185–86, 355, 361–65, 370, 405. *See also* /ch/; /k/; /s/; /sh/
caffe +, 153
Campbell, A., 97, 207, 208
[*cancell +*, *cancel*], 171
cata-, 65
Caxton, William, 209–10, 352, 408, 417
cc, 76, 397. *See also* /ch/; /k/
cch. *See* /k/
Cedilla, 405
+ ceit, 267
[*+ ceive*, *+ cept*], 44–45, 56, 267
+ cess, 402
/ch/, 206, 209, 407; = *c*, 412; = *cc*, 412; = *ch*, 71, 412–15; in clusters and concatenations, 413, 414–15; palatalized spelling of, 412, 415–17; after reduced vowels, 413, 415; = *s*, 412; vs. /sh/, 410–11, 412, 415–16; after short vowels, 413–14, 415; shortening rules and, 413, 414; at simple boundaries, 413–14; spell-

ings of, 412–17; = *t*, 412, 415–17; = *tch*, 412–14, 415; = *tsch*, 412; after vowel digraphs, 413, 415
ch, 71, 110, 212. *See also* /ch/; /k/; /sh/
[*chancell +*, *chancel*], 171
Chancery English, 14
Chaucer, Geoffrey, 13, 14
Chaytor, H. J., 21
Checked vowels. *See* Vowel sounds
chlor +, 358
chm. *See* /m/
Chomsky, Carol, xxv, 4
Chomsky, Noam, and Morris Halle, xxv, 4, 30, 52, 131, 211, 409
chor +, 358
+ chron, 358
chrys +, 358
cht. *See* /t/
chth. *See* /th/
ck, 9, 72, 76, 210. *See also* /k/
Clanchy, M. T., 21
Clipping, 36, 61, 282
Closed syllables. *See* Vowel lengthening and shortening
cn. *See* /n/
co-, 178, 179
Code, in orthography: and environment, 5–9; and performance, 4–9, 22, 139
Coelements. *See* Sets and coforms
Coforms. *See* Sets and coforms
col-, 177, 178, 446
com-, 28, 34, 177, 178–81, 311, 428, 433, 446, 453
Complex boundaries, 329. *See also* Assimilation; Duplicative addition; Twinning Rule; *and individual consonant sounds*
Complex long *u*. *See* /yū/
Complex words, 12, 86–87
Compound words, 12, 56–57, 73, 75, 80, 87, 164–65, 332, 336, 341, 349, 354, 383, 428, 453
con-, 177, 178, 179, 181, 433
Concatenations. *See* Consonant concatenations
Connate groups, 45–46
Conservative analogy, 11–12, 75, 80, 96, 104, 112, 118, 121, 122, 124, 135–36, 139–41, 155, 159–60, 162, 173, 174, 194, 220, 276, 278, 353, 411, 425, 429, 431; Third Syllable Rule and, 139–41; twinning and, 173. *See also* Analogy
Consonant clusters, 71, 72, 74–75, 210; cumulations, 72; doublet equivalents, 72;

Consonant clusters (*cont'd*)
  doublets, 72, 76–77, 210, 363; simplifications, 55, 72; tight, 74, 331, 336, 340,
  348, 353, 362–63, 366–67, 370–72, 382,
  385–86, 402, 406, 414–15, 419, 427–28,
  433, 445, 452–53. *See also* Doublet constraint; Final doublet constraints; Initial
  Doublet Rule; Mixed Voicing Rule;
  Triplet Rule
Consonant concatenations, 71, 73, 75–76,
  210. *See also* Doublet constraint; Mixed
  Voicing Rule; Triplet Rule
Consonant digraphs, 71–72, 163, 209–10
Consonant letters, 210–12. *See also* Alpha-
  bet; Consonant digraphs
Consonant sequence rules, 71–80, 89
Consonant sounds, American English, 206,
  210–12; voiceless vs. voiced, 73–74; vs.
  vowel sounds (*see* Vowel sounds)
Content. *See* Meaning and content
Continental *i*, 91, 104, 152, 262, 271
Contractions, 373
Convergence, 48, 149, 153, 159–60, 192, 194,
  222, 249–51, 258–59, 280–81, 285, 308,
  321–26, 350, 355–56, 431, 444, 446. *See
  also* Analogy; Mixed convergence; /ur/
  convergence
Cooper, Christopher, 145
Coote, Edmund, 145
cor-, 177, 178, 311, 453
[*corall +, coral*], 171
Correctness, 25–26, 27–29
Correspondences, sound and spelling, 10,
  14–17, 22–24, 26–27, 31. *See also individual sounds*
coun-, 179
cq. See /k/
cqu. See /k/
Craigie, William, 14, 20, 87
crotch +, 414
[*crumm +, crumb*], 424
[*crystall +, crystal*], 171
cs. See /ks/; /s/
ct, 72. *See also* /t/
cten +, 345
Cumulations. *See* Consonant clusters
[*curr +, +cur*], 172

/d/, 206, 327–28, 337–38; = *bd*, 339; = *d*,
  327–28, 337, 339–41, 342; = *dd*, 327–28,
  337, 341–42; = *ddh*, 339; = *dh*, 339; =
  ed, 338; = *ld*, 338–39; in clusters and
  concatenations, 340; at complex boundaries, 341; after long vowels, 341; after
  reduced vowels, 342; after short vowels,
  340, 341–42; shortening rules and, 340; at
  simple boundaries, 339–40; spellings of,
  338–42; after vowel digraphs, 340
d, 207; flapped, 338. *See also* /d/; /j/
Daneš, Frantisek, 6
[*dazz +, daze*], 150
dd, 76. *See also* /d/
ddh. See /d/
de-, 15, 194, 262
Demands, in orthography, 4, 5–9, 12–13,
  29–31, 51, 162, 461–62
demi-, 263
Dental stops, 327. *See also* /d/; /t/
Dentals, before /ù/ and /yù/, 299
Derivational suffixes. *See* Suffixes
De-stressing. *See* Stress
Dewey, Godfrey, xxviii–xxix
dg, 72, 210. *See also* /j/
dge, 76. *See also dg*
dh. See /d/
di- (assimilation of *dis-*), 193–94
Dialects, 13–14, 23–24, 40, 201–3
dif-, 193, 383
Digraphs. *See* Consonant digraphs; *and
  individual vowel digraphs and individual
  consonants*
Diphthongs, 53, 250, 301–6
dis-, 78, 177, 193–94, 383
Dis-integration, in orthography, 17–18, 20,
  103, 334. *See also* Integration
Dissimilation, 334; and lost /r/'s, 449
Distribution rules, 82–87. *See also* Final *s*
  Rule; Final *z* Rule; Short Word Rule;
  y-to-*i* tactics
Disyllables, iambic and trochaic, 123–24
Dixon, Robert, 4
dj. See /j/
Dobson, E. J., xxix, 204, 213, 217, 219, 220,
  221, 222, 228, 229, 230, 235, 239, 240,
  241, 243, 307, 322, 339, 351, 360, 376,
  380, 381, 388, 389, 399, 410, 417, 424, 425,
  426, 430, 435, 440, 457, 458
Dolby, J. L., and H. L. Resnikoff, 123, 316,
  451
Doublet consonants. *See* Consonant clusters
Doublet constraint, in consonant clusters
  and concatenations, 77–79, 180–81, 184,
  189, 194, 331, 340, 348, 354. *See also*
  Mixed Voicing Rule
Doublet equivalents. *See* Consonant
  clusters

dt. See /t/

[*duell +, duel*], 172

Duplicative addition, 100, 328, 332, 336, 341, 349, 354, 383, 393, 400, 403, 428, 433–34, 442, 446, 450, 453

dvi +, 340

/dw/, 74

dwo + (Indo-European root), 346

/dz/, 74

/dzh/, 407, 421

/e/, 203; = *ae,* 221; = *ai,* 220; = *ay,* 220; = *e,* 217–19; = *ea,* 219–20; = *ei,* 220–21; = *eo,* 221; history of, 217, 219, 220–21; = *ie,* 220; shortened VCV and, 218–19; spellings of, 217–21; = *u,* 221; VC# and, 218; VCC and, 217–18; word-final, 220

/ē/, 203, 211; = *ae,* 268–70; = *agh,* 270; = *ah,* 270; = *ay,* 270; = *e,* 260–62; = *ea,* 264–67; = *ee,* 264–67; = *ei,* 267–68; = *eo,* 270; = *ey,* 268; history of, 258–59; = *i,* 91, 104, 152, 262–64; vs. /i/, 91; = *ie,* 267–68; = *oe,* 268–70; spellings of, 260–70; VC# and, 261, 264; VCC and, 262, 264; VCrV and, 261; VCV and, 260, 263, 264; V.V and, 260–61, 262, 263, 264; = *y,* 262

/ə/ (schwa), 149–51, 152, 153, 203; /i/ and, 222–23; vs. /u/, 242

/əl/: = *ile,* 152; = *le,* 149–51

e, 136–37, 207, 211, 212. *See also* /ä/; /ā/; /e/; /ē/; /i/; /y/

e- (assimilated form of *ex-*), 181, 182

e + (initial particle), 48–49

ea. See /ā/; /e/; /ē/; /i/

-ean, 260

ear. See /âr/; /êr/; /ôr/; /ur/

eau. See /ō/; /yū/

ec-, 182, 368, 372

Ecriture, 22

-ed (noun suffix), 40

-ed (verb suffix), 7, 33, 34, 40, 61, 166, 338, 343

Edh. *See* Runes

ee, 81, 94, 157–58. *See also* /ā/; /ē/; /i/

-ee, 94

eer. See /êr/

-eer, 317, 318

ef-, 181, 383

-efy, 276

ei. See /ā/; /ē/; /i/; /ī/

eigh. See /ā/

eir. See /âr/

Element boundaries. *See* Boundaries; Complex boundaries; Merging

Elements, 32–39; bound, 32–33, 36; free, 32–33, 36; vs. morphemes, 33; nonterminative, 32–33, 37–39, 46–47, 170–72; syllables and, 59–60; terminative, 32–33, 37–39. *See also* Bases; Particles; Prefixes; Sets and coforms; Suffixes

em-, 187–88

Emery, Donald, 25, 27, 166, 168, 440, 441, 450

en-, 177, 187–88

-ence, 49, 59, 434

-ency, 434

English alphabet. *See* Alphabet

enn +, 432

-ent, 59, 434

Environment, and code, in orthography, 5–9

eo. See /e/; /ē/; /ō/

-eous, 260

/êr/ field, 204, 315, 454; = *aer,* 318; = *ear,* 313, 317; = *eer,* 313, 317; = *eir,* 318; = *er,* 316; = *ier,* 313, 318; = *ir,* 316, 318; = *irr,* 316; spellings of, 316–18; = *yr,* 318

er. See /âr/; /êr/; /ur/

-er (agent suffix), 40, 54, 60, 166, 171, 318. *See also -our*

-er (comparative), 34, 60, 167

err. See /âr/

-ery, 141

-es. See [*-s, -es*]

-esce, 398

-ess, 405

-est, 34, 167

et. See /ā/

-et, 347

-etic, 116

-ette, 347, 348

-ety, 81, 273

Etymological analysis. *See* Explication

Etymological demand, 12–13, 17–20, 47, 51, 461, 462

eu, 459. *See also* /òi/; /ū/; /yū/

-eum, 260

Euphonic *e*. See *e +*

eur. See /ur/; /ùr/; /yùr/

Evans, John, 145

ew, 212. *See also* /ō/; /ū/; /yū/

ex-, 49, 177, 181–83, 192, 368, 372, 383, 390, 404

[*excell +, excel*], 171

Explicata, immediate vs. mediate, 44–45

Explication, 28, 32–66, 462; accessibility
in, 32, 37, 51–52; boundaries in, 56–63;
elements in, 32–33; vs. etymological
analysis, 50–51; vs. generative grammar,
51–52; mediate and immediate explicata,
44–45; particles in, 33, 47–49; vs. phonological analysis, 52–55; primes in, 36–
37; processes in, 32; semantic relationships in, 55–56; sets and, 39–47; spelling
act and, 49–50; summarized, 66
extra-, 371
ey. See /ā/; /ē/; /ī/

/f/, 180, 206, 374–75; in clusters and
concatenations, 378–80, 382; at complex
boundaries, 380, 383; = f, 377–78, 380,
381–82, 384; = ff, 377, 380, 381, 383–84;
= ft, 378, 380; = gh, 274, 378, 379–80;
history of, 377–78; = lf, 72, 378, 380;
after long vowels, 380, 382; = ph, 20,
210, 377–79; = pph, 379; after reduced
vowels, 380, 384; after short vowels,
380–81, 382–84; shortening rules and,
380, 382; at simple boundaries, 378–79,
380, 381; spellings of, 378–84; vs. /v/,
374–75; after vowel digraphs, 380, 382;
word-final, 380, 381
f, 93, 207. See also /f/; /v/
fac+, 46
far+, 46
feas+, 46
+fect, 46
Feedback, positive and negative, 5–9, 22,
40
+feit, 46, 229
+fer, 56, 168–70, 323
fet+, 46
fett+, 46
+fex, 46
ff, 76. See also /f/
ffe, 76, 381
fg, 75
[+fic, +fy], 46
+fice, 46
Final doublet constraints, 38, 76–77
Final e, 145–60; deletion of, 26, 28, 38, 70,
154–60; fossil, 148–54, 253–54, 381, 401,
415, 431, 432, 444; functions of, 96–97,
103–4, 145–54; history of, 99, 103–4;
insulating, 147–48, 238, 253, 290, 394–95;
long vowels and (see VCV); soft c and g
and, 70, 146–47, 155–56, 238, 406; Short
Word Rule and, 88–89, 148; in VCV, 145,

148–49, 151–54; in Ve#, 145; voiced th
and, 147, 386; in word-final le, 149–51
Final s Rule, 82–83, 148
Final z Rule, 83–84, 148, 392
Fisher, John, 14, 207
+fit, 46
/fl/, 74
[flamm+, flame], 427
Flap Rule, 338
Flapped d, 338
Flapped t, 342–43
[flocc+, flock], 172
fluor+, 321
Folk etymology, 18–19, 51, 60, 192, 274,
343, 387, 429
Fossils: n's in French adoptions, 6–7. See
also Final e
Fowler, H. W., 268–69, 390
/fr/, 74
Free elements. See Elements
Free vowels. See Vowel sounds
French fossil e's. See Final e
Fricatives, before /ū/, 298. See also Palatal
sibilants; Simple fricatives
Front stops, 327–49. See also /b/; /d/; /p/;
/t/
ft, 74. See also /f/
/fth/, 334
-ful(l), 77, 79, 243, 383, 441
Full assimilation. See Assimilation
+fy. See [+fic, +fy]

/g/, 206, 207, 350; = ckg, 352; in clusters
and concatenations, 353–54; at complex
boundaries, 354; = g, 350, 352–54, 355,
436; = gg, 350, 351, 352, 354–55; = gh,
209–10, 350, 352; = gu, 350–51; before
le, 355; after long vowels, 354; after
reduced vowels, 355; after short vowels,
353, 354–55; shortening rules and, 353;
at simple boundaries, 352; spellings of,
350–55; = tg, 352; after vowel digraphs,
354; = x, 350, 351–52
g, 207; soft and hard, 146–47, 350–51, 353,
417. See also /g/; /j/; /zh/
Gelb, I. J., 207
[gemm+, gem], 171
Generative grammar. See Explication
geo-, 260
Gestalt psychology, 29–30, 31, 461
gg, 72, 76, 351, 417–18. See also /g/;
/j/
gh, 71, 102, 111, 209–10, 212, 239–40,

247–48, 255, 271, 274, 286, 294, 345–46, 352, 378. *See also* /ā/; /ē/; /f/; /g/; /ī/; /k/; /ō/; /t/; Velar fricative

ght, 102, 237, 239–40, 274. *See also* /t/

Glides, 411, 415, 416, 431, 457, 459–60

[*glott+*, *+glot*], 171

gm. See /m/

gn, 15, 20, 72, 103, 180, 275, 299. *See also* /n/

Goody, Jack, 17, 22, 462

Gould, Stephen Jay, 7–8

[*gramm+*, *gram*], 174, 427

Grammatical content. *See* Meaning and content

Graphemes, 207

Graphotactics, 69. *See also* Tactics and tactical rules

Great Vowel Shift, 213, 219, 247, 249, 256, 259, 271, 280, 288, 292

Grimm, Jacob, 97

gu, 350–51

Gumb, Raymond, 10

/gw/, = *gu*, 351, 457

[*gymn+*, *gymnasi+*, *gym*], 63–64

/gz/, = *x*, 74, 351–52, 370

/h/, 23, 206; *a* vs. *an* before, 390; in clusters, 386; = *h*, 386–87, 388–89; spellings of, 386–90; = *wh*, 71–72, 387–88, 389. *See also* /hw/

h, 62, 178, 207, 211, 212, 343–44, 389–90. *See also* /h/; /hw/

Haas, W., 207

Halle, Morris. *See* Chomsky, Noam

Hanna, Paul R., Jean S. Hanna, R. E. Hodges, and Erwin H. Rudorf, Jr., xxviii, 4, 214, 217, 223, 231, 241, 244, 251, 260, 272, 281, 284, 289, 299, 302, 303, 316, 327, 328, 337, 342, 350, 356, 376, 380, 384, 386, 391, 396, 397, 400, 405, 407, 412, 417, 426, 429, 437, 439, 447–48, 456

Hard *c*. See *c*

Hard *g*. See *g*

Hart, John, 3

hatch+, 414

Havelock, Eric, 17, 461, 462

Head vowels, 90

Heller, Louis, and James Macris, 23

hier+, 319

High short *o. See* /ȯ/

High short *u. See* /u̇/

Hodges, Richard (17th c.), 104

Hodges, Richard (20th c.), 4. *See also* Hanna

Holdouts, 4, 10, 30–31; to /a/ = *a* correspondence, 215–16; to assimilation of *ad-*, 189–91; to assimilation of *com-*, 180–81; to assimilation of *ex-*, 182; to assimilation of *syn-*, 198; to doublet constraint, 78–80; to final *e* deletion, 156–57, 158–59; to Final *s* Rule, 82–83; to Final *z* Rule, 84; to Initial Doublet Rule, 76; to Mixed Voicing Rule, 75–76; to *oi* vs. *oy* distribution, 302–3; to Short Word Rule, 89; to soft *g*, 146–47; to Stress Frontshift Rule, 129–30; to Suffix *-ic* Rule, 116–18; to Suffix *-id* Rule, 120–21; to Suffix *-ion* Rule, 119; to Suffix *-ish²* Rule, 122; to Suffix *-it* Rule, 120; to Suffix *-ity* Rule, 114; to Suffix *-ule* Rule, 122; to Third Syllable Rule, 134–38; to Twinning Rule, 174–76; to VC# pattern, 94; to VCC pattern, 101–7; to VC*le*# pattern, 105–6; to VCV pattern, 107–8, 112, 127–30; to V.V pattern, 93; to *y*-to-*i* tactics, 84, 86–87

Holmberg, Borje, 213

homeo-, 260

-hood, 242

[*horr+*, *+hor*], 172

Householder, Fred, 11, 17, 23

hu, = /w/, 456

Hultzen, Lee, 72

/hw/, 23, 458; = *wh*, 71–72, 388–89

hydr+, 47–48

Hyphens, 77, 78, 165, 179, 383

/i/, 203; = *a*, 151–52; = *ai*, 279; = *e*, 222, 228; = *ea*, 229; = *ee*, 229; = *ei*, 229; history of, 222; = *i*, 152–53, 154, 222, 223–26; = *ie*, 229; = *o*, 228; in shortened VCV, 224–25, 227; spellings of, 223–30; stressed and unstressed, 151–53, 154, 222–23; = *u*, 228–29; = *ui*, 229–30; *v* and, 224; in VC#, 224, 227; in VCC, 223, 226–27; = *y*, 84–85, 222, 226–27

/ī/, 203; = *ai*, 279; = *ay*, 279; = *ei*, 278; = *eigh*, 278; = *ey*, 279; history of, 271–72; = *i*, 152–53, 154, 272–76; = *ie*, 278; = *oy*, 279; spellings of, 272–79; = *uy*, 279; in VCC, 271, 275, 277–78; in VC*l*V and VC*r*V, 274–75, 277; in VCV, 272, 276–77; in V*e*#, 273; in V.V, 272–73, 277; = *y*, 85, 276–78

i, 16, 20, 118–19, 136, 207, 208, 459–60; *j* and, 207, 208, 417; before suffixes, 47, 57–59, 132; vowel and consonant, 208; *y* and, 58, 84–87, 207, 208, 271–72. *See also* Continental *i; /e/; /i/; /ī/; /y/; y-to-i* tactics
-i, 81, 273
+ i + (particle), 47–48, 57–59, 86–87
-ia, 137–38, 263
-ial, 43
Iambic disyllables. *See* VCV
-ian, 263
*i-*before-*e* pattern, 220, 229, 267
[*-ible, -ibil +*], 47. See also *-able*
-ic, 34, 65, 115–18, 127, 161, 172–73, 174, 215, 218, 220, 224, 227, 234, 330, 335–36, 340, 347, 353, 364, 365, 366, 382, 419, 427, 432–33, 444–45, 452
-ical, 366
-ication, 366
-icose, 366
-ics, 372
-id, 219, 330, 335–36, 347, 353, 365, 419, 427, 444, 452
-idae, 121, 270
-ide, 272
ie, 95, 157. *See also /ē/; /i/; /ī/*
-ier, 318
ier. See /êr/
-ies, 375
ieu. See /yū/
iew. See /yū/
-iff, 373–74, 384
-ification, 366
-ify, 276
ii, 81–82
il-, 186, 446
-ile, 152, 272
Ill-formed spellings, 26–27
im-, 186, 428
Immediate explicata. *See* Explicata
in- (in), 177, 186–87, 191, 316, 428, 446, 453; *en-* and (see *en-*)
in- (not), 34, 177, 186–87, 316, 428, 446, 453
-ine, 152–53, 263, 272
-ineae, 270
Inflectional suffixes. *See* Suffixes
-ing, 34, 36, 40, 155, 166, 167, 437
Initial Doublet Rule, 20, 76
Initial particle. *See e +*
Insulating. *See* Final *e;* Final *s* Rule; Final *z* Rule; *u; v*
Integration, in orthography, 4, 5–9, 17–20, 40, 69–70, 81–82, 83, 85, 89, 100, 103, 126, 127–28, 129, 170–72, 190, 195–96, 231–32, 356, 361, 362, 367, 407–8, 422, 430. *See also* Dis-integration; Periphery vs. center
-ion, 28, 36, 39, 40, 41–42, 43, 44, 47, 118–19, 129, 132, 224, 262, 263, 347, 353, 365, 416, 419, 422, 432–33, 434, 460
[*-ionn +*], 47
-ior, 262, 263
-ious, 262, 263
-ique, 263
/īr/, 318–19; = *ier,* 319–20; = *ir,* 319; spellings of, 319–20; = *yr,* 319
ir. See /êr/; /īr/; /ur/
ir-, 186, 453
irr. See /êr/
-ise. See -ize
-ish[1] (forms adjs.), 121, 409
-ish[2] (forms verbs), 121–22, 173, 219, 409, 427, 432–33, 444, 452
-ism, 34, 395
-ist, 34, 64; *-st* coform of, 65
-it, 120, 219, 224, 330, 335–36, 340, 427, 452
-ite, 28, 154, 272
-ition, 119
-itis, 272
-ity, 34, 112–15, 133, 161, 173, 215, 218, 224, 234, 262, 340, 347, 353, 365, 377, 402, 427, 432–33, 444, 452, 460; *-ety* coform of, 81
-ium, 137–38, 264
-ive, 40, 373–74
-ization, 394
-ize, 34, 83, 87, 272; *-ise* coform of, 65, 83, 272; *-ze* coform of, 65

/j/, 47, 206, 208, 407; in clusters and concatenations, 418, 419, 420–21; = *d,* 407, 417–18, 420; = *dg,* 417–18, 420; = *dj,* 417–18; = *g,* 146–47, 417–18, 419–20, 421; = *gg,* 351, 417–18; history of, 417–18; = *j,* 417–18, 420–21; after long vowels, 418, 420; palatalized spelling of, 417–18, 420; after reduced vowels, 418, 420; after short vowels, 418, 419, 420; and shortening rules, 418; at simple boundaries, 418–19, 420–21; spellings of, 417–21; after vowel digraphs, 418, 420; /zh/ and, 146, 421–22
j, 93, 207, 208, 209, 417–18, 460. *See also* /j/; /zh/
Jespersen, Otto, xxix, 12, 23, 34, 87–88, 91, 97, 103, 104, 114, 131, 133, 135, 139, 180, 204, 213, 217, 219, 220, 221, 222, 228, 229, 230, 231, 232, 233, 234, 235, 237, 239, 240, 241, 243, 245, 246, 247, 249, 250,

256, 258, 259, 270, 274, 275, 277, 280, 281, 285, 289, 291, 292, 297, 301, 307, 319, 322, 325, 327, 339, 341, 343, 351, 355, 356, 360, 373, 376, 378, 380, 381, 385, 387, 388, 389, 391, 397, 399, 400, 409, 410, 411, 413, 417, 421, 424, 425, 426, 430, 435, 443
[*jogg* +, *jog*], 150
Johnson, Samuel, 279, 334, 369, 417
Jones, Daniel, 344
[+*journ*], 186
ju, = /w/, 456

/k/, 206, 207, 350, 436, 437, 438; = *c,* 355–56, 357, 361–62, 363–70, 398, 436; = *cc,* 356; = *cch,* 356, 358; = *ch,* 20, 49–50, 71, 355, 356–58, 436; = *ck,* 70, 356, 361–62, 368–70; in clusters and concatenations, 366–68; = *cq,* 360; = *cqu,* 360; = *gh,* 361; history of, 355–56; = *k,* 70, 355–56, 361–65, 366–68, 436; = *kg,* 361; = *kh,* 356, 361; = *kk,* 356; = *lk,* 356, 360–61; after long vowels, 361, 363; = *q,* 356, 358–59; = *qu,* 355, 356, 358, 359–60; after reduced vowels, 361, 364, 366, 369–70; = *sc,* 361; after short vowels, 361–62, 363, 365, 368–69; shortening rules and, 361, 365; spellings of, 356–72; word-final, 70; = *x,* 360
k, 207. *See also* /k/; *k*-insertion rule
k-insertion rule, 31, 47, 361–62, 368, 370
kal +, 363
Katz, David, 29
/kd/, 75
Kenyon, John, and Thomas Knott, 91, 204–5, 223, 262, 335, 388, 410, 416, 458–59
ker +, 363
Kerek, Andrew, 23
kg. See /k/
kh. See /k/
+*khana,* 64
Kim, Suksan, 97, 100
kk, 76. *See also* /k/
kl, 74
klept +, 363
Klima, Edward, 42
kn. See /n/
Knott, Thomas. *See* Kenyon, John
Koffka, Kurt, 29–30
Kohler, Wolfgang, 29
/kr/, 74
/ks/, 74, 370–72
/kt/, 74, 361, 366

Kurath, Hans, 53, 97, 205
/kw/, 10, 106–7, 355, 358–60, 457
kwi + (Indo-European root), 63
kwo + (Indo-European root), 63
kym +, 363
kyph +, 363

/l/, 79–80, 204, 206, 211, 212, 232, 233, 239, 241, 439; in clusters and concatenations, 442, 445; at complex boundaries, 166–68, 442, 446; = *l,* 439, 440–42, 444–46, 447; = *ll,* 170–71, 440–43, 445, 446–47; = *ln,* 439, 440; after long vowels, 442, 445–46; after reduced vowels, 442, 447; after short vowels, 441–43, 444–45, 447; shortening rules and, 442, 444–45; at simple boundaries, 170–71; = *sl,* 439–40; spellings of, 439–47; after vowel digraphs, 442, 445, 446; word-final, 38, 77, 166–68, 440–43, 444
l, 93, 101–2, 207, 439; vs. *ll* spellings, 166–68, 440–41. *See also* /l/; /r/
Labials, before /yù/, 297–98
Ladefoged, Peter, 74, 206
Langue, 22
Lass, Roger, xxvi; and John Anderson, 100
Laszlo, Ervin, 9
Lax vowels. *See* Vowel sounds
/lb/, 74
ld, 97, 98, 101–2, 258, 268, 271, 275, 280, 285. *See also* /d/
le#, 149–51. *See also* VC′C′*le*
[*leng* +, *long*], 437
-*less,* 77, 405, 446
-*let,* 34
Letters. *See* Alphabet
Levins, Peter, 145
Levitt, Jesse, 23
Lexical simplification, 61
lf, 72. *See also* /f/
-*like,* 77, 272
Linell, Per, 52
Linking *i* and *o* particles. *See* Particles
Linksz, Arthur, 270
Liquids, 74, 79–80, 211, 298, 348, 439–55. *See also* /l/; /r/
lk, 101–2. *See also* /k/
ll, 76, 77, 101–2, 170–71, 264, 459. *See also* /l/
lm, 101–2, 424–25
ln. See /l/
+*log(ue),* 351
Long *a. See* /ā/

Long consonants. *See* Old English
Long *e*. *See* /ē/
Long *i*. *See* /ī/
Long *o*. *See* /ō/
Long *u*: complex (*see* /yū/); simple (*see* /ū/)
Longest Common String. *See* Principle of
    Longest Common String
Low back vowels. *See* /ä/; /ò/; Vowel
    sounds
Low short *o*. *See* /ä/
Low short *u*. *See* /u/
lt, 101–2, 285
lv, 380. *See also* /v/
[*ly* +, *lyse*, +*lyte*], 64–65
-*ly*, 34, 36, 262, 446

/m/, 180, 206, 423; = *chm*, 426; in clusters
    and concatenations, 427–28; at complex
    boundaries, 428; before /f/, 180; = *gm*,
    423, 425–26; = *lm*, 423, 424–25; after
    long vowels, 428; = *m*, 423, 426–28, 429;
    = *mb*, 54–55, 72, 423–24; = *mh*, 426;
    = *mm*, 423, 426, 427, 428–29; = *mn*,
    423, 425; = *mp*, 426; after reduced
    vowels, 429; after short vowels, 427, 429;
    shortening rules and, 427; at simple
    boundaries, 426–27; = *sm*, 426; spell-
    ings of, 423–29; = *tm*, 426; before *v*, 180;
    after vowel digraphs, 428
m, 100, 207. *See also* /m/
mamm +, 427
[*mann* +, *man*], 432
Marchand, Hans, 34
mark +, 363
/mb/, 74
mb, 54–55, 72, 97, 98, 102, 271, 275, 280,
    328. *See also* /m/
McLuhan, Marshall, 21
Meaning and content, 35, 51, 55–56
[*medall* +, *medal*], 170
Mediate explicata. *See* Explicata
-*ment*, 79, 434
Merging, 55, 59–60, 61–63, 109, 236, 295,
    449
mess +, 402
[*metall* +, *metal*], 38, 39
Metathesis, 225, 389, 458–59
mh. *See* /m/
Miege, Guy, 145, 421
Minims, 108, 245–47
Minimum and maximum simplicities, in
    orthography, 29–30, 31
mis-, 79

[+*miss*, +*mit*], 39, 45–46, 56, 402
Mixed convergence, 196–97, 216, 221, 229,
    230, 270, 275, 334, 357, 358, 389, 449,
    457
Mixed Voicing Rule, 73–76, 193, 195,
    370–72
mm, 76. *See also* /m/
mn. *See* /m/; /n/
mon +, 49
Monaghan, E. J., 132
Morphemes, vs. elements, 33
Morphophones, 202–6, 307
Mossé, Fernand, 97, 100, 133, 207, 258, 271
mp. *See* /m/
mps, 72
Mulcaster, Richard, 3–4, 5, 8, 13–14, 17, 30,
    31, 103, 145, 203, 208–9, 463
myrmec +, 326

/n/, 206, 232, 423, 429; = *cn*, 431–32; in
    clusters and concatenations, 433; at
    complex boundaries, 15, 433–34; = *gn*,
    20, 72, 429, 430–31; = *kn*, 429–30; after
    long vowels, 430–31, 433; = *mn*, 429,
    431; = *n*, 429, 432–33, 434–35; = *ng*,
    432; = *nn*, 429, 433–35; = *pn*, 429, 431;
    after reduced vowels, 20, 28, 434–35;
    after short vowels, 432–33, 434; shorten-
    ing rules and, 432–33; at simple bound-
    aries, 432; spellings of, 429–35; after
    vowel digraphs, 433
n, 100, 207. *See also* /n/
Nasals, 74, 423–38. *See also* /m/; /n/; /ŋ/
/nd/, 74
nd, 97, 98, 102, 268, 271, 275
Negative feedback. *See* Feedback
neo-, 260
-*ness*, 79, 405, 433–34
Nessly, Larry, 52
neur +, 321
Newman, Stanley, 112
Ney, James, xxviii
/ŋ/ (eng), 10, 70, 206, 353, 423; history of,
    435; = *m*, 436; = *n*, 10, 435–37; = *ng*,
    10, 435, 437–38; spellings of, 436–38
ng, 353, 432. *See also* /ŋ/
/ŋg/, 74, 435
nn, 76. *See also* /n/
[*noi* +, +*noy*], 303
Nonterminative elements. *See* Elements
Nonterminative suffixes. *See* Suffixes
Norman scribes, 13–14, 108, 208–10, 355,
    358, 373, 383, 391, 408, 413, 457, 458

/ò/, 203, 231, 442–43; = a, 239; = au, 237–38; = aw, 236–37; before C#, 236–37; before CC, 236, 237; before CV, 236, 238; = o, 238–39; = oa, 240; = ou, 239–40; spellings of, 236–40. See also /ä/

/ō/, 203; = au, 281, 286; = eau, 281, 286; = eo, 287; = ew, 286–87; history of, 280–81; = o, 280–83; = oa, 280, 281, 284; = oh, 286; = oo, 286; = ou, 281, 285–86; = ough, 281, 286; = ow, 281, 284–85; spellings of, 281–87; VCC and, 101–2, 104, 283, 446; Ve# and, 281; VClV and, 283; VCV and, 281; V.V and, 281; word-final, 282–83

o, 207. See also /ä/; /aù/; /i/; /ò/; /ō/; +o+; /u/; /ù/

o- (assimilated form of ob-), 195, 196

+o+ (linking particle), 33, 47–48, 49

oa. See /ò/; /ō/

oar. See /ôr/

ob-, 177, 195–96, 336, 356, 372, 383

oc-, 195, 356, 372

-ock, 369–70

oe, 95, 158. See also /ē/; /ō/; /ū/

-oecia, 270

of-, 195, 383

og. See ogue

og-, 195

ogue, 238–39

oh. See /ō/

/òi/, 203; = eu, 303; = oi, 20, 302; = oy, 302; = uoy, 303; history of, 301; spellings of, 302–3

oi. See /òi/

-oid, 302

Old English: long consonants in, 97; Third Syllable Rule in, 133. See also Vowel lengthening and shortening

omni-, 34

O'Neill, Wayne, 205

Ong, Walter, 17, 461, 462

Onions, C. T., 19

oo, 299. See also /ō/; /u/; /ù/; /ū/

oor. See /ôr/; /ùr/

op-, 195, 336

Open syllables. See Vowel lengthening and shortening

/ôr/ field, 204, 454; = aor, 315; = ar, 313, 314; = arr, 313; = aur, 315; = ear, 315; = er, 315; = oar, 314; = oor, 315; = or, 311–13; = orr, 311–12; = our, 314–15; spellings of, 311–15; /wôr/ = war, 313

or. See /ôr/

-or, 54. See also -er

Orm, 97, 341, 381

orr. See /ôr/

Orthographic concepts, 52–55

-os+, 47

Oswalt, Robert, xxv, 4, 91, 96, 112, 131, 135, 140

ou, 81. See /aù/; /ò/; /ō/; /u/; /ù/; /ū/

ough. See /ō/; /ū/

our. See /ôr/; /ur/; /ùr/

-our, 54

-ous, 47, 59

ow, 81, 212, 303–5. See also /ä/; /aù/; /ō/

/p/, 201, 206, 327–28; = bp, 334–35; in clusters and concatenations, 336; at complex boundaries, 336–37; = gh, 334; after long vowels, 336; = p, 327–28, 333, 335–36, 337; = ph, 334; = pp, 327–28, 333–34, 335, 336–37; after reduced vowels, 337; after short vowels, 335–37; shortening rules and, 335–36; at simple boundaries, 335; spellings of, 333–37; after vowel digraphs, 336

p, 207, 425, 426. See also /p/

[+pair, pare], 26–27

Palatal sibilants, 407–22. See also /ch/; /j/; /sh/; /zh/

Palatalization, 23, 44, 47, 58, 407. See also /ch/; /j/; /sh/; /zh/

para-, 64

[parcell+, parcel], 171

Parole, 22

Parsons, Talcott, 9

Partial assimilation. See Assimilation

Particles, 32, 33, 47–49, 56–59; initial, 48–49; linking, 47–48, 234–35; nontactical, 47. See also Etymological demand; +i+; k-insertion rule; +o+; Palatalization; Phonetic demand; Twinning Rule

Partridge, Eric, 34, 48, 50, 149, 179, 195, 266, 437

Pattern and regularity, 4, 5–12, 14–20, 24, 25–26, 27–31, 32, 39–40, 41, 62–63, 69–70, 82–87, 91, 112, 123–24, 161–62, 168–70, 439, 440–41; subelemental and subsyllabic, 62–63. See also Rules and ruliness; Strings; Tactics and tactical rules; VCC; VCV; etc.

pb. See /b/

+peat, 57

[pencill+, pencil], 171

[penn+, pen], 171, 432

Pennant, 19
Penzl, Herbert, 355
Performance. *See* Code
Periphery vs. center, in orthography, 6–7, 17–20, 40, 81–82, 85, 100, 126, 127–28. *See also* Integration
Perrin, Porter, 179
Persistent long *u*. See /ū/
[*personn* +, *person*], 172, 174
+ *pete*, 28, 37, 38
ph, 71, 111, 210. *See also* /f/
+ *phile*, 379
+ *phobe*, 379
Phonemes, 11, 201–3, 207
Phonemic spelling, 3–4, 13–14, 201–3
Phones, 11, 201
Phonetic demand, 12–20, 47, 461–62
Phonetic spelling, 3–4, 13–14, 201–3
Phonotactics, 69. *See also* Tactics and tactical rules
phot +, 379
phth. *See* /t/; /th/
phys +, 379
[*pistill* +, *pistil*], 171
+ *piter*. *See* [+ *pter*, + *piter*]
pleur +, 321
[*plumm* +, *plumb*], 427
pn. *See* /n/
pneum +, 431
Position, in Latin, 99–100
Positive feedback. *See* Feedback
pp, 76. *See also* /p/
pph. *See* /f/
pre-, 262
Preemption, 12, 14–17, 113, 114, 115, 117, 120–21, 131–33, 134–38, 139–41, 155, 172–73, 174–75, 183, 291. *See also* Holdouts
Preferred regularity. *See* Principle of Preferred Regularity
Prefixes, 32–34, 35, 36, 48, 57, 105, 177–98
Primes, 36–37, 140–41
Principle of Preferred Regularity, 25–26, 147, 157, 166–67, 168, 170, 218, 441
Principle of Longest Common String, 57
Prins, A. A., xxix, 213, 217, 219, 220, 221, 222, 231, 233, 240, 245, 247, 250, 259, 271, 280, 285, 289, 297, 301, 307, 322, 327, 351, 373, 378, 385, 388, 409, 443
pro-, 36, 46
Processes and procedural rules, 9–10, 32. *See also* Assimilation; Final *e* deletion; Palatalization; Simple addition; Twinning Rule

ps. *See* /s/
psamm +, 399
pseud +, 399
psil +, 399
psor +, 399
psych +, 399
psychr +, 399
/pt/, 74
pt. *See* /t/
[+ *pter*, + *piter*], 19, 192
Pulgram, Ernst, 207

q, 207, 208, 356, 457. *See also* /k/; *qu*
qu, 10, 95, 106–7, 355, 356, 437, 457. *See also q*
questionn +, 174
Quirk, Randolph, et al., 34

/r/, 79–80, 204, 206, 211, 232, 439; in clusters and concatenations, 450, 452–53; at complex boundaries, 450, 453; = *l*, 449; after long vowels, 450, 453; = *r*, 447–48, 450–53, 454–55; after reduced vowels, 322, 451, 454–55; = *rh*, 20, 71–72, 76, 447, 448–49; = *rps*, 449; = *rr*, 447–48, 450–51, 452, 453–54; = *rrh*, 76, 449, 451; after short vowels, 450–52, 454; shortening rules and, 450, 451–52; spellings of, 447–55; after vowel digraphs, 450, 453; = *wr*, 447–48
r, 207. *See also* /r/
[*raill* +, *rail*], 172
Rapaport, Anatol, 9
Rask, R. K., 97
/r/-colored vowels, 307–26
re-, 33, 177, 262
'*re*, 315
Read, Charles, 32
Reduced vowels, xxvi, 83, 90–91, 168, 203; /i/ and, 222–23; vs. /u/, 241, 242. *See also individual consonant sounds*
Registers, 20, 38, 171, 197
Regularity, in orthography. *See* Pattern and regularity; Rules and ruliness
/rg/, 74
rh, 76, 212. *See also* /r/
Roberts, A. Hood, 72
Roman alphabet, 207–9
rps. *See* /r/
rr, 76. *See also* /r/
rrh, 76, 212. *See also* /r/
+ *rrhage*, 76
+ *rrhagia*, 76

+ *rrhagic*, 76
+ *rrhagy*, 76
+ *rrhaphy*, 76
+ *rrhea*, 76
+ *rrheuma*, 76
+ *rrhexis*, 76
+ *rrhinia*, 76
Rudorf, Erwin H., Jr. *See* Hanna
Rule of Syllabicity, 59–60, 65, 449
Rules and ruliness, 4, 9–10, 24, 25–26, 29–
31, 38, 42–44, 51–52, 56–59, 91, 112,
159–60, 161–62. *See also* Flap Rule; Processes and procedural rules; Rule of Syllabicity; Tactics and tactical rules
Runes, 209; ash (*æ*), 209, 213, 259; edh (*ð*),
209, 210, 384; ligature (*œ*), 258; thorn (*þ*),
209, 210, 384; wen (*ƿ*), 208, 209; yogh
(ȝ), 97, 209, 459–60
+ *rupt*, 61

/s/, 146, 201, 202, 206; = *c*, 146, 397, 400,
405–6; in clusters and concatenations,
16, 400, 402, 406; at complex boundaries, 400, 403–4; = *cs*, 400; history of,
397; after long vowels, 400, 403; = *ps*,
397, 399; after reduced vowels, 401, 404–
5; = *s*, 16, 397, 400–405; = *sc*, 397–98;
= *sch*, 397, 400; after short vowels, 400,
401, 402, 404; shortening rules and, 400,
402; at simple boundaries, 400, 401–2;
spellings of, 397–405; = *ss*, 397, 400–
402, 403–5; = *st*, 380, 397, 399–400;
= *sth*, 391, 397, 400; = *sw*, 397, 400;
after vowel digraphs, 400, 402–3; = *z*,
84, 397, 399
s, 93, 207, 208–9; word-final, and final *e*,
82, 148, 394–95, 401, 404–5. *See also* /s/;
/sh/; /z/; /zh/
[-*s*, -*es*], 15, 33, 34, 39, 40, 59–60, 75, 80,
82, 395
-*s'*, -'*s*, 34, 395
[*sacc* +, *sac*], 171, 356
saf +, 383
Šaljapina, Z., and V. Ševoroškin, xxvii
Samuels, Michael, 14, 23
Sapir, Edward, 16
[*satch* +, *sack*], 414
Saussure, Ferdinand de, 16, 22
sc. See /k/; /s/; /sh/
sch. See /s/; /sh/
schsch. See /sh/
Schwa. *See* Reduced vowels
sci +, 411–12

Scragg, D. G., 389
Scribes. *See* Norman scribes
se-, 262
Self-regulation and self-reorganization, 5–9,
31, 40, 461
Semantic content. *See* Meaning and
content
Semantic demand, 12–13, 14–17, 461–62
semi-, 262, 263
Semivowels, 74, 211, 456–60. *See also* /w/;
/y/
-*sen*, 302–3
Sets and coforms, 33, 38, 39–47, 58–59, 177,
462
/sh/, 44, 47, 206, 407; = *c*, 407, 409–10, 412;
= *ch*, 407–8; vs. /ch/, 410–11, 412, 415–
16; palatalized spellings of, 44, 407; = *s*,
407, 409–11; = *sc*, 407, 409–10, 411–12;
= *sch*, 407–8; = *schsch*, 408;
= *sh*, 407, 408–9; spellings of, 44, 407–
10; = *ss*, 407, 409–10, 411; = *t*, 407, 409–
10; = *x*, 407, 409–10; vs. /zh/, 410
sh, 71, 111, 210, 212. *See also* /sh/
Shakespeare, William, 21
-*ship*, 409
Short *a. See* /a/
Short *e. See* /e/
Short *i. See* /i/
Short *o*, 53, 203, 204–6, 231–40. *See also*
/ä/; /ò/
Short *u*, 53, 203, 204. *See also* /u/; /ù/
Short vowels. *See* Vowel sounds; *and
individual consonant and vowel sounds*
Short Word Rule, 76, 87–89, 148, 236, 276,
279, 340, 352, 401, 451
Shortening rules, 112. *See also* Stress
Frontshift Rule; Suffix rules; Third
Syllable Rule
Sibbald, 19
Sibilants. *See* Palatal sibilants
Silent final *e. See* Final *e*
Silent letters, 54–55, 328, 337–38, 343–46,
352, 389–90, 423–24
Silent reading, vs. reading aloud, 21–22
simil +, 177
Simple addition, 12, 65, 80, 100, 140, 155,
156, 157–58, 162–68, 170–72, 174–75, 178,
180, 182, 183, 185–87, 189, 190, 193, 194,
195, 196, 197, 198, 229, 260–61, 262, 273,
281, 398, 418. *See also* Duplicative
addition
Simple boundaries, 56–59, 329. *See also
individual consonant sounds*

Simple fricatives, 373–406. *See also* /f/; /h/;
/s/; /th/; /<u>th</u>/; /v/; /z/
Simple long *u*. *See* /ū/
Simplicity, in orthography. *See* Minimum
and maximum simplicities; Unity
-sis, 64–65
sk, 74, 361, 362, 363
Skeat, Walter, 18, 50, 61
Skousen, Royal, 23
sl. See /l/
/sm/, 74
sm. See /m/
Smith, Henry Lee, xxxi, 202, 205, 307
Smith, Philip, and R. G. Baker, 23, 32
Smith, Thomas, 3
/sn/, 74
[*snugg*+, *snug*], 150
Soft *c. See c*
Soft *g. See g*
son+, 432
sonn+, 432
soph+, 379
Sounds, American English, 201–6; distinctive-feature analysis of, 211–12. *See also*
Consonant sounds; Vowel sounds
/sp/, 74
Speech, vs. writing, 14–17, 21–22
Spelling process, 49–50
Spelling pronunciations, 22–24
Spelling reform, 30
Spellings: accepted, unaccepted,
unrecorded, 27–29, 30; well- and ill-
formed, 26–27. *See also* Variant spellings
spr, 72
ss, 76, 82, 104. *See also* /s/; /sh/; /z/
sse, 76
/st/, 74
st, 104, 264, 265, 267, 268, 380, 416. *See
also* /s/
-st. See -ist
Standardized spelling, rise of, 8, 21–22, 24
Status words, and adaption, 20
Stems, 35–37, 162–68. *See also* Primes
-ster, 303
sth. See /s/
+*stice,* 59
stit+, 59
Stops, 206, 327–49, 350–72. *See also* /b/;
/d/; /g/; /k/; /p/; /t/
Strang, Barbara, 97
[*streng*+, *strong*], 437
Stress, 49; and de-stressing, 151–54; noun/
verb stress pairs, 168; in strings, 90–93,

94, 127–28; and suffix rules, 112–13, 115–
18, 120–21, 133; and twinning, 161, 162,
164, 165–74
Stress Frontshift Rule, 112, 127–28, 214–15,
218, 224, 234, 244–45, 246, 330, 335, 340,
347, 353, 365, 377, 393, 395, 419, 427, 432,
444, 445, 452; holdouts to, 129–30
Strings, 90–91; /r/-colored vowels and, 307–
8; VC*e* (*see* VCV, and final *e*). *See also*
VC#; VCC; VC′C′*le*; etc.
Stubbs, Michael, xxv, 4, 17, 23, 462
su-, 184
sub-, 34, 57, 78–79, 177, 183–86, 245, 336,
341, 356, 372, 383, 453
Subelemental and subsyllabic patterning.
See Pattern and regularity
suc-, 183, 356, 372
sud-, 341
suf-, 183, 383
Suffix rules, 112–22, 127; twinning and, 161,
172–73. See also *-ic; -id; -ion; -ish²; -it;
-ity; -ule*
Suffixes, 32–33, 34–35, 36, 57–59, 112–22;
derivational and inflectional, 34–35; nonterminative, 46–47. *See also individual
suffixes*
sug-, 183
sum-, 183
[*summ*+, *sum*], 427
[*sumpt*+, +*sume*], 36, 37, 39–41
sup-, 183, 336
super-, 34, 184
sur- (assimilated form of *sub-*), 183–84, 453
sur- (over, above), 184, 324
sus-, 184
/sw/, 74, 457, 458
sw. See /s/
sy-, 198
syl-, 198
Syllabic *l. See* /əl/
Syllabicity. *See* Rule of Syllabicity
Syllables: elements and, 59–60; boundaries
for, 59–60, 61–63, 71–72
sym-, 198, 428
syn-, 177, 197–98, 428
Systems and systematicity, xxv, 4, 5–9, 12–
13, 30–31, 155, 159–60, 461

/t/, 206, 327–28; = *bt,* 17–18, 342, 344; =
cht, 342, 346; in clusters and concatenations, 348; at complex boundaries, 349;
= *ct,* 342, 345; = *dt,* 342, 345; = *ed,*
342, 343; flapped, 342–43; = *ght,* 345–46;

after long vowels, 348; = *phth*, 346; = *pt*, 342, 344–45; after reduced vowels, 349; after short vowels, 347–48, 349; shortening rules and, 347–48; at simple boundaries, 346–47; spellings of, 342–49; = *t*, 327–28, 342, 346–48, 349; = *th*, 342, 343; = *tt*, 327–28, 342, 346, 349; = *tw*, 342, 346; after vowel digraphs, 348

t, 207; in Latinate verbs, 61–62. *See also* /sh/; /t/; /zh/

-*t* (verb suffix), 7

+*tach*, 413

Tactics and tactical rules, 9, 69–141; /r/-colored vowels and, 307–8. *See also* Consonant sequence rules; Distribution rules; Shortening rules; Strings; Vowel Doublet Rule

[*tann*+, *tan*], 171

tch, 72, 77, 210. *See also* /ch/

techn+, 358

Tense vowels. *See* Vowel sounds

Terminative elements. *See* Elements

[*terr*+¹, +*ter*¹] (earth), 172

[*terr*+², +*ter*²] (fright), 172

/th/, 147, 206; = *chth*, 385; in clusters and concatenations, 385; history of, 384–85; = *phth*, 385; spellings of, 385–86; = *th*, 385; = *tth*, 385

/th̲/, 206, 384; = *th*, 147, 385–86

th, 62–63, 71, 108–10, 147, 209, 210, 212. *See also* /t/; /th/; /th̲/

theor+, 37

Thesaurarium Trilingue Publicum, 89

Third Syllable Rule, 112, 129, 131–41, 175, 239, 291, 330, 333, 335, 340, 347, 353, 365, 377, 382, 395, 402, 414, 419, 427, 432, 444, 445, 452; conservative analogy in, 139–41; in Latinate disyllables, 138–39, 227, 234; in Old English, 133, 225, 226, 235; preemptors of, 134–38; short vowels and, 214, 218, 224, 227, 234, 239, 245, 246; VCVV and, 135–38; V.V and, 135

Thorn. *See* Runes

Tight clusters. *See* Consonant clusters

tm. See /m/

[*tonsill*+, *tonsil*], 161, 171

Trager, George, xxxi

trans-, 34, 78

Triplet Rule, 77, 158, 383, 396, 447

Trochaic disyllables. *See* VCV

tsch. See /ch/

/tsh/, 407, 416

tt, 72, 76. *See also* /t/

tth. See /th/

/tw/, 74

tw. See /t/

Twinning Rule, 9, 15, 25, 26, 31, 38, 47, 76, 96, 140, 150, 161–76, 212, 332, 337, 341, 349, 354, 375, 383, 393–94, 400, 403, 428, 433, 442, 446, 450, 453; American vs. British, 167–68; final *l* and, 440; holdouts to, 174–76; nonterminative bases and, 170–72; stress and, 162, 164, 165–70, 173–74; suffix rules and, 161, 172–73; VCC and, 162

tyrann+, 432

/u/, 203, 204; = *o*, 245–47; = *oo*, 247; = *ou*, 247–48; spellings of, 244–48; = *u*, 244–45; in VC#, 244, 245, 246; in VCC, 244, 245, 246; in shortened VCV, 244–45, 246–47

/u̇/, 203, 204, 241; history of, 241; = *o*, 243; = *oo*, 242; = *ou*, 243; spellings of, 241–43; = *u*, 242–43; in VCC, 242

/ū/, 203, 211; = *eu*, 295–96; = *ew*, 295; history of, 288–89; = *o*, 288, 291–92; = *oe*, 293; = *oo*, 288, 289–90, 291; = *ou*, 288–89, 293–95; = *ough*, 294; persistent, 105, 114–15, 118, 120, 122, 124, 134–35; spellings of, 289–96; Third Syllable Rule and, 291; = *u*, 288–89, 290–91; = *uh*, 296; = *ui*, 296; = *uo*, 296; VCV and, 289–90; Ve# and, 290–91; V.V and, 291; = *w*, 296; and /yū/, 297

u, 136, 207, 208, 211, 212, 245–46, 459; insulating, 229, 350–51; and *v*, 81, 208; word-final, and final *e*, 20, 95–96, 147, 350–51. *See also* /e/; /i/; /u/; /u̇/; /ū/; /w/; /yū/

ue, 95–96, 157

ugh. See /yū/

uh. See /ū/

ui. See /i/; /ū/; /yū/

-*ule*, 122, 330, 353, 365

-*um*, 64

un-, 34, 36, 177, 245

Unaccepted spellings, 27–29

Unigraphs, 90

Unintegrated elements. *See* Integration; Periphery vs. center

Unity, in orthography, 10–13, 41, 45–46, 139–40, 159–60. *See also* Conservative analogy; Variety

Unrecorded spellings, 27–29

uo. See /ū/

uor. See /ùr/

uoy. See /òi/

/ur/ convergence, 454; = *ear,* 325; = *er,*
  323; = *eur,* 326; history of, 321–22; = *ir,*
  324; = *irr,* 324; = *our,* 325; spellings of,
  323–26; = *ur,* 324; = *urr,* 324; /wur/
  = *wor,* 323; = *yr,* 326; = *yrr,* 326

/ùr/: = *eur,* 321; = *oor,* 321; = *our,* 321;
  spellings of, 320–21; = *uor,* 321; = *ur,*
  320

ur. See /âr/; /ur/; /ùr/; /yùr/

-*ure,* 153–54, 242, 266

uu, 81

uy. See /ī/

/v/, 180, 206, 207–8, 246; in clusters, 376;
  and /f/, 373–74; = *f,* 373–74, 376; history
  of, 373–75; after long vowels, 376; = *lv,*
  376, 380; spellings of, 375–77; after
  reduced vowels, 377; after short vowels,
  376, 377; shortening rules and, 377; = *v,*
  373–75, 376–77; = *vv,* 375–76

v, 93, 207, 208, 373–77; vs. *u,* 208, 246; in
  VCV, 128–29, 218–19, 225, 234; word-
  final, and final *e,* 147, 375. *See also* /v/

Vachek, Josef, 6, 17, 207

Variant spellings, 21–22, 25–26; *c* and *s,*
  406; *f* and *ph,* 379; *l* vs. *ll,* 439, 440–41; *r*
  vs. *rr,* 450

Variety, in orthography, 10–11, 13–14, 140.
  See also Unity

VC# string, 93–94, 97, 140, 162, 163, 165,
  172–73, 174, 176, 214, 218, 224, 227, 233,
  234, 244, 245, 246, 261, 264, 369, 381,
  401

VCC string, 31, 47, 88, 90, 96–98, 100–107,
  112, 113, 121–22, 140, 162, 214, 217–18,
  223, 226–27, 233, 239, 242, 244, 245, 246,
  328–30, 332, 337, 341–42, 349, 354, 368,
  383, 394, 396, 404, 413, 415, 420, 429,
  434, 447, 454; holdouts to, 101–7, 262,
  271, 283; vs. VCV, 96–98, 99, 129, 150,
  162. *See also "in clusters and concatenations," under individual consonant sounds*

VC'C'le string, 80, 106, 329, 331, 333, 337,
  342, 349, 355, 361, 368–69, 380, 384, 394,
  400, 401, 404. See also *le#*

VCe# string. *See* VCV, and final *e*

VCle string, 105–6, 251–52, 274–75, 277,
  283, 299, 368–69

VCrV string, 106, 251–52, 261, 274–75, 277,
  283, 299

VCV string, 90, 96–98, 107–11, 112–15, 123–
  30, 140, 141, 162, 307; and final *e,* 107–8,
  145, 148–49, 151–54, 159–60; in iambic
  disyllables, 123; with long head vowels,
  114–15, 118–19, 120, 122, 123–26, 129–30,
  134–38, 140–41, 145, 151–53, 154–57, 251,
  253–54, 260, 263, 264, 272, 276–77, 281,
  289–90, 299 (*see also individual consonant sounds*); with short head vowels, 69,
  112–14, 115–16, 118–19, 120–22, 127–30,
  131–33, 138–39, 146, 147, 151–54, 214–15,
  218–19, 224–26, 227, 233, 234–35, 242–43,
  244–45, 246–47 (*see also individual consonant sounds*); in trochaic disyllables,
  123–26, 127–30; *v* in (see *v*). *See also*
  VCC

VCVV string, 119, 135–38

V*e*# string, 94–96, 145, 157–58, 273, 281,
  290–91, 299

Velar fricative, in Old English, 209, 247–48,
  255, 271, 274, 278, 286, 294, 345. See
  also *gh*

Velar stops. *See* /g/; /k/

Velars, before /yù/, 297–98

velle +, 38

Venezky, Richard, xxv, xxvii, 4, 17, 30, 53,
  71, 205, 307, 316, 409

Visual bias, growth of, 13, 21–24

[*voc +,* *+ voke*], 363–64

Voiced and voiceless consonants, 73–74,
  327

Vowel digraphs. *See individual vowel
  digraphs and individual consonants*

Vowel Doublet Rule, 81–82, 86

Vowel lengthening and shortening, 97–98,
  125–26, 258–59, 271, 275, 280

Vowel letters, 210–12. *See also individual
  vowel letters*

Vowel sequence rules, 81–82. *See also*
  Vowel Doublet Rule

Vowel sounds, American English, 74, 203–
  6, 210–12; free and checked, 53, 205;
  head, 90; lax and tense, 53, 205–6; low
  back, 204–6, 231–40; /r/-colored, 307–26;
  short and long, 53, 97–98, 203, 219. *See
  also individual consonant and vowel
  sounds*

Vowel unigraphs, 90

Vowels, vs. consonants, 210–12, 426, 459

vv, 76. *See also* /v/

V.V string, 91–93, 115, 118, 135, 140, 242–43,
  252, 254, 260–61, 262–64, 272–73, 277,
  281, 291, 299

VVC'C' string, 100

/w/, 206, 208, 211, 212, 232, 233, 239, 313, 400; = *hu*, 456; = *ju*, 456; = *o*, 456; = *ou*, 456; spellings of, 456–59; = *u*, 456, 457; = *w*, 456, 458–59; = *wh*, 71–72, 458–59
w, 81, 207, 208, 212, 296. *See also* /w/
Walker, J., 104
war. See /ôr/
-ward, 236
Watkins, Calvert, 346
Watt, Ian, 462
Webster, Noah, 132, 213, 370
Weir, Ruth, 4
Well-formed spellings, 26–27
Wen. *See* Runes
werg- (Indo-European root), 448
wergh- (Indo-European root), 448
werp- (Indo-European root), 448
Wertheimer, Max, 29
West Germanic gemination, 100
wh, 62–63, 71–72, 212. *See also* /h/; /w/
Whorf, Benjamin Lee, 72
-wise, 272
/wôr/. *See* /ôr/
wor. See /ur/
Word-final doublets, 76–77
Word-initial doublets, 76
wr, 212. *See also* /r/
wreg- (Indo-European root), 448
wreik- (Indo-European root), 448
wreit- (Indo-European root), 448
Writing: public uses of, 24; vs. speech, 16–17, 21–22, 461
Written Standard English, 14, 21–22, 23–24, 203
wrizd- (Indo-European root), 448
/wur/. *See* /ur/
Wyld, Henry, 10–11

x, 74, 89, 100, 163, 207, 351–52, 370–71, 436–37. *See also* /g/; /k/; /sh/; /z/

/y/, 206, 211, 212, 456; = *e*, 459; = *i*, 459–60; = *j*, 460; = *ll*, 459; spellings of, 459–60; = *y*, 459; = *z*, 459–60

y, 207, 208, 211, 212, 226–27. *See also* /ē/; /i/; /y/
-y 157, 262, 373, 375
y-to-*i* tactics, 37, 58, 65, 84–87, 157, 208, 262–63, 273, 277, 278. See also *i*
ye, 96
-yer, 459
Yogh. *See* Runes
yr. See /ur/
yrr. See /ur/
/yù/, 241, 242–43
/yū/, 203, 288, 297–99; = *eau*, 300; = *eu*, 300; = *ew*, 299; history of, 297; = *ieu*, 300; = *iew*, 300; spellings of, 299–300; vs. /ū/, 297–99; = *u*, 299; = *ugh*, 300; = *ui*, 300; VCC and, 299; in VC*le* and VC*r*, 299; VCV and, 299; V*e#* and, 299; V.V and, 299
/yùr/, 320; = *eur*, 321; = *ur*V, 320–21

/z/, 202, 206; in clusters, 15, 392, 393, 395; at complex boundaries, 392, 393–94; = *cz*, 391; history of, 391; after long vowels, 392, 393, 396; after reduced vowels, 392, 394, 396; = *s*, 15, 16, 391–92, 394–97; after short vowels, 392, 393, 394, 395; and shortening rules, 392, 393, 394, 395; at simple boundaries, 392, 393, 395; spellings of, 391–97; = *ss*, 391–92, 394–96; = *sth*, 391; = *ts*, 391; = *tz*, 391; after vowel digraphs, 392, 393, 396; word-final, 392, 394–95; = *x*, 391; = *z*, 391–94, 396–97; = *zz*, 391–92, 393–94
z, 93, 100, 207, 208, 391–94, 459–60; word-final, and final *e*, 83–84, 148, 392. *See also* /z/
-ze. See *-ize*
Zettersten, Arne, 72
/zh/, 44, 206, 407; = *g*, 146, 422; history of, 421–22; = *j*, 422; vs. /j/, 146, 421–22; palatalized spellings of, 44, 422; = *s*, 422; vs. /sh/, 410; spellings of, 422; = *t*, 422; = *z*, 422
zz, 76, 83–84. *See also* /z/

American English Spelling

Designed by Ann Walston.

Composed by Village Typographers, Inc.,
in Times Roman.

Printed by Thomson-Shore, Inc.,
on 50-lb. Glatfelter Smooth Antique offset.
Bound by John H. Dekker and Sons, Inc.,
in Joanna Arrestox.